NEARLY
EVERYTHING
IMAGINABLE

Studies in Latter-day Saint History

An imprint of BYU Studies and the
Joseph Fielding Smith Institute for Latter-day Saint History

Brigham Young University
Provo, Utah

NEARLY EVERYTHING IMAGINABLE

THE EVERYDAY LIFE OF UTAH'S MORMON PIONEERS

Edited by

Ronald W. Walker
Doris R. Dant

Brigham Young University Press

This volume inaugurates the Smith Institute and BYU Studies series
Studies in Latter-day Saint History.

Previous BYU Studies Monographs

The Truth, The Way, The Life:
An Elementary Treatise on Theology

The Journals of William E. McLellin, 1831–1836

Hearts Turned to the Fathers:
A History of the Genealogical Society of Utah, 1894–1994

Mormon Americana:
A Guide to Sources and Collections in the United States

Behind the Iron Curtain:
Recollections of Latter-day Saints in East Germany, 1945–1989

Coming to Zion

Life in Utah: Centennial Selections from BYU Studies

The First Mormon Temple:
Design, Construction, and Historic Context of the Kirtland Temple

Letters of Minerva Teichert

No part of this book may be reproduced in any form or by any means
without permission in writing from the publisher. For information about
subscribing to *BYU Studies*, a quarterly multidisciplinary LDS journal,
write to: BYU Studies, 403 CB, PO Box 24098, Provo, Utah 84602-4098.

Library of Congress Cataloging-in-Publication Data

Nearly everything imaginable : the everyday life of Utah's Mormon pioneers /
    edited by Ronald W. Walker, Doris R. Dant.
        p. cm. — (Studies in Latter-day Saint history)
    Includes bibliographical references (p.) and index.
    ISBN 0-8425-2397-9
    1. Utah—Social life and customs—19th century. 2. Mormons—Utah—Social
life and customs. I. Walker, Ronald W. (Ronald Warren), 1939- II. Dant, Doris
R. III. Series.
F826 .N43 1999
979.2'02—ddc21

                                                                98-58057
                                                                CIP

Printed in the United States of America
10 9 8 7 6 5 4 3 2 1

To the Saints whose everyday lives
laid the foundation

TABLE OF CONTENTS

Preface

This book began with a discussion among colleagues. At the time, The Church of Jesus Christ of Latter-day Saints was about to celebrate the 150-year anniversary of the arrival of the Mormon pioneers in Utah. Also, Brigham Young University's Joseph Fielding Smith Institute for Latter-day Saint History was searching for a theme for its upcoming annual symposium. My friends at the Smith Institute wondered if we might combine both: hold a symposium that would commemorate the founding of the Mormon settlements in Utah.

During this discussion, I argued that few subjects in early LDS history were more important and more neglected than the everyday life of Utah's Mormon pioneers. Although the last fifty years have seen a dramatic flowering of Mormon history (over eight thousand titles have been produced since the end of World War II), most works focused on such traditional topics as LDS institutional history, prominent LDS men, and events in mainstream Mormonism, particularly those occurring in Salt Lake City. While these topics are important and admirable, I hoped that the Smith Institute might use its sesquicentennial symposium to do something more innovative. I wanted to celebrate the life of the "ordinary" Saint—the men, women, and children whom President J. Reuben Clark once called "pioneers of the last wagon train."[1]

An irrevocable law governs a staff discussion such as I describe: the most outspoken voice receives the committee assignment. It was not surprising, then, that I was asked to head the Smith Institute committee that sponsored the symposium "Everyday Life in Pioneer Utah," held at Brigham Young University in March 1997. The hope of our committee, which included my Smith Institute friends, Jill Mulvay Derr, Richard L. Jensen, Carol C. Madsen, and Marilyn R. Parks, was ambitious. We wanted our symposium to serve as a call to scholars to do more work on the subject of Mormon and Utah everyday life. We also wanted this plea to have a lasting and concrete result. Therefore, from the beginning we hoped that the papers presented at our conference would be published.

But what kind of a book would be the result? Usually, published symposia papers tend to be narrow and scholarly and therefore have limited appeal. They also tend to have the rough edge of preliminary writing. We wanted to achieve something different. At a time when so much history is written for historians—scholars speaking to scholars—we wanted to reach out to the general reader. Accordingly, we sought articles of broad appeal written by scholars with a reputation for fine writing. We also requested that Doris Dant join us as a co-editor. Doris, who for many years has served as executive editor of *BYU Studies,* brought to the publishing task a careful eye for detail. She has also helped many of us improve our writing, especially in tightening our prose, a necessary procedure in a book as large as this one. As always, brevity is style, and Doris has helped us to be reasonably brief.

The title of our book, *Nearly Everything Imaginable,* has meaning on several levels. The phrase, taken from Jill Mulvay Derr's essay on pioneer food and diet, suggests both the difficulty and the variety of pioneer living. The phrase also suggests the book's broad methods and sources. Without too much exaggeration, we can claim using "nearly everything imaginable" to reconstruct the past: biography, comparative study, cultural history, demography or statistical analysis, eulogy, folklore, geography, literary deconstruction, material culture study, narrative history, musicology, photography, local history, oral history, and sociology. In short, this book not only argues that more "everyday history" should be written, it also provides an example of the various approaches by which such a study can be undertaken. In a modest way, this book is intended as a methods handbook.

We continue this expansive theme with a broad choice of article topics divided into six sections: Prologue, Mormon Village, Rhythms of Pioneer Life, Life Cycles, Pioneer Lives, and Epilogue. The Prologue section contains Elder Marlin K. Jensen's eulogy of the "uncommonly heroic" common Saint. Elder Jensen, a member of the LDS Church's First Quorum of the Seventy, provides many examples of early pioneer devotion but none more moving than Warren Marshall Johnson's travail at his Lonely Dell outpost on the Colorado River. Johnson's letters are certain to become classics in LDS literature. Richard Lyman Bushman, currently Gouverneur Morris Professor of History at Columbia University, introduces a different but related theme. Bushman considers the cultural bequest of Joseph Smith and concludes that the Prophet was less interested in the sheen and polish of refined culture than in reinforcing a hardy, honest spirit among his people. In Bushman's view, early Mormon culture was a species of straightforward, caring religion manifested in the life of Mormonism's founder. It was a legacy by which Utah's Saints governed their daily lives.

The second section of the book deals with the topic of the "Mormon village," a distinguished and long-standing staple of Mormon scholarship. The topic is at least as old as Richard T. Ely's influential essay, "Economic Aspects of Mormonism," *Harpers Monthly Magazine* 106 (April 1903): 667–78. Ely, a prominent turn-of-the-century social scientist, called for an end to sectarian controversy about the Mormons and urged the serious study of their economic and social life, including their village communitarianism. Of the several post–World War I social scientists who responded to this call, the most important was probably Lowry Nelson, himself a product of Mormondom's Castle Valley hamlet of Ferron, Utah. Nelson's case studies of Mormon town life helped to define the concept for a later generation of scholars.[2]

Three articles pick up on this theme. My own article, "Golden Memories: Remembering Life in a Mormon Village," goes beyond the usual physical and sociological description of the village to reveal some of its inner relationships. In order to do so, I have used "old-timer" oral histories and autobiographies gathered during the 1930s and allowed these accounts to describe the life these villagers once lived. The result is a nostalgic portrait of the warmth and purpose of Mormon community life.

University of Utah history professor Dean L. May uses a different method to reach a similar conclusion. In an essay drawn from his book, *Three Frontiers: Family, Land, and Society in the American West, 1850–1900* (New York: Cambridge University Press, 1994), May compares the Mormon town of Alpine, Utah, with the farming districts of Sublimity, Oregon, and Middleton, Idaho. According to May, the cultural assumptions of each community helped to determine its social behavior. In the case of Alpine, the Mormon ideals of community and cooperation led to a society that was "harmonious, orderly, unified, and compassionate."[3]

In a third essay about Mormon community life, Richard Neitzel Holzapfel and David A. Allred test a behavioral model proposed by sociologist Rosabeth Moss Kanter, who has argued that the establishment of successful utopian communities generally follows a consistent pattern, which Kanter distills into a series of descriptive social "mechanisms." Applying Kanter's model to the behavior of the settlers of Utah Valley, a cluster of Mormon towns fifty miles south of Salt Lake City, Holzapfel and Allred conclude that the Mormons were successful colonizers largely because of the influence of their religion on the practical aspects of daily life. Thus, a common denominator unites each of these essays: the religious quality of Mormon town life made the Mormons more oriented to the ideals of cooperation, community, and sharing and less accepting of the ideals of individualism and self-seeking.

The next two sections of the book explore Mormon everyday life from a variety of viewpoints, some relatively new to Mormon studies. Andrew H. Hedges discusses the challenges of early homemaking; Richard Cracroft, Mormon hymns; Larry V. Shumway, pioneer dancing; and Jill Mulvay Derr, pioneer food. William G. Hartley examines worship activity. His essay, a summary of many years' research and writing, is especially important because of religion's central role in the Mormon settlements. Claudia L. Bushman provides an additional dimension to Mormon pioneering by examining the tension between Relief Society ideals and the daily reality. Also included in this section are two photographic essays, Richard G. Oman's on Mormon regional furniture and Carma de Jong Anderson's on dress. With the exception of the Bushmans and Oman, whose careers respectively have been centered in eastern universities and the Museum of Church History and Art in Salt Lake City, these authors are associated with Brigham Young University.

The fourth section of the book deals with "life cycles"—the successive stages of maturing life. Four articles discuss the neglected topic of early Utah childhood and adolescence. Writer Susan Arrington Madsen and former assistant LDS Church historian and University of Utah history professor Davis Bitton use pioneer youth diaries to suggest what coming of age in early Utah may have been like. In turn, BYU history professor Brian Q. Cannon's article on the Mormon practice of adopting or indenturing Native American children reminds us that pioneer Utah involved more than one culture and that Mormons and Native Americans struggled to reach some kind of uncomfortable accommodation. In yet another article dealing with the life stage of

Gems from the Teachings of Church Leaders
Elder Vaughn J. Featherstone on the Monumental Work of the Pioneers

"The glory of God is portrayed in the lives of the Latter-day Saint pioneer men, women, and children who placed all they had on the altar. They were prepared to give everything, including their lives. These pioneers forged lives that were fired white hot in the crucible of some of the most difficult suffering and tests. This was a magnificent generation of common, ordinary souls who were brought together through their faith in God and who moved forward to meet danger and trials. They were given a monumental work to do, and they did it."

("Following in Their Footsteps," Ensign, July 1997, 8)

("Helping in Their Lessons," *Ensign*, July 1987)

youth, James B. Allen, also a former LDS assistant historian, discusses school life. The topic, for all of its importance, has surprisingly received little attention from popular and academic writers alike.

The life cycle section also contains an important article about pioneer married life. Using a computerized database of LDS genealogical records and state vital records, University of Utah professors Lee L. Bean, Geraldine P. Mineau, and Ken R. Smith examine early Utah married life from an entirely new perspective—how such factors as pioneering, agrarian life, and LDS religious practice affected the life expectancy of married couples. The authors' statistical analysis concludes that Utah pioneering reduced longevity, a trend that was most pronounced among rural women, non-LDS, and Mormons who were less religiously "active" in their church. The report of Bean, Mineau, and Smith is another example of the important demographic research on early Utah life being completed at the University of Utah. During the last twenty years, researchers there have published a succession of studies on such topics as early Utah fertility, family size, longevity, nuptiality, migration, mortality, and widowhood, often within the context of LDS plural marriage. The result has been a more accurate profile of nineteenth-century daily life, as old and facile judgments give way to new, statistically based evidence.

The life cycles section ends, fittingly, with Richard Jackson's article on Mormon cemeteries—the inevitable end to mortal journey. During his career, Jackson, a BYU professor of geography, has repeatedly addressed the theme of Mormon life within the context of geography, of the natural, physical setting. Here Jackson provides a fresh view—that Mormon cemeteries furnish a window to the larger culture of everyday Saints.

The book concludes with two final sections. "Pioneer Lives" reminds readers that Mormon daily life can often be best seen by examining individual lives biographically. Harriet Horne Arrington warmly traces the life of her ancestor, Joseph Horne, one of Mormonism's first converts and an early Utah settler. Arrington's sketch tells of the primitive conditions in Salt Lake City's pioneer fort, the hardship that the Mormons faced when scouting out the land, and the challenge of carving out a successful career in Utah. John W. Welch's biographical sketch of his ancestor, John Welch of Paradise, Utah, captures the warp-and-woof detail of an "ordinary" life being lived when Utah's pioneering era was drawing to a close. Last, the dean of Mormon historians, Leonard J. Arrington, presents a biographical sketch of his progenitors that has several untraditional shades: his progenitors were latecomers who arrived on the railroad and, after first not prospering, returned East before getting a second wind at settling in the West. Arrington's recital is interesting both on its own account and also because of what it tells of the background of one of Mormonism's leading twentieth-century intellectuals.

In the book's last section, William A. Wilson discusses contemporary folklore. Wilson argues that the stories that people tell about the past are important not so much for what they reveal about historical events but for what they reveal about the people themselves: present-day folklore conveys present-day ideas and attitudes. We put Wilson's article at the end of our book because it suggests a wider truth. While historical studies like those presented in this book may be more precise than the lore of the people, inevitably all study of the past will bear the traces of what might be called "presentism." Thus, we allow Wilson's essay to confess our frailty and outlook. While the contributors to this book are respected scholars, no doubt their work collectively reflects the respectful attitude that most of them feel for the Mormon tradition. Broader and perhaps more hostile perspectives of the Mormon pioneer past can be found elsewhere.

Our authors would probably wish me to be explicit about another point. Some of the essays in this book are preliminary. They represent research that is ongoing; while introducing topics, they do not exhaust them. These essays are presented in the spirit of LeRoy R. Hafen, a distinguished Mormon historian of another generation, who, impatient with scholars who researched endlessly but never brought their work to publication, cited a proverb: "Alas for those who never sing; but die with all their music in them."[4] In contrast, this volume sings with the strains of pleasing melodies, although in some cases complete symphonies await composition.

Not only does this book examine many topics which have previously received only slight scholarly attention, it also begins a new publishing venture. This book appears in a new series published by the Brigham Young University Press and called Studies in Latter-day Saint History. Studies in Latter-day Saint History unites the resources of the Joseph Fielding Smith Institute for Latter-day Saint History with those of *BYU Studies* in what promises to be a fruitful collaboration. We are honored that our volume has been chosen as the first book of this new series.

We also acknowledge the professional assistance that we have received. The Studies in Mormon History general editor, John W. Welch, extended interest and support. Members of the *BYU Studies* staff verified facts and citations; the expertise of Jed Woodworth and David Allred was particularly valuable in this endeavor. Karl F. Batdorff and Amy Bingham helped prepare the illustrations for our two photographic essays. We thank Ron Read and his colleagues at the Museum of Church History and Art for their contributions to Richard Oman's essay and for the photographs appearing on the dust jacket. Richard Holzapfel selected many of the book's other illustrations, drawing upon his extensive knowledge of the holdings of Utah's archives. We also express appreciation to Bjorn Pendleton of BYU's Instructional Technology Center for his artful dust-jacket design and to Amy Bingham, who in addition to assisting with the book's graphics, indexed the manuscript. A special reward in the scholarly heaven must await those who volunteer for and complete such a chore.

—Ronald W. Walker

Notes

1. J. Reuben Clark Jr., "They of the Last Wagon," *Improvement Era* 50 (November 1947): 704–5, 747–48. Reprinted as "To Them of the Last Wagon," *Ensign* 27 (July 1997): 34–39.

2. For Nelson's early publications, see *A Social Survey of Escalante, Utah,* Brigham Young University Studies, no. 1 (Provo, Utah: Brigham Young University, 1925); *The Utah Farm Village of Ephraim,* Brigham Young University Studies, no. 2 (Provo, Utah: Brigham Young University, 1928); "The Mormon Village: A Study in Social Origins," *Proceedings of the Utah Academy of Sciences* 7 (1930): 11–37, reprinted in Brigham Young University Studies, no. 3 (Provo, Utah: Brigham Young University, 1930); and *Some Social and Economic Features of American Fork, Utah,* Brigham Young University Studies, no. 4 (Provo, Utah: Brigham Young University, 1933). Nelson's research on the Mormon settlements in Alberta was published in Carl A. Dawson, "The Mormons," pt. 3 of *Group Settlement: Ethnic Communities in Western Canada,* Canadian Frontiers of Settlement, vol. 7 (Toronto: Macmillan, 1936), 175–272. All these studies were eventually republished in Lowry Nelson, *The Mormon Village: A Pattern and Technique of Land Settlement* (Salt Lake City: University of Utah Press, 1952).

3. See page 85.

4. LeRoy R. Hafen, "Joys of Discovery—Historical Research and Writing," *BYU Studies* 7, nos. 3 and 4 (1966): 183.

PROLOGUE

Street scene of St. George, Utah, about 1876. C. E. Johnson, photographer.

Upon These We Bestow More Abundant Honor

Elder Marlin K. Jensen

Almost fifty years have passed since President J. Reuben Clark Jr., on the occasion of the centennial of the pioneers entering the Salt Lake Valley, delivered an unforgettable general conference sermon praising the common pioneers of that era.[1] To epitomize the segment of unheralded and largely unknown men and women who trekked west and helped found the Great Basin Kingdom, President Clark chose to pay tribute to those of "the last wagon." While acknowledging the greatness and the indispensable role of Brother Brigham and the other giants of those early days of the State of Deseret and Utah Territory, President Clark elected to eulogize "those who trod after where those giants led."[2]

The Place of the Commonplace in History

This approach by President Clark not only made for grand elocution and enduring literature, it was also historiographically commendable. Dale L. Morgan, the eminent Utah historian who focused on the nineteenth century, identifies the issue precisely:

> Conflict makes news, and news makes history, yet men live rich and quiet lives outside the boiling currents of their times, and who shall say whether the thousand existences in quiet do not more nearly express the shape of human experience than the fiercely spotlighted existence that survives as history.[3]

In December of 1905, in a brief but delightful editorial on "commonplace things" in the *Juvenile Instructor,* President Joseph F. Smith stated the principle this way: "Those things which we call extraordinary, remarkable, or unusual may make history, but they do not make real life."[4] This is an important lesson to learn because even

Courtesy LDS Church Archives

Salt Lake City in 1863. Visible behind the fence surrounding Temple Block are the "Old" Tabernacle (built in 1852) and the bowery.

today we are tempted to dote on the "headline" events of the *Church News* at the expense of a more fundamental and accurate understanding of the true spirit of our times.

Going back in time 150 years and capturing "real life" in pioneer Utah is a difficult, but very worthwhile, pursuit. The essence of real life can best be distilled from the commonplace happenings in the lives of the ordinary people of those times. To come to know such people—their sturdiness, their constancy, their daily routines, their struggles, their accomplishments, their courage and faith—is to come to know our history in a very practical and wonderful way. I believe it is also to come to know ourselves.

HISTORICAL SOURCES

To put meat on the bones of ordinary pioneers, one must prospect through the abundance of primary historical sources left by very busy people who nonetheless seem to have had a sense of their own destiny and, in many cases, a desire to record the daily occurrences and musings by which that destiny was being shaped. A perusal of journals, letters, autobiographies, and other records of the ordinary people of the day reveals common threads of both action and attitude. (I must parenthetically admit at this point that, as challenging as it has always been for me personally to be a regular journal keeper, I harbor at least a slight suspicion, if not the outright hope, that those who consistently accomplished this task in pioneer times may have been a little more than ordinary!) I wish to examine from the record a few lives that I believe are representative of the common Latter-day Saints. Hopefully these accounts will give us an appreciation for the texture of those times at the "real-life" level.

JOHN BENNION

If life's meaning can best be found in its dailiness, what does the record show regarding the routine of common people in early Utah?

The journals of John Bennion are instructive concerning the male side of this question. Born in Wales in 1820 and converted to the faith in Liverpool, Bennion immigrated to Nauvoo in 1842 and arrived in the Salt Lake Valley in October 1847. He settled in 1850 at a bend in the Jordan River along what is now Forty-Eighth South in the Taylorsville-Bennion area of Salt Lake County.

For over twenty years, from 1855 to the day before sustaining a fatal injury on his horse on August 31, 1877, Bennion made terse but almost daily entries in his journals. The month of January 1855 is typical:

Jenuary 1855

Mon 1st	I with my family attended a party at the school house, day very windy
Tues 2nd	Jobing at home, Snow Storm
Wed 3rd	Do [ditto] at home very windy
Thur 4th	Do at home, very windy
Fri 5th	Cutting willows to put around yards
Sat 6th	hauling willows, Sammy went to town
S 7th	at meeting morning & evening at the School house. Sammy returned found no cattle had lodged at Bro Tarbets
Mon 8th	Tending my Stock, & went up to night School
Tues 9th	Do & Sent home Betsy Griffiths, pleasent weather
Wed 10th	Was out north hunting cattle with Sam R [diarist's oldest son] we rode all day without Success
Thurs 11th	at home taking care of the Sheep attended the prayr meeting in the evening
Fri 12th	went to the city with team had some buissness & to search for the cattle missing
Sat 13th	returned home not finding the cattle
14th S	attended Sunday School twice & meeting in the morning, at home in the evening
Mon 15	Jobing at home
Tues 16	Do
Wed 17	at home finishing the Sheep cot[e] Bp Hunter came out this evening
Thur 18	Selected out his last Springs lambs and devided them I took twelve & he 29 he paying me the differance
Fri 19	herding the Sheep, while I went to the fort, the crows killed two lambs
Sat 20	herding the Sheep
S 21	Attended the Sunday School & meeting

Mon 22	herding the Sheep & Cattle
Tues 23	went to the City recieved instructions to settle with the individuals of the ward four [individuals] I took back to Immigration on tithing
Wed 24	herding the Sheep & Cattle
Thur 25	herding the Sheep & Cattle
Fri 26	jobing at home untill evening, when I went to attend a party at Jno Pugmire
Sat 27th	went to mill with a grist [portion of grain taken to a mill to be ground]
S 28	Attended Sunday School & meeting twice
Mon 29	took logs to mill and got my grist Paid five dollers to —Sanderson
Tues 30	hauling adobies to the fort
Wed 31	Do Do[5]

As one reads these and thousands of other similar notations made by Brother Bennion, a pattern of life emerges that is probably quite characteristic of the ordinary people of those times and yet is very inspiring to the modern mind. There is the relentlessness of daily labor, the concern for and closeness of family, the quest for education, and the welcome respite provided by the Sabbath and other prescribed rituals of worship. There is also a sense of making life as convenient and comfortable and happy as circumstances will permit. Permeating all these entries appears to be a conviction that what was being done is in accordance with divine will. There is also a quiet confidence that whatever one's particular role is in the Lord's grand design, regardless of whether that role is large or small, it has significance and value.

John Bennion was a common man, and yet his constancy in the mundane labors of life certainly prepared him well for eternity. It also gives lasting credibility to the dying declaration he made to his wife Mary Turpin Bennion: "All I have to say to my family is, do as I have told you, *all the day long.*"[6]

PATTY BARTLETT SESSIONS

I have chosen to help us see women's lives during those early years in the Salt Lake Valley through the eyes of Patty Bartlett Sessions. Sessions kept a daily record for forty-two years, commencing in 1846.

From other sources, we learn of her early life in Maine, her baptism in 1834, and her migration with her family to Far West, Missouri, in 1837. In succession, Sessions and her family were then forced to flee from Far West to Nauvoo, from Nauvoo to Winter Quarters, and then to the valley of the Great Salt Lake in the Big Company of 1847: "Go 14 miles . . . got into the valley it is a beautiful place my heart flows with gratitude to God that we have got home all safe lost nothing have been blessed with life and health I rejoice all the time."[7] She was then fifty-two years old.

The record of her daily rituals over those forty-two years reveals a common, but very fascinating, woman. For instance, as with most of the early Saints who had been taken "one of a city and two of a family," Sessions always lamented the fact that her children David Junior and Sylvia had stayed behind in Iowa. On May 31, 1846, Sessions made this poignant entry: "When I think that Sylvia and David . . . is not coming tears fall from my eyes as fast as the drops of rain from skies for I can now give vent to my feelings by weeping O Lord comfort my poor wounded heart."[8]

Sessions's first husband, David, died in 1850. When John Parry, a Welshman whose wife had died crossing the plains, started to court her, a spirit of optimism began to creep into her writing. On December 9, 1851, she wrote that chopping wood "is very hard."[9] By December 14, 1851, she had married Mr. Parry and with refreshing honesty recorded, "I was married to John Parry and I feel to thank the Lord that I have some one to cut my wood for me."[10] Now there's a love story with which the soap operas would struggle.

The range of Sessions's activities and her versatility over the years covered by her journals are amazing. As a midwife, she delivered hundreds of babies. She was an efficient businesswoman, who, besides her midwifery, established a profitable venture selling seeds and seedlings. She was frugal, yet she willingly tithed to the Lord.

During her later years, she founded the Patty Sessions Academy in Bountiful and provided schooling for her grandchildren and other children whose parents could not afford to pay school expenses. She was also active in community affairs, helping start the Council of Health in 1848 and presiding over a society established in 1854 to help clothe the Native Americans. This group evolved into a formal Relief Society. As lofty as all of these activities sound, such involvements occupy only a small portion of her journals. Far more prominent are

Courtesy LDS Church Archives

Patty Bartlett Sessions: midwife, businesswoman, philanthropist—a "common" Saint.

the references to washing, ironing, and housework. She seems to have forever been cooking, spinning, weaving, knitting, crocheting, and sewing for herself and others. She was also frequently busy planting, harvesting, and preserving.

Unwittingly, perhaps, Sessions even wrote her own epitaph. The editor of Sessions's journals, Donna Toland Smart, to whose research I owe my knowledge of Sessions and much of what I have shared, has written that a single, tattered scrap of webbing was found pressed between pages of an 1842 medical book Sessions owned. Cross-stitched thereon in bold red letters and decorated with forest-green squiggles are two simple words: "Remember me."[11] That we will.

A Unique Spirit

Reviewing journals like those of John Bennion and Patty Bartlett Sessions may prompt some to argue that, except for a few controversial issues during the latter part of the nineteenth century, the history of Utah and her peoples is just the same as that of every other state. I beg to differ. I believe the Utah pioneers, the common Saints of those times, possessed a unique and overriding spirit of consecration and allegiance to a cause and to the inspired leaders of that cause. That spirit sustained them through unbelievable hardships and motivated them to lay their time, their talents, and everything else they had on Zion's altar. I think this spirit is unique in the annals of U.S. history.

Charles Lowell Walker

A case in point is Charles Lowell Walker. Born in 1832 in England, he converted to Mormonism as a teenager and immigrated to St. Louis, Missouri, in 1849. He came to Salt Lake City in 1855 and established

The Patty Sessions Academy. Established in Bountiful, the academy provided tuition-free schooling for Patty's grandchildren and for children who would not have had an education otherwise.

a home and began to prosper. He married in the fall of 1861. At the age of thirty, having lived in Utah for seven years, Brother Walker experienced a most interesting Sabbath on the nineteenth of October 1862. His diary entry for the day reads:

> [It was a] Pleasant [day]. Went up to the Bowery. Brother D[aniel] Spencer and H[eber] C Kimball gave us some good exhortations pertaining to our duties. At the close of the meeting 250 men were called to go to the Cotton Country [in southwestern Utah]. My name is on the List . . . and was read off the Stand. At night I went to a meeting . . . of those that had been called. Here I learn'd a principle that I shant forget in a while. It showed to me that obedeance was a great principle in Heaven and on earth. Well[,] here I have worked for the last 7 years thro heat and cold, hunger and adverse circumstances, and at last have got me a home, a Lot with fruit trees just beginning to bear [which] look pretty. Well[,] I must leave it and go and do the will of My Father in Heaven who over rules all for the good of them that love and fear him, and I pray God to give me Strength to accomplish that which is required of me in an acceptable manner before him.[12]

For the next three weeks, Charles Walker and his wife prepared to move south. They received no special subsidy to give up their home or to supplement their move to what later came to be called Dixie. On November 11, Walker wrote, "I have to sell a great many things almost for nothing as I cannot haul them and many take the advantage of my circumstances in putting their price on my articles . . . but I am bound to go by the help of the Lord."[13] The next day, he wrote, "The house looks desolate. The things all sold."[14] The following day was the day of departure. On November 13, 1862, he wrote:

> I left my home, friends, relatives, and acquaintances and started out to perform my Mission. Many came and wished me good bye with tears in their eyes and blessed me, wished me well and were sorry I was going to leave as I had lived amongst them and with them for over 7 years. This was the hardes[t] trial I ever had and had it not been for the gospel and those that were placed over me I should never [have] moved a foot to go on such a trip, but I came here not to do my own will but the will of those that are over me, and I know it will all be right if I do right.[15]

Two and a half weeks later, on December 9, 1862, he arrived at his destination. Creating images that today's St. George Chamber of Commerce would consider defamatory, he wrote:

> St. George is a barren looking place. The soil is red and sandy. On the north ranges a long[,] high[,] red rocky bluff. On the East is a long

Courtesy LDS Church Archives

George A. Smith, for whom St. George, Utah, was named.

black ridge of volcanic production. On the west the same. On the south runs the Virgen river, a shallow, rapid stream from which a great portion of the land is irrigated. To look on the country, it [is a] dry, parched, barren waste[,] with here and there a green spot on the margin of the streams. [It is] very windy, dusty, blowing nearly all the time. The water is not good, and far from being palatable. And this is the country we have to live in and make it blossom as the Rose. Well[,] it[']s all right; we shall know how to appreciate a good country when we get to it, when the Lord has prepared the way for his People to return and build up the waste places of Zion.[16]

It was a difficult life. There is almost no way for us today truly to appreciate what it meant to be a prisoner in that time and place. On the Fourth of July 1869, Brother Walker wrote:

I think without exception this is the dullest Fourth I ever saw. Bread is scarce and meat and butter are out of the question, and it seems as tho in working and contriving to get a morsel to eat[,] it taxes our energies to the uttermost. Times are very dull and nothing much doing except slaving on the ditches and dams.[17]

Walker was a desert poet and, despite great adversity, retained an admirable sense of humor. In 1873 he sang this lighthearted song to Elder George A. Smith, who was visiting the Saints in the town that was his namesake. The song describes the sense of accomplishment the Saints felt in pioneering Dixie:

Oh[,] what a desert place was this
When first the Mormons found it.
They said no white man here could live
And Indians prowled around it.

Twas said the land[,] it was no good,
And the water was no gudder,
And the bare Idea of living here
Was enough to make one shudder.

Now green Lucern in verdant spots,
Bedecks our thriving City.
Whilst vine and fruit trees grace our lots
And floweretts sweet and pretty,
Where once the grass in single blades
Grew a mile apart in distance.
And it kept the crickets on the go
To pick up their subsistence.

The Sun it is so scorching hot
It makes the water siz, sir.
And the reason why it is so hot,
'Tis just because it is, sir.
The [wind] like fury here does blow
That when we plant or sow, sir,
We place one foot upon the seed
And hold it till it grows, sir.[18]

Between each verse, Walker sang the following chorus, which contains a prophetic promise that just might redeem him for public relations purposes:

Muskeet, soap root,
Prickly pears, and briars.
St. George ere long will be a place
That every one admires.[19]

While indeed the tangible work of the St. George pioneers was admired, another kind of compensation awaited those who faithfully consecrated their all to the Lord's cause. After a number of years struggling in the valley of the Virgin River, Brother Walker wrote his feelings in inspired verse regarding the rewards in store for the faithful:

Dearest children, God is near you,
Watching o'er you day and night,
And delights to own and bless you,
If you strive to do what's right.
He will bless you, He will bless you,
If you put your trust in Him.

This, of course, is hymn number ninety-six in our hymnbook. It portrays in words what Brother Walker's life portrayed in deeds.

Courtesy LDS Church Archives

St. George, Utah. Charles Walker, who lived there from 1862 to 1904, described it upon his arrival as a "dry, parched barren waste." Photograph by C. R. Savage.

Charles Lowell Walker lived in St. George until his passing in 1904. Along with many others called to the cotton mission in St. George, he eventually progressed and prospered. But others in nineteenth-century Utah were called to offer enormous expenditures of time, human toil, and suffering in the sugar, iron, and lead missions, which were all essentially economic failures. In our modern vernacular, most of those wonderfully common folk simply hung in there.

WARREN MARSHALL JOHNSON

Another story illustrating how uncommonly heroic the common Saints often were is the account of Warren Marshall Johnson. Brother Johnson was born in 1838 in New Hampshire. He was raised a

Methodist and received enough education that he was sought as a schoolteacher in later life. In 1866 he left Boston with a couple of adventurous friends who wanted to find their pot of gold in California. Johnson, who was slight of build and somewhat sickly, decided the change of scenery might be good for his health, and he joined his friends for their overland venture. Following the Oregon Trail, they got to Idaho, where Johnson's health broke. His illness was so serious that he sought the closest medical help—which was in Utah. He found himself under the care of Dr. Jonathan Smith in Farmington, Utah. As he convalesced at Dr. Smith's home, he discovered that Mormons were not so odd after all and began to investigate the gospel. Not only did he acquire a testimony of the gospel, but he also found love in his relationship with Dr. Smith's daughter Permelia. That fall of 1866, Johnson became a Latter-day Saint.

The following year, he was ordained an elder and called to serve in the Muddy Mission, which was centered in what was thought to be southern Utah but is now southern Nevada. The environment there is more sterile and inhospitable than that of St. George. Two years after taming the reluctant land enough to have prospects of a future, Johnson left St. Thomas, which is now under Lake Mead, and returned to Farmington, where he married Permelia Smith in 1869. She returned with him to St. Thomas, where he taught school. Two years later, after a government survey had indicated that the Muddy settlements were in Nevada, the enterprise was abandoned. Johnson and his wife, with many of the other Muddy settlers, moved to Long Valley, Utah, to the community that was to be called Glendale, near Bryce Canyon. Here he married a second wife, Samantha Nelson.[20]

In the same year that Warren Johnson moved to Glendale, John D. Lee moved to the mouth of the Paria River, where he established the Church-owned ferry at the base of the deep canyon walls of the Colorado River. The ferry was to be the main point of transit between Utah and the Arizona Mormon settlements. When John D. Lee left the area, his replacement could not handle the rugged environment and died of exposure, leaving no one to run the ferry.[21]

At that time, Warren Johnson was a counselor to the bishop of the ward in Long Valley, as well as a schoolteacher in Glendale. His bishop asked Johnson to move to the ferry and temporarily man the operation until a permanent ferryman could be employed. The thirty-seven-year-old Johnson apparently readily accepted. He took his first wife, Permelia, and their first child to the ferry site in March 1875. It was bleak. Lee's Ferry was one of the most remote outposts of the system of Mormon towns and villages. The major settlements along the Little Colorado River in Arizona would not flourish for another decade, meaning river clients were not plentiful. Lee's wife had named their log-home site Lonely Dell. And indeed it was lonely. When the Johnsons arrived, the domicile that awaited them was the empty cabin of his deceased predecessor, whose coffin had been made with the front door and the only table in the dwelling. Not much else greeted them, but they made do.

The frail schoolteacher became a ferryman, farmer, stockman, and, later, postmaster. The year after moving to Lonely Dell, Johnson brought his second wife and their four-day-old son from Glendale to the Colorado River. His "temporary" assignment became a mission lasting twenty-one years.

Sixteen years after moving to Lee's Ferry, Warren Johnson wrote a letter to President Wilford Woodruff that describes his personal sacrifice and tragedy:

Lee's Ferry Ariz July 29/1891

President Wilford Woodruff

Dear Brother

It has occurred to me that you ought to know how affairs are going at this place, which is my excuse for intruding on your time, which I know is fully occupied with other affairs.

Last spring I divided my family, according to your counsel, a portion of them moving to Kanab for the purpose of schooling my children. In May 1891 a family residing at Tuba City, [Arizona] came here from Richfield, Utah, where they had spent the winter visiting friends. At Panguitch they buried a child, and without disinfecting the wagon or themselves, not even stopping to wash the dead child's clothes, they came to our house, and remained over night, mingling with my little children, and the consequence was [that] in 4 days my oldest boy and my first wife, was taken violently ill with a fever and sore throat.

We knew nothing of the nature of the disease [which was likely diphtheria—an upper-respiratory disease that affects the throat and lungs and can attack the heart muscle], but had faith in God, as we are here on a very hard mission, and had tried as hard as we knew how to obey the word of Wisdom, and attend to the other duties of our religion, such as paying tything, family prayer &c &c, that our children would be spared. But alass, in 4½ days he choked

Courtesy LDS Church Archives

Wilford Woodruff, to whom Warren Johnson confided his family's trials with illness and death.

to death in my arms. Two more were taken down with the disease and we fasted and prayed as much as we thought it wisdom[,] as we had many duties to perform here. We fasted some 24 hours[,] and once I fasted 40 hours, but all of no avail for both my little girls died also. About a week after their death my fifteen year old daughter Melinda was stricken down and we did all we could for her but she followed the others, and three of my dear girls and one boy has been taken from us, and the end is not yet. My oldest girl 19 years old is now prostrate with the disease, and we are fasting and praying in her behalf today. We have become better acquainted with the nature of the disease, than at first, and we are strongly in hopes she will recover, as two already have, that came down with it. I would ask for your faith and prayers in our behalf[,] however. What have we done that the Lord has left us, and what can we do to gain his favor again[?]

> Yours in the gospel
> Warren M Johnson[22]

"What have we done that the Lord has left us, and what can we do to gain his favor again?" The pathos of Johnson's plea rings in the mind and heart of anyone who has ever suffered personal tragedy. This ordeal caused Johnson's family to vacillate between hope and despair week after week during the summer of 1891. Johnson's touching letter to his friend Warren Foote the month after his letter to President Woodruff portrays Johnson's commitment to God and the scope of one man's experience with severe trials. I believe this letter is one of the finest pieces of religious literature we have in the Church, and I quote it with a feeling of reverence for Johnson and his family.

Lee's Ferry, Arizona
Aug 16, 1891

Warren Foote

Dear Brother,

Your kind and welcome letter [of June 25, 1891] was received a long time ago. I was surprised at receiving it for I had no idea that any of my friends would take the trouble to write during my affliction. Rest assured that I shall ever feel grateful to you for the words of comfort your letter conveyed to us. It seemed almost as though God had forsaken us, and that he had turned a deaf ear to our fasting and prayers and anointing and administering the ordinances of the gospel to the sick, for it was all of no avail, and four of my dear children are now lying in their graves. It is a fearful blow for us, for you know that ever since I heard the gospel, I have tried as much as the average of our brethren to live up to the principals thereof. I have tried to pay my tithing, obey the Word of Wisdom, attend to the family devotions, and teach my children correct principles; and God promised if we would do so the destroyer should pass by us. There are unseen influences around us that are trying to cause me to lose faith in God and to make me feel that there is no use to continue to pray, for He will not hear my prayers, that there is no use for me longer to obey the Word of Wisdom, or anoint with oil and lay on hands to rebuke disease, for the promise that when we do so, they will recover, does not apply to us. When I look around and see others that do not pay tithing, attending meetings only once in a while, and do not have family prayers, and they are blessed in their families in health and a plenty of this worlds goods to allow them to live at ease; it is hard indeed for me to see the hand of God in the death of my children and especially after obeying the call of the Priesthood in coming out here and for 16 yrs., having one of the hardest missions that was ever the lot of a member of this church to perform. You can imagine how I feel, as you know how I have tried to live, and the implicit faith I had in the gospel and the promises of God to those who have tried to be faithful.

However, I do not [always] feel that way[,] only at times, for there are other spirits or influences around us that say to me, that God is the Father of the spirits of my children, and that He loves them as well as I do, and that he knows definately better than I do what is best for them and us. God has said that "He would have a tried people in the last days," and those who desire to do right will have to pass through greater trials than those who are not trying to reach the highest glory. Brother Foote, I feel well when I look at it in the above light and especially when I think of the influences we have felt when my children died. It did not seem like death, and even when they were breathing their last, we could not feel bad, there was such a heavenly influence in the room. And also the looks of the children after death, almost a smile on their lips, I never saw anyone look as beautiful as they did after death. Joseph Stewart was here when Minda died and several times he remarked, "She's as pretty as a doll." I know they are happy now, and I hope I shall not give way to the spirits of evil, but that I may live so that bye and bye I can go and dwell with them. I can assure you, however, that it is the hardest trials of my life, but I set out for salvation and am determined that it is through the help of my Heavenly Father that I hold fast to the iron rod, no matter what troubles come upon me I have not yet slackened in the performance of any of my duties, and hope and trust that I shall have the faith and prayers of my brethren, that I may live so as to receive the blessings, you having authority, have placed on my head. I often think how much better off I am today, than when I lived on the Muddy with no one but myself to look after, and I feel to thank God for all this.

May God bless you, Brother Foote in all your labors.

Yours in the Gospel
Warren M. Johnson[23]

Warren Marshall Johnson's faith endured. Subsequent events in his life further demonstrate his commitment to the kingdom. In 1895, four years after the death of his children, Johnson with the Kanab Stake president was inspecting land in Fredonia, Arizona, as a potential homesite for Johnson's family in preparation for his release from the ferry mission. Both were riding on the top of a stack of hay that shifted when the wagon lurched, throwing them to the ground. The stake president landed on his feet, but Warren Johnson slammed into the ground at the base of his spine. While he did not realize the extent of the injury for some time, Warren Johnson was paralyzed from the waist down for the rest of his life.

One might think this good man would have applied for medical retirement. But not so. Almost inconceivably, four years after the accident, he decided to start over again—this time in the fledgling Mormon colonies in Alberta, Canada. Lying in the back of a wagon driven by his wife, he left the Arizona/Utah border and slowly bumped and rocked northward. The two stopped in Salt Lake City on their way, and after counseling with Church leaders, they changed their objective to the new Mormon settlements in the Big Horn Basin in north central Wyoming. The following year, the rest of their family left

Kanab and joined them. Johnson soon became the settlement's presiding elder as well as its postmaster. But the winter of 1901–2 was a severe one. His animals were nearly destroyed, and his health was broken. He died in the spring of 1902.

Virtue Is Not Hereditary

One could cite anecdote upon interesting anecdote to support the proposition that the common Saints of pioneer times were in truth very often quite uncommon people. Even as we are thrilled and hopefully motivated by the majesty of their lives and eagerly press into our family history centers to confirm our relationships to them, it behooves us to remember "those of the last wagon" and President Clark's eloquent reminder that virtue is not hereditary. Fifty years ago, he stated it this way:

> In living our lives let us never forget that the deeds of our fathers and mothers are theirs, not ours; that their works cannot be counted to our glory; that we can claim no excellence and no place, because of what they did, that we must rise by our own labor, and that labor failing we shall fail. We may claim no honor, no reward, no respect, nor special position or recognition, no credit because of what our fathers were or what they wrought. We stand upon our own feet in our own shoes. There is no aristocracy of birth in this Church; it belongs equally to the highest and the lowliest.[24]

The Value of Pioneer History

One might profitably ask what purpose Church history is to serve, particularly for a people consciously striving to become like him with whom, as Moses records, "all things are present" (Moses 1:6). And yet the Lord wasted no time in informing the newly ordained Prophet Joseph that "there shall be a record kept" (D&C 21:1) and later declared to the Kirtland Saints that they should "obtain a knowledge of history" and "this for the salvation of Zion" (D&C 93:53).

Perhaps we can never completely know of things as they are and as they are to come unless we also know them as they were (D&C 93:24). Thus, with a deeper appreciation of the common Saints in times past, those of us who are the common Saints of this generation will be encouraged and motivated to "act well our parts."[25]

Certainly times have changed, and our challenges are vastly different from those of our nineteenth-century counterparts. Where once

Swedish converts, Johan Johnasson Broberg (1830–1918) and Eva Catherine Andersson Broberg (1837–1907), lived out their "common" lives in a Mormon settlement in Cache Valley, Utah. This photograph was taken around 1900.

the pioneers hungered for contact and correspondence, we now wish there were a way to escape the relentless reach of email. Where once finding a morsel to eat taxed their energies "to the uttermost," we now struggle in a surfeited world to stay even remotely close to our recommended body weight. Where once considerations of nature and the economy tended to drive the Saints together and unite them, our relative independence in such matters has produced centrifugal forces in our lives that threaten the sociality of the Saints.

Nevertheless, the basic bottom line of our religious life remains the same: whether to choose good over evil and whether to follow God's plan or reject it. In this respect, my personal experience is that the common Saints of the present day are doing very well. Three short illustrations will support my contention.

Modern-Day Common Saints

The first illustration is drawn from an experience I recently had attending a stake conference in the East. During the Saturday evening session, a tall and graceful young mother spoke on her family's attempts (with six children ranging from a sixteen-year-old to five-year-old twins) to hold meaningful family home evenings. Her talk was engaging and helpful, but even more intriguing was the reaction of her husband, whom I easily picked out in the congregation because of his obvious adoration for his attractive wife. When my turn to speak came, I mentioned that I felt she had a husband who "only had eyes for her" and commented on what a blessing that was. A few days later, a six-page, single-spaced letter came to me from that grateful husband, telling me just why his eyes were so single to his wife's glory.

What unfolded is a classic pioneer story set in modern times. A story of two BYU athletes—he an outstanding football player and she a basketball star—falling in love, marrying in the temple, and then embarking on an odyssey that rivals anything the nineteenth century produced. The tale involves leaving family, living in foreign countries and contending with foreign languages, filling demanding Church callings, and enduring long distances, difficult births, seriously ill children, the death of loved ones, and the adoption of a deceased sister's children. I will let the adoring husband speak briefly for himself:

> You noted that I only have eyes for my wife. How could I not? She teaches me each day by her example of love and devotion to that which is right, and by her willingness to serve. She has accepted every Church assignment ever presented to her. She left her home and family to live with me, moved all over the world, brought six special spirits into this world and is raising them right, made every house we have lived in into a real home, taught the gospel with the love and compassion that only a woman and mother can, and never complained that life is too hard, or that we live too far away. She holds the family record for coaching undefeated basketball teams for my sons, she having three blemish free seasons and me never even getting to the championships with the team I coached when she was too pregnant to do so. I have known the humility of having my oldest son ask that Mom coach his team rather than Dad! On warm afternoons I come home to find her working with my kids on their basketball skills in the driveway. She then gets up every morning at 5 AM to cook a warm breakfast and fix fresh lunches for my older boys before they go off for their early morning Seminary.[26]

The second experience occurred while my family and I served between 1993 and 1995 in the New York Rochester Mission of the Church. During that time, we once received from the Membership

Department a separate information sheet on each of five thousand "lost members" of the Church whose last known addresses were within the boundaries of our mission in New York. We were to distribute the sheets to the appropriate areas, and the missionaries would visit the last known addresses of each of the lost members. The program called for the missionaries to knock at each of five thousand doors, inquire regarding the current whereabouts of the lost members, express interest in their welfare, and also ask whether the person answering the door had ever heard of the Church. It was a great way to locate lost members (of which there are far too many) and also to find interested people to teach. However, before I distributed the five thousand sheets, I felt I needed some way to establish accountability with the missionaries, so I called the Membership Department in Salt Lake City to ask if they could print a master list. The sister with whom I spoke was very obliging and told me she would send a list that very day.

Then she surprised me by saying, "By the way, I know who you are." I asked how so. "Because," she said, "when you moved to Rochester, I sent your family's membership records to the Brighton Ward."

"Well," I asked, "why would you remember our family?" "Because," she answered, "Roger Jenkins called our department to see if we had promptly sent your records on to New York."

"Do you know Roger Jenkins?" I asked. "Do I know Roger Jenkins," she replied. "Everyone here in the Membership Department knows Brother Jenkins!"

Then she said something I shall never forget, even if I live a million years. "If every ward membership clerk in the Church were like Brother Jenkins, we would have no lost members."

Oh, how my heart burned within me at that moment. How I wished for the integrity and concern for the welfare of souls that the humble (call him "common" if you wish) membership clerk of my home ward possesses. I hope in the hereafter to flutter up to wherever Brother Jenkins will be and occasionally shine his shoes.

Finally, I recently completed and sent to Brigham Young University a letter of recommendation for one of the missionaries with whom we served in New York. He was seeking admission for spring semester. Before writing my recommendation, I read the brief instructions at the top of "Form E," which directed that "to help us distinguish between exceptional applicants, please provide specific examples that differentiate this student from others."

Immediately, I knew I was in trouble. The wonderful young elder who had asked me to recommend him was not "exceptional," and I was not sure he could be "differentiated" from other students in any significant way. In short, it occurred to me that he was just a common Saint of these latter days, a fairly average young man diligently living the gospel and preparing for life. And yet, I wanted in every honest way I could to boost his chances for admission. I gave it my best effort by writing something like this:

> To Whom it May Concern:
>
> I wish I could report that this wonderful young man were "exceptional" and list all the reasons why. But the fact is, he is probably just about average in grades, intelligence, and performance. However, this much I can say—I have six daughters and I am convinced that if he married any one of them (which I would welcome) she would never go hungry; she would usually be happy; and she would most likely, under his guidance, end up living eternally with her Father in Heaven and her husband and family. Quite honestly, it is on the backs of men and women like him that the Lord from the beginning has built his kingdom. Please make room at BYU for a "common" Saint!

I have not yet heard whether my unorthodox approach did more good than harm.

The Apostle Paul may have had the "common Saint" in mind when he wrote the Corinthians and compared the Church and its various officers or parts to the human body:

> But now hath God set the members every one of them in the body, as it hath pleased him.
>
> And if they were all one member, where were the body?
>
> But now are they many members, yet but one body.
>
> And the eye cannot say unto the hand, I have no need of thee: nor again the head to the feet, I have no need of you.
>
> Nay, much more those members of the body, which seem to be more feeble, are necessary:
>
> And those [members] of the body, which we think to be less honourable, upon these we bestow more abundant honour; and our uncomely parts have more abundant comeliness. (1 Cor. 12:18–23)

I am convinced that upon those common Saints of all ages who "think they are less honorable" God will eventually "bestow more abundant honor." God will always need and have a few "noble and great ones" (D&C 138:55), but he will also always need the common Saints to follow them and to "go and do" (1 Ne. 3:7). Both are equally important and necessary in bringing to pass his eternal purposes.

I pray that whatever our part, we will do it well and to His glory. In the name of Jesus Christ, Amen.

Marlin K. Jensen is a member of the First Quorum of the Seventy of The Church of Jesus Christ of Latter-day Saints. The author acknowledges the assistance of the Church Historical Department staff, particularly Ronald O. Barney and William W. Slaughter of the Archives Division.

NOTES

1. J. Reuben Clark Jr., "They of the Last Wagon," *Improvement Era* 50 (November 1947): 704–5, 747–48. Reprinted as "To Them of the Last Wagon," *Ensign* 27 (July 1997): 34–39.

2. Clark, "Last Wagon," 704.

3. Dale L. Morgan, *The Great Salt Lake* (Albuquerque: University of New Mexico Press, 1973), 325.

4. Joseph F. Smith, "Common-Place Things," *Juvenile Instructor* 40 (December 15, 1905): 752.

5. [Mildred Bennion Eyring, comp.], *Bennion Family History,* 5 vols. [Salt Lake City: Bennion Family Association, 1931–68], 3:2–3, Archives Division, Historical Department, The Church of Jesus Christ of Latter-day Saints, Salt Lake City (hereafter cited as LDS Church Archives).

6. *Bennion Family History,* 4:468; italics added.

7. Donna Toland Smart, "Patty Bartlett Sessions, Pioneer Midwife," in *Worth Their Salt: Notable but Often Unnoted Women of Utah,* ed. Colleen Whitley (Logan: Utah State University Press, 1996), 4. I express appreciation to Donna Toland Smart, to whose research I owe my knowledge of Patty Bartlett Sessions. She has edited and published *Mormon Midwife: The 1846–1888 Diaries of Patty Sessions* (Logan: Utah State University Press, 1997).

8. Smart, "Patty Bartlett Sessions," 5.

9. Smart, "Patty Bartlett Sessions," 7.

10. Smart, "Patty Bartlett Sessions," 7.

11. Smart, "Patty Bartlett Sessions," 12.

12. Charles Lowell Walker, *Diary of Charles Lowell Walker,* ed. Karl Larson and Katharine Miles Larson, 2 vols. (Logan: Utah State University Press, 1980), 1:239.

13. Walker, *Diary,* 1:240.

14. Walker, *Diary,* 1:240.

15. Walker, *Diary,* 1:240.

16. Walker, *Diary,* 1:241.

17. Walker, *Diary,* 1:294.

18. Walker, *Diary,* 1:369, 370.

19. Walker, *Diary,* 1:369.

20. P. T. Reilly, "Warren Marshall Johnson, Forgotten Saint," *Utah Historical Quarterly* 39 (winter 1971): 6.

21. Reilly, "Warren Marshall Johnson," 7.

22. Reilly, "Warren Marshall Johnson," 19.

23. "Warren Marshall Johnson: Father."

24. Clark, "Last Wagon," 748.

25. The inscription "What-E'er Thou Art, Act Well Thy Part" inspired Elder David O. McKay on his mission. James B. Allen, "McKay, David O.," in *Encyclopedia of Mormonism,* ed. Daniel H. Ludlow, 4 vols. (New York: Macmillan, 1992), 2:871.

26. [Name withheld] to author, February 26, 1997.

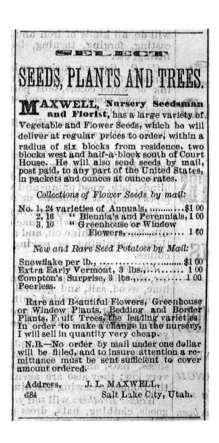

Was Joseph Smith a Gentleman?
The Standard for Refinement in Utah

Richard Lyman Bushman

Frances Trollope, mother of the novelist Anthony Trollope, came to America in 1827 with her husband, a failed barrister and farmer, to open a fancy-goods shop in Cincinnati. While her husband kept shop, Frances traveled about the country, observing the American scene. After still another business failure, the Trollopes returned to England, and in 1836 Frances Trollope published *The Domestic Manners of the Americans.* Although it was an immediate hit in England and was subsequently translated into French and Spanish, the book infuriated readers in the United States. Everywhere Mrs. Trollope looked, she had found vulgarity, which she depicted in broad, humorous strokes. On the steamboat that carried the Trollopes up the Mississippi from New Orleans, the respectable passengers dined together in what was called "the gentleman's cabin," a compartment "handsomely fitted up, and the latter well carpeted," she said, "but oh! that carpet! I will not, I may not describe its condition. . . . I hardly know any annoyance so deeply repugnant to English feelings, as the incessant, remorseless spitting of Americans." Her feelings were equally riled by the table manners of the so-called gentlemen, who included among their number a judge and men with the titles of general, colonel, and major.

> The total want of all the usual courtesies of the table, the voracious rapidity with which the viands were seized and devoured, the strange uncouth phrases and pronunciation; the loathsome spitting, from the contamination of which it was absolutely impossible to protect our dresses; the frightful manner of feeding with their knives, till the whole blade seemed to enter into the mouth; and the still more frightful manner of cleaning the teeth afterwards with a pocket knife, soon forced us to feel that . . . the dinner hour was to be any thing rather than an hour of enjoyment.

Ordinary people appeared still more degraded to her eyes: "All the little towns and villages" seen from the deck of the steamboat were "wretched-looking in the extreme. . . . I never witnessed human nature reduced so low, as it appeared in the wood-cutters' huts on the unwholesome banks of the Mississippi." She was surprised to find that the mayor of Memphis was "a pleasing gentleman-like man"; to her he seemed "strangely misplaced in a little town on the Mississippi."[1]

Trollope wrote with an ideological grudge. She candidly announced in the preface that in describing "the daily aspect of ordinary life, she has endeavoured to shew how greatly the advantage is on the side of those who are governed by the few, instead of the many." In other words, aristocratic England had it all over democratic America. She wanted her countrymen to see "the jarring tumult and universal degradation which invariably follow the wild scheme of placing all the power of the state in the hands of the populace."[2] But if ideology gave a special edge to her writing, her standard for measuring democratic degradation was by no means unique. Travelers from France and Spain, from New England, Philadelphia, and New York—virtually everyone who ventured into the western portions of the country—asked Trollope's question: how civilized were the inhabitants of the new regions? Though the answers varied, the question was the same. Where did the manners of the people put them on the scale of civilization? Were they ladies and gentlemen or barbarians?

The West came under particular scrutiny because of the common belief that civilization fell away as one ventured farther into the wilderness, the home of the savage tribes. Easterners feared that civilized manners were stripped from migrants to the unsettled frontier, reducing them slowly but surely to barbarism. In other words, history reversed itself as people migrated west; they returned to the primitive condition of humanity before civilization had developed. Horace Bushnell, the illustrious Congregational preacher and theologian in Hartford, Connecticut, delivered a despairing sermon on the West entitled "Barbarism the First Danger."[3]

Sermons like Bushnell's made clear that the measurement of civilization in the West was of more than academic interest. In a democratic nation where power is in the hands of the populace, the western states were in danger of coming under the control of barbarians who would not only govern their own regions but send representatives to the Congress of the United States. Reports that guests at Andrew Jackson's 1829 inaugural stood in muddy boots on damask chairs and generally trashed the White House sent terror through the civilized East. Jackson seemed to head the vanguard of western barbarians taking power in the nation's capital. Josiah Quincy, the Bostonian who later visited Nauvoo, said of General Jackson's administration that it "swept away much of the graceful etiquette which was characteristic of the society as I saw it." In the face of the onslaught, "social barriers" were demolished "by the unrefined and coarse."[4]

The question of refinement cut even more deeply in Utah in the early days when the governance of the territory was at issue. The Latter-day Saints worked with a double handicap in striving to win respect from eastern travelers: in addition to the usual doubts about civilization in the West, the visitors were skeptical about Mormon religious fanaticism. Travelers came expecting that the poor credulous fools who submitted to the rule of Brigham Young would lack education, manners, taste, and intelligence—in short, would be as degraded as the woodcutters Trollope sighted along the banks of the Mississippi. The Saints for their part had a lot at stake in proving the travelers wrong. If they could not persuade visitors of their religious beliefs, the Mormons at least wanted to demonstrate their refinement. Besides respect from eastern cultural centers, control over their government hung in the balance. William Warner Major's fanciful portrait of Brigham Young sitting amid columns and elegant furnishings, every inch the polished gentleman, epitomized the campaign to demonstrate Mormon refinement (fig. 1).

This cultural struggle affected the way early Utahns presented themselves to the world and the way history has been written ever since. From the mid–nineteenth century on, Mormons in telling their story have emphasized cultural respectability. The history of "refinement in the wilderness," as this narrative might be called, has appeared in formal histories and been elaborated in Mormon folktales. The history succeeds because it does rest on a factual base. Like the "suffering pioneer" narrative of Utah history, real stories can be told in support of this point of view. We have accounts of pioneers eating crickets and of water dripping from sod roofs to prove the pioneers really did suffer. We also have records of barrels of fine china being carried across the plains to show that the Mormon settlers brought civilization to barren Utah. The Daughters of Utah Pioneers museum is an impressive monument to this history—the story of a refined and enlightened people driven to the West, where they reestablished civilization in the desert.

Although the story of Utah refinement is myth in the good sense of being an overarching story that grew from people's view of the world as well as from the reality of their lives, it is a myth with truth to it. My own grandmother, largely a twentieth-century person to be sure, started life sewing overalls in a ZCMI factory, and yet on her husband's salary as a shoe salesman, she turned her house on the lower avenues in Salt Lake City into a tiny palace of taste and homemade beauty. She not only believed the civilization-in-the-wilderness myth, she lived by it, changing the material conditions of her life to conform to the story.

This mingling of myth and reality means that historians should not disregard these traditional narratives and try to replace them with their own versions of the "truth" based on supposedly hardheaded research. We do not want to demolish a narrative that has proven so fruitful, but rather to test its limitations and develop its analytical power. We can usefully ask, for example, how civilization-in-the-wilderness history accounts for the large portion of the population that did not live by this myth so far as we can see. George Anderson's photos, while documenting much refinement, also inform us that gentility did not prevail everywhere in Utah, even by the 1890s. People lived in shacks as well as mansions, and we can imagine that still more shabbily dressed people lived in crude cabins in rough and tough areas of the state where Anderson never ventured.

In the unadulterated refinement-in-the-wilderness narrative, these rough Utahns are often looked on as unfinished Latter-day Saints on whom the gospel had not yet worked its refining influence. In time, the uplifting spirit of the Mormon religion, plus a little prosperity, would civilize crude farmers and turn their cabins into comfortable and refined houses. Refinement, in other words, was thought to be the natural destiny of good Mormons, an integral part of Latter-day Saint culture. Besides entering into Utah through middle-class American culture, refinement came to Utah through Mormon religious beliefs. In this view, "everything virtuous, lovely, or of good report, or praiseworthy" in the thirteenth article of faith must refer to good manners, decorated houses, well-kept gardens, and handsome clothes—the marks of refinement. The improvement of domestic manners and beautification of houses and yards was an aspect of personal salvation, as I think my grandmother surely believed, so that every good Mormon was on the way to becoming genteel.

If refinement was part of the religion, the foundations would have been laid down by Joseph Smith in Kirtland and Nauvoo, where Mormon culture was born. In those places, the fundaments for most of

Courtesy Museum of Church History and Art

FIG. 1. William Warner Major (1804–1854), *Brigham and Mary Ann Angell Young and Their Children* (1845–1851). Oil on board, 25" x 33". This painting elevates Brigham Young to the status of a refined country gentleman. The typical standard of refinement in Utah, however, was less opulent.

later Mormonism were constructed. The city plans of the early Mormon gathering places in the East, for example, were models for Salt Lake City and other Utah towns with their wide streets, square blocks, and town house lots for farmers. The precedents for genteel living should have been established at the same time. If refinement was basic, Joseph Smith would have spoken of it and what is more lived by it. Hence the relevance of the question: Was Joseph Smith a gentleman?

The modern depictions of Joseph Smith rarely show him as anything but a gentleman. With few exceptions, he appears in high collar with white stock and a dark suit (fig. 2); the only contemporaneous picture shows him in the uniform of a general. We can scarcely conceive of him otherwise, because if not a gentleman he would have been coarse, hardly a fitting character for a religious leader. The natural inclination today is to think that refinement and religion must intermingle. Living in a century when the American middle class has absorbed the standards of genteel culture, we have trouble imagining that gentility could ever be considered alien to true religion.

In the eighteenth century, however, before the middle class as we know it had come into existence, gentility was thought of as a sinful extravagance for the population as a whole, best left to the gentry and the European aristocracy. Benjamin Franklin felt guilty about replacing a plain earthenware bowl with chinaware for his breakfast bread and milk, and he chided plain workmen who tried to appear like gentlemen by living beyond their means.[5] Lorenzo Dow, the great evangelist after whom Brigham Young's brother was named, made fun of all genteel practices. Dancing schools came right out of Babylon, Dow said, and were actually little more than places "where people were taught 'the important art of hopping and jumping about.'" He condemned the promoters of "Polite Literature" in the form of romances and novels, which caused people to neglect the Bible. Peter Cartwright, a pioneer Methodist preacher in the first half of the nineteenth century, told of a fashionably dressed man who could not find forgiveness until "with his hands he deliberately opened his shirt bosom, took hold of his ruffles, tore them off, and threw them down in the straw; and in less than two minutes God blessed his soul."[6] Writing in his memoirs in 1856, Cartwright mourned how Methodist simplicity had been lost as the century had gone on. He loved the early days when Methodists "dressed plain; attended their meetings faithfully, especially preaching, prayer and class meetings; they wore no jewelry, no ruffles," and "parents did not allow their children to go to balls or plays; they did not send them to dancing-schools."[7] A good Methodist in other words was plain, not fancy, avoiding fashionable dress in the belief that gentility stood in the way of heartfelt religion.

Joseph Smith came out of that tradition. Before his visions set him on another course, he was "partial to the Methodist sect," at a time when plain living was still their way (JS—H 1:8). Emma was a Methodist, as were Brigham Young and many other early converts. They would have understood the passage in the revelation called "the law of the Church" that commanded the Saints to "let all thy garments be plain, and their beauty the beauty of the work of thine own hands" (D&C 42:40). Those words would have made sense to Joseph Smith, who did not grow up among genteel people. Not "well-bred" in the conventional sense of being reared as a gentleman, he was part of the mass of log-cabin people to whom the Whig politicians appealed in the log-cabin campaign of 1840. For the larger part of his boyhood, his parents, poor tenant farmers, resided among the lower ranks of the social order, the class of people that included Abraham Lincoln's family. The Smiths were dirt farmers, who worked with their hands at

FIG. 2. Pino Drago (1947–), *Monday, 24 June 1844, 4:15 A.M.: Beyond the Events*, 1987. Oil on canvas, 56" x 47". In this modern painting, Joseph is depicted as a refined gentleman in genteel surroundings.

a time when genteel culture belonged to white-collar workers who labored with their minds.

But the Smiths' lowly social position and Joseph's connection with the Methodists do not tell the whole story of his upbringing. Complicating this picture of a plain-folks family was the spread of middle-class gentility in the first decades of the nineteenth century, touching the lives of many farm people including Joseph Smith's mother. More attuned to cultural pressures than others in the family, Lucy Smith had social ambitions. Around 1819, when the Smiths finally got land of their own in Manchester after fourteen years of tenant farming, she hoped to find a place among the village middle class. Soon after they built their cabin, she happily accepted an invitation to take tea with "some wealthy merchants wives and the minister's lady." Her pleasure turned to chagrin, however, when one of the women innocently declared that "Mrs. [Smith] ought not to live in that log house of her's any longer she deserves a better fate." "Interpreting the comment as a slight," Lucy turned on the circle and excoriated the women for the failings of their husbands and children. Although the Smiths lived in a cabin, she wanted it known that they were the moral equals of anyone in town. As Lucy told the story, she came off the victor in this clash between moral values and gentility, and yet moral respectability was not enough for her. In the next entry, Lucy noted that "about this time we began to make preparations for building a house. The family hired a carpenter to construct a frame house with parlor and central hall," the classic design for middle-class genteel dwellings—even though the ensuing debt overwhelmed their resources and led to the loss of their farm.[8] Lucy wanted a genteel house badly enough to stretch their resources to the breaking point.

Besides his mother's influence in rearing him, Joseph also came under the influence of genteel culture through a few of the early converts. Sidney Rigdon, though afforded only a common school education while he grew up on his father's farm in Pennsylvania, consumed books voraciously while preparing to be a Baptist preacher and retained everything. As the minister of a "respectable" Pittsburgh congregation, he was exposed to middle-class, urban values, which he brought with him into the LDS Church.[9] Refinement was never a major theme of his preaching, but he did find a place for good manners and comely appearance. In an article called "The Saints and the World," published in the *Messenger and Advocate* in 1836, he outlined the work of building Zion and then posed a question: "Now let me ask the saints of the last days, what kind of people must you be, in order that you may accomplish so great a work?" How was Zion to "become the joy and the praise of the whole earth, so that kings shall come to the brightness of her rising?" The people of Zion needed to shine. "Surely, it will be by her becoming more wise, more learned, more refined, and more noble, than the cities of the world, so that she becomes the admiration of the great ones of the earth." Zion would attract attention "by the superiority of her literary institutions, and by a general effort of all the saints to patronize literature in our midst, so that the manners of the saints may be properly cultivated, and their habits correctly formed." Besides the people themselves, "her buildings will have to be more elegant, her palaces more splendid, and her public houses more magnificent." "Neither are we to leave out of the question," Rigdon went on, "the dress of the saints, for this supplies a place also in effecting this great object; the beauty and neatness of their dress is characteristic of the degree of refinement, and decency of a society. The nobles of the earth would not be likely to admire disgraceful apparel, untastefully arranged." Without all this, Zion could not become "the joy and praise of the whole earth."[10]

Although a strong endorsement for refinement, Rigdon's article fell short of making it an article of faith. He promoted correct manners, beautiful dress, and elegant buildings more as means to an end than as a basic value. His aim was to win the admiration and support of earthly powers, not to make the Saints over into ladies and gentlemen as a good in itself. In other moods, Mormon preachers could show their doubts about gentility. A *Times and Seasons* article in support of baptism by immersion expressed doubt about the willingness of refined people to get themselves wet all over. "Enlightened and refined society are not so vulgar as to go down into the water to be baptized. How ridiculously absurd it would be to lead one of the elite of the popular world, muffled in silks and satins, down into the dark waters of the great Mississippi."[11] Lorenzo Dow's and Peter Cartwright's skepticism about fashionable people echoes in those sentences. An old-style ambivalence about gentility is found in Mormonism along with Rigdon's enthusiasm. Refinement was at one moment a desirable polish to make the Saints shine in the world's eyes and at another a worldly pride that hindered acceptance of the gospel.

How did Joseph Smith navigate these crosscurrents in Mormon culture? The eyewitness depictions of the Prophet show him in many lights but not usually as a standard polished gentleman. Some come close. Emily Partridge Young, one of Joseph's wives, said, "He was all that the word *gentleman* would imply—pure in heart, always striving for right, upholding innocence, and battling for the good of all."[12] While attaching admirable qualities to the term "gentleman," Emily Young said nothing about the fine manners usually connected to gentility. The Masonic grandmaster who came to Nauvoo in March 1842 for the installation of Masonic officers was surprised at the man he met. Instead of an "ignorant and tyrannical upstart," Joseph Smith was "a sensible, intelligent, companionable and gentlemanly man."[13]

Most observers agreed with the grandmaster that Joseph was "a fine-looking man," but they did not consider him a gentleman. When Joel Hills Johnson met Joseph in 1831, the Prophet himself said, "I suppose you think that I am [a] great green, lubberly fellow," and Johnson observed that the phrase "was an exact representation of his person, being large and tall and not having a particle of beard about his face."[14] A Vermont girl who saw him in Kirtland in 1833 said, "He would better have answered to the character of a 'Davy Crockett,' than to the leader of a band who professed to be followers of the Saviour of mankind."[15] Charlotte Haven, a girl from New Hampshire, lived in Nauvoo through most of 1843. Not a Mormon, she viewed the Prophet with a jaundiced eye. She saw "a large, stout man, youthful in his appearance, with light complexion and hair, and blue eyes set far back in the head," making no note of either polish or crudity in his appearance. His speech was another matter. She had expected, she said, "to be overwhelmed by his eloquence" and was disappointed. He spoke in "a loud voice, and his language and manner were the coarsest possible. His object seemed to be to amuse and excite laughter in his audience." By comparison, Sidney Rigdon struck Haven more favorably: "He has an intelligent countenance, a courteous manner, and speaks grammatically." She judged him "by far the ablest and most cultivated of the Mormons," an indirect comment on the little she knew about Joseph Smith.[16]

Haven's reaction to Joseph Smith's speech was unusual. No one called him a polished speaker, but most were impressed with his effectiveness. Parley Pratt said Joseph was "not polished—not studied—not smoothed and softened by education and refined by art," and yet "he interested and edified, while, at the same time, he amused and entertained his audience; and none listened to him that were ever weary with his discourse." His enemy Eber Howe, the antagonistic Painesville, Ohio, newspaper editor, granted that Joseph was "easy, rather fascinating and winning."[17] He had a great knack for the telling rejoinder when he came under verbal attack. A female preacher who came across Joseph in 1831 challenged him to swear in the presence of God that an angel from heaven showed him the golden plates. Joseph replied gently, "I will not swear at all." She demanded, "Are you not ashamed of such pretensions? You, who are no more than an ignorant ploughboy of our land!" Joseph meekly said, "The gift has returned back again, as in former times, to illiterate fishermen."[18]

The comparison with Christ's illiterate fishermen may have summed up Joseph's idea about himself. He did not pretend to oratory and eloquence; fine speeches were left to Sidney Rigdon. Joseph thought of himself more as a plain person with a gift. If called upon, he could get a crowd to laugh, as he seems to have done in Charlotte Haven's hearing, but his tongue also gave forth the mysteries of godliness when he chose. Eliza R. Snow, a refined, graceful person herself who wrote poetry and taught a "select school" for young ladies, lived with the Smiths and watched Joseph's " 'daily walk and conversation.' " She found that "his lips ever flowed with instruction and kindness," though capable of "severe rebuke" when moved to defend his people.[19]

"Gentleman" was not the word Josiah Quincy used to describe Joseph. Son of the Harvard College president and soon to be mayor of Boston himself, Quincy was a thoroughgoing Brahmin when he and Charles Francis Adams paid a call on Joseph Smith in May 1844. Quincy was not unattentive to the question of gentility. In the collection of sketches taken from his journal, Quincy preceded the account of his Nauvoo visit with the story of Andrew Jackson's visit to Boston to receive an honorary degree from Harvard while he was president of the United States. Quincy opened his sketch by rebutting the judgment common among Bostonians that "General Jackson was not what you would call a gentleman!" To the contrary, Quincy declared, "the seventh President was a knightly personage" and "vigorously a gentleman in his high sense of honor and in the natural straightforward courtesies which are easily to be distinguished from the veneer of policy." Quincy put forward this claim against the prevailing intolerance of Jackson by "the Brahmin caste of my native state."[20] Presumably, he had the nerve to say the same of Joseph, whom he greatly admired, had he seen gentlemanly qualities in the Prophet.

Instead he found another basis for his admiration. Joseph appeared to Quincy as a great vital force. He compared Joseph to the Rhode Island congressman, Elisha Potter, whom Quincy had met in Washington in 1826. The two of them, Quincy said, emanated "a certain peculiar moral stress and compulsion which I have never felt in the presence of others of their countrymen." Potter, a giant of a man in physical bulk, had "wit and intelligence" in proportion to his size. Though not as large, Joseph left a similar impression. "Both were of commanding appearance, men whom it seemed natural to obey." Potter carried about him "a surplus of vital energy, to relieve the wants of others": "I well remember how the faces about Miss Hyer's dining table were wont to be lighted up when he entered the room." Quincy in passing spoke of Potter as "a gentleman," a word he never applied to Joseph, but the impressive qualities of both of them had nothing to do with refinement.[21]

Quincy and Adams dropped in on Joseph Smith unannounced early one morning. Their steamboat had stopped at the Nauvoo landing after midnight, and they were about to continue upstream after they discovered there was no room at "General Smith's tavern," but a room was found in an old mill that had been converted into a house. They swept "a small army of cockroaches" from the coverlet and slept through night in their dressing gowns. The next morning after driving two muddy miles, they saw the Prophet by a three-story frame house surrounded by a white fence:

> Preëminent among the stragglers by the door stood a man of commanding appearance, clad in the costume of a journeyman carpenter when about his work. He was a hearty, athletic fellow, with blue eyes standing prominently out upon his light complexion, a long nose, and a retreating forehead. He wore striped pantaloons, a linen jacket, which had not lately seen the washtub, and a beard of some three days' growth. This was the founder of the religion which had been preached in every quarter of the earth.

While the incongruity of Joseph's appearance and his religious pretensions struck Quincy as slightly humorous, it did not trouble Joseph. Later in the morning before he accompanied the two visitors on a tour of Nauvoo, Joseph changed into a broadcloth suit, but he had seen no need to dress up earlier to appear on the streets of the city. On this day, he had left off the white stock of the modern portraits and had not bothered to shave his face. The role of prophet, which he never stepped out of, did not require him to appear in the garb of a gentleman. Nor was he embarrassed when caught in undress by two finely attired visitors.

And yet his presence impressed Quincy. "A *fine-looking man* is what the passer-by would instinctively have murmured," he said of the Prophet, "but Smith was more than this, . . . one could not resist the impression that capacity and resource were natural to his stalwart person." Linking him to Potter again, Quincy observed that "of all men I have met, these two seemed best endowed with that kingly faculty which directs, as by intrinsic right, the feeble or confused souls who are looking for guidance." The comment reduced the Nauvoo Mormons to mixed-up weaklings but without devaluing Joseph's character. Although disbelieving everything Joseph said and considering his comments "puerile," Quincy could not resist "the impression of rugged power that was given by the man."[22]

Joseph did not come among his working-class followers as John Wesley did, appearing as an aristocrat with fine skin and smooth hair that awed and inspired common people. On an ordinary day, Joseph stepped out of his house in striped pantaloons, a dirty jacket, and a three days' growth of beard. Nor did he reside in a splendid mansion. After getting by in a cramped log house for three years in Nauvoo, he moved into the Mansion House, where there was more space to entertain visitors.[23] Fenced with white pickets, as Quincy noted, and probably painted, the house was certainly well above the average Nauvoo residence and yet did not function as a mansion when Quincy and Adams visited. Sold to a tavern keeper in January 1844 to help with Joseph's debts, the house did not have the amenities of a mansion on this particular day. As he set about to entertain his distinguished visitors, he was not able to usher them into a parlor where genteel people always entertained important guests; Joseph had to hunt for a space to even sit down.[24] Avoiding the "comfortless" barroom, Joseph opened one door occupied by a woman in bed, shut it, and ran upstairs to another room where three men were sleeping in three beds. The next room had two sleeping occupants, but "the third attempt was somewhat more fortunate, for we had found a room which held but a single bed and a single sleeper. . . . Our host immediately proceeded to the bed, and drew the clothes well over the head of its occupant. He then called a man to make a fire, and begged us to sit down." Without embarrassment, Joseph then discoursed on the Church's history and prospects.[25]

The incident occurred a little over a month before the Prophet's death. Nauvoo had grown into a large city, about as large as Chicago. Migrants were pouring in at a ferocious rate, and a huge temple was under construction on the bluff overlooking the town. Still, at this late date, Joseph could not entertain important visitors in a parlor, the essential architecture of a gentleman. He talked to them in his pantaloons, sitting in a bedroom next to a concealed (and likely startled) sleeper huddled under the covers. Much as they admired the Prophet's intelligence and personal force, Quincy and Adams could never write a report on Joseph Smith's refinement.

Joseph Smith himself recognized the incongruity and had taken strong measures to end it. Like Sidney Rigdon, he believed the Saints should show a polished face to the world. A January 1841 revelation commanded the Saints to build a hotel at the same time as the temple was going up, "that the weary traveler may find health and safety while he shall contemplate the word of the Lord" (D&C 124:23). Joseph put the case more bluntly when he later was pressing the city to step up its efforts. "There is no place in this city," he told a conference in April 1843, "where men of wealth, character and influence from abroad can go to repose themselves, and it is necessary we should have such a place."[26] He foresaw the arrival of figures like Quincy and Adams and knew they deserved better than a bed covered with cockroaches and a parlor shared with a covered sleeper. Lyman Wight and George Miller got busy in the summer of 1841 to raise money and bring down lumber from Wisconsin to raise the massive structure. The plans called for a three-story brick building composed of two wings, each 120 by 40 feet, enough space for seventy-five rooms plus a suite for Joseph and his family.[27]

In the end, the hotel construction was more than the Saints could manage at the same time as the temple. The hotel was never completed, though not for want of effort on Joseph's part. He insisted the hotel was of equal importance with the temple, though sentiment was all against him. "The building of the Nauvoo House is just as sacred in my view as the Temple," he told the workers in February of 1843. "I want the Nauvoo House built. It *must* be built. Our salvation [as a city] depends upon it." As he put it, the Lord had commanded, " 'Build a Temple to my great name, and call the attention of the great, the rich, and the noble.' " But when they came to see the temple, they would ask, "Where shall we lay our heads? In an old log cabin."[28] But the rhetoric was in vain. In the summer of 1843, the project was abandoned with the hotel only partly up, and the next May, Quincy and Adams had to stay in a shanty.

As a comment on the Mormon attitude toward gentility, the failed Nauvoo House made the point exactly. The large plan, the great effort, Joseph's pleadings with the workmen, all attested to his serious interest in presenting his people favorably. How else, as Sidney put it, "is Zion to become the joy and the praise of the whole earth." Nothing about the city or the Saints should bring shame to the work, moving Joseph to put the hotel, rhetorically at least, on a par with the temple. But when resources ran out, Nauvoo House construction stopped while the Saints worked on the temple up to the last second before their departure, determined to complete it at any cost. Refinement and beauty were means to an end, not, like the temple, the greatest good itself.

Warren Cowdery stated the Mormon position in an 1837 essay on "Manners" in the *Messenger and Advocate.* "I make it a point of morality," Cowdery wrote, "never to find fault with another for his manners. They may be awkward or graceful, blunt or polite, polished or rustic, I care not what they are if the man means well and acts from honest intentions."[29] Joseph Smith would have endorsed those sentiments. He said that he loved a man better "who swears a stream as long as my arm yet deals justice to his neighbors and mercifully deals his substance to the poor, than the long, smooth-faced hypocrite." He spoke of himself as "a huge, rough stone rolling down from a high mountain," polished only when it chipped off a corner by striking something.[30] John D. Lee, a rough-hewn man himself, said Joseph's "countenance was that of a plain, honest man, full of benevolence and philanthropy and void of deceit or hypocrisy."[31]

Joseph Smith's hopes for elevating his people followed along the same line. He certainly did not want to leave them mired in vulgarity and coarseness. Jackson County frontiersmen shocked him in 1831 with their "degradation, leanness of intellect, ferocity, and jealousy"; he mourned for those "who roamed about without the benefit of civilization, refinement, or religion."[32] Joseph envisioned cultural development for the Saints but not exactly in terms of genteel polish. He used another vocabulary for the assembly that gathered in April 1841 to lay the foundation stones for the Nauvoo temple. The crowd's demeanor lifted his spirits, because he heard no profane language and saw no intoxication:

> We will say we never witnessed a more imposing spectacle than was presented on this occasion, and during the sessions of the conference. Such a multitide of people moving in harmony, in friendship, in dignity, told in a voice not easily misunderstood, that they were a people of intelligence, and virtue and order; in short, that they were *Saints;* and that the God of love, purity and light, was their God, their Examplar, and Director; and that they were blessed and happy.[33]

Those were Joseph's words—intelligence, virtue, order, friendship. Nothing about dress, posture, fine manners, fashion. He was more interested in character than personality.

The refinement-in-the-wilderness histories of Utah then must be put in a broader context. Refinement there was most certainly, but more as a product of spreading middle-class gentility than as a result of Mormon teachings. In Mormon culture, refinement was more an aspect of hospitality and public relations than of religion itself. The campaign for gentility conducted in the pages of the *Woman's Exponent* in the 1870s was as much political as moral. Among the Mormons, the highest human ideal was not refinement. The grim bearded faces and gaunt female forms in Anderson's photographs were not incomplete Saints as the history of refinement implies. Joseph could have sat among them, dressed in workman's clothes, and chatted as comfortably as he talked with visiting Brahmins. He cared more that his people were honest and loyal, true to one another and their faith, than that they throw off gleams from a polished surface. If they slid their food into their mouths on a knife blade, he would not have objected. He never pretended to be a polished gentleman himself and valued a host of other qualities above good manners. From Liberty Jail in March 1839, he pled with the Saints for a reformation of everyone, "both old and young teachers and taugh[t] both high and low rich and poor bond and free Male and female." What he wanted from them was something far simpler and more difficult than refined manners. "Let honesty and sobriety, and cander and solemnity, and virtue, and pureness, and meekness, and simplisity, Crown our heads in every place."[34] He would have asked the same of farm families in desert cabins and of well-dressed ladies and gentlemen on the streets of Salt Lake City.

Richard Lyman Bushman is Gouverneur Morris Professor of History at Columbia University.

NOTES

1. Frances Trollope, *Domestic Manners of the Americans* (New York: Howard Wilford Bell, 1904), 16, 19–20, 21–22, 25.

2. Trollope, *Domestic Manners*, vi, vii.

3. Richard L. Bushman, *The Refinement of America: Persons, Houses, Cities* (New York: Alfred A. Knopf, 1992), 386–88.

4. Josiah Quincy, *Figures of the Past*, new edition (1883; Boston: Little, Brown, 1926), 229–30.

5. Bushman, *Refinement of America*, 184–85.

6. Quoted in Bushman, *Refinement of America*, 314, 317.

7. Quoted in Bushman, *Refinement of America*, 319.

8. Bushman, *Refinement of America*, 425–26.

9. Richard S. Van Wagoner, *Sidney Rigdon: A Portrait of Religious Excess* (Salt Lake City: Signature Books, 1994), 4–5, 10–11, 29.

10. Sidney Rigdon, "The Saints and the World," *Messenger and Advocate* 3 (December 1836): 421.

11. "Baptism—the Mode of Its Administration . . . ," *Times and Seasons* 4 (September 15, 1843): 321.

12. Hyrum L. Andrus and Helen Mae Andrus, *They Knew the Prophet* (Salt Lake City: Bookcraft, 1974), 173.

13. Joseph Smith Jr., *History of The Church of Jesus Christ of Latter-day Saints,* ed. B. H. Roberts, 2d ed., rev., 7 vols. (Salt Lake City: Deseret Book, 1971), 4:566 (hereafter cited as *History of the Church*).

14. Andrus and Andrus, *They Knew the Prophet*, 29.

15. Elizabeth Allen, *Sketches of Green Mountain Life; with an Autobiography of the Author* (Lowell, Mass.: Nathaniel L. Dayton, 1846).

16. William Mulder and A. Russell Mortensen, eds., *Among the Mormons: Historic Accounts by Contemporary Observers* (New York: Alfred A. Knopf, 1958), 118–19, 120, 123.

17. Quoted in Fawn Brodie, *No Man Knows My History: The Life of Joseph Smith* (New York: Alfred A. Knopf, 1945), 103.

18. Quoted in Brodie, *No Man Knows My History*, 103–4.

19. Linda King Newell and Valeen Tippetts Avery, *Mormon Enigma: Emma Hale Smith: Prophet's Wife, "Elect Lady," Polygamy's Foe, 1804–1879* (Garden City, N. Y.: Doubleday, 1984), 61.

20. Quincy, *Figures of the Past*, 296.

21. Quincy, *Figures of the Past*, 231–33.

22. Quincy, *Figures of the Past*, 320–22.

23. Robert Flanders, *Nauvoo: Kingdom on the Mississippi* (Urbana: University of Illinois Press, 1965), 175.

24. A month later, John C. Calhoun Jr. visited Joseph in Nauvoo and was entertained in a "drawingroom." Brian Q. Cannon, ed., "John C. Calhoun, Jr., Meets the Prophet Joseph Smith Shortly before the Departure for Carthage," *BYU Studies* 33, no. 4 (1993): 777.

25. Quincy, *Figures of the Past*, 322.

26. *History of the Church*, 5:328.

27. Flanders, *Nauvoo*, 182–83.

28. *History of the Church*, 5:285.

29. Warren Cowdery, "Manners," *Messenger and Advocate* 3 (February 1837): 463.

30. *History of the Church*, 5:401.

31. Quoted in Brodie, *No Man Knows My History*, 125.

32. *History of the Church*, 1:189.

33. *History of the Church*, 4:331.

34. Dean C. Jessee, ed., *The Personal Writings of Joseph Smith* (Salt Lake City: Deseret Book, 1984), 397.

Mormon Village

Center Street in Provo, Utah, 1875. George Taylor, photographer.

Golden Memories: Remembering Life in a Mormon Village

Ronald W. Walker

For the past fifty years, scholars have written about the "Mormon village"—the archetypical Mormon pioneer frontier community. As a result, we know about its ideals (unity, cooperation, equality, and religious striving). We know about its physical layout (rectangular streets often laid off at the cardinal points of the compass) and its pattern of settlement (homes and gardens on village lots with agricultural fields and livestock nurtured several miles away). We even know that the Mormon village left a distinctive mark on the landscape (unkept outbuildings, pervasive water ditches, and poplar trees providing shade and a sense of order).[1] But what was daily life in the Mormon village like?

Fortunately, we can begin to answer that question, too. During the 1930s, the Federal Writers' Project of the Works Progress Administration (WPA) collected autobiographies, sketches, and questionnaire responses from Utah's surviving pioneers. Later, the state-controlled Utah Writers' Project continued the process. Because of these two successively running government projects, from 1935 to 1943 over nine hundred pioneers left personal accounts of life in a Mormon village. Through them much can be learned of village life.[2]

Most respondents were Mormons. Forty percent were women, an unusually high proportion for a nineteenth-century data cohort (population group). The majority had been children during the pioneer era: about 30 percent were born before 1850, another 30 percent in the 1850s, and still another 30 percent in the 1860s. Still more important, most WPA respondents were drawn from the rank and file and lived their lives in Utah's new or outlying pioneer settlements. Their stories describe the fabric of everyday frontier life.

Like many old-timers before and since, the respondents had firm opinions. Syria Allen, a longtime citizen of Huntington, Emery

County, thought that "the old days was pretty hard picken."[3] Circleville's Thadius Fullmer agreed. Utah was "a hell of a country," he said. It was a "dry and arid" place "fit [only] for the Indians."[4] James Ivie, descended from a family of Indian fighters, was equally terse about the early days: "Can't forget them—wouldn't like to relive [them]."[5]

Yet, despite fully acknowledging the difficulties of pioneering, the WPA respondents were remarkably upbeat about their past. Ellen Lee Woodard, an Iron County resident, remembered "happy days,"[6] and Elvira Lance, comparing pioneer conditions with succeeding times, believed that frontier life was "happier and more contented."[7] Julia Hills Johnson concurred: "There is more conveniences to day," she acknowledged, "but the olden days were by far the best."[8]

Were these appraisals simply "golden memories"—a case of passing years and nostalgia softening reality—or had pioneer life offered something special? When explaining themselves, many of the pioneers spoke of human relationships. "Early days were hard to get along but pleasant to live because all were so kind and friendly to one another," said Manti resident Dorothea Jorgensen.[9] Amy Carline Phillips also spoke of congeniality: in early days people "helped one and another" and lived like "one happy family."[10] In turn, James Munroe Redd believed that the old-timers were "really more happy and contented" because they were "more social and co-operatively inclined."[11]

This refrain appears in anecdote after anecdote as the old pioneers mentioned the sharing, neighborliness, and cooperation that once bound them together.

Helping Newcomers

When the Saints arrived in Utah, friends, relatives, or even self-appointed greeters might meet them at Emigration Square (or later at a local railroad depot).[12] Mary Ann Richards remembered her father frequently welcomed emigrants and invited them to his home for dinner.[13] Eliza Burgess Briggs recalled such kindness firsthand. When she and her mother arrived in Ogden, they received a basket of food and an invitation to stay in the home of a couple they had met earlier while traveling to Utah. To ease what must have been a crowded condition, Eliza and her mother soon found other accommodations by trading domestic work for housing and food.[14]

Other immigrants told of receiving produce, large cans of milk, or even sections of beef on arriving in Utah.[15] The Swiss immigrants of

1861 were given more extended aid. Counseled to settle in southern Utah but without the means to do so, the Swiss were transported in relay fashion by each community on the road.[16] Adelaide Jackson Slack told another story. After her father baptized relatives in England and convinced them to emigrate, he welcomed them into his Toquerville home. "We had twenty two at the table all one winter," said Adelaide, counting family members and recently arrived converts. "We were glad to have them."[17]

Charles Twelves and his family—survivors of the ill-fated Martin handcart party of 1856—were first lodged at the Salt Lake City tithing office. Then local settlers escorted the family to Provo, where they were given a small log house. The next spring Twelves's father, hoping to improve the family's circumstance, built an eight-by-ten-foot dugout that burrowed four feet in the ground. The dwelling was "comfortable," Twelves reported, although sleep was at first difficult because of disturbing night visits by wolves.[18]

Townspeople tried to see after the newcomers' needs. The people at Kanab welcomed new settlers with a party.[19] If the new arrivals came too late in the season to grow their own crops, the established pioneers shared their own harvest.[20] The Biblical precedent of "gleaning the fields" was sometimes followed. Or the immigrant poor might be aided by giving them the less-desirable parts of a slaughtered animal—the paunch, head, feet, or liver.[21]

William John Hill appreciated the help of Ogden leader James Brown ("a kind neighbor and friend"), who brought the Hill family food and wood after they arrived in Utah in the early 1850s.[22] In another example of assistance in Ogden, Joseph Perry lodged the nine-member Hadley family in a surplus adobe house. Unfortunately, the Hadleys did not stay put. They moved into a cabin owned by Pat Jackson, promising Jackson one of their sons would do live-in work to help with the rent. But Jackson reportedly fed the boy "soap grease scraps" and eventually forced the Hadleys to leave.[23] If the Hadleys' version of events is accurate, not all established settlers were "Saints."

Many newcomers were greenhorns who needed help with basic frontier routines. After settling in Panguitch, stonemason and English convert Henry Excell had one misadventure after another. During his first attempt to handle a team of oxen, he drove too close to a kiln, dislodged several bricks, and spooked his oxen into running home. "This was my first and last experience driving an ox team," he recalled. Henry's subsequent attempt as a fieldhand initially went no better. He was unable to channel irrigation water until a local settler showed him how.[24]

Sometimes Church leaders would ask a local family to help feed a recently arrived widow and her children. It was an assignment that could severely tax resources. "My heart swells with pride," Martha Cragun Cox wrote of her mother's treatment of one widow family, "when I remember that the wheat cake[s] for the Atkin's children was just as large as ours, and the half pint of milk each morning and evening was never stinted in favor of her own little ones."[25] One time the Cragun and Atkins' flour supply was reduced to one small baking. James Cragun left for the fields without breakfast, and his wife, Eleanor, went to gather "greens"—the wild bulbs and grasses that many pioneers used when no other alternative seemed possible. Still the Cragun family shared with the Atkins. Soon, however, the family flour sack was mysteriously replenished. Apparently, becoming aware of the situation, neighbors anonymously contributed in the families' behalf.

Sharing Supplies

The Cragun experience was not unusual. According to Ernest Munk, a central Utah settler, "People were liberal [with their means] and would divide what they had."[26] Further, the practice of dividing out commodities made economic sense. Without stores to sell goods or much money to buy what might be available, this practice was a means of market distribution, especially if something "extra good or unusual" were available.[27] The custom equalized society: "In sharing with each other every one was the same," remembered Henry O. Jensen of Scipio.[28]

Whatever the reasons, sharing was so common that it became a routine of life. Sometimes the articles traded were as simple as a start of yeast or coals taken from one hearth to another.[29] Or they might be planting seed, farm equipment, or edibles like milk, butter, and cheese.[30] Meat was a commonly shared commodity, perhaps because there was no alternative. Without refrigeration a recently slaughtered animal could spoil before it was eaten.[31] Besides, the people may have been further motivated by knowing that any item given would likely bring something in return.

Sometimes the shared item was so unusual that pioneers remembered it years later. When Owen Clark found a bear lodged in the cliffs near Cannonville, he killed it and offered the meat to all comers.[32] Elizabeth Yates of Scipio secured an extravagantly expensive pound of

Courtesy LDS Church Archives

Wagon camp, ca. 1870. In this scene, men camping in Salt Lake Valley prepare to share a meal. Sharing was a way of life rather than a mere polite gesture; at times a pioneer's survival might depend on it. Charles R. Savage, photographer.

sugar from St. Louis—a rare pioneer delicacy—and doled it out for six months: "If there was anyone sick in town she made it a point to send a taste of sugar."[33] After Apostle George Q. Cannon sent a box of apples to the mother of Ann Elizabeth Melville in Fillmore, each of the Melvilles' neighbors received one. Ann Elizabeth kept her apple on the mantle shelf, taking only an occasional bite.[34]

The pioneers sometimes spoke of sharing items that the current Latter-day Saint interpretation of the Word of Wisdom proscribes. To get a fresh supply of tobacco, Rensselaer Kirk traveled one hundred miles to Cortez, Colorado, only to learn that the store had just a dollar's worth in its inventory. Worse, as Kirk returned home, many of his friends on the trail wanted a share. Upon completing his 200-mile journey, Kirk had no more tobacco than when he began.[35]

Another incident involved tea. After Mrs. Henderson of Cannonville provided milk to visiting miners, the men appreciatively gave her a half a package of tea. Rather than hoarding the difficult-to-obtain commodity, Henderson divided it with the other five families in the village, reserving an equal portion for herself. Her sacrifice, she said, gave her "as much pleasure" as "anything [she] had ever done."[36]

During the hard times of 1854–55, when the territory seemed close to famine, the Colvin farm of Payson was one of the few not ravaged by grasshoppers. The Colvins were therefore in a position to give their neighbors a daily ration of cornmeal.[37] At Wellsville another grasshopper infestation (they were common in pioneer times) prompted similar charity. The Leatham family, remembering that they "nearly starved" during the natural disaster that had once afflicted them, for many years maintained a large bin of flour with an open invitation to any needy family.[38]

In St. George, Church leader David Cannon regularly traded food to needy men in exchange for their work, even when his family could do the tasks themselves.[39] Mr. Greenwell of West Weber had the reputation of never turning away a request for meat, and at Christmas he traditionally slaughtered three or four "good beef cattle" and then asked the local LDS bishops to make a distribution to the needy regardless of their religion or race.[40] In southern Utah, a settler approached Mr. Shumway, a local rancher, with a confession. He had been hungry and had killed one of Shumway's range cattle. "If you get hungry again, kill another cow," said Shumway.[41]

Sarah Chaffin told a story of her family's charity while her father served a Church mission. Before leaving Utah, her father gave a neighbor five dollars, with the instruction to use it to help the Chaffin family through any hard times. When those times arrived, the neighbor arranged for the Chaffins to pick up twenty-five pounds of flour, and the Chaffin boy was dispatched to get it. As he made his way home, hard-pressed neighbors asked for a share, and the boy complied. An old man even followed him to the door. "If I had a pint of gold, I would give it to you for a pint of flour," he pleaded. Again, the request was met, which brought criticism from the local "block teachers." If the family went hungry, they thought, it would be their own fault. In fact, the Chaffins were forced to pick serviceberries to get through the season.[42]

The pioneers' generosity, usually personal and spontaneous, was reinforced by the teachings and practices of the LDS Church. Provo settler George Thomas Peay remembered that Church leaders made sharing a standing "order."[43] Another pioneer recalled that during worship services, members of the congregation regularly discussed community needs and acted on them.[44] One local Mormon leader regularized charity by passing a "community basket" through his ward; members of his congregation either placed commodities in the basket or removed them, whatever their circumstance. A more common practice was for a bishop to receive in-kind tithes and "fast-offerings" and then dispense these commodities to the poor.[45] And in times of special need, some local bishops levied quotas on surplus grain, which then was distributed to those in want.[46]

NURSING EACH OTHER

Illness and disease required a special kind of giving. Because most frontier communities had neither doctors nor hospitals, women provided the nurturing—and some had remarkable records of service. The southern Utah village Tonaquint depended on Sophronia Carter, who on one occasion visited the cabin of a bedridden woman. Sophronia found the nearby Santa Clara River was rapidly rising. In order to save her friend's life, Sophronia carried the woman through waist-deep, raging water. During her career as a pioneer nurse, Sophronia helped "hundreds of needy people in sickness and suffering."[47]

When typhoid fever struck a family near Sarah Joy Surrage's home in Weber County, she worked tirelessly. First the neighbor's seven-year-old boy died, and Sarah prepared the body for burial. Then the disease claimed the life of the mother. When Sarah's own family became infected, she struggled to save both families but lost one of her daughters. "I went without sleep so long that I finally got so I hardly needed sleep," she remembered. After the epidemic ran its course, Sarah was asked to raise her neighbor's family and did so.[48]

These nurturing women were remarkable. The Sanpete nurse-midwife Artemesia Draper Anderson reported that in one eight-month period, she traveled 1,033 miles by horse and another 347 miles by "other conveyances." During her career, Artemesia delivered more than two thousand babies—her last being twins, whom she midwifed when eighty years old.[49] Annie Hermin Cardon Shaw, yet another nurse-midwife, practiced in Weber County. Once while traveling to deliver a child, Annie fell and injured her head. She nevertheless bound up her injury, delivered the baby, and returned home; later a silver plate was placed in her skull to fuse the bones. On another occasion, Annie was summoned to deliver a child shortly after having given birth herself. Friends put Annie on a featherbed and took her by covered wagon to fill the appointment.[50]

WORKING TOGETHER

Another measure of the pioneers' group spirit was their work and social routines. These were topics that the WPA old-timers spoke about repeatedly and with great enthusiasm, because to them, pioneering meant working and playing together. Livy Olsen remembered that when the people settled Spring City they joined to root out brush and to plant crops—everyone did the tasks for which they were "best adapted." The cleared land was then divided into five- to ten-acre parcels and given to individual families. The method allowed the land to be settled quickly "for the common good."[51]

A Fairview settler told of a community work project that became a part of local lore, perhaps because it so aptly characterized the people and their times. Every able-bodied man and boy agreed to work on the "City Ditch" canal "till it would carry water." Spring crops apparently could not be planted until a reliable water source was established. However, as the men dug their ditch, they encountered an unyielding hardpan. Orville Cox, who from the outset of the project had been more of an observer than a worker, finally walked away from the work gang. His apparent desertion made the men furious. "We didn't swear," remembered one of the crew, only "because the bishop was there."[52]

The next morning, however, Cox was back on the job with several teams of oxen and a strange-looking contraption that was part plow and part battering ram. Working through the night, he had taken a fourteen-foot log and attached a thumblike appendage that carried a crowbar. Next, along its sides, he inserted oak sticks designed for holding and positioning. With the oxen pulling the device and the men steering it, Cox's machine easily carved through the hardpan: four passes and the hardpan was gone. Later Cox explained why he had left the crew without giving an explanation. He was not the bishop, he said, and besides, the men would only have laughed at his idea. His way was best. "Just shut up and do, and when a bunch of men see a thing working they'll believe."[53]

Mads Anderson Jr., an early Mt. Pleasant citizen, remembered the community work that he and his father completed as part of the prevailing social contract. Father and son worked on roads connecting the various Sanpete County communities and still other roads extending into the canyons. Although not owning any livestock and therefore not gaining any direct advantage, the Anderson family also built fences, including the five-mile Lane Fence, which was designed to contain the community's cow herd. These projects were done "without compensation" and "for public benefit."[54]

Another joint project was the construction of a community fort, often the first structure of a new village. These multiuse buildings protected the new settlers from Native Americans while at the same time providing a temporary school, meetinghouse, and home. Fort living could be difficult. Quarters were cramped and infested with mice, bedbugs, and the neighbors' dogs. Yet settlers found compensation for these trials. "While living in the fort we were just one large family," Mary Henrie Cooper recalled. Mary liked the sense of equality such a life brought.[55]

During the second stage of village pioneering, settlers moved from the fort to village lots. This was the time for cabin building and for the construction of a community center that would serve as a church and school. At Circleville, the community center began with each family delivering three hewed logs to the building site and then working to raise the building. To furnish the interior and hire a teacher, the Circleville citizens levied a 2 percent property tax, which according to the chairman of the building committee brought no outward complaint. "The settlers were a common class of people, and it was easy to get their cooperation in anything for the betterment of the community," he reported.[56]

Pioneering also meant other kinds of cooperation. To provide livestock with winter feed, the boys and men of the village joined to clear snow from the range. In summertime they helped each other in their respective fields. And there were cabin and barn raisings. These festive occasions, which drew neighborhoods and perhaps the entire village together, typically began in the late afternoon and continued until the work was done. "What if there were a few of the gossipy items of the day considered," said one of the old-timers defensively. "No harm was intended. [Besides,] a wonderful lot of work [was] done." An evening dinner and dance generally concluded these labors.[57]

Black Hawk War militiamen, July 1866. Militia duty was a civic responsibility of all men age fourteen and up. The men pictured here served during an eight-year conflict between the Mormon settlers and factions of the Ute, Paiute, and Navajo tribes unified under the leadership of Black Hawk. *Left to right, bottom row:* Henry Snell, Edward D. Woolley Jr.; *middle row:* William Goforth, Solomon F. Kimball, Jasper Conrad; *top row:* Alma Pratt, Conrad Wilkinson, William B. Dougall. Charles R. Savage, photographer.

Another joint activity was militia duty. Every man fourteen years or older was formally enrolled, but women were also involved. In 1866, the villagers of Virgin reacted quickly when Navajo raiders took more than fifty head of cattle. Old men and boys shelled corn for horse feed; the young men corralled horses, prepared saddles, and cleaned guns; and women and girls prepared provisions. By midnight the militiamen left the town and, joining the "minute men" of another community, reclaimed some of their stock. Usually, the clever Navajo marauders were not so easily thwarted.[58]

Age often determined the kind of militia duty that was performed. Boys carried dispatches, performed guard duty, and patrolled streets and corrals; elderly men maintained outposts and scouted; and older teens and young men fought.[59] Whatever their roles, militiamen were made to understand that militia duty was an important civic responsibility. When Thomas Hull of Franklin, Idaho, refused a militia call in order to remain with his wife, who had recently delivered a child, Church leaders found Hull's behavior unacceptable. Ensuing angry words led to his excommunication.[60]

Militia drills sometimes combined pleasure with duty when wives and children camped near the drilling grounds. After the men completed their military work, the citizens might dance, enjoy horse races and footraces, and hold other sporting activities. One "Military Day" in Provo lasted three days.[61] At Kanarra a militia drill continued for a week.[62] Still another at Harmony drew three thousand people, who enjoyed a "big parade," band music, horse racing, and a speech delivered by Elder Lorenzo Snow, who was dressed in military regalia.[63]

The village women also worked together—and enjoyed themselves in the process. Catherine Larsen remembered picking wild currants on the upper Sevier River with some of her neighbors. A noon picnic briefly relieved the tedium of work, but the most happy part of the day was the wagon ride home when the berry pickers' "merry songs filled the clear evening air." Such singing made "life worth while" and turned something that was "a necessity" into "leisure time fun."[64]

Women's work often meant making cloth. Hannah McFarland Bingham remembered picking wool from her neighborhood's wire fences and washing it. Hannah then invited friends to her home to card the fabric. The evening concluded with refreshments—Johnny cake or a molasses cookie served with milk or water. These occasions were "very happy time[s]."[65]

Haying on the Blue Creek ranch, ca. 1900. Although some of these men may be hired hands, harvesting was often a communal affair.

Next the wool had to be spun. This task called for another round of parties, restricted in size because few homes could hold more than five spinning wheels.[66] If a larger group was desired, the local schoolhouse or the hostess's yard might be used.[67] Wherever the location, games, songs, and, most importantly, friendly competition lightened the activity: who could spin the most skeins? At noon the women stopped for "dinner" and in the evening for "supper," when the men arrived. A dance normally ended the day. "Those were sure good times," Danish convert Eliza Othilda Christensen Jorgensen recalled.[68]

If the ladies were not carding and spinning together, they were weaving, sewing, grating vegetables, braiding rugs, or quilting together—the latter being a pioneer favorite pastime. The eight women who gathered in Pernilla Anderson's single-room dugout in Santaquin finished a quilt in a day.[69] At Nephi some of the women periodically quilted together for several weeks. Then, the "great number" of completed quilts were distributed on the basis of productivity with the fastest worker receiving the most.[70] One youngster never forgot the expectation of a coming work party. "We will have a real good dinner today with cookies and cake, too," she remembered telling her younger brother.[71]

The young men and women did the harder work, like husking corn.[72] Husking parties often began at twilight, when six or eight lanterns were hung around the large piles of accumulated corn.[73] "Then the crowd would gather and begin the work, or fun, for it was fun," insisted one participant.[74] A competition might be held to determine who could do the most work.[75] Or perhaps the color of the corn might be made into a game. If a girl found a rare red ear, it was evidence that she would be the first of the girls to marry. If a boy found one, it meant he was about to lose his girlfriend.[76] There were variations. Occasionally the special red ear gave a boy the right to kiss a girl—a "simple past time [that] afforded a great deal of pleasure for the hard working people."[77]

Another popular work-pastime was fruit drying. Rachel Brown's father purchased apples and then required Rachel and her friends to peel and cut them for drying.[78] Eliza Burdett Horsepool remembered that participants at her parties processed more than a dozen bushels of peaches in a single evening. While the girls cut the fruit, the boys managed the pans and placed the sliced peaches on roof sheds to dry.[79] Again, a hint of romance was often in the air. Some parties allowed a boy and a girl to leave the well-lit cabin to spread the fruit in the dark.

This was a "real treat," remembered one pioneer, because it gave a couple a rare chance at privacy. On such nocturnal adventures, "lots of sparking [romantic flirting] was done by all."[80]

Sometimes a single incident united villagers and encouraged them to work together. Rebecca Wilson told of a young man who was suddenly called on a preaching mission but had no suit to wear. "That [became] a busy week," she recalled. "One Sunday the wool was on the sheep's back. By the next Sunday it had been clipped, cleansed, corded, spun, woven, and made into a splendid suit and was on the back of the missionary as he delivered his farewell address in the little church house, [and] then [he] left on his religious pilgrimage to the 'nations of the earth' to carry the Gospel Light to those who sat in darkness."[81]

The settlers at Mayfield, Sanpete County, joined to defeat an incursion of cattlemen. Although the local Anderson family had already "taken up" the strategic land at the mouth of a local canyon, they had not "proved" their homestead rights by building a cabin on the site and living there. Hoping to exploit this oversight, the cattlemen began to construct a cabin and warned the villagers that the uplands were no longer available for use. Within a day, the local settlers began and finished a cabin, and a Mormon family slept in it that night. The Andersons retained the land because the "town gave their support."[82]

COURTING AND VISITING

Even courting was done in groups. Young men and women "didn't go in couples but everybody went together, and they had lots of fun, singing and laughing," remembered Martha Horspool Hellewell.[83] The important thing was to be a part of a crowd—a group of like-minded friends who readily associated with each other.

Laura Smith Hadfield recalled her crowd's activity in the small southern Idaho town of Elba. The young people assembled at a moment's notice.

> We would go outside and look over the country and see whose house had a light in it (we burned coal oil lamps in those days), and then we would ride over there and spend the evening. If the house was dark we knew the folks were not home. . . . It was nothing for nearly all of us to arrive at the same place in an evening without any previous arrangements. It took nearly the whole community to make a good crowd. Sometimes we would have to stay all night on account of the blizzards. I have known them to stay for two or three days.[84]

Social visiting was a part of the pioneer way.[85] On Sundays and during the winter season when fieldwork eased, parents might load their families into a wagon, drive to a neighbor's home, and spend the day.[86] During such visits, the women "brought their knitting," for outfitting a family with clothes required constant effort.[87]

"Visiting" also allowed neighbors to catch up on the news, which sometimes meant group reading of national newspapers and magazines.[88] Henrietta Wilson recalled the big brush fires built near her home that furnished reading light during the Civil War.[89] In fact, some neighborhoods organized reading clubs that shared the cost of Pony Express "war extras." While she was reading to such a group, Martha Cragun Cox remembered that neighbor John Dalton questioned her pronunciation of the word "Chicago." "That word is 'She-car-ger,' little girl," Dalton said, tapping his cane on the floor. But Martha, unable to see Dalton's pronunciation in the word, continued with her own way.[90]

CELEBRATING TOGETHER

The celebrations of the pioneers also manifested a community spirit. Even a person's birthday might be observed "like one big family," said Olive Cheney Aldous. Olive's mother shaped molasses dough into figurines, fried them in lard, and apparently distributed them to villagers.[91] One birthday that was widely observed was Brigham Young's. This celebration was remembered as "very important" and "commonly" commemorated, perhaps with an extended family picnic to a local canyon.[92]

President Young's scheduled tours of the territory were another cause for community celebration. "Everyone looked forward" to them, insisted several of the pioneers, with "long hours" spent in preparation.[93] In southern Utah, the women wove material for new dresses and then searched the countryside for roots from which to extract suitable dyes. Their "desire had been fulfilled" if they marched in their new clothes, perhaps shoeless, in a local parade honoring the visiting Church dignitary.[94]

An impressive ten buggies might constitute President Young's entourage, the Church leader himself riding in a "white top" drawn by a span of splendid horses. As the procession entered a village, children sometimes scattered welcoming flowers. Handshakes followed. "I will never forget how soft and nice his hand was," said Diantha Olsen Newton, obviously expecting a palm hardened by pioneer toil.[95] And during his tours, Brigham Young offered advice down to the slightest detail. In Sanpete County, the President told settlers not to root out the sagebrush that lined the road: apparently he believed that these plants possessed some kind of salubrious quality.[96] At Huntsville he encouraged the Saints by promising their crops and fruit would prosper despite a short growing season.[97] The tours usually included community singing, speeches, and hearty meals.

Some pioneers celebrated May Day by erecting a traditional maypole and decorating it with red, blue, and white stripes made from discarded garments.[98] As the pioneering era drew to a close, Thanksgiving was also observed.[99] However, pioneer holidays were generally restricted to four: Christmas, New Year's Day, Independence Day, and Pioneer Day.

The pioneers infrequently spoke of Christmas trees and Christmas caroling. Rather, they recalled putting up stockings, exchanging a simple gift, or eating an apple, a molasses cookie, or a plain-tasting cake.[100] Many Christmas customs involved neighbors. A serenading fife-and-drum band might tour the neighborhood in an ox-drawn wagon.[101] Or village children might pass from house to house chanting "Christmas gift, Christmas gift"—usually enough to win them a small reward. On one such occasion, a woman dispensed a yard of calico, which an enterprising girl could make into an apron.[102]

The most important social Christmas activity was an evening dance. Sometimes these parties continued without interruption until dawn. Sometimes they recessed for several hours in the late evening so that supper parties could be held in nearby homes. One woman served as many as fifty couples during one of these intermissions.[103] Whatever the arrangement, the Christmas evening dance began the winter social season, which then continued at least until New Year, when another major dance was held. During these final days of December, there might be a flurry of dancing, candy pulls, singing, and amateur dramatics.[104]

The Mormons' two summer holidays, Independence Day (July 4) and the much more actively celebrated Pioneer Day (July 24), were closely bunched together and therefore observed in much the same manner. For many women and children, July was a time for new clothes. Pernilla Anderson received a new summer dress each year.[105] Jane Sprunt Warner Garner sewed special suits for her three boys and then colored them with a "greenish-yellow" dye extracted from rabbit brush.[106] Diantha Olsen Newton's mother prepared calico dresses for her girls, with straw hats and blue-ribbon streamers serving as accessories.[107]

Courtesy LDS Church Archives

An 1873 illustration depicting "Brigham Young on His Travels." President Young's annual trips through the territory not only provided him an opportunity to be among the people but were also long-awaited events for residents, who had a chance to see their leader and to join in on the parades, banquets, and socials associated with his arrival in each Mormon pioneer communty.

Preparations might also include a new speakers' platform for the meetinghouse or new log benches. Martha Canfield remembered the scrubbing: "Everything was made clean and tidy."[108] For the upcoming events, some villages erected outdoor "boweries," shaded areas made by placing cottonwood branches, with their green leaves still intact, over a raised network of poles.[109] Other holiday preparations included the selection of men to serve on the planning committee and, most importantly, a community "marshall." An Independence Day or Pioneer Day marshall was a man of local distinction, often voluble and good-humored, who directed the hour-by-hour program of events.

The holiday was often announced by the local fife-and-drum band, which began its serenading at daybreak and continued until midmorning. A pioneer band was important to villagers—"the life of all entertainments"—explained one pioneer, attracting people from miles around to hear them play.[110] But if a band were unavailable, the day might be heralded by gunfire, which continued during the summer holidays until dusk. There were other expedients. In 1852, after some of the Provo boys bragged about having the honor of waking the populace, a rival group hid the cannon and woke the village by banging on an anvil.[111] Following the early morning noise, communities

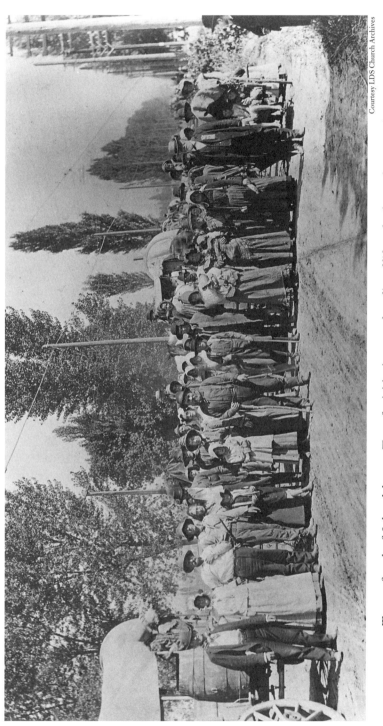

Twenty-fourth of July celebrants. Town festivities improved quality of life and enhanced community cooperation. For the two July celebrations, pioneers usually dressed in their best. Date unknown.

celebrated Independence Day with a flag raising around a liberty pole, followed by patriotic speeches.

Pioneer Day had its own speeches. But instead of extolling national values, Pioneer Day orators praised the Mormon pioneers, who were also commemorated with parading wagons, handcarts, and sometimes mounted Native Americans. The children of the village usually joined the march, which generated among them great excitement. Olive Cheney Aldous, a native of Uintah in Weber Country, remembered her anticipation:

> My sister and I were to march in the parade and we went barefooted because we didn't have shoes. Mother had made me a sunbonnet out of an old summer coat of father's and it was all starched so nice. I felt so dressed up. [As we traveled to the village], I said, "Now Pa, make the oxen trot like horses." He replied, "Oxen were not made to trot like horses but just to draw." I was so afraid that we would be late for the parade. The martial band led and we marched all around town.[112]

In addition to speeches and parades, the WPA old-timers remembered footraces, horse races, greased pig chases, greased pole climbing, baseball, skits, and parodies. Several decades after the event, Hannah Hanson Huntsman still recalled Charles Lambert's satire of the song "Love among the Roses," which Lambert renamed "Love among Big Noses." Said Huntsman's interviewer, "Judging from the excessive laughter which she indulged in while telling it," the parody "must have been an extravaganza of an outstanding nature."[113]

Another frequent activity was a sham battle between the pioneers and Native Americans, which generally concluded on a happy note when the two groups of actors made peace. (In reality, the original settlers and natives fought few pitched battles and still fewer that deserved commemoration.) One such pioneer-and-native pageant proved tragic. Rehearsing an Independence Day program in Provo in 1879, Albert Park was killed when a fellow actor shot him with a supposedly harmless wad of tissue.[114]

A Pioneer Day celebration in Ogden narrowly avoided a much greater tragedy. Organizers invited two thousand children to watch a cannon firing and, hoping for the loudest possible noise, put wet grass and sand into the gun's barrel instead of the usual blank charge. When the cannon exploded, it showered debris over the area, including a twenty-five-pound piece that crashed through the roof of a nearby tailor's shop. But neither there nor among the densely packed

PIC-NIC PARTY

AT THE

HEAD WATERS

OF

BIG COTTONWOOD.

PRES. BRIGHAM YOUNG *respectfully invites* ~~George Laubt~~ *and family to attend a Pic-Nic Party at the Lake in Big Cottonwood Kanyon on*

Friday, 24th of July.

REGULATIONS.

You will be required to start so as to pass the first mill, about four miles up the Kanyon, before 12 o'clock, on Thursday, the 23rd, as no person will be allowed to pass that point after 2 o'clock, p.m. of that day.

All persons are forbidden to smoke cigars or pipes, or kindle fires, at any place in the Kanyon, except on the camp ground.

The Bishops are requested to accompany those invited from their respective Wards, and see that each person is well fitted for the trip, with good, substantial, steady teams, wagons, harness, hold-backs and locks, capable of completing the journey without repair, and a good driver, so as not to endanger the life of any individual.

Bishops will, before passing the first mill, furnish a full and complete list of all persons accompanying them from their respective Wards, and hand the same to the Guard at the gate.

GREAT SALT LAKE CITY, July 18, 1857.

Invitation from Brigham Young to a picnic on July 24, 1857, celebrating the tenth anniversary of the pioneers' arrival in Utah. During this celebration, the Saints were informed that the U.S. Army had been deployed against them.

children were there injuries. "It was sure a miracle but not one of those children were hurt," said a local citizen.[115]

Independence Day and Pioneer Day celebrations also featured afternoon dinners, sometimes served on long tables under the temporary boweries.[116] During the later pioneer period, a favorite menu was barbecued lamb followed by molasses cake. Sometimes a jug of beer or a barrel of wine was present "for those who cared to indulge."[117] Intoxicants may have been responsible for the killing of a Native American during a celebration staged by the Panguitch citizens. Purportedly wishing to "scare" the Indian by shooting through the Indian's hat, a settler fired "too low." The man was sent to prison for the shooting.[118]

DANCING

Independence Day and Pioneer Day usually ended with a dance— no doubt the single most important social activity of the pioneers. Perhaps the reason that they so universally enjoyed dancing was because it reflected their ideals. "There was no class distinction," recalled one pioneer. "Everyone had an equal good time and part."[119] Indeed, dancing allowed all members of the society to join together, whatever their status or age.[120] Most communities even accepted infants at their dances, and by the time children reached the age of four or five, they were seasoned performers.[121]

In the winter season, dances might start after a lecture or dramatic production at the local schoolhouse, which perhaps led some settlers to give dancing the unusual name of "spelling school."[122] On the other hand, large summer dances were usually held outside on a piece of flat ground, perhaps under a bowery. To prepare for a dance, the soil was packed and then swept.[123] Smaller dances, summer or winter, were held in any home large enough to accommodate a single quadrille of four dancers.[124]

In most rural areas, admission to a dance was paid with commodities. Wheat, corn, squash, potatoes, or even chickens might do.[125] Nancy Higgins, a southern Utah settler, remembered that a barefoot suitor called at her home with a pumpkin under one arm ("he looked quite differently from what the young men of today do").[126] The lack of shoes added to the rustic atmosphere; at some rural dances, nine out of ten dancers went barefoot.[127]

The dances included reels, quadrilles, schottisches, polkas, mazurkas, and an occasional waltz. Other dances were identified as the "Trolli-Hopsie" and the "Danish Slide-off."[128] Round dances in which couples paired off were restricted, especially in Utah's early times. For music, most communities depended on either the fiddle or accordion, but variations included the guitar, flute, and small organ, any of which might be played with an accompanying fiddle.[129] Some communities boasted a small orchestra, like Sanpete County's "Westenshow Orchestra," which had two violins, two bass fiddles, and a second bass.[130] However, smaller dancing parties were sometimes required to "make do." On these occasions, settlers used a comb covered with paper or they whistled, sang, or clapped. Sometimes they provided rhythm with a device called the "bones"—a percussion instrument formed from pairs of thin strips of bone or wood held between the fingers.[131] Musicians and the "floorwalker" (also known as the "caller" or "prompter") were paid from the commodities gathered at the door or perhaps with a load of wood.

Clearly, dancing was an important activity that the pioneers took seriously. Many community dances gave prizes to the best dancers on the floor, and despite pioneer scarcity, some settlers used their hardearned means to attend a dancing school. "Every one wanted to be a good dancer," explained Edwin R. Lamb.[132] And later, when the oldtimers looked back on their early days, dancing brought pleasant memories. "In the candle light we would dance and swing, making the light flicker in the breeze caused from the swishing of our skirts," reminisced one former enthusiast.[133] Indeed, dancing was one of the reasons that the pioneers, without the "means of [modern] luxuries," nevertheless had "a good time and enjoyed [them]selves more than most folks seem to do today." That, at least, was the judgment of Weber County resident Mary Ann Geertsen.[134]

CONCLUSION

How unique were the Mormon social and group values? Many of the activities the Mormons relished—their charities, work and party bees, neighborly visits, community holidays, and their unrelenting round of dances—had counterparts throughout America, especially in rural and frontier areas. Perhaps the characteristics that set Mormon communities apart were the degree to which these acts were practiced and the religious content that filled the Mormons' daily frontier life. The Mormon village system was designed to facilitate group life, while Mormonism itself, as a new religious movement, infused its converts with a sense of mission that made pioneering virtually a sacrament. These two factors made what happened in the LDS Intermountain West unusual, if not unique.

We should not be surprised, therefore, if the old-timers looked back on their experiences with satisfaction. Pioneering had been a struggle, but Mormon group life gave their lives meaning and warmth. This is doubtless the reason why so many of the pioneers were emphatic about having had *good* times despite *hard* times. They believed that they had helped each other, borne each other's burdens, and lived a life that was broader than individual wants and material accumulation. Indeed, their recollections speak of a society full of social bonds that our own troubled generation can look back on with gratitude and envy.

Ronald W. Walker is Senior Research Historian at the Smith Institute for LDS History and Professor of History, Brigham Young University. He is indebted to his research assistant, Joseph Richardson, who completed preliminary research and prepared an early draft.

NOTES

1. For a sampling of the literature on Mormon village life, see Wilford Charles Bailey, "The Social Organization of the Mormon Village" (Ph.D. diss., University of Chicago, 1955); Reed H. Bradford, "A Mormon Village: A Study in Rural Social Organization" (Ph.D. diss., Louisiana State University, 1939); Richard V. Francaviglia, *The Mormon Landscape: Existence, Creation, and Perception of a Unique Image in the American West* (New York: AMS Press, 1978); Edward A. Geary, "For the Strength of the Hills: Imagining Mormon Country," in *After 150 Years: The Latter-day Saints in Sesquicentennial Perspective*, ed. Thomas G. Alexander and Jessie L. Embry (Provo, Utah: Charles Redd Center for Western Studies, 1983), 72–94; Edward A. Geary, *Goodbye to Poplarhaven: Recollections of a Utah Boyhood* (Salt Lake City: University of Utah Press, 1985); Richard H. Jackson, "The Mormon Village: Genesis and Antecedents of the City of Zion Plan," *BYU Studies* 17, no. 2 (1977): 223–40; Richard H. Jackson and Robert L. Layton, "The Mormon Village: Analysis of a Settlement Type," *Professional Geographer* 28 (May 1976): 136–41; Dean L. May, "The Making of Saints: The Mormon Town as a Setting for the Study of Cultural Change," *Utah Historical Quarterly* 45 (December 1977): 75–92; Dean L. May, *Three Frontiers: Family, Land, and Society in the American West, 1850–1900*, Interdisciplinary Perspectives on Modern History, ed. Robert Fogel and Stephan Thernstrom (New York: Cambridge University Press, 1994); Lowry Nelson, *The Mormon*

Village: A Study in Social Origins, Brigham Young University Studies, no. 3 (Provo, Utah: Research Division, Brigham Young University, 1930); Charles S. Peterson, "A Mormon Town: One Man's West," *Journal of Mormon History 3* (1976): 3–12; and Michael S. Raber, "Family Life and Rural Society in Spring City, Utah: The Basis of Order in a Changing Agrarian Landscape," in *Community Development in the American West: Past and Present Nineteenth and Twentieth Century Frontiers,* ed. Jessie L. Embry and Howard A. Christy (Provo, Utah: Charles Redd Center for Western Studies, 1985), 135–62. Several of Wallace Stegner's essays in *Mormon Country* (New York: Duell, Sloan and Pearce, 1942) also address Mormon village life.

2. For background on the WPA project, see Larry Malmgren, "A History of the WPA in Utah" (master's thesis, Utah State University, 1965).

3. Syria Allen [b. 1863], Personal History, 3:3, Pioneer Biographies. About half of the WPA pioneer materials were autobiographies and sketches; the rest were responses to the WPA questionnaire. The WPA materials are found in several repositories, including the collection entitled "WPA Biographical Sketches" at the Utah State Historical Society, Salt Lake City, Utah (hereafter cited as Bio. Sketches). A microfilm collection of this material is available under the title of "Utah Pioneer Biographies" (hereafter cited as P. Bios) at the Family History Library of The Church of Jesus Christ of Latter-day Saints, Salt Lake City. Since these collections have overlapping, but different, content, I have used both while researching and writing this paper. Citations from the Biographical Sketches include page numbers whereas the Pioneer Biographies collection citations provide microfilm reel and page number. When quoting responses to the WPA questionnaire (available in both collections), I listed the appropriate question number, as in question 74. Finally, in order to give a rough idea of the chronological experience of the pioneers, I have provided birth dates in brackets. Birth dates are taken mainly from the WPA registers and are unverified.

4. Thadius Fullmer [b. 1853], Questionnaire, question 74.

5. James T. Ivie [b. 1850], Personal History, 3, Bio. Sketches.

6. Ellen Lee Woodard [b. 1867], Questionnaire, question 74.

7. Elvira M. Wing Lance [b. 1865], Questionnaire, question 74.

8. Julia Hills Eager Johnson [b. 1855], Questionnaire, question 67.

9. Dorothea Jorgensen [b. 1856], Personal History, 16:4, P. Bios.

10. Amy Carline Davis Phillips [b. 1851], Personal History, 23:3, P. Bios.

11. James Munroe Redd [b. 1863], Personal History, 4, Bio. Sketches.

12. Nancy Elizabeth Bethers Smith [b. 1837], Personal History, 2, Bio. Sketches.

13. Mary Ann Parker Richards [b. 1839], Personal History, 4, Bio. Sketches.

14. Eliza Burgess Briggs [b. 1859], Personal History, 6:1, P. Bios.

15. Rose Berry West [b. 1862], Personal History, 1–2, Bio. Sketches; Rose Berry West [b. 1862], Personal History, 29:1, P. Bios.

16. John Staheli [b. 1857], Personal History, 27:2, P. Bios; Edward R. Frei [b. 1845], Personal History, 10:1–2, P. Bios.

17. Adelaide Jackson Slack [b. 1868], Personal History, 25:4, P. Bios.

18. Charles Twelves [no b. date], Personal History, 1–2, Bio. Sketches.

19. Arze Adams [b. 1865], Questionnaire, question 53.

20. Hilda Miller Olsen [b. 1875], Questionnaire, question 24; Hilda Miller Olsen [b. 1875], Personal History, 1–2, Bio. Sketches.

21. Mons Peterson [b. 1861], Questionnaire, question 20.

22. William John Hill [1838], Personal History, 4, Bio. Sketches.

23. Lorenzo Hadley [b. 1851], Personal History, 12:7–8, P. Bios.

24. Henry Excell [b. 1858], Questionnaire, question 34.

25. Martha Cragun Cox [1852], Personal History, 15–16, Bio. Sketches.

26. Ernest Munk [b. 1858], Personal History, 20:2, P. Bios.

27. Ephraim Young Moore [b. 1879], Questionnaire, question 24.

28. Henry O. Jensen [b. 1871], Personal History, 15:1, P. Bios.

29. Polly Ann Eliner Taylor [b. 1856], Questionnaire, question 24.

30. Seed: Jordan H. Brady [b. 1863], Questionnaire, question 24; farm equipment: Pernilla Anderson [b. 1850], Questionnaire, questions 26–27; and dairy products: Isaac H. Grace [b. 1857], Questionnaire, question 24.

31. Malona May Moore [b. 1875], Questionnaire, question 24; Jerusha Baxter Maughan [b. 1859], Questionnaire, question 18; Charles South [b. 1835], Questionnaire, question 24.

32. Owen W. Clark [b. 1860], Personal History, 7:1, P. Bios.

33. Willis Eugene Robison [b. 1854], Questionnaire, question 20.

34. Ann Elizabeth Melville Bishop [b. 1856], Questionnaire, question 67.

35. Rensselaer Lee Kirk [b. 1859], Questionnaire, question 34.

36. William Jasper Henderson [b. 1863], Questionnaire, question 24.

37. Lydia Ann Colvin Taylor [b. 1851], Questionnaire, questions 15, 24, and 74.

38. Mary Evans Williams Leatham [b. 1851], Personal History, 18:4, P. Bios.

39. David H. Cannon Jr. [b. 1860], Questionnaire, question 24.

40. John [Jack] Greenwell [b. 1868], Personal History, 11:5, P. Bios.

41. Richard Franklin Shumway [b. 1868], Personal History, 25:2, P. Bios.

42. Sarah M. Chaffin [b. 1815], Personal History, 3, Bio. Sketches.

43. George Thomas Peay [b. 1861], Questionnaire, question 24.

44. Peter Peterson [b. 1860] and Celestia M. Terry Peterson [b. 1860], Personal History, 23:3, P. Bios.

45. August Sorenson Mackelprang [b. 1851], Questionnaire, question 24. Fast offerings required village members to fast the first Thursday of each month and donate the uneaten food to the local storehouse.

46. William Olson [b. 1853], Questionnaire, question 24; Livy Olsen [b. 1856], Personal History, 22:6, P. Bios; Soren Peter Sorensen [b. 1854], Questionnaire, question 24.

47. Sophronia Carter [b. 1841], Personal History, 2, Bio. Sketches.

48. Sarah Joy Bennington Surrage [b. 1854], Personal History, 27:2, P. Bios.

49. Artemesia Draper Anderson [b. 1857], Personal History, 3:5–6, P. Bios. Also see *Our Pioneer Heritage,* comp. Kate B. Carter, 20 vols. (Salt Lake City: Daughters of Utah Pioneers, 1958–77), 6:549.

50. Annie Hermin Cardon Shaw [b. 1861] related these incidents about her mother in Personal History, 4–5, Bio. Sketches.

51. Olsen, Personal History, 22:13.

52. Ephrasia Cox Day [b. 1854], Personal History, 1–2, Bio. Sketches. The incident is published in Carter, *Our Pioneer Heritage,* 9:580–81.

53. Day, Personal History, 1–2. See Carter, *Our Pioneer Heritage,* 9:580–81.

54. Mads Anderson Jr. [b. 1863], Personal History, 3:2–3, P. Bios.

55. Mary Henrie Cooper [b. 1866], Questionnaire, question 74.

56. Fullmer, Questionnaire, question 34.

57. Ezekeil Johnson [no b. date] and Julia Hills [no b. date], Personal History, 31, Bio. Sketches. The document is actually a series of "Ancestral Sketches and Memoirs" written by Mary Julia Johnson Wilson, who was born in Johnson's Fort (Enoch), Utah, November 13, 1862.

58. James Jepson Jr. [b. 1854], Personal History, 15:3–5, P. Bios.

59. James H. Jennings [b. 1853], Personal History, 15:6, P. Bios.

60. Thomas Hull III [b. 1837], Personal History, 1, Bio. Sketches.

61. Moses Leon Burdick [b. 1861], Questionnaire, question 53.

62. Cannon, Questionnaire, question 53.

63. Moroni Spillsbury [no b. date], Personal History, 27:2, P. Bios.

64. Catherine C. Larsen [b. 1856], Personal History, 18:3, P. Bios.

65. Hannah McFarland Bingham [b. 1863], Questionnaire, question 34B.

66. Diantha Olsen Newton [b. 1869], Personal History, 3, Bio. Sketches.

67. Martha Canfield [no b. date], Personal History, 3, Bio. Sketches.

68. Eliza Othilda Christensen Jorgensen [b. 1858], Personal History, 16:2, P. Bios. The judgment was shared by many pioneer women. "We enjoyed being together," said Alvaretta Faroquine Robinson. "We would spin . . . just for the fun of it." Alvaretta Faroquine Robinson [b. 1854], Questionnaire, question 34.

69. Pernilla Anderson [b. 1850], Questionnaire, question 34.

70. Grace, Questionnaire, question 34.

71. Naomi Read [Reed?] Cowan [b. 1857], Personal History, 4, Bio. Sketches.

72. Thomas C. Groneman [b. 1860], Questionnaire, question 34.

73. Hanah Johnson [b. 1870], Personal History, 16:2, P. Bios; Annie Peterson Jensen [b. 1875], Personal History, 15:2, P. Bios.

74. Jensen, Personal History, 15:2.

75. Bingham, Questionnaire, question 34B.

76. Annie Peterson Jensen [b. 1875], Questionnaire, question 34.

77. Grace, Questionnaire, question 34.

78. Rachel A. Brown [b. 1876], Personal History, 6:2, P. Bios.

79. Eliza Burdett Horsepool [b. 1857], Personal History, 4–5, Bio. Sketches.

80. Hannah Hanson Huntsman [b. 1865], Questionnaire, question 34.

81. Mary Julia Johnson Wilson [b. 1862], Personal History, 32, Bio. Sketches.

82. Taklla Amanda Anderson (Mattson) Luke [b. 1866], Personal History, 3, Bio. Sketches.

83. Martha Horspool Hellewell [b. 1860], Personal History, question 34.

84. Laura Smith Hadfield [b. 1858], Personal History, 6, Bio. Sketches.

85. Olive Cheney Aldous [b. 1851], Personal History, 5, Bio. Sketches; A. Y. Duke [b. 1860], Questionnaire, question 22.

86. Moore, Questionnaire, question 34; see also Duke, Questionnaire, question 22.

87. Annie George Miles [b. 1859], Questionnaire, question 34.

88. Fanny Young Clyde Wall [b. 1860], Questionnaire, question 44.

89. Henrietta Wilson [b. 1851], Personal History, 30:1, P. Bios; see also Lydia Ann Taylor, Questionnaire, question 44.

90. Cox, Personal History, 17–18.

91. Aldous, Personal History, 5–6.

92. Lucinda Alvira Pace Redd [b. 1864], Questionnaire, question 53; Nancy Elizabeth Darrow Higgins [b. 1865], Questionnaire, question 53.

93. Israel Nielson [b. 1848], Personal History, 21:7, P. Bios; Olsen, Personal History, 11–12. Also see Ann Eliza Pehrson [b. 1853], Questionnaire, question 53; and Andrew Oman [b. 1866], Questionnaire, question 53. For background of Young's tours, see Gordon Irving, "Encouraging the Saints: Brigham Young's Annual Tours of the Mormon Settlements," *Utah Historical Quarterly* 45 (summer 1977): 233–51.

94. Maggie Cragun [no b. date], Personal History, 7:3, P. Bios.

95. Newton, Personal History, 3–4.

96. Newton, Personal History, 3–4.

97. Matilda Olson Sprague [b. 1854], Personal History, 5, Bio. Sketches.

98. John Henry Ward Lister [b. 1861], Questionnaire, question 74. See also Malinda Rhoads Morgan [b. 1863], Questionnaire, question 53; and Isaiah Cox [b. 1859], Questionnaire, question 53.

99. Alice Ann Langston Dalton [b. 1865], Personal History, 3, Bio. Sketches; Chrystine Carlile Giles [b. 1848], Questionnaire, question 53; Julia Ann Wright Petty [b. 1847], Personal History, 23:3, P. Bios; Joseph E. Taylor [b. 1860], Personal History, 28:5, P. Bios.

100. Mary Jane Perkins Wilson [b. 1870], Personal History, 30:4, P. Bios; Walter Slack [b. 1868], Personal History, 25:4, P. Bios.

101. Aldous, Personal History, 6.

102. Shaw, Personal History, 5–6.

103. John H. Earl [b. 1855] and Ada Arville Burk Earl [b. 1857], Personal History, 9:4, P. Bios.

104. Phillips, Personal History, 23:3.

105. Anderson, Questionnaire, question 53.

106. Jane Sprunt Warner Garner [b. 1863], Personal History, 5, Bio. Sketches.

107. Newton, Personal History, 2–3.

108. Canfield, Personal History, 2.

109. Marinda Allen Ingles [b. 1857], Personal History, 5, Bio. Sketches; Robert Nelson Watts [b. 1849], Questionnaire, question 53; Madora Browning Weaver [b. 1856], Questionnaire, question 53.

110. Jennings, Personal History, 15:5.

111. Cyrus Sanford [b. 1813], Personal History, 25:3, P. Bios.

112. Aldous, Personal History, 6.

113. Huntsman, Questionnaire, question 53.

114. Groneman, Questionnaire, question 34; Joseph Park [b. 1852], Questionnaire, question 34; Mary Ann Bolitho [b. 1856], Personal History, 5:2, P. Bios. Some sources place the incident several years earlier.

115. Taylor, Personal History, 28:7–8.

116. Weaver, Questionnaire, question 53.

117. Canfield, Personal History, 2; James Herman Tegan [b. 1858], Questionnaire, question 53.

118. David James Shakespear [b. 1861], Questionnaire, question 34.

119. Edwin R. Lamb [b. 1831], Personal History, 2, Bio. Sketches.

120. Anderson, Questionnaire, question 22.

121. Hadfield, Personal History, 6.

122. Jennings, Personal History, 15:2.

123. Garner, Personal History, 4.

124. Polly Berthena Huntington [b. 1849], Questionnaire, question 22.

125. Garner, Personal History, 4.

126. Higgins, Questionnaire, question 22.

127. Henderson, Questionnaire, question 22.

128. Lamb, Personal History, 2; Henderson, Questionnaire, question 22; Peterson and Peterson, Personal History, 23:2; Taylor, Questionnaire, question 74.

129. Nielson, Personal History, 21:4; Peterson and Peterson, Personal History, 23:2; Elisha Wilbur [b. 1847], Questionnaire, question 4; Taylor, Questionnaire, question 74.

130. Mary Louise Wintch [b. 1858], Personal History, 30:2, P. Bios.

131. Henderson, Questionnaire, question 22; Surrage, Personal History, 27:3; Alma Lutz [b. 1841], Personal History, 18:5, P. Bios; Hadley, Personal History, 12:12.

132. Lamb, Personal History, 2; Robert Green [b. 1860], Questionnaire, question 22.

133. Garner, Personal History, 4.

134. Mary Ann Geertsen [b. 1854], Questionnaire, question 22.

It Takes a Village:
Social Character in Rural Settlements

Dean L. May

Shortly before her death, Caroline Henrietta Lind Adams, whose third child was born in Alpine, Utah, called her twelve children to her bedside. She gave them advice, bid them farewell, and then sang a song to remind them that life's purposes transcend the personal and even the familial—one of the oldest Mormon folk themes:

> Now let us rejoice in the day of salvation.
> No longer as strangers on earth need we roam.
> Good tidings are sounding to us and each nation,
> And shortly the hour of redemption will come,
>
> We'll love one another and never dissemble,
> But cease to do evil and ever be one.
> And when the ungodly are fearing and tremble,
> We'll watch for the day when the Savior will come,
>
> When all that was promised the Saints will be given,
> And none will molest them from morn until ev'n,
> And earth will appear as the Garden of Eden,
> And Jesus will say to all Israel, "Come home."[1]

She took the solemn occasion to remind the crowd at her bedside that they were not just her children, but also her contribution to the ongoing task of building the Mormon Zion and to admonish them to take up the charge with zeal. They had been, by virtue of their upbringing in a Mormon village, endowed with powerful and important defenses against the ills of our late-twentieth-century society. Such an upbringing required a village.

The power of Mormon village life is particularly evident in my study *Three Frontiers*. The first of the frontiers is the farming district of Sublimity in the Willamette Valley of Oregon; the second, the Mormon village of Alpine, Utah; and the third, the farming district of Middleton, Idaho, twenty miles west of Boise. Sublimity, Alpine, and Middleton each began in successive decades: the 1840s, 1850s, and 1860s, respectively. And the settlers of each district brought to the West their own cultural baggage—their own understandings of the purposes and character of family, of land and land ownership, and of community. The result was three strikingly different societies.

THREE PATTERNS OF SOCIAL ORGANIZATION

The Sublimity, Oregon, folk distributed themselves thinly across the landscape, aggregating in neighbor-kin clusters that admitted little social world beyond that visible from the front stoop of their stately frame houses. Habits brought with them from the South and Midwest encouraged the forming of intense family and close neighbor ties. To all appearances, these ties constituted the community in which the greater part of their lives was played out. For them, as for historian Steven Hahn's up-country Georgia yeomen, "families seemed particularly inclined to locate near one another,"[2] and "when family did not reside nearby, yeomen reached out to other farmers in the area, creating bonds of community."[3]

Yet the breadth of those bonds created in Oregon was limited and local. There is little evidence of a wider identification with the civil jurisdiction and trading center of Sublimity. Rather, the citizens considered themselves primarily part of scattered local farm districts, such as Whiteaker, McAlpin, or Victor Point.[4] Even worship took place principally in family-neighborhood groups. Moreover, their world, again like that of Hahn's up-country yeomen, was one where the household was the setting of most of the production and consumption, where much of all trade and barter took place within the kin-neighbor group, and where each household's first preoccupation was assuring that it could produce enough to sustain its members until the next harvest.[5] Though their farms were enormous by Alpine standards, averaging almost three hundred acres to Alpine's fifteen, the Sublimity folk farmed only a tenth of their land. The rest they planned to pass on to their children and children's children, thereby creating a base for dynastic continuity.

In Alpine taking up land was more an economic necessity than an effort to acquire a base for perpetuating a dynasty. Most of the settlers there had been factory operatives or craftspeople in their native England. Their conversion and migration had severed kin connections. Thus, the key institution in Alpine was not the family, but the

Church-village community—the center of social life and the motivating and driving force behind politics and cooperative economic endeavors. Neighbors and kin in Alpine met more often in the meeting-house than in their parlors, the favorite meeting place of Sublimity folk. The lines of a poem written by an Alpine native express their preference well: "A church arose of sturdy native stone, / And five hundred people proudly called it home."[6] While Sublimity settlers dispersed themselves into an expansive physical space, Alpine settlers contracted into a compact settlement surrounding the church, which they saw as their home. Where the structure of Sublimity was made up of fairly autonomous clusters of neighbors and kin, Alpine's social structure comprised the whole population of the village.

In early Middleton, Idaho, neither the land, as in Sublimity, nor the community, as in Alpine, provided a base for social organization and cohesiveness. Middleton was initially settled by gold seekers and Civil War refugees. Women were nearly as rare in the farming as in the mining districts of the territory, and neither family nor community were vital institutions for the founding population. Early visitors found that

Courtesy Blanche Devey Bennett

Built in 1872, this 37' x 60' rock church also served the people of Alpine, Utah, as a schoolhouse until 1900. The citizenry spent so much time in this building they "called it home." This Sunday School group was photographed in 1916 on the north side of the church.

Middleton people interacted principally at the local flour mill (at times it served as the post office), the saloon, the racetrack, and dances.

If Sublimity society can be represented by small nodes of neighbor-kin groups that dot the landscape and Alpine by an extensive, tightly woven community net, early Middleton would seem to be a series of points spread along the river with but a few faint lines connecting families into neighborhoods or a broader community. Middleton seemed in some measure to embody what Alexis de Tocqueville feared might happen in America: "Where family pride ceases to act, individual selfishness comes into play. When the idea of family becomes vague, indeterminate, and uncertain, a man thinks of his present convenience; he provides for the establishment of his next succeeding generation and no more."[7]

DIFFERENT SENSES OF SOCIAL ETHICS AND SENSIBILITY

This short paper cannot possibly recount the many consequences of the three patterns of social organization I have described. My model, however, suggests that from different cultural assumptions about the purposes and meanings of land, family, and community, there arise different patterns of production, marketing, and consumption, different roles for women, different ways of dealing with deviance and violence, and different senses of obligation to ancestors, to progeny, and to others in the society. What I would like to do in the space remaining is describe, as I see it, how the character of human interaction in the three societies created different senses of social ethics and sensibility. The contrast will highlight some of the unique and powerful social structures of nineteenth-century Mormon villages like Alpine, so let me begin with Alpine, using specific families to illustrate the broader patterns.

In 1870 when a U.S. census taker made the Alpine rounds, the William and Julia Strong household consisted of eight people: the couple, age 38 and 34, and six children ranging from Don, 13, to baby Estella, not quite a year old. The family farmed thirty acres, twice as much as the town's average. They also kept a garden lot in town and had a team of horses, 3 milk cows, 2 oxen, 4 calves or steers for beef, 12 sheep, and 2 hogs. Their granary stored 240 bushels of wheat, 200 of corn, and 80 of oats. They kept 250 pounds of potatoes in the root cellar behind the house, and that year Julia had churned 100 pounds of butter and spun 20 pounds of wool to work into socks and sweaters against the hard Alpine winter. The family no doubt had other commodities that were not reported—chickens, eggs, carrots, onions, and other garden vegetables. Yet, after contributing 10 percent of their harvest to the bishop's storehouse and saving enough for their own needs, they had very little to trade. Indeed, they may have had to draw upon the storehouse in April or May to make it through until the clumps of pie plant (rhubarb) pushing through the wet soil could be harvested and radishes, lettuce, beets, peas, and new potatoes would bring color and variety once again to their bland winter diet.

At the same time, four hundred miles northwest in Middleton, the census taker found the settlers Moses and Emmaroy Fowler, 39 and 36 years old, who had no children but had taken in Emmaroy's blind brother, William; her mother, Matilda Douglas; and Moses' sister Elizabeth. Their farm appeared to be a successful commercial operation. On 160 improved acres, they harvested 1,600 bushels of spring wheat, 2,000 of oats, and 200 of barley and produced 400 pounds of butter from the milk of their seven cows. Of course, Fowler needed help in running so extensive an operation and had paid $300 for farm equipment and $1500 in wages to the young men who helped him. The Fowlers, however, produced no hay, pork, wool, corn, potatoes, or garden vegetables.[8] They apparently sold their grain for cash at nearby mining camps and used the proceeds to buy the food and clothing needed for their household.

That same summer, there were six people in the household of George and Elizabeth Hunt of Sublimity, Oregon. The Hunts were about the same age as the Strongs and Fowlers, 39 and 36, and had a daughter and two sons—Georgianna, 12; Melanchthon, 10; and Jeptha, 8. A twenty-two-year-old hired hand, E. F. Perkins, lived with them. They farmed 35 of their 640 acres, harvesting a ton of hay; 100 bushels of wheat, 250 of oats, 100 of potatoes, and 300 of apples; 200 board feet of lumber; and a clip of 400 pounds of wool from their 80 sheep. They also kept 20 hogs, 6 horses, and 25 head of cattle and churned 300 pounds of butter from the cream. They harvested less wheat and fewer potatoes than the Strongs but had two fewer mouths to feed and could buy any supplies they lacked by selling or bartering surplus hogs, cattle, wool, apples, and timber.[9] By relying on beef, hams, and bacon, they could feed themselves well enough through the mild Oregon winters. If flour became scarce in the spring, Elizabeth could readily borrow from her sister-in-law, Temperance Downing, who lived on the next farm and would have saved a good winter's supply from the 800 bushels of wheat her husband, John, had harvested that year.

The Strongs, Fowlers, and Hunts each typify the predominant mode of production in their districts—the first barely subsistent, the second expansively commercial, the third aiming first to provide for the family, though with a clear intent to grow a surplus of certain crops for market sale. These patterns of production imply differing attitudes towards the land and its uses. But more generally, they may also define different contexts for human interaction within the three societies.

Alpine people met, discussed, planned, and worked with one another in voluntary associations on a daily basis. Yet the subsistence character of their economy meant that they seldom met at the marketplace. Most families had little to buy or sell. The variety and paucity of crops produced on each farm indicate that the main aim was to produce enough to provide until the next harvest. When exchange took place, it was most often a cup of flour for an egg, a skein of yarn for a hen, or a mess of beans for a pan of potatoes—not five hundred bushels of wheat for one thousand dollars.[10] In time of need, residents could seek assistance from the bishop's storehouse, where a variety of the commodities donated as tithing were kept for redistribution to the poor. But material exchange most commonly occurred in the contexts of neighborly borrowing and lending among households (done principally by women) or contributions to or assistance from the tithing house, which, being administered by the bishop and Relief Society president, was sanctified and removed from worldly bargaining and advantage seeking.

The significance of this cooperative interdependence is profound. If it were possible to peer into Alpine on a Saturday afternoon in the 1870s and observe each meeting of the townspeople, we would find a striking pattern. William Strong might be soliciting books from Albert Marsh for the Alpine City Library Association. Julia, noted for her fine voice, would perhaps be rehearsing a song to sing at the funeral of the Devey baby, Albert, who lived just three months. Ten or fifteen Relief Society sisters might also be rehearsing, and others preparing a luncheon for the Devey family. Bishop McCullough would be checking that the meetinghouse was draped in white and making last-minute preparations before conducting the funeral. Some residents would be shopping at the Alpine Cooperative Store for needles, thread, or tea. A few with some surplus—John Moyle, Angelia Vance, Thomas Carlisle, or James Wiley—might be hauling vegetables, milk, butter, or eggs to the railroad station at American Fork for shipment to Salt Lake City or to mining camps up American Fork Canyon or in the Salt

Lake Valley. The youth of the Alpine Literary Society could be enjoying a canyon outing. Elsie Booth might have organized an activity for the smaller children, while Richard T. Booth and John Vance might be discussing plans for a future Sunday School picnic.

We would see that people were interacting with others outside their household almost everywhere we looked and that most were engaged in or planning voluntary activities. Certainly some household members would be carrying out the tasks necessary for physical survival—producing, feeding, clothing, housing, and exchanging— but these occupied a relatively small part of person-to-person contacts outside the household. And each time people met and talked—when the Deveys asked Julia to sing at baby Albert's funeral; when Albert Marsh agreed to give a half-day's work to the library fund; when Elsie Booth took twenty or thirty children on a canyon walk, teaching them to identify shooting stars and Indian paintbrush or to make oboelike whistles from joint grass beside the streams; or even when the men and women of the town sang together weekly in a choir—each time these encounters took place, connecting strands of vaguely defined outward obligation were being teased out, twisted, and in time securely tied. The obligations were never made contractual or explicit, and in their very indeterminate quality lay their power. For who can determine when they have repaid the debts owed to those who took time from life-sustaining activities to teach embroidery, literature, or that the meadow lark sings "Alpine is a pretty-little-place!" The Alpine people, without quite willing it or realizing it, were constructing a web of obligation, gratitude, and affection that held residents emotionally and, hence, physically to the town.

The Sublimity economy was much like that of Alpine, though by custom more than by hard necessity. While the people took pride in having fine homes and thrifty farms and were alert to markets, mines, and other means to better themselves, the first aim of each family was independence. They grew a variety of crops on their farms, and at first only a few farmers, like John Downing, native of Pennsylvania, moved aggressively into producing staples. Most of the others were content to farm only enough of their great tracts of land to feed themselves and provide a modest surplus to sell. They resisted the tendency of growth and progress to rob leisure and autonomy from their lives. From the reminiscences we have, theirs seems a convivial society, a people who enjoyed getting together for family events and holidays. They valued neighbors more than profits and tried to keep a reasonable balance between them.

George Hunt told his daughter a moral tale that says much about his values. An early family, the Fieldses, found a tract of land to squat on and set up camp under a great fir tree that stood beside the pioneer road. The family raised a few sheep, kept to themselves, and let neighbors know they wanted to be left alone. One day, passers-by noticed no signs of life and, investigating, found every member of the family dead or sick from a fever. The rescuers discovered fifteen hundred dollars in cash sewed in the pillow ticks—the probable reason for the Fieldses' unfriendliness. The family "would not make friends, for fear they would be robbed." Sarah Hunt Steeves concluded:

> Thus this family, supposed to have been poor, except for their sheep, starved to death or died of neglect, with plenty of funds for their needs, right in camp.
>
> For years the old fir tree stood guard over the place of this ill-fated camp, when a fire laid it low and then this old fallen monarch was still pointed out and the story told of the pioneer folk who lost their lives, probably because they refused their neighbors' friendship.[11]

The story is powerful and eloquent. The sacred fir tree initially offered promise in spite of the family's aloofness, yet, alas, it, like the Fields family, was burned and wasted after they chose money over neighborliness, the profane over the sacred. Worldliness had destroyed the once proud "monarch," and its rotting hulk became a warning to those who passed that way.

But the sin of the Fieldses was their aloofness from neighbors, not from all who came by. If there is a single word that best captures the social mentality of the Sublimity folk, it is *clannish*. They had a strong sense of common identity within the neighbor-kin group (they were often, after all, blood relatives). And they dotted the Waldo Hills with small, powerful communities that provided admirably for the social, moral, and physical needs of their members. Like the people of Alpine, they interacted principally in social, volunteer settings that spun threads of connection and obligation. But the span of these threads was short, restricted to a relatively small group. And while it was imperative to offer hospitality to all, those not of the clan were rarely given access to their small world. Relations with the outside were formal, contractual, and commercial.

If we were to look in on the Sublimity people in the 1870s, then, we would see frequent, close, familial, human contact within each of the small communities spread across the landscape. Georgianna Hunt, sixteen, might well be helping for a day at Cinderella Darst's, whose husband, Paul, has suddenly died of "apoplexy," leaving her with two daughters and an infant son, Charles, born shortly after his father's death. Elizabeth Hunt could be tending the family store, selling needles, tea, or tobacco to Margaret Downing, wife of John's brother, James, or to another neighbor lady, Elizabeth Shanks. Or she might be attending her sister-in-law Temperance Hunt Downing, whose chronic illness would lead to her death in 1876. On a Saturday or Sunday, George would be drilling the local men in a militia exercise. Or there might be a Sabbath service at the Rock Point school that many of the neighbor folk would attend. For at least a few months each year, the Whiteaker children, representing perhaps ten or fifteen families, most of them kin, would attend the school at Rock Point, their parents boarding the teacher, each a few weeks at a time. In any given household, one might find members of a neighbor household canning, assisting with a barn raising, helping thresh the wheat, knitting, or simply passing the time.

Certainly, as in Alpine, neighbors occasionally called upon one another to borrow a cup of flour, a dozen eggs, or other things they found suddenly in short supply. Yet the effort each household made to be independent of all others minimized such exchanges. As in Alpine, the people met each other far more often in the voluntary, sociable activities and settings that fostered indeterminate, and hence enduring, feelings of mutual affection and obligation. But as noted, these interactions were limited principally to small neighbor-kin groups.

In Middleton all but a few families lived in homes on their land, where the nearest neighbor would be half a mile or more away. The expansive distribution of homes in the Middleton district diminished not only neighborhood friction and petty irritation but also convivial socializing. In the Idaho district, people relatively rarely met and worked together in voluntary association.

It is thus no surprise that, were we to peer in on Middleton in the 1870s, it would be strikingly different from both Alpine and Sublimity. We would see dozens of freight wagons going to and from the mill, laden with grain they had bought from the farms of Fowler and his neighbors or with barrels of flour as they left to make their way to the Boise Basin or Owyhee mines. Each stop of a wagon would involve contact and negotiation. Fowler might frown a bit when the miller, Sam Foote, tells him that the price paid for wheat at the mill has dropped. John Eggleston and Dan Jury would be arranging to ship their abundant barley harvest to a brewery in Boise. John Kerr would be hauling potatoes to Silver City or contracting with William Hemingway to do it for him. A cluster of men waiting their turn to unload might be discussing whether wheat or oats would be best for planting this season. Who has horses to sell (James Thomas), or milk, butter, and cheese (G. Wooten), or beef (Jacob Plowhead)? Has the water gone down enough for freighters to bypass Perry Munday's ferry (and save three dollars per wagon on a round-trip to the Owyhee mines)?[12]

A good deal of other exchanges took place as well. Since farmers commonly specialized in no more than a few crops for commercial sale, many households had to purchase or trade with others for eggs, butter, vegetables, and other goods. No doubt much of this exchange took place informally between households, as in Alpine and Sublimity. But merchandising seems also to have played a considerable role in Middleton. In 1865, William Montgomery and V. R. Fuller opened a store in the village. In 1870 there were two stores, one run by Perry Munday, and another by James Stevenson and Abner Packard.[13] Edward Shainwald came to Middleton about 1877 to open yet another mercantile business. Trucking and bartering from farm to market, from home to home, and from store to home were the common activities that brought Middleton people into contact with one another.

We would, of course, see amusements and recreation. Here and there across the valley, and surely at John Eggleston's fine home, evening dances would occasionally be held, perhaps with Moses Fowler's blind brother-in-law, William Douglas, setting the pace with his fiddle. On Sunday there would be horse races, with much good-natured banter, a few bets placed, and occasional detours to J. H. Holland's saloon for a beer or shot of whiskey.[14] Also, on some Sundays, four or five Methodist families would worship together at Central Park, and in homes and schoolhouses elsewhere in the district, others would listen to sermons by itinerant or visiting city pastors. On almost any day, we would see men chatting in the saloon, the mill, the two stores, the blacksmith shop, and the butcher shop about local politics, commodity prices, and social events.[15]

Yet it may be significant that the settings for this socializing were principally commercial and male. We find no record of library associations, literary clubs, children's organizations, women's societies, choirs, or militias. Almost everywhere in Middleton, production and marketing constituted the content and setting of social interaction. These contacts were no doubt amiable, not meanspirited or grasping, and the nexus of each was mutual, not just personal, advantage. Yet every man weighed his own strength in the negotiation and tried to maximize his profit in the deal that was struck. Moreover, once the exchange took place and the accounts were settled, that was the end of the matter. The ties that might bring the negotiators together again were expectations of future opportunity, not unbounded strands of affection and past obligation.

No doubt, thousands of personal, noncommercial exchanges took place over decades within Sublimity's neighbor-kin groups or in the Alpine community, and these supported, at least for a time, a significant social convergence among the people there. In Middleton such exchanges were relatively rare. Divergence was the Middleton norm from the beginning. In 1900, only 4 percent of Middleton's 1870 population remained (11 of 281), compared to 32 percent of Alpine's people (73 of 210).

Still, lest Sublimity or Alpine folk take too much comfort from the contrast, we must acknowledge that their visions of what they were building in the West ultimately were not fully realized. Had we asked George Hunt and many of his Sublimity neighbors what they would expect to find there a hundred years hence, they would have imagined a mosaic of extended family groups living independently and comfortably on adjoining thrifty farms, bound to the land and to one another by a common family heritage. In fact, a family descended from George Hunt does still live on part of his land. But the rest are scattered. A cemetery on the land that went to his daughter, Sarah, a plot that George Hunt declared was to be "a family burying ground forever for the heirs of my body and all descendants of my body," is lost, its hallowed ground plowed and built upon.

Alpiners also had a dream, and though driven by religious faith, it was as centered in this world as were the dreams of their contemporaries in Oregon and Idaho. They had chosen to flee from the Babylon of industrial capitalism to "the mountains of Ephraim,"[16] where, led by God's anointed, they could build a society that was harmonious, orderly, unified, and compassionate—a people fit "for the coming of the Lord Jesus," as Brigham Young put it.[17] Their deepest desire was to find community so that "no longer as strangers on earth need we roam."[18] Alpine still exists. Its founders built a village and came to understand that it takes a village to give human beings a sense of purpose, place, and continuity in life. Strongs, Healeys, and Nashes still live there in considerable numbers. Much rootedness and much mutual care and sharing are still found there. In one sense, it may not matter much to old Alpiners that their fields are now covered with expensive homes, for the land never had for them the magic that it had for George Hunt and his neighbors. Land was, as for Middleton folk, a way to make a living. Yet old-timers speak with regret of the day the ward was divided. They look askance at subdivisions that flout the orderly line of the old streets with their predictable names, and they regret that their children no longer can afford to live in Alpine; real-estate developers and wealthy urbanites have pushed land values beyond the reach of the community's children.

An early Middleton settler, Junius Wright, found his first summer in Middleton "pleasant and profitable" and so determined to stay for a time. "Agriculture and allied enterprises soon established a foundation for progressive prosperity," he remembered. In fact, he and other Middleton folk had no particular social vision beyond "progressive prosperity" when they came. They were fleeing from a war and seeking comfort from its ravages in the promise of riches.[19] They found good land free and farmed it fully and profitably. Despite hard times (those in the '80s costing William Montgomery his place), many prospered. If they did very well, like Wright, they moved on. If they did poorly, like Montgomery, they moved as well. Those who stayed found it hard to found and maintain institutions that would free them from their world of getting and spending. Each person and each family made it on their own and ultimately took satisfaction in having done so. They were beholden to no one. They could turn the rich resources of the unsettled West to their own ends, and it was no one's business but their own.[20] They were among the thousands that built the New West of the 1860s that is with us still.

The men and women who founded Sublimity and Alpine had dreamed dreams and seen visions. Their stories are poignant and powerful for what they dreamed and for where they failed. As the paths of individuals within Sublimity, Alpine, and Middleton diverged ever more, the nature of the societies they built merged—first Sublimity, then, gradually, Alpine, turned toward Middleton's call—to a life lived for the moment, to comfort and plenty, to privacy, and to self.

Dean L. May is Professor of History at the University of Utah.

Notes

This essay draws from Dean L. May, *Three Frontiers: Family, Land, and Society in the American West, 1850–1900*, Interdisciplinary Perspectives on Modern History (New York: Cambridge University Press, 1994). I have drawn principally from chapters four, five, six, and seven of the book in preparing this paper. Permission to include portions of *Three Frontiers* in this publication has been granted by Cambridge University Press.

1. "Now Let Us Rejoice," in *Hymns of The Church of Jesus Christ of Latter-day Saints* (Salt Lake City: The Church of Jesus Christ of Latter-day Saints, 1948), no. 3; "Caroline Henrietta Lind Adams," in Jennie Adams Wild, "Builders of Alpine," manuscript in possession of Mrs. Wild, Alpine, Utah.

2. Steven Hahn, *The Roots of Southern Populism: Yeoman Farmers and the Transformation of the Georgia Upcountry, 1850–1890* (New York: Oxford University Press, 1983), 53.

3. Hahn, *Roots of Southern Populism,* 54.

4. See also Hahn, *Roots of Southern Populism;* Orville Vernon Burton, *In My Father's House Are Many Mansions: Family and Community in Edgefield, South Carolina,* Fred W. Morrison Series in Southern Studies (Chapel Hill: University of North Carolina Press, 1985); and Robert C. Kenzer, *Kinship and Neighborhood in a Southern Community: Orange County, North Carolina, 1849–1881* (Knoxville: University of Tennessee Press, 1987).

5. The discussion of what constitutes sufficient production for subsistence and for market has produced an extensive literature. See Bettye Hobbs Pruitt, "Self-Sufficiency and the Agricultural Economy of Eighteenth-Century Massachusetts," in *William and Mary Quarterly,* 3d. ser., 41 (July 1984): 333–64; Carole Shammas, "How Self-Sufficient Was Early America?" *Journal of Interdisciplinary History* 13 (autumn 1982): 260–62; James A. Henretta, "Families and Farms: *Mentalité* in Pre-Industrial America," *William and Mary Quarterly,* 3d ser., 35 (January 1978): 3–32; Michael Merrill, "Cash Is Good to Eat: Self-Sufficiency and Exchange in the Rural Economy of the United States," *Radical History Review* 4 (1977): 67–68; and James T. Lemon, *The Best Poor Man's Country: A Geographical Study of Early Southeastern Pennsylvania* (Baltimore: John Hopkins Press, 1972).

6. La Von Alice Brown Carroll, "Alpine," in Jennie Adams Wild, *Alpine Yesterdays: A History of Alpine, Utah County, Utah, 1850–1980* (Salt Lake City: Blaine Hudson Printing, 1982), iv.

7. Alexis de Tocqueville, *Democracy in America,* ed. Phillips Bradley, 2 vols. (New York: Alfred A. Knopf, 1945), 1:49–50.

8. 1870 U.S. Manuscript Census for Utah County, Utah, and Ada County, Idaho; Tax Lists for Utah County in 1870; manuscript of the U.S. Agricultural Production Census for Ada County for the same year. The Idaho tax lists, unlike those in Utah, do not contain production information for field crops.

9. U.S. Manuscript Census for 1870; Oregon State Census for 1865. Oregon tax lists contain no information on field crops, and the manuscript of the U.S. Agricultural Census has apparently been lost or destroyed.

10. The two-dollars-per-bushel price is from a list of standard prices for farm commodities published in 1863 at the central tithing office in Salt Lake City under Brigham Young's endorsement. This attempt to introduce stability into an often erratic price structure may have been unique to Utah. Bishops were to pay out and receive commodities from their local tithing office at the administered price, which thus set levels of prices within the economy generally.

11. Sarah Hunt Steeves, *Book of Remembrance of Marion County, Oregon, Pioneers, 1840–1860* (Portland: Berncliff, 1927), 70.

12. The names given are of those who the marshals taking the U.S. Agricultural Census for 1870 recorded as having harvested large quantities of the commodities mentioned. Perry Munday advertised his ferry in the *Boise Semi-Weekly Democrat*, December 19, 1868.

13. Informants for the Dunn and Bradstreet company were optimistic about Stephenson's prospects, vouching for his "good habits & attit[tude]. Char[acter]. and bus[iness] habits excellent. Strongly honorable. . . . Will undoubtedly pay any debt he may contract." Reporting on Munday and a partner, Enoch Reese, however, they wrote, "Their char[acter] for hon[esty] is not very good & it is very diff[iccul]t to collect of them." The firm was "constantly pinched & slow pay. In present shape are more or less at mercy of cr[editor]s." See the Dun & Bradstreet book abstracting reports sent to them by informants, "Oregon & Utah Territories, 1869–1873" on "J. M. Stephenson & Co., Middleton, November 20, 1869" and "Western Territories, Vol. II, . . . 1871–1876," on "P. Munday & Co., Middleton March 25, 1872." All are in the manuscripts collection of the Baker Library, Harvard University, Cambridge, Mass.

14. Eggleston's facilities were described in *Boise Tri-Weekly Statesman*, November 21, 1868. The musical talents of Will Douglas are mentioned in Jennie Cornell, "Pioneers of Canyon County," book 2. Judge Milton Kelly of Boise described a visit to the J. H. Holland saloon in *Boise Tri-Weekly Statesman*, November 4, 1876.

15. Thomas Carlisle operated a small store in his Alpine home as early as 1867, and the Alpine Cooperative store was opened in 1868. Except for the stores, Alpine had no other businesses that could serve as a setting for local talk and gossip.

16. "Ye Elders of Israel," in *Hymns*, no. 319.

17. "Thirteenth General Epistle of the First Presidency," in *Messages of the First Presidency*, comp. James R. Clark, 6 vols. (Salt Lake City: Bookcraft, 1965), 2:184 (October 29, 1855).

18. "Now Let Us Rejoice," in *Hymns*, no. 3.

19. Junius B. Wright, Reminiscences, Idaho State Archives, Boise.

20. Interestingly, political scientist Robert Blank sees Idaho as having a political culture that is unusually individualistic. Robert H. Blank, *Individualism in Idaho: The Territorial Foundations* (Pullman: Washington State University Press, 1988).

A Peculiar People: Community and Commitment in Utah Valley

Richard Neitzel Holzapfel and David A. Allred

Historical geographer Wilbur Zelinsky identified seven religious regions in the United States in an important 1961 essay.[1] As one would expect, the region for The Church of Jesus Christ of Latter-day Saints was centered in Utah and extended outward. Concerning this region, one geographer of religion noted, "Nothing elsewhere in the nation compares with the dominance of the Latter-day Saints in the intermountain area."[2] Utah County in particular is one of the most religiously inclined large population counties in the nation. By 1985, the Provo-Orem area had the highest rate of church membership out of 215 major metropolitan areas in the United States.[3] The trend continues both countywide and in the Provo-Orem area as we enter into a new millennium.

The effort to create a new society and culture on the Utah Valley frontier began when the first Latter-day Saints arrived in 1849. They established enduring colonies throughout the county. Their success was based on the settlers' commitment to their church and to the vision held by Joseph Smith and Brigham Young, a vision based on building the kingdom of God and establishing Zion. The commitment to achieve these utopian aims was based in the first place on a spiritual confirmation of the truth of the message of the Restoration. That commitment was then strengthened and at times renewed during the process of building Zion.

Commitment "Mechanisms"

Sociologist Rosabeth Moss Kanter postulates that achieving sufficient strength and solidarity in a utopian society is based primarily on how members become committed to the community's values and endeavors and to each other. Committed members work hard, participate actively, and demonstrate an intense loyalty to the community.

Further, since a utopian community represents an attempt to establish an ideal social order within the larger society, the smaller group must vie with the outside for the members' loyalties. Retaining members, achieving group cohesiveness, and establishing social control are three major areas in which any effort to establish a new society must be successful.[4]

Communities that are successful in these areas take specific measures to build the commitment of their members. Kanter identifies six such commitment mechanisms practiced in utopian societies, six "specific ways of ordering and defining the existence of a group":[5] sacrifice, investment, renunciation, communion, mortification, and transcendence.[6] These mechanisms correspond in many instances to concrete practices and conditions in nineteenth-century Mormon society in Utah Valley. This paper briefly reviews those practices and conditions, relating them to Kanter's model to describe ways in which the Saints' commitment to the utopian vision of establishing the kingdom of God on earth was strengthened and sustained in Utah Valley.

SACRIFICE

When members of a community sacrifice for the community, their commitment to the group increases. Kanter explains this phenomenon with the psychological principle "the more it 'costs' a person to do something, the more 'valuable' he will consider it, in order to justify the psychic 'expense' and remain internally consistent." She further points out that many religions view sacrifice as an offering to God, an act that can make a believer "more worthy of the deity."[7] Living on the frontier, following the Word of Wisdom, and accepting mission calls are among the sacrifices made by the nineteenth-century Latter-day Saints in Utah County.

FRONTIER LIVING. Kanter observes that in utopian communities, austere living conditions strengthened commitment among members: "Members' struggles symbolized the importance of the shared endeavor, for the venture was of more consequence to them than material comfort."[8] When members sacrifice extravagant or sometimes even comfortable living, their priorities change, and the community becomes more important than self.

The history of the Latter-day Saints is one of sacrifice. From the first call to move the Church to Kirtland until the end of the colonization of territorial Utah, members of the Church were repeatedly asked to move to the frontiers of civilization and to forgo the conveniences of established society. The first settlers to come to Utah Valley were Mormons, who in 1849 established Fort Utah at present-day Provo on the banks of the Provo River. Within a year, several other settlements in Utah Valley were begun: Alpine, American Fork, Lehi, Payson, Pleasant Grove (Battle Creek), and Springville. Other settlements followed.[9] Many of the valley's settlers left another frontier community, Salt Lake City, only to start over in Utah County.

In establishing each of these cities, the settlers traded comfort for loyalty to the cause that had lead them or their parents to the Rocky Mountains in the first place. Their sacrifices served to deepen their societal commitment because the community was all they had; commitment to the community was at times a matter of survival. When hordes of grasshoppers began destroying Spanish Fork's crops in 1855, John Lowe Butler recorded, "Sometimes the whole settlement would turn out men, women and children and try to drive them in the creeks or rivers." After the crickets were gone, the community quickly planted again: "The folks watered [the crops], and cut it for hay. If

Ackerman Lith. 379 Broadway N.Y.
Courtesy R. Q. Shupe, San Juan Capistrano, California

Fort Utah. Settled in 1849, Provo became the religious, economic, social, and political center of the Mormon colonization efforts in Utah County. The fort itself functioned as a means of protection against possible Native American attack. In addition, the cooperative efforts in building the fort and maintaining life there during the first years of settlement helped establish and maintain individual and group commitments to the mountain Zion.

they had not, some of their cattle would have starved to death that winter for the feed was all destroyed by the grasshoppers."[10] Community commitment not only aided short-term survival; it also led to all but one of the valley's settlements surviving into the twentieth century, an unusually high percentage when compared to those of other western territories.

WORD OF WISDOM. Interestingly, another sacrifice characteristic of many utopian communities is abstinence from one or more of the following: coffee, tea, tobacco, and alcohol. Sometimes mandated "under a variety of ideological guises," Kanter explains, such "sacrifice aided commitment."[11]

Although not always followed at the time, the Word of Wisdom was increasingly emphasized by Church leaders in early Utah County. Of secondary importance during the 1850s and 1860s, it grew in significance and by the 1870s was becoming a test of faithfulness. Even lay members stressed its importance. For example, Thomas Higgs spoke on the subject in July 1878 at a meeting in Payson:

> We ought to live pure that our tabernacles may be fit to be receptacles for the Holy Spirit.... He touched on the use of tobacco ... and [its] effects on the Human system and spirituous liquors also and its effects[. I]t was distructive [*sic*]in its nature[. T]he use of these things was a bad practice[. S]moking of the cigarette inhaling the smoke and sending it out through ... the nose and ears it tainted the whole system and effected the blood in a destructive manner. Our course ought to be worthy of emulation and especially those holding responsible positions in the Church of God[. H]e exhorted all to be pure and upright in our walk and conversation.[12]

Apparently even those who had already shown their commitment to the community were encouraged to live the Word of Wisdom. In stake conference, William Paxman chastised members who had already sacrificed much: "Many elders boasted of their age in the Church, of being acquainted with the Prophets Joseph and Brigham, and of journeying and suffering with the saints; yet they have not learned to have sufficient faith to overcome their appetites."[13] As a sacrifice required of all and as one with both a physical and a spiritual dimension, observance of the Word of Wisdom built commitment to the doctrines of the Church.

MISSION CALLS. Another sacrifice expected of early Utah Valley society was either serving a Church mission or supporting those on missions. Many men left their families for a time to proclaim the gospel in distant parts of the world. Their families sacrificed to help them serve one or more of these missions. When Elias Blackburn departed from Provo in 1859 for a mission to Great Britain, he left four wives and eleven children under eleven years of age (including four one-year-olds). Elias put his family in the care of Elisha Goff, an unmarried brother-in-law, and trusted Goff and the community to help his family provide for themselves. In case of crisis, block teachers or aid from ward members or the storehouse could be called on.[14] During Elias's absence, tragedy struck; he learned that a child born to his wife Elizabeth had died. He recorded in his journal, "[The child] <u>Had Lived to Walk and talk and then Died & I had not Seen it</u>—God Bless and <u>Comfort the Dear bereft</u>—God help me to Continue to preach the gospel in a <u>foreign land</u>." The grief associated with the child's death (and the fact that Elias never saw the child) strengthened the family's religious commitment. Elias's journal entry continues, "I wrote to my Wife a Comforting letter telling her that we must all be <u>tried and Live So as to meet the Dear one in heaven</u>."[15]

INVESTMENT

The investment of an individual's resources into a community is another mechanism that strengthens commitment. Kanter observes that in the process of investing money, time, and talents members buy "a share in the proceeds of the community and . . . hold a stake in its continued good operation."[16] Investment efforts helped unite the inhabitants in Utah County. The Saints contributed to their community by gathering to Zion and then by giving tithes and offerings and living the Law of Consecration.

THE GATHERING. In encouraging members to invest their resources in the cause, many successful communities asked members to live together. According to Kanter's research, six of seven successful utopias banned nonresident members.[17] The Latter-day Saints also gathered together; throughout the nineteenth century, this was a major doctrine of the Church. To facilitate the building of a community of Saints in the West, the Church organized the Perpetual Emigrating Fund, a revolving fund that helped perhaps 30,000 poor converts immigrate to the United States between 1849 and 1887.[18] Funds given to Saints to immigrate were viewed as loans; while repaying their debt, community members sacrificed to enable more converts to come to Zion and strengthen the community.

Of the many Saints that immigrated west, one group, the Icelandic Saints, was specifically sent to Utah County. Between 1856 and 1860, sixteen converts from Iceland settled in Spanish Fork.[19] By 1900 about 370 Icelanders had come to Utah, and all but one initially settled in Spanish Fork.[20] One of the early Icelandic converts, Gundy Erasmus-dottir Haflidasson, was baptized in 1853 and arrived in Spanish Fork in 1859. She left behind her unbaptized family, hoping that someday they would join her. Fourteen of her descendents did make the trip before she died in 1888.[21]

In Spanish Fork, the gathering provided strength to the community as emigrants came from Wales, England, and Denmark, as well as from Iceland. Without doubt, the principle of gathering provided many of the human resources necessary to have communities in Utah County. The blending of cultures in the county was not without its struggles. Some Icelanders experienced cultural prejudice including pejorative labels, such as "lousy Icelander" and "Black Danishman"; exclusion, such as not being allowed to bless the sacrament in church; or the "intangible feeling" of discrimination in the community.[22] Nevertheless, at other times, the community celebrated their differing cultures. One Fourth of July, each nationality paraded in traditional clothing to "show the handiwork of the fatherlands."[23]

TITHES AND OFFERINGS. The chief means of providing resources to expand the kingdom of God was members' donating time, cash, and property. Tithing and fast offerings provided the principle ways for members to contribute. Tithing included an initial payment of a tenth of all of one's goods plus subsequent payments of a tenth of one's increase. Further, a tithe of time for work projects was often required. Fast offerings were also encouraged.[24] The items donated to the local bishops' tithing houses in Utah County were used to help support Church work projects; to take care of needy Latter-day Saints in the community, such as the disabled, the widows, and the families of men who were on Church missions; and to help care for the Native American people in the region.

By giving money and time to the community, donors strengthened their own commitment to the community, and their donations made the community stronger. Investing in the community also helped the Church provide for its members, which would consequently make members loyal to the community. As one biography of an early Provo bishop explains, "All kinds of people are found in a ward: some are widowed, some aged, some ill, some poor. Bishop Blackburn was responsible for all of these. He provided for them out of the tithing produce. . . . He strengthened them with love as well as with food and clothing."[25]

In addition to the tithe of time required, members had priesthood responsibilities and Church callings to fulfill, especially after 1860 when the auxiliary organizations began forming in Utah County.[26] While serving as a bishop in Lehi, Abel Evans was once asked to perform a priesthood blessing with one of his counselors, Lorenzo Hatch, who recorded the following:

> Friday night I was called out of bed to go and administer to John Catlin's wife. The devil caused her to bark like a dog. We cast the spirit out. Brother Abel Evans was with me. We administered to her, and she appeared well and comfortable, but as soon as we were gone the devil commenced again and they sent for Abel. He stayed all night and kept her right till morning.[27]

Sacrificing a night's sleep may not have been the norm for the Saints in Utah County, but such an effort is indicative of the type of time sacrifice required of the people. Asking members for such investments in their church and community strengthened their commitment, making them feel a part of something worth such sacrifices.

RENUNCIATION

Through the commitment mechanism of renunciation, a communal society ensures that the loyalty of its members lies with the community. Kanter lists three groups that societies may ask the individual to renounce: the outside world, a spouse, and the family.[28] Latter-day Saints were asked to renounce the outside world and to some extent traditional marriage.

THE SAINTS AND THE OUTSIDE WORLD. In order to successfully establish a community away from the dominant culture, a group must insulate itself from the pressures exerted by the larger society. Once in Utah Valley, isolated from the dominant American culture, the Saints attempted to create a new society. This effort was radical in concept and powerful in its resolve. Pioneer experience in Utah County can be understood only in light of their powerful desire to establish God's kingdom on the earth. Additionally, the struggle to establish permanent settlements on the Utah Valley frontier must be seen in light of the Saints' efforts to escape from the calamities they believed were about to fall upon the nations of the earth.[29] Mormon pioneers born and raised in Utah did not have to break with traditional culture as their parents did, but they were forced to demonstrate the same dedication in a uniquely Mormon world.

The process of renouncing the outside world, Kanter suggests, is facilitated by geographic isolation. She gives these criteria for isolation: the community is located more than five miles away from others, has few nonmember residents, and is not located near a waterway or railroad.[30] The Great Basin fulfilled all these requirements until 1869, when the transcontinental railroad was completed. Yet even after the railroad came to Utah, the gathering of early LDS converts to the frontier may be seen as a means of detaching an individual from other cultural options and attaching the person to the community.

Additional insulation derives from the use of language. Kanter points out that terminology can contribute to successful renunciation of the outside world as members refer to themselves as "good" and the outside world as "evil."[31] Utah County residents used language in a similar way, referring to themselves as "Saints" and the outside world as "Babylon."

POLYGAMY. In utopian societies, the traditional marriage relationship could supersede loyalty to the community and was therefore an affiliation frowned upon by utopian communities. By emphasizing either celibacy or free love, those communities renounced the closeness and fidelity of the traditional marriage.[32]

Plural marriage was one way the Latter-day Saints renounced the outside culture.[33] Early Utah County Saints viewed polygamy as a divine command for their community and practiced it, many times, only after receiving spiritual confirmation of the doctrine. In addition to its spiritual dimension, polygamy widened the community members' circle of loyalty and concern beyond a single spouse. Richard Van Wagoner noted that polygamy "greatly improved the cohesiveness of the larger Mormon community." Further, "group violation of what had been conventional behavioral norms served to weld the Saints into a new fraternity of people—'a peculiar people.'"[34] Whether one practiced plural marriage or simply continued supporting the Church, which sanctioned it, this type of renunciation was reinforced.

Practicing polygamy not only served to separate the Saints from the outside world, making them a community, at times it was also a form of renunciation on a personal level. By living the law, a woman renounced some of her claim to her husband. One child of a polygamous marriage recalled, "My mother was a very lonely woman. When my father died, my mother was only thirty-eight, and she lived to be ninety-one. She lived most of her life without him. Even then [when he was alive] she was sharing him with another woman."[35] It is easy to

Courtesy Beth Olsen, Pleasant Grove, Utah

William Wadley had three wives, two of whom had died by the time this photograph was taken in Manila, Utah, ca. 1897. Here William, in the center with a hat at his feet, and his wife, Isabelle McKay Wadley, standing at his left, pose with a friend and Wadley children, grandchildren, and daughters-in-law. Plural marriage was once both a demonstration of commitment to the Mormon effort and a mechanism that strengthened individual commitment to the group.

see that such a test would serve either to deepen or destroy a woman's commitment to the community's values.

The number of individuals and families involved in polygamy varied from community to community and from decade to decade. An emphasis on plural marriage during the Mormon Reformation increased the number of those practicing it so that on March 5, 1857, Church leaders in Salt Lake City cautioned President James Snow of Provo to use his position to stop promoting plural marriage so forcibly.[36] No matter the extent of its practice, polygamy both required and built commitment to the Church and therefore to the community.

COMMUNION

The Latter-day Saint settlements in Utah County were characterized by centralization and by a high degree of participation and involvement in the everyday life of the community. This interaction generally occurred in the form of assignments from the stake or ward leaders as well as participation in Church rituals and ordinances and in various kinds of meetings for all age groups. The interaction between individuals is important ground on which community is enhanced. Kanter describes many areas that provided opportunities for communion. Five that apply to the focus of this paper include community planning and work, community holidays, songs, ritual, and enduring persecution.[37]

COMMUNITY PLANNING AND WORK. The vast majority of early settlers participated in cooperative efforts in their communities—some informal and others formal. Colonization, like missionary work and immigration, required the closest kind of cooperation. For example, the success and survival of the Mormon settlements in Utah County derived in large part from the vast irrigation systems that spread throughout the valley. That system was built because the Church was able to organize labor, supply capital, plan construction, and claim ownership of all the water in the name of the community. Further, from the time of the first settlement forts, organized groups of pioneers dug canals, constructed roads, built fences, planted a variety of crops, erected private and public buildings, and laid the groundwork for subsequent village life. All in all, Mormon cooperation made the colonization of the well-watered valley a very successful venture for the pioneers.[38]

Historian Dean May comments on how community efforts affected Alpine residents: "Their incessant interaction in voluntary associations helped to diminish a sense of self or even family. It drew them out and beyond into what they saw as a community of Saints, a City of God on earth, represented in their experience by the life they knew in Alpine."[39] The merging of ecclesiastical, social, economic, and political responsibility facilitated the establishment of viable communities in Utah County—shaped more by administrative decisions and group planning than by the market forces so typical in other western regions (mining camps, cattle towns, and rural trading centers). The focus on community built a commitment to it.

COMMUNITY HOLIDAYS. For most Mormon citizens in the county, Pioneer Day represented "a birthday, an independence day, and a thanksgiving day."[40] It was also a holiday that especially built commitment to the community. Summarizing sociological research on community celebrations, Steven L. Olsen explains that such festivities can "bind individuals to a community and engage them in the celebration of its past, confirmation of its present, and anticipation of its future."[41] Although Utah County citizens celebrated national holidays, such as the Fourth of July, residents developed a calendar punctuated with specific dates memorializing their own history. "Pioneer Day served as one of the Latter-day Saints' prime mechanisms for preserving and expressing their ideology[,] . . . solidifying their society and the roles of its members, and maintaining awareness of their history."[42]

The city of Lehi's celebration of Pioneer Day in 1860 included a toast that focused on bringing the people together, in part to encourage and instruct them concerning their societal roles: "The noble Sons and fair Daughters of Zion—may the former grow up as the sturdy oaks of the forest which bend to ever[y] storm but never break; may the virtue and graces of the latter shine as the stars of the firmament and be as a halo around Zion."[43] In addition to providing an opportunity to express such ideology, the day also built communion by giving the participants a chance to celebrate. In the afternoon "dancing commenced and continued till midnight with much glee and good feelings with all."[44]

SONGS. Both music and poetry held a strong position in the Mormon pioneer culture, and one of their functions was to build community.[45] From 1835 onward, the Church had hymnbooks containing many distinctive Mormon hymns. A popular hymn since 1836, "The Spirit of God," captures some of the uniqueness of life as a Latter-day Saint. A little-known verse, used well into the Utah period, compared the Church to ancient Israel and gave the community of Saints a model to emulate:

> Old Israel, that fled from the world for his freedom,
> Must come with the cloud and the pillar amain,
> A Moses and Aaron and Joshua lead him,
> And feed him on manna from heaven again.[46]

Church music historian Michael Hicks observes that both the lyrics and music of "The Spirit of God" made it a moving and strident hymn to those who sang it, a hymn that reaffirmed commitment to the community.[47]

"The Spirit of God" was surely sung in Utah County, but other examples also reveal the role music and poetry had in building community. In 1886, American Fork resident William Grant was preparing to go to prison for polygamy. Stepping off the train in Provo to "take my Trial," Grant was handed a note with a poem written by a friend:

> Do not despair dear brother
> For God in whom you Trust—
> Has untold blessings now in store
> Awaiting all the Just— . . .
>
> Receive these few simple breathings
> And should they aid or cheer—
> God be praised he is the giver—
> May we all his name revere.

Grant recorded the poem in his journal and after it wrote, "This poem is a pleasure and help to me and I verily believe it helped me during my Trial." A few days later, about 250 people gathered at Grant's house in American Fork for dinner, speeches, and "recitations, songs and poems."[48] To a man soon to be imprisoned and separated from his family, such lyrical expressions of support would have reminded Grant of the reasons he was willing to suffer for his faith and surely strengthened his resolve to do so.

RITUAL. Latter-day Saints punctuated their calendar with sacred ordinances associated with various phases of their lives. In addition to their transcendent spiritual value, these rituals had the power to more fully commit the community members to the values of the group. In many of the rituals or ordinances, the member made covenants to God, and through these covenants, the member promised, in effect, to be committed to the LDS community's values, norms, and practices.

Blessing of young infants, baptism and confirmation of older children, and ordination to priesthood for men were some of the religious rituals performed in all the LDS settlements. Days when the ordinances took place were special, and while somewhat different from current practice (now usually tied to a specific birthday), the rites of passage for children were always remembered. In Cedar Fort, children were baptized at "the south corner of the block and across the street north of the rock fort." Pieces of "lumber were placed on each side of the ditch, and then a dam was placed in the ditch, until the water was backed up deep enough" to perform baptism by complete immersion. At the Sunday worship service (sacrament meeting), the children were then confirmed members of the Church, the ordinance being under the direction of the local bishop, who was in charge of all religious activity in the community. Later, a hole in a nearby field (called "Doby Hole" because the mud was used to make adobes before the site was abandoned) was used for a number of years as the town baptismal site. Baptisms were held at this site every one or two years.[49]

Marriage was another commitment-building ritual. Although local bishops performed civil marriages with a Mormon flavor, the Church taught that a man and woman should make a covenant with each other through a religious ceremony performed in specially dedicated rooms—as had been done in the Nauvoo Temple (1845–46). Previous to being married, converts received their "washings and anointings" and "endowments" in the Endowment House on Temple Block, taking upon themselves religious vows. Residents of Utah County made the trip north to Salt Lake City to receive these special ordinances or received them before moving to Utah County. The endowment ordinance not only acted as a rite of passage for recently arrived converts and immigrants but also bound these individuals and families to the Church through covenant.

The LDS prayer circle, known as the "true order of prayer," was associated with temple ritual.[50] The special ceremony required the participants, usually dressed in white temple clothing, to pray in a circle at a specially dedicated altar. Away from the Endowment House and temple, participants met in dedicated rooms of private residences in pioneer communities. (If the community was significantly large, several circles were organized.) For example, George A. Smith organized a prayer circle in Provo on July 13, 1857, choosing John Riggs as president and William Marsden as clerk.[51] The weekly meetings included time for instruction, prayer, and discussion.

On a community level, an important aspect of these special prayer circles was the bonds of loyalty and fellowship they engendered. First, new members were received into the group by unanimous vote of support. Each meeting, members were required to state their feelings about each other. When problems arose, time was spent to reconcile the parties, even if it meant that several meetings were required to do so. Finally, the weekly prayers themselves often had the effect of softening feelings and of developing a sense of brotherly love and harmony among the participants.[52]

ENDURING PERSECUTION. Kanter cites persecution as an event that will build communion among members of a group.[53] Suffering for a cause endears the cause to an individual. Much has been written about the persecution of the Saints throughout the history of the Church. Many early Utah County residents had lived through the violence in Missouri and Illinois. Many more had endured persecution in their homelands before emigrating to Utah. The Utah War and the anti-polygamy crusade mounted further opposition against the Church. Through these trials, the Saints learned to band together.

During the 1857 Utah War, the Saints in Utah County were asked to help the many inhabitants of the northern communities who were relocating south to avoid Johnston's Army. The community in Provo responded during this time of persecution. Elias Blackburn recorded in his journal, "The roads are crowded with the Saints moving South. . . . Very busy dealing out provisions to the public hands. I am feeding 100 men, all hard at <u>work</u>."[54] Blackburn's biographers observe, "The unconditional acceptance and care for [the Saints moving south] . . . is a measure of the unity and applied Christianity practiced in the Church, especially in time of crisis."[55]

MORTIFICATION

Kanter's fifth mechanism, mortification, describes the means community members employ to change and mold themselves in order to fulfill the aims of the group. Mortification "provide[s] a new identity for the person that is based on the power and meaningfulness of group membership."[56] For nineteenth-century Latter-day Saints, this process was aided by discipline and spiritual differentiation.[57]

DISCIPLINE. In disciplining its members, a society provides both guidelines for behavior and feedback to individuals to help them conform to the standards of the community. The mid-1850s especially saw discipline used to increase commitment. The emphasis on such doctrinal teachings as the Word of Wisdom and polygamy varied from time to time, but during the Mormon Reformation, which climaxed during the fall of 1856, religious zeal increased the attention given both doctrines. Discipline mandated that members keep their covenants. At its peak, the reformation resulted in a large-scale program of rebaptism and rededication to religious principles, including personal cleanliness and community order.

The principal architect of the reformation, First Presidency Counselor Jedediah M. Grant, came to Provo in July 1855 and delivered a fiery sermon to the local Saints, previewing the coming religious tidal wave. Grant said that "the Church needs trimming up, and if you will search, you will find in your wards certain branches which had better be cut off." He continued, "The kingdom would progress much faster, and so will you individually, than it will with those branches on, for they are only dead weights to the great wheel. . . .

I would like to see the work of reformation commence, and continue until every man had to walk to the line." The main message of the reformation was "purify yourselves, your houses, lots, farms, and every thing around you on the right and on the left, then the Spirit of the Lord can dwell with you."[58]

John Young, a Church leader from Salt Lake City, arrived in the fall of 1856 on a preaching and teaching tour of the county. Starting at Spanish Fork in late September, Young and his assigned group of home missionaries held conferences in several county communities. The conference at Pleasant Grove at the end of October serves as a typical example. For two days, in scenes reminiscent of Protestant religious revivals, Young and his companions urged members of the congregation to repent of their sins and confess.

After sufficient time had been given to confession, Young and his companions offered rebaptism to the group. Following the baptismal and confirmation service, the congregation again met for further spiritual edification. At times, the outpouring of feelings and emotions included speaking in tongues. The meeting was finally dismissed amid great rejoicing.

Home missionaries, whose assignment included visiting the homes of individual members, became an important means of maintaining the high level of religious enthusiasm in Utah County. A catechism was introduced, which was to be used during home visits. As the reformation progressed, the catechism, which dealt with a variety of items from observance of the Ten Commandments to family prayer, expanded to include as many as twenty-seven questions, including one about bathing regularly.[59]

The reformation also emphasized marriage, including plural marriage. This emphasis, often preached by local home missionaries, led to some problems. Utah County resident Mary Jane Mount Tanner noted that "every single person was expected to marry, and a great many unsuitable marriages were made, many which were afterwards dissolved for it was a time of general religious excitement."[60] Heber C. Kimball, a member of the Church's First Presidency, wrote James Snow of Provo, "We do not wish this matter [plural marriage] forced."[61]

The full impact of the reformation cannot be known, but church attendance and donations to help the poor and to maintain Church programs increased. Numerous letters to Brigham Young inquiring about confessions and forgiveness also suggest that many residents during that period committed themselves to be better Saints and neighbors.[62]

Nevertheless, some of those concerned with the excesses of the Church's spirited reform decided to leave Utah. Certainly, discontent in Zion was nothing new, but for a sizable number, the reformation was a clarion call to flee the Mormon kingdom, where religion permeated the lives of most settlers. Social integration of those of other faiths and former Mormons continued to cause difficulty and misunderstandings on occasions, especially for those who publicly attacked the solidarity of the Church. Certainly, as a member of a minority, life was challenging, and if the individual or group was a vocal critic of the Church, additional stresses were experienced. Those who left removed opposition to the ideals of the community and in so doing solidified the community.

SPIRITUAL DIFFERENTIATION. In order for individuals to pattern their lives after a community's standards, a model of success must be offered. Kanter points out that many successful utopian communities have a "type of stratification . . . which distinguishe[s] members on the basis of their achievement in living up to group standards." The distinguishing characteristic is group morality rather than intellect or skill. Differing levels of success in the community are evident and provide members with a standard to emulate.[63]

Several of these conditions existed in nineteenth-century Utah County. Being a religious society, the valley's inhabitants placed emphasis on moral behavior. Prominent Church leaders such as Abraham O. Smoot, Elias H. Blackburn, George A. Smith, and others were widely respected and served as positive models of moral living. For example, the obituary of Elias H. Blackburn extols his service to the Church and his example to the Saints:

> As a pioneer and missionary he has been excelled by few, his whole life has been one of service to God and loyalty to his associates. . . . Honesty, humility, loyalty to the Lord and His servants is the record he has made in life; and he leaves behind for the emulation of his kindred and many friends a pious, beautiful career.[64]

As the Saints strove to perfect their lives—a process of mortification— examples such as Blackburn's served as models of commitment.

TRANSCENDENCE

Kanter's final mechanism for creating commitment is transcendence. Members of a community need to believe that the organization of which they are a part can give meaning, structure, and coherency to

Courtesy LDS Church Archives

Old and new tabernacle, Provo, ca. 1880. Because they housed meetings of all kinds, these structures functioned as symbols of both Church and civic authority in Utah Valley. Upper corners of the photograph have been restored.

their lives. Martin Buber described this process as "a longing for that *rightness,* . . . which of its very nature cannot be realized in the individual, but only in human community."[65] Both the doctrine and the leaders of a community can provide the transcendence required to unify a community and provide meaning to members' lives.[66]

DOCTRINE. Church doctrine gave early Utah County Saints access to the "rightness" Buber describes. Manifestations of this doctrine prevailed in the community; daily experiences were imbued with religion. To these Church members, Mormonism was not just a Sunday religion but an entire way of life.

One aspect of Mormon doctrine that bestowed life with purpose and meaning was a belief in patriarchal blessings. Latter-day Saints found comfort through these priesthood blessings. On October 29, 1878, Susannah Summers Higgs of Payson received a blessing from Levi W. Hancock, an LDS patriarch who was visiting family members in Utah County. The first section of the blessing identified one of the purposes of possessing a copy of the blessing:

> Sister Susannah I place my hands upon thy head and will bless thee as I am moved by the holy spirit. That thou mayest look upon the same and be benefited through thy prayers of faith that the prom[p]tor of the same may be rooted and grounded in thy mind and [that] it might be strengthening to thy faith.[67]

These inspired pronouncements promised blessings and offered solace and strength to the receiver, often predicated upon commitment to the Church as evidenced by obedience to the Lord's commandments.

Further, the early Saints of Utah County believed they were building Zion and the kingdom of God on the earth. Their everyday work, when viewed in this light, was vitally important. They also had the plan of salvation, which answered fundamental questions about the purpose of life and the events before and after life on earth. These doctrines blessed the Saints and made commitment to the cause a privilege.

LEADERSHIP. The leadership of the community provided transcendence by administering the divine doctrine and directing the path of the Church day to day. Many utopian communities are founded by a strong, charismatic leader and a hierarchy of authority to interact with the members of the community. If the founder died, many times the successor had been acquainted with the founder and may have even been designated by him. The top leader of a society and his hierarchy administer the workings of the community within the context of the group's ideology.[68] The leaders that Utah County Saints followed, Joseph Smith and Brigham Young, fulfill many of Kanter's requirements for building community through charismatic, powerful leaders.

The Church authorities in the county—Apostle George A. Smith and stake (during the period, a countywide Church unit) presidents Isaac Higbee, James C. Snow, Dominicus Carter, William Miller, Abraham Owen Smoot, and Edward Partridge—also played significant leadership and community-building roles during the nineteenth century. They often served as both the religious and civic leaders of the communities and county.

For example, Smoot came to Utah County when he was called by Brigham Young to be the ecclesiastical and civic leader in the region and served in numerous ways from 1868 until his death on March 6, 1895. When Smoot died, thousands thronged into the Provo Tabernacle—a fitting testimonial to his enduring legacy.

The leading Church officials were represented on a local level by the bishop. The bishop facilitated such priesthood activities as visiting the Saints at home each month. A bishop was responsible for seeing that a school was established for the young people. Additionally, he coordinated construction of canals, roads, and public buildings and supervised social activities in the community. Bishops also performed such typical religious duties as conducting marriages and funerals. They coordinated directives from Salt Lake concerning mission calls, public work activities requests, and the collection of Church donations. In Summit Creek (present-day Santaquin), Bishop George Halliday instructed a group of ward teachers that they were to pray with each family and "be kind and patient, in their enquiries and questions. . . . [and] urge upon the Parents the necessity of looking after their Children and not allow them to parade the streets at night and watch over them, and keep them, out of mischief."[69]

These multifaceted duties constituted a daunting task, especially when the term of service for a bishop was often as much as a decade or more. For example, Henson Walker of Pleasant Grove served for 10 years; Aaron Johnson of Springville, 18 years; David Evans of Lehi, 28 years; Leonard Harrington of American Fork, 32 years; and Lorenzo Argyle of Lake Shore (as presiding elder and bishop), 33 years. Bishops were also required to support their own families.[70]

Like bishops, many of the Relief Society leaders remained in their callings for extended periods of time. Mary John, an emigrant from Wales, was called as the Provo Third Ward Relief Society secretary for 10 years. She was then called as a counselor in the Utah Stake Relief Society organization and later served as the president for 21 years.[71]

Men and women such as these provided leadership to the members around them and strove to build commitment among them, a commitment based on transcendent doctrines taught by a prophet of God.

THREE DEFENSIVE MEASURES

Because Kanter's commitment mechanisms often overlap, an example of how they worked together in Utah County is in order.

As the transcontinental railroad made its way closer to Utah and as the mining frontier expanded in their midst, Church leaders became concerned about the negative effects integration with the national economy would certainly have. Brigham Young recognized that if the Saints became integrated into the national market economy, they would become mere suppliers of raw materials—forced to repurchase their own products in manufactured form at a comparative disadvantage.

President Young announced three programs to help unify the Saints against the encroachment of the dominant American culture in the late 1860s and early 1870s: first, a cooperative program of buying, transporting, and selling of merchandise; second, the organization of local Schools of the Prophets for adult male members of the Church; and finally, the reestablishment of the Relief Society for the adult female members of the Church. These plans both increased the investment of the Saints in their mountain haven and enhanced communion among the inhabitants.

THE COOPERATIVE MOVEMENT. Although some cooperatives were functioning earlier, most cooperatives started after Brigham Young established the Zion's Cooperative Mercantile Institution (ZCMI) as a parent store in Salt Lake City in October 1868.[72] Thousands of Utah County residents became stockholders in their local cooperatives, many of which were directed by local priesthood leaders.[73] As much out of religious duty as from good business sense, local Utah County stores were either bought out or went out of business as Latter-day Saints began to support the cooperative movement. The ZCMI "all-seeing eye" and the inscription "Holiness to the Lord" soon became familiar symbols on storefronts throughout the valley as ZCMIs appeared in Alpine, American Fork, Benjamin, Cedar Fort, Fairfield, Lehi (two stores), Goshen, Payson, Pleasant Grove, Provo (three stores), Salem, Santaquin, Spanish Fork, and Springville.[74]

The cooperative movement expanded to include a number of businesses besides mercantile stores. Taking the lead from ZCMI, local cooperatives restricted dividends in order to promote cooperative sawmills, tanneries, molasses mills, furniture shops, butcher shops, and other such establishments. One of the most significant of these cooperative manufacturing institutions was the Provo Cooperative Woolen Factory, the first and most important manufacturing establishment in the territory. The construction generated employment for people throughout Utah County, payment being made in stock. Completed in spring 1872, the cost of building was estimated to be $155,000. The first cloth was manufactured in June 1873.[75]

Following the establishment of the cooperative movement, Brigham Young called for the establishment of the united order—a movement more communal than anything yet advanced in Utah. In spring 1874, LDS Church leaders Wilford Woodruff and Erastus Snow

Provo Cooperative Woolen Factory, ca. 1875. One of the most important cooperative efforts in Utah County, the cooperative woolen mill in Provo provided employment and essential products for a community dedicated to economic, social, political, and religious independence.

organized united orders in Provo (April 26), Lehi (April 28), and
Cedar Valley (April 28). Additional united orders were organized on
the same day in Pleasant Grove, American Fork, and Alpine (April 27)
and in Santaquin (date unknown), Goshen (date unknown), Payson
(May 1), Spanish Fork (May 2), Springville (May 3), Cedar Fort (May 3),
and Fairfield (May 3).[76]

LOCAL SCHOOLS OF THE PROPHETS. The second aspect of the
Church's effort to thwart encroachment by American society was
the establishment of local Schools of the Prophets. Originally insti-
tuted in the Church by Joseph Smith in Kirtland, Ohio, in the 1830s,
the organization was revived in 1868. Soon it spread to the principal
settlements throughout the territory (Provo on April 15, 1868; American Fork on July 22, 1868; and Payson on September 20, 1868). The
School of the Prophets acted as an integral part of the community in
which it functioned, resembling an economic or political planning
conference in addition to a religious group.

Such a school exerted tremendous influence as it organized, conducted, and controlled local and territorial elections. This process is
illustrated in Provo when Smoot "proposed to take into consideration
the nomination of candidates to be elected as County officers at the
next general election" in August 1868. He hoped those chosen would
"be sustained here and at the Polls." Apparently, bishops from all the
Mormon settlements in the county were in attendance, as they were
given responsibility to "see to the election in their settlements, that the
same is carried on as the Law directs." Just as in the Church, individuals did not seek political positions; rather, the school leaders selected
persons from the populace to serve in these positions and asked
people to sustain them (vote for them).[77]

REESTABLISHMENT OF THE RELIEF SOCIETY. At the same time the
men were organizing into the School of the Prophets, the women
began to assemble together in meetings that would further unify the
Saints in Utah County.[78] The Relief Society, originally founded in
Nauvoo in 1842, had been largely inactive (1844–66) except for a brief
period in the 1850s. In December 1866, Eliza R. Snow was assigned to
reestablish the Relief Society as a fundamental part of every ward
throughout the territory. Within three years, seventeen Relief Societies were organized in Utah County.

The Relief Society women in the county fostered a myriad of programs for community development, including a silk industry and a
wheat storage program. In addition, the women built Relief Society

halls and granaries on property purchased with their own funds. The Society not only strengthened relationships among the women, but also met their spiritual and emotional needs. In Goshen, the minutes indicate that "Sister Eliza R. Snow arose and blessed the sisters with the gift of tongues. Sister Mary Dodds [second counselor in the Goshen Relief Society presidency] interpreted consisted of blessing the sisters and to teach the youth of Zion."[79]

Sometimes responding apathetically to a community request, as William G. Hartley notes later in this volume, Church members in Utah Valley experienced both ups and downs in their commitment. The above measures were taken at a time when loyalty to the Church was waning.[80]

CONCLUSION

The daily life experiences of Latter-day Saints on the Utah Valley frontier demonstrate how religion and its infusion into every aspect of life (economic, political, educational, and social) radically shaped the contours of the social reality in Utah County. The pervasive presence of the Church ensured that the Saints building cities in the wilderness were also building a utopia based on the revelations and doctrines of the Church. Within the community of Saints thus established, commitment was strengthened and renewed through the mechanisms Kanter describes—sacrifice, investment, renunciation, communion, mortification, and transcendence. The power of this commitment continues to be felt in Utah County, where numerous LDS chapels and two temples attest to the faithfulness of the valley's Saints.

Richard Neitzel Holzapfel is Assistant Professor of Church History and Doctrine, Brigham Young University. David A. Allred is an M.A. candidate in English at Brigham Young University.

NOTES

1. Wilbur Zelinsky, "An Approach to the Religious Geography of the United States: Patterns of Church Membership in 1952," *Annals of the Association of American Geographers* 51 (June 1961): 163–64, 193.

2. Samuel S. Hill, "Religion and Region in America," *Annals of the American Academy of Political and Social Science* 480 (July 1985): 135.

3. Rodney Stark and William Sims Bainbridge, *The Future of Religion: Secularization, Revival and Cult Formation* (Berkeley: University of California Press, 1985), 70.

4. Rosabeth Moss Kanter, *Commitment and Community: Communes and Utopias in Sociological Perspective* (Cambridge: Harvard University Press, 1972), 2, 43, 76–82.

5. Kanter, *Commitment and Community*, 75.

6. See Kanter, *Commitment and Community*, 75–125.

7. Kanter, *Commitment and Community*, 76.

8. Kanter, *Commitment and Community*, 79.

9. See "Mormon Expansion by Decade," in Wayne L. Wahlquist, ed., *Atlas of Utah* ([Ogden, Utah], and Provo, Utah: Weber State College and Brigham Young University Press, 1981), 90–91.

10. John Lowe Butler, Autobiography, cited in William G. Hartley, *My Best for the Kingdom: History and Autobiography of John Lowe Butler, a Mormon Frontiersman* (Salt Lake City: Aspen Books, 1993), 274–76.

11. Kanter, *Commitment and Community*, 77.

12. Payson Ward, Utah Stake, Historical Record, 1875–1879, July 7, 1878, Archives Division, Historical Department, The Church of Jesus Christ of Latter-day Saints, Salt Lake City (hereafter cited as LDS Church Archives).

13. Journal History of the Church, December 4, 1883, 6, LDS Church Archives, microfilm copy in Harold B. Lee Library, Brigham Young University, Provo, Utah.

14. Voyle L. Munson and Lillian S. Munson, *A Gift of Faith: Elias H. Blackburn, Pioneer, Patriarch, and Healer* (Eureka, Utah: Basin/Plateau, 1991), 121–22.

15. Elias H. Blackburn, Journal, cited in Munson and Munson, *A Gift of Faith*, 134.

16. Kanter, *Commitment and Community*, 81.

17. Kanter, *Commitment and Community*, 80–81, 82.

18. David F. Boone, "Perpetual Emigrating Fund (PEF)," in *Encyclopedia of Mormonism*, ed. Daniel H. Ludlow, 4 vols. (New York: Macmillan, 1992), 3:1075.

19. Elva Simundsson, *Icelandic Settlers in America* (Winnipeg, Manitoba: Queenston House Publishing, 1981), 2.

20. LaNora Allred, "The Icelanders of Utah," typescript, 10, 20, available through the Icelandic Association of Utah, Spanish Fork, Utah.

21. Helga Thorderson Evans, "Vestmannaeyjar's Children: An Icelandic Saga of Love, Hope, and Faith," typescript, 4, 50, 54, in possession of Byron Geslison, Spanish Fork, Utah. For more information on the family, see "Gundy Haflidasson—Family," in *Our Pioneer Heritage*, comp. Kate B. Carter, 20 vols. (Salt Lake City: Daughters of Utah Pioneers, 1958–77), 7:502–9.

22. Allred, "The Icelanders of Utah," 32.

23. Thorteim Jonsson, letter, trans. Svava Anderson, cited in Allred, "The Icelanders of Utah," 25.

24. See William G. Hartley, "Common People: Church Activity during the Brigham Young Era," in this volume.

25. Munson and Munson, *A Gift of Faith*, 36–37.

26. See Hartley, "Common People."

27. Lorenzo Hatch, Journal, cited in Ronald D. Dennis, *Indefatigable Veteran: History and Biography of Abel Evans, a Welsh Mormon Elder* (Provo, Utah: Rhydybont Press, 1994), 197.

28. Kanter, *Commitment and Community*, 82–92.

29. See Grant Underwood, *The Millennarian World of Early Mormonism* (Urbana: University of Illinois, 1993); Dan Erickson, "Joseph Smith's 1891 Millennial Prophecy: The Quest for Apocalyptic Deliverance," *Journal of Mormon History* 22 (fall 1996): 1–34.

30. Kanter, *Commitment and Community*, 83.

31. Kanter, *Commitment and Community*, 84.

32. Kanter, *Commitment and Community*, 86–89.

33. Technically, Mormons practiced polygyny—the practice of a man marrying more than one woman.

34. Richard S. Van Wagoner, *Mormon Polygamy: A History* (Salt Lake City: Signature Books, 1989), 103.

35. Oara Cluff Pace, interview, 10, as cited in Jessie L. Embry, *Mormon Polygamous Families: Life in the Principle,* Publications in Mormon Studies, ed. Linda King Newell, vol. 1 (Salt Lake City: University of Utah Press, 1987), 131.

36. Brigham Young to James Snow, March 5, 1857, Brigham Young Papers, LDS Church Archives; as cited in Paul H. Peterson, "The Mormon Reformation" (Ph.D. diss., Brigham Young University, 1981), 132.

37. Kanter, *Commitment and Community*, 91–103.

38. Many historians, including Leonard J. Arrington, Davis Bitton, and Thomas G. Alexander, have discussed in detail this part of the story. This study utilizes their insights and conclusions as the foundation of the discussion that follows. See, for example, Leonard J. Arrington, "Economic History of a Mormon Valley," *Pacific Northwest Quarterly* 46, no. 4 (October 1955): 97–107.

39. Dean L. May, *Three Frontiers: Family, Land, and Society in the American West, 1850–1900,* Interdisciplinary Perspectives on Modern History, ed. Robert Fogel and Stephan Thernstrom (New York: Cambridge University Press, 1994), 243. See also Dean L. May, "It Takes a Village: Social Character in Rural Settlements," in this volume.

40. Steven L. Olsen, "Pioneer Day," in Allan Kent Powell, ed., *Utah History Encyclopedia* (Salt Lake City: University of Utah Press, 1994), 424.

41. Steven L. Olsen, "Celebrating Cultural Identity: Pioneer Day in Nineteenth-Century Mormonism," *BYU Studies* 36, no. 1 (1996–97): 161.

42. Olsen, "Celebrating Cultural Identity," 174. See also Olsen, "Pioneer Day," 424.

43. "Twenty-Fourth at Lehi," *Deseret News,* August 1, 1860, 176.

44. "Twenty-Fourth at Lehi," 176.

45. See Richard H. Cracroft, " 'Oh, What Songs of the Heart': Zion's Hymns as Sung by the Pioneers," in this volume.

46. "The Spirit of God," in *Sacred Hymns and Spiritual Songs, for the Church of Jesus Christ of Latter-day Saints,* 14th ed. (Salt Lake City: George Q. Cannon, 1871), no. 244.

47. Michael Hicks, conversation with Richard Holzapfel, Provo, Utah, October 22, 1998.

48. William Grant, *Biographical Sketches of the Life of Wm. Grant, Written by Himself, at American Fork, Utah, Commenced May 21, 1882,* microfiche, 98–100, Special Collections, Harold B. Lee Library, Brigham Young University, Provo, Utah (hereafter cited as BYU Archives). The information about the gathering at Grant's house is from a clipping from the *Enquirer* that was pasted into Grant's journal.

49. Margery J. Peterson, *Our Roots Grow Deep: A History of Cedar Valley* (American Fork, Utah: Lyndon W. Cook, 1990), 4-2-4-3.

50. Bathsheba W. Smith, "Recollections of the Prophet Joseph Smith," *Juvenile Instructor* 27 (June 1, 1892): 345, cited in D. Michael Quinn, "Latter-day Saint Prayer Circles," *BYU Studies* 19, no. 1 (1978): 79–105.

51. "Record of President John Rigg's Prayer Circle," BYU Archives.

52. Quinn, "Latter-day Saint Prayer Circles," 104–5.

53. Kanter, *Commitment and Community,* 102–3.

54. Elias H. Blackburn, Journal, as cited in Munson and Munson, *A Gift of Faith,* 97.

55. Munson and Munson, *A Gift of Faith,* 92.

56. Kanter, *Commitment and Community,* 103.

57. The term "spiritual differentiation" is used in Kanter, *Commitment and Community,* 108–10.

58. Jedediah M. Grant, in *Journal of Discourses,* 26 vols. (Liverpool: F. D. Richards, 1855–86), 3:60–61, July 13, 1855.

59. For a list of questions in the catechism and a discussion of the reformation see Paul H. Peterson, "The Mormon Reformation of 1856–1857: The Rhetoric and the Reality," *Journal of Mormon History* 15 (1989): 59–87.

60. Mary Jane Mount Tanner, Autobiography, 105, LDS Church Archives, cited in Peterson, "The Mormon Reformation," 117.

61. Heber C. Kimball to James Snow, March 6, 1857, Brigham Young Letterbooks, LDS Church Archives.

62. Peterson, "The Mormon Reformation," 114.

63. Kanter, *Commitment and Community,* 108–9.

64. "Loa, Close of Brilliant Career: Patriarch Elias H. Blackburn Lays Down Life's Labors at 81," *Deseret Evening News,* April 16, 1908, 8, cited in Munson and Munson, *A Gift of Faith,* 329.

65. Martin Buber, *Paths in Utopia,* trans. R. F. C. Hull (Boston: Beacon Hill, 1958), 7, cited in Kanter, *Commitment and Community,* 113.

66. See Kanter, *Commitment and Community,* 111, 113–25.

67. Susannah Summers Higgs, "Patriarchal Blessing," October 29, 1878, in possession of Susannah Broberg Langenheim, Glendale, California.

68. Kanter, *Commitment and Community,* 116–20.

69. "Historical Records and Minutes," Summit Creek Branch, Utah Stake, October 25, 1875, LDS Church Archives.

70. Bishops, along with stake priesthood leaders, did receive a portion of the tithing collected. This process helped defray expenses but was never intended to provide a living for the leader. On a practical level, perishable goods could be utilized by the bishop, who spent much of his time dealing with tithing-in-kind to make sure that donated items were not wasted.

71. C. B. P., "Sketch of Sister Mary John," *Woman's Exponent* 34 (February 1906): 55.

72. Leonard J. Arrington, Feramorz Y. Fox, and Dean L. May, *Building the City of God: Community and Cooperation among the Mormons* (Salt Lake City: Deseret Book, 1976), 91–92.

73. Canceled stock certificates, 1869–1946, Zion's Cooperative Mercantile Institute, LDS Church Archives.

74. Arrington and others, *Building the City of God*, 412–13.

75. Arrington and others, *Building the City of God*, 107.

76. Arrington and others, *Building the City of God*, 412–13.

77. Provo School of the Prophets, Minutes, July 20, 1868, typescript, 60, Utah State Historical Society.

78. Summary based on Jill Mulvay Derr, Janath Russell Cannon, and Maureen Ursenbach Beecher, *Women of Covenant: The Story of Relief Society* (Salt Lake City: Deseret Book, 1992), 83–126; Maureen Ursenbach Beecher, "Relief Society (1884)" and "Eliza R. Snow's Relief Society Travels (1880–1881)," in *Historical Atlas of Mormonism*, ed. S. Kent Brown, Donald Q. Cannon, and Richard H. Jackson (New York: Simon & Schuster, 1994), 104–7.

79. Goshen Ward, Santaquin-Tintic Stake, November 12, 1881, [p. 2], "Relief Society History, 1881–1931," LDS Church Archives.

80. See Hartley, "Common People."

RHYTHMS

Street scene of Ogden, Utah, about 1873. Milan P. Warner, photographer. Taken from a stereograph, the images have been combined to produce a fuller view.

FIG. 1. Pioneer wagon, ca. 1870. After months of traveling in a wagon, families often used the wagon as an extension of their new home. It was not uncommon to find a wagon in the yard serving as an extra bedroom for months following the establishment of a log home or dugout.

Battle of the Homefront: The Early Pioneer Art of Homemaking

Andrew H. Hedges

On a visit to a local historical site some time ago, I walked through several buildings that had been restored and decorated to look like the homes where Utah's early Mormon settlers had lived. While I was struck with how small these houses were and with the number of children raised in them, I was also impressed with the craftsmanship of the early Saints and their obvious ability to effectively use the natural resources of their new location. Similarly, I gained appreciation both for the difficulties attending the performance of even the simplest household tasks and for the Saints' industry and ingenuity. Nevertheless, I ended my tour with the somewhat smug feeling that pioneer life was not that much different from my own. While the pioneers may have lacked some of the modern conveniences we enjoy today, their accommodations were nevertheless quite adequate, their food plentiful, and their lives relatively uncomplicated. Overall, pioneer life looked rather quaint and cozy.

I have since learned that while the reproductions I saw on that tour are more or less accurate they reflect pioneer life in its later years, after the Saints had time to accumulate the finer things of life and refine their everyday processes. Almost wholly lacking from the tour were reproductions of the Saints' living conditions upon their arrival in Utah and descriptions of the challenges they faced over the next several years—even decades in some of the more remote settlements—as they sought to establish themselves in the Great Basin and surrounding territory. The snug little cabins I walked through followed many years of primitive shelters, backbreaking labor, scarcity, and want.

This essay focuses on the pioneers' home life during these difficult early years and on their efforts to establish homes and provide for their families under less-than-ideal conditions. While both men and women engaged in this undertaking, the bulk of the everyday tasks within the home fell on the shoulders of the women. They, more than the men, took responsibility for attending to the children's needs, for planning and making meals out of the available foodstuffs, and for creating a home—a real home—out of whatever shelter was available at the moment. While the men's duties and responsibilities took them to the front lines of various battles outside of the home, pioneer women served on the front lines of their own wars and skirmishes—engagements that, while not as exciting perhaps as an Indian war or foreign mission, were every bit as important to the building up of Zion. Their story, the battle of the home front, needs to be told.

SHELTER

An appreciation for the accomplishments of pioneer women begins with an understanding of what structures and shelters served as "houses" in early Utah. Very few people had a home waiting for them when they arrived in the territory or the time, tools, and means to build or buy one immediately upon their arrival. The same held for those who were called to settle outlying areas years later. Under such conditions, it is no surprise to learn that the first "house" many immigrants found themselves occupying was the same "house" they had occupied coming across the plains: their wagon (fig. 1). Hannah Nixon's experience in this regard was a common one. Moving to Salt Lake City from a small settlement on the Jordan River, she and her family moved their wagon box onto the floor of an unroofed, one-room house and spent the winter of 1851–52 living there. Although they built a two-room house the following spring, a subsequent call from Brigham Young to settle St. George required them once again to make their wagon their home until a more permanent house could be erected.[1] At least a few families continued to utilize the trusty wagon box even after such a home had been built; Joseph Fielding's family, for example, which arrived in the Salt Lake Valley in 1848, elected to sleep in their wagons even after they had erected a one-room log cabin.[2]

Pioneers who settled along the banks of streams frequently constructed crude shelters of the willows that grew in such places. Such "willow shanties" were far from comfortable; Hannah Crosby, for example, who helped settle Bunkerville on the Virgin River, noted how poorly these shelters protected their inhabitants from the "exceedingly hot" Dixie summers.[3]

Cooler by far, but complete with their own set of problems, were the dugouts a number of immigrants used. As the name suggests, a dugout was constructed by digging a short, broad trench horizontally into the side of a hill or an embankment. The trench comprised the walls and floor of the home and was covered with brush, branches, canvas, and the like for a roof. Of necessity, such shelters were generally quite small; Uhan Parson, for example, an early settler of Huntsville, recorded that his family of seven lived for a time in a dugout whose dimensions were a mere twelve by fourteen feet.[4]

Ann Howell Burt has left us with a lengthy and vivid description of life in such a dwelling. A native of Glamorganshire, Wales, Ann immigrated to America as a child in 1851, came west to Utah in 1852, married, and found herself living in a dugout in summer 1863. "The neighbors," she recorded in her journal, "call it the Castle of Spiders and it is well named, for I never saw so many reptiles and bugs of all kinds." She continued:

> For several mornings I was puzzled to find my milk-pan skimmed; could not understand what could have done it. So the other evening I sat down behind the door, with my knitting, to watch proceedings, and what was my surprise to see a huge bull-snake come crawling out from the head of our bed and swaying gracefully toward my crude cupboard, began to skim my cream. Now I cover my milk tightly.[5]

Things did not improve over the course of the summer, as subsequent entries indicate:

> This is a hideous place. Some days ago, I killed a rattlesnake with my rolling pin, as he came crawling down the steps. I was just cooking supper and the baby was on the floor or rather the ground, for we have no other floor. I was badly frightened. . . . A few days ago, while keeping the flies off the baby's face as he slept on an improvised bed on the floor, I discovered, to my horror, a large tarantula crawling toward the child. I seized the broomstick, thrust the end of it at the tarantula and when it took hold of the thing which was provoking it I hurriedly put it into the fire.[6]

Ann's last journal entry about her dugout experience speaks volumes: "We are going to move away from here," she wrote. "I am weary from fighting all these reptiles."[7]

The next level of sophistication beyond the dugout was the well-known log cabin. Notwithstanding the favorable press these dwellings have received, they were generally far from snug and inviting (fig. 2). With lumber at a premium, most were equipped with nothing more

Fig. 2. Samuel and Mary Bunting family, 1869. Union Pacific Railroad photographer A. J. Russell captured a Latter-day Saint pioneer family living in Kaysville, Utah, thus preserving cultural information about living conditions on the Utah frontier. Some-times identified as a polygamist family, Mary and Samuel Bunting pose with other family members. Mary is standing behind her husband in the doorway; they are surrounded by Mary's mother, her three sisters, and five nieces and nephews.

than dirt floors that could be cleaned—if such a word is appropriate—
only by wetting the dust and sweeping it out with a homemade broom.[8]
As if that were not enough of a trial, Mary Horne, one of the pioneers
of 1847, reminds us that the timber out of which these cabins were constructed was full of bedbugs and that during the first few years of settlement in the Valley, "mice were very troublesome." These uninvited
houseguests intruded in such numbers, she continues, that the settlers

> could see their ground floor tremble as [the mice] ran about under
> their covered trails. And when the stones at the corners [of the cabins]
> supporting their roofs, loosened and fell by the rain, the frightened
> mice ran in hordes. Sometimes as many as 60 would be caught before
> going to bed. [The pioneers] had to make their own traps, and one
> contrivance was a bucket full of water with a board sloped at each end,
> balanced on the edge, and greased. This caught dozens of mice.

Mary closes her account of this infestation by noting that "the first cat
and her progeny were invaluable."[9]

The early Saints learned from the records kept by trappers, mountain men, and early explorers that Utah was a desert. Accordingly,
they built their early cabins with the understanding that the roofs need
not necessarily be impervious to rain. Before experience taught them
to do otherwise, they made cabin roofs by placing a layer of grass and
weeds, "then a good layer of earth," over poles placed as close together
as possible.[10] The finished product was almost flat. Although noted
for its warmth, it apparently did little more than slow the rain—which
came in torrents at times. Leaking roofs turned the Saints' homes,
with their dirt floors, into muddy messes. As one unfortunate sister
recalled, "We had rain out of doors and a mud-fall in the house, for the
continued fall of rain so thoroughly soaked the earth over head that
the downpour was mud, *good-honest-mud.*" She continued:

> You can imagine the condition our beds and bedding were in, as
> long as there was a dry spot, we would move it there, but after a
> while there was no dry spot. One of the family had a babe nine days
> old, she stayed in bed till it was soaked through, then she was placed
> in a chair before the fire with an umbrella over her head.[11]

Mary Horne noted that "the flags and dirt formed but a slight protection [against the rain], and it was a strange sight to see [the people]
sitting at their tables or on the bed, their heads covered with an
umbrella while the rain was coming through the roof long after it had
ceased outside."[12] Melting snow had the same effect on the small
cabin Williamena McKay lived in at Huntsville while her husband

served a mission to Arizona. The snow caused the cabin's chinking to dislodge, turning its earthen floor to mud.[13]

Perhaps the most enduring house the earliest settlers could build out of native materials was one of adobe or rock (fig. 3). These were generally better insulated against both the cold and the heat than other shelters, they did not disintegrate in the rain, and they generally provided an effective barrier against the incursions of wildlife. Accordingly, many families built and lived in such homes when conditions permitted. Despite their obvious advantages, however, rock and adobe houses came with their own sets of problems. As Louise Thalmann Hasler, a Swiss immigrant, learned, building an adobe home took a tremendous amount of time and labor. In order to finish just two of the planned six bedrooms of their adobe home over the course of one summer, she had to work side by side with her husband in bringing the adobes from the drying yard into the building lot, unloading them, and placing them on the growing walls. With winter coming on, she laid the shingles on the roof while her husband did the carpentry work inside. The house was ready for habitation by December. Two months later, having done everything from hefting adobes to roofing her home over the course of her pregnancy, Louise gave birth to a healthy son.[14]

Courtesy Utah State Historical Society

FIG. 3. Mormon family in front of their adobe home in Utah.

Not everyone who attempted to build such a home fared as well as Louise and her husband did. Work progressed so slowly on the rock home Hannah Nixon's family was trying to build, for example, that winter caught them with no more than a one-room cellar in which to stay along with another family.[15] Similarly, winter burst upon Williamena McKay of Huntsville and her family when only part of their five-story rock home was completed. Heavy snows subsequently caved in that part of the roof they had managed to finish and even toppled some of the rock walls.[16] Such problems could plague these homes even after they were supposedly finished, a lesson Rachel Burton learned the hard way when the east wall of her adobe home, in which she had been living for several months, caved in during a windstorm.[17]

While dugouts, shanties, cabins, and adobe or rock dwellings constituted the principal types of homes for the Saints, circumstances occasionally required them to live in other structures as well. Eva Beck and her family, for example, who immigrated from Germany in 1863, spent their first winter in Lehi living in a former chicken coop.[18] Similarly, Lucina Boren of Wallsburg lived in an empty granary in Heber during hostilities associated with the Black Hawk War.[19] Such structures were utilized for both relatively infrequent and short periods of time but constituted an important aspect of the Saints' housing prospects all the same.

Moves and Limited Resources

The Saints faced at least two other challenges that compounded the difficulties of establishing a home in early Utah. First, many families, either in response to formal mission calls or their own search for greener pastures, made several moves over the course of their lives in the West. Those making a move frequently left established homes and occupations and started afresh. Such moves were generally done by wagon (even as late as the early 1900s) and could be tiring, difficult, and hazardous (fig. 4). While many, if not most, early homemakers faced this challenge at least once in their lives, others faced it far more frequently. Nanna Anderson, for example, moved some twenty times by wagon over the course of her married life and lived everywhere from Canada to Arizona before she finally prevailed upon her husband to settle down.[20]

Second, the resources and materials that could be used to furnish these homes were extremely limited and primitive. Rag wicks in a dish of grease and, later, candles constituted the light source for these early homes; rope "springs" and straw-filled mattresses answered for beds. Other furnishings were just as humble, and the small stove, single table, two chairs, and straw bed that comprised the sum total of Rachel Burton's home furnishings in 1856 were probably quite representative of what most young couples could expect to possess at the time.[21]

Clearly, turning a house into a home under such conditions was no small feat. As we have already seen, it required courage enough to kill a rattlesnake with a rolling pin, endurance enough to haul adobes while pregnant, and self-control enough to withstand plagues of mice and insects occurring on a biblical scale. As the umbrellas in the cabins demonstrate, the ability to improvise was also in heavy demand. All of these virtues, and especially the last, became even more important when the early Saints faced special occasions or extraordinary circumstances. Even though the appropriate materials were not always on hand, holidays, with their special traditions, still needed to be celebrated; babies continued to be born; and sick people still needed medical care. These and other special circumstances had to be addressed as appropriately as possible, and more often than not, the responsibility for doing so lay with the women of the Church.

A little creativity allowed pioneer women to accomplish great things with their limited resources (fig. 5). Sarah Gladhill recalled how her mother, in an attempt to make Christmas more special in their Ogden home during the 1860s, would "take a picture she had brought with her from Philadelphia and not having a frame for it she would take a piece of dark cloth and bind it and hang it up, taking down the one she had put up the Christmas before as it would be fly specked and dirty."[22] Similarly, when Christmas found the pioneers of San Juan County camped in wagons at Hole-in-the-Rock, mothers managed to save the day by filling the children's stockings—which were carefully hung from the wagon wheels—with parched corn and cookies baked in a Dutch oven.[23]

The same creativity, mixed with a liberal dose of grit and determination, allowed women like Leora Campbell, one of the first settlers in Liberty, to successfully meet more harrowing challenges. While her husband was away and she was living in a log cabin with no windows and only a hole in the sod roof for a chimney, Leora went into labor just as "an awful storm came up." "The rain came down in torrents," she recorded.

> Our house leaked all over, not clear water but mud. There was a place from about the middle of the bed to the head that did not leak. My

husband's grandmother was living with us that winter. She put me crosswise of the bed, and put her featherbed over me to keep me dry. She put her quilts under the bed to keep them dry. Wet boards were laid down on my bed for me to lie on. A sheet was hung up to the head of the bed to keep out the wind and one across the foot of the bed.... Thus I gave birth to the first white child born in Ogden Valley."[24]

MEALS

Pioneer women usually assumed responsibility for preparing meals for the family. This was no easy task in early Utah. Prior to the coming of the railroad, stoves and specialized utensils for preparing food were scarce, as their weight and bulk frequently prevented their being hauled across the plains in wagons. Primitive means of preservation meant that only a few types of foodstuffs could be imported from the outside as well, and initially, pioneers used much of their supply as seed for the following year rather than for food. Poor yields due to crickets and droughts continued to limit the amount of the harvest the Saints could use for food. Mary Horne reported that three years passed before her family grew enough vegetables that they could spare some for the table.[25]

The net result of these forces was that early pioneer women again faced the all-too-familiar problem of making do with what little they had on hand. Many, predictably enough, utilized a wide variety of native plants—including the famed sego lily bulbs, milkweed shoots, "marrowfat peas," wild parsnips, currants, pigweed greens, and even mushrooms—as they sought to supplement their families' diets.[26] Conditions slowly improved as the Saints perfected irrigation techniques, obtained a greater variety of seeds, and grew accustomed to the region's unpredictable weather, but native plants continued to be a staple in outlying areas like Liberty—where Leora Campbell and her husband ate nothing but sego lily roots "for three or four days at a time"—well into the 1860s. After the poor harvest following the entrance of Johnston's Army into the territory in 1858, Saints like Ann Burt turned again to roots even in more centrally located areas.[27]

Under such conditions, the ability to improvise was at a premium. Water mixed with parched barley, wheat, and even peas substituted for coffee; cornstalks and watermelons were processed into molasses. Settlers ate the rinds of melons after having first boiled them in molasses.[28] Ingenuity, coupled with a strong stomach, became even more important during the lean winter months, when supplies were

Fig. 4. Mormon family, ca. 1867. After their arrival at the LDS Church headquarters in Salt Lake City, many immigrants loaded wagons again and made a trek to a far-flung settlement. Once they arrived in the new settlements, living conditions were in many cases primitive. Note the mismatched team and condition of the horse.

Fig. 5. Utah pioneer home, ca. 1870. A Mormon mother and child pose inside their log home in a pioneer settlement in Utah. Conditions on the Utah frontier were Spartan for many individuals until much later, but this scene could be duplicated well into the late nineteenth century.

Courtesy Utah State Historical Society

low and the chance for outside aid fell off to almost nothing. Mary Horne recalled one family whose stores gave out midwinter but who had a ready supply of fresh milk. Allowing a portion of each day's milk to stand and thicken, they would then mix it with fresh milk and "eat it for bread." This constituted their sole source of subsistence for six weeks.[29] Ann Burt noted in her diary how one family tried to enhance its meager supply of flour over the winter of 1855–56 by mixing it with sawdust—a failure, it turned out. She also recorded the desperate straits of her own family. "We were given a piece of meat by Brother V.," she wrote.

> He had been up in the mountains and carried home a couple of dead animals that had died of starvation during the cold winter. Well, there was not much meat to it, and when it was boiled it was black; still it satisfied our hunger. . . . Oh for a few of the good things we had at home![30]

Even when enough food was on hand, the monotony of the fare could challenge even the best cook's skill. While waiting for her fiancé to arrive in the Valley, Maren Nielson, a convert from Denmark, had her first taste of boiled wheat and fried jackrabbit, a dish which "tasted rather good," she reflected, although it "was different than anything I had ever eaten." The dish lost its savor for both Maren and her young family in Sanpete County, however, for it became their standard supper fare. Virtually every night for years, according to her record, she had nothing but wheat and jackrabbit to prepare for her family's supper, until the dish she had once enjoyed became positively distasteful to her. Her family, predictably enough, was similarly affected, to the point that one of her sons, when asked to give the blessing over yet another meal of wheat and rabbit, gave the "prayer" in the following verse:

> Rabbit young, Rabbit old,
> Rabbit hot, Rabbit cold,
> Rabbit tender and Rabbit tough.
> Oh please, Dear Lord,
> We've had enough.[31]

Many pioneer women endured these privations through several months of pregnancy—a fact few historians have appreciated. Unlike today, when well-stocked grocery stores are open around the clock, early Utah women in the so-called delicate condition had to nourish themselves with what they had on hand. At times this could be painfully little, as the story of a woman named Gatha illustrates.

Conceiving shortly after her arrival in the Valley in the fall of 1847, Gatha and her husband lived on rations of a half pound of flour and corned beef over the winter and were reduced to eating thistle greens and buttermilk by the time spring arrived some months later. To make matters worse, Gatha spent the spring days walking beside a team of oxen while her husband followed the plow behind. She did have the good fortune to obtain a piece of bread from the midwife as her due date approached, and some obliging neighbors—"whose kindness," she wrote, "I shall never forget"—gave her a little more. But nothing she ate over the entire course of her pregnancy ever amounted to the "full enjoyable meal" her body needed.[32] Gatha was fortunate in that her baby, despite the privations, was a "plump healthy child," but many women were not so lucky.

CLOTHING AND BEDDING

It was also the pioneer women's responsibility to see that their families had adequate clothing, bedding, sheets, and the like. This, too, was a difficult task in the early days and continued to present a challenge in remote settlements long after a variety of textiles and finished articles of clothing were available in Salt Lake City. In the absence of commercially produced cloth, women again relied on the materials they had on hand to make suitable fabric at home. While a few families were fortunate enough to live both where and when cotton was grown, many of the early Saints, at least for a time, made their textiles from wool or flax. This could be a time-consuming process; flax, for example, had to be soaked in water for some six weeks after it had been picked before it could be spun into thread and then woven into usable cloth. Taking a cue from their Native American neighbors, pioneer women learned how to use native plants like squaw bush to dye their material. And after all this, of course, women did the actual sewing of the clothing or bedding by hand. The whole process was so labor intensive and time consuming that Maren Nielson of Sanpete County routinely worked "all day and most of the night" to keep her growing family in clothes.[33]

Family members commonly needed articles of clothing made or repaired when none of the materials generally used to do so were immediately available. In these cases, pioneer women again relied on their industry and ingenuity to meet the demand. If necessary, cow or even buffalo hair, which pioneers had carefully collected from sagebrush and preserved as they journeyed west, could substitute for wool. In a pinch, women used animal skins to patch men's pants; in times of great need, they even used such skins to make full garments.[34] Old clothes, and even clothes still in use, were frequently altered and pressed into service. Maren Nielson, for example, regularly made her daughters' dresses from her own old clothes, while Hans Christensen's wife parted with one of her skirts in order to furnish her husband with a much-needed pair of pants.[35]

HOME NURSING

As if making a shelter livable, preparing meals, and seeing that their families were properly clothed were not enough, women regularly shouldered the added burden of caring for sick children and husbands. Large families, the prevalence of disease, and inadequate medical care and supplies combined to make this one of the most challenging duties for pioneer homemakers. Recounting an experience to which many women today can probably relate, Hannah Nixon of St. George recalled how her little Mary, ill from Dixie's unrelenting summer heat, "used to cry till I didn't know what to do . . . I felt like I would go crazy, so when I got so I couldn't stand it no longer I picked her up and went out with her and sat down and cried so she stopped squalling and wanted to know what is the matter Mama."[36] These times were made all the harder when military duty, Church callings, and missions took husbands out of the homes for extended periods of time, leaving their wives—who were frequently ill themselves—to take care of a sick family alone. Such times could test even the most proven Saints. After finding herself and four children gravely ill shortly after her husband left on his second mission to California, Sarah Rich, wife of Charles C. Rich and no stranger to affliction, admitted that "to be left alone . . . with a sick family was rather trying."[37]

Caring for sick children was also one of the most heartbreaking duties pioneer women faced, as days or weeks spent caring for a sick little one all too frequently ended with the child's death. After the strain of caring for seven children with whooping cough during her family's first winter in Cache Valley, for example, Henrietta Williams had to face burying two of them.[38] The number of children a family might lose through disease was staggering at times. Rachel Robinson buried seven of her twelve little ones, while of the ten children Teresa Duncan brought into this world, six died before adulthood—four of them dying from diphtheria within one week of each other.[39]

INCOME

While the men generally took primary responsibility for providing for their families' economic needs, Utah's pioneer women at times shouldered part of this load as well. With their husbands' resources taxed to the utmost with Church work, farming, and building a house of some sort for their families, women like Sarah Rich and Mary Perkins would have been hard-pressed to furnish their homes adequately had it not been for the initiative they showed in selling eggs, butter, preserves, and dried fruit.[40] Polygamous wives sometimes found it necessary to supplement what their husband could spare for each of his families; for example, Ellen Gunderson—who joined the Church in Denmark, immigrated to Utah, and married A. C. Nielson as a second wife in 1880—supported herself by selling rugs and carpets she wove.[41]

Wives of husbands who had been called on missions found themselves in similar circumstances, and the records clearly indicate that being the wife of a missionary entailed far more than writing weekly letters. Hannah Romney's situation was a common one. After her husband was called on a mission to England, Hannah learned how to make gloves to support herself and her baby. Finding the market for gloves somewhat depressed at the time, she took up nursing, sewing, washing, "or any kind of work," she wrote, "that I could do honestly." Hannah found herself in the same situation again eleven years later, only this time she had five children to support. Taking advantage of the construction of the St. George Temple, this good mother, who was concerned that her growing family be "educated and clothed to correspond with the society we mingled with," again went to work, this time by washing and sewing for the temple workmen. Washing "all day from sunup to sundown" earned her a dollar.[42]

These, of course, are just some of the challenges Utah's early homemakers faced in their efforts to raise families far from the centers of civilization. Women fulfilled numerous other duties as well, including farm work, Church responsibilities, medical care, and education. A full discussion of all that pioneer women undertook would require a book-length treatise. Little of what they accomplished came easily. Insects, snakes, snow, mud, sun, and disease fought them at every turn, and at times it probably seemed as if all nature had channeled its forces against them. This was especially true in their efforts to establish homes in the wilderness, and any history of the period that fails to acknowledge the challenges they faced in their everyday lives as mothers and wives is woefully incomplete.

MOTIVATION TO ENDURE

Why, one might legitimately ask, did these women endure all that they did? What helped them carry on under such trying circumstances? To answer that they had no choice would be as wrong as it would be simplistic, for opportunities to leave certainly existed. While no small number took advantage of these opportunities, a far greater number did not. Again, why? A few reflections from Ann Burt, one of the women I have quoted extensively, provide what I think is the clue.

In October 1854, at a time when living in Utah promised little more than hard work and hunger, Ann's husband decided to leave the company of the Saints for California. When Ann, who was pregnant at the time, refused to accompany him, he promptly sold the house she was living in and left. At this critical point, Ann received a letter from a wealthy, childless uncle living in her native land of Wales, a place she loved and missed so much that her every attempt to sing "Home Sweet Home" ended in tears. In his letter, Ann's uncle informed her that if she would return to Wales, he would make her the sole heir of his extensive wealth and property. Homeless and homesick, without a husband, destitute, and expecting a baby, Ann nevertheless refused the offer. Her brief explanation for so doing, written shortly after her husband left, should be considered a classic among the early Saints' statements of faith. "He wanted me to accompany him," she recorded in her diary, "but I could not think of it. It may be better there in a way, but we have come here for the Gospel's sake, and here I intend to stay and weather it out with the rest of the Saints."

"We have come here for the Gospel's sake, and here I intend to stay and weather it out with the rest of the Saints." In this short sentence, we learn both how and why she and thousands of other Latter-day Saint women faced the rigors of pioneer life. As we have seen, creativity and diligence helped pioneer women meet the challenges they encountered in the valleys of the mountains. Patience, too, and the ability to improvise were important attributes. But Ann Burt's words tell us that more important than everything else in determining how successfully these wives and mothers would provide for their families in the face of opposition was a firm testimony of the gospel and an unswerving determination to be true to that testimony at all costs. As disagreeable, even fatal, as the bugs, snakes, mud, and disease may have been, they paled into relative insignificance alongside these simple, yet powerful, convictions.

Andrew H. Hedges is Assistant Professor of Church History and Doctrine at Brigham Young University.

NOTES

1. Hannah Isabell Fawcett Nixon, "Biography of Hannah Isabell Fawcett Nixon," first-person account, typescript, 2, 10, Library Archives, Utah State Historical Society, Salt Lake City (hereafter cited as Historical Society Archives).

2. Rachel Fielding Burton, "Autobiographical Sketch," typescript, Archives Division, Church Historical Department, The Church of Jesus Christ of Latter-day Saints, Salt Lake City (hereafter cites as LDS Church Archives).

3. Hannah A. Crosby, "Sketch of the Life of Hannah A. Crosby, Daughter of Edward and Emily Abott Bunker," typescript, 5, Historical Society Archives.

4. Uhan Parson, "Brief Sketch of the Life and Experiences of Uhan Parson," holograph, Historical Society Archives.

5. Sophy Valentine, *Biography of Ann Howell Burt* (Brigham City: n.p., 1916), 24.

6. Valentine, *Biography of Ann Howell Burt,* 24.

7. Valentine, *Biography of Ann Howell Burt,* 25.

8. Eva Christine Beck Zimmerman Harrison, Autobiography, in *Our Pioneer Heritage,* comp. Kate B. Carter, 20 vols. (Salt Lake City: Daughters of Utah Pioneers, 1958–77), 8:50.

9. Mrs. Joseph Horne [Mary Isabella], "Migration and Settlement of the Latter Day Saints," typescript, 19, Historical Society Archives.

10. Gatha, "Personal Reminiscences," *Woman's Exponent* 21 (April 1, 1893): 149.

11. Gatha, "Personal Reminiscences," 149.

12. Horne, "Migration," 16.

13. Williamena McKay, Autobiography, LDS Church Archives.

14. "Arthur Davis Hasler, a Swiss American Limnologist," *Swiss American Historical Society Newsletter* 23 (November 1987): 15–16.

15. Nixon, "Biography," 10.

16. McKay, Autobiography.

17. Burton, "Autobiographical Sketch."

18. Harrison, Autobiography, 8:50.

19. Lucina Mecham Boren, Journal, in *Treasures of Pioneer History,* comp. Kate B. Carter, 6 vols. (Salt Lake City: Daughters of Utah Pioneers, 1952–57), 6:317–18.

20. Nanna Ameilia Erickson Anderson, Autobiography, in Carter, *Our Pioneer Heritage,* 3:208–15.

21. Burton, "Autobiographical Sketch." Similarly, Hannah Romney and her husband began housekeeping with "a small cook stove, a bed, three chairs, a small table and enough dishes for three," while Mary Little began married life with "a feather bed, pillows and quilts . . . a few dishes . . . a bake oven, and camp kettle." Hannah Hood Hill Romney, Autobiography, in Carter, *Our Pioneer Heritage*, 5:266. See also Mary Jane Lytle Little, "A Biographical Sketch of the Life of Mary Jane Lytle Little," in "Autobiographies of Thomas Evans, Priscilla Merriman Evans, James A. Little, Mary Jane Lytle Little," typescript, 93, Special Collections, Harold B. Lee Library, Brigham Young University, Provo, Utah (hereafter cited as BYU Archives).

22. Elvera Manful, "Sarah S. Moulding Gladhill," Pioneer Personal History, typescript, 8, Historical Society Archives.

23. Mary Jane Perkins Wilson, "Pioneer Personal History," typescript, Historical Society Archives.

24. Leora Margyann Talmadge Campbell, Autobiography, in Carter, *Our Pioneer Heritage*, 4:54-55.

25. Horne, "Migration," 17.

26. Histories of the period are rife with accounts of people using such items for food. The above list was compiled from "Biography of Henrietta E. C. Williams and Enoch Burns," typescript, 15, BYU Archives; and Nixon, "Biography," 3.

27. Campbell, Autobiography, 4:55; Valentine, *Biography of Ann Howell Burt*, 22.

28. Horne, "Migration," 15, 19.

29. Horne, "Migration," 17.

30. Valentine, *Biography of Ann Howell Burt*, 21.

31. Maren Kristine Nielson, Autobiography, in Carter, *Our Pioneer Heritage*, 11:303-4.

32. Gatha, "Personal Reminiscences," 149. Similarly, Hannah Romney of St. George finished out one of her pregnancies having little more than "dry bread with a little vinegar sweetened with sugar" to eat. Romney, Autobiography, 5:267.

33. Nielson, Autobiography, 11:304.

34. Horne, "Migration," 22.

35. Nielson, Autobiography, 11:304; Hans Christensen, "Memoirs of Hans Christensen," typescript, 20, Historical Society Archives.

36. Nixon, "Biography," 13.

37. Sarah Dearman Pea Rich, Autobiography, LDS Church Archives.

38. "Biography of Henrietta E. C. Williams," 24-25.

39. Campbell, Autobiography, 4:39; Teresa Ann F. Urie Duncan, Journal, in Carter, *Our Pioneer Heritage*, 9:431.

40. Wilson, "Pioneer Personal History"; Rich, Autobiography.

41. Nielson, Autobiography, 11:307.

42. Romney, Autobiography, 5:265, 268.

"Oh, What Songs of the Heart": Zion's Hymns as Sung by the Pioneers

Richard H. Cracroft

Oh, what songs of the heart
We shall sing all the day,
When again we assemble at home.[1]

The hymns of the Latter-day Saints have always been crucial to the spiritual expression of individual Saints as well as to the collective expressions of the Mormon people. Hymns—defined as sacred and spiritual "songs of the heart" addressed to deity—gladden the soul by enabling formal, lyrical expression of one's profoundest spiritual feelings. But they also do much more, for hymns assist in organizing and interpreting LDS history,[2] framing LDS beliefs, and expressing LDS hopes, expectations, and ideals.[3] Hymns, then, are vital in transforming the Latter-day Saints into more than a sect, denomination, or church, for hymns provide part of that spiritual and cultural glue which has congealed the Latter-day Saints into a people.

Hymns have served the Latter-day Saints in much the same way that stories serve nations and peoples. Cultural pundit Neil Postman describes the power of stories: "A story provides a structure for our perceptions; only through stories do facts assume any meaning whatsoever. . . . [Human beings] require a story to give meaning to their existence. Without air, our cells die. Without a story, our selves die."[4] Similarly, LDS hymns lend form, meaning, and purpose to Latter-day Saint theology and assist the Saints in "mak[ing] sense out of the world";[5] they frame, as seen by peering through Mormon spectacles, a Mormon cosmos.

Nevertheless, it seems to me that, despite the affinity present-day Saints may feel with their forefather and foremother Saints, the hymns as sung by the Mormon pioneers meant something compellingly different to them than the same hymns mean to us or will mean to our great-grandchildren.

As this closer look at a handful of nineteenth-century LDS hymns of Zion makes clear, the men and women who pioneered and settled Utah Territory between 1847–1890 brought to these hymns a different *Weltanschauung,* or worldview, an almost unique personal and collective history, and thus a remarkably different perspective. The hymns are packed with specific cultural and religious allusions, references, meanings, feelings, and responses that are at a remove from the purview of the contemporary Latter-day Saint. In framing and giving expression to recent, familiar, and immediately past events, these hymns were, for the Saints, instant history. The impassioned lyrics of these hymns, set to soul-stirring music, resonated and reverberated within and among the pioneer Saints with an immediacy, pertinence, and anticipation regarding recent events, familiar circumstances, and imminent expectations.

The pioneer Saints hymned the events of the Restoration and the modern-day gathering of Israel; they heralded the imminent millennial reign of Jesus Christ; they cheered the restoration of the holy priesthood as part of the restoration of all things; they mourned their martyred prophet while being empowered by his witness; they prayed for freedom from oppression and persecution; they urged one another to keep the vision pure, to remain true to the faith; they sang of their Latter-day Saint doctrines and beliefs, from "work for the dead" and temple sealings for the living to consecration, tithing, the Word of Wisdom, and the plan of redemption and exaltation; they shouted praises for newly revealed holy scriptures and continuing communications with the heavens; they sang of their duty to call on the inhabitants of Babylon to repent, be baptized, and flee to Zion; and above all, they praised the tender mercies of their God who had led his chosen Israel to Zion, "freedom's last abode," and they stood "all amazed" at the Atonement of the Lord Jesus Christ.

While Latter-day Saints hymn the same themes today, the pioneer Saints did it first; and they did it with a fervor and faith that, although still extant among the Latter-day Saints, may seem, comparatively, more subdued, less confident, less sure of the imminence of Christ's Second Coming, more jaded by the insistent incursions into faith of a secular and materialistic world, and certainly less militant and more mainline Christian.

EMERGENT THEOLOGY

The hymns the pioneers sang stand as artifacts that, when imaginatively probed, yield insight, some recovery, and greater understanding of the different world of the Mormon settlers of Utah Territory. Reflected in their hymns is the Saints' on-the-cusp excitement at the emergence of newly restored theology. There is no question about it: Mormon hymns broke new ground because Latter-day Saint doctrines are unique. Whether singing Joseph Townsend's "The Iron Rod"[6] about the vision of a prophet named Nephi or hymning Joel Johnson's "The Glorious Gospel Light Has Shone" about vicarious work for the dead, the Saints could soon confound any lurking Gentile with a plethora of Mormon allusions and images—sung *shibboleths*. Consider, for example, these excerpts from verses two and three in Johnson's 1841 hymn:

> As Christ to spirits went to preach
> Who were to prison led,
> So many Saints have gone to teach
> The gospel to the dead.
> And we for them can be baptized,
> Yes, for our friends most dear,
> That they can with the just be raised
> When Gabriel's trump they hear.[7]

We hymn these doctrines today but without the sense of dissonance jarring with the teachings of other Christian churches.

PERENNIAL FAVORITES, DIFFERING WORLDS

An examination of the perennially popular Mormon hymns "The Morning Breaks," "Redeemer of Israel," "The Spirit of God," "O My Father," "Praise to the Man," and "Come, Come, Ye Saints" makes evident that Mormon hymns reveal not only the pioneer Saints' exultation in their restored theology, but also their strong faith and remarkable confidence in the inevitable triumph of the kingdom of God and their collective vision of themselves as God's chosen Israel.

"THE MORNING BREAKS." Written by Parley P. Pratt (1840) and set to the tune "Hudson," composed by Mormon convert George Edward Percy Careless (1864), "The Morning Breaks" expresses in moving lyrics Mormon joy at the recent Restoration of the gospel. It stirs the heart of the convert and helps keep vivid among the Saints God's "strange act" (Isa. 28:21) in leading, individually and collectively, the children of the promise out of obscurity and sin into salvation and righteousness:

> The morning breaks, the shadows flee;
> Lo, Zion's standard is unfurled!
> The dawning of a brighter day
> Majestic rises on the world.
> . . . .
> Thus Zion's light is bursting forth
> To bring her ransomed children home.[8]

We sing these words with fervor but not with quite the same fervor of men and women who have laid their all on the altars of a brand-new Zion.

"REDEEMER OF ISRAEL." The Saints' vibrant optimism, confidence, and gratitude to the Father for touching common lives, all expressed in "The Morning Breaks," are likewise evident in "Redeemer of Israel." Written by W. W. Phelps, the hymn first appeared in 1832 in *The Evening and the Morning Star,* a Jackson County, Missouri, LDS newspaper. This adaptation of Joseph Swain's "Oh Thou, in Whose Presence My Soul Takes Delight"[9] underscores the concerns of the Saints with recent mob oppression in Jackson County, persecution to which Phelps and his printing press had fallen prey. As with other hymns, however, this hymn is layered with Mormon history, incorporating as it does new meanings arising from the later persecutions of the Saints—the hostilities in Missouri and Nauvoo, the forced exodus into the Mountain West, the U.S. military invasion in the Utah War of 1857–58, and the 1874–1890 polygamy raids on Mormon Zion by the U.S. government. Note in the second and third verses the multiple layers of meaning as they would occur to Saints fleeing the latest persecution:

> We know he is coming
> To gather his sheep
> And lead them to Zion in love,
> For why in the valley
> Of death should they weep
> Or in the lone wilderness rove?
>
> How long we have wandered
> As strangers in sin,
> And cried in the desert for thee!
> Our foes have rejoiced
> When our sorrows they've seen,
> But Israel will shortly be free.

Typically, the Saints end the hymn with this confident rallying cry in the fourth verse: "Fear not, and be just, / For the kingdom is ours. / The hour of redemption is near."[10]

Comparing Phelps's Mormon adaptation with Swain's first, second, and third verses is instructive regarding the focal points of Latter-day Saint faith, expectations, and concerns in 1832. Wrote Swain in the original hymn, which appears in the 1820 *Repository of Sacred Music:*

> O thou in whose presence my soul takes delight,
> On whom in afflictions I call,
> My comfort by day and my song in the night,
> My hope, my salvation, my all.

> Where dost thou at noontide resort with thy sheep,
> To feed on the pastures of love,
> For, why in the valley of death should I weep,
> Alone in the wilderness rove.

> O why should I wander an alien from thee,
> Or cry in the desert for bread,
> My foes would rejoice when my sorrows they see,
> And smile at the tears I have shed.[11]

To his adaptations, Phelps added a verse, now excluded, which again underscores the remarkable faith and confidence—even cocksureness—of the fledgling Mormon people:

> The secret of heaven, the myst'ry below,
> That many have sought for so long,
> We know that we know, for the Spirit of Christ
> Tells his servants he cannot be wrong.[12]

"**THE SPIRIT OF GOD.**" This optimism and confidence roll through Phelps's most Mormon, beloved, and enduring hymn, "The Spirit of God." Apparently an original composition, the hymn was first titled "Hosanna to God and the Lamb" and was published in Emma Smith's 1835 hymnal. The hymn was sung in March 1836 at the dedication of the Kirtland Temple and has been sung at all temple dedications since. "The Spirit of God" hosanna-shouts the LDS doctrines of millennialism, the restoration of all things, and continuing revelation, proclaiming that "the veil o'er the earth is beginning to burst," that "the visions and blessings of old are returning, / And angels are coming to visit the earth"—thus enabling expansion of the Saints' knowledge of God, who is "restoring their judges and all as at first." The Saints look forward to the imminent coming of Jesus Christ and the beginning of the Millennium, when "Jesus descends with his chariot of fire" to the welcoming hosannas of his people.[13]

One of two verses, as recorded in the 1835 hymnal but omitted from the recent hymnbook, reflects priesthood ordinances as practiced in the early Church:

> We'll wash, and be wash'd, and with oil be anointed
> Withal not omitting the washing of feet;
> For he that receiveth his PENNY appointed,
> Must surely be clean at the harvest of wheat.[14]

"O MY FATHER." One of the most beloved doctrinal hymns to emerge from the Nauvoo era is "O My Father" by Eliza R. Snow. Probably the best-loved and best-known hymn of Mormonism, "O My Father" was written and published in 1845, sixteen months following the death of Joseph Smith, Snow's husband in plural marriage. The hymn, which, then and now, would confound most Gentiles with its doctrines, became an important formulation of doctrine for nineteenth-century Latter-day Saints. Originally titled "Invocation, or the Eternal Father and Mother,"[15] "O My Father" is a storied hymn reflecting, on one level, Eliza R. Snow's forlorn condition following Joseph Smith's death, as a single (actually widowed), forty-one-year-old woman dependent upon the Stephen Markham family. On another level, the hymn reflects Snow's attempt to comfort Zina D. Huntington, the loss of whose mother had led Zina to ask Joseph Smith, shortly before his death, "Shall I know my mother when I meet her in the world beyond?" The Prophet Joseph had responded, "Yes, you will know your mother there,"[16] and then expounded, on a third level, upon the resurrection and the relationship of mortals to each other and to a Heavenly Father and Mother, concepts about which Joseph would elaborate in the King Follett Discourse (1844). From these precious insights arose the inspiration for "O My Father"[17] and the powerful truth—now part of the warp and woof of Mormonism but at that time startling, new, and visionary—that "Truth is reason; truth eternal / Tells me I've a mother there."[18]

"PRAISE TO THE MAN." The assassination of the Prophet Joseph Smith Jr. and his brother Hyrum on June 27, 1844, immediately spawned a number of hymns in honor of the murdered prophet, thereby introducing a new theme into Mormon hymnody. Of these hymns in honor of the Prophet Joseph, the most popular continues to be "Praise to the Man," by W. W. Phelps.[19] The wrathful line in the second verse that formerly read, "Long shall his blood, which was shed by assassins, / Stain Illinois while the earth lauds his fame," was gentled in the 1927 hymnal to "Plead unto heav'n, while the earth lauds his fame."[20] The original wording of that line, along with the tone of the hymn, reflects an immediacy and a personal and group pain that present-day Saints, while sympathetic, may not fully comprehend.

Written and published within a few weeks of Joseph's death, the hymn recounts recent events in Mormon history, reveals something of the in-your-face belligerence that characterized the Gentile-Mormon conflict and makes clear the determination of the harried and harassed Saints to press on despite the loss of their prophet. They sound their confidence in the eventual triumphant day when, "mark our words," they seem to say, " 'millions shall know "Brother Joseph" again.' "

The hymn was originally sung as a dirge, slowly and mournfully, to the tune "A Star in the East," rediscovered in the 1950s by the Ames Brothers and recorded in their best-selling "My Bonnie Lassie." The hymn enabled pioneer Saints not only to mourn their fallen leader, but also to use any occasion of its singing to testify to those who "knew not Joseph" (Ex. 1:8) of his prophetic virtues and divine calling. Whether or not "millions" would know Brother Joseph again, thousands of Saints who had known him well would bring to the hymn the immediacy and grief arising from firsthand acquaintance with the murdered prophet— emotions not as possible 150 years after the tragedy at Carthage.

"COME, COME, YE SAINTS." "Come, Come, Ye Saints," the great hymn of the trek across the plains to the valleys of the Wasatch, has become the signature hymn of the Mormon people. In recounting the story of the trek, "Come, Come, Ye Saints" not only encourages the Saints along the Mormon Trail to "gird up your loins; fresh courage take" but also describes the mythic mortal and spiritual journey of every Latter-day Saint, of every child of God, out of Babylon to Zion, from the profane to the sacred, from darkness into light.

Every seasoned Saint can tell the story behind this hymn's composition. Several days west of Nauvoo, William Clayton heard that his wife Diantha, who had been unable to travel, had borne him a son. He recorded on April 15, 1846, "This morning I composed a new song—'All is well.'"[21] Again and again, the hymn voices the hopes of a driven people:

> We'll find the place which God for us prepared,
> Far away in the West,
> Where none shall come to hurt or make afraid;
> There the Saints will be blessed.

We'll make the air with music ring,
Shout praises to our God and King;
Above the rest these words we'll tell—
All is well! All is well!

And should we die before our journey's through,
Happy day! All is well!
We then are free from toil and sorrow, too;
With the just we shall dwell!
But if our lives are spared again
To see the Saints their rest obtain,
Oh, how we'll make this chorus swell—
All is well! All is well![22]

"Come, Come, Ye Saints" evoked intense personal meanings in virtually every Mormon pioneer, resounding, as it did so well, the literal and spiritual journeyings of the Saints and testifying of the individual and collective sacrifices that Joseph Smith taught were demanded by God of every Saint. For Mary Goble Pay (1843–1913), a single phrase of the hymn took on terrible meaning. At age thirteen, Mary Goble and her family left England and eventually joined the 1856 handcart companies already under way. Early on, a little sister became ill and died; after they joined the other companies, her brother froze to death; her baby sister who was born on the plains died of starvation after six weeks; and finally, just before the company arrived in Salt Lake City, her mother died. Mary survived but lost all ten toes to the cold. She recalls the night before her mother gave birth to a little girl on the frozen plains and gives new and chilling meaning to the hymn:

> We traveled on till we got to the Platt River. That was the last walk I ever had with my mother. We caught up with Handcart companies that day. We watched them cross the river. There were great lumps of ice floating down the river. It was bitter cold. The next morning there were fourteen dead in camp through the cold. We went back to camp and went to prayers. We sang the song "Come, Come, Ye Saints, No Toil Nor Labor Fear." I wondered what made my mother cry. That night my mother took sick and the next morning my little sister was born. It was the 23rd of September. We named her Edith and she lived six weeks and died for want of nourishment.[23]

One of the few LDS hymns adapted by other faiths, "Come, Come, Ye Saints" appears in the Protestant *New Church Hymnal*,[24] with lyrics attributed to "Avis B. Christiansen, based on William

Clayton." The Protestant adaptation highlights the historicity of the LDS version by changing the charged third verse, which reads:

> We'll find the place which God for us prepared,
>   Far away in the West,
> Where none shall come to hurt or make afraid;
>   There the Saints will be blessed.

Christiansen's adaptation describes a heavenly rather than an earthly resting place:

> God hath prepared a glorious Home above
>   Round His throne, for His own,
> Where they may rest forever in His love
>   Toil and tears all unknown.
> There they shall sing eternal praise
>   To Him who saved them by His grace.
> Through heaven's courts the song shall swell,
>   All is well, All is well!

The earlier Protestant version that William Clayton adapted as "Come, Come, Ye Saints" is a so-called white spiritual of the "dying Christian type." Entitled "All Is Well," that version is closer in meaning and lyrics to the *New Church Hymnal:*

> Weep not my friends, weep not for me, All is well;
>   My sins are pardoned, I am free; All is well.
> There's not a cloud that doth arise,
>   To hide my Saviour from my eyes;
> I soon shall mount the upper skies—All is well.[25]

The differences are at once profound and obvious.

HYMNS OF GATHERING, PREACHING, AND REJOICING

In the hymns of Zion that called pioneer Saints to gather, to preach the gospel, and to rejoice in Zion, we find again the characteristic Latter-day Saint urgency, immediacy, excitement, and exultation that moved so many to such commitment and sacrifice.

GATHERING AND PREACHING. As early as 1831, the Lord was sounding the call through the Prophet Joseph Smith to "gather ye together. . . . Go ye out from Babylon, . . . gather ye out from among the nations," and "flee unto Zion" (D&C 133:4, 5, 7, 12). It is virtually impossible for twentieth-century Saints to comprehend the sacrifice involved in tearing up roots and moving one's family to pioneer unimproved land, first in New York, then Ohio, then Missouri, then Nauvoo, then the Salt Lake Valley.

The pioneer Saints gathered because they believed that God had commanded them to do so. And as they went, they sang Cyrus H. Wheelock's hymn written in 1851, "O Babylon, O Babylon, we bid thee farewell; / We're going to the mountains of Ephraim to dwell." Sung to the borrowed tune "Long, Long Ago" by Thomas H. Bayly, "Ye Elders of Israel" is one of the most enduring of gathering and missionary hymns. Its stirring cadences were especially suited to the accompaniment of local chapters of Pitt's Brass Band as they played for departing Mormon missionaries. This hymn had—and still has— the spiritual power to move men to leave their hard-won farms and growing families to cross the world in search of "the righteous, where'er they may be" and bring them "to the mountains of Ephraim to dwell":

> Ye elders of Israel, come join now with me
> And seek out the righteous, where'er they may be—
> In desert, on mountain, on land, or on sea—
> And bring them to Zion, the pure and the free.

Then the refrain: "O Babylon, O Babylon, we bid thee farewell; / We're going to the mountains of Ephraim to dwell."[26] The expectant millennialism of the Latter-day Saints gave missionary work and the gathering to Zion great urgency and high priority, as Eliza R. Snow wrote:

> The time is far spent; there is little remaining
> To publish glad tidings by sea and by land.
> Then hasten, ye heralds; go forward proclaiming:
> Repent, for the kingdom of heaven's at hand.[27]

Consequently, nearly every pioneer company gathering to Zion records meeting a party of Mormon missionaries heading east toward the mission field.

REJOICING IN ZION. At the heart of the Mormon hymns is Zion and an intense longing for a refuge at once tangible and spiritual. Even before the Latter-day Saints fled to the Rocky Mountains, the idea of Zion was firmly fixed in their imaginations. Present-day Saints are hard pressed to comprehend what it meant to put down one's roots at last in the Zion of God and raise one's voice in praise to God for the security of "our mountain home so dear."[28] As children of Israel, the Saints planted their ensign on Ensign Peak (Mt. Zion) and thereby took part in fulfilling the prophecies of Isaiah. In the music of Ebenezer Beesley and the words of Joel Hills Johnson, they sang from their valleys in the Wasatch while looking up to towering, sheltering mountains:

> High on the mountain top
> A banner is unfurled.
> Ye nations, now look up;
> It waves to all the world.
> In Deseret's sweet, peaceful land,
> On Zion's mount behold it stand![29]

Weary with their settle-plant-and-flee existence, the pioneer Saints sang, no doubt with a different kind of fervor and with greater relief than contemporary Saints can muster, Charles Penrose's "O Ye Mountains High":

> In thy mountain retreat, God will strengthen thy feet;
> Without fear of thy foes thou shalt tread;
> And their silver and gold, as the prophets have told,
> Shall be brought to adorn thy fair head.

Praising the mountain retreat, "sacred home of the prophets of God" with its "vales of the free," President Penrose, who had himself made the trek from England to Utah and eventually held a position in the First Presidency, reminds the Saints of the first Zion:

> O Zion! dear Zion! home of the free,
> Tho thou wert forced to fly to thy chambers on high,
> Yet we'll share joy and sorrow with thee.[30]

Perhaps no other hymn so lyrically expresses the feelings of the Saints about Zion than "For the Strength of the Hills," wonderfully adapted from English poet Felicia D. Hemans by Edward L. Sloan to fit like a glove the history and circumstances of the Saints:

> For the strength of the hills we bless thee,
> Our God, our fathers' God;
> Thou hast made thy children mighty
> By the touch of the mountain sod.
> Thou hast led thy chosen Israel
> To freedom's last abode;
> For the strength of the hills we bless thee,
> Our God, our fathers' God.
>
> At the hands of foul oppressors,
> We've borne and suffered long;
> Thou hast been our help in weakness,
> And thy pow'r hath made us strong.

Amid ruthless foes outnumbered,
In weariness we trod;
For the strength of the hills we bless thee,
Our God, our fathers' God.

Thou hast led us here in safety
Where the mountain bulwark stands
As the guardian of the loved ones
Thou hast brought from many lands.
For the rock and for the river,
The valley's fertile sod,
For the strength of the hills we bless thee,
Our God, our fathers' God.[31]

At the end of the twentieth century, the historical context of these words is muted, gentled, or nonexistent for those who have never lived "amid ruthless foes outnumbered" or "borne and suffered long" "at the hands of foul oppressors." When the pioneers sang this song, the immediate past became the joyful present and future in the Zion of God.

Songs of the Trials of Establishing Zion

Of that Zion "far away in the West,"[32] Eliza R. Snow warned the European Saints, "Think not when you gather to Zion your troubles and trials are through." Utah Territory was indeed "a good place to make Saints," Brigham Young said, as he undertook to direct some eighty-five thousand emigrants streaming in from Europe over three decades to various settlements up and down the Mormon Corridor. The Saints, he explained, are "like the potter's clay," people who "have got to be ground over and worked on the table, until they are made perfectly pliable and in readiness to be put on the wheel, to be turned into vessels of honor."[33] It would not be long before the potter's-wheel experience of the gathering Saints would appear in their hymns, as President Young called them to Dixie and Las Vegas, Carson City and Santa Clara, Cedar City and Paragonah, and Cache Valley, Orderville, and San Bernardino. A handful refused to go, many of them complained, but most of them went.

A call to southern Utah was considered a sentence, not a blessing in disguise. Some unfortunate recipients of this call sang hymns to remind them of their dream of Zion, and some, instead of cursing Brigham, sang songs like "Once I Lived in Cottonwood," about their plight:

Oh, once I lived in Cottonwood and owned a little farm,
But I was called to Dixie, which did me much alarm;
To raise the cane and cotton, I right away must go;
But the reason why they called on me, I'm sure I do not know.

I yoked old Jim and Bolly up all for to make a start,
To leave my house and garden, it almost broke my heart.
We moved along quite slowly and often looked behind,
For the sand and rocks of Dixie kept running through my mind.

The hot winds whirl around me and take away my breath;
I've had the chills and fever till I'm nearly shook to death.
"All earthly tribulations are but a moment here;
And, oh, if I prove faithful, a righteous crown I'll wear."

My wagon's sold for sorghum seed to make a little bread;
And poor old Jim and Bolly long ago are dead.
There's only me and Betsy left to hoe the cotton-tree;
May Heaven help the Dixie-ite wherever he may be![34]

In his journal, Thales H. Haskell Sr., suffering in Utah's Dixie from dam breaks on the Virgin River and washed-out ditches, cleverly parodied the hymn "Come Let Us Anew":

Our life on the stream
The Old Virgin I mean
    Glides swiftly away
But the contrary ditch
Still refuses to stay

Included in his rough journal entry is the frustrated refrain: "By the Patience of Job / And no rain from above."[35]

Hymn from the Utah War

After ten years of being left alone in the mountains, by which time the Saints were able to put down permanent roots, encroachment began. On July 24, 1857, as the Saints celebrated in Little Cottonwood Canyon their tenth anniversary of arriving in Utah (see p. 66), they were informed by Abraham O. Smoot and Porter Rockwell that the U.S. Army was on the march to invade and put down rebellion in Utah Territory: the Saints were at war with the United States, and the Utah War of 1857–58 was on. President Young recalled the missionaries, recalled the settlers from the perimeters of the territory, and put the Saints on war footing.

Local squads of the Nauvoo Legion drilled and paraded through the centers of Utah's villages and hamlets; the local contingent of Pitt's Brass Brand paraded up and down the square—if they had one; and they all sang "Up, Awake, Ye Defenders of Zion," another hymn by Englishman Charles W. Penrose and the rallying war song of the Utah War, sung to the tune of "The Red, White, and Blue." Note in the hymn the specific references to atrocities against the Mormons, and pay special attention to both the fierce wording applied to the federal troops and the treasonous words of the last stanza, in which Penrose proclaims, "Soon 'the Kingdom' will be independent." I show in brackets the gentling emendations of the 1985 hymnal:

(1857 version, as printed in 1863)	(1985 redaction)
Up, awake, ye defenders of Zion!	
The foe's at the door of your homes;	
Let each heart be the heart of a lion,	
Unyielding and proud as he roams.	
Remember the wrongs of Missouri;	[trials of Missouri]
Forget not the fate of Nauvoo.	[the courage of Nauvoo]
When the God-hating foe is before ye,	[the enemy host is . . .]
Stand firm, and be faithful and true.	
	[Chorus added using last two lines of each verse]
By the mountains our Zion's surrounded;	[By His power is Zion . . .]
Her warriors are noble and brave,	
And their faith on Jehovah is founded,	
Whose power is mighty to save.	
Opposed by a proud, boasting nation,	[In each soldier a brave heart is beating]
Their numbers, compared, may be few,	[Tho our]
But their union is known through creation,	[We'll not rest till our foes are retreating]
And they've always been faithful and true.	
Shall we bear with oppression for ever?	[entire verse omitted]
Shall we tamely submit to the foe,	
While the ties of our kindred they sever?	
Shall the blood of the prophets still flow?	
No! The thought sets the heart wildly beating;	
Our vows, at each pulse we renew,	
Ne'er to rest till our foes are retreating,	
While we remain faithful and true!	
Though, assisted by legions infernal,	
The plundering wretches advance,	[plundering foemen]
With a host from the regions eternal,	
We'll scatter their hosts at a glance!	
Soon "the Kingdom" will be independent;	
In wonder the nations will view	
The despised ones in glory resplendent;	[Our Zion in . . .]
Then let us be faithful and true![36]	

For those who know the intent of these words, this war hymn meant to rally Mormon troops to warfare with the United States Infantry seems a rich incongruity when sung in Mormon wards near July Fourth and Twenty-fourth as patriotic alternatives to "America the Beautiful" or "My Country, 'Tis of Thee" and in honor of the United States of America—the seat of "the God-hating foe" and "plundering wretches."

SUNDAY SCHOOL HYMNS

The Deseret Sunday School Union had an incalculable influence on the hymning of the Latter-day Saints. The Sunday School hymn reflected a sea change in Mormon hymnody made necessary by the rising generation of errant or straying youth who "knew not Joseph" (Ex. 1:8) or Brigham and who had not been called upon to sacrifice for the kingdom of God. In teaching the youth of Zion to "choose the right,"[37] to live righteous lives, the hymn became an aid in teaching Latter-day Saint values and lifestyle as well as theology. While present-day Saints can identify with numerous teachings in the hymns, many members distance themselves from certain quaint, outdated, and often unintentionally humorous hymns.

The Sunday School, formally established by the Church in 1866, featured, for the next century, weekly hymn practice, which included churchwide teaching of a hymn of the month, often newly minted. The new hymn would be published along with other new hymns in the *Juvenile Instructor*, also founded in 1866 as the official publication of the Deseret Sunday School Union Board. The Sunday School not only placed the didactic hymn at stage center for much of the pioneering and settlement era but also stimulated the writing of hymns throughout the Church.

The fervor of the call to attend Sunday School, held at ten each Sabbath morning (sacrament meeting usually being held at seven each Sunday evening), is seen in the several somewhat-dated Sunday School songs still included in the 1985 hymnbook: "Welcome, Welcome, Sabbath Morning," "Thanks for the Sabbath School," "We Meet again in Sabbath School," and "Come Away to the Sunday School." Gone forever is "Never Be Late," one of the favorite but time-worn Sunday School hymns of the settlement era:

> Never be late to the Sunday School class,
> Come with your bright sunny faces;
> Cheering your teachers and pleasing your God—
> Always be found in your places.

Never be late, never be late;
Children remember the warning:
Try to be there, always be there
Promptly at ten in the morning.[38]

Joseph L. Townsend and William Clayson, two Sunday School workers in Payson, Utah Valley, teamed up to write dozens of Sunday School hymns. To their stirring hymns, many of them militant and martial, such as "Hope of Israel" and "O Thou Rock of Our Salvation," the Deseret Sunday School Union added such hymns of moral uplift and caution as "Scatter Sunshine," "There Is Sunshine in My Soul Today," and "I'll Be a Sunbeam for Jesus."

As one who was a child on the Arizona Mormon frontier, President Spencer W. Kimball would recall with pleasure a sentimental bit of doggerel, "Don't Kill the Birds," which he had learned in Sunday School nearly eight decades earlier. Though the hymn was long ago dropped from the hymnal and may have made little impression on others, its admonitions deeply and personally impressed young Spencer and later influenced his adult attitudes about the environment and human stewardship:

Don't kill the little birds, that sing on bush and tree,
All thro' the summer days, their sweetest melody.
Don't shoot the little birds! The earth is God's estate,
And He provideth food for small as well as great.[39]

Similarly, Mormon boys up and down the settlements learned and sang, often in Sunday School opening exercises, in soprano or falsetto, Evan Stephens's "A 'Mormon' Boy." The hymn became a part of those youths' lives, and they never forgot the experience of singing their righteous pride at being Latter-day Saint boys destined to enjoy, as deacons, more priesthood power "than the Pope at Rome":

A "Mormon" boy, a "Mormon" boy, I am a "Mormon" boy.
I might be envied by a king, For I am a "Mormon" boy.[40]

Another of the frequently sung Sunday School hymns to come from the early Sunday Schools and Primary associations is Eliza R. Snow's "In Our Lovely Deseret," set to the tune of George F. Root's popular Civil War song, "Tramp, Tramp, Tramp," about a captured Union soldier—"In my prison cell I sit / Thinking, Mother dear, of you"[41]—which Sister Snow transformed into a distinctively Mormon hymn, now dated by its parochial views:

In our lovely Deseret,
Where the Saints of God have met,

There's a multitude of children all around.
They are generous and brave;
They have precious souls to save;
They must listen and obey the gospel's sound.

Chorus: Hark! hark! hark! 'tis children's music—
Children's voices, oh, how sweet,
When in innocence and love,
Like the angels up above,
They with happy hearts and cheerful faces meet.

That the children may live long
And be beautiful and strong,
Tea and coffee and tobacco they despise,
Drink no liquor, and they eat
But a very little meat;
They are seeking to be great and good and wise.[42]

President Spencer W. Kimball recalled for a general area conference his personal association with this hymn:

> I remember the song "In Our Lovely Deseret." . . . I can remember how lustily we sang: "Hark! Hark! Hark! 'tis children's music, / Children's voices, O, how sweet. . . ." . . . I remember we sang: "That the children may live long, / And be beautiful and strong." I wanted to live a long time and I wanted to be beautiful and strong—but never reached it. "Tea and coffee and tobacco they despise." And I learned to despise them. . . . The song goes on: "Drink no liquor, and they eat / But a very little meat." I still don't eat very much meat. "They are seeking to be great and good and wise." And then we'd "Hark! Hark! Hark!" again.[43]

As the century waned, the pioneers grew older, the settlements became towns and cities, the influence of the East encroached, and Zion was threatened with increasing inactivity among the young people. Attempting to interest and activate a flagging youth, the Sunday School began publishing, late in the century, hymns like "True to the Faith" by Evan Stephens.[44] The congregation would pledge to be "true to the faith that our parents have cherished, / True to the truths for which martyrs have perished" and, in another popular Sunday School hymn, would stand up to declare themselves in singing "Who's on the Lord's side? Who?"

Conclusion

As we have seen, the hymns of the pioneer Saints spoke directly to them in tones, accents, and images that described their daily lives, recent history, tribulations as a people, and their faith in God. Hymns

helped the Mormon pioneers to see themselves as children of God
who were hard at work fulfilling ancient prophecy, building Zion, and
making meaningful sacrifices for the kingdom of God. In a way peculiar to their times and seasons, the Mormon pioneers gleaned strength
and courage, resilience and tenacity from the association-laden hymns.
Their vision renewed by their worship services, of which hymns were
a part, they returned to their homes to fight the good fight, stave off the
latest drought, dig yet another well, plant a promising crop, and "hold
to the rod, the iron rod."[45] Somehow, singing their hymns, their songs
of the heart, helped bring their Zion cause, their people's turbulent
past, their formidable present, and their visionary destiny into saintly
focus and enabled them, once more, to make their chorus swell, "All is
well! All is well!"

Richard H. Cracroft is Professor of English and Director of the Center for the Study
of Christian Values in Literature at Brigham Young University.

NOTES

1. "Oh, What Songs of the Heart," in *Hymns of The Church of Jesus Christ
of Latter-day Saints* (Salt Lake City: The Church of Jesus Christ of Latter-day
Saints, 1985), no. 286 (hereafter cited as *Hymns*).
2. For example, "Joseph Smith's First Prayer," in *Hymns*, no. 26.
3. See also Mary D. Poulter, "Doctrines of Faith and Hope Found in Emma
Smith's 1835 Hymnbook," *BYU Studies* 37, no. 2 (1997–98): 32–56.
4. Neil Postman, "Learning by Story," *Atlantic Monthly* 264 (December
1989): 122.
5. Postman, "Learning by Story," 122.
6. *Hymns*, no. 274.
7. *Hymns*, no. 283.
8. *Hymns*, no. 1.
9. George D. Pyper, *Stories of Latter-day Saint Hymns* (Salt Lake City:
Deseret News Press, 1939), 96.
10. *Hymns*, no. 6.
11. Quoted in Karen Lynn Davidson, *Our Latter-day Hymns: The Stories
and the Messages* (Salt Lake City: Deseret Book, 1988), 35–36.
12. Emma Smith, comp., *A Collection of Sacred Hymns for the Church of the
Latter Day Saints* (Kirtland: F. G. Williams, 1835), no. 6.
13. *Hymns*, no. 2.
14. Smith, *A Collection of Sacred Hymns,* no. 90.
15. Eliza R. Snow, *The Personal Writings of Eliza Roxcy Snow,* ed. Maureen
Ursenbach Beecher (Salt Lake City: University of Utah Press, 1995), 109.

16. Pyper, *Stories of Latter-day Saint Hymns,* 4.

17. See also Davidson, *Our Latter-day Hymns,* 294; and Jill Mulvay Derr, "The Significance of 'O My Father' in the Personal Journey of Eliza R. Snow," *BYU Studies* 36, no. 1 (1996–97): 84–126.

18. *Hymns,* no. 292.

19. Pyper, *Stories of Latter-day Saint Hymns,* 97–100.

20. Davidson, *Our Latter-day Hymns,* 55–56.

21. William Clayton, *William Clayton's Journal* (Salt Lake City: Deseret News, 1921), 19.

22. *Hymns,* no. 30.

23. Richard H. Cracroft and Neal E. Lambert, eds., *A Believing People: Literature of the Latter-day Saints* (Provo, Utah: Brigham Young University Press, 1974), 144; italics added.

24. *New Church Hymnal* (n.p.: Lexicon Music, 1976), no. 324.

25. *New Church Hymnal,* no. 324. See also Albert C. Ronander and Ethel K. Porter, *Guide to the Pilgrim Hymnal* (Philadelphia: United Church Press, 1966).

26. *Hymns,* no. 319.

27. *Hymns,* no. 266.

28. *Hymns,* no. 33.

29. *Hymns,* no. 5.

30. *Hymns,* no. 34; *Deseret News 1997–98 Church Almanac* (Salt Lake City: Deseret News, 1996), 44.

31. *Hymns,* no. 35.

32. *Hymns,* no. 30.

33. Brigham Young, in *Journal of Discourses,* 26 vols. (Liverpool: F. D. Richards, 1855–86), 4:23, August 17, 1856.

34. Cracroft and Lambert, *Believing People,* 254–55.

35. Thales H. Haskell Sr., Diary, typescript, 41, Special Collections, Harold B. Lee Library, Brigham Young University, Provo, Utah.

36. *Hymns,* no. 248; Davidson, *Our Latter-day Hymns,* 255. The hymnal in which this song first appeared is *Sacred Hymns and Spiritual Songs for The Church of Jesus Christ of Latter-day Saints,* 12th ed., rev. (Liverpool: George Q. Cannon, 1863), 73–74.

37. *Hymns,* no. 239.

38. *Deseret Sunday School Song Book: A Collection of Choice Pieces for the Use of Sunday Schools, and Suitable for Other Occasions,* 3d ed. (Salt Lake City: Deseret Sunday School Union, 1899), 158.

39. *Deseret Sunday School Song Book,* 6th ed. (Salt Lake City: Deseret Sunday School Union, 1907), 185; Spencer W. Kimball, "Strengthening the Family—the Basic Unit of the Church," *Ensign* 8 (May 1978): 47–48.

40. *Deseret Sunday School Song Book,* 122–24.

41. Davidson, *Our Latter-day Hymns,* 307.

42. *Hymns,* no. 307.

43. Kimball, "Strengthening the Family," 47.

44. *Hymns,* no. 254.

45. *Hymns,* no. 274.

Meadow Ward pulpit, Joseph H. Fisher (1856–1940), Meadow, Utah, about 1884, wood and paint loaned by Meadow Ward, Mervin Beckstrand, bishop. The focal points for religious furniture in meetinghouses and tabernacles were usually pulpits and sacrament tables because LDS liturgy focuses on preaching, teaching, and a very straightforward blessing and passing of the sacrament. Cloth usually draped the sacrament tables, so these pieces of furniture typically received only simple decoration. The pulpits, which were prominently placed in the center of the podium, were usually the most elaborate piece of furniture in the meetinghouse or tabernacle. Occasionally the pulpit was ornamented with symbolic forms that reminded the congregation of their religious community and spiritual commitments.

The symbolic carving on this pulpit reminded the Saints in the Meadow Ward that they were to love each other and work together to build Zion by making the desert blossom as a rose. Note how Fisher spells out the word "Welcome" with twigs and branches, a message that greeted the Saints of Meadow each week as they came to their church meetings. Fisher was a pioneer in Meadow. He was on the town council and later served as the stake patriarch.

The Homemade Kingdom: Mormon Regional Furniture

Richard G. Oman

I believe in going into the mountains and cutting down the timber, framing it into proper shape, and then manufacturing the various articles of furniture that we need; . . . make the furniture here.

—John Taylor[1]

Unlike most furniture traditions, Mormon regional furniture is not defined by style. Because it embodies the connections between a religious faith and a furniture tradition, it is defined by principles, beliefs, practices, and history of The Church of Jesus Christ of Latter-day Saints in the nineteenth and early twentieth centuries. Mormonism embraces the physical with the spiritual.[2] This furniture tradition demonstrates how the spiritual and the physical were integrated by the Saints' translating religious principles from the abstract to the concrete, from faith to wood and paint.

By looking at this tradition, we also learn something about the nature of Church leadership in the nineteenth century, especially that of Brigham Young. The Saints were strongly encouraged to be involved in "home manufacture"[3] of furniture. But individual style was left up to the craftsmen. Brigham Young, himself a furniture maker, could have dictated a particular style as the Shakers of the eastern and midwestern U.S. had done.[4] He had the skills, position, and authority to have done so. But he chose not to. Accounting for this stylistic openness is the flexibility of such operating beliefs as "teach them correct principles and they govern themselves," "magnify your calling,"[5] and "if there is anything virtuous, lovely, or of good report or praiseworthy, we seek after these things" (A of F 13).

Nevertheless, some may see nineteenth-century Latter-day Saints as a tightly regimented group that were individually allowed little personal freedom and expression by their leaders. The vast aesthetic diversity within the Mormon regional pioneer furniture tradition challenges those assumptions. Unity came from commitment to the overriding goals of building Zion and preparing for the Second Coming of the Lord. But in working toward those goals, much space was left for individual and cultural aesthetic diversity, creativity, and initiative. Some have seen early Utah Mormonism as an isolated monolith directed from the top down. If such had been the case, perhaps the biggest threat to Latter-day Saint culture would have been stagnation and atrophy. But the great variety within the furniture of this material culture tradition belies that interpretation as well.

Perhaps the expressions of adaptability, flexibility, and openness to differing ideas in furniture also exemplifies Mormonism's ability to continually expand and absorb. The Church in Utah Territory expanded to accept new converts from many different backgrounds and cultures throughout the nineteenth century. These people were forged into a unified people and their furniture traditions in many cases absorbed rather than discarded.

With the coming of the transcontinental railroad in 1869, the Mormon regional furniture tradition should have been killed off, for Latter-day Saints were no longer isolated by geography and transportation from large eastern furniture factories. The usual national pattern was for small cottage industries to wither in the face of the larger and more efficient eastern factories. But there were actually more furniture makers in Utah in 1870 than there were in 1860.[6] And methods new to furniture making were tried; one of the Mormon responses to this external challenge from large eastern factories was the successful Brigham City cooperative furniture factory.

Although local furniture making eventually began to slow down, it nonetheless continued for many years. For example, there are many Eastlake-style pieces of handmade Mormon furniture. This is a style that was very popular in this country from the mid-1870s to the 1890s, many years after the coming of the railroad. Though furniture was imported into Utah after the coming of the railroad, Mormon regional furniture continued to be made long after economic determinism should have rung its death knell. The strong religious foundation for the tradition helped keep the furniture-making tradition going.

The actions of English convert Henry Dinwoodey help illustrate this point. In Salt Lake City, he established a small furniture factory that specialized in making chairs. Prior to the arrival of the railroad in 1869, Dinwoodey went on a buying trip and ordered large quantities of furniture from the eastern furniture factories. The first train that arrived in Utah carried that furniture. Dinwoodey continued making furniture, but the bulk of his business shifted to selling imported furniture.

When the Manti Temple was nearing completion in 1888, Dinwoodey donated several pieces of furniture for its furnishing. Handwritten on the bottom of two little stools is a very telling message: "Homemade and Presented by Henry Dinwoodey to the Manti Temple April 23, 1888." By this time, Dinwoodey was a very busy and financially successful businessman. He had excellent connections with the top furniture factories in the East. He certainly could have afforded to import the best furniture American factories could produce as presentation pieces to the Manti Temple. But he chose to make the pieces himself (or perhaps to have one of his local hired craftsmen make it). Why? My assessment is as follows: For many years, Church leaders had linked "make the furniture here"[7] to the religious goal of building Zion. "Home manufacture" was an act of religious commitment.[8] This elevated the making of furniture to an act of faith. And when it came to furnishing a place as sacred as a temple, "homemade" trumped "imported," even if imported furniture could have been more visually spectacular. Though Dinwoodey had been selling eastern furniture to the general public in Salt Lake City for many years, a personal gift to a temple was an act of religious consecration. The furniture needed to have a profound spiritual meaning. Being homemade infused those little stools with that meaning. How else can we interpret a wealthy, spiritually committed furniture dealer presenting homemade furniture to a temple almost twenty years after he began importing furniture from eastern factories?

The following text is an edited and occasionally expanded version of some of the title, section, and caption texts from the exhibition *The Homemade Kingdom: Mormon Pioneer Regional Furniture* that was displayed at the Museum of Church History and Art from March 6, 1998, to January 18, 1999. This exhibition describes the furniture tradition as being intimately linked to missionary work and gathering, expanding Zion, provident living, religious and temporal cooperation, and—as a way of expressing the importance of homes and families and churches—beautifying Zion.

GATHERING SKILLS AND IDEAS

Hundreds of furniture makers converted to the restored gospel in the nineteenth century. Many of these converts were skilled craftsmen who had been apprenticed and trained in their local communities. Called to gather to Zion, these new converts came to Utah bringing their tools, skills, and aesthetic traditions with them—but very little furniture. Among these converts, especially those from the British Isles and Scandinavia, were the craftsmen who would create the Mormon pioneer regional furniture tradition.

The gathering to Zion assembled new ideas and styles as well as people. Latter-day Saint religious beliefs made it easy to assimilate these new styles because good skills and knowledge were seen as part of the gospel and as revelations from the Lord. The result was many furniture styles often existing side-by-side in the pioneer communities, illustrating how converts from a variety of different cultures were fused into a single people without giving up the best of their former furniture traditions.

> *(Mormonism) is making rapid progress. . . . Furthermore, its converts are not made from the lowest ranks; those sought and obtained by the Mormonite apostles are mechanics and tradesmen . . . who are remarkable for their moral character.*
>
> —*The Athenaeum* (a non-LDS London newspaper), April 3, 1841

> *Let us . . . gather all the knowledge . . . bestowed on the nations home to Zion.*
>
> —Brigham Young, in *JD*, 8:280, June 3, 1860

English-made vernacular Sheraton-style chair, Lancashire, England, about 1840–60, ash with rush seat, collection of Kenyon and Gina Kennard. This chair's style is typical of that area of England from which the Cottams, who were early chair makers, came. Lancashire was the center of the textile industry in England. Textile mills needed wooden spindles that required the wood-turning skills used in making chairs. So the town of Waddington supplied many of those spindles along with chairs for the industrial workers of the area.

Utah-made vernacular Sheraton-style side chair, attributed to John Cottam Sr. (1792–1878) or John Cottam Jr. (1823–1903?), Salt Lake City, 1865, cottonwood, painted to simulate hardwood, and rush. This chair came out of a house just a couple of blocks from the Cottam home in the northwest section of Salt Lake City. The Cottams were early LDS convert chair makers who came from Waddington, Lancashire, England, a town famous for making chairs with elaborately turned parts.

Ohio-made tablet-top Windsor side chair, maker unknown, probably northeastern Ohio, about 1840–60, poplar, pine, and paint. This chair style goes back to Baltimore, where English cabinetmaker Thomas Shereton's designs were applied to American vernacular chairs. This hybrid style then moved into western Pennsylvania and from there to the Kirtland area of Ohio. Latter-day Saint chair makers in the area, such as the Whiting family, made chairs in this style, as they did later in Utah and Arizona.

Collection of Kenyon and Gina Kennard

Utah-made tablet-top Windsor side chair, Great Salt Lake Public Works, Salt Lake City, 1856, pine grained to look like mahogany. The Public Works were a Church-owned-and-operated collection of workshops established to help build religious and public buildings as well as provide products for homes and businesses in the area. The Public Works also employed recently arrived skilled craftsmen until they could find other places of work. The early supervisors of the woodworking shops were older converts who had joined the Church in Kirtland, hence the Ohio style of the chairs.

Utah-made rustic-style rocking chair, maker unknown, Utah, 1860–90, pine painted to simulate mahogany. The style of this chair goes back to the border region of nineteenth-century Scotland, where it was called a Caithness chair. This style was consciously made to look very rustic. Many Scottish convert furniture makers came to Utah in the nineteenth century.

Slogbord, Anderson (no dates), Mt. Pleasant, Utah, 1870–90, wood and paint, collection of John Todd. The slogbord is a very traditional Swedish sofa. The maker of this piece came from the area of Stockholm, Sweden, where he made railroad cars. In Mt. Pleasant, he farmed and built furniture. Anderson lived in one of the oldest houses, which was built on the foundation of the original pioneer fort.

EXPANDING ZION

After they arrived in Salt Lake City, converts were frequently sent out to colonize other areas in Utah Territory as well as Canada and Mexico.[9] The settlers in all these colonies continued to look to Salt Lake City as their capital even if that capital was hundreds of miles away. People with specific skills selected to establish a self-sustaining colony—furniture makers, blacksmiths, schoolteachers, musicians—were called as settlement missionaries by Church leaders and sent out in wagon trains to colonize new areas.[10] Because little furniture could be taken, there was a constant demand for new furniture to be made in the new settlements. In this way, different styles of furniture were spread throughout Zion.

The life of Ralph Ramsay, one of the finest pioneer furniture makers, illustrates this experience.[11] Ramsay grew up in northern England. A very talented young man, he went to London to perfect his skills as a furniture maker and woodcarver. Then Ramsay joined the Church and left London for the small, isolated city of Salt Lake, a move not designed to enhance his career.

However, in Salt Lake City he did well. Ramsay's talent attracted the attention of President Brigham Young. Brother Brigham hired him to help create Eagle Gate, carve the beehive on the Beehive House, and construct and carve the casing for the Salt Lake Tabernacle organ as well as various pieces of furniture for the Beehive and Lion Houses. Then Ramsay was called on a mission by Brigham Young to provide leadership for the Richfield cooperative and to supervise the making of furniture in the area.

From Richfield, Ramsay moved to St. Johns, Arizona, to the Mormon colonies in Mexico, and finally to the small Mormon village of Snowflake, Arizona. For a talented, upwardly mobile artist-craftsman, this pattern of moving would make no economic or career sense. But put into the Latter-day Saint context of making religious covenants of consecration, obeying prophetic leadership, building Zion, and responding to mission calls, Ramsay's acts are reasonable and even predictable.

Leave the heavy furniture behind. In reference to timber for making our bed steads and other articles of furniture, we can find plenty of it. We want every mechanic to take with him his tools.

—Erastus Snow, 1861, cited in Florence S. Jacobsen, "Restorations Belong to Everyone," *BYU Studies* 18, no. 3 (1978): 282

Secretary desk, Alma "Almy" Warr (1855–1940), Kamas, Utah, about 1900, pine and paint. This is one of the best examples of decorative painting and stenciling on Mormon regional furniture. Scott and Lucina Lewis commissioned Almy Warr, a fellow resident of Kamas, to make this piece for their home. Born in England, Warr was probably a house-builder and decorator because many of the decorative wooden elements of this desk appear to be pieces left over from interior architectural moldings.

Drop-leaf expandable kitchen table, maker unknown, proba-bly Sanpete County, Utah, 1865–85, wood hand grained to look like mahogany. Latter-day Saints often had large fami-lies. This table could easily be expanded to accommodate many people.

PROVIDENT LIVING

Furniture makers were encouraged to refine their skills and teach others. Craftsmanship was sanctified among the Saints. They were also encouraged to make do with what they had or could create. Because natural resources for building furniture were limited, European painting techniques such as graining, brought by convert immigrants, were used to transform local woods like pine and cottonwood into furniture that had the appearance of rare hardwoods. Graining was usually done in four steps:

1. The piece of furniture was given a base coat of paint to seal the wood. Paint was thin bodied and usually made by hand.
2. A ground coat of paint was applied. This coat varied depending upon the type of grain that was being simulated.
3. A darker coat of paint was put over the ground coat, and while it was still wet, this coat was manipulated with combs, rags, brushes, or even the fingertips. This process created patterns by removing some of the wet paint.
4. When the paint was dry, a coat of varnish, oil, or shellac, often into which a small amount of pigment had been added, was put on as a final sealer.

Learn . . . how to get timber from the kanyons, . . . how to hew stone and bring them into shape and position to please the eye and create comfort and happiness for the Saints. These are some of the mysteries of the kingdom.

—Brigham Young, in *JD,* 10:25, October 6, 1862

Chest of drawers, A. Swensen (1834–?), Mt. Pleasant, Utah, January 30, 1873, pine hand grained to look like mahogany. Mt. Pleasant was a favorite settlement for many Scandinavian convert emigrants in the nineteenth century. Many of these settlers brought cabinetmaking skills with them from the Old World. The use of turned columns, scooped molding, carved feet, and skillful graining all denote the work of a well-trained Norwegian cabinetmaker and carpenter. This chest is signed and dated by the maker.

Table, maker unknown, Mt. Pleasant, Utah, about 1875, pine hand grained to look like walnut parquetry. This table is made of large pine boards even though it appears to be made of intricate walnut parquetry. This graining is among the most skillfully done on any piece of Mormon regional furniture. The painting and style of this table indicate the experience and training of a Scandinavian convert. The style of the curved legs indicate that it was probably a Scandinavian folk version of a much earlier French design. Scandinavians, particularly Swedes, were greatly enamored with French culture. This table reflects that interest being brought to pioneer Utah.

Kitchen table, maker unknown, Manti, Utah, about 1875, pine hand grained to look like mahogany, collection of John Todd. Not all graining was an attempt to replicate the actual grain pattern of real wood. This piece is a highly expressive version of mahogany that is done with just a few bold brush strokes.

Washstand, William Bell (1816–1886), Salt Lake City, about 1860, pine hand grained to look like mahogany and marble, loaned by the Beehive House. The painting on this washstand is a superb example of mahogany graining and marbleizing. The artist was doing his best to replicate the actual appearance of hardwood and marble. The maker was one of our finest pioneer furniture makers. Bell, a native of northern England, was trained in London. After joining the Church and emigrating to Salt Lake City, he worked for many years making furniture for Brigham Young. This piece was made for Emmeline F. Young, whereupon four other wives of Brigham also had Bell make washstands for them.

Blanket chest, maker unknown, probably Sanpete County, Utah, about 1865, pine hand grained to look like mahogany. Chests like these were used for the storage of extra bedding. All the painting on this is original except the top, which has been retouched.

Cooperation and Self-Reliance

The furniture in this section is from the Salt Lake Public Works and the Brigham City Mercantile and Manufacturing Association, which operated a successful furniture factory. In attempting to build Zion, the Saints' self-sufficient religious commonwealth, some cooperative manufacturing and marketing organizations like the one in Brigham City, Utah, were developed under direct Church sponsorship. Enterprises like this helped the Saints to be less dependent upon goods imported from the East and reinforced the religious imperative for economic independence from the outside world. These institutions and values helped prolong the Mormon regional furniture tradition.

Brigham City was among the most successful nineteenth-century LDS manufacturing cooperatives. At one time almost thirty different departments besides the furniture factory existed in the co-op. Among them were a tannery, a blacksmith shop, a planing mill, and a woolen mill. Because several people worked in the co-op factory, individual workers could specialize in different furniture building tasks. For this reason, all of the painting on furniture produced at this co-op is similar.

Many branches of industry have been organized here to help to sustain each other, to labor for the good of all, and to establish cooperation in the midst of the Church in this place.

—Brigham Young, in *JD*, 17:115, June 26, 1874

How long do you think it would take if we were all producers, and converting the raw materials into useful articles, to become a selfsustaining people?

—Erastus Snow, in *JD*, 19:186, June 3, 1877

Utah-made gondola Windsor side chair, Great Salt Lake Public Works, Salt Lake City, about 1855, wood and paint. This chair was made in the Church-owned and operated Salt Lake Public Works. The tan painting appears to be a later overpainting. Most of the Public Works chairs of this style are hand grained to look like mahogany.

China cupboard, probably made by the Brigham City cooperative furniture factory, Brigham City, Utah, about 1875, pine hand grained to look like walnut and burl. This piece was owned by Lorenzo Snow, who directed the establishment of the Brigham City cooperative. Family tradition says that this cupboard was made in that co-op. This previously stripped piece was totally regrained by Ronald Wheat in 1997. He based his regraining upon the original style of the Brigham City co-op.

Headboard, Brigham City cooperative furniture factory, Brigham City,
Utah, about 1875, pine, hand grained
to look like walnut and burl, collection
of Brigham City Museum Gallery.

Pie safe, Brigham City cooperative
furniture factory, Brigham City,
Utah, about 1875, pine, hand
grained to look like walnut, and
tinned sheet metal, collection of
Lorenzo and Elma Hansen. Pie safes
were used for food storage. The per-
forated tinned panels allowed air circulation but kept out the flies. Notice
the graining and the decorative turn-
ings on this small utilitarian piece,
indicating an attempt to go far beyond necessity in order to beautify
the piece. Christian and Elizabeth
Hansen, who operated the dairy for
the Brigham City co-op, commissioned this pie safe. Elizabeth used it
for storing freshly baked goods to
feed the large crew at the dairy.

Beautifying Zion

Creating beautiful furniture was part of the integration of faith, religious activity, and beauty. The Saints were admonished to begin by beautifying with their own hands the immediate environment of their homes, gardens, cities, and temples until Zion would become like the Garden of Eden and a fit place for the return of the Savior. Creating beauty was an act of learning, worship, and faith that helped the maker become more like the Creator.

Early Latter-day Saints did not have an ascetic view of life. They enjoyed comfort, beauty, and fine craftsmanship. Brigham Young set the standard by commissioning furniture that demanded the best locally available design and craftsmanship. This had the effect of raising the standards for furniture making throughout Zion.

Homes were sacred buildings for the settlers, who took care to furnish their homes with beautiful "homemade" furnishings. Furniture was usually decorative rather than austere. Even utilitarian items like flour bins were finished to look like fine furniture. Beautification of the home helped create a peaceful and spiritual place for raising children and was also an expression of spiritual commitment to building Zion.

It is our duty to adorn and beautify [our home] to make it so lovely and attractive that angels may condescend to visit it.

—John Taylor, in *The Gospel Kingdom,* comp. G. Homer Durham (Salt Lake City: Bookcraft, 1943), 283–84

Beautify every place with the workmanship of our own hand.

—Brigham Young, in *JD,* 17:53, May 3, 1874

Meal bin, maker unknown, location unknown, 1865–85, wood (hand grained to simulate bird's-eye maple), metal, and porcelain. Meal bins were used to store flour or meal. Since few houses had the luxury of a separate pantry space, bins were usually placed in the kitchen. The decoration of these bins frequently went far beyond utilitarian needs. Often they were made to look like fancy desks. This piece is decorated to look like a cylinder desk made of bird's-eye maple.

Reclining armchair, William Bell (1816–1886), Salt Lake City, before 1869, wood, fabric, and metal, collection of John Todd. This chair has an adjustable back and a slide-out footrest. Made for Brigham Young, this is one of the earliest examples of a reclining chair, far preceding a better known model by Bell's countryman William Morris. Such innovation and comfort was encouraged by Brigham Young.

Inlaid parlor table, George Kirkham (1852–1923), Salt Lake City, about 1893, various woods, collection of Leo Fox. George Kirkham made this table for his wife Mary out of small scraps of wood he brought home from working on the finish woodwork of the Salt Lake Temple. A convert cabinetmaker, builder, artist, and musician from England, Kirkham also worked on the St. George and Manti Temples.

Mormon couch, Ole Swensen (no dates), Manti, Utah, after 1870, wood hand grained to look like walnut. These pieces of furniture often did double duty as couches during the day and beds at night. The hand graining simulates mahogany. This couch is in a modified Empire style that was a little old fashioned at the time it was made.

Regency couch, attributed to William Bell (1816–1886) and Ralph Ramsay (1824–1905), Salt Lake City, 1856, pine, grained to look like rosewood, and fabric. Bell became Brigham Young's chief furniture maker. Brigham even gave Bell a building lot from the corner of his farm. In 1869, Brigham sent Bell to the small town of Heber City because there was a need there for a furniture maker. This couch was commissioned by Brigham Young for the Lion House. It is English Regency, a style popular when Bell and Ramsay started their apprenticeships in England, but it was becoming old fashioned by the time the couch was made. This is the finest couch ever made in pioneer Utah. Most of the finish on this piece is original. After later extensive overpainting was removed, inpainting was done by Wallace Budd. The fabric is copied from a small piece of original upholstery fabric found on the couch.

Richard G. Oman is Senior Curator, Museum of Church History and Art. Several years in the making, *The Homemade Kingdom* resulted from the efforts of many people, including Kenyon Kennard, who provided significant curatorial and interpretive input based upon many years of passionate interest and research on furniture in both America and Great Britain; Steve Olsen, who helped frame the theological, historical, and anthropological context; and Susan Rhondeau and Lois Cook, who helped with research. All photographs in this essary are provided courtesy Museum of Church History and Art. Unless otherwise noted, all furniture items are in the museum's collection.

NOTES

1. John Taylor, in *Journal of Discourses,* 26 vols. (Liverpool: F. D. Richards, 1855–86), 17:68, May 7, 1874 (hereafter cited as *JD*).

2. See Steven L. Olsen, "The Mormon Ideology of Place: Cosmic Symbolism of the City of Zion" (Ph.D. diss., University of Chicago, 1985).

3. Home manufacture was defined as local and regional manufacture as opposed to importation from the eastern factories.

4. Even the color of paint for particular types of furniture pieces (chairs, beds, tables, and so on) was carefully delineated in the sect's Millennial Laws. See Malcolm Jones, "Shaker: Decorative Arts," in *The Dictionary of Art,* ed. Jane Turner, 34 vols. (New York: Macmillan, 1996), 28:542–43. For a more complete description of this tradition, see Edward D. Andrews and Faith Andrews, *Religion in Wood: A Book of Shaker Furniture* (Bloomington: Indiana University Press, 1966).

5. Joseph Smith, cited by Erastus Snow, in *JD*, 24:159, June 24, 1883. Brigham Young said, "Will you try to magnify your calling?" Brigham Young, in *JD*, 3:245, March 16, 1856.

6. Kenyon Kennard is currently compiling a dictionary of Mormon furniture makers that documents this point.

7. John Taylor, in *JD*, 17:68, February 1, 1874.

8. Heber C. Kimball, in *JD*, 5:10, July 5, 1857.

9. See George A. Smith, in *JD*, 90:202, October 20, 1861; and Dale F. Beecher, "Colonizer of the West," in *Lion of the Lord: Essays on the Life and Service of Brigham Young,* ed. Susan Easton Black and Larry C. Porter (Salt Lake City: Deseret Book, 1995).

10. Thomas Cottam, an English convert chair maker, was typical. He was among the first to receive colonization mission calls to settle Utah's Dixie. One of the finest chair makers in the Mormon commonwealth, Cottam helped build the St. George Tabernacle and made many of the chairs for the St. George Temple. Charles S. Cottam, *Brief History of Thomas Cottam,* in possession of author.

11. All the information on Ralph Ramsey is from Ralph Ramsay, Reminiscences and Journal, microfilm of holograph, and from Ralph Ramsay, Scrapbook, 1963–1970, photocopy of holograph, both in LDS Church Archives.

Mormon Clothing in Utah, 1847–1900

Carma de Jong Anderson

Being so far removed from the styles of the pioneer period, we sometimes have difficulty understanding early Mormon clothing. For example, what we often see in the LDS historical films made before 1998 are ensembles spurious in cut and colors and quite underaccessorized. For accurate information about what early Mormons would have worn according to their social status and economic ability, I have analyzed and photographed clothing collections all over America and in England, Scotland, Wales, and Ireland.

Mormon letters and journals yielded information about clothing's various sources, uses, textiles, colors, and trims. The terminology of the 1800s, however, is quite different from what is familiar to us. Who among us would immediately understand such terms as *pantalets* versus *pantaloons,* a *palto,* or Brigham Young's *warmus?* (I venture to say a warmus was probably a comfortable woolen coat smock worn by a farmer or craftsman.) In today's textile terminology, *muslin* has a connotation of crudeness, but in the nineteenth century, this term referred to all weights of fine, white cotton—elegant fabrics. Even the words *smock, frock,* or *smock-frock* carried a completely different meaning for pioneers and were solely in the male domain until about 1900. The *frac* referred to in French fashion terms meant a heavily tailored frock coat for a man's day wear. *Engageantes,* another little-known term, refers to connecting sleeves worn under the flaring sleeves of the 1840s called *pagodas.* Even the use of a top hat differs from modern preconceptions; it was not exclusively for formal wear for most of the pioneer years but remained in a man's wardrobe as a work hat for the field when the hat became old and damaged.

The difficulty of learning about clothing is increased by a scarcity of photographs and artifacts, such as accessories, pieces of clothing, and scraps of antique fabrics. Photography did not exist until 1839, when French painter Louis-Jacques-Mandé Daguerre invented the process of creating permanent pictures on metal plates. But daguerreotypes and other photographic images and portraits before 1860 are too scarce to rely upon for a thorough knowledge of historic clothing design among Mormon members. Fortunately, remarkably helpful portraits and scenes can be found in photography collections that contain materials from the broader American and British culture of the 1840s and '50s.

Today there is virtually no folk clothing left from nineteenth-century Utah. True to the immigrant spirit, the European Saints wanted their clothing to match that of the American Mormons. When their traditional folk clothing wore out, it was replaced with the constantly changing international style of clothing worn by the majority of the Church members in the West. Clothing rags (as well as good fabric scraps) were absorbed into rugs or quilts or processed for paper. Emulating the larger social group created for immigrants a comfortable feeling of fitting in, but it did have some tragic effects. For over a hundred years, Mormons continued to lose age-old skills, beautiful styles, and interest in displays of ethnic origins.

The clothing ensembles shown in this photo essay often contain one to three original parts. The other items of each ensemble have been faithfully reproduced so that the textile fibers, weaves, colors, and prints—and most importantly the cut of the pattern—appear original and so that accessories are authentic. All these details had to be drafted from the visual and structural information I have obtained from handling and photographing actual clothing. The ensembles in this photo essay are as accurate as I could presently make them, although after four decades of diligent research I still find bits of startling new knowledge even in my casual reading.

In this photo essay, carefully chosen local models with original pioneer hairstyles provide insight into how some of our pioneer ancestors, ages two to seventy, might have appeared. Certainly these images are preferable to conjuring up images for paintings or sculptures by drawing from memories of children's book illustrations.

Carma de Jong Anderson is Director of the Costume Institute of Utah and serves as costume designer/reproducer of historic sites for the LDS Church, Exhibits Department, and the restorations done through the Museum of Church History and Art. She also teaches a workshop on early Mormon clothing in the Department of Theatre and Media Arts at Brigham Young University.

PLATE 1. Mormon grandmother

Double puffs on these flamboyant "Marie" sleeves add to the importance of a shirred-front dress with a high V neckline. Such shirring began to fall out of fashion by the end of the 1850s. An elegant floral calico print is seen with the formal apron removed. Worn throughout the nineteenth century, this original 1840 apron is cross-barred cotton batiste, a fabric likely from France or Switzerland, trimmed in hand-knitted lace edging and insertion. A very common, flat straw hat covers the customary day cap, which was given less and less ruffling as this fashion waned before the Civil War. Many women who wore fashionable small, hollow gold beads in Nauvoo continued to use them for decades afterward. For dancing parties, a lace collar would be added and the day cap left at home. This dress's very full skirt would be held out further with layers of petticoats and a small hoop.

PLATE 2. Salt Lake City dentist

Dressed for hot weather in his international styled, finely tailored clothing, Alexander Neibauer, a Berlin-trained dentist, is dutifully making home visits. The light, unlined linen coat, typical of what Neibauer might have chosen, was sewn totally by hand in the 1840s. A fine topper with beaver fur in the felt makes a stiff and proper hat, originally from London. The dentist's silk tie, a button-on "stock" tie, matches the standard black hat . The trousers are cream wool with silk striping.

PLATE 3. Welsh immigrant of the 1840s

The revered folk clothing of commoners in Wales is still celebrated and preserved. A red wool "short gown" over a chemise is comfortable with a neck shawl of softest lamb's wool. Under a black-red-and-gray-striped skirt are additional petticoats, each of a different fabric—gorgeously embroidered cotton *(broidery anglaise),* gray linen, and black flannel. Very fine Irish crochet trim is on her tubular calf-length pantelets, which cover black, clocked (figured) stockings. Women's best shoes of the mid-1800s had the same high, heavy heels with large buckles as pirates wore centuries before on the Spanish galleons. A woman's necessary white day cap, with lappets hanging, is under the tall-crowned felt hat, typically worn by both men and women.

PLATE 4. Irish colleen

A poor young girl from Ireland wears a tiny shawl of brown jacquard pinned around the low neckline of her chemise to keep her warm enough to scrub clothing in tubs outdoors or sit in the chilly doorway of a cabin to make lace in the bright daylight. Irish lace produced in the mid-1800s was often a minuscule, crocheted pattern, only 25 percent of the size seen today. Her large shawl of red, green, and brown is soft warm wool, her only coat against winter's blast. Spun, woven, and dyed at home, a green-and-black-plaid flannel skirt (usually called a petticoat) is layered over other serviceable linen or wool petticoats, and the girl's heavy leather oxfords have nailed and pegged soles.

PLATE 5. Former gardener from Staffordshire

Tough, linen coat smocks were worn on ships to Zion and across the plains to Utah as the customary raincoat, warm coat, and work uniform that kept a man's other clothing clean. The smock features rows of intricate, stretchy smocking on the front, back, and sleeves. Sections of rose-garden embroidery proclaim this immigrant's former occupation. Sadly for this form of decoration, when an embroidered garment wore out from the rigors of building the West, there was never time to replace it with a similarly decorated garment, and the use of an embroidered badge of occupation died out. This immigrant relishes a flowery neckerchief and an ancient top hat from Hanley, England, which would have been a cast-off from his former employer.

Mary Ann Abel might have worn a prairie dress such as this in 1853 when she arrived in Utah with her husband Elijah and three children. This dress is an original high-quality cotton twill with a resist print grounded in black. It makes an ample wrapper dress (for maternity or travel) of about 1850–65 with a plain front yoke and bone buttons. Bishop sleeves are so full they require the usual shortening tuck on the inside arm seam to prevent them from falling too low. The smoothly braided palm-leaf hat is also original, about 150 years old, with pale ribbons added.

PLATE 7.
Fancy Eastern convert

A young miss from Boston or Philadelphia in the early 1850s is ready for visiting and dancing in a voluminous skirt trimmed in gauged pleating on hemline, shoulders, and pagoda sleeves. Typical V-shaped flanges have piped edges flaring over the shoulders, a style that persisted from the late '40s through the '50s. Collar and engageantes (the absolutely necessary attachable undersleeves) are of cotton batiste embroidered white on white. Wealthy, faithful converts from the Eastern States and Upper Canada had lovely accessories: silk shawls, fashionable bonnets with gauzy lace scarves draped over them, gloves, and clocked stockings, each kept meticulously in place. Cotton fabric, still fairly high priced in America, was considered a fine textile when well woven and printed. Its common competitors were the great varieties of silks in most people's wardrobes.

PLATE 8.
Colonizing
blacksmith

PLATE 9.
Scottish
fisherlassie

In a split-legged leather apron, a hardy pioneer bent the iron for wagon-wheel rings, cornered the wagon boxes, and shoed horses. A simple collarband was most commonly seen on work shirts of the mid–nineteenth century. The shirt is of soft cotton with black and brown woven together, the same colors as the heavier, striped trousers of linen and wool. While the smith dodges sparks from the forge, trouser legs are tucked into calf-high, square-toed boots. A soft-leather pilot cap with a considerable brim keeps some of the sparks out of the blacksmith's hair.

Leaving behind their grueling jobs of hauling fish to sell in villages by the North Sea, young women immigrated to the western territory. The usual thick, wool short gown covers a long-sleeved underchemise and layers of linen and wool-flannel petticoats. This lassie's outside petticoat is pinned up on the sides to keep it out of the mud of Utah farms. Wooden-soled shoes, the only kind that would last in wet sand and surf, serve as well for Utah chores. White wool stockings add a modicum of comfort. A Scottish brooch is placed at the front neckline every work day, preserving a touch of femininity during intensive labor.

PLATE 10. Immigrant farmers   A grandson helps his aged British grandmother through the snow of mountain country. Settlers brought their typical farmer's jackets, or *paltos;* this one has pieced corduroy cuffs and collar as accent on gray-and-white homespun tweed. These garments are nearly always unlined and are therefore not equal to high altitude storms. The man's painted black straw hat has a modish square crown and adds a little dignity for men who cannot afford dark felt. The linsey-woolsey trousers are broadfall style; they button up horizontally across the front, onto the waistband, and never have pockets in the back. Grandmother's shawl is wool in greenish-brown, black, and white, with an original red, knitted winter hood. Her striped stockings are held up under the knees by nonelastic garters woven out of tape. An outer petticoat is vertically striped gray-and-red wool, often seen among the weavers in Welsh communities.

PLATE 11. Midwife on call

Accustomed to sudden emergencies, this midwife will put on her large apron and walk or ride a horse to a cabin wherever and whenever she is needed. She is wearing her bright, abstracted calico print of the 1840s, accented by turquoise piping on the shoulder flange and cuffs. Her fine, big sunbonnet is wired buckram covered in cheap polished cambric, with crown and curtain made of pieced scraps of heavy black silk. Midwives habitually brought along their knitting or sewing to occupy themselves during hours of waiting and carried extra bread or other foods to the family of the woman in "confinement."

PLATE 12. Daughter of Switzerland

A charming child displays her Swiss village origin. The Heber Valley in Utah was colonized by many Swiss and Dutch immigrants, and their traditional clothing and customs died hard. Some huge dairy cows in Midway were still wearing decorated Swiss bells as late as the 1970s. This little girl's *mieder* has ribbon lacing up the front and creative strapping over the shoulders. Symmetrical embroidery designs in blues and white make the back view as interesting as the front; the back is shown off during folk dances. A superfine, cotton-batiste apron displays the famous Swiss machine embroidery available in the last half of the nineteenth century and is embellished with crocheted edging and flowers. Quality silk ribbons are buttoned and bowed around puff sleeves. The clogs are required for seasonal slush. With typical Germanic orderliness, all the girl's blond hair is stylishly braided around her head.

PLATE 13. Rocky
Mountain family

Woven in a cheerful green, a symbol of fertility, this miniature plaid makes a cool wrapper, or prairie dress, for wear in grain fields and orchards. The pioneer mother's apron is tied around her higher and higher each month. After the baby comes, the dress will continue to be worn, for a prairie dress is ideal for a nursing mother. Jet buttons are on the high yoke, and hooks close the lower front opening. Sun and rain protection comes from a very broad-brimmed hat of braided straw; the mother's little boys wear a pilot cap and a small felt hat. The older son is wearing a common skeleton suit; he simply buttons the form-fitting parts together at the waistline. The suit is carefully pieced out of nonmatching fabrics, indicating the family's poor textile resources. The younger boy literally lives and sleeps in his soft cotton smock of blue, red, and white woven together, making a comfortable shirtlike garment the color of wild purple gentians.

Original knitted lace insertion and edging on cross-barred batiste (see plate 1)

Original silky cotton twill, resist painted (see plate 6)

Original hand-woven Danish wool, men's vesting as facing (see plate 15)

An original foundation lace with darned design (see plate 27)

Pleated trim on pagoda sleeve, modern fabric typical of 1840s (see plate 7)

Original heavy gray flannel embroidered in red wool (petticoat worn under Danish skirt, see plate 15)

PLATE 14. Close-ups of fabrics

PLATE 15. Dane from Alborg

PLATE 16. The ubiquitous piper

This folk clothing is one of the hundreds of varieties seen on Scandinavian converts from smaller villages. Women in Alborg favored the giant, red-silk bow of this original small calico cap with wool padding, lined in red lamb's wool fabric for a cold climate. A traditional striped skirt in a particularly rain-resistant goat wool was spun, dyed, woven, and sewn by hand. Heavy silk-tape binding on the hemline secures the brown jacquard vesting fabric pieced together for a hem facing. The black-banded skirt was made *at least* 150 years ago but is likely 200 years old. With corset-like sections and a front-hooked opening, the sea-blue moiré bodice is trimmed in black, and the apron with black silk lace. Both items are reproductions.

In Utah the stubborn Scottish community long remained culturally cohesive against all forces of assimilation. For example, Robert D. Young always entertained in full kilt regalia. When he was a young man, the whole territory knew his skill at dancing, especially the sword dance. Other Scots rendered lively versions of ancestral legends, doggedly holding onto their heavy brogues. This kilt's close-fitting wool jacket with silver buttons echoes past generations of kilted soldiers. The bagpipes would have been an expensive item in pioneer days.

PLATE 17.
Susa Young Gates

This pastel, printed-cotton dress was made by Brigham Young's daughter when she was sixteen years old and living in Salt Lake City. It features opulent tiers of ruffles sewed to a strong, ugly calico print base for the skirt—paradoxically saving expensive cloth at the same time that the dress was lavishly decorated with ruffles edged in black silk ribbons. Susa used knotted, black silk fringe, which could have come from a worn-out piece of her mother's clothing. The fitted, boned bodice has a black silk jacquard bow that lies over the bustled skirt in back. A young woman of social rank would have definitely worn a corset, and the model wears Susa's crinoline, the required wire cage held together with heavy, cotton tapes to shape the skirt and bustle in back. Sleeves with pagoda layers over balloon gathers were very fanciful for a young woman in 1869.

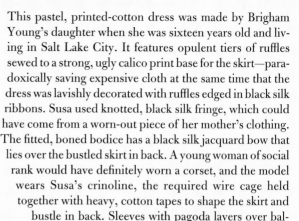

In the finery of the 1870s, Maude Adams, "America's darling" redheaded actress, returned occasionally to the place of her birth, Salt Lake City. This raspberry-red jacquard silk, representative of what she might have worn, has a pleated train and bustle and a high Victorian collar closed with numerous gold buttons. An original black silk cape is edged in velvet and lined in royal-blue silk, quilted for a chilly night. Sumptuous ostrich plumes are combined in a long-tasseled boa and matching plume for the high hairstyle draped in silk-velvet roses. Long gloves and a copper beaded reticule, reminding us of finery supported by Utah's growing mineral wealth, complete her evening attire.

PLATE 18. An actress

PLATE 19. Traveler to the capital

In 1891 several Utah women traveled to Washington, D.C., to attend the first meeting of the National Council of Women. There, on behalf of the Relief Society and YLMIA, they presented their credentials and applied for membership in the council. Although the women waited in suspense for a time, the organizations were admitted by a unanimous vote. Here one of the representatives is shown in her traveling attire. Her plum-colored wool suit, embellished with black-silk braid on gigot sleeves and jacket, has a lovely lingerie blouse *(waist)* with a fine Irish-lace neckpiece. Black fur trimming accents the pillbox hat with a wired, silk rosette high in back.

Fine tailoring was the hallmark of clothing in the nineteenth century. This man's coat (which was always worn with a vest) is a dense fabric of elegant nap. A beaver top hat was used only formally in the 1890s. President Cannon wears it for an evening promenade in downtown Salt Lake City with his tiniest (size two and "feisty") wife. This is her original couturier dress in clay-colored bengaline silk, accented by acid-green silk velvet. The very high collar is cut out in V shapes, front and back, with only cords of green velvet circling the neck. Black felt is turned upward into the 1890s vertical tricorn hat, decorated with sprays of silk flowers, called artificials. The period shoes with pointed toes lace up almost to the calf.

PLATE 20. Mr. and Mrs. George Q. Cannon

PLATE 21. Victorian lingerie

By the 1880s and '90s, many lovely fabrics were readily available in Northern Utah stores. With silk crepe, bengaline, and crepe de chine, as well as silky satins made, after 1889, of the new rayon fibers, women and girls with sewing skills could duplicate the elegance of East Coast items brought to the Wasatch slopes. A large number of local residents in Utah were adept at producing both bobbin and needle lace, along with tatting and crocheting. In addition, machine-made laces were easily obtained on the market. This nightgown-nightcap combination came from Lehi. It features rich faggot-pointed trimming in crocheted edging beautifully executed on silk crepe fabric.

PLATE 22. Wealthy toddler

An early Salt Lake black velvet jerkin with pleats, set-in waistband, and gilded buttons up the back is worn with white linen pantalets, patent leather slippers, and a velvet tam. Jaunty red silk plaid makes the hatband and cockade for a bit of silver jewelry—a modish cap for a boy with the comforts of money in 1875 in the center of Mormonism. Many a moppet was trained to walk with this parlor toy, a push donkey still covered in the last remnants of his mohair fur.

At the turn of the century, Clarence Marcellus Barker departed for a mission in Sydney, Australia, two to three months' travel from North Ogden, Utah. His narrowly fitted, double-breasted coat is in an elegant, heavy, silk novelty weave. It was black, is now faded to a dark green, and had possibly been his father's coat in the 1880s. Matching corded silk covers the buttons. A very stiff, high collar is attached to a pleated-bosom shirt. Smooth oxfords and linen trousers are selected for the humid South Seas. A fashionable bowler releases some of the missionary's romantic curls, and leather gloves with a silk umbrella are fashionable, but necessary, accessories for his adventures.

PLATE 23. Elder Clarence Marcellus Barker

PLATE 24. Mormon artist

In his one black suit, John Hafen traveled to France in 1891 for training; he was accompanied by other LDS artists who wanted to paint creditable murals for Mormon temples. Leaving a large family on his farm in Springville for a year, he used every moment of his Church-funded trip to study from the best teachers and see museums as far away as Italy. A simple smock like this one was the only protection Hafen had from the staining paints in the studios of the Julian Academy; no gentleman student would be anything but fully dressed while working in class.

PLATE 25. Damsel on a picnic

Fifty years after Amelia Bloomer and other women attempted "bloomer dresses" and years after Brigham Young's attempt at a bifurcated style of dress for Zion (which did not catch on with Utah ladies), the new-fangled, pleated bicycling bloomers expressed a Utah girl's emerging freedom in athletics. This woman's sailor scarf adds a mannish touch to the Gibson girl blouse, and a typical sailor hat of Salt Lake City, 1900, fits the goose as well as the gander. Authentic no-nonsense, leather high tops make sturdy knockabout shoes for groves and streams where friendly groups cavort and take the air at the start of a new century.

Celebrating the teletype announcement of Utah's union with the United States, an 1896 citizen wears her dark-green suit with shirred bands and silk piping. The blouse, called a waist, is cream netting and lace with gigot sleeves under the jacket and pouter-pigeon center-front gathering. Large brooches and fancy belt buckles were as popular in the 1890s as they had been in the 1830s. Approaching the end of Queen Victoria's life, some hats were enlarged markedly into new designs; this is a statehood-period hat in black velvet.

PLATE 26. Celebrant of Utah statehood

PLATE 27. Bridesmaid and beau

His cap of 1900 is white linen, golf style; her hat is a miniature straw, decked out in peach roses. His coat is a blue-and-white-striped seersucker, closing high with only the top button; her dress is shadow-striped sheer cotton with geometric blue figures. His narrow tie under a stiff choker collar is silver-blue silk; her sash is pale-blue satin with a bustle bow. The two-piece dress, extensively restored, has balloon sleeves flounced in wide, white lace with darned designs, matching the long, shawl-collar trim. Around the voluminous skirt is a twelve-inch flounce with many yards more of lace. Her white parasol for the garden party is decorated, under and over, with peach lace and chiffon.

Plate 1. Model: Vivian Best, who produced her own dress and cap. Apron from the Winifred Bowers collection in the Costume Institute of Utah. Photo: *Deseret News,* Ravell Call.

Plate 2. Model: Devon Hokansen. Trousers, collection of Roberta James; doctor's valise, collection of Carolyn Peters Driggs. Ensemble: Carma de Jong Anderson. Photo: Joseph R. Putnam Photography.

Plate 3. Model: Merilee Forcha Crandall in clothing reproduced by Carma de Jong Anderson. Photo: baciPhotography, Brett Crandall.

Plate 4. Model: Nancy Kensinger. Ensemble: Carma de Jong Anderson. Photo: baci-Photography, Brett Crandall.

Plate 5. Model: Garrett Fry. Smocking by Karen Johnson; embroidery by Carma de Jong Anderson. Photo: *Deseret News,* Ravell Call.

Plate 6. Model: Judelka Castro. Ensemble: Carma de Jong Anderson. Photo: Joseph R. Putnam Photography.

Plate 7. Model: DaJe Garfield. Prize-winning ensemble designed and produced by Betty Robinson. Photo: *Deseret News,* Ravell Call. Rear view: baciPhotography, Brett Crandall.

Plate 8. Model: Douglas Merrill, a demonstrator docent at the Museum of Church History and Art, Salt Lake City. From seventeen costumes produced for "Pioneer Profiles" by Carma de Jong Anderson. Photo: Joseph R. Putnam Photography.

Plate 9. Model: Mairie Gairnes McCloud. Reproduction by Carma de Jong Anderson of clothing pictured in an 1844 calotype photograph from Scotland. Photo: baciPhotography, Brett Crandall.

Plate 10. Models: Nicholas James Ivie and Dottie McKinlay Packer. Ensembles: Carma de Jong Anderson. Photo: Richard L. Anderson.

Plate 11. Model: Connie Moss Knight, a docent at the Museum of Church History and Art, Salt Lake City. Ensemble: Carma de Jong Anderson. The bonnet is a copy of an original in the Historical Society of Newton, Ohio. Photo: Joseph R. Putnam Photography.

Plate 12. Model: Katherine Helena Hamblin. Ensemble: Carma de Jong Anderson. Photo: *Deseret News,* Ravell Call.

Plate 13. Models: Nicole Riley with sons Jackson and Joshua. Dress produced by Roselle Anderson Hamblin in lightweight India cotton gingham; boy's smocking by Nancy West. Ensembles: Carma de Jong Anderson. Photo: *Deseret News,* Ravell Call.

Plate 15. Model: Julia Patch. Skirt and cap from Danish immigrants, the Lars Christensen family of Lehi, Utah. Ensemble: Carma de Jong Anderson. Photo: *Deseret News,* Ravell Call.

Plate 16. Model: Jared McCloud with his own pipes and kilt at the Utah State Historical Society Centennial fashion show, 1997, produced by Carma de Jong Anderson. Photo: *Deseret News,* Ravell Call.

Plate 17. Model: Rachel Rosa Lee Hamblin. Putty-colored silk spoon bonnet from an unknown source; dress and crinoline from the collection of Carma de Jong Anderson. Photo: Royal Photography, Trent Farnsworth.

Plate 18. Model: Sarah Marshall. Ensemble: Carma de Jong Anderson. Photo: baciPhotography, Brett Crandall.

Plate 19. Model and tailor: Diane Taylor-Taylor; braiding by Delna Macfarland. Ensemble: Carma de Jong Anderson. Photo: Olan Mills. Facts in caption from Carol Cornwall Madsen, "'The Power of Combination': Emmeline B. Wells and the National and International Councils of Women," *BYU Studies* 33, no. 4 (1993): 649.

Plate 20. Models: Brian Cannon and Jeannette Higginson. Kidskin shoes from Sanpete County, Utah; hat design by Carma de Jong Anderson for PBS film, *Let the Women Vote,* Louise Degn, Producer-Director. Photo: *Deseret News,* Ravell Call.

Plate 21. Model: Janae Padilla. Lingerie from the Lars Christensen collection; kid slippers with silk pompoms from the Carolyn Peters Driggs collection. Ensemble: Carma de Jong Anderson. Photo: Joseph R. Putnam Photography.

Plate 22. Model: two-year-old Reese Rasband. Jerkin from estate of Nettie Woodbury Miller, donated to the Costume Institute of Utah by Elizabeth Reiser; donkey from collection of Marilyn Chapman. Ensemble: Carma de Jong Anderson. Photo: Joseph R. Putnam Photography.

Plate 23. Model: Pieter Marshall. Coat in possession of Elder Barker's daughter, Phyllis Barker Van Wagenen. Ensemble: Carma de Jong Anderson. Photo: Joseph R. Putnam Photography.

Plate 24. Model: Miles L. Watters. Ensemble: Carma de Jong Anderson. Photo: *Deseret News,* Ravell Call.

Plate 25. Model: Megan Ahrendes. Sailor scarf courtesy Clyde E. Sullivan. Ensemble: Carma de Jong Anderson. Photo: *Deseret News,* Ravell Call.

Plate 26. Model: Patricia Nelson Tanner, wife of Utah Congressman Jordan Tanner. Tanner's mother, Annie Atkin Tanner, owned the hat. Suit and blouse constructed by Vivian Best; designed by Carma de Jong Anderson. Photo: Joseph R. Putnam Photography.

Plate 27. Models: Stefani Knudsen and Randy Mott. Dress from the collection of Winifred Bowers. Ensembles: Carma de Jong Anderson. Photo: baciPhotography, Brett Crandall.

Dancing the Buckles off Their Shoes in Pioneer Utah

Larry V. Shumway

In our more appreciative moments, we wonder at the magnificence of human spirit that the pioneers exhibited in their struggles against all odds to carve a meaningful and civilized life out of a forbidding wilderness. Of the many factors contributing to the pioneer successes, I will consider here but two—dance and its associated music. The records left by the pioneers make it clear that dance and dance music played a more significant role in the successful pioneering of Utah than is generally acknowledged. Music and dancing relieved the harshness of the pioneers' living conditions and helped develop the sense of community common to Mormon settlements.

Although musical entertainments other than dancing were to be found as well—in private or informal evenings at home with family and friends or in the more formal settings of socials, picnics, and holiday programs—from the pioneer era well into this century, most community musical activity centered around dancing. Sometimes dances were held in the open air but more often in homes or public buildings. In urban areas, such as Salt Lake City and Ogden, public halls dedicated to dancing and theatricals were built quite early and were heavily patronized. Out in the rural settlements, people danced first in homes, then churches and schools, and later in public halls. Dances were held regularly, usually on Friday evening, but were also given in connection with any number of national and local celebrations and events—the Fourth of July, Twenty-fourth of July, Thanksgiving, Christmas, Easter, election eve, harvesttime, barn raisings, and even ball games or school plays.[1] In addition to the dancing and convivial atmosphere, many people were interested in the music itself and would attend a dance simply to listen.

SOCIAL DANCE IN NINETEENTH-CENTURY AMERICA

In mid-nineteenth-century America, dancing had a spotted reputation at best. Given the strict Christian underpinnings of Utah
pioneer society, many may find it remarkable that dancing was a widespread, Church-sanctioned activity. However, in this penchant for
dancing, the pioneers shared much with the larger society, where,
since the late eighteenth century, dancing had become a popular form
of entertainment.

Prior to the Revolutionary War, country dances, whose origins go
back to the peasant dancing of medieval Europe, were popular among
the lower classes in the new colonies. The upper classes danced the
minuet and gavotte, imitating the courtly balls popular in Europe, but
also enjoyed genteel versions of traditional country dances. After the
Revolutionary War, courtly dancing declined because of its strong
association with monarchy and privilege, while the various forms of
country dancing—both genteel and popular—continued.[2] The popular forms of country dancing, however, were not accepted by the upper
classes, who did not consider them to be refined, nor were they usually
done in reputable places. Indeed, as Charles Hamm points out, "in
almost every mention of country dancing, there is a link to some sort of
impropriety: drinking, gambling, intimacy between the sexes."[3]

Thus, dancing in public places came in for heavy criticism by
numerous moralists and the clergy, a response that, in one form or
another, has continued to the present time. Although censure against
dancing was particularly strong in Puritan New England, dance was
tolerated there by high society, sometimes even with a grudging
approval on the grounds that it could be something of an art form that
would give a certain elegance and polish to the young lady or gentleman. Proponents argued that dancing would teach the youth genteel
manners and give them a graceful carriage and bearing as well as a
sense of social self-confidence.[4]

In the South, the migration to America had been more for economic than religious reasons, and the resulting wealth and sense of
class required of its people a social polish that included fashionable
and graceful dancing. Thus, dancing became an educational must for
the gentleman or gentlewoman. Grand balls became gracious affairs to
showcase the graceful gentility of upper-class breeding, and mixed
dancing was very much accepted. Dances encompassed all the trap-
pings of high society the new country could muster.[5]

About this time in England, dancing had become very popular among the middle class, and as large numbers of immigrants came to the United States from the British Isles, those tastes accompanied them to the New World. For them, dancing was seen as a good form of recreation.

During the nineteenth century, despite the persistent climate of religious censure, mixed social dancing became acceptable throughout most of American society. In many areas, the population was sparse and spread out, and an occasion for dancing was something looked forward to and savored for as long as possible. Sometimes, however, dancing led to overly exuberant celebration and disruptive behavior, fueled by consumption of liquor, which seemed to bear out the contention of the persistent critics of dancing that it was an activity surely leading to sin and all its consequences.[6]

The dance forms of the eighteenth and nineteenth centuries were basically figure or pattern dances, most commonly called cotillions or quadrilles. Some of the step patterns could be quite complicated, and, as these dance forms gradually became more acceptable, dancing masters began to appear in many eastern cities and towns to give the necessary instruction. Since many of the step patterns were hard to remember, the practice of one of the musicians calling out the figures arose in the early nineteenth century. This custom helped the dancers considerably, probably making dancing more fun and more accessible to the general population.

Nauvoo Leaders' Views on Dancing

Dancing parties were common among the Mormons during the Nauvoo period (1839–46), which, given the varying background and expectations of its citizens, raised some real questions in the minds of many about the propriety of the practice. In an 1844 letter to the editor of the *Times and Seasons*, "a father and elder in Israel" requests a clarification of the Church stance on dancing.[7]

The reply from the editor, probably written by Elder John Taylor, was included in the same issue and began with the following observation:

> We have always considered that there existed on the minds of the religious community, a great deal of unnecessary superstition in relation to dancing, but perhaps this feeling is engendered more through other associations and evils connected with it, than from the thing itself. There certainly can be no harm in dancing in and of itself, as an abstract principle, but like all other athletic exercises,

it has a tendency to invigorate the system and to promote health. . . . Therefore, looking at dancing merely as an athletic exercise, or as something having a tendency to add to the grace and dignity of man, by enabling him to have a more easy and graceful attitude, certainly no one could object to it. So much then for dancing as a science.[8]

The editor traces the record of dancing in the scriptures, quoting from 2 Samuel 6:13–15, where David dances before the Lord with all his might. He then observes that while dancing "was adopted for the purpose of celebrating the praise of God," the dancing of the day was not that kind, for "we never heard God's name praised, nor his glory exalted in any of them. Nor do we think that there is the least desire to glorify God in the dancing of the present day . . . and that it has not a tendency to glorify God, or to benefit mankind." In conclusion, he reiterates the neutrality of dancing and focuses rather on the contexts of time and place:

> As an abstract principle . . . we have no objections to [dancing]; but when it leads people into bad company and causes them to keep untimely hours, it has a tendency to enervate and weaken the system, and lead to profligate and intemperate habits. And so far as it does this, so far it is injurious to society, and corrupting to the morals of youth. Solomon says that "there is a time to dance:" but that time is not at eleven or twelve o'clock at night, nor at one, two, three or four o'clock in the morning.[9]

Three ideas emerge from the editor's reply, which would form the basis for later policies governing dancing in Mormon Utah pioneer communities: First, dancing, as an exercise, tends to "invigorate" the body and promote health and well-being if done in moderation. Second, dancing has a "tendency to add to the grace and dignity of man, by enabling him to have a more easy and graceful attitude." And third, dancing, illustrated in the scriptural record as a "part of the service to God," should be conducted in a proper atmosphere of piety and loving sociality, without which the evils stemming from dance, as per its critics, could become a real possibility.

After the assassination of Joseph Smith some three months later, however, the Church leaders felt the need to discourage worldliness and excess of frivolity, believing that dancing and other amusements had the tendency to distract people from the real and pressing needs of the hour. These grim and somber times prompted a sternly worded epistle from the Council of the Twelve over the signature of Brigham

Young. The letter was published in the *Times and Seasons* and pointed the Saints' attention to what was required of them:

> In order to do this [build the kingdom] we must not only be industrious and honest . . . but we must abstain from all intemperance, immorality and vice of whatever name or nature; we must set an example of virtue, modesty, temperance, continency, cleanliness and charity. And be careful not to mingle in the vain amusements and sins of the world. . . . Among the most conspicuous and fashionable of these we might mention, balls, dances, corrupt and immodest theatrical exhibitions, magical performances, etc., all of which are apt not only to have an evil tendency in themselves, but to mingle the virtuous and vicious in each others society; nor for the improvement of the vicious, but rather to corrupt the virtuous. . . . And so far at least as the members of the church are concerned, we would advise that balls, dances, and other vain and useless amusements be neither countenanced nor patronized; they have been borne with, in some instances heretofore for the sake of peace and good will. But it is not now a time for dancing or frolics but a time of mourning, and of humiliation and prayer.[10]

This statement may appear to be a general indictment of dancing, and it certainly is a warning of the ill effects of worldly and unfettered revelry in the public dances. Yet subsequent events, as well as statements by Brigham Young, indicate that this deep concern was more for the time, place, and especially the environment in which dancing was done. Under Brigham Young's approval, dancing resumed in Nauvoo[11] and continued around evening campfires after a hard day on the pioneer trail.

BRIGHAM YOUNG'S VIEWS ON DANCING

Because many early members of the Church came from the strict religious traditions that looked with disfavor on dancing, the widespread practice of dancing among the Mormon pioneers is very surprising. Equally surprising is that the person who, more than any other, shaped the Mormon view of dancing and gave it its peculiar stamp of approval was Brigham Young. President Young was a New Englander raised in a strict household where "to listen to the sound of a violin was an unforgivable sin," yet, as Elizabeth Haven Barlow notes, "later President Young became a wonderful dancer and loved all sorts of art and music."[12]

Dancing always had the Church leaders' blessing, but with it also came their admonishment to preserve a proper atmosphere and attitude.[13] Every occasion was to be opened and closed with prayer, and the people were to be unrelentingly vigilant in keeping out worldly influences, particularly liquor, rowdy behavior, and suspicious strangers who might bring harm to the community. This type of setting is what Brigham Young envisioned as necessary for dancing to fulfill its *raison d'être*—providing the wholesome recreation requisite for physical, mental, and social growth. In a speech entitled "Recreation and the Proper Use of It," delivered at the Legislative Festival on March 4, 1852, Brigham Young once again articulated his view toward the practice of dancing:

> I want it distinctly understood, that fiddling and dancing are no part of our worship. The question may be asked, What are they for, then? I answer, that my body may keep pace with my mind. My mind labors like a man logging, all the time; and this is the reason why I am fond of these pastimes—they give me a privilege to throw every thing off, and shake myself, that my body may exercise, and my mind rest. What for? To get strength, and be renewed and quickened, and enlivened, and animated, so that my mind may not wear out. . . . I do not wrestle, or play the ball; all the exercise I do get is to dance a little.[14]

Speaking on another occasion, President Young emphasized that dancing under the right auspices was not only good for the people but was also as wholesome an activity as any sport—the only requirement for purity being a proper attitude:

> If you want to dance, run a footrace, pitch quoits or play at ball, do it, and exercise your bodies, and let your minds rest. . . . If you wish to dance, dance; and you are just as much prepared for a prayer meeting after dancing as ever you were, if you are Saints. If you desire to ask God for anything, you are as well prepared to do so in the dance as in any other place, if you are Saints. Are your eyes open to know that everything in the earth, in hell, or in heaven, is ordained for the use of intelligent beings? . . . Those who cannot serve God with a pure heart in the dance should not dance. [15]

In the matter of the training and education of his own children, President Young said the following:

> I had not a chance to dance when I was young, and never heard the enchanting tones of the violin, until I was eleven years of age; and then I thought I was on the high way to hell, if I suffered myself to linger and listen to it. I shall not subject my little children to such a course of unnatural training, but they shall go to the dance, study

music, read novels, and do anything else that will tend to expand their frames, add fire to their spirits, improve their minds, and make them feel free and untrammeled in body and mind.[16]

A number of times, President Young chastened the critics of dancing by offering the following opinions on the prevalent religious censure of fiddling and dancing: "Tight-laced religious professors of the present generation have a horror at the sound of a fiddle. There is no music in hell, for all good music belongs to heaven";[17] "every decent fiddler will go into a decent kingdom";[18] and "I have heard many a minister say that there were no fiddles in heaven. At that time I did not understand as I do now, for I now know that there are no fiddles in hell. There may be many fiddlers there, but no fiddles; they are all burned that go there."[19]

The fruits of Young's policies in encouraging dancing are summarized nicely by his daughter, Susa Young Gates:

> People would have had in those grinding years of toil, too few holidays and far too little of the spirit of holiday-making which is the spirit of fellowship and socialised spiritual communion, but for Brigham Young's wise policy. He manifested even more godly inspiration in his carefully regulated social activities and associated pleasure than in his pulpit exercises. He kept the people busy, gave legitimate amusements full sway and encouraged the cultivation of every power, every gift and emotion of the human soul.[20]

In an article that appeared in the *Utah Musical Times* not long after Brigham Young's death, the authors list once again the positive aspects of dancing that were envisioned by President Young and that more or less reflect the popular attitudes toward dancing at the time:

> A social dance is certainly one of the best things to drive away dull care, disperse sour and sombre feelings, dispel melancholy thoughts, banish hypochondriacal ideas, and infuse in a company a spirit of cheerfulness, geniality, affability, and kindly courtesy. It will also do much to abolish bashfulness, awkwardness, and boorishness in social intercourse . . . and to impart a more satisfying self-possession and ease and repose of deportment, and a very desirable self-collectedness of manner, when in company. . . . Further than this, dancing is physically a most beneficial exercise, and if people generally were accustomed to dance frequently, but in moderation, there would not be so much heard of terrible suffering from indigestion, biliousness would be banished, and dyspepsia would measurable be destroyed.[21]

Saints were "encouraged to conduct and attend their own dances,"[22] rather than to go to the places where public dances were held. In this way, they could control the atmosphere and thereby let the act (or art) of dancing be unhindered in filling its role as a wonderful means of recreation and wholesome social interaction. To be sure, controversy about dancing continued, even down into this century, but usually centered on whether the conditions of Brigham's pronouncements were being met in actual practice.

DANCING IN UTAH TERRITORY

After the pioneers arrived in the Great Salt Lake Valley and began spreading out into numerous settlements, dancing continued as a favored activity. Mary Isabella Horne, who arrived in the valley in October 1847, three months after the first pioneers, notes that the first year was hard, but during the second year, "we had more time for amusements . . . , having our social parties, dancing parties, etc."[23]

The celebration dance on the Twenty-fourth of July 1868 in Coalville was typical of celebrations in territorial Utah:

> At daybreak the citizens were serenaded by the brass and martial bands. At nine o'clock everyone was at the Church where speeches, singing and oration finished the forenoon program. At 2 P.M. dancing commenced and continued until the grey morning light dawned. All was peace and joy.[24]

In keeping with Brigham Young's stated views about proper atmosphere, the pioneers strove to make their celebrations and their dances "harmonious," "well-ordered," and "conducted with decorum and propriety." Dances were opened and closed with prayer. A floor manager was employed to make things go smoothly—limiting the number of dancers to the space available and making sure that everyone who wanted to had a chance to dance. He was also arbitrator, arbiter, and occasionally bouncer as he sought to keep civility at a proper level. Sometimes dances were stopped because of unruly or untoward behavior.[25]

The sociality and community spirit engendered by dancing made the activity even more desirable. In a letter to his sister in England, John Barker writes, "We have been to several dancing parties and expect to go to more this winter, for all in the town mix together and enjoy each others company & friendship."[26]

Dances were for the whole family; so that no one need stay at home, even babes in arms were brought and put to sleep in bedrooms, on benches, or even in beds made on the floorboards of a carriage or wagon: "Often a lady was compelled to leave the floor—her baby was crying. No mother remained at home on account of children, except in cases of sickness. Babies were brought along and beds were arranged on seats with coats and shawls for coverings."[27] In this setting, there was no generation gap—children learned about being part of the community and the adult world and its expectations for them in the future. They also picked up a sense of dancing—its forms and steps.

Important elements of dancing included knowing the proper steps and the etiquette associated with dancing, such as properly asking a partner to dance and giving a correct thank-you. As early as 1850, Brigham Young asked George Wardle to conduct a dancing school so people would get proper training in the art of dancing. A wheelwright by trade, Wardle had been an "ardent student of music in his native England," and thus equipped, he began instruction, first in Marcy Thompson's log cabin[28] and later in a dance hall he constructed in 1851 on Second West between North and South Temple. The hall was a social center for a number of years,[29] and President Young and other leading Church authorities were among Wardle's students.[30] Eventually, President Young asked Wardle to go to Provo to start a dancing school and later to go to Midway for the same reason.

Knowing the proper dance steps was important, and, in order to enable everyone to participate, a knowledgeable person commonly took time at a dance to teach the steps. As a resident of early Kanab reports, "Edwin Ford, who after 1873 played his violin at all dances, also called for the cotillions. It is said he expected the participants to dance the figures correctly, and if anyone made a mistake he would stop the music, give instructions, and then begin the music again."[31]

Though whole families attended community dances, on special holidays such as the Fourth or Twenty-fourth of July, Christmas, or New Year, an afternoon dance was often held just for children. During the 1876 Fourth of July celebration in Cedar City, there was "dancing by the children in the afternoon and by the adults in the evening. Peace and good order did everywhere abound throughout the whole day."[32] Of the same day in Paragonah, an observer writes, "We had a very pleasant celebration of the Fourth. . . . Dancing commenced at 1 o'clock for the children, and in the evening adults indulged in the same way, which was kept up until a late hour. The whole affair went off very pleasantly."[33] Another diarist in Mt. Carmel in Kane County wrote:

> At two P.M. the little folks assembled and occupied a few hours in dancing. Then they gave way for the more elderly ones, who occupied the time to good advantage until midnight when the dance was dismissed and all went home in peace, feeling well satisfied.[34]

While children's dances were for the young ones' amusement, they were also viewed by Church authorities as an opportunity to teach the steps as well as proper dancing manners and etiquette to the children. In a letter to the officers of the children's Primary Association in Farmington, Aurelia Spencer Rogers, then the president of the association, requests such instruction: "I regret very much not being able to attend the children's party, knowing they will have a fine time, especially if they observe good order. And to have order, there should be some regulations in regard to their dancing."[35] She then lays out in some detail a number of such regulations, which, if followed, would teach the children proper dancing habits and manners.

In a reminiscent account, Emma B. Lindsay remembers the setting in which Brigham Young conducted dances and also mentions his abilities as a dancer:

> During the holidays, I well remember my father taking my sister Rebecca and me to a dance at the old Social Hall on State Street at Salt Lake City. . . . I remember seeing President Brigham Young, his fine appearance and how he danced. He was very light on his feet and good at dancing. I also remember the order maintained during the dance.[36]

Emmeline B. Wells notes that during President Young's visits to the large home of Isaac Chase "there would soon be a Cotillion, Money Musk, Sir Roger de Coverley, or a Schottish Reel. Pres. Brigham Young was a famous dancer, and certainly one of the most graceful pictures of all those popular men of the olden time."[37]

As a child in Nephi, Utah, in the 1860s, Charlotte Evans Adams was thrilled when, at a party given in honor of his visit to that town, President Young "asked her to dance with him for he was such a graceful dancer, executing the intricate figures of the Lancers, quadrille, and Schottische so beautifully."[38] With regard to the benefits of dancing, the famed English traveler Richard Burton notes that among the Mormons "dancing seems to be considered an edifying exercise. The Prophet dances, the Apostles dance, the Bishops dance."[39]

Dancing Venues in Pioneer Utah

Lack of a large, enclosed space for dancing did not deter the pioneers from dancing. If nothing else was available, they would dance in the open air, but as time and means became available, they built various structures either specifically for dancing or for a variety of purposes, including dancing.

Boweries. Of necessity, dancing was an open-air activity during the trek across the plains, but as dancing continued to be a favored activity in the Great Salt Lake Valley, the Saints began to find more agreeable venues for their dances. The earliest pioneers in the Salt Lake Valley built two boweries—large, temporary structures that were basically arbors. The boweries were used for public functions, including dancing. The first notable event celebrated by the Saints in the valley was the "harvest feast" of 1848, held at the "second" bowery at about Fourth West and Fourth South. The harvest feast was a celebration and dance to give thanks for the fruits of the Saints' labors of the first year in their new home.

> On the 10th of August we held a public feast under a bowery in the center of our fort. This was called a harvest feast; we partook freely of a rich variety of bread, beef, butter, cheese, cakes, pastry, green corn, melons, and almost every variety of vegetable. Large sheaves of wheat, rye, barley, oats and other productions were hoisted on poles for public exhibition, and there was prayer and thanksgiving, congratulations, songs, speeches, music, dancing, smiling faces and merry hearts. In short, it was a great day with the people of these valleys, and long to be remembered by those who had suffered and waited anxiously for the results of a first effort to redeem the interior deserts of America, and to make her hitherto unknown solitudes "blossom as the rose."[40]

Private Homes. As new pioneer settlements began to be established farther and farther from Salt Lake City, the settlers took with them the same expectations for dancing and other social occasions. Realizing the importance of entertainment as a means of keeping people's spirits high and of promoting community social cohesion, President Young chose the personnel for each pioneer company with a careful eye to providing a full complement of skills necessary for its success. Thus he selected not only a variety of artisans, but musicians as well; groups of Saints sent to settle an outlying area were seldom without a fiddler.

With few resources at first, dances and other parties took place in private homes. In fact, in both Salt Lake City and in the outlying communities, commodious homes of leading citizens furnished most of the dancing space. In Salt Lake City, the home of Isaac Chase, built in Liberty Park (ca. 1853–54), was a very popular site for parties and dancing, especially among young people. According to Emmeline B. Wells, the Chases were warm and hospitable hosts and entertained many guests and visitors, young and old, some of whom would just drop by:

> At that time there were not many houses convenient for dancing, but the big kitchen, or living room at Chases', with its wide open fireplace, and big stout andirons with blazing logs across in wintertime and the great crane swung high, and the pot-hooks with kettles hanging, was a bright picture and when one came in cold from the sleigh, the fireplace was in itself like a great welcome. Sister Chase always had the spinning wheel, with some soft, white rolls, and the old fashioned reel with a skein of yarn on it, and the table put out of the way somewhere. The floors had no carpet to be removed, nor any waxing to be done, and if the fiddlers came, or even one, Jesse Earl, was sure to be there if there was to be a gathering of young folks, and it seems to me that John Gleason had a fiddle, too. . . . There were no restrictions about time, and it was often in the early morning hours when the young people wended their way homeward. [41]

Pioneer Emma B. Lindsay of Taylorsville records that "many dances were held at our home; the only music was that of the violin. Sometimes step dances were part of our entertainment. We also held dances at Wm. Parker's home. One room was all that they had. When the dance was held, beds and other furniture were taken out." She also remembers other dances when "a mid-night supper was served and then dancing continued a while after. Some of the girls who had two dresses would change them at this point, and then finish the dance in a different attire."[42]

The dances often included not only the usual ones done in the United States, but also "'step dancing' or later, 'Toe dancing' when some of the old dances learned in Scotland or Ireland were danced by those who had learned them in their childhood."[43] In Tooele the Saints danced even when a fiddler was not available:

> The first dancing party occurred in Bishop Rowberry's house on Christmas Day 1849. Josiah Call whistled and someone had a Jews Harp, and that furnished the music. In the summertime a bowery was built and especially on the evenings of July Fourth and July 24th

they danced, sometimes all night. The dances were opened and closed with prayer.[44]

This reference to the music for the dance being furnished by a whistler is echoed by Charles R. Bailey in the following note in his diary in 1859:

In Wellsville we had a dance on Christmas night and New Years also; our meetinghouse was very small—14x16 and our music was very scarce only one violin and there was too many for the house so we divided up and one part went to Brother John Maughan's house but when we got there we had no music so I was called to make music for the dance being a good whistler. I had to do my best. John Maughan and Brother Frank Gunnell did the calling. We had a good time all the same but in those days I could make as good music as a flute or piccolo.[45]

Dancing was such an important social event that some people even built their homes with one especially large room to accommodate dancers. Josie Patterson notes that her father built such a home in Salt Lake City before being called to go to Arizona.[46] Aaron Johnson, the first bishop of Springville, Utah, who settled the area with some thirty other families, "built a larger adobe house in the spring of 1852 . . . [that] was the only place for several years that was large enough for meetings, dances and public gatherings."[47] "During the winter of 1852–53, . . . Johnson told the boys that if they would furnish fuel and lights, his large front rooms could be used for dancing."[48] They immediately organized some sleds to carry the wood and after several trips to the forest had gathered a number of cords of firewood. Myrtle H. Conover records:

Levi Curtis secured the "Assembly Rooms" for cotillion parties which were held weekly during the winter. Levi and James O'Banion were the fiddlers. Old and young would gather for dancing; everybody came early and left about the midnight hour. The bedrooms opening from the hall were generally filled with babies snugly tucked away, while the mothers enjoyed the dance. . . . The huge fireplaces at either end of the hall were piled high with dry cedar fagots, the flames from which, seemingly endowed with the spirit of the dance, leaped and danced up the chimneys with a roar that laughed the winter blasts to scorn. Candles held in place by three nails driven into wooden brackets were ranged high along the walls. . . . Tickets were paid for in any kind of produce that the fiddlers could be induced to accept. Usually a couple of two-bushel sacks could be seen near the door, into which the dancers deposited their contributions. . . . The New Year of 1853 was danced in with extra ceremony; more candles were furnished and another fiddler, William Smith, procured.[49]

The townspeople of Clarkston, on the Bear River, also contributed to a private home to make it suitable for dancing. Catherine H. Griffiths notes that in 1863 "when the people first settled Clarkston, they didn't have any place for public gatherings. William Steward had the largest house in the settlement so the citizens told him that they would put in a lumber floor if he would let them use it for dances. This he did and the dancing began."[50]

Further south, in Beaver, John Mathews "built his home knowing that he would be called upon to offer it for such purposes [dancing]. He built partitions between certain rooms that could easily be moved, making a larger space for dancing and other functions. Needless to say, many parties were held here."[51] When homes were used for dancing, the furniture and carpeting were all moved out, leaving room for one or two squares. Often the fiddler would stand in the doorway so that people in two or more rooms could hear the music.[52]

In the small community of Washington, near St. George, dance parties were held at private homes "until the large meeting house was built in 1877. Bishop Covington's home had two stories; the upper story, which consisted of one big room with a fireplace, was reached by an outside stairway; here dances could be held without people having to invade the privacy of Bishop Covington's living quarters."[53]

PUBLIC BUILDINGS. As settlements became more established, churches and schoolhouses were built, and they became the places for dancing. Though many were small and some had dirt floors, the buildings sufficed for a people who would have their entertainment. A typical story was recorded in the community of Fillmore, where they completed the new schoolhouse in late 1851, and everyone attended the first dance:

> It had one big room and was made of cottonwood logs with a large fireplace in one end, rude benches made of split logs and a dirt floor that was sprinkled and swept before each social event. On the evening of the first dance, the whole town turned out to enjoy the event. The light from the fireplace and candles revealed the happiness these early pioneers felt in thus being able to enjoy a sociable time together. Their hardships were forgotten for the time as the musicians tuned up their fiddles and banjos. The evening

began with prayer, then Brother Hiram Mace, the dance master, taught some step-dancing to the younger people, after which everybody, old and young, joined in the square dancing.[54]

The occasional alternative to the dirt floor was one made of logs sawed lengthwise and laid closely together:

> Sometimes a dance would be given in some home which boasted a "puncheon floor." Most floors were the hard-packed earth; but when the good man of the house possessed both gumption and logs, he could set sawed-off logs close enough in the dirt to make quite a respectable flooring, called puncheon. Then came the dance! It was some job, you may be sure, to turn a "pigeon wing" on that uneven, bumped-up surface. But it could be done and it was done.[55]

Orderville offers a view of how dances took place in that communal settlement. The large dining hall, where the whole community ate their meals in three shifts (first the men, then women, then children),[56] became their dance hall. Charles William Carroll, who moved there in 1878, recalls:

> We had dances in the dining hall. We would shove all the tables against the walls and shave soap on the floor to make it smooth. . . . We had good music for our weekly dances. Brother Covington and Lon Cox would trade off with the fiddle. That was all the instruments we had, but we thought it was great.[57]

HALLS BUILT PRIMARILY FOR DANCING. In addition to the boweries, during the first years in the valley an enclosed public space large enough to accommodate dancing was constructed at some hot-water springs located several miles north of the temple lot. The area was known as Warm Springs:

> In the summer of 1850, a commodious bath house was built over the springs, boarding in one inner pool for women, an outer one for men and boys, with several private rooms fitted with wooden bath tubs. . . . The Bath House was dedicated with prayer and religious services on November 27, 1850. The morning service was followed by a great afternoon and evening celebration of feasting and dancing. . . . In front of this Bath House was an adobe cottage for the caretaker, and soon an immense dancing hall, also built of substantial adobe, was added, with a roomy dining-room and equipped with kitchens, all fitted with benches and tables. Public parties and even theatrical entertainments were given here, even after the completion of the Social Hall.[58]

The following July, Warm Springs was the site of a state ball and supper given in honor of the chief justice visiting the territory from the United States.[59] At least one wedding also took place there that year, as described by the bride, Rachel Simmons:

> We were married on the 18th of December 1851 in what was called the Warm Springs Bath House. It was at that time the largest and best place for large parties. It was a fashionable place. I had as nice a wedding as could be had in those days. . . . After the ceremony, we had supper, then danced until next morning.[60]

The most famous recreational facility of the early pioneers was the Social Hall, located on State Street in the center of Salt Lake City between South Temple and First South. It was a substantial building, measuring 40' x 80' and made of adobe with a shingle roof. The ground floor was used for theatricals and was built with a sloping floor leading down to the stage. The basement floor, on the other hand, was designed for dancing, parties, and banquets. The hall was formally opened and dedicated on New Year's Day 1853, with Heber C. Kimball calling the meeting to order and Amasa Lyman offering the dedicatory prayer. There were congratulatory speeches, musical numbers, and recitations, but "a ball was the main feature of the evening."[61]

Courtesy LDS Church Archives

Streetcar at the Warm Springs bathhouse, ca. 1875. Built in 1850, Warm Springs provided public facilities for bathing and soon after for dancing as well.

Courtesy BYU Archives

Social Hall, Salt Lake City, 1858. A ball was the highlight of the dedication of the Social Hall in 1853. The basement was designed for dancing, and the ground floor was used for theatricals.

On November 29, 1855, a special dance was held in the Social Hall to welcome back missionaries returning from foreign lands. Jedediah M. Grant of the First Presidency directed the proceedings, noting that

> those missionaries that cannot dance, and do not try, we shall consider have not fulfilled their missions this evening. He then led off in the dance, which he executed in right good earnest. The whole company caught the electric spark, and "good earnest" characterized the exercises of the evening. . . . When the evening was well advanced, and the party had exercised themselves much in the dance, President Grant addressed the returned missionaries.[62]

As communities developed throughout the territory, buildings dedicated primarily to public entertainments gradually began to be built. Following the Warm Springs model, some were built next to water and featured trees, flowers, and lawns in garden settings where people could enjoy the natural beauty while partaking of good food and dancing. Many resorts with dancing pavilions were built around Utah Lake at American Fork, Pleasant Grove, Geneva, and Lincoln Beach, to name a few.

Near Manti in 1873, Daniel Funk even created a man-made lake by diverting the water of Six Mile Creek into what was known as the Arapene Valley. Though it presented a number of engineering problems, in the end his lake covered seventy-five acres at a depth of twenty feet. In this previously dry area, he planted six thousand fruit and shade trees, as well as a variety of vegetables, notably sugarcane and melons. He built dance pavilions both on shore and over the lake where "the hard working people of southern Utah" could come for wholesome entertainment.[63]

In nearby Sevier county, a family-enterprise, do-it-yourself dance hall was constructed by musician Lars Nelson (later Neilson) in the mid-1880s. He had grown "tired of playing for entertainments in boweries, hay barns, log cabins, churches and large front parlors."

> The dance hall was a modest frame building about 100 feet long and 40 feet wide, facing west, overlooking the pasture lands. . . . The dance floor was made of smooth planed boards on which generous amounts of candle wax was whittled, then polished to a slick gloss by the sliding, dancing feet. . . . The place was reached by following a narrow dirt road which hugged the curving mountainside from Glenwood to Annabelle.
>
> The first ball was a rousing success. Curious people who had watched the building proceedings with growing interest came from surrounding towns, filling the hall to capacity. The hillside was covered with wagons, buggies, horses and mules. A strict dance manager allowed no rough antics to be carried on . . . although sometimes the quick quadrilles, whirling and jumping polkas might be considered rough. People came expecting amusement, and the Neilsons' reputation as entertainers fulfilled their expectations.[64]

This dance hall was unique in that the music was provided entirely by Lars and his family. Their antics and sheer musicianship contributed substantially to the hilarity and the entertaining atmosphere of the dances.[65]

One dance hall with a singularly unique building feature was the American Fork Opera House built in 1883. It was modeled somewhat after the Salt Lake Theater, built in 1862, and was constructed in a T-shape with each part measuring 40' x 80'.

> [The] unique feature of the building was the movable floor which could be raised and lowered to accommodate the particular type of entertainment. . . . One end of the floor swung on a mammoth hinge secured in the front section of the foyer. Huge iron screw jacks,

Courtesy BYU Archives

Saltair, ca. 1897–1900. The queen of all early Utah entertainment facilities was located on the south shore of the Great Salt Lake. Saltair advertised the world's largest dance floor.

operated by hand, raised the opposite end of the floor flush with the stage area, thus permitting the full expanse of the stage floor and auditorium to be used for dancing and similar entertainments. When theatricals were to be presented, the auditorium floor was lowered on the same jacks.[66]

Opera houses were built in a number of other communities as well, and at least one, the St. George Opera House, shared the same feature of a moveable floor.[67]

In 1893 the queen of all pioneer entertainment facilities, Saltair, was built on the shores of the Great Salt Lake. It was the ultimate recreational resort for the area's citizens, and in size and scope it had no peer in the United States at that time. The dancing pavilion itself was 140' x 250', with a roof supported by an iron framework that left no pillars or other obstructions on the floor. A railway brought hundreds of recreation seekers to Saltair daily, and activities continued into the night, since the structure was "lighted with 1,250 incandescent and forty arc lights, giving the place a fairylike appearance as they were reflected in the placid waters of the lake on a calm summer night."[68]

PIONEER DANCE MUSIC

The music used in dancing consisted largely of traditional tunes from Scotland and Ireland, where they had accompanied reels, jigs, and hornpipes. These were lively tunes in either duple time 2/4 (2/4 or 4/4) or triple time (6/8), and they were played primarily on the fiddle, accompanied occasionally by whatever other instruments might be available, including the accordion, flute, guitar, reed organ, harmonica, or banjo. In the absence of any of these instruments, whistling or even humming through a comb covered with paper might be employed. In Salt Lake City were several wind bands that often provided music for dancing.

The fiddle, however, was undoubtedly the instrument of choice because of its large repertoire of tunes and because, as an instrument, it offered those things most necessary for dancing: a clear and carrying sound; droning, which gave a semblance of harmony; and, just as importantly, a driving rhythm that gave dancers the impetus to move their feet.[69] To be sure, fiddlers ranged tremendously in talent from those who could merely scrape out a tune to those whose music had the touch of the artist. But the sound of a fiddle worked magic in the minds of those who loved a dance; the better the fiddler, the more profound the inspiration for dancing and its enjoyment.

With the appearance of dancing masters came collections of music to be used, a number of which are still extant. Many of them contain tunes transcribed for the piano and show a simplified melody line with a rudimentary harmony line in the bass clef. This description does not mean the music of the pioneers was simple—traditional fiddle tunes that survive today show a singular musical sophistication, often featuring interesting tunes as well as rhythmic and ornamental nuances that almost defy notation.

A TOUCH OF ELEGANCE ON THE FRONTIER

The lively nature of the dances—reels, jigs, two-steps, marches, and quadrilles—required lively music. Little wonder then that one attractive aspect of dancing was the exercise it gave its participants. On the horizon, however, was a dance that was destined to have a great impact on the pioneers and bring to them both controversy and a touch of elegance that was lacking in the more vigorous forms of dancing. The dance was the waltz with its attendant set of variations.

Walk Along John to Kansas

A typical quadrille tune. Sometimes known as "Rabbit, Where's Your Mammy?" this tune features a nonstandard tuning. Transcription courtesy Larry V. Shumway.

The waltz arrived in the United States about the turn of the nineteenth century and soon became popular. However, it was met immediately with cries of outrage and shock at the untoward familiarity of a couple dancing in closed position, closely facing each other—especially if they were not married or were married to someone else. For some, including many social arbiters, the dance was simply vulgar. For the moralists and clergy, its consequences were more dire: "When the young gentlemen put their arms about the ladies' waists and whirled them about the room, the older generation warned the girls that they would lose all modesty and self-respect, and predicted where such intimacies would lead."[70] This kind of controversy followed the waltz wherever it went.

There was also a second type of criticism, not of the dance itself, but rather of the simplistic way in which it was being taught and danced. This criticism came from numerous dancing masters whose life's work had been to teach not only the dance steps, but more particularly the graceful use of the body while dancing. For them dancing was not just the proper steps, but rather a discipline to develop strength of muscle and grace of carriage and bearing, which in turn would lead to the cultivation of the social graces that attend people of culture. The waltz steps themselves were not difficult to learn, and upstart teachers of the waltz and the popular dance crowd seemed satisfied to learn only the steps. Thus, a whole host of the other important little things that were supposed to accompany dancing lessons—the cultivation of which led to airs and graces—were never learned, and this deficit was anathema to the traditional dancing masters.

The older Utah pioneers knew about the waltz and frowned on it as being in poor taste. To their generation, it was absolutely scandalous, but for the younger set it was an intriguing dance requiring strength and grace, but, more to the point, it allowed a new familiarity between the sexes as they danced. In his account of dances in the town of Fillmore in the 1850s, Dean Robison notes that in the first dances held in the newly completed schoolhouse "everybody, old and young, joined in the square dancing. Only dances that required the gentleman to take the hands or one arm of his lady were allowed. At this time waltzing was considered in poor taste, as it permitted too much familiarity between partners."[71] Sometime later, thanks to two young men who had spent some time in Salt Lake City, the waltz was introduced to Fillmore:

> Two lads, Wise and Leigh Cropper . . . had been to Salt Lake City attending school and were eager to demonstrate a new dance they had learned. . . . The Dan Olson Orchestra . . . played the music "Blue Danube Waltz," and the first waltz ever danced in Millard County was expertly executed by the two Cropper boys and their partners. It was the first time a boy had ever been allowed to take a girl in his arms when dancing. Before the evening was over, everyone in the hall had tried the new dance.[72]

There were frequent admonitions from the pulpit against the waltz, and in many places it was censured and stopped altogether.[73] An 1877 statement on round dancing was issued over the signature of President John Taylor in what was known as the "Epistle of the Apostles": "We do not wish to be too restrictive in relation to these matters, but would recommend that there be not more than one or two permitted in an evening."[74]

Obscured by all the raucous contentions over the waltz was the elegance of the music and of the dance itself when done well. Waltz music differed substantially from the lively tunes used for the reels and quadrilles. It was smoother flowing, sweeter sounding, and moved at a more graceful tempo, calling to mind the beauty of music rather than

Courtesy BYU Special Collections, Harold B. Lee Library

The Ether Blanchard family, Springville, Utah, 1902. *Left to right:* Achilles Blanchard, Ether and Sylvia Blanchard, and Margaret Goff. Achilles holds the homemade harp he constructed from a bicycle frame. Ether holds his fiddle. The instruments were important enough to the Blanchards to be included in this formal family portrait. George Edward Anderson, photographer.

a driving rhythm. The feeling of variety that the waltz music brought was as welcome as the dance itself.

Over a period of some years, resistance to the waltz and its music gradually faded, and soon after the turn of the century, as the pioneer period came to a close, the dance became universally popular. Its potential for showing "the graceful use of the body and the [proper] deportment of the ballroom"[75] became increasingly apparent, inspiring people's efforts to learn to waltz properly. In many areas, the ability to waltz well became almost a visual index of a person's attainment of social grace.

The pioneer mentality and sentiment regarding dancing continued well into the mid-twentieth century in numerous communities throughout the Great Basin. New dance forms, notably the foxtrot, displaced the older formation dances more and more, but older dances such as the Virginia Reel or schottische remained a part of an evening's activity. Such dances may be found in some communities even today. Their music and forms are still in the memory of the older generation, and sometimes they are trotted out on special occasions commemorating town history or for an old folks' party, conjuring up memories of stirring music and moving forms immersed in an atmosphere of warm communal and spiritual convivality.

Larry V. Shumway is Associate Professor of Humanities and Music, Brigham Young University. A longer version of this article that includes information on dances held during the stay at Winter Quarters and the trek across the plains was published in *BYU Studies* 37, no. 3 (1998): 6–50.

Notes

1. See also Ronald W. Walker, "Golden Memories: Remembering Life in a Mormon Village," in this volume.

2. See Thornton Hagert, program and liner notes, bibliography and discography for sound recording, *Come and Trip It: Instrumental Dance Music, 1780s–1920s*, no. 293 of the Recorded Anthology of American Music (New York: New World Records, 1978), 1–2.

3. Charles Hamm, *Music in the New World* (New York: W. W. Norton, 1983), 69.

4. Joseph E. Marks III, *America Learns to Dance: A Historical Study of Dance Education in America before 1900* (New York: Exposition Press, 1957), 25–26.

5. Marks, *America Learns to Dance,* 62.

6. Hamm, *Music in the New World,* 69. See also Andrew Karl Larson, *I Was Called to Dixie* (Salt Lake City: Deseret News Press, 1961), 458–60.

7. "To the Editor of the *Times and Seasons," Times and Seasons* 5 (March 1, 1844): 459.

8. "To the Editor," 459.

9. "To the Editor," 460.

10. Brigham Young, "An Epistle of the Twelve, to The Church of Jesus Christ of Latter-day Saints:—Greeting," *Times and Seasons* 5 (October 1, 1844): 669.

11. It is not clear exactly when the Saints resumed dancing in Nauvoo, but Brigham Young records one interesting incident of dancing in the Nauvoo Temple on December 29, 1845:

> The labors of the day [in the temple] having been brought to a close at so early an hour, viz.: eight-thirty, it was thought proper to have a little season of recreation, accordingly Brother Hanson was invited to produce his

violin, which he did, and played several lively airs accompanied by Elisha Averett on his flute, among others some very good lively dancing tunes. This was too much for the gravity of Brother Joseph Young who indulged in dancing a hornpipe, and was soon joined by several others, and before the dance was over several French fours were indulged in. The first was opened by myself with Sister Whitney and Elder Heber C. Kimball and partner. The spirit of dancing increased until the whole floor was covered with dancers, and while we danced before the Lord, we shook the dust from off our feet as a testimony against this nation. (Joseph Smith Jr., *History of The Church of Jesus Christ of Latter-day Saints,* ed. B. H. Roberts, 2d ed., rev. 7 vols. [Salt Lake City: Deseret Book, 1971], 7:557.)

12. Elizabeth Haven Barlow, Autobiography, quoted in *Our Pioneer Heritage,* comp. Kate B. Carter, 20 vols. (Salt Lake City: Daughters of Utah Pioneers, 1958–77), 19:319.

13. For additional information about dancing among the early Mormons, see Karl E. Wesson, "Dance in The Church of Jesus Christ of Latter-day Saints, 1830–1940" (master's thesis, Brigham Young University, 1975); Leona Holbrook, "Dancing as an Aspect of Early Mormon and Utah Culture," *BYU Studies* 16, no. 1 (1975): 117–38; and Michael Hicks, *Mormonism and Music: A History* (Urbana: University of Illinois Press, 1989), especially chapter 5, "Going Forth in the Dance."

14. Brigham Young, in *Journal of Discourses,* 26 vols. (Liverpool: F. D. Richards, 1855–86), 1:30–31, March 4, 1852.

15. Brigham Young, in *Journal of Discourses,* 6:148–49, December 27, 1857.

16. Brigham Young, in *Journal of Discourses,* 2:94, February 6, 1853.

17. Brigham Young, in *Journal of Discourses,* 9:244, March 6, 1862.

18. Brigham Young, in *Journal of Discourses,* 8:178, September 9, 1860.

19. Brigham Young, in *Journal of Discourses,* 10:313, June 10, 11, 12, and 13, 1864.

20. Susa Young Gates, *The Life Story of Brigham Young* (New York: Macmillan, 1930), 266.

21. *Utah Musical Times* 2 (February 1, 1878): 169.

22. Dean Chesley Robison, "Utah Pioneer Recreation Centers," in Carter, *Our Pioneer Heritage,* 8:426.

23. Mary Isabella Horne, "My Pioneer Home," in Carter, *Our Pioneer Heritage,* 1:125.

24. "Celebrations in Utah Territory—1868," in Carter, *Our Pioneer Heritage,* 12:22.

25. See Larson, *I Was Called to Dixie,* 458–60; Kenner C. Kartchner, *Frontier Fiddler: The Life of a Northern Arizona Pioneer,* ed. Larry V. Shumway (Tucson: University of Arizona Press, 1990), 158–60.

26. John Barker, quoted in "Letters of John H. Barker," in Carter, *Our Pioneer Heritage,* 4:90; italics added.

27. "Lest We Forget the Pioneer Christmas," in Carter, *Our Pioneer Heritage,* 15:195.

28. "George Wardle—Musician," in Carter, *Our Pioneer Heritage,* 2:492.

29. Andrew Jenson, "Salt Lake City Sixteenth Ward," *Encyclopedic History of The Church of Jesus Christ of Latter-day Saints* (Salt Lake City: Deseret News Publishing, 1941), 751.

30. "George Wardle—Musician," 2:492.

31. "Kane County," in Carter, *Our Pioneer Heritage,* 8:470.

32. C. J. Arthur, "Centennial Celebrations," in Carter, *Our Pioneer Heritage,* 20:12.

33. "Centennial Celebrations," 20:12–13.

34. "Centennial Celebrations," 20:14.

35. Aurelia Spencer Rogers to President and counselors of the Primary Association of Farmington, n. d., quoted in "The Primary Association," in Carter, *Our Pioneer Heritage,* 15:162.

36. Emma B. Lindsay, "Christmas When I Was a Girl," in Carter, *Our Pioneer Heritage,* 20:186.

37. "Told by Emmeline B. Wells," in Carter, *Our Pioneer Heritage,* 14:535.

38. Charlotte Evans Adams, quoted by Jesse Archibald Atkinson in "Brigham Young—His Wives and Family," in Carter, *Our Pioneer Heritage,* 1:447.

39. Richard Burton, *The City of the Saints* (New York: Alfred A. Knopf, 1963), 253.

40. Parley P. Pratt Jr., ed., *The Autobiography of Parley P. Pratt,* 4th ed. (Salt Lake City: Deseret Book, 1985), 335.

41. "Told by Emmeline B. Wells," 14:534–35.

42. Emma B. Lindsay, quoted in "That They May Live Again," in Carter, *Our Pioneer Heritage,* 8:170.

43. "That They May Be Remembered," in Carter, *Our Pioneer Heritage,* 18:164.

44. "That They May Be Remembered," 18:164.

45. Charles R. Bailey, quoted in "That They May Be Remembered," in Carter, *Our Pioneer Heritage,* 18:159.

46. Matilda Josephine Anderson Patterson, "Personal Journal and Other Writings of Matilda Josephine Anderson Patterson," typescript, 3, copy in possession of author.

47. Venna A. Reese, "Utah County," in Carter, *Our Pioneer Heritage,* 1:163.

48. Myrtle H. Conover, "Springville," in Carter, *Our Pioneer Heritage,* 8:488.

49. Conover, "Springville," 8:488–89.

50. Catherine H. Griffiths, quoted in Ann Godfrey Hansen, *Wood Stoves and Woolen Stockings* ([Salt Lake City]: Covenant Communications, 1991), 113.

51. "Pleasure—Beaver, Utah," in Carter, *Our Pioneer Heritage,* 8:455.

52. Merle Kartchner Shumway, personal communication with author, summer 1987.

53. Larson, *I Was Called to Dixie,* 458.

54. Robison, "Utah Pioneer Recreation Centers," 8:473.

55. Gates, *The Life Story of Brigham Young,* 253.

56. Charles William Carroll, quoted in Elsie C. Carroll, "Stories of Long Ago," in Carter, *Our Pioneer Heritage,* 1:192–93.

57. Carroll, quoted in "Stories of Long Ago," 1:192–93.

58. Gates, *The Life Story of Brigham Young,* 262.

59. Orson F. Whitney, *History of Utah,* 4 vols. (Salt Lake City: George Q. Cannon and Sons, 1892), 1:459.

60. Rachel Emma Woolley Simmons, "Journal of Rachel Woolley Simmons," in *Heart Throbs of the West,* comp. Kate B. Carter, 12 vols. (Salt Lake City: Daughters of Utah Pioneers, 1939–51), 11:165.

61. "Social Hall," in Carter, *Our Pioneer Heritage,* 5:216.

62. George D. Watt, "Returned Missionaries' Party in the Social Hall," *Deseret News,* December 19, 1855, 325.

63. Ingrid Jolley Stringham Hardy, "Funk's Lake—Sanpete County," in Carter, *Our Pioneer Heritage,* 2:188–89.

64. Lela N. Fackrell, "Sevier County," in Carter, *Our Pioneer Heritage,* 8:477–78.

65. Fackrell, "Sevier County," 8:478.

66. Relva Booth Ross, "Recreation—Utah County," in Carter, *Our Pioneer Heritage,* 8:485–86.

67. Mabel Jarvis, "Utah's Dixie," in *An Enduring Legacy,* comp. Lesson Committee, 12 vols. (Salt Lake City: Daughters of Utah Pioneers, 1977–89), 4:363.

68. "Great Salt Lake Beach Resorts," in Carter, *Our Pioneer Heritage,* 2:152–53.

69. The term *fiddle* is generally understood as an old generic term for bowed lutes, in this case for violins. There is no substantial difference between a fiddle and a violin, though occasionally the former are homemade and thus of a somewhat rougher workmanship. "Fiddling" refers specifically to a style of playing the violin in which there are techniques, particularly in the bowing, which account for the fiddle "sound." Fiddle music is characterized by pervasive offbeat accents and often droning, which is playing the melody on one string with the bow also touching another, usually open, string.

70. Marks, *America Learns to Dance,* 76.

71. Robison, "Utah Pioneer Recreation Centers," 8:473.

72. Robison, "Utah Pioneer Recreation Centers," 8:473.

73. See Davis Bitton, "Those Licentious Days: Dancing among the Mormons," *Sunstone* 2 (spring 1977): 16–27.

74. Quoted in Larson, *I Was Called to Dixie,* 461. The context of this quote was a set of rules laid down by the St. George Stake high council to govern dancing in the stake, one of which stated their opposition to "round dancing, and in regard to waltz, schottische, or polka, or any other dance embracing the features of these dances" (461).

75. Marks, *America Learns to Dance,* 76.

Some of the Native and Introduced Wild Plants
Gathered by the Pioneers

Common name	Genus and species	Location and other information
Greens, bulbs		
dandelion	*Taraxacum*	perennial, in lawns and waste places
lamb's-quarter*	*Chenopodium album*	annual, usually 1–2 ft. high, valleys and foothills, disturbed sites
lucerne	*Medicago*	valleys and foothills, disturbed sites
pigweed	*Amaranthus*	annual
redroot	*Amaranthus retroflexus*	annual, 1–6 ft. high, in cultivated fields and waste places
sego lily	*Calochortus nuttallii*	5–6 inches below surface, on dry plains, foothills, and canyons, 4,400–7,000 ft.
stinging nettle	*Urtica dioica (or breweri)*	1–6 ft. high, along rivers and streams and in other wet sites, in mountains
turnip	*Brassica campestris*	in waste places, escaping from cultivation
wild onion	*Allium*	in dry soil in open fields, mountainsides
Fruits		
chokecherry	*Prunus virginiana (or melanocarpa)*	shrub or small tree, 10–16 ft., along streams, valleys to upper canyons
currant	*Ribes aureum*	5–12 ft. high, along streams and fence rows, occasionally in foothills
elderberry	*Sambucus coerulea*	bushy or treelike, 6–15 ft. high, in mountain valleys
gooseberry	*Ribes inerme*	along mountain streams
ground-cherry	*Physalis longifolia*	perennial, 1–3 ft. high, stream banks and rich soil
raspberry	*Rubus leucodermis*	2–6 ft. high, in mountain valleys
serviceberry	*Amelanchier alnifolia*	shrub, 3–15 ft. high, in dry soil on hillsides
strawberry	*Fragaria*	perennial, rich soil in light shade in meadows and along streams, some species in mountain meadows
wild rose (hips)	*Rosa*	bushy or climbing shrubs, some species in mountains

*Also called pigweed.

SOURCES: A. O. Garrett, *Spring Flora of the Wasatch Region,* 5th ed. (Salt Lake City: Stevens and Wallis, 1936), Richard J. Shaw, *Vascular Plants of Northern Utah: An Identification Manual* (Logan: Utah State University Press, 1989), and Stanley L. Welsh and Glen Moore, *Utah Plants: Tracheophyta,* 3d ed. (Provo, Utah: Brigham Young University Press, 1973).

"I Have Eaten Nearly Everything Imaginable": Pioneer Diet

Jill Mulvay Derr

George Washington Brown, a member of Brigham Young's 1847 vanguard company, recalled how Shoshones in the Salt Lake Valley cautiously welcomed the newcomers with food. Initially, wrote Brown, "the Indians seemed to be afraid of us. . . . It wasn't many days before some of them came into camp and gave the men some dried service berries and crickets to eat."[1] Food would continue to be an important factor in Mormon relations with Utah's native peoples. Likewise, over the next twenty or thirty years, as Mormon settlers greeted companies of immigrants with everything from turnips and melons to plum cakes and feasts, food would mark the end of the pioneer journey and the beginning of relationships in a new land.

In a different sense than we ordinarily suppose, the way to a person's heart is often through the stomach. Eating may be a routine part of life, but because nourishment is absolutely essential, the study of food in any given culture takes us quickly beyond cook fires, gardens, bins, and cellars to the people themselves. For example, contemporary historians have studied the impact of the frontier and of technological advances on the American diet, but they have also considered such questions as the role of food in affirming social status, provoking domestic conflict, and defining secular and religious rituals.[2] The journals and reminiscences of Utah pioneers are filled with references to lacking, obtaining, preparing, sharing, and relishing food. This brief survey of pioneer diet reveals that food is a fascinating lens through which one can view Utah's pioneer men and women, a lens that might be used to much greater advantage by historians.

THE INITIAL STRUGGLE TO PROCURE FOOD

In their temporary settlements along the Missouri River during the winter of 1846–47, the Latter-day Saints had already experienced the difficulty of nourishing thousands of people in the wilderness. There they had gathered, hunted, planted, and traveled to frontier outposts to replenish the limited provisions they had brought with them. Similar patterns are evident in the initial settlement of the Great Basin. The advance pioneer company entered the Salt Lake Valley on July 22, 1847, with instructions from Brigham Young to begin planting immediately. On July 23, committees staked off an area 20 by 40 rods to plant beans, corn, and buckwheat; built a dam and cut irrigation trenches; mowed grass; and started a turnip patch. The next day, a five-acre potato patch was plowed, and seed potatoes planted. Two days later, corn was planted and irrigated. By July 31, a thirty-five-acre lot had been planted with corn, oats, buckwheat, potatoes, beans, and "garden seed."[3] Other committees attempted hunting and fishing but met with little success.

Mary Isabella Horne, who arrived in the Salt Lake Valley in October 1847, later summarized the Saints' difficulty procuring food during the first year or two in the Great Basin:

> The cattle being worked down were very poor. The beef had to be boiled all day to make it tender enough to eat. Our cow had to work in the yoke, and consequently went dry, so we had neither milk nor butter. I had to make gruel out of shorts for my children to break their bread in for supper and breakfast. We had a little meat for dinner, no vegetables, but a few segoes and parsnips which the boys dug.

She welcomed the chance to feast upon venison after someone shot a stray deer that had jumped the fence into the Old Fort. She knitted fishing skein for men who went to the Jordan River to fish and wove together willows and brush to fence off a garden in front of her dwelling, where she planted flowers and vegetables, which "finally grew." At first, she recalled, "very few vegetables could be eaten; they must go to seed for another year." Melon, pumpkin, and squash vines were productive, so, wrote Mary Isabella, "we had melon preserves and squash butter. For coffee, beans, peas, and sliced carrots were used, with a little molasses boiled in it for sweetening. In this way, everyone kept busy. We had only time to make friendly calls on each other to see how we succeeded under difficulties."[4]

Mary Isabella also testified that "the Lord preserved us in health in a wonderful manner during those trying times." She remembered when "swarms of crickets took possession of our fields, covering our grain like a black pall. Starvation stared us in the face." She witnessed the miraculous coming of gulls

> to save our crops in this barren valley, where we were one thousand miles from any supplies in the East, and seven hundred miles from the west. We must have starved if the Lord had not sent us deliverance. When the crops were gathered we held a grand Harvest Home, all joined in praise and thanksgiving to our Heavenly Father for His protection and blessings upon us. Our crops were light, still we had some to spare to the emigrating Saints when they came in. Wheat was traded for flour and a few groceries, and with a little milk and butter occasionally, and our melon preserves, helped us out the next year, though we had to be very economical to make our provisions last until another harvest.[5]

Horne's description reflects the comments of dozens of other Utah pioneers with regard to how they procured food and what they ate. Their diaries and reminiscences indicate that they gathered wild roots, bulbs, and greens when food was scarce; usually struggled to get enough flour; raised vegetables and fruits and processed many of their own foods; ate the meat of domestic and wild fowls and animals as well as fish; and suffered severe crop failures due to grasshoppers, crickets, and drought. The pioneers cooperated and shared with friends and neighbors and often with strangers, and they felt and acknowledged the protecting hand of the Lord in providing them with food.

Irregular Harvests

The pioneer experience with food was complex and irregular. Some communities were plagued by drought or grasshopper infestations when others were not. Plentiful harvests in any community might follow or be followed by severe shortages. For example, after the settlers' difficulties during the first two years of settlement, the harvest of 1850 was abundant and increased each of the following four years. Susannah Clark wrote to her mother from Pleasant Grove in October 1851:

> We are all well and enjoying the blessings of a new world, with plenty around us to eat and plenty to spare. . . . We have been blessed with raising a good crop this year. We raised fourteen acres of good wheat, which will make about 400 bushels, one acre of oats (35 bushels), two acres of corn (60 bushels), half an acre of potatoes (100 bushels), half an acre of squash and pumpkins (10 wagon loads), fifteen bushels of beets and other vegetables in proportion. George has raised all this himself, excepting harvest.[6]

Wild Plants Used for Food

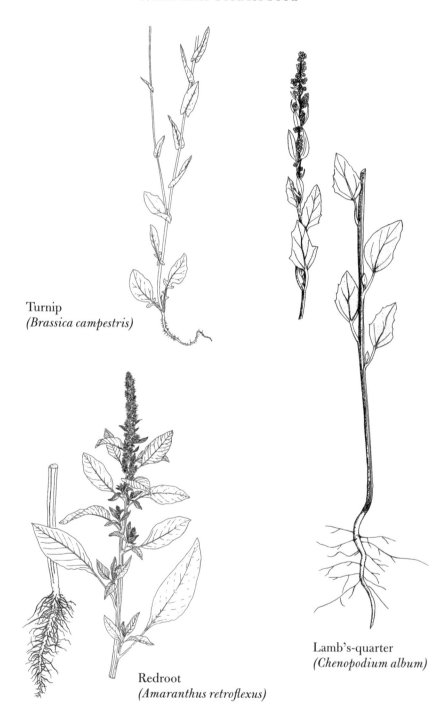

Turnip
(Brassica campestris)

Redroot
(Amaranthus retroflexus)

Lamb's-quarter
(Chenopodium album)

Polly Berthena Huntington, too, recalled that "by the time we reached Springville in 1852 the people who had already settled there had succeeded in raising sufficient grain and vegetables so that food was available for all. Fish were plentiful in the nearby streams and we did not suffer for the necessities."[7] By contrast, Christian Stucki remembered a time in Santa Clara when "many were facing starvation" because flour was so scarce. His father was sick from living for weeks on pigweed greens and roots, and Christian could remember seeing him go along the street, "so weak he had to take hold of the fence." When he arrived at the home of a neighbor who had just been to Salt Lake to trade dried peaches for flour, he received a sack of grain and a loaf of freshly baked bread, "which he tore to pieces and ate ravishly with trembling hands."[8] Long before the end of the century, however, Utah pioneers succeeded in building a varied and adequate food supply based on different combinations of gathering, home production and processing, hunting and fishing, and trading and buying.

The Gathering of Roots, Bulbs, and Greens

When food was scarce, pioneers like Brother Stucki gathered greens and roots as a necessity, whereas in times of plenty, these items were used to supplement other foods. Levi Jackman, who arrived with the pioneer company of July 1847, found himself short of rations and decided to search for the thistle roots he had seen local Indians eat. "I only regretted that I could not get enough of them. They tasted mutch like parsnip," he noted in his journal.[9] Isaiah Moses Coombs recalled that following the bad harvests of 1854–55, great care had to be taken to preserve the stores of grain. "Greens, wild roots, etc., were freely eaten by all classes so as to spin out the bread stuff until the harvest of '56."[10] According to William Rigby, bad harvests persisted in Lehi during 1856 and 1857, and as a result, he wrote, "my wife and I ate so many weeds during the summer that our skin became tinted with green."[11] Mary Henrie Cooper remembered that her mother would never eat pigweed and dandelion greens because she had "had to live on them for several weeks one time."[12]

When Barbara Gowans moved to Tooele with her parents and grandparents in 1856, wild greens were part of her diet. She recalled going with her grandmother "along the ditch where the willows grew to gather nettles to eat. She would tell me to grip them hard, then they would not sting." The family simmered the nettles three times in fresh water to make them edible. Barbara could "remember sitting down to eat nothing but greens. We used nettles, pigweed, and redroot."[13] Harmon Gubler recollected eating pigweed and lucerne during his childhood in Santa Clara. "We would walk for miles to find some of the lucerne so that we could have it to eat," he said.[14] One St. George family lived for six weeks on nothing but boiled lucerne "without even salt or pepper."[15] Others remembered gathering dandelion greens, lamb's-quarters, wild mushrooms, rose hips, turnips, onions, and artichokes. Isaiah Cox, whose family was among the early settlers of St. George, ate "wild cane which grew along the stream."[16]

The bulb of the sego would later be memorialized as the food which kept Utah's earliest settlers from starvation, and indeed dozens of pioneers recounted hungrily searching for sego and other roots.[17] "Mother told us one day that she didn't have a thing for us to eat," recalled Lorenzo Hadley, "so my brothers and I went out and dug segoes. Mother thought they would cook up like a potato but they didn't because they boiled all away and just made the water thick. We put salt on it though and lived on it for two weeks."[18] Some families found that boiling sego and other wild bulbs and roots in milk made a nourishing, healthful beverage.[19]

The same wild greens and roots that curbed hunger in hard times were in better times considered a delicacy. "We considered pigweed greens a des[s]ert," declared John Hyrum Barton, who grew up in Iron County.[20] "The Segos we children gathered and ate just as a delicacy," recalled David H. Cannon Jr., noting that "some people ate them at the table, prepared into some very tasty dishes."[21] Isaiah Cox dug sego bulbs and remembered that "another choice wild delicacy which we dug along the river bottom was the grass nut," similar to the sego bulb but larger.[22]

BERRY PICKING

For many pioneers, the gathering of wild berries was even more memorable than the gathering of roots, bulbs, and greens. "Before we could raise any fruit, the fields abounded with ground Cherries growing spontaneously, which we appreciated as a great favour from the Giver of all good," wrote Lucy Meserve Smith about her early years in Provo. Taking with her the two sons of her sister wives, she used to go before sunrise about a mile into the field and "pick a five galon can full of the precious fruit and go back in time to eat our breakfast." What the family did not eat, they sold "for a good price as fruit was scarce every where in the Territory."[23]

Wild Fruits Gathered by the Pioneers

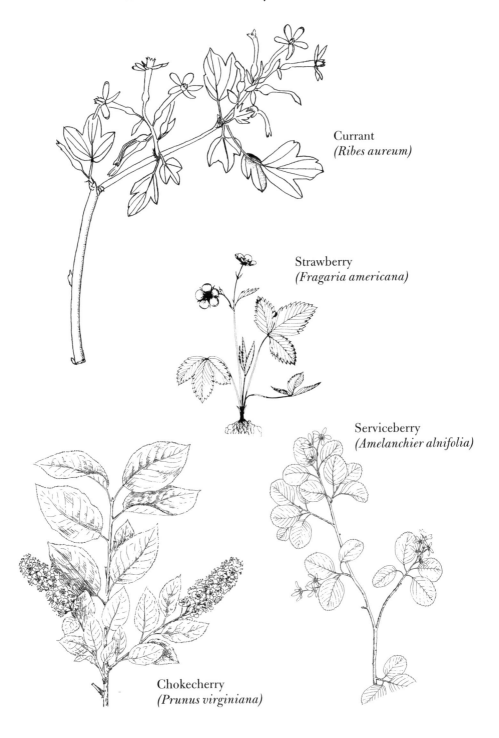

Currant
(Ribes aureum)

Strawberry
(Fragaria americana)

Serviceberry
(Amelanchier alnifolia)

Chokecherry
(Prunus virginiana)

"The whole country was covered with wild berries," recalled Hyrum Allen, "namely Service, Chokecherries, currants, Raspberries, Strawberries, gooseberries." They were "very thick" and of a "large and delicious flavor," he reported.[24] It took some time for settlers to become familiar with their various characteristics, however. Wilson Howard Dusenberry and a companion went to the mountains to help drag logs down and "picked a lot of elderberries as we were thirsty and hungry. Was as sick as I conveniently could be . . . learned not to eat raw elderberries."[25]

Many hands made lighter work of berry gathering. Catherine C. Larsen remembered:

> When we lived at Sevier, we used to go gathering wild currants, both kinds black and yellow . . . on the banks of the Sevier River. Then we would plan to pick berries in the canyon. A group of neighbors would get in the wagon and plan to be gone for the day. We would be off early and be up the canyon before it got too hot. There was a scramble for the best bushes. One could hear a merry buzz and see a group of busy people getting berries for the winters fruit supply. At noon we all put our lunch together and had a real picnic. Then we were soon back to work. Some of them would knock the fruit off on clothes lain under the bushes and others were busy gathering what they could by hand. As the sun neared the western hills we would put our things in the wagon and start for home. You could always hear a bunch of berry pickers as they neared home, their merry songs filled the clear evening air and this is how we made life worth while. These outings were of a necessity as well as part of our leisure time fun.[26]

The Pursuit of Something Sweet

Wild berries could be dried or made into preserves for winter use. Carl Evirt Jensen of Manti remembered gathering berries in a large bucket all summer long. His mother used molasses to make them into preserves. "Lots of times," he said, "we would have thirty gallons of molasses and preserves, in the cellar for winter use."[27] At first, sweet syrups were made by boiling down squash and beets. "We used to raise beets and made beet molasses for a sweet," Mary Stapley Bringhurst recalled, remembering with fondness the vinegar pies made on special occasions with a savory filling of vinegar, beet molasses, and flour.[28] Provo pioneers recorded washing sweet sap off the leaves of cottonwood trees along the Provo River—"sugar the thickness of a knife edge"—and boiling it down into syrup and sugar.[29] Juice also could be squeezed out of cornstalks and boiled down into syrup.

Sugar was the one item that pioneers consistently mentioned as unavailable or terribly expensive. One or two pounds of sugar would be made to last a family one year. "It was used only as medicine for the babies," Isaiah Cox explained.[30] Jane Sprunt Warner Garner recalled her mother returning from a three-day journey to Salt Lake City to get the family's "first sugar. It was brown sugar and carefully hoarded in a sugar bowl with a cloth tied over it, to be used only on special occasions, generally when company came and we children got very little of it."[31] Although scarce, brown sugar was cheaper and more readily available than white.

In the early 1850s, instead of importing large quantities of expensive sugar, Brigham Young and Church officials imported sugar-beet seed and machinery in hopes of setting up a sugar works in the area south of Salt Lake City now known as Sugar House. While the cultivation of sugar beets was no problem, the imported machinery could not be made to produce sugar, and by 1856 the enterprise was decidedly a failure.

Still intent on minimizing imports, President Young advocated production of sorghum cane, which settlers in several areas succeeded in raising. Syrup extracted from sorghum stalks (termed by some settlers "sugar cane") could be boiled down to thick molasses, and sorghum seed could be used as grain. "Many of the farmers made their own pure molasses from the sugar cane they raised," Alma Chambers remembered.[32] Fannie Ellsworth Greenwell described how "the juice was squeezed from the sugar cane by running it through large wooden rollers. The juice was then boiled in the large vats of tin. My father had three of these vats and the juice was boiled first in one and then in the second and then into the third vat for the last boiling. He had large homemade wooden spoons to stir the molasses with and wooden dippers to dip it with."[33] Fannie's father may well have been the owner of a sorghum mill, one powered by water, perhaps, or one with power "furnished by a boom pole, pulled with one horse." Such mill owners often took every tenth gallon for their work.[34]

Molasses was used in fruit preserves, pies, cakes, cookies, and candy. James J. Adams, who went to Parowan in 1851, said his family used molasses and "a little honey, when we got bees. I remember the first cake mother made out of sugar, we wouldn't hardly taste it, as it looked so different from what we were used to."[35] Until a sugar-beet factory was successfully established at Lehi in 1891, molasses "remained the principal source of sweet in the territory."[36]

GRAINS AND BREADS

While grain was rarely as scarce as sugar, the struggle to get it was a more conspicuous part of the pioneer experience in Utah. Families did what they could to obtain corn, wheat, or other grains and get them ground into meal or flour. For two centuries, corn had been the white settlers' first crop on the westering American frontier, just as it had been the staff of life for generations of Native Americans.[37] Likewise, corn was the first principal grain in most of Utah's early households. "I can well remember when flour was Ten Dollars per hundred, and hard to get at that," recalled Mary Julia Johnson Wilson. "Most everybody lived on corn meal, as we generally had better luck raising corn, and could even grind it in the old coffee mill, a household implement which most every family had in those days."[38] Graters could also be used for coarsely grinding corn. Manomas Lavina Gibson Andrus remembered that "after about the first year" her family could raise quite a bit of corn. However, her father "would always manage to have a little flour for her mother to have bread to eat because she was sick, but we children usually had to eat Johnny Cake."[39] Isaac H. Grace from Nephi remembered that "corn meal bread was used extensively to replace flour or white bread. This type of bread was not very well liked, but became a necessity over white bread." His mother often required that "each of the children must eat two slices of corn bread before they could have one slice of white."[40]

Some families raised their own wheat, but the majority seem to have bought wheat or flour or traded goods or services for these essential commodities. Men, women, and children also gleaned wheat after farmers had harvested their fields.[41] Millesant London Osborn Parks, who was separated from her husband, arrived in Utah in 1852 with her five children and settled in Bountiful, where she had some difficulty providing for her family: "She and her children would glean wheat then grind it between two flat rocks. She would then make biscuits, giving each child one and a cup of milk for the day's allotment of food."[42] During their first autumn in Payson, John Hafen's family "gleaned wheat, enough to furnish food for the winter," and the next fall, they gleaned some seventy-five bushels of wheat.[43] Elizabeth Horrocks Baxter's mother "often went barefooted and without breakfast to glean wheat from the fields and then at night would take her gleanings to be ground in the Taylor Mill at Riverdale. She had to crawl across a narrow bridge to get to the mill and had to wait her turn for grinding, yet she was happy in being able to bring home a pan full of flour as compensation for her day's work."[44] Henry Excell, who did not come to Utah until 1882, nonetheless remembered going to the fields and gleaning after the harvester "to get wheat for my winter flour. One fall six of us did this under a partner ship. Each night we would stack our daily gleanings in the same stack. When we finished gleaning, the thrasher thrashed our stack free, which turned out one hundred bushels of good wheat. The wheat was taken to the miller and ground into flour, and then divided in six equal parts."[45]

Barley was also frequently used. It was the first grain that ripened in the spring. "We had a small coffee mill and it went all around in the fort for the people to grind their barley in," recalled Olive Aldous. "Then they would make mush with it. I tried to eat a bowl full with milk on but I just couldn't swallow it."[46] When John Hock Hinton moved to Dixie with his family, they used their coffee mill to grind grain or sorghum cane seed for making bread. The mill was "also used by all their neighbors for the same purpose."[47]

Various alternatives were used to extend the wheat supply. Mixing cane seed with flour made it last longer. The mother of Margaret Warner Williams Wood learned from the Indians to dry roots and greens to grate and mix with flour for bread.[48] Utah's native peoples often ground crickets and grasshoppers to mix into bread or added sunflower seeds they had gathered. Martha Ann Clinger Boren remembered eating "bread made from bran with a very little flour mixed in to hold the bread together. When we could not get flour we made bread without. Often mother would scorch some flour which we would make into a mush. We thought this mush the best food, as the taste was different from the bran bread."[49] Pioneer families sometimes reserved some wheat whole rather than grinding it into flour, soaked the grain overnight in water, and then boiled it for cereal. Because boiled wheat took so long to chew and proved very filling, some families believed it extended their supply of wheat. Lumpy dick, made by slowly adding white flour to boiling water until it is thick like mush, was standard fare in many families and even relished when served with milk and sweetening.[50]

Homemade breads of all varieties lingered long in the memories of the pioneers. Saleratus (sodium or potassium bicarbonate), often washed from the soil, could be cleaned and mixed with sour milk or buttermilk for biscuits. Bread was sometimes made with "salt risin'," or corn meal mixed with hot water and salt and allowed to ferment. Other bakers used flour yeast, flour mixed with water and sweetener and allowed to ferment.[51] Mary Wilson recalled that "the neighborhood yeast center was a regular part of the community setup of those early days."[52] Apparently flour yeast could be a stimulating treat. Eleanor C. Bruhn composed in memory of her younger years an "Ode to Aunt Salena's Yeast."

> We recall our pail, with our flour to trade
> For the grandest beverage that ever was made.
> No doubt you're wondering—"what is the drink"
> But many'll agree when they stop to think;
> Whether bound for the west or for the east
> No drink is finer than Aunt Salena's yeast.
>
> Our mother would measure our sugar or flour,
> And send us forth, at the evening hour.
> We'd get our yeast for the homeward trip,
> And often, too often, we'd steal a sip.
> And when we'd return mother would say,
> "Salena's getting stingier day by day."[53]

Bread and cake were often baked in a "skillet," which might be better described today as "an iron Dutch oven or low built iron pot with three legs, which elevated it above the coals or fire, and with a sunk in heavy iron lid, tight-fitting, so that the coals could be placed on the top to insure the necessary heat."[54] Thomas Samuel Bladen remembered ending a tiring day's work with a hard, dry crust of bread, which he dipped in the ditch to soften, but he also recalled more plentiful times, when "they could have a spot of molasses in the center of their slice of bread . . . and they would eat all around the spot of molasses first and save the piece with molasses on for the last precious bite."[55] Jane Garner took to West Weber's one-room, white schoolhouse a lunch of bread and molasses. "I can tell you it tasted good by luncheon time when the molasses had soaked well into the bread," she affirmed.[56] Many families had bread spread with lard for lunch or ate a supper of bread and milk. Rosina Mueller Beacham remembered how her family would put their broken bread "in hot water and make a stew out of it." She also described the treat her father baked in their oven, which he had "made out of rocks." He "made a ladle out of a board about 14 or 16 inches in diameter. It was round and had a handle.

We would mix batter out of flour and cream, put some salt and chopped onions in it and an egg. We would put this on the ladle and slip it off into the oven. It made a very good cake," she recalled.[57]

Utah Vegetables and Fruit

According to historian Richard Hooker, Americans traditionally "disdained any vegetable cookery other than boiling,"[58] but early Utahns, like their eastern and western counterparts, still raised and consumed them. The annual Deseret State Fair in 1858 included a vegetable department, which "was not very full" but featured "excellent and choice" samples of squashes, pumpkins, beets, carrots, onions, potatoes, peas, beans, artichokes, tomatoes, corn, parsnips and other roots that were "not to be excelled in any country."[59] Some vegetables were stored in root cellars; others were preserved in brine. However, pioneers did not remember vegetables with the ebullient affection they reserved for Utah fruit.

Melons seem to have been raised with immediate success and were proudly presented as gifts to arriving immigrants and to President Brigham Young as he traveled throughout the territory.[60] Mary Isabella Horne credited Leonora Taylor with being "among the first, if not the very first, to plant apple and fruit seeds. The trees were transplanted on their lot in the Fourteenth Ward, where they grew to be very large trees, and produced fine large fruit of excellent flavor."[61] The Fruit Committee of the Deseret Agricultural and Manufacturing Society presented to the *Deseret News* a lengthy report of fruit exhibited at the 1858 State Fair, including such apple varieties as Sweet Mountain Home, Mountain Chief, Fall Spice, Lake, Hamilton Tart, Hamilton Sweet, Green Winter, Big Red, Geninton, and Yellow Bell Flower. The committee encouraged more cultivation of grapes, noted "fine specimens of Apricots," and recommended the fine flavor and reliability of the Pottawotamie strawberry. The plum and prune trees, it noted, "were few and the trees young." Pear trees were not mentioned in the report, but peaches were praised and the planting of peach pits recommended since "several who have tried it here . . . have produced trees far superior to the parent."[62]

When C. N. Teeter of Idaho visited Salt Lake City in August 1863, he was delighted to have arrived "just in the nick of time to get all the fruit I can eat." He rhapsodized about Utah peaches: "There is no end to the peaches this city affords, in fact the whole city with the exception of the business portion is one vast peach orchard, and they have just begun to ripen nicely and in size and quality they cannot very well be surpassed. I ate some yesterday that measured seven and a half inches in circumference."[63]

Many of Utah's pioneers fondly remembered the abundance of peaches. Harmon Gubler's family bought one and a half acres in Santa Clara that had "three rows of peach trees on it. . . . We used to dry peaches by the tons for use in the home."[64] Peach cuttings and apple peelings, like berry gatherings, were popular social occasions. "We had what we called peach cuttings," recalled Elizabeth Horrocks Baxter. "A bunch of us would gather together and pick the peaches and then cut them in half and spread them out on the roofs to dry. After our work was done we would have a dance or candy pull."[65] Mary Jane Lambson Davis recorded that her family "dried a great deal of fruit. I dried peaches and traded them at the store for the material to make my wedding dress." She noted that "it was a real luxury to have a dress of store goods."[66]

Preserving the precious harvest was critical for winter well-being. Berries, currants, peaches, apples, and other fruits were easily dried in the warmth of Utah's summer sun. "We would string the musk melons up on a long string and let them dry," recalled Harmon Gubler. "Some people used to dry water melons, but we never did because they would dry up to almost nothing."[67] Drying fruit had other disadvantages. "When the fruit, apples and peaches were out on the scaffolds, flies rested on them in clouds. It was the bane of dried fruit. And though they were thoroughly washed before they were used in the winter, the memory of that black cloud of flies would be forever bright," declared Hannah Hanson Huntsman of Fillmore. "Even after the people started to selling dried fruit to other places our consciences hurt us till we quit."[68] It is not clear whether or not the cheesecloth often used to cover drying fruit made the process less distasteful to Hannah.

In addition to being dried, fruit could be preserved in barrels, crockery, and tins. Polly Huntington of Springville recalled that "preserved fruit" was an important early industry there. Using sorghum as a preserving medium, the women would pack the preserves in fifteen-gallon barrels manufactured by Springville cooper Suminum Blanchard. "The settlers of Sanpete County were good customers for both the sorghum and the preserved fruit as they had been unable to raise sugar cane in their section," Polly recalled.[69] In Parowan the jars made by a local potter were used for preserving fruit.[70] Laura Smith Hadfield, whose family mostly dried fruit, recalled that her mother also "used to preserve fruit by putting it in cans, putting a lid on, and then sealing it with sealing wax."[71]

Inexpensive glass jars with self-sealing lids, invented in 1859 by John L. Mason, became widely available in the 1860s. Home bottling or canning quickly became popular among Utah women, in part perhaps because of contemporaneous Mormon emphasis on all forms of home production and manufacturing. For many families, picking or buying large quantities of fruit to bottle at home became a harvesttime ritual. Hannah McFarland Bingham of Ogden recalled how "at canning time the women would get together and drive out to North Ogden or Nob Hill . . . to get their peaches. . . . When they went to North Ogden, they would drive a span of mules and it would take them all day."[72]

John Henry Ward Lister remembered a cannery in St. George where settlers around the area purchased fruit. Eventually, other commercial canneries came to Utah. Commercially canned or tinned fruits, vegetables, and fish became increasingly available after the Civil War, but "consumers could not be certain that they were purchasing really safe cans with properly cooked foods until the 1920s."[73]

BARNYARD PROVISIONING AND MEAT PRESERVATION

John Hyrum Barton said his orchard in Paragonah "furnished every kind of fruit and berries that could be raised." "We always had good food," Barton remembered. He seems to have relished variety, boasting, "For meat I have eaten nearly everything imaginable: Pork, beef, mutton, chicken, vension [*sic*], duck, rabbit, sage hen, mtn squirrell, mtn hare, mtn sheep, antelope, horse meat, geese and even porcupine."[74] Meat, poultry, and fish—staples of the pioneer diet—were sometimes easier to come by than flour. On April 8, 1849, six months after her arrival in the Great Salt Lake Valley, Eliza Marie Partridge Lyman cooked her remaining flour and had "no prospect of getting any more untill after harvest." Nine days later, her brother Edward brought her "a quarter of beef [and] also drove our cow Frosty to us so that we can have some milk."[75] Utah's pioneers actually exported horses and cattle.[76]

Families able to acquire cows, pigs, or chickens stabilized their food supply. Thomas Briggs, who arrived in Utah in 1864, declared himself prosperous once he and his wife "had two fat pigs in the pen." Pigs must have been very popular since Briggs noted that at the April 1868 general conference President Brigham Young advised the Saints "to eat less pork and more fowl and fish."[77] Barnyard provisioning was widespread because it required neither intensive labor nor large tracts of land. "Everyone had their own cows and had what butter, cheese and milk they wanted. They raised their own pigs and had what meat they wanted," recalled Hyrum Allen of Huntsville.[78]

Harriet Maria Young Brown "just couldn't get along without butter," so when she and her husband helped settle the Muddy, "she dug a hole in the sand large enough to hold a milk pan, wet the sand, put a pan of milk in the hole and covered it with another pan. She then spread a canvas over it and kept the cloth wet. As soon as the cream came to the top, she skimmed if off and churned it into butter."[79] Others had butter with less effort, except for the tedious churning, and many remembered how plentiful butter, cheese, and eggs became over the years. Laura Smith Hadfield, who grew up in Farmington, affirmed that "food was no object . . . as we all had plenty. You couldn't even give eggs or butter away."[80]

With only three cows, Isaac Grace's family in Nephi did not have sufficient milk to make cheese, so they borrowed from a neighbor the use of his cows for a week in exchange for a small quantity of milk and butter, getting enough extra milk to "manufacture cheese on their homemade cheese press."[81] In October 1853, the editor of the *Deseret News* noted receiving "a cheese, from the MANTI SISTERS, of San Pete county; weight . . . we think from 75 to 85 lbs." He added: "God bless those dear sisters with life, health, and abundance of the good things of earth, so that next year they make cheese twice as BIG."[82] Butter, cheese, and eggs were important bartering commodities in many communities, where, as Olive Aldous recalled, "there was lots of exchanging going on but not much money in circulation."[83]

Annie Clark Kimball described her family's adobe home, built in the 1870s, with "its thirty-foot deep windlass well which kept food supplies deliciously cold when suspended near the crystal water in a strong basket."[84] The wells and springhouses could keep dairy products cool but were usually not cold enough to preserve meat. Because fresh meat attracted flies and rodents, it could not be stored near fresh milk and butter in an insulated milk house.[85] Fresh pork, mutton, and beef could be eaten immediately and might be shared with family and friends. It was a treat to be sure, but it could be quite tough—"tougher than a boiled owl," as Eliza Lyman described beef brought by a neighbor in 1849.[86] Without refrigeration beef could not be aged, and cooks, therefore, faced the challenge of making tough meat tender with carbonate of soda, perhaps, or by long and slow simmering.

Beef and pork could be preserved through salting down or through corning in a brine of salt, saltpeter (potassium nitrate), and brown sugar or molasses. Elizabeth Baxter told how her father "would go out on the prairie and watch where some cattle were starving to death and when one died he would butcher it and get a piece of the meat and go down to Great Salt Lake to get salt to preserve it."[87] Fruit could be mixed with cooked meat and preserved in mincemeat. The slaughtering of hogs furnished sausage, bacon, and hams to be "cured" in the smokehouse as well as lard for pies, cakes, and frying.[88]

Hunting and Fishing

In many pioneer families, hunting and fishing were critical to the food supply. "Fish and game have always been plentyful here in Utah," John Henry Ward Lister observed. Indeed, because "there were no game laws then," it was "a hunters and fishers paradise."[89] During some periods of scarcity, fish were a particularly important commodity. Peter Madsen arrived in Salt Lake City in 1854 and moved immediately to Provo, where, in 1855, he witnessed the terrible infestation of crickets or grasshoppers. "So thick did they descend that they fairly darkened the sun," he recalled. The black hoards destroyed most of the promising small crop along the Provo River and then "made their way to the shores of Utah Lake which they attempted to cross and were drowned by the wagon loads. Many of them were eaten by the fish." He recounted how shortly thereafter the people were saved by the fish:

> People came to the lake. From Sevier on the south to Salt Lake on the north, they came with wagons and barrels and salt prepared to take fish home with them for food during the winter months. Their crops were destroyed and they were weak from hunger. . . .
>
> They all camped along the river near where it empties into the lake and we made preparations to supply them with mullet and trout which were quite plentiful at that time. Having been accustomed to fishing in Denmark when a boy, I was prepared for this important duty of furnishing food for starving people, and I will always remember the scene along the river bank after the first day's catch had been distributed. The campers were in little groups

around the campfires where they were broiling fish on hot coals and eating them with relish that only those who have been through an experience of this kind can appreciate.

The bishop of Provo sent men to help and all day and all night the fishing went on. The Saints came and remained on the river until they had enough fish salted to last them during the winter; then they left for their homes to give others room who were equally needy. For weeks the work went on. Nobody ever asked who did the work or who received the fish. We were all comparatively equal in those days and all we asked was enough to eat until we could raise crops to supply us food. I have always regarded this as one of my greatest opportunities for doing good.[90]

David Moore remembered plenty of fish in the Ogden area, as well as an abundance of wild chickens, ducks, and geese. He recounted how they "would roast turkeys by tying a string to the turkey's legs and hangin[g] it from a nail in the mantle. They would then get up a good fire and give the turkey a twirl over it." Moore said he "couldn't see how people could ever go hungry unless it was the lack of ammunition."[91]

During the early years, particularly, such a lack was likely. James Moss remembered feasting upon the jackrabbits in Grass Valley that were destroying his family's crops—after his parents "called for the Indians to come and kill the rabbits with their bows and arrows."[92] "It was sure hard for us to get enough to eat during those times when the grasshoppers were so bad," recalled Lorenzo Hadley. "There were plenty of wild duck and chickens around here but we didn't have much am[m]unition. Daddy only had a few loads left after our trip over the plains." The resourceful fourteen-year-old Lorenzo "found a piece of lead that we had fetched from England . . . hammered this out flat and cut some small pieces out for shot and loaded the gun and went down to Greenwell's slough in West Weber where the ducks were thick." It was the first time he had ever shot a gun, but he killed a total of nine ducks, and he and his brother "cleaned up four or five of them for mother to cook for us that night." Lorenzo soon found people willing to pay him fifteen cents a piece for dressed ducks. "That fall," he recalled, "I shot and sold enough ducks to buy myself a suit of clothes worth fifteen dollars besides buying all my am[m]unition."[93] Hunting, like home production of foods, could be an important source of income. Albert Garrison Garner of Huntsville recalled hunting deer and selling their hams "for 9¢ per lb. to Elec Brewer of Ogden who then sold them to miners in Montana." Garner "also hunted Pine

Hens and sold them to a man (by the name of Berdsley) who ran the Rail Road Hotel in Ogden."[94]

THE STRUGGLE WITH HUNGER

Some pioneers who grew up in Utah in the last half of the nineteenth century never recalled struggling for food. "Some stories were told of how people had to eat roots to keep alive but I knew of no one but who had plenty to eat, maybe not much of a vari[e]ty, but they had plenty of what they raised," declared Brigham Dalton of Rockville. Even he, however, recalled the rationing of flour in hard times.[95] Inevitably, those who struggled with shortages and hunger remembered and remarked with emotion on their experience.

Begging for food was likewise painful, though it seems to have come more easily for children. Elizabeth Baxter was nearly three when she and her impoverished family were returning to Ogden after staying in Spanish Fork during the population's move south in 1858. "We didn't have much to eat and I went begging," she recollected frankly, remembering tasting butter for the first time when one woman gave her hot biscuits with butter.[96]

Asking to borrow flour when her family had none was difficult for Harriet Weaver Taylor's mother, who "had never had to do anything like that over in England." Harriet's mother "took a little brass kettle and went down to a neighbor," asking the lady who came to the door if she could borrow a little flour to be returned in a day or two when the family received flour. But, recalled Harriet,

> the lady said that if she loaned flour out that way, that she would soon be in the same fix as mother. Mother was terribly hurt and turned and started for home. The lady must have felt ashamed because she called to her to come back, but mother wouldn't go back, she said, "Too late!" The next day we had 200 pounds of our own flour come. Those surely were hard times.[97]

Stories of refusal to share, food theft, or ungrateful recipients are far outnumbered by accounts of generosity and gratitude.[98] Edward Frei's father, "a very reserved man," cried when his neighbor gave him half a sack of flour to feed his hungry children. As he left for home, the neighbor's wife called him back and "turned a dipper full of nice warm biscuits on a napkin" for the Frei children.[99] "The people as a whole were very good about dividing their food supplies with their neighbors. This fact saved many families from going hungry,"

Isaiah Cox affirmed.[100] David Cannon recollected many occasions when he saw his father "trade food to some needy person for work, when he could easily have done all of his own work himself."[101] Mary Cooper proudly emphasized her hometown's reputation for sharing: "Some of the men used to say, if a family was in need of food, clothing or a place to live during the winter, they came to Panguitch because they knew they would be taken care of."[102] George Washington Brown and his wife Wealtha hauled threshing machinery into the Uintah Basin one fall and were sent enough flour and pork to help them make it through the winter. "We kept on loaning out our flour until we had none for our own use," Wealtha recalled. The pork George had cut up and stored "in the wheat at the Co-op granary" also disappeared. "Well, people got so hungry that someone had helped themselves to most of it but I dont blame them, they were hungry."[103]

The Blessing and Protection of the Lord

If, indeed, among Utah's pioneers it "was a universal practice to be generous"[104] and "a common thing in those days to see one neighbor divide her last pan of flour with her neighbors,"[105] it was in some measure because Latter-day Saints believed they were building Zion, where God's people would be "of one heart and one mind" and where there would be "no poor among them" (Moses 7:18). They labored in the Great Basin desert, they believed, by God's appointment and with his approval. "The Lord was with those early day pioneers and provided ways and means for them to exist," William Bethers testified.[106] Accounts of seagulls devouring crickets came to symbolize the numerous occasions and varied ways divine intervention furnished hungry Saints with food.

Sometimes the miracle came through the ministerings of an inspired brother or sister. At the end of her family's journey across the plains, Margaret McNeil Ballard recalled, their food "gave out," and they arrived in Ogden in October 1859 without a cent and very weak with hunger. Seeing a pile of squash in a field, Margaret's mother sent her to beg for some at the home nearby. The old woman who answered Margaret's knock at the door said, "'Come in, come in, I knew you were coming and have been told to give you food.' She gave me a large loaf of fresh bread," Margaret recounted, and later "she came and brought us a nice cooked dinner."[107]

In other instances, nourishment wondrously appeared to sustain a hungry person or family, calling to mind the manna provided the wandering children of Israel or the feeding of the Prophet Elijah by ravens (Ex. 16:14–35; 1 Kgs. 17:6).[108] Abigail Cox Heaton recounted how her parents, who helped settle Manti, were amply supplied with food until a summer when "droughts left them almost in the throes of famine." Like other families in Manti, the Coxes lived on greens that summer until even they became so sparse that "women and children fairly scoured the land for greens." Abigail's young brother Walter returned one afternoon with a "few spindly weeds" that "were scarcely enough for one person, let alone a family of seven, and the children were crying for food." That night, "the family prayed in humility for something to eat." The next morning, they knelt again in prayer before a reluctant, but obedient, Walter left to search for greens. According to Abigail's account, he was successful:

> In a short time he returned to the dugout with a basket of crisp stalky greens; even his mother was amazed. He was almost breathless as he told her of having found a large patch of the luscious weeds just as if they had been planted in rows, and on the same ground where many had been searching the previous day. Never had they eaten such good greens, and for days the people of the Manti Valley gathered baskets of greens that seemed to satisfy their hunger and even, some claimed, put flesh on them.[109]

Utah's pioneers gradually built a food supply steady enough to see them through hard times and assure future abundance. They later reflected with pride on the hard work and resourcefulness that forged the tradition they bequeathed, a tradition that included helpfulness and sharing and a humble acknowledgment of God's hand in their survival and achievement. After all, they were witnesses to the fulfillment of the Lord's ancient promises that in the last days his house "shall be established in the top of the mountains . . . and all nations shall flow unto it," that "the desert shall rejoice, and blossom as the rose," and, further, that "in this mountain shall the LORD of hosts make unto all people a feast of fat things" (Isa. 2:2; 35:1; 26:6).

Jill Mulvay Derr is Research Historian at the Smith Institute for LDS History and Associate Professor of Church History at Brigham Young University. The author gratefully acknowledges Jennifer Jacob's assistance with initial research for this article. Plant illustrations are based on Richard J. Shaw, *Vascular Plants of Northern Utah: An Identification Manual* (Logan, Utah: Utah State University Press, 1989); Stanley L. Welsh and Glen Moore, *Utah Plants: Tracheophyta,* 3d ed. (Provo, Utah: Brigham Young University Press, 1973); and Stanley L. Welsh, Michael Treshow, and Glen Moore, *Guide to Common Utah Plants* (Provo, Utah: Brigham Young University Press, 1964).

NOTES

1. "George Washington Brown—Frontiersman," in *Our Pioneer Heritage,* comp. Kate B. Carter, 20 vols. (Salt Lake City: Daughters of Utah Pioneers, 1958–77), 2:496.

2. Richard J. Hooker, *Food and Drink in America: A History* (Indianapolis: Bobbs-Merrill, 1981) provides a helpful chronological overview punctuated with interesting details. Joseph R. Conlin, *Bacon, Beans, and Galantines: Food and Foodways on the Western Mining Frontier* (Reno: University of Nevada Press, 1986), illustrated with excellent photographs, examines the frontier food of miners in several western locations, from scant provisions to cookhouse, saloon, and restaurant meals. Jacqueline Williams, *Wagon Wheel Kitchens: Food on the Oregon Trail* (Lawrence: University Press of Kansas, 1993) considers the equipment, supplies, and meals of westering pioneers and draws from the diaries of some Latter-day Saint women. Jacqueline B. Williams, *The Way We Ate: Pacific Northwest Cooking, 1843–1900* (Pullman: Washington State University Press, 1996) is a topically arranged treatment of food in the Northwest, rich in details relevant to pioneer Utah and complete with some recipes. David W. Miller discusses the impact of technology on American food consumption in "Technology and the Ideal: Production Quality and Kitchen Reform in Nineteenth-Century America," in *Dining in America, 1850–1900,* ed. Kathryn Grover (Amherst: University of Massachusetts Press; Rochester, N.Y.: The Margaret Woodbury Strong Museum, 1987), 47–84.

Numerous local and regional studies of food range widely from recipes to home production to domestic and marketplace issues. For example, the Daughters of Utah Pioneers published a compilation of early Mormon recipes, "The Pioneer Cook Book," in *Our Pioneer Heritage,* 5:117–64. Janet Alm Anderson, *Bounty: A Harvest of Food Lore and Country Memories from Utah's Past* (Boulder, Colo.: Pruet Publishing, 1990), features memorable photographs, recipes, remedies, and reminiscences from Utah State University's Special Collections and Archives, Logan, Utah. Janet Bruce, "Of Sugar and Salt and Things in the Cellar and Sun: Food Preservation in Jackson County in the 1850s," *Missouri Historical Review* 75, no. 4 (1981): 417–47, is filled with information that applies to a much broader setting. *Foodways in the Northeast: The Dublin Seminar for New England Folklife, Annual Proceedings, 1982,* ed. Peter Beenes (Boston: Boston University, 1984) includes among other articles Daphne L. Derven, "Wholesome, Toothsome, and Diverse: Eighteenth-Century Foodways in Deerfield, Massachusetts," 47–63, which draws upon account books to identify varieties of foodstuffs and their peak periods of consumption, and Laurel Thatcher Ulrich, "It 'went away shee knew not how': Food Theft and Domestic Conflict in Seventeenth-Century Essex County," 94–104, which carefully examines seven court cases of theft of food by servants and neighbors.

3. Manuscript History of Brigham Young, 1846–47, ed. Elden J. Watson (Salt Lake City: Elden J. Watson, 1971), 563–65, 568.

4. Mary Isabella Horne, "My Pioneer Home," in *Our Pioneer Heritage,* 1:123–25, reprinted from *Juvenile Instructor* 29 (March 15, 1894): 181–85.

5. Horne, "My Pioneer Home," 1:125.

6. Susannah Clark to Ann Dalley, October 23, 1851, cited in "Life in the Valley," in *Our Pioneer Heritage,* 3:251.

7. Polly Berthena Huntington [b. 1849], Questionnaire, question 20, WPA Biographical Sketches, Utah State Historical Society, Salt Lake City, Utah (hereafter cited as Bio. Sketches). Ronald W. Walker graciously shared with me his notes from this collection and encouraged my further research in this remarkable source of recollections of the pioneer experience. The sketches fall into two categories: narratives and answers to a standardized WPA questionnaire. The narratives I have entitled "Personal History"; the answers to the questionnaire, "Questionnaire." Page numbers accompany the narratives; question numbers accompany the questionnaire. To give a chronological sense of the pioneer experience, I have included the year the pioneer was born in brackets. These dates come from the register to the collection and are unverified. Since almost all quotations in this paper come from WPA transcriptions, typographical errors should not be interpreted to reflect the spelling of pioneers. All references in this article to Bio. Sketches refer to the Utah State Historical Society's WPA collection.

8. Christian Stucki [b. 1859], Personal History, in Casper Gubler [b. 1835], Personal History, 3, Bio. Sketches.

9. Levi Jackman, "A Short Sketch of the Life of Levi Jackman, 1797–1876," 43, typescript, Special Collections, Harold B. Lee Library, Brigham Young University (hereafter cited as BYU Archives).

10. Isaiah Moses Coombs, Diary, cited in *Our Pioneer Heritage,* 1:345.

11. William F. Rigby, Diary, cited in *Our Pioneer Heritage,* 4:251.

12. Mary Henrie Cooper [b. 1866], Questionnaire, question 33, Bio. Sketches.

13. Barbara Gowans Bowen, Autobiography, in *Our Pioneer Heritage,* 9:414.

14. Harmon Gubler [b. 1856], Personal History, 3, Bio. Sketches.

15. Sylvester Earl [b. 1862], Personal History, 2, Bio. Sketches.

16. Isaiah Cox [b. 1859], Questionnaire, question 33, Bio. Sketches.

17. Brian Q. Cannon examines the experiences of Utah's early settlers with the sego lily and the flower's evolution into a cultural icon in "The Sego Lily, Utah's State Flower," *Utah Historical Quarterly* 63 (winter 1995): 70–84.

18. Lorenzo Hadley [b. 1851], Personal History, 7, Bio. Sketches.

19. Olive Cheney Aldous [b. 1861], Personal History, 2, Bio. Sketches.

20. John Hyrum Barton [b. 1868], Questionnaire, question 33, Bio. Sketches.

21. David H. Cannon Jr. [b. 1860], Questionnaire, question 33, Bio. Sketches.

22. Cox, Questionnaire, question 33.

23. Lucy Meserve Smith, "Historical Narrative," quoted in Kenneth W. Godfrey, Audrey M. Godfrey, and Jill Mulvay Derr, eds. *Women's Voices: An Untold History of the Latter-day Saints* (Salt Lake City: Deseret Book, 1982), 264–65. The original holograph is in Special Collections, Marriott Library, University of Utah, Salt Lake City.

24. Hyrum Allen [b. 1862], Questionnaire, question 23, 73, Bio. Sketches.

25. Wilson Howard Dusenberry, Diary, cited in *Our Pioneer Heritage,* 1:237; ellipses in original.

26. Catherine C. Larsen [b. 1856], Personal History, 3, Bio. Sketches.

27. Carl Evirt Jensen [b. 1863], Personal History, 2, Bio. Sketches.

28. Mary [Stapley] Bringhurst [b. 1865], Personal History, 1, Bio. Sketches.

29. William Samuel Bethers [b. 1843], Personal History, 2, Bio. Sketches. See also Lucy Meserve Smith, "Historical Narrative," 264.

30. Cox, Personal History, 2.

31. Jane Sprunt Warner Garner [b. 1863], Personal History, 4, Bio. Sketches.

32. Alma D. Chambers [b. 1858], Questionnaire, question 20, Bio. Sketches.

33. Fannie Ellsworth Greenwell [b. 1862], Personal History, 3, Bio. Sketches.

34. Chambers, Questionnaire, question 34.

35. Luella A. Dalton [b. 1842], Personal History, 2, Bio. Sketches.

36. Leonard J. Arrington, *Great Basin Kingdom: An Economic History of the Latter-day Saints, 1830–1900* (Lincoln: University of Nebraska Press, 1966), 117–20, 390.

37. Conlin underscores the importance of corn to western pioneers. Conlin, *Bacon, Beans, and Galantines,* 12.

38. Mary Julia Johnson Wilson, "Biographical Sketches and Memoirs of Mary Julia Wilson of Hillsdale, Garfield County, Utah, Hills," 22, in Ezekiel Johnson [b. 1862], Personal History, Bio. Sketches.

39. Manomas Lavina Gibson Andrus [b. 1842], Personal History, 2, Bio. Sketches.

40. Isaac H. Grace [b. 1857], Questionnaire, question 23, Bio. Sketches.

41. Leaving grain in the field to be gleaned by the poor was a long-standing tradition with biblical antecedents. (See Lev. 19:9–10.)

42. Edith H. Terry, "Millesant London Osborn Parks," in *Our Pioneer Heritage,* 2:337.

43. John Hafen [b. 1856], Personal History, 1, Bio. Sketches.

44. Elizabeth Horrocks Baxter [b. 1856], Personal History, 2, Bio. Sketches.

45. Henry Excell [b. 1858], Questionnaire, question 34, Bio. Sketches.

46. Aldous, Personal History, 2.

47. John Hock Hinton [b. 1839], Personal History, 4, Bio. Sketches.

48. Margaret Warner Williams Wood [no. b. date], Questionnaire, question 33, Bio. Sketches.

49. Martha Ann Clinger Boren [b. 1846], Questionnaire, question 20, Bio. Sketches.

50. "Puddings," in *Our Pioneer Heritage,* 5:158.

51. Williams discusses different varieties of yeast in *Wagon Wheel Kitchens,* 9–14.

52. Mary Julia Johnson Wilson, "Ancestral Sketch and Memories of Mary Julia Johnson Wilson, 1776–1877," 20, typescript, BYU Archives.

53. Eleanor C. Bruhn, "Ode to Aunt Salena's Yeast," in *Our Pioneer Heritage,* 1:559.

54. Wilson, "Ancestral Sketch," 20.

55. Thomas Samuel Bladen [b. 1852], Personal History, 1, Bio. Sketches.

56. Garner, Personal History, 3.

57. Rosina [Mueller] Beacham [b. 1866], Personal History, 2–4, Bio. Sketches.

58. Hooker, *Food and Drink in America: A History,* 356.

59. W. G. Mills, "Deseret State Fair," *Deseret News,* October 13, 1858, 139.

60. Historian's Office Journal, March 13, 1851, and August 24, 1861, manuscript, Church Archives.

61. Horne, "My Pioneer Home," 1:124.

62. L. S. Hemingway, "Fruit Culture," *Deseret News,* October 6, 1858, 134.

63. C. N. Teeter, "Four Years of My Life," typescript, Idaho State Historical Society, as quoted in Conlin, *Bacon, Beans, and Galantines,* 49.

64. Gubler, Personal History, 3.

65. Baxter, Personal History, 4.

66. Melissa Jane Lambson Davis, "A Pioneer Story," in *Our Pioneer Heritage,* 12:109.

67. Gubler, Personal History, 3.

68. Hannah Hanson Huntsman [b. 1865], Questionnaire, question 20, Bio. Sketches.

69. Huntington, Questionnaire, question 29.

70. John Henry Ward Lister [b. 1861], Questionnaire, question 20, Bio. Sketches.

71. Laura Smith Hadfield [b. 1858], Personal History, 3, Bio. Sketches.

72. Hannah McFarland Bingham [b. 1870], Personal History, 5, Bio. Sketches.

73. Williams, *The Way We Ate,* 118.

74. Barton, Questionnaire, question 20.

75. Eliza Marie Partridge Lyman, Journal, April 8 and 17, 1849, quoted in Godfrey, *Women's Voices,* 248, 250. The original holograph journal is located in the Historical Department of The Church of Jesus Christ of Latter-day Saints, Salt Lake City.

76. Arrington, *Great Basin Kingdom,* 135–36.

77. Thomas Briggs, Diary, cited in *Our Pioneer Heritage,* 3:285, 287.

78. Allen, Questionnaire, question 18.

79. Bessie Spencer Bateman, "Precious Butter," in *Our Pioneer Heritage,* 2:252.

80. Hadfield, Personal History, 6.

81. Grace, Questionnaire, question 24.

82. "Valley Products," *Deseret News,* October 15, 1853, 2.

83. Aldous, Personal History, 4.

84. Annie C[lark] Kimball, "Happy Adobe Homes," in *Our Pioneer Heritage,* 1:134.

85. See Williams, *The Way We Ate,* 132–33.

86. Eliza Marie Partridge Lyman, Journal, May 25, 1849, cited in Godfrey, *Women's Voices,* 253.

87. Baxter, Personal History, 3.

88. Williams, *The Way We Ate*, 134–40. See also Bruce, "Of Sugar and Salt and Things in the Cellar and Sun," 424–34.

89. Lister, Questionnaire, question 32; Barton, Questionnaire, question 32; Excell, Questionnaire, question 32.

90. Clara Madsen Taylor, "Peter Madsen, Veteran Fisherman of Utah Lake," in *Our Pioneer Heritage*, 2:176–77.

91. David Moore [b. 1851], Questionnaire, question 18, 32, Bio. Sketches.

92. Lucille C. Jones, "Fanny Elizabeth Goodman Moss," in *Our Pioneer Heritage*, 3:86.

93. Hadley, Personal History, 8.

94. Albert Garrison Garner [b. 1858], Questionnaire, question 31, Bio. Sketches.

95. Brigham Dalton [b. 1863], Personal History, 1–2, Bio. Sketches.

96. Baxter, Personal History, 2–3.

97. Harriet Weaver Taylor [b. 1859], Personal History, 6, Bio. Sketches.

98. For example, the journal of Henry W. Sanderson mentions the theft of two sacks of his flour in the Salt Lake Valley in the summer of 1847, in account of "Caroline (Emmeline) Sessions," in *Our Pioneer Heritage*, 1:502. Ephrasia Cox Day, born in Fairview in 1854, recalled rationing of bread "the first ten years" and complained, "We had to give our supper each day to some English people and the thing that got me they were not a bit careful with their foods and would waste too much." Ephrasia Cox Day [b. 1854], Personal History, 1, Bio. Sketches.

99. Edward R. Frei [no b. date], Personal History, 2, Bio. Sketches.

100. Cox, Questionnaire, question 23.

101. Cannon, Questionnaire, question 24.

102. Cooper, Questionnaire, question 24.

103. Wealtha Ann Reynolds Brown [b. 1858], Pioneer History, 2-3, Bio. Sketches.

104. Chambers, Personal History, question 24.

105. Earl, Personal History, 2.

106. Bethers, Personal History, 2.

107. Margaret McNeil Ballard, Diary, cited in *Our Pioneer Heritage*, 3:201.

108. After the widow of Zarephath shared the last of her meal with Elijah, she was blessed with continuing divine sustenance, and her own "barrel of meal wasted not, neither did the cruse of oil fail, according to the word of the LORD" (1 Kgs. 17:16).

109. "The Lord Will Provide," in *Our Pioneer Heritage*, 7:566–67.

COMMON PEOPLE: CHURCH ACTIVITY DURING THE BRIGHAM YOUNG ERA

William G. Hartley

"The people constitute the power and reality of the Kingdom of God." That fundamental truth, voiced by LDS pioneer bishop Leonard W. Hardy in 1861, is often ignored in Mormon history, which tends to concentrate on Church leaders and programs.[1] Of 150,000 Latter-day Saints over whom Brigham Young presided during his three decades in Utah, barely 1,000 served as leaders from bishopric level up to General Authorities—a ratio of 149 to 1.[2] How did the 149,000 Saints who were not leaders practice their religion?

In 1860 a Salt Lake City bishop reported that most in his ward were "just as faithful as they knew how to be, others as much the reverse, neglecting almost every duty."[3] What did being "faithful" mean back then? What did the bishop have in mind when he said "every duty"? Or, applying today's terminology, what did it mean in Brigham Young's day to be "active in the Church"?

To be "active in the Church" today is to attend Sunday meetings somewhat regularly, to fulfill a calling, and, if fully committed, to hold and use a temple recommend. By contrast, during Utah's first two decades, the Saints did not go regularly to any church meetings, and ward buildings were too small to allow most members to attend sacrament meeting. For most of that early period, men, women, and children had no Sunday School, Relief Society, Mutual, Primary, or ward priesthood meetings to attend nor auxiliary callings to fill. Saints had no temples needing their attendance for proxy ordinance work. Therefore, what constituted "being a good Mormon" back then? What follows is an attempt to answer that question.

Courtesy LDS Church Archives

Construction of the first tabernacle, later known as the Old Tabernacle, began in 1851. Dedicated on April 6, 1852, it was used until 1870 and eventually replaced by the Assembly Hall. This daguerreotype was taken sometime in 1853 by Marsena Cannon.

SIZE OF STAKES AND WARDS

Stake and ward sizes varied dramatically. Brigham Young had no more than 13 stakes to oversee at one time until he expanded the total to 20 stakes just before he died in 1877. Those 20 stakes averaged 12 wards apiece, but 8 stakes had more than 14 wards, and the dominant Salt Lake Stake, where one-fourth of the Church membership lived, had 35 wards.

When Brigham Young died, gathered Zion included 104,000 Saints living in 240 wards. Wards averaged 81 families and 432 members per unit. But Salt Lake Stake's wards were larger than most, averaging 566 members. And wards in the Utah (Utah County) Stake were even larger, averaging 808 members each.[4]

CHURCH ATTENDANCE

Believers who gathered to Zion lived in villages and towns for educational, social, cultural, and religious purposes. There they belonged to specific wards and stakes and could attend church meetings. The types of meetings, their frequency, and their procedures varied according to local circumstances and habit. "Going to meeting" was more optional then than it is today.

SUNDAY MEETINGS. From the first pioneers' first week in Great Salt Lake Valley, leaders provided each Sunday a general (not ward) church meeting or two. When settlements formed outside the valley, the same pattern continued. The norm by the mid-1850s was two public meetings on Sunday conducted for the entire settlement, not just for a ward. Both meetings, usually at 10 A.M. and 2 P.M., were held so that speakers could address the Saints. The afternoon meeting became the people's sacrament meeting.

In Salt Lake Stake, the main Sunday meeting took place on Temple Square. On Sunday afternoons, some of the valley's Saints gathered for the stakewide sacrament meeting and to hear the General Authorities preach. At first the attendees met only during good weather, under a brush-covered bowery. Then the Church built the "Old" Tabernacle, seating capacity 2,500 (less than half of the city's population). It was replaced in 1867 by the "New" Tabernacle, seating capacity of 8,000 (still not quite half of the city's population), which still stands on Temple Square.[5] Other multiward settlements that did not have tabernacles continued the tradition of settlement-wide outdoor Sunday meetings.

During winter months, however, outdoor meetings could not be held, so the Salt Lake Valley and outlying wards conducted their own services in homes or in ward meetinghouses, after such were erected. Even the Old Tabernacle, when it was in use, proved to be too cold during the winter to host the Sunday general meetings. It appears that cold weather caused settlement-wide sacrament meetings to become ward meetings, a major development in the worship history of the Saints. In 1867, because wards by then were conducting Sunday Schools on Sunday mornings, leaders ceased holding the downtown Tabernacle Sunday morning general meeting.[6]

For the Saints who attended, the Sunday services provided varying calibers of speakers, a chance to partake of the sacrament, and sometimes impressive inspiration. An eighteen-year-old diarist in Smithfield, Cache County, commented about her Sunday activities on April 21, 1867:

> I have been to two meetings to day. Have listened to the pleasing word of God spoken by His servants and have been much instructed and comforted thereby. Oh! That the honest in heart everywhere might listen to such teaching! Could they do otherwise than to understand and believe.[7]

Martha Spence Heywood, who had no children to care for during most of these years, attended church services regularly in Salt Lake and then in Payson when she went down there as an early settler. She noted on Thursday, May 4, 1854, the monthly fast day, that she "attended forenoon and afternoon meetings and felt much benefited thereby." She added that "there was quite a good attendance of females," which implies that such was unusual and worth noting.[8] Among reactions to meetings she recorded in her diary are these: "Today we had a good meeting," "Had a good meeting this forenoon," "Had some good speaking," and "Had a good meeting."[9] Of two Sunday meetings in Salt Lake's bowery, years apart, she noted, "Enjoyed the remarks of Joseph Young in reference to keeping the Sabbath holy," and "Truly comforted and instructed by the preaching" that provided "a variety of good instruction."[10]

Sunday meetings in most settlements were well attended—but only if judged by how full the meeting facility was. If measured by the percentages who "went to church," those meetings were poorly attended. One Salt Lake City ward reported that of its 181 families, only 31 were regularly represented at Sunday meetings, and 97 of the families, or 50 percent, were "perfectly indifferent."[11] Historian Ronald W. Walker points out that "'going to meeting' clearly was not a popular nineteenth-century pastime."[12]

Several factors account for the early Utah Saints' light attendance at Sunday services. The primary cause was inadequate meeting halls. In most areas, the first meetinghouses were too small for everyone in the ward to be seated for Sunday meetings. The Toquerville chapel, for example, was a 20' x 16' adobe house, the size of some family rooms in today's suburban homes, too small to serve the settlement's nineteen families.[13] Though small buildings might be full on a Sunday, the majority of ward members were not in attendance. In 1856, Elder Wilford Woodruff mentioned "wards where they are so crowded." Many meetings, he said, are "as full as people can be" so that "many of the ward have to go home."[14]

In 1861, Brigham Young recommended the building of "substantial Halls in the different wards."[15] In the following sixteen years, many wards built new meetinghouses, but often the new structures were still too small. In 1877, for example, Salt Lake City's twenty-first ward designed a new meetinghouse that was about 28' x 43'[16]—enough space to seat only about 180 people. Some communities did build large churches, such as the 85' x 40' edifice Kaysville Ward built by the

Courtesy BYU Archives

Going to meeting was impossible for many children in early Utah wards. Because LDS Church meetinghouses like this one in Provo were too small to hold everyone, children often stayed at home while their parents attended meetings. Sometimes even adults could not find a seat and had to go home.

early 1860s, which could seat 900 Saints. Curtains divided its basement into four classrooms.[17] Ogden built a tabernacle, in use by the late 1850s, that could seat 1,200.[18] Nevertheless, as late as 1877, the *Juvenile Instructor* reported that many children had never partaken of the sacrament because "in many places the meeting houses are too small for them to meet with the grown people, and therefore they have to stop at home while their parents attend meeting."[19]

Often, the first meeting places were either members' homes or simple one-room, log assembly halls.[20] Not only were they small, but often they were crudely finished and uncomfortable. Gunnison Ward's first meetinghouse was 20' x 40', built of logs, with a roof of willows, straw, and earth. The walls were chinked and plastered with mud and whitewashed on the inside. Floorboards did not fit very closely together. Benches were "formidable slabs" with four legs attached. A crude pine table stood in one corner.[21]

In Tooele "the first public house was built in 1854," John Alexander Bevan recalled. He also described its lack of amenities:

It was 28 ft. long by 18 feet wide, a log-house with a dirt roof. A fireplace in each end stood lengthwise, north and south, facing the east. There was one small door, and two small windows in front. The chimneys were built of adobe. The fireplaces were large, so that the wood could be stood up in them endways, and make a big fire to give both heat and light. The head of each family made a bench for his family to sit on. These benches were usually made of slabs, with four legs put in on the round side of the slab. . . . Besides the fire for light, they had tallow candles, home-made, and each family was supposed to furnish a candle. The house was used for all purposes, both religious and otherwise. It was the schoolhouse, the meeting house, and the amusement hall. It had a pulpit on the west side near the center. This pulpit, or stand, was about large enough to hold three men.[22]

Local meetinghouses, no matter the size, discouraged attendance by being too hot, too cold, or too smoky. Boweries and other buildings became unbearably hot during summer months. In St. George the first bowery proved to be "too small" for general gatherings. "On every side the assemblies were exposed to the rude blasts of the hot summer, and the deep chilling atmosphere of the winter season."[23] But the new bowery, 85' x 45', while large and neat, suffered from frequent windstorms that blew dust through the willows into the faces of the assembled faithful. Charles L. Walker attended a conference on May 4, 1866, at which "I heard little of what they said, for the wind roared through the willows that covered the bowery, with such violence that it was almost an impossibility to hear the speaker." Two days later, men nailed "wagon covers round the bowery to protect [attenders] from the gale." St. George had a meeting hall, but "it would seat only about a hundred people." Finally, in 1869, a spacious tabernacle opened for Sunday meetings, although it was unfinished. Meetings were held in the basement, for the building exterior was not finished until 1871; the interior, not until 1875.[24]

In 1869, Provo's tabernacle had a new stove that smoked up the room. "I do the best I can when the Stove is red hot," the custodian said. "I put the Coal in quick, but cannot prevent the smoke and flame coming out when the door is opened."[25] Two years later, during a cold December, "several members of the Choir were complaining because of the coldness of the Meeting House." "Unless the room is warmed," a bishop warned, "the people will stay at home."[26]

Other life realities hindered men, women, and children from going to meetings. In that premicrophone era, attenders at the outdoor meetings and in the Old Tabernacle and other larger meetinghouses had trouble hearing and understanding the speakers. On some Sundays, travel to meetings over dirt roads in uncovered wagons was unpleasant and even impossible because of mud, ice, rain, wind, dust, snow, or scorching sun. Sickness and small children kept many Saints home from meetings, especially the mothers. Martha Spence Heywood's excuse for missing her Salt Lake City ward's sacrament meeting one Sunday in January was because of "the bad walking," meaning mud or snow or water, and "the close atmosphere of the house."[27] Farm chores and irrigation turns had to be done, even on the Sabbath. Saints in farming regions developed a pattern of not attending meetings during busy summer months, a practice that lingered into the twentieth century. Also, foreign-speaking immigrants sometimes stayed home from English-speaking sacrament meetings.

Poor quality meetings, too, contributed to nonattendance patterns. Smaller communities lacked enough speakers to give variety to the meetings year after year. Women, it appears, rarely spoke in sacrament meetings. Available speakers often were not good speakers. Therefore, within a few years, a ward's meetings became repetitious and often boring. Illustrating the "dull meeting" problem is Provoan Sidney Alexander Pace's recollection that

> we were in the habit of going into meeting on Sunday and if the speaker was not lively enough, fifteen or twenty of us young boys would get up and walk out of meeting and go down by Bishop Loveless's home . . . They used to have large straw stacks and here we went to have our fun. . . .
>
> . . . The Bishop . . . gave me a good fatherly talk and gave me a mission to work with the young boys of the ward and get them into meeting and keep them there. He said he didn't care how I did it but he wanted me to do that for him. . . . By the end of a month's time all the boys would stay in meeting until it was out.[28]

To improve sacrament meetings, the Church called men to be home missionaries to travel in assigned regions and speak in ward meetings and at special conferences.[29]

A lack of fervor among work-distracted Saints likewise lowered the attendance. Lackluster attendance at Provo Tabernacle afternoon meetings in 1872 caused stake president Abraham O. Smoot to ask block teachers

> to report why the people do not come to meeting, the turn-out is unwarrantable. . . . Provo ought to fill this house to overflowing but they do not[,] only when the President [Brigham Young] comes; then they turn out for curiosity. I feel that the people do not enjoy the spirit of their religion.

Smoot continued, "There has not been too much preaching, or to[o] lengthy meetings," he said, adding that "a healthy man who complains of two meetings, is weak in the faith." Three years later the problem persisted, so President Smoot decided to "call the regular meetings wether the people attended or not and thus free himself from all blame."[30]

At the end of 1860, bishops for Great Salt Lake City's twenty wards gave verbal reports at the biweekly bishops meeting, telling of the wards' number of families, attitudes, and participation. The comments dealing with meeting attendance are summarized here (what is notable is that the bishops' perspective seems to have been not what percentage of members attended but how full the meetinghouse was):

> Meetings well attended on Sunday, some few "on the background."
>
> Meeting well attended.
>
> Weekly meeting pretty well attended, fast meeting but few attend.
>
> Sunday meeting well attended, fast meetings not so.
>
> Sunday night meetings and on fast day well attended.
>
> Fast meeting well attended.
>
> Monthly fast meeting well attended, at which they bless their children.
>
> Good spirit toward attending meetings.
>
> Good spirit prevails, meeting well attended.
>
> Meeting tolerably well attended; "some who have lived in the ward six years have never been seen at a meeting, and yet call themselves saints."
>
> People generally very slack in going to meeting.
>
> No place for holding meetings.[31]

In some LDS meeting halls, men sat on one side and women on the other, a strange practice not yet well researched. The Old Tabernacle, for a period of time, had a partition running through the center, separating the sexes—women on the north, men on the south. The practice continued in the New Tabernacle, according to an 1867 visitor there—women sat in the middle seats, men in the side seats along the walls. The Parowan Ward meetinghouse was similarly segregated, women on the east side, men on the west.[32] How extensive this practice was is not known.

LDS religious life was centered in the ward and its religious meetings. To outsiders ward sacrament meetings often seemed irreverent, informal, and lacking in good speeches and admirable music. But for many Saints, these ward meetings provided inspiration and appreciated instruction.[33]

WARD SUNDAY EVENING AND MIDWEEK PRAYER MEETINGS. In many wards, small numbers of Saints gathered in someone's home for a Sunday-night and a midweek-night prayer meeting. These meetings, which continued throughout the Brigham Young period, primarily featured testimony sharing, singing, and praying rather than preaching.[34] Women as well as men spoke. In Nephi's early days, Martha Spence Heywood sometimes attended the ward's prayer meetings. On Sunday evening, October 12, 1851, she noted that "we met together for worship and had a good meeting" at which two men spoke and then "Sister Gifford spoke a few words and I followed her."[35]

"It stormed so fast Wednesday evening that we had no prayer meeting," she diarized on February 16, 1851, in Salt Lake. "Our prayer meeting last Sunday evening to Brother Leonard's was full and very good." Regarding a Sunday evening prayer meeting in Nephi, Martha Spence Heywood noted, "Our prayer meeting did not amount to much." But on another occasion, she wrote that "we had a very good prayer meeting."[36]

WARD FAST MEETINGS. Continuing a practice started in Nauvoo, wards held fast meetings on the first Thursday of every month. Workers had to leave their jobs for two hours or more to attend. To facilitate their attendance, Church leaders at times sternly reminded LDS employers to close their doors during the fast meeting hour. In 1874 a gathering of bishops discussed the "very imperfect way" members treated fast meetings. Presiding Bishop Hunter regretted that "so many failed to appreciate the blessings of our fast meetings." One bishop responded that "our man servants and maid servants should be allowed to go, and our stores and workshops closed, to give all a chance."[37] Two years later, Bishop Hunter reported that for the first time the Salt Lake Stake's public works closed on fast-day morning and would continue to do so in the future so that public workers could attend fast meetings. One of Bishop Hunter's counselors, Bishop Leonard W. Hardy, added that he believed those who failed to attend fast meetings should pay a double fast offering. "All the Merchants in the Church ought to close their stores on that day and give the clerks a chance to go to meeting," he urged.[38] One month later, the bishops agreed that a petition be drawn up that requested city merchants to close for three hours on fast days. What resulted from this plan is not known.[39]

PRIESTHOOD-RELATED MEETINGS. In early Utah, high priests groups and elders quorums were few and served little more purpose than for the men to come together for testimony bearing or talks about the gospel. Most ordained men held the office of seventy and belonged to one of the general quorums of seventy. Because nearly all of the men sent out as missionaries were ordained as seventies prior to leaving, they needed to join a seventies quorums when they returned. Seventies quorums were numbered quorums so that a man belonged to the Sixteenth Quorum, for example, and when he moved, he still belonged officially to that quorum. By the 1860s, Utah had more than sixty such quorums. These were not stake entities, nor were they necessarily linked to a locality. Gradually, seventies belonging to various quorums who lived in the same locality started to meet together in a "mass" quorum for testimony bearing or instruction but not for assignments to do local Church work. During this period, seventies quorum meetings generally saw low attendance.

Where they existed at all, priesthood quorums were stake entities. Stake-level priesthood gatherings included separate monthly meetings for high priests and seventies. Priesthood holders met with their stake quorum officers, who gave instruction and gospel explanation, but the meetings consisted primarily of the men in attendance bearing testimonies. As recorded in the quorum minute books for several of the stakes and settlements, quorum leaders' admonitions indicate that attendance at these meetings generally was less than leaders wanted.[40]

The functions of deacons, teachers, and priests were performed primarily by Melchizedek Priesthood holders. Revelation affirms that "those holding the Melchizedek Priesthood can act in all the offices of the Aaronic Priesthood" if called upon and set apart for that office,[41] so the bishops and stake Aaronic Priesthood quorum presidencies "called and set apart" such men to be *acting* priests, *acting* teachers— the home teachers of that day—and *acting* deacons.[42] Hence they were termed the "acting priesthood"—meaning those called into active service. The rest were reserves.[43]

Wards held acting teachers meetings once or twice a month, at which the teachers reported to the bishop about their visits to ward members. These meetings were that generation's equivalent to our modern ward priesthood meetings. Sometimes the group was referred to as a teachers quorum.

To prepare the ward meetinghouse for meetings and, under the direction of the bishop, aid the poor, wards had a few acting deacons. Deacons meetings in larger population areas were monthly stake meetings. In more isolated settlements, deacons, if they met at all, generally attended the acting teachers meetings.

GENERAL CONFERENCES AND STAKE CONFERENCES. Saints' meeting schedules included "going to conference." Thousands flocked to Great Salt Lake City twice a year to attend LDS general conferences. (Again, the percentage of total LDS members in Utah who attended general conference was very low.) Traveling in wagons, buggies, and carts, on horseback, on foot, and later by train, many used the trip for spiritual renewal as well as for shopping and renewing friendships. That general conferences sometimes were crowded is shown by Martha Spence Heywood's comments on April 6, 1856. She went to conference at the bowery but found there a "dense crowd," so she went back home.[44]

Quarterly conferences, which were not then termed stake conferences, were held in several different settlements, including American Fork, Bountiful, Farmington, Kaysville, Provo, Tooele City, Fillmore, and Spanish Fork. But they were held between November and January and from June to August, Church leaders apparently letting general conference serve as the other two conferences per year. By the mid-1860s, St. George held stake conferences each May and November. Many special conferences were held whenever General Authorities passed through a settlement.[45]

Dixie's premier diarist, Charles L. Walker, regularly attended local church meetings. He particularly enjoyed a stake conference held in St. George on May 4, 1872. Resident Apostle Erastus Snow, who was serving as the stake president, "spoke in a powerful and very interesting manner on the Power and Authority of the Holy Priesthood. It was rich and very edifying. I could have listened to him all day; it was meat and drink to my soul, and I felt as tho I had a rich feast of spiritual food."[46]

Saints had opportunities in most stakes to attend stake conferences. By the mid-1850s, the Davis Stake was holding twice yearly conferences, no two in a row in the same community. On March 14 and

15, 1857, for example, the conference took place at Kaysville. Nine men spoke during the two days.[47] In some other stakes, the conferences were held less regularly.[48]

SLOW INCREASE IN WARD MEETINGS AND CALLINGS

During the first two decades of the pioneer period, LDS men, women, and children had no church meetings to attend other than the Sunday general worship meetings, prayer and fast meetings, stake conferences, or acting teachers meetings. For most wards during this period, the only ward priesthood officers were the bishopric, the acting teachers quorum, and a few acting deacons. Well into the 1860s, the vast majority of "active" Latter-day Saint adults never held a ward job. Without Relief Societies, Sunday Schools, Mutuals, and Primaries, wards had few positions available for anyone to fill. As a result, most ward members held no ward jobs. The turning point was the third decade, when ward meetings and activities increased as the four auxiliary organizations were introduced one by one. Thus only gradually, with the advent of Church auxiliaries, did service in ward positions become a regular part of the committed Mormon's life.

The following beginning dates for Lehi's ward organizations reveal the lack of opportunity for ward jobs that existed for two-thirds of the Brigham Young era:[49]

Bishopric	1851
Elders quorum	1858
Seventies quorum	1862
Sunday School (tried in 1851, died out)	1866
Relief Society	1868
Teachers quorum	1869
High priests quorum	1869
Deacons quorum	1871
Young Ladies Retrenchment Association	1875
Young Men's Mutual Improvement Association	1875
Primary Association	1878

MALES WITH PRIESTHOOD OFFICES, NO DUTIES. In 1852, 2,200 of Utah's 12,000 total number of residents (men, women, and children) held a priesthood office—or one-fifth of all the people. By 1877, a quarter of a century later, the ratio stood about the same, 22,000 out of 104,000 total. Assuming that about half the total population was above age fifteen and that half of these were males, then the 22,000 who held priesthood offices comprised almost all the males over age fifteen.

However, even though most male adults held a priesthood office, most did not have specific duties to perform. The men were expected only to be ready to accept calls to be acting teachers or to fill proselyting missions if and when such calls came.

In 1852 some 40 percent of priesthood bearers were seventies, and 20 percent were elders. (Seventies then were Melchizedek Priesthood officers, seventy to a quorum, in dozens of quorums that functioned like stake quorums; they were not comparable to today's First and Second Quorums of Seventy, whose members are General Authorities.[50]) By 1877, however, the elder-to-seventy ratio had reversed, and 41 percent of priesthood bearers were elders and 20 percent seventies. The percentages of high priests (14) and Aaronic Priesthood (24) remained unchanged throughout the period.[51] On average, an LDS ward in 1877 had 13 high priests, 19 seventies, and 38 elders, or 70 Melchizedek Priesthood bearers out of 432 members. It had 6 priests, 6 teachers, and 10 deacons, for 22 Aaronic Priesthood bearers total.[52]

Most lesser priesthood bearers were adults, not boys.[53] The Church had no expectation that a boy should advance through the ranks—deacon to teacher to priest—or that a boy needed to hold a priesthood office at all. Most young males were ordained first to the Melchizedek Priesthood in their late teens or early twenties to be an elder or seventy.[54]

ACTING TEACHERS. The first ward callings were the bishoprics, including clerks, and then the acting teachers, but only a select dozen or score of men served as acting teachers in a ward. Bishoprics and this corps of teachers "shouldered the ward's leadership and performed its labor."[55]

During Brigham Young's presidency, Melchizedek Priesthood men handled almost all Aaronic Priesthood work in Utah, doing "double duty" by acting in both priesthoods.[56] One older man who was a seventy served as an acting priest in one ward and an acting teacher in two wards and was in the stake's deacons quorum presidency.[57] Another man, an elder, was also both an acting deacon and an acting teacher.[58] Bishop Hunter often exhorted priesthood men to "magnify both priesthoods."[59] The statement "I was an Elder before I was a deacon" was easily understood during the pioneer period.[60]

A man called to be a teacher was expected to visit a big set of families living in the ward. As ward populations grew, he was assigned a companion so that teachers could visit in pairs. Some teams were assigned to visit all the families in a given block, giving rise to the "block teacher" designation. They visited monthly in many wards but only quarterly or randomly elsewhere. A survey in 1870 shows that LDS wards had between eighteen and twenty-four block teachers each, and each team visited between eight and twenty families. Bishops met monthly, or sometimes biweekly, with their acting teachers to receive reports and give assignments.[61]

Then, as now, end-of-the-month visits were common. In 1864, Bishop Hardy complained about teachers who "put off their visits through the wards to the very last evening before they have to give in their report, this hurrying way of visiting, failed to accomplish the design of a Teachers duty."[62]

By assignment from the bishops, teachers did more than pay visits to members' homes. They settled some disputes, helped the needy, collected fast offerings, obtained needed resources, and administered the sacrament.[63]

RELIEF SOCIETIES. After being shelved in Nauvoo, Relief Societies were organized for a brief period in the 1850s by women in some wards primarily to assist needy Native Americans in their neighborhoods. But no more than three or four societies survived the "Move South," the northern Saints' 1858 evacuation to more southerly settlements, a response to the threat of Johnston's army.[64] For most LDS women, the Relief Society program was not reorganized until 1867, fully twenty years after the first Saints entered Utah. Therefore, for a full generation, women, most of whom did not attend sacrament meetings regularly, at best attended weeknight prayer meetings. For them, religion was concentrated on interactions at home and with neighbors rather than centered around formal, weekly church attendance.[65]

By the late 1860s, Relief Societies were started in most wards, giving women "church work" to do. Provo's third ward Relief Society commenced on December 2, 1868, by voting in twenty-two members. Mary Jane Tanner, the bishop's wife, was the first president. Each week the sisters met in a different house. They debated whether or not to have two separate society meetings, one a prayer meeting and the other a quilting meeting. At first they tried one meeting at which they had prayer and a hymn and then quilted and sewed. But the atmosphere became too relaxed and gossipy, the minutes note, so they began holding both types of meetings weekly. For a long time, attendance was good at quilting meetings but "very low" at prayer meetings.[66]

Relief Societies copied the priesthood organization in several respects. They called women to be teachers, like the block teachers, to visit the sisters in the ward. They called a few sisters to be deaconesses, doing the work ward deacons did—making the meeting place ready and comfortable for each week's meeting.[67] Because of the existence of ward Relief Societies, a dozen or more women in each ward received "church callings" to serve in positions in the wards.

SUNDAY SCHOOLS FOR CHILDREN. In the early 1850s, Sunday Schools began sporadically in wards here and there, founded by concerned local individuals rather than Church leaders. Richard Ballantyne started the first one in 1849 when fifty youth, ages eight to fourteen, met in a special room added to his home. Other individuals copied him, so that independent Sunday Schools sprang up in most wards. Provo started a Sunday School in 1852, which operated off and on. In 1860 the school started meeting in the Third Ward meetinghouse—one Sunday School for four Provo wards. Finally, in 1876 each ward organized its own Sunday School.[68] A Sunday School started in Lehi in 1851 but "was not permanently organized until 1866."[69] In fall 1856, Bishop John Rowberry in Tooele decided his ward needed a Sunday School "for the benefit of the Rising Generation." He appointed Eli Lee to run it, so "Bro. Lee immediately commenced operations by collecting a few of the children together on Sunday mornings, and instructing them, assisted by his wife. For some time, but little progress was made." By 1857 the school had eight classes—five taught by men and three by women.[70]

In 1866, Elder George Q. Cannon launched the *Juvenile Instructor* to help the Sunday Schools, and in 1872 he became the Church's first general superintendent of all the Sunday Schools. By the 1870s, two hundred Sunday Schools involved nearly fifteen thousand youth and adults. Sunday Schools created ward positions that Saints could be called to fill. For the first time, women and children participated directly in a Sabbath meeting as teachers and students, and many men became officers and teachers. Songs, prayers, scripture lessons, catechisms, and recitations were all part of the school. So, too, were examination days, like one Salt Lake bishop Frederick Kesler attended when he found "the house was well fild, the pieces ware well spoken & a Large No. of presants ware given out as Reward of merit which consisted in some verry choice Books."[71]

A revealing picture of Sunday School activity appears in the first statistical report the Deseret Sunday School Union compiled.[72] Their data are for the quarter ending September 15, 1872. In twenty Utah counties and one Idaho stake, the Church had 190 Sunday Schools, of which 149 had reported. These 149 enrolled 13,373 pupils—5,964 boys and 7,409 girls—and had 1,408 teachers—687 men and 721 women. Following are the courses of study and the number of classes taught in each:

New Testament	330	Bible	118
Alphabet	206	Miscellaneous	72
First Reader	202	Doctrine & Covenants	54
Second Reader	202	*Juvenile Instructor*	52
Book of Mormon	129	Theology	28

Adults were not the only ones to stay home from Sunday School; so did older youths and young adults. William Dunbar of the Salt Lake City Twentieth Ward became concerned for the ward's young people ages sixteen through twenty-two because

> as a general thing the class I am referring to do not attend Sunday school. They consider that they are too old, that they know too much, or that it is rather humiliating to associate with children; and, with a few exceptions, those I mean are not of the kind who have read the Bible. . . . They must not expect to study "Mormonism" by reading novels, but they must read the Bible, Book of Mormon, Doctrine and Covenants, Millennial Star, Orson Pratt's Works, the Voice of Warning and many others. These are the works our children must study if they ever find out for themselves the truth of the principles of "Mormonism."[73]

EFFORTS TO HELP THE "UNCHURCHED" YOUTH. For two decades, most LDS parents in Utah raised their children without the help of Church programs. This generation of parents believed that their children would grow up to be righteous by virtue of living in Zion and away from Babylon. "No thought was bestowed upon their spiritual culture," Eliza R. Snow confessed, with the result that "we had Infidels among them; children of good parents."[74] Children born in the faith, another leader said, "did not seem to value it like those who had left everything for its sake."[75]

LDS records show that adults complained about a variety of misbehaviors by adolescent boys: rowdyism, vile language, reckless horseback riding, throwing rocks through windows, vandalism, fighting, intoxication, smoking, spitting tobacco juice on church floors, gang behavior, and Sabbath breaking.[76] Adults complained about girls "retailing scandal," drinking tea, being lazy, desiring inappropriate fashions, dancing improperly, dating Gentiles, and relishing novels.[77]

Most teens did not attend Sunday School, believing it was for little children. But in the 1870s, recruitment pushes increased teenage Sunday School enrollments. One teacher said that twenty young men in his class "were exceeding rough" at first "but now they attended regularly and their minds were awakened." Another remarked that his class grew from 2 to 110 in two years and that "rowdyism was being dispensed with." Another report said that "the Sabbath School had a great effect to restrain boys from whiskey, tobacco and bad habits" and that the boys "were more polite and amenable to good advice."[78]

Some of the teenage girls began to receive indirect training and to be further involved in the Church when they started receiving calls to teach the children in Primary following its creation two years after Brigham Young's death.

Leaders, being parents themselves, created additional programs to prevent the young folks from growing up unindoctrinated, untrained, and unappreciative of their religion.[79] Valuing their young people, they launched mutual improvement programs for young women in 1869 and for young men in 1875. The weekly meetings of the YWMIAs and YMMIAs featured "intellectual exercises," "suitable amusements," and programs intended to build testimonies, improve manners, and overcome deficiencies in members' educations.[80]

Illustrating the start-up of youth movements is the Salt Lake City Seventeenth Ward. Its Young Ladies Cooperative Retrenchment Society began in 1870 with nineteen young women as members and a married woman as president. This group resolved to reform in many specific areas: to read Church books, to obey the Word of Wisdom, to remove right-hand gloves when partaking of the sacrament, and to not "retail scandal." Leaders stressed proper dress standards for the girls, some of whom had received their endowment: dressing neatly and plainly, avoiding tight lacing, eschewing long trains or "dresses so short that the tops of our high shoes could be seen," not mutilating temple garments by cutting off the sleeves and collars, not turning garments down "from their shoulders" to go to parties, and not wearing shawls gentile style or bonnets made after gentile patterns.[81]

The ward's retrenchment attendance sagged. One reason was that some girls said "they do not have any thing to retrench in they do not wear ruffles and frills," so why come? The organization folded, then resurrected in 1873. But by 1875 the girls had wearied of meetings where the woman president called on them to stand up and say something. "It seems that we can not say any thing where we are in our meetings," one honest girl said, "but we can talk freely when out of doors." "I think I could speak better if there was no older Sisters present," confessed another. Miss Addie Clayton put the problem in a nutshell: she "hated to refuse to speak yet hated to speak." One effort to boost attendance seemed guaranteed to create guilt in the girls: "If we do not come to meeting," an officer said, "our guardian angel cannot come, and they love to come and converse together."[82]

President Brigham Young's 1875 ban on round dancing stirred up the girls. Some approved a resolution to quit round dancing, some abstained from voting, and some voted in favor of the resolution but with reluctance. Clarissa Smith "presumed there was no girl that like[d] round-dancing as well as she did yet she had said she would quit so she would. The temptation was great." Another pledged "to try by the help of the Lord to quit round dancing, although it was hard." Addie Clayton did not vote because she feared she might break the promise. There was no harm in round dancing, she reasoned, "if harm was not made of it." Jennie Russell pledged, "by the help of the Lord," to quit round dancing and also tea and coffee. Lizzi Smith "liked tea & coffee but was going to stop that & round dancing." One girl liked the dancing ban because she never could get the step right and appreciated an excuse to quit trying.[83]

The Seventeenth Ward's Young Men's Mutual held its first meeting on November 2, 1875. Their purpose for organizing was "to learn all they could in regard to the principles of our religion" and to practice public speaking and explaining "our views and ideas." Members participated in discussions, talks, lectures, readings, declamations, and the sharing of personal essays. Discussion topics included the "first principles," Word of Wisdom, and signs of the times. For new participants, it was "the first time that most of them had ever stood before a congregation."[84]

By 1877 a main feature of the YMMIA meetings was questions and answers. An assigned person brought in a question on any religious, scientific, or historical subject. The executive committee assigned a member, someone other than the question raiser, to be the answerer. If no one could answer a particular question, the committee, which included the bishop, would consult with Church authorities "except on Scientific or Historical subjects." Among questions raised were "How high was the tower of Babel?" "Was Moroni a spirit or resurrected being?" "What is the difference between a Republican and a Democrat?" and "When was the first locomotive made?"[85] About twenty young men normally attended the ward's YMMIA meetings.[86] Late in 1877, the Seventeenth

Ward's YMMIA and YLMIA agreed to hold joint meetings once a month, an innovation that enlivened both organizations.

PRIESTHOOD FOR YOUNG MEN. As part of the multipronged effort to strengthen the youth, priesthood leaders labored on a modest scale to place boys into priesthood harness during the mid-1870s. Salt Lake Stake President Angus M. Cannon wanted bishops "to draw the young men into positions in the Priesthood and thus an excellent experience, and, at the same time, preserve them from evil associations." He personally had noticed a "marked improvement" in his own sons after they were ordained.[87] Priesthood service, proponents argued, like involvement in the auxiliaries, would help keep boys from evil practices while inculcating skills to qualify them for adult church service. To care for meetinghouses, deacons were specifically advised to clean the building; keep dust off the seats; polish the stove; carry in coal; light the fires; have the sacrament trays, table, and clothes clean and neat; usher people to their seats; help keep order during church services; and even clean the "back-houses"—apparently the outhouses.

MORE MEETINGS, MORE WARD JOBS. In his handwritten history of Gunnison Ward, Bishop Christian Madsen explained the evolution in meetings, which provided the opportunity for more people to hold positions in their wards:

> In regard to the Ecclesiastical arrangements, there was of course separate meetings both forenoon and afternoon, untill Sunday Schools were introduced. which afterwards occupied the Sunday forenoon. All the year round. In winter time there was Sunday and Thursday night meetings, besides the meetings of Acting Priesthood and Quorums.

By November 1877, Gunnison Ward had the following schedule of meetings:[88]

Saturday afternoon:	Priesthood and associations
evening:	Aaronic Priesthood
Sunday 10–12 A.M.:	Sunday School
2–4 P.M.:	Sacrament meeting
4–6 P.M.:	Bishop and acting teachers meeting
Wednesday evening:	Scandinavian meeting
Thursday evening:	Two prayer meetings
One evening a week:	Amusements
One day a week:	Juvenile choir
	Adult choir

SAINTS AND ORDINANCES

THE SACRAMENT. The day after the arrival of Brigham Young in Salt Lake Valley, a Sunday, the advance company partook of the sacrament; in the next few years, the sacrament was sometimes administered only once a month.[89] By the mid-1850s, however, the Saints had the opportunity to partake of the sacrament weekly in the area-wide sacrament meetings.

Twice during the Brigham Young years, the sacrament was withheld for short periods. Once was for several months during the Mormon Reformation when the Saints were given time to repent and make restitution prior to renewing their covenants. The other interval came during the Utah War period, 1857–58, when the sacrament was withdrawn while the federal army established itself in Utah. Some of the leaders' concerns about holding Sunday meetings are indicated by instructions given October 1858; bishops were told that "if there are any meetings, let them be prayer meetings" and not preaching services where speakers might say something offensive to the occupation army. "Be careful to controul all that may be said," Presiding Bishop Edward Hunter cautioned, "for an enthusiastic Mormon is more dangerous than an Apostate." Finally, early in August 1859, Brigham Young recommended that local leaders start holding public Sunday meetings again "in all the wards once a week at least." That November, Presiding Bishop Hunter expressed gratitude "for the privilege of again having the sacrament administered in the Tabernacle."[90]

During sacrament meetings, the sacramental water was passed down the rows in a "common cup." These containers were goblets or glasses—tiny individual cups were not introduced until 1911. In 1852 the General Authorities wanted to obtain a special set of sacrament glasses and plates for use in the Sunday afternoon downtown services. They asked members to contribute silver from which to make sacrament vessels. Very quickly they collected silver coin worth $149 and several pounds of silver watch cases, spoons, rings, and other "ornaments." The silver was melted down and then cast by silversmith Israel Barlow to form twelve silver cups. Then in 1855, leaders obtained "six new silver bread baskets." In 1873, Salt Lake City's ninth ward dedicated its "silver service for the communion table," purchased with members' donations. Provo wards spent more than four years trying to raise enough through donations to buy a nice sacrament serving set for use in the Provo Tabernacle.[91]

For many years, the methods for blessing and passing the sacrament varied from ward to ward. Often, bishops personally administered the sacrament, both in their own wards and in the settlement-wide sacrament meetings. One bishop noted in 1874 that "at 2 PM I administered the sacrament in the New Tabernacle assisted by my 2 council[ors] and [Acting] Teachers." Some wards blessed bread and water first, then passed both at the same time. In other wards, bishops decided "to bless the bread and water at the Sacrament according to the universal custom" instead of "blessing both before distributing either." While

Before the introduction of individual cups in 1911, the sacrament water was passed in communal goblets. This sacrament serving set was used in the rock church built in 1872 in Alpine, Utah. SOURCE: Jennie Adams Wild, *Alpine Yesterdays* (Salt Lake City: Blaine Hudson Printing, 1982).

bread and water passed through the congregation, speakers continued their talks. In a valleywide 1854 sacrament meeting in Salt Lake City, for example, after the opening song and prayer, the bread was blessed, and while it passed around, Brigham Young preached a sermon. Then he stopped in midsermon, "blest the contents of the cup," and resumed his talk while the water goblets passed around.[92] An opinion on whether the congregation should kneel was issued in 1868, when Presiding Bishop Hunter told bishops he preferred the "kneeling posture," which "was much more seemly to his mind, than standing as at present."[93]

A few small cases of "misconduct" during the sacrament needed correcting. "Instead of the saints taking a sip of water, at the sacrament and then passing it," one leader complained, "they indulged in the habit of drinking too freely, with the view of quenching their thirst."[94] Some men and women kept their hats on in church, especially in cool weather, and women wore gloves. Bishops were told in 1867 that because "the gentlemen were required to uncover their heads while partaking of it [the sacrament]" as a sign of respect "the ladies should be required to take off their gloves."[95]

Local leaders wondered if children should receive the sacrament during Sunday School time. "In settlements where there are Meeting Houses sufficiently spacious to admit of children attending the public meetings on Sunday afternoon, we suggest that they be encouraged to go there," the First Presidency advised local leaders. But where meeting-houses were too small, bishoprics should serve the sacrament weekly to the Sunday School children.[96] As children usually did not attend the afternoon sacrament meetings, leaders introduced the sacrament into Sunday School. Bishop Kesler's diary noted the innovation: "I visited our Ward Sunday School & spoke a few minets while the Sacrement was passing around, it being the 2nd time that it had been administered unto our children in the Sunday Schools."[97]

BAPTISMS. Almost all baptisms in early Utah took place outdoors in streams or lakes. LDS records identify but few baptismal fonts any-where in Utah. In October 1856, the First Presidency dedicated a baptismal font located near the Endowment House in Salt Lake City. A year later, two Apostles helped dedicate a baptismal font in the city's fourteenth ward.[98] In 1861, Brigham Young had a large wagon boarded up to make a font a few rods east of his schoolhouse. About 10' x 12', it had two dressing rooms attached. The President dedicated it September 4, 1861, then told the ward bishops "they were quite welcome to use it for Baptizing, instead of the creek."[99]

In 1875 the Presiding Bishop asked Frederick Kesler, a millwright, to build a new baptismal font for a group baptism of Native Americans then visiting Salt Lake City. With boards and pipes, he built the font to run east to west so the officiator would stand facing south, letting the candidate rise facing east, as in the Resurrection.[100] Kesler installed his font to have running, not standing, water, for he believed that baptisms should be, like Jesus' was, in running water.[101]

In 1877 leaders urged parents to baptize children when they turned eight, even in winter, rather than waiting several months. Although children might be "afraid of the cold water," the ordinance should not be postponed.

REBAPTISMS. Newcomers to Zion learned upon arrival that they should be rebaptized as an initiatory rite wherein they covenanted and committed to the new religious setting and society they were join-ing. It was "a kind of standing ordinance for all Latter-day Saints who emigrate here,"[102] following the example set by Brigham Young's 1847 pioneer company.[103] In October 1854, a bishop with thirty-two Dan-ish families in his ward reported that on a prior Sunday 107 Danes, some of whom were from other wards, were rebaptized.[104] "When Brethren first come in here," Presiding Bishop Hunter instructed in 1856, "they should be rebaptized and set to work."[105]

During Brigham Young's presidency, leaders provided Utah Saints with three opportunities to be rebaptized: during the consecration movement in 1854, the "Mormon Reformation" in 1856–57, and the united order movement in the mid-1870s. On these occasions, Saints were asked to search their souls and repent sufficiently to be worthy of being baptized once again. During the reformation, almost all adult Saints were rebaptized. For example, some five hundred Saints in the Kaysville Ward—nearly every member of the ward—accepted rebaptism.[106] During the united order campaign, leaders judged that the members seemed to be in a "stupor" and needed to be awakened through renewing their covenants. The Twelve set the example by being rebaptized and preached the necessity of the "elders renewing their covenants with the Almighty by rebaptism"; women were to do the same.[107]

Rebaptisms took place for other reasons. Ill people were rebaptized to renew their health. People found guilty of serious sin were not cut off from Church membership if they were contrite but were instead instructed to be rebaptized.[108]

TEMPLE ENDOWMENTS AND MARRIAGES. Prior to 1877, Church activity did not involve participation in temple ordinances other than receiving one's own endowments, being married, witnessing marriages, and doing some baptisms for the dead. Endowments were given in the upper floor of the Council House in Salt Lake City from 1851 to 1855, at the Endowment House in Salt Lake City from 1855 until 1877 and even later (until 1889), and in the St. George Temple starting in 1877. Men and women rarely went to these sacred places after receiving their own endowments and being married.[109]

Most of the adult Saints in Brigham Young's time obtained their temple endowments. A total of about seventy thousand adults lived during the three decades studied here. From 1851 to 1876, 43,952 Saints received their endowments—about 70 percent of the total number of adults.[110] Another sizable percentage of adults had been endowed in Nauvoo.

In May 1855, when the Endowment House first opened, the First Presidency strongly encouraged Saints to keep the house busy.[111] Wards received quotas to fill on assigned days, so bishops sent unendowed men and women there to receive the ordinances.

Even youths were sent. "We would like to see many of the young and sprightly young persons, who are strict to obey their parents," said Endowment House director and First Presidency Counselor Heber C. Kimball.[112] Records of the Kaysville elders quorum for 1865 show that thirty-six of its first members became elders while in their teens, most being ordained at the Endowment House prior to receiving the endowment.[113]

A bishop asked Brigham Young in 1877 at what age girls might receive endowments, and the prophet replied that "if naturally ripe and early development of mind and body" a girl at twelve could, but "as a general rule 15 is old enough."[114] One age study involves the Endowment House records for 1870, 1872, 1877, and 1878 and the St. George Temple endowment records for 1877 and 1878.[115] These records show that teenagers, particularly girls, commonly received their endowments at young ages. For all recipients under age 30, the average age for receiving endowments was 22 for men and 19.5 for women. However, the most popular age for receiving endowments was 17 for women, followed by 18, 16, and 19. For men, the most popular age for receiving endowments was 23, followed by 24, 20, and 22. Of 1,085 endowments checked in the samples, one in three, or 373, were teenage recipients. A few youths received endowments at 9, 12, and 13, but the youngest age when *significant* numbers of endowments were given was 14 for both boys and girls.

A sampling of Endowment House marriage records for the year 1870 shows that endowment age corresponded with marriage age for girls. That year, the commonest age for girls to marry was 17, and the average was 18. A few girls as young as 12 received temple marriage sealings. For women under age 24, the average marriage age was 18, but the average age of the men they married was 25, a difference of seven years. This age gap is smaller than that found by Dean May for Kanab during the 1870s, where women married at the average age of 19 and men at 29. The gap is larger by three years than the age difference Larry Logue found for marriages in St. George, where women and men married at age 19 and 23 respectively.[116]

Scholars continue to refine our estimates of the incidence of plural marriage. Findings vary in terms of total percent of families involved, depending upon time period and what communities were studied. Larry Logue's research shows that in St. George nearly 30 percent of households were involved in polygamy in 1870, and 33 percent were in 1880. All recent evidence conclusively shows that most LDS adult men and women in Utah between 1847 and 1877 were monogamists, not polygamists.[117]

Patriarchal Blessings

It was common practice for Saints to obtain patriarchal blessings. Patriarchs often traveled in circuits so people could receive their blessings. Recipients paid a small fee to reimburse the patriarch for his traveling expenses. Sometimes Saints received two or more patriarchal blessings in their lifetimes. Within three weeks of arriving in the Salt Lake Valley in 1850, for example, Martha Spence Heywood sought for and received her blessing from Patriarch John Smith. Three years later, she received a second blessing from a Brother Cazier. Many, like Sarah Dugard Crowther, received a patriarchal blessing in Nauvoo and a second one in Utah.[118]

Proselyting Missions

Church missionary records show that during the entire 1847–77 period only 2,657 men entered the mission field—less than one thousand per decade. In 1877, by comparison, Utah had perhaps twenty thousand adult males (a few thousand who lived in the time under discussion had died by 1877). Thus, in terms of missionary service, at best only one man in ten—but probably no more than one in twenty—filled a Church proselyting mission. Salt Lake City's sixteenth ward had 113 families in 1857, or at least one hundred adult males. But during the 1860 to 1877 period, only twelve men left from that ward on proselyting missions—suggesting a rate lower than 10 percent.[119] This small percentage counters an image we have popularized that says because the men were so often called away on missions significant numbers of women ran farms and families, developing their independence and abilities in new ways.[120]

Personal Religion and Worthiness Standards

Saints knew what constituted being a "good Mormon," even if they lived below their own expectations. They understood that they should practice the basics of Christian behavior: be honest; do not kill, steal, lie, or commit adultery; read scriptures; pray; have family prayer; help the poor; attend church meetings; and teach the gospel in the home. To "teach the principles of the Gospel of Christ to their children at least 10 minutes every day" was one covenant parents in Gunnison made in recommitting to live the united order.[121]

BUILDING UP ZION. All who "crossed the plains," "gathered to Zion," and then built up Zion were considered good Latter-day Saints until they proved otherwise. "Abide among his saints," the First Presidency urged.[122] The faithful were those who stayed in Zion and obeyed admonitions against going to California or backtracking on the Mormon Trail. They built up Zion by erecting homes, developing farms, caring for their cattle, digging irrigation systems, maintaining village roads, constructing meetinghouses, and helping neighbors. Those willing to physically strengthen the Mormon settlements were considered such stalwarts that problems they might have with smoking, drinking, profaning, Sabbath breaking, and even immoral living did not normally cost them their standing in the community and the Church.[123] Citing Brigham Young, Daniel H. Wells taught,

> "Go to with your mights and build up the kingdom of God, by quarrying the rock, by bringing the timber from the kanyons [sic] and making it into lumber, by making adobies, mixing the mortar, burning the lime, and drawing from the elements around us the material necessary to beautify, and build up, and to exalt in every way those principles that essay to establish righteousness over the whole earth." If the word is to build forts, build them; if to raise grain, raise grain.

He added that in his opinion a "woman that makes a yard of cloth accomplishes a good work towards building up the independence of the kingdom of God, and by her works her faith is made manifest."[124]

CATECHISMS. Members had no annual temple worthiness interviews through which Church leaders could monitor, encourage, and even enforce behavior. So what leverage did the Church have to help members behave righteously? Two Church programs seem to have filled that function: the general rebaptism campaigns noted above and catechisms,[125] which ward teachers or local leaders used to interrogate the members in a manner somewhat like that of the modern temple recommend interview.

John Jaques published a catechism for children in 1854, which became widely used throughout the Church up through the 1890s, even in Europe, Hawaii, and Samoa. It was primarily doctrinal but included two chapters on commandments—the Ten Commandments and the Word of Wisdom.[126]

During the Mormon Reformation, members were asked a series of questions about their righteousness. The questions dealt with both negative and positive behaviors, the negative ones being murder, adultery, betraying fellow Saints, bearing false witness against a neighbor, becoming drunk, stealing, lying, incurring debts with no intention to pay, underpaying hired help, coveting, profaning, and speaking against LDS leaders and teachings. On the positive side, members were asked if they labored faithfully for their wages, paid tithes, kept the Sabbath, and attended ward meetings. Men were expected to preside in their families.[127]

In addition, various reformation leaders spoke out against specific activities they believed offended the Spirit. Novel reading was one. Another was having more enthusiasm for socials than for worship meetings: David Ivins of Utah County, speaking to a meeting of bishops in Salt Lake City, said there was "one class of the people fill the Ball Room and, and [sic] another class attend prayer meeting."[128]

WORTHINESS REQUIREMENTS. The Church had general requirements or expectations regarding worthiness for individuals seeking to obtain their endowments. One year after the Endowment House opened, its director, President Heber C. Kimball, advised the bishops regarding who they should recommend by letter to come for endowments. His requirements for both men and women follow:[129]

> Pay tithing from year to year.
>
> Pray in your families.
>
> Do not speak against the authorities of the Church and kingdom of God.
>
> Do not steal.
>
> Do not lie.
>
> Do not swear.
>
> Do not interfere with the neighbors' things or spouses.
>
> Respect presiding officers and bishops.

When the St. George Temple opened early in 1877, Saints wishing to go there needed to obtain a recommend from their bishops, who had received blank recommend forms for that purpose. The printed recommend form read, "I hereby recommend [blank] as a faithful member of the Church, having paid full Tithings and donations, and as being worthy of receiving (here state the ordinances desired in the Temple), if endorsed by Prest. B. Young."[130]

Another set of worthiness requirements was framed during the united order enlistments in the mid-1870s. One set of united order rules said the member should refrain from swearing, "adultery, whoredom, and lust," vulgar and obscene language and conduct, being contentious or quarrelsome, speaking evil of others, being selfish, wearing a "foolish and extravagant fashion," and buying items from abroad that were being made in Utah. On the positive side, they should pray with their families morning and evening, pray privately, keep the Word of Wisdom "according to the Spirit and meaning thereof," treat family members with kindness and affection, seek the salvation of all mankind and good for all, observe personal cleanliness, keep the Sabbath day holy, return what is borrowed, patronize members of the order, foster and encourage the production and manufacturing of all consumer goods, be simple in dress and manners, labor for mutual benefit, perform labor honestly and diligently, and sustain with faith, works, and prayers those in charge of the united orders.[131]

TITHING. Leaders firmly believed that the best way of judging people is by the spirit they show in the settling of their tithing. As leaders taught regularly in sermons and LDS publications, tithing involved three parts: (1) an initiatory tithe of all one possessed when he or she started paying tithing, usually at the time of conversion; (2) a tithe of increase and income; and (3) a labor tithe.[132] Labor tithing originated in Nauvoo. For every ten days that a man and his team did not work for income, such as days spent in riding and leisure, he was expected to work one day for the Church as labor tithing. Or, he could use labor tithing to substitute for paying tithing in kind.[133]

Leaders constantly counseled members to be punctual and strict in paying tithing and offerings to the poor.[134] By the mid-1850s, the Saints paid tithes to their bishops and settled with the bishop at year's end. Late in 1860, when Salt Lake City's bishops gave verbal report about their wards, most of them commented about the spirit of tithe paying.[135] They made summary statements like these:

> Good desire to settle tithing in season.
>
> Good spirit toward tithing.
>
> Most of ward felt well especially toward tithing.
>
> Hard to get donations.
>
> Good spirit to pay tithing.
>
> Good feeling regarding tithing.

Bishop Alonzo Raleigh, and no doubt other leaders, "believed it would come in the course of events that Tithing would be a matter of fellowship, just as much as stealing or drunkenness is now."[136]

However, in 1852, President Young explained that non–tithe payers were not to be subjected to Church discipline. "There is no compulsory or arbitrary power to be exercised over the brethren, in order to coerce the payment of tithing," he instructed.[137] But he sometimes wished that non–tithe payers could be disciplined. In 1868 he told bishops that he "really wished they would cut off from the church those members who did not pay their tithing." In September 1876, he stressed how strongly he believed that every "good Mormon" must be a tithe payer: "What is a fact, we have become so dull and indifferent, that men are permitted to remain in the church who gave way to habits of intoxication and never pay a cent of tithing, although Jehovah told Joseph that Tithing was a standing law for ever."[138]

We do not know how many Saints did or did not tithe. But the percentage of tithe payers exceeded at least 40 percent of the adults.[139] Tithing records for Spring City show that between 82 and 94 percent paid some tithing during the 1860–68 period.[140]

FASTING AND FAST OFFERINGS. Because of the Lord's stern admonition that the Church take care of the poor and needy, fast offerings became almost as basic an obligation for practicing Mormons as their tithes. On occasion, members were warned that "those who failed to pay their offerings were not entitled to the sacrament."[141]

At first, LDS members brought their fast offerings to the meeting-house. Offerings were food items rather than cash, and bishops distributed the donated food to the needy in the ward, sometimes assisted by the acting priesthood. Later, the bishops assigned deacons or teachers to pick up food donations from the members' homes. In 1871 a Salt Lake City bishop told of "his method to send the teachers round on a fast day morning from house to house, and by these means he obtains sufficient to sustain the poor."[142] In 1876 the Aaronic Priesthood young men in Payson, Utah, collected "about 150 lbs of flour, 2 sacks of potatoes, 2 quarts of Dried fruit 15 or 20 lbs of Meat and 5c in money." The Payson Aaronic Priesthood members gave considerable help in the 1870s to one needy lady in the ward, Sister B——. Some boys were sent to purchase a cow for her, others to gather wood for her stove. They regularly brought her flour. They gathered fast offerings for her benefit. They plowed land for her and planted some lucerne for her cow.[143]

At times, members participated in special fasts. "Today all the inhabitants of Cache Valley are required to hold a solemn Fast," a young Cache Valley woman wrote in 1868, "and pray to Him who heareth righteous prayers, that the grasshoppers may not destroy the crops."[144]

WORD OF WISDOM. John Jaques's catechism posited that good members were expected to obey the Word of Wisdom. However, the Word of Wisdom never became a binding law on Brigham's Saints.[145] For example, moderate drinking was allowed, although drunkenness was not tolerated.

In October 1851, Salt Lake Valley bishops discussed the Word of Wisdom. One bishop noted that tithing was a test of fellowship (although not a matter for Church discipline), but the Word of Wisdom was not. Bishop Edward Hunter's counsel on the Word of Wisdom was "as much as possible observe it" and teach the upcoming generation to do it.[146] His counsel to bishops eight years later regarding liquor was that men should "either take it moderately or let it alone entirely."[147] Regarding tobacco, President Young said it was injurious, "but since it is so extensively used, and many seem to place upon it as high a value as bread, why not raise it here, and stop its immense importations."[148]

At the April 1867 conference, President Young instructed bishops that "every Elder in Israel must know that whiskey, tobacko [*sic*], tea and coffee are not good for them to take" and that "he sometimes felt like making the observance of the Word of Wisdom a matter of fellowship, but it would be thought severe."[149] So, he assigned the bishops to ask members to obey the Word of Wisdom. They did, with good results, at least temporarily. Two weeks later, Salt Lake Valley bishops reported that the majority of Saints had been obeying the Word of Wisdom since conference. "Others were gradually leaving off their use," they said, except "some whose advanced years and long usage, deemed it unwise to abstain."[150] Less than a year later, Bishop Hunter "rejoyced at the general observance of the word of wisdom," at least in Great Salt Lake Valley.[151] The late-1860s campaign brought a slight improvement that was short-lived. Obedience to the Word of Wisdom did not become a binding worthiness behavior until the twentieth century.

MORALITY. Married adults guilty of adultery were dealt with harshly, usually excommunicated. Personal and LDS records for the Brigham Young period do not mention youthful sexual immorality, so its extent cannot be known or guessed. At the dawn of the 1870s, one leader boasted that "our young live virtuously until they marry," a standard youths knew they should not violate.[152] Occasionally, teenage girls were victimized by older men, such as stepfathers or masters in the houses where the girls lived as servants. Youths guilty of having consensual sex before marriage received reprimands and loss of religious reputations rather than excommunications. However, they were expected to marry to "make things right." When premarital sex sins were confessed only after the couple had married, forgiveness often came with confession and rebaptism and without excommunication. One young man, for example, "committed himself previous to his endowments" and then married the young woman. The authority hearing the case noted that the Church had been "lenient" with such cases in the past, so the apology of the man was accepted and he was forgiven by being rebaptized.[153]

MISCELLANEOUS CHURCH ASSIGNMENTS AND EXPECTATIONS

To be a member was to deal with appeals to help with a number of Church projects. Perhaps the assignment families accepted that had the most far-reaching impact was to fill calls from Church leaders to uproot and move out to colonies the Church was establishing.

But Church members also frequently filled short-term assignments. Well known is the late in 1856 appeal that drew heroic responses from volunteers who rescued the handcart people trapped by Wyoming snows. When a gathering of Spanish Fork Saints heard the call for help, thirteen "young and able bodied men" volunteered and rushed five wagons and teams toward Wyoming.[154] Between 1861 and 1868, hundreds of men and youths from all over Utah went east as volunteers manning scores of "down and back" wagon trains that brought thousands of immigrants to Zion. Kaysville Ward members, for example, drove nine teams in 1868. A year earlier, that same ward provided thirteen teamsters and teams that hauled thirty-nine loads of cut rock to the Salt Lake Temple site. When the Church asked for men to help fill labor contracts for transcontinental railroad construction jobs, men from dozens of wards responded.[155] Appropriately, life sketches by or about men who filled such assignments describe the pride the men felt for giving such assistance to the Church and its members.

Members heard many requests and instructions. Devout members obeyed, and the less faithful disregarded them. Saints were asked in the mid-1850s to consecrate their properties to the Church and, in the 1870s, to pool their properties into united orders. Members offered much resistance to the latter effort, causing President Young to admit a year before his death that "he had been inspired by the Gift and power of God to call upon the saints to enter into the united order, or order of Enoch, and that now was the time, but he could not get the people to enter into it. He had cleared his skirts if he never said another word about it."[156]

In the late 1850s, Saints were told not to exchange their products with the United States army stationed at Camp Floyd. Early in 1861, President Young

> asked the Question, whether there was any harm in taking Wheat, Butter, Eggs, &c to Camp Floyd to sell to our enemies. He answered Yes, for such persons would weep and lament as long as Eternity lasts, if ever they are saved in the Kingdom of God, and the blight inflicted on their Character in the sight of Heaven and all Holy Beings, will never be obliterated.[157]

At times, profanity became a problem. Perhaps the worst outbreak was in 1868–69 among LDS men in railroad construction crews. Their language bothered President Young so much that he asked bishops "to cut off from the Church any man, who has been working on the railroad, and indulged in cursing, swearing or drunkeness [sic]." He was determined "that no man shall have the fellowship of the saints who takes the name of God in vain, and indulges in wickedness."[158]

When the Church developed, published, and taught the Deseret Alphabet, members felt obligated to try to learn how to read it. By late 1869, "most of the wards" in Salt Lake City "were using [Deseret Alphabet] books either in their day or Sunday schools."[159] Another expectation outside the usual was for Saints to accept diverse nationalities. In 1864, for instance, Brigham Young remarked

> on the oneness, and unity that should exist among the saints of God, to cast under our feet every feeling of national prejudice, that inasmuch as the saints have been gathered from different nations, baptized into one faith, and received of the same spirit, we should learn to cherish towards them the kindest of feelings, as saints of God, regardless of the nation that gave them birth.[160]

LEADERSHIP AND FOLLOWERSHIP

Any claim that the early LDS priesthood leaders were dictators who cracked whips, making the Saints jump, is doubly mythical—about the nature of both the leaders and the followers. Utah's early LDS settlers were not docile sheep easily led anywhere. Southerners, New England Yankees, Scots, Welsh, British, and Scandinavians had inbred streaks of independence that let them balance personal and family needs with Church needs, the scale tipping one way one time and the other way at other times.

Illustrative is Provo's situation between 1868 and 1872, as revealed in minutes of the bishops' meetings in that city.[161] With a charge to "build up Provo" and "make Provo one of the centres of attraction," Brigham Young sent Abraham O. Smoot to Provo in 1868 to be a mayor and what we would now call a stake president. But Smoot found he could not budge the bishops much and that they, likewise, had trouble making the Saints respond to their requests.[162] Smoot met twice monthly with the bishops of the five Provo wards to consult, monitor, and admonish. He instructed that the minutes of those meetings "record all that we do and who does" and "whether we respond to the calls made upon us or not"; the record shows plodding progress at best.[163]

After one year in office, Bishop Smoot felt frustrated by Provoans' unresponsiveness. "When has there been a job completed in this place[?]" he charged. "What is the reason we are not united enough and confidence is lacking[?]" Month by month, year by year, apathy smothered many of his calls for progress, causing him to complain in 1872, "Turn any way you will and ask what you will and you get nothing in any of our public calls."[164] Among public calls not well responded to were those to construct the Provo Canyon road, build a new tithing house, erect adequate meetinghouses and schools, finish off the tabernacle grounds with a well and outhouses, build and operate the woolen mill in Provo, erect adequate schools, and carry out cooperation-type projects. Even a rather simple community effort like obtaining sacrament vessels for the Provo-wide sacrament meetings floundered for over four years.[165]

When Brigham Young and the School of the Prophets pushed cooperative merchandising, Smoot tried to gain Provo's support for the idea. "As we have a head that must dictate," Smoot said of Brigham Young, and "as Bishops and Teachers, we must instruct the people on these things, give the Co-operative System your influence and support." But after laboring for a year to convert the people, one bishop reported that "there is quite an opposition to Co-operation and the [woolen] Factory."[166] Smoot added, "We have not more than 10% of the people who are in favor of or believe and act in Cooperation."[167] As if testifying to disprove charges of priesthood dictatorship, Smoot lamented:

> I would not of myself keep calling on the people to cooperate, build factory, &c. only that the burden is laid upon me by the Priesthood and I want to carry it out. There is a few of clear brain that can see

the good of this, but the masses do not see the point, and I think they are getting tired of hearing me talk about it. I would not say another word only as I am required. If the Bishops of Provo and the County do not help me I am left alone. I do not know that there is anything said in the meetings of the people in favor of Cooperation, Factory, &c. I can occasionally hear of it being preached down. I want the Bishops to help me.[168]

The bishops' meeting minutes reveal four causes for Provo's slowness to make projects happen. First, Provo had a good share of "hard people" who possessed traditional English independence. A favorite Mormon motto was "mind your own business," and common people applied that to strangers, neighbors, and Church leaders alike.[169] Second, bishops lacked respect among the Saints. Smoot arrived at a time when leaders' influence had waned for some reason. "Heads here have not the proper influence," Smoot noticed. "I think I can see a feeling of distrust in the people to any measure proposed by authority, and while this lasts with the people we are dead ducks." Provo had good people "disposed to be good Mormons, but they are filled and troubled with doubts and fears." Although bishops "are rising in the esteem of true men in the kingdom," he said, still they lacked "the necessary persuasive powers" to motivate their people.[170] Third, and perhaps more important than the other factors, Provoans had limited resources. Leaders constantly assessed and taxed the people and called for donations for Church projects, apparently beyond the people's ability to pay. "We are poor" was a complaint bishops heard when soliciting funds or goods.[171] The fourth hindrance was leadership style. Bishops rarely minded Smoot's "snubbing our ears and stirring us up to our duties." But rather than dictate, Smoot functioned democratically, feeling that "the bishops as a body are really legislators for Zion." He encouraged but did not demand results from bishops holding lifetime tenure. Bishops, in turn, lacked bargaining power with members, unlike today's leaders who can deny temple recommends to unsupportive Saints.[172]

EBBS AND FLOWS OF COMMITMENT

Historian Richard Bushman observed that often our published LDS histories describe well the conflict between the Church and the world but pay little attention to the tensions between God and the Church.[173] In past dispensations, the faith of God's chosen people ebbed and flowed, and the Saints' commitments during the Brigham Young years traced out similar ups and downs.

One decade, the 1870s, provides a case study. It was a decade when the Church experienced much "progress"—gaining railroad connections, opening a temple, founding united orders, creating new auxiliary programs, welcoming a continuous stream of immigrants, and restructuring stakes, wards, and quorums. But of spiritual health and progress during that decade, leaders became unusually critical as indicated by their sermons and comments during meetings.

Early in 1871, Presiding Bishop Hunter warned that the people's indifference towards their duties "almost deprived them of their fellowship." He observed that "many were getting sleepy and falling away from the faith."[174] Bishop William Thorne of Salt Lake was "satisfied with his brethren that the people were asleep and did not feel that interist [*sic*] in the work that they should."[175] Minute books are sprinkled with such judgmental phrases as "there needs to be a wakening up and a shaking of the dry bones," time to wake up from "our lethargy," "Mormonism is at low ebb," "the great necessity of a reformation," "things have been at loose ends," "people were all drifting," and "the darkest time since the Church was organized."[176] In May 1874, one officer reported that "Bro. Brigham told us if we drifted further we should be over the precipice."[177]

To counter slackness and to bring greater faith and dedication, Church leaders introduced new programs and projects. But apathy blunted these reform efforts. Regarding the united orders, one Salt Lake bishop confided in his diary, "I am sorry to see so mutch [*sic*] opposition manifested towards the united order as thare is in this city it betokens no good & in consequence of which we may be made to se[e] mutch sorrow and affliction."[178] Reacting to poor support for temple projects, Brigham Young bluntly chastised the Saints; he "spoke sharply of the tardiness of the people in living our religion and he said we were nigh ready to be spewed out of the mouth of the Lord."[179]

Another reform tool in mid-decade was rebaptism. Members were requested to repent and reorder their lives preparatory to renewing their commitments to the Church by being rebaptized. Presiding Bishop Hunter had high hopes for the plan: "We have been in a lukewarm state for a long time, and he did not know of anything more suited to our present condition than rebaptism."[180] A high priests quorum officer put it plainly: he "compared the Church to day like unto a ship after a long voyage, in a Dry Dock for repairs and needing it."[181] A year after the rebaptism push, however, the general feeling was that it had not done much to improve the people.[182]

Not all leaders felt so judgmental. Bishop Alonzo Raleigh, for example, said in 1875 that "he did not think a greater proportion were apostatizing, and giving way to Drunkenness and Debauchery, than they did do at Nauvoo, or since the first organization of the church."[183]

Records for the 1870s identify many who did right when too many around them were careless. One is John Picknell, an older man. Noting the critical spirit some members manifested towards Brigham Young, he counseled, "Don't find fault, especially with the president, he may do wrong, as well as we, it matters not what those over us may do, its none of our business. If they give us the priesthood, & they apostatize the next day it dont matter to us, we are right if we do right!"[184]

When some priesthood bearers complained they were too busy to attend quorum meetings, Brother Picknell chided them:

> You say you have not much time to come to meeting, how much time do you suppose I've to do? I've Seventies', Priests' Teachers' & Deacons' meetings to attend. Teacher in two wards, a Priest in one, [prayer] circle meetings to attend &c I'm out almost every night in the month. I'm after the pay! I can't afford to lose it.[185]

Reacting to unfaithfulness around him, he warned that "one half [of the Church] will turn away, let it not be you nor me" and then added the folksy but straightforward truth: "Every tub must stand on its own bottom."[186]

Stalwarts also are seen in Salt Lake City's seventeenth ward Relief Society minute book, which records the sisters' responses to a terrible epidemic in the 1870s that took the lives of many of their children. Determined to unite their faith by praying privately in their homes, they proposed that

> at ten o'clock of each day, we retire to a quiet place and pray, that our faith may be concentrated, that we may have wisdom and faith sufficient by our united prayers to stay the diptheria which is now raging among our children, and that on Thursday we abstain from food until after prayers.[187]

Salt Lake City's Eighth Ward assigned Samuel D. Chambers, a former Mississippi slave, to serve as an assistant to the deacons, who took care of the ward meetinghouse and did ushering. A regular guest at the stake deacons meetings, more than once he was the *only* person there other than the stake officers. His testimonies, which quorum clerk Thomas C. Jones recorded, impressed his fellow deacons, most of whom were adults. Samuel joined the Church at age thirteen while a slave in Mississippi. Although lacking contact with the Church for a quarter century, he maintained his testimony. Becoming a free man in 1865, he earned enough money to gather to Zion in 1870 at age forty. His fervor is felt in his recorded testimonies given between 1873 and 1877: "I'm glad that I ever took upon me the name of Christ." "The knowledge I received is from my God. It is a high and holy calling, without the testimony of God we are nothing." He enjoyed serving the Church because he "did not come here [to Utah] to sit down and be still." His desire was to "be active in doing what he can for the building up of the kingdom of God." He attended meetings, ushered at the tabernacle, tithed fully, and endured as a stalwart until his death in 1929 at age ninety-eight.[188]

Just before President Brigham Young died in August 1877, he expressed his wish that the Saints gathered in Zion lived their religion better. "It is a marvel that the Lord did not scatter this people to the four winds," he observed. "It would have been done but for the prayers and faith and works of the humble saints"—the John Picknells, the Seventeenth Ward sisters, and the Samuel Chamberses of the Church.

William G. Hartley is Associate Research Professor at the Smith Institute of LDS History, Brigham Young University.

Notes

1. Presiding Bishopric Minutes of Bishops Meetings, 1851–84 (hereafter cited as Bishops Minutes), February 28, 1861, Archives Division, Historical Department, The Church of Jesus Christ of Latter-day Saints, Salt Lake City (hereafter cited as LDS Church Archives).

2. The 1,000 figure is conservative. Only about 1,250 bishops served in Utah wards during the entire nineteenth century, so for the Brigham Young period, there might have been half that many. Stakes never numbered more than seven, and wards more than about 100 until 1877—just weeks before Brigham Young died. Thus, counting General Authorities (First Presidency, the Twelve, the first Council of Seventy, and Patriarchs), stake presidencies, and bishops, the total is probably under 1,000. For the tally of nineteenth-century bishops, see Donald Gene Pace, "Community Leadership on the Mormon Frontier: Mormon Bishops and the Political, Economic, and Social Development of Utah before Statehood" (Ph.D. diss., Ohio State University, 1983), 80.

3. Bishops Minutes, November 22, 1860.

4. For a detailed population census of Utah Saints in 1877, see chart in William G. Hartley, "The Priesthood Reorganization of 1877: Brigham Young's Last Achievement," *BYU Studies* 20, no. 1 (1979): 27.

5. In late 1853, the city had 5,979 residents; see a bishops' census report in B. H. Roberts, *A Comprehensive History of The Church of Jesus Christ of Latter-day Saints, Century One,* 6 vols. (Provo, Utah: Corporation of the President, The Church of Jesus Christ of Latter-day Saints, 1965), 4:18, n. 39; Salt Lake Valley's population in 1870 was 18,337, according to Allen Kent Powell, "Population," in *Utah History Encyclopedia,* ed. Allen Kent Powell (Salt Lake City: University of Utah Press, 1994), 432; also see "Tabernacle" and "Tabernacles," in Andrew Jenson, *Encyclopedic History of The Church of Jesus Christ of Latter-day Saints* (Salt Lake City: Deseret News Publishing, 1941), 858, 860.

6. William G. Hartley, "Mormon Sundays," *Ensign* 8 (January 1978): 23.

7. Journal of Louisa Lula Greene, holograph, April 8, 1867, microfilm, LDS Church Archives.

8. Juanita Brooks, ed., *Not by Bread Alone: The Journal of Martha Spence Heywood, 1850–56* (Salt Lake City: Utah State Historical Society, 1978), 100, entry for May 4, 1854.

9. Brooks, *Not by Bread Alone,* 51, February 2; 56, April 12; 61, June 22; and 70, October 12, 1851.

10. Brooks, *Not by Bread Alone,* 59, June 8, 1851; 127, June 8, 1856.

11. Bishops Minutes, September 1, 1870.

12. Ronald W. Walker, "'Going to Meeting' in Salt Lake City's Thirteenth Ward, 1849–1881: A Microanalysis," in Davis Bitton and Maureen Ursenbach Beecher, eds., *New Views of Mormon History: A Collection of Essays in Honor of Leonard J. Arrington* (Salt Lake City: University of Utah Press, 1987), 154.

13. Hartley, "Mormon Sundays," 19–25.

14. Miscellaneous Minutes File, January 27, 1856, Brigham Young Papers, LDS Church Archives. See also Joseph Heinerman, "The Mormon Meetinghouse: Reflections on Pioneer Religious and Social Life in Salt Lake City," *Utah Historical Quarterly* 50 (fall 1982): 340–53.

15. Bishops Minutes, February 14, 1861.

16. "Utah News," *Millennial Star* 39 (August 13, 1877): 527.

17. G. D. Watt, "Dedication of the Kay's Ward Meeting House," *Deseret News Weekly,* September 30, 1863, 81; William Blood, Diary, September 27, 1863, LDS Church Archives.

18. Milton R. Hunter, comp. and ed. (for Daughters of Utah Pioneers, Weber County Chapter), *Beneath Ben Lomond's Peak: A History of Weber County, 1824–1900* (Salt Lake City: Deseret News Press, 1944), 448–49.

19. "Editorial Thoughts," *Juvenile Instructor* 12 (June 15, 1877): 138.

20. Members in Mendon, a town settled in 1859, met first in private homes, then in a log meetinghouse built in 1860, and next in a rock meetinghouse opened in 1866; see Doran J. Baker, Charles S. Peterson, and Gene A. Ware, eds., *Isaac Sorensen's History of Mendon: A Pioneer Chronicle of a Mormon*

Settlement (Salt Lake City: Cache County Historical Preservation Commission and Utah State Historical Society, 1988), 29, 30, 50. For another key source regarding LDS meetinghouses, see "Meetinghouses," chapter 5 of C. Mark Hamilton, *Nineteenth-Century Mormon Architecture and City Planning* (New York and Oxford: Oxford University Press, 1995), 77–91.

21. Christian A. Madsen, "Holiness to the Lord: A History of Gunnison, Utah," typescript by Edith J. Romney, 3, included with Gunnison Ward Historical Record, LDS Church Archives.

22. John Alexander Bevan, "The Early History of Tooele," typescript, 11, LDS Church Archives.

23. *The Veprecula,* September 15, 1864, quoted in Andrew Karl Larson, *"I Was Called to Dixie": The Virgin River Basin; Unique Experiences in Mormon Pioneering* (Salt Lake City: Deseret News Press, 1961), 565–66.

24. Larson, *"I Was Called to Dixie,"* 566, 569.

25. "Record of Business Meetings of the Bishop's and Lesser Priesthood of Provo City" (1868–75), January 19, 1869, LDS Church Archives (hereafter cited as Provo Bishops Minutes).

26. Provo Bishops Minutes, December 6, 1870.

27. Brooks, *Not by Bread Alone,* 49, January 19, 1851.

28. "Biography of Sidney Alexander Pace, as Told by Himself," typescript, LDS Church Archives.

29. A. Glen Humphreys, "Missionaries to the Saints," *BYU Studies* 17 (autumn 1976): 74–100.

30. Provo Bishops Minutes, June 29, 1869; April 23, 1872.

31. Bishops Minutes, November 22, December 6, 1860.

32. Wilford Woodruff, *Wilford Woodruff's Journal, 1833–1898, Typescript,* ed. Scott G. Kenney, 9 vols. (Midvale, Utah: Signature Books, 1983–84), 5:269–70 (January 2, 1859); Daniel Sylvester Tuttle, *Reminiscences of a Missionary Bishop* (New York: Thomas Whittaker, ca. 1906), 346; "Parowan Restores Old Church Hall," *Deseret News,* December 4, 1939, 5; A. Barnett, "'We Must Do Right and Be Guided by the Priesthood': A Study of the Parowan Meeting House and Its Role in the Mormon Community, 1860–1890," typescript, 51–52.

33. Heinerman, "Mormon Meetinghouse," 350–53; Davis Bitton, "Early Mormon Lifestyles; or the Saints as Human Beings," in *The Restoration Movement: Essays in Mormon History,* ed. F. Mark McKiernan, Alma R. Blair, and Paul M. Edwards (Lawrence, Kans.: Coronado Press, 1973), 298–302.

34. Walker, "'Going to Meeting,'" 142.

35. Brooks, *Not by Bread Alone,* 70, October 12, 1851.

36. Brooks, *Not by Bread Alone,* 53, February 16, 1851; 71, October 19, 1851; 103, June 22, 1853.

37. Bishops Minutes, September 24, 1874.

38. Bishops Minutes, June 1, 1876.

39. Bishops Minutes, June 29, 1876.

40. Author's observation based on reading dozens of quorum minute books of that time period, available in the LDS Church Archives.

41. Bishops Minutes, December 7, 1882.

42. Bishop Adam Spiers labeled it a "provision made" to allow the higher priesthood to officiate in the lesser. Tenth Ward, Salt Lake Stake, General Minutes, Teachers Report Meetings, 1874–80, November 6, 1874, LDS Church Archives.

43. William G. Hartley, "Brigham Young and Priesthood Work at the General and Local Levels," in Susan Easton Black and Larry C. Porter, eds., *Lion of the Lord: Essays on the Life and Service of Brigham Young* (Salt Lake City: Deseret Book, 1995), 338–70.

44. Brooks, *Not by Bread Alone,* 120.

45. Journal History Index listings for "conferences" and "special conferences" for the 1849–77 period; A. Karl Larson and Katharine Miles Larson, *Diary of Charles Lowell Walker,* 2 vols. (Logan: Utah State University Press, 1980), entries in vol. 1 for May and November 1866–72.

46. Larson and Larson, *Diary of Charles Lowell Walker,* 1:343.

47. Journal History of the Church, March 14, 1857, LDS Church Archives.

48. Hartley, "Mormon Sundays," 23.

49. *Lehi Centennial History, 1850–1950, Part 1* (Lehi, Utah: Free Press Publishing, 1950), 155–60.

50. Seventies quorums were general quorums directed by the seven-man First Council of the Seventy. Some thirty-three quorums were organized before the Saints left Nauvoo. Most men called as missionaries during the nineteenth century were ordained to the office of seventy and belonged to seventies quorums after they returned. In time the Church had hundreds of seventies quorums, which became stake entities during most of the twentieth century. The First Quorum of Seventy, reconstituted in 1976, became a General-Authority-level quorum whose members replaced the Assistants to the Twelve. Stake seventies quorums were phased out in October 1986, leaving the First Quorum, and later a Second Quorum, also General Authorities, as the only bodies of seventies in the Church. An in-depth history of the seventies, written while they were stake quorums, is James N. Baumgarten's "The Role and Function of the Seventies in L.D.S. Church History" (master's thesis, Brigham Young University, 1960). Also see S. Dilworth Young, "The Seventies: A Historical Perspective," *Ensign* 6 (July 1976): 14–21.

51. Compare priesthood totals in the 1852 Church census with priesthood totals in the 1878 census figures I charted in my study "Priesthood Reorganization of 1877," 27.

52. William G. Hartley, "Ordained and Acting Teachers in the Lesser Priesthood, 1851–1883," *BYU Studies* 16 (spring 1976): 375–78.

53. Hartley, "Ordained and Acting Teachers," 378.

54. William G. Hartley, "From Men to Boys: LDS Aaronic Priesthood Offices, 1829–1996," *Journal of Mormon History* 22 (spring 1996): 100, 105.

55. Walker, "'Going to Meeting,'" 150.

56. Bishops Minutes, May 26, 1861. Presiding Bishop Hunter called on those present "holding the Aaronic Priesthood to magnify both Priesthoods."

57. Salt Lake Stake, Deacons Quorum Minutes, 1873–77, December 14, 1875, LDS Church Archives (hereafter cited as Salt Lake Deacons Minutes). The man was John Picknell.

58. Salt Lake Deacons Minutes, January 27, 1877.

59. Presiding Bishopric, Lesser Priesthood Meeting Minutes, 1855–78, January 5, 1861, LDS Church Archives (hereafter cited as General Aaronic Priesthood Minutes).

60. Matthias Cowley, Salt Lake Deacons Minutes, May 26, 1877.

61. Bishops Minutes, June 23, 1870.

62. Bishops Minutes, December 1, 1864.

63. Eighth Ward, Salt Lake Stake, General Minutes, 1856–75, January 7, 1857, LDS Church Archives.

64. Jill Mulvay Derr, Janath Russell Cannon, and Maureen Ursenbach Beecher, *Women of Covenant: The Story of Relief Society* (Salt Lake City: Deseret Book, 1992), 63, 75–82.

65. Derr, Cannon, and Beecher, *Women of Covenant,* 71, 82.

66. Provo Third Ward, Utah Stake, Relief Society Minutes, LDS Church Archives.

67. Regarding deaconesses, see the following Salt Lake City wards' Relief Society minutes in the LDS Church Archives: Eleventh Ward Relief Society Minutes, 1869–79 (Eliza R. Snow reorganized the society on March 3, 1869, and said the presidency should set apart deacons and other officers); Eighth Ward Relief Society Minutes, 1874–82 (entries during 1872 show nine women served as deacons, and in 1878 the deaconesses were reorganized and a new deacons' president installed); and the Fifteenth Ward Relief Society Minutes, 1855–73 (on January 1, 1873, four ladies filled the office of deacon).

68. *Jubilee History of Latter-day Saints Sunday Schools, 1849–1899* (Salt Lake City: Deseret Sunday School Union, 1900), 431–32, 452–56.

69. *Lehi Centennial History,* 158.

70. Tooele Branch, Sunday School Records, LDS Church Archives.

71. Frederick Kesler, Diary, typescript, June 21, 1874, Frederick Kesler Papers, Special Collections, Manuscripts Division, Marriott Library, University of Utah, Salt Lake City.

72. *Jubilee History,* 44–45.

73. William C. Dunbar, in *Journal of Discourses,* 26 vols. (Liverpool: F. D. Richards, 1855–86), 17:16, 18–19, 21, January 4, 1874.

74. Mrs. L. D. Alder, "R. S. Reports," *Woman's Exponent* 6 (February 15, 1878): 138.

75. Salt Lake Deacons Minutes, February 8, 1876.

76. Davis Bitton, "Zion's Rowdies: Growing Up on the Mormon Frontier," *Utah Historical Quarterly* 50 (spring 1982): 182–95; Bishops Minutes, June 28, 1877; *Juvenile Instructor* 7 (September 28, 1872): 155; Salt Lake Deacons Minutes, April 14, 1874; Bishops Minutes, December 20, 1860; January 15, 1874; Southern Utah Mission, St. George Stake, Lesser Priesthood Record Book A, January 27, 1877, LDS Church Archives; Salt Lake Deacons Minutes, March 7, April 13, and September 14, 1875; Kanab Ward, Kanab Stake, General

Minutes, Ward Teachers Report Minutes, 1872–81, February 16, 1873, LDS Church Archives; Provo Bishops Minutes, August 17, 1869; June 7, 1870; and February 28, 1871; General Aaronic Priesthood Minutes, February 5, 1876; November 2, 1867.

77. For examples, see Salt Lake's Seventeenth Ward Young Ladies Cooperative Retrenchment Society minutes for the 1870s, LDS Church Archives.

78. School General Board Minutes, February 4, 1873, LDS Church Archives.

79. See "Primary," "Sunday School," "Young Men," and "Young Women" entries in *Encyclopedia of Mormonism,* ed. Daniel H. Ludlow, 5 vols. (New York: Macmillan, 1992); *Jubilee History;* Susa Young Gates, *History of the Young Ladies' Mutual Improvement Association of The Church of Jesus Christ of Latter-day Saints, from November 1869 to June 1910* (Salt Lake City: Deseret News, 1911); Clarissa A. Beesley, "The Young Women's Mutual Improvement Association," *Improvement Era* 38 (April 1935): 243, 264–65, 271; and Carol Cornwall Madsen and Susan Staker Oman, *Sisters and Little Saints: One Hundred Years of Primary* (Salt Lake City, Utah: Deseret Book, 1979).

80. "'Helps' to the Priesthood," *Contributor* 1 (November 1879): 36–37.

81. "Seventeenth Ward, Salt Lake Stake, Y.L.M.I.A. Minute Book, 1870–92," October 28, November 10, December 22, 1870.

82. Salt Lake Seventeenth Ward, Young Ladies Retrenchment, June 8, 1871; November 17, 1875; January 17, 1877; December 15, 1875; September 13, 1876.

83. Salt Lake Seventeenth Ward, Young Ladies Retrenchment, February 7, 1877.

84. "Seventeenth Ward, Salt Lake Stake, Y.M.M.I.A. Minute Book, 1875–87," microfilm of manuscript, November 16, 1875, and minutes for the 1875–80 period, LDS Church Archives.

85. "Seventeenth Ward, Y.M.M.I.A. Minute Book," March 5, 1877; April 17, 1877; April 10, 1877.

86. "Seventeenth Ward, Y.M.M.I.A. Minute Book."

87. Salt Lake Stake Historical Record Book, 1876–80, November 3, 1877, LDS Church Archives.

88. Report filed for stake conference, November 28, 1877, in Madsen, "History of Gunnison," 195–97.

89. Bishops Minutes, February 25, 1852, comments concerning Salt Lake's Thirteenth Ward.

90. Bishops Minutes, October 28, 1858; December 9, 1858; August 4, 1859; November 24, 1859; Brigham Young to George A. Smith, January 26, 1857, in Journal History, January 26, 1857.

91. Journal History, April 18, 1852; Thomas Bullock Minutes, March 25, 1855, LDS Church Archives; Salt Lake City Ninth Ward Record of Members, January 26, 1873, LDS Church Archives; Provo Bishops Minutes, September 10, 1868; March 12, 1872.

92. Kesler, Diary, July 4, 1874; Bishops Minutes, January 18, 1852, and June 30, 1856; George Goddard, Journal, microfilm of holograph, LDS Archives, vol. 18, March 17, 1876, 47; Salt Lake Stake, Minutes, LDS Church Archives, September 17, 1854.

93. Bishops Minutes, April 2, 1868.

94. Bishops Minutes, June 15, 1865.

95. Bishops Minutes, February 21, 1867.

96. Circular of the First Presidency, July 11, 1877, in *Messages of the First Presidency,* comp. James R. Clark, 6 vols. (Salt Lake City: Bookcraft, 1965), 2:289.

97. Kesler, Diary, August 12, 1877. On July 10, 1877, the *Deseret Evening News* published a notice from the Presiding Bishopric requesting bishoprics to "administer the Sacrament of the Lord's supper to Sunday School children in their respective wards, or deputize the authorities of the schools to attend to it." "Local and Other Matters," *Deseret Evening News,* July 10, 1877.

98. Journal History, March 23, 1857.

99. Bishops Minutes, August 1, 1861.

100. Kesler, Diary, March 27, 1875.

101. In 1881, Bishop Edwin D. Woolley "spoke in favor of a running stream of water for baptising." Bishops Minutes, February 17, 1881.

102. Orson Pratt, in *Journal of Discourses,* 18:160–61, July 18, 1875.

103. Woodruff, Diary, August 6, 1847; C. Edward Jacob and Ruth S. Jacob, eds., *The Record of Norton Jacob* (Salt Lake City: Norton Jacob Family Association, 1949), entry for August 8, 1847.

104. Bishops Minutes, October 24, 1854.

105. Bishops Minutes, August 12, 1856.

106. Journal History, September 15, 1856.

107. Bishops Minutes, July 1 and 15, November 4, 1875.

108. Orson Pratt, in *Journal of Discourses,* 18:160–61, July 18, 1875; D. Michael Quinn, "The Practice of Rebaptism at Nauvoo," *BYU Studies* 18 (winter 1978): 226–32; H. Dean Garrett, "Rebaptize," in *Encyclopedia of Mormonism,* ed. Daniel H. Ludlow, 5 vols. (New York: Macmillan, 1992), 3:1194.

109. Martha Spence Heywood received her endowment in the Council House on April 16, 1851. See Brooks, *Not by Bread Alone,* 57, April 20, 1851.

110. Endowment House Record, Endowments, 1851–76, microfilm, Special Collections, Family History Library, Salt Lake City.

111. Andrew Jenson, "Endowment House," in *Encyclopedic History of The Church of Jesus Christ of Latter-day Saints* (Salt Lake City: Deseret News, 1941), 230.

112. One such assignment was for Dry Creek, American Fork, Pleasant Grove, and Provo to send twenty people each to receive endowments and Springville to send forty. See Heber C. Kimball to the Bishops of Utah, May 19, 1856, in Journal History, May 19, 1856.

113. Kaysville Ward, Davis Stake, Elders Quorum Minute Book, 1865–77, 1865, LDS Church Archives. To cite one example, Ephraim P. Ellison was endowed on March 24, 1865, when he was fourteen; see Ephraim P. Ellison, Daybook, May 5, 1929, copy in author's possession.

114. Bishop Christian A. Madsen, "Holiness to the Lord: A History of Gunnison, Utah," holograph, 124, microfilm, included with Gunnison Ward Historical Record, LDS Church Archives.

115. Endowment House Record, Endowments, 1870–72, 1876–79, and Sealings of Couples, January to March 1870; St. George Temple, Endowments, 1877–78, microfilm, LDS Genealogical Department.

116. Endowment House Record, Sealings of Couples, January to March 1870; Dean L. May, "People on the Mormon Frontier: Kanab's Families of 1874," *Journal of Family History* 1 (winter 1976): 182; Larry Logue, *A Sermon in the Desert: Belief and Behavior in Early St. George, Utah* (Urbana and Chicago: University of Illinois Press, 1988), 56. Logue's statistics are for 1861–80 marriages.

117. Logue, *Sermon in the Desert,* 49.

118. Brooks, *Not by Bread Alone,* 34, October 27, 1850; 100, May 4, 1853; William G. Hartley, *Kindred Saints: The Mormon Immigrant Heritage of Alvin and Kathryne Christenson* (Salt Lake City: Eden Hill, 1982), 58, 64.

119. *Book of Remembrance of the Sixteenth Ward, Riverside Stake* (Salt Lake City: Sixteenth Ward Book of Remembrance Committee, 1945), 16, 83.

120. Missionary Record, I and II, manuscript, LDS Church Archives. My figures support Dean L. May's estimate that half of 1 percent of Church members filled missions, in his "A Demographic Portrait of the Mormons, 1830–1980," in *After 150 Years: The Latter-day Saints in Sesquicentennial Perspective,* ed. Thomas G. Alexander and Jessie L Embry (Provo, Utah: Charles Redd Center for Western Studies, 1983), 56.

121. Madsen, "History of Gunnison," 156 (February 1, 1877).

122. First Presidency, "A Word to the Saints," in Clark, *Messages of the First Presidency,* 2:110 (February 19, 1853).

123. Historian Jessie Embry has noted that "people in early Utah saw little reason to separate church and state. Taking care of the community cattle herd, completing the irrigation project, and trading at the Church's cooperative store were considered religious duties." Jessie L. Embry, "'All Things unto Me Are Spiritual': Contrasting Religious and Temporal Leadership Styles in Heber City, Utah," in *Community Development in the American West: Past and Present Nineteenth and Twentieth Century Frontiers,* ed. Jessie L. Embry and Howard A. Christy, Charles Redd Monographs in Western History, no. 15 (Provo, Utah: Charles Redd Center for Western Studies, 1985), 165.

124. Daniel H. Wells, sermon, September 10, 1861, in Journal History, September 10, 1861.

125. Davis Bitton, "Mormon Catechisms," LDS Church Historical Department, Task Papers in LDS History, no. 15, Salt Lake City. In the General Bishops Meetings, sentiment favored tolerating adults not obeying Word of Wisdom but expecting youths to live it.

126. See John Jaques, *Catechism for Children: Exhibiting the Prominent Doctrines of The Church of Jesus Christ of Latter-day Saints* (Salt Lake City: George Q. Cannon, 1870). For its many editions, see entries under Jaques in Chad L. flake, ed., *A Mormon Bibliography, 1830–1930: Books, Pamphlets, Periodicals, and Broadsides Relating to the First Century of Mormonism* (Salt Lake City: University of Utah Press, 1978).

127. Gustive O. Larson, "The Mormon Reformation," *Utah Historical Quarterly* 26, no. 1 (1958): 53–55.

128. Bishops Minutes, February 25, 1852.

129. Journal History, May 19, 1856; Edward Kimball, "Temple Recommend Questions as Indicators of Changing Value Emphasis," typescript, in possession of Edward Kimball.

130. Included in letter from A. K. Thurber to Bishop C. A. Madsen, March 9, 1877, in Madsen, "History of Gunnison," 165.

131. Madsen, "History of Gunnison," 62–64.

132. William G. Hartley, "Ward Bishops and the Localizing of LDS Tithing, 1847–1856," in Davis Bitton and Maureen Ursenbach Beecher, eds., *New Views of Mormon History: A Collection of Essays in Honor of J. Arrington* (Salt Lake City: University of Utah Press, 1987), 96–114. When Brigham Young was asked how much labor tithing was due from a man with three sons between the ages of fifteen and twenty, he replied, "One tenth of their time." Bishops Minutes, October 8, 1855.

133. William G. Hartley, "Edward Hunter: Pioneer Presiding Bishop," in *Supporting Saints: Life Stories of Nineteenth-Century Mormons,* ed. Donald Q. Cannon and David J. Whittaker (Provo, Utah: BYU Religious Studies Center, 1985), 283.

134. Circular of the First Presidency, 2:288.

135. Bishops Minutes, November 22, December 6, 1860.

136. Bishops Minutes, January 19, 1860.

137. Brigham Young, postscript to Edward Hunter, "Circular," [1852], copy in Library Division, Historical Department, The Church of Jesus Christ of Latter-day Saints, Salt Lake City.

138. Bishops Minutes, November 12, 1868; September 21, 1876.

139. Hartley, "Localizing of LDS Tithing," 96–114.

140. Michael S. Raber, "Family Life and Rural Society in Spring City, Utah: The Basis of Order in a Changing Agrarian Landscape," in Embry and Christy, *Community Development in the American West,* 144.

141. Bishops Minutes, October 28, 1869.

142. Bishops Minutes, December 7, 1871.

143. Payson Ward, Utah Stake, Priests [and Aaronic Priesthood] Minutes, December 26, 1876, LDS Church Archives. Regarding care for the needy lady, see minutes for April 12, June 7, 1876; February 28, March 28, June 6, 1877.

144. Journal of Louisa Lula Greene, July 6, 1868.

145. Paul H. Peterson, "An Historical Analysis of the Word of Wisdom" (master's thesis, Brigham Young University, 1972); Leonard J. Arrington, "I Have a Question," *Ensign* 7 (April 1977): 32–33; Robert J. McCue, "Did the Word of Wisdom Become a Commandment in 1851?" *Dialogue* 14 (fall 1981): 66–77; Thomas G. Alexander, "The Word of Wisdom: From Principle to Requirement," *Dialogue* 14 (fall 1981): 78–88.

146. Bishops Minutes, October 13, 1851.

147. Bishops Minutes, May 26, 1859.

148. Bishops Minutes, April 1863.

149. Bishops Minutes, April 4, 1867.

150. Bishops Minutes, April 18, 1867.

151. Bishops Minutes, March 26, 1868.

152. George Q. Cannon, in *Journal of Discourses,* 13:208, October 9, 1869.

153. St. George Stake, Lesser Priesthood Minutes, August 25, 1877, LDS Church Archives.

154. George Hicks, "A History of Spanish Fork," typescript, Special Collections and Manuscripts, Harold B. Lee Library, Brigham Young University, Provo, Utah, 10. See also Rebecca Bartholomew and Leonard J. Arrington, *Rescue of the 1856 Handcart Companies,* Charles Redd Monographs in Western History, no. 11 (Provo, Utah: Charles Redd Center for Western Studies, 1992), 8.

155. William G. Hartley, *To Build, to Create, to Produce: Ephraim P. Ellison's Life and Enterprises, 1850–1939* (Layton, Utah: Ellison Family Organization, 1997), 69–77.

156. Bishops Minutes, September 21, 1876.

157. Bishops Minutes, April 6, 1861.

158. Bishops Minutes, March 4, 1869.

159. Bishops Minutes, December 9, 1869.

160. Bishops Minutes, October 7, 1864.

161. Provo Bishops Minutes, 1868–1872.

162. Provo Bishops Minutes, November 10, 1868; November 23, 1869.

163. Provo Bishops Minutes, April 2, 1868.

164. Provo Bishops Minutes, July 14, 1872.

165. Provo Bishops Minutes, November 23, 1869; July 14, 1872; and minutes from 1868 to 1872.

166. Provo Bishops Meetings Minutes, November 23, 1869.

167. Provo Bishops Minutes, October 15, 1869 [1868]; November 23, 1869.

168. Provo Bishops Minutes, November 23, 1869.

169. Provo Bishops Minutes, November 23, 1869.

170. Provo Bishops Minutes, October 15, 1869 [1868]; November 10, 1868; March 29, 1870.

171. Provo Bishops Minutes, May 21, 1872.

172. Provo Bishops Minutes, March 1, 1870; September 10, 1868; July 20, 1869; August 17, 1869; November 21, 1871.

173. Richard Bushman, "Faithful History," *Dialogue: A Journal of Mormon Thought* 4 (winter 1969): 17–18.

174. General Aaronic Priesthood Minutes, 1857–77, June 1871.

175. General Aaronic Priesthood Minutes, November 3, 1870.

176. Salt Lake Deacons Minutes, December 23, 1876; General Aaronic Priesthood Minutes, September 7, 1870; Salt Lake Stake, High Priests Quorum Minute Book, 1865–1904, LDS Church Archives, May 29, 1875 (hereafter cited as Salt Lake High Priests Minutes); General Aaronic Priesthood Minutes, July 3, 1875; Salt Lake High Priests Minutes, May 30, 1874; Salt Lake Deacons Minutes, June 9, 1874.

177. Salt Lake Deacons Minutes, May 12, 1874.

178. Kesler, Diary, June 28, 1874.

179. Kesler, Diary, June 3, 1875. Kesler is responding to President Young's statement, recorded as, "Unless we lay aside our covetousness and wickedness God will spew us out of his mouth." See Bishops Minutes, June 3, 1875.

180. Bishops Minutes, November 8, 1875.

181. Salt Lake High Priests Minutes, October 30, 1875.

182. Salt Lake Deacons Minutes, April 11, 1876.

183. Bishops Minutes, December 30, 1875.

184. Salt Lake Deacons Minutes, September 11, 1876.

185. Salt Lake Deacons Minutes, December 14, 1875.

186. Salt Lake Deacons Minutes, June 9, 1874.

187. Salt Lake City Seventeenth Ward, Relief Society Minutes (1871–84), manuscript, May 22, 1879, LDS Church Archives.

188. [William G. Hartley], "Saint without Priesthood: The Collected Testimonies of Ex-Slave Samuel D. Chambers," *Dialogue* 12 (summer 1979): 16–18; William G. Hartley, "Samuel D. Chambers," *New Era* 4 (June 1974): 46–50.

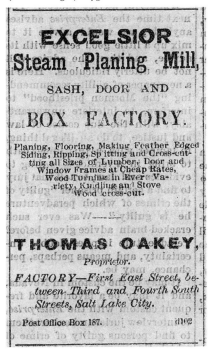

THE WOMAN'S EXPONENT.

EMMELINE B. WELLS, ... Editor.

Published semi-monthly, in Salt Lake City, Utah.
Terms: One copy one year, $2.00; one copy six months,
1.00. Ten copies for the price of nine. Advertising
rates: Each square, ten lines of nonpareil space, one
time, $2.00; per month, $5.00. A liberal discount to
regular advertisers.

Exponent Office, corner of South Temple, and First
East streets, opposite Eagle Gate. Business hours from 10
a.m. to 5 p.m. every day except Sunday.

Address all business communications to
Publisher WOMAN'S EXPONENT,
Salt Lake City, Utah.

SALT LAKE CITY, JULY 1, 1878.

THE WOMEN OF UTAH.

In the United States and Great Britain, the women of this people are a popular subject of conversation. What is said of them would, we are told, make volumes were it written. Domestic drudges, ignorant, low and vulgar, is the verdict passed upon them as a body. They have no opinions, they are not in possession of intelligence, isolated and kept in subjection, required to fulfill only menial relations even in marriage; these and a thousand other absurdities are palmed off upon those who are uninformed on the subject and are accepted as genuine truths. Occasionally some person or persons, are wise enough to investigate for themselves while visiting Utah and not to put off with somebody's "say so." But these cases are so rare comparatively, that the general public are not much enlightened on the subject. Some self-evident facts are now understood concerning this people; because the condition of the country has established them; it was formerly known as a desert, it is now full of flourishing towns, this is apparent; with schools, manufactures, churches, railroads and all the facilities for cultivation and improvement. The Latter-day saints are known as the pioneers and motive power in these great changes. Is it consistent to suppose that men have accomplished so much towards beautifying and improving a country associated with women of inferior calibre? No! The mothers, wives and daughters have been and are, co-workers in all these infinite and arduous undertakings. They have labored incessantly, in the interests of their families, to use an elevating and refining influence; and that which would tend to peace and good will. To-day they occupy a position of which they may justly be proud, notwithstanding all the aspersions cast upon them.

To be sure their educational opportunities in the past, and the advantages of "so called polite society," have not been such as women of the world fancy, but shut up in their mountain home, free from the evil influences which prevail to an alarming extent in more densely populated and older communities, they have developed other capabilities and powers of mind that have given them strength of character and personal attributes calculated to raise them in the scale of intellect and intelligence, beyond those who spend so much time and devote their precious God-given talents to the frivolities and accomplishments of fashionable life, which all tend to weaken instead of strengthening character.

The peculiar circles, and experiences of Mormon life have had a tendency to make women self-helpful, and self-reliant, and have given them indomitable energy, and undaunt-

ed courage, and these characteristics prepare them to use more discreetly any trust or confidence reposed in them. They are fully aware that any antagonism or defiance towards men, would hinder instead of helping them, that both must co-operate together for the mutual benefit of all, for "woman is not without man nor man without woman in the Lord," and they are engaged in the Lord's work. The men of this community were anxious woman should have the "franchise" believing it to be just and right that she should have every opportunity to represent her own cause. The many responsibilities placed upon the sisters of this Church should awaken them to the necessity of becoming conversant with the subject of laws, governments, and the history of nations past and present, in order that they may use the ballot judiciously, and vote understandingly, as well as to maintain other privileges and rights which they enjoy. One can not be too well informed in regard to the laws of nations and the relations of countries. No woman should content herself with a simple assertion from another, and feel she has no time to read, or study and inform herself, or attend the meetings held among the sisters for general instruction. By prudently economizing time, every woman in the enjoyment of average health, whatever her domestic cares may be, can find some time for personal culture, and it will promote health and happiness both. A better knowledge of one's self, of the relations of individuals to each other, and their duty to God, with fervent faith in His holy Gospel, will fit man and woman for the truest enjoyment. There attainments can never be reached by sitting idly down and waiting, they demand diligent and constant action, and a rightful exercise of all the faculties of one's nature.

HOME AFFAIRS.

In the issue of EXPONENT June 1st, the report of agriculture at Rockville should have stated five ounces of silk worm eggs instead of dozen, and instead of silk-worms for sale, it should read silk worm eggs.

LETTERS, ESSAYS, Relief Society Reports, and other items laid over until another issue. The Quarterly Conference occupies considerable space but we feel that it is essential to the particular in publishing these minutes for the benefit of the various societies.

MOST of the Sunday Schools of the different wards in the city have been recreating and rusticating in the rural gardens in the vicinity, of late, giving the children a fine opportunity for a day's pleasure in the open air, with a variety of amusements to add to their enjoyment.

In COMPANY with Mrs. M. I. Horne, Mrs. S. M. Heywood and Mrs. B. W. Smith, we visited the Relief Society at Mill Creek, and Sugar House Ward on Tuesday June 25th. Excellent meetings at both places with a full attendance of men as well as women. The sisters are becoming more and more alive to the exigencies of the times and encouraging home industries, storing grain and all good works.

THE ROYAL Baker, a pamphlet compiled by the New York Cooking School, will give you directions for making every variety of bread, griddle cakes, puffs, muffins, waffles, tea-biscuits, buns, crackers, toasts, pastry, pies and puddings, dumplings, fritters and pancakes, meat pies etc.; it contains 594 recipes how to make the different kinds of articles mentioned. It would be valuable to housekeepers as reference.—Price 10 cts.

THE TABERNACLE Choir will give a concert in the Tabernacle on the Fourth of July, under the supervision of Mr. Careless, leader of the Choir, whose well known talent for directing and arranging will give it popularity. Mrs. L. Careless, Miss S. E. Olsen, Messrs. B. B. Young, Mark Croxall, J. J. Daynes and other vocal and instrumental performers will take part in the performance. The proceeds are to be donated towards the building of the New Tabernacle.

MISS DORA H. BYON, of London, England, a lady traveling for pleasure, made us a social call on Monday June 24, to see and hear something of Mormons and Mormonism. Miss Byron has been making a tour of the United States and Canada, has used well against our people, especially the condition of our women; she evidently intends to see and hear for herself. She is interested in the woman's movement, and expresses herself as being astonished to see so much good being done by Mormon women.

ELDER J. F. WELLS, Pres't. of the Central Committee of the Y. M. M. I. A., and Elder M. H. Hardy, his Counselor, are about to start on a tour into the country in the interest of the young peoples' Associations. They will interest themselves specially in seeking to advance the spiritual and educational interests of the territory. They will visit Morgan, Summit, Rich and Bear Lake Counties, returning by way of Cache, Box Elder, Weber and Davis Counties, making it a point to meet with all the Associations wherever practicable. God speed and bless them in their efforts for culture and higher development among the young people.

ON MONDAY, at 12 o'clock, June 10, we went in company with Miss E. R. Snow, to the United States Court-room, with Sister Annie Musser who desired to procure her second naturalization papers. We found it to be a very easy matter to accomplish, and nothing unpleasant whatever connected with it, and would advise all the sisters who have not yet become citizens to make no delay whatever, and "go and do likewise." There are many good and sufficient reasons why women should become naturalized as well as men, and our sisters should comprehend it. To all the sisters who have not done so we would urge upon them the propriety of attending to it while there is so good an opportunity.

MISS ELIZA R. Snow and Mrs. Zina D. Young are making a tour in the interest of the Relief Societies and Retrenchment Associations through portions of Utah, Juab and Sanpete Counties. They left Salt Lake City on Monday morning June 17, held a meeting at American Fork at 2 o'clock p. m. the same day, and again in the evening, at Pleasant Grove on Tuesday, at Mona on Wednesday, at Nephi on Thursday, and from thence proceeded to Fountain Green in Sanpete Co. The meetings at all points were numerously attended and much interest awakened on the subjects of home industries, especially silk-culture, also storing grain, and other departments of labor among the sisters.

SISTER VIENNA JAQUES who resides in the 12th Ward of this city, and whose name is mentioned in one of the revelations in the Book of Doctrine and Covenants, was ninety-one years old on Monday June 10. The next day she accompanied the Old Folks Excursion to Ogden. She is in excellent health and feels as if she might yet live many years. She lives entirely alone, never having had any

FIG. 1. This page of the July 1, 1878, *Woman's Exponent* informs us that a year's subscription costs $2.00. The first article claims that Mormon life has made the women "self-helpful, and self-reliant." However, the women know that "any antagonism or defiance towards men, would hinder instead of helping them, that both must co-operate together for the mutual benefit of all."

REPORTS FROM THE FIELD:
THE WORLD OF THE *WOMAN'S EXPONENT*

Claudia L. Bushman

Perhaps some of you have seen Tom Stoppard's recent play *Arcadia,* which considers the problems of historical research. The action takes place in two time periods in the drawing room of Sidley Park, an English country home. The first action occurs in 1809 and involves redesigning a garden, making a mathematical discovery, and dueling to satisfy a breach of honor. All of these activities create documents. The second action takes place in the present day and involves scholars who re-create the past from these documents, using all their hopeful sleuthing and intellectual cunning to shape a plausible picture. Because we have seen the past and understand the real truth, we know when the scholars go astray—as scholars often do. The documents speak, but they do not explain.

I am involved in a similar exercise today and probably am also susceptible to error as I attempt to interpret some documents of our recent past. I want to paint a picture of everyday life in Salt Lake City a century ago, using issues of the *Woman's Exponent* from 1878, the earliest volumes in the collection of the Huntington Library.

My premise is this: The *Woman's Exponent,* which was neither owned nor controlled by the Church, both described and created the Mormon woman of the last quarter of the nineteenth century. The *Exponent* described Mormon women because it had to keep in touch with reality in order to be credible, but it also tried to create an ideal Mormon woman so as to mold real women into something higher and better. I am searching for clues to everyday life in this prescriptive document, always aware that people write not the obvious but the should-be and the unusual. I am trying to interpret beyond what is actually written, for as Yogi Berra said, "You can observe a lot just by watching."

The audience of the *Woman's Exponent* was the Mormon woman in urban Salt Lake and in settlements in all directions. The paper prescribed what she should be doing and how she should feel about it and told her the news worth knowing as well as encouraged her to tell her own story in the idiom offered by the paper. The *Exponent* constructed a Mormon female image in which Mormon women could see themselves as they were and as they should be.

At the same time as it spoke to Mormon women, the *Exponent* also had a serious diplomatic mission to the outside world. It presented an image of female Mormondom to counter the view of Mormon women as ragged, downtrodden wretches that was so prevalent in the national media. While addressing Mormon women, the *Exponent* also spoke to the greater public. As a result, it was a public-relations machine persuading the scornful East that Mormons were respectable and should be admitted to the union. The *Exponent*'s focus was much broader than that of our contemporary Church periodicals.[1]

I will give examples of the *Exponent*'s description of the Mormon woman's role, suggesting the degree of image versus reality, looking for clues that tell us how closely Mormon women lived up to the ideal stereotypes. Then I will consider how these women were portrayed to readers outside Mormon circles. You may disagree with my conclusions.

PRESCRIPTIVE IMAGE VERSUS REALITY

The *Woman's Exponent* is a text that projects a certain world, not *the* world, but *a* world, an upbeat, enthusiastic woman's world with many voices. No single voice takes precedence. The obedient, earnest, and triumphant reports from the Relief Society and other Church auxiliaries, with synopses of talks from leaders, comprise the most unified voice, but that voice gets no emphasis. We have a great deal of suffrage and women's rights rhetoric, some homegrown, some copied from the wider eastern rights press, which projected a different type of woman's world. We also have personal voices, the little essays of sisters with a point to make, as well as bits of information copied from all over. There are many voices here.

The dimensions of the *Exponent*'s world are very broad. We hear about George Eliot's latest novel[2] and "the Coronation stone" in England's Westminster Abbey.[3] The *Exponent* tells us how many men were arrested for crimes in New York City.[4] We tour Kentucky's Grand Crystal Cave and see its mummies.[5] English laws are described.[6] An

FIG. 2. Long-term editor of the *Woman's Exponent,* Emmeline B. Wells depicted an upbeat, enthusiastic woman's world where thrift and home industry were practiced, woman suffrage was promoted, and independence and refinement were encouraged. Wells was photographed by C. M. Bell in Washington, D.C., on January 14, 1879.

eclipse of the sun is observed.[7] These references go into geography, literature, history, even to the universe, places that women stuck on the Wasatch Front with few books cannot be expected to visit. The *Exponent* projects a very wide world with Zion at the center. But these references broaden the scope of acceptable thoughts for women, producing the rest of the world for their consideration. They also display the wide erudition and interests of Mormon women to those outside Utah.

SELF-IMPROVEMENT AND THE GENERAL GOOD. That women should improve their minds is a steady theme. Mary Jane Crosby of East Bountiful writes that "an hour's reading each day in some useful book, helps prepare a woman for future work and lifts her out of a daily routine of housework." Her comments justify and prioritize learning, which "lifts her" above daily routine to be a Mary rather than a Martha. Mary Jane asserts that "there is no branch of education that woman may not undertake"—a heroic, triumphant note. But she quietly qualifies that to say, "All should be taught the . . . need and utility of adapting themselves to the circumstances in which they are placed." The message is to dream big dreams but maneuver in limited space. Feeling compelled to justify her learning to the majority who are living the "daily routine of housework," she says that reading helps in treating others well and in teaching children.[8] Individual learning, presented as a private pastime, must really be for the general good.

This emphasis on the unified general good, "to cultivate a spirit of oneness,"[9] countered the emerging individuality of the age. The Hyde Park Relief Society reports their activities, "as we wish always to be numbered with those your paper represents."[10] Eliza R. Snow reports happily on the textile factory in Brigham City, "truly the hive of Deseret, and its people are the working bees."[11] (Why has no one noted that comparison to an insect is demeaning?) This subordination of the self to the greater work, a major theme of Mormondom, was under heavy attack from the rising consumer culture and so required constant iteration. Sarah Sudweeks of Circle Valley, Pinto County, works out this theme with sinister implications: "Can we become the working bees in the hive of Deseret, if we do not accomplish our part of the labor that is assigned us to do, that we can keep everything in its proper place, that the moths cannot find place among us; for what keeps outside the hive cannot spoil the honey, but it is the canker that is inside that gnaws the vitals and lops the branches."[12] Unity is in jeopardy.

TENSION BETWEEN REFINEMENT AND THRIFT. The strongest voice in the *Woman's Exponent* is the prescriptive voice of the Relief Society, urging an agenda of thrift and home industry. Brigham Young states this position in his pungent prose: "I want the sisters to say to themselves, and then to their daughters, sisters and friends, 'We will wear that which we will make, or we will wear nothing; we will make what we wear on our heads; we will make our own hats and bonnets.'" Going into debt would pauperize the whole community, so "let us sustain ourselves."[13] The reports from the field, obtained as the Relief Society leaders toured the Mormon settlements, show long lists of specific tasks attempted and achieved. Mulberry shoots had been set out to feed silkworms. Grain had been gathered and stored, hats braided, shares in the cooperative stores purchased, and money donated to the temples.

Some women had even invested in the publication of Edward Tullidge's *Women of Mormondom,* which they read at meetings. This collection of biographies unified the readers against the demonized outsiders, as the women vicariously suffered with the early Saints, identifying with them as victims. In the late 1870s, women faced the current form of persecution—the loss of the vote. A woman from West Weber identified "the same spirit of persecution" abroad as "when the saints were scattered and driven." Her heart "burn[ed] with resentment towards those who ought to protect a mere handful of peaceful, loyal citizens."[14] Surely those words were written as much for the East as for Mormondom. The St. George women perhaps went farther: "The bitter persecutions, the heart-rending trials, of our sisters . . . wake a responsive chord, and call forth the holiest sympathies of the hearts of the mothers and daughters of Zion, and sets before them bright and illustrious examples, worthy of imitation. Their records will assuredly stand forth . . . to the condemnation and everlasting shame and disgrace of their vile, fiendish persecutors."[15] Here is the Relief Society's image of themselves: virtuous, persecuted grain savers against the hard world.

What of the actuality? The *Exponent*'s depiction of all Mormon women engaged in hard, communal labors is likely exaggerated. I think that if we added up all the grain saved, the silk made, and the good work done and divided it among the groups that reported their endeavors, the results would be disappointing.

References to silk reflect hope rather than accomplishment. Sister Wadroup of Centerville submitted a "specimen" of silk ribbon, the only actual silk mentioned in these pages. We are told that the success of the silk enterprise will depend upon the people, for if they do not plant many mulberry trees, "there will not be many cocoons, and consequently there will not be material for the loom." This declaration is a threat, a warning, rather than a boast of accomplishment.[16]

As for the grain, we get frequent references to small stores because of poor wheat land. H. M. from Gunnison (fig. 3) notes that women don't like to glean wheat, preferring to contribute bushels from their

SHOULD WE GLEAN?

It is to the daughters of Zion, to the faithful, the humble, the meek and the lowly, that I would appeal in favor of gleaning; for none but such will value it as a privilege to out in perhaps, a very warm summer day, and gather the golden heads of grain left in the field.

In the short time since the sisters were first told to store up grain, a great amount of breadstuff has been laid up, with which fact, all who read the EXPONENT are well acquainted. The readers of the EXPONENT will also remember that our beloved and departed Prophet, President Brigham Young, in a meeting with the sisters at Ogden, said "Let the sisters glean." It is not for me to say who should glean, and who should not, "Wisdom is justified by her children," but sisters, let none of us think that it doesn't mean us, if we possibly can go.

Some will say "I will rather give a bushel of wheat, than go out to glean." That is a very good substitute for gleaning, provided you cannot go; but, it does not quite cover the ground, sisters, unless such is the case. The wheat we glean to store up for Zion, is clean, pure, plump wheat; it is not taken from our husbands' granaries; it is clear, positive, real gain, at the same time we yield obedience to the command of a kind Heavenly Father. Let us, who know the will of our Father, labor while yet it is day, for no one knoweth how long Providence will vouchsafe such bountiful harvests as we have been permitted to reap for a succession of years. It has been spoken by holy prophets, modern, as well as ancient, that famine will smite the earth and its inhabitants. And how often have we not shrank from the mere thought of the terrible sufferings that are yet to come upon blind, disobedient, ungrateful mankind.

To those, (if any there be) whose hands are so soft, white and tender, that their owners feel as if they can not possibly expose them so, or, they have not been "raised" to do such work, I would say read the beautiful little story, of a few months back, in the EXPONENT, entitled "Two pairs of hands." Let us all re-read, if we do not remember, such spirited, inspiring articles as "Sisters be in earnest," and "The Grain Question," and not allow ourselves to forget that the time is short, and getting shorter every day in which to prepare for the great day of the Lord's vengeance.

The history of storing grain by the Relief Society of this place, commenced in '75, under the most favorable auspices. Our Bishop made it a topic for public speaking in our Sabbath meetings, by himself and the leading brethren, till in a few weeks everybody in town was familiar with it, and the way was paved for the sisters whose duty it became to gather donations for Zion's Relief Fund. With all our available means, except twenty-five dollars with which we purchased a share in the publication of the Woman's Book, we bought up wheat; the brethren and sisters all donating liberally, besides, soon swelled the pile. And when the idea of gleaning by the Relief Society and Y. L. M. I, A. was mentioned, our Bishop called for volunteers at every Sabbath meeting as long as gleaning was kept up, to take the gleaners to the field and back, which was responded to by many of our brethren, the bishop attending in person several times, making us feel that they took a lively becoming interest in the endeavors of the sisters. Those who volunteered to convey the gleaners, met at the place appointed, at 8 o'clock, a. m., twice a week, and shortly after we rolled out of town a very happy company. We did not "stand," nor indeed, "sit" on ceremonies, but we did sit down on our empty sacks which, filled in the evening, with headings afforded us very comfortable seats. After gleaning from 9 till 12 a. m., we availed ourselves of the "squatters' right," and how we did enjoy our dinner! The good things brought by the sisters who had plenty, were freely divided with those who had less, making the nooning a very enjoyable affair. We knew very well it would be naughty to lay down the farmer's lucerne, and empty his cellar for milk, so we did not do it. And though we enjoyed our dinner immensely, we did not forget that gleaning was object number one, of which our well filled sacks bore ample evidence.

One of our most delicate and refined sisters went out with us and gleaned, quite sure of a severe headache, and on returning home, told us with becoming pride, that she had had no headache, and said she, "I thought gleaning was something so hard, so different from what it is."

I have no doubt that gleaning would be very hard to carry on to any great extent, if the brethren did not give it their support; if the gleaners were left to walk to the field, and carry their filled sacks home, after eight or nine hours gleaning; if the gleaners were a small minority, instead of a great majority of the sisters, old and young of a place; if they were scoffed at, instead of honored, encouraged and supported in it. By gleaning too many hours a day, and too many days a week, it becomes irksome. But it takes faith, hope and charity to glean for Zion.

May God bless those who have gleaned, those who will glean hereafter, and those who would cheerfully glean if they but "could," and all who lend their influence and efforts to the great object of filling the store-houses of the Lord.

H. M.

Gunnison, July, 1878.

FIG. 3. An appeal to "the daughters of Zion, to the faithful, the humble, . . . for none but such will value gleaning as a privilege." (August 1, 1878.)

husbands' granaries, but, she urges, "the wheat we glean to store up for Zion, is . . . clear, positive, real gain, at the same time we yield obedience to the command of a kind Heavenly father." She also makes it clear that gleaning is a trial for the refined woman: "One of our most delicate and refined sisters went out with us and gleaned, quite sure of a severe headache, and on returning home, told us with becoming pride, that she had had no headache."[17]

The tension between refinement and pioneer industry is repeatedly set out, the one fashionable and tempting, the other the right thing to do. When Eliza R. Snow asked that the Relief Society women in Farmington who had manufactured their own hats rise, many stood. But, Eliza reports, "not so many [stood] as one would expect in a settlement where straw material is abundant."[18]

"Mary" explores this tension, regretting that women complain now when in the past they really had something to complain about. Nevertheless, she details the pride of the days when women made their own dresses. They "spun and wove all day and cut [their] cloth at night" to make "good serviceable dresses" kept for best the first year. "Do you remember sisters how much pains was taken in dyeing, how carefully the sage brush was boiled in the big kettle and set with alum or copper as to make the requisite shades for plaiding; and how proud we were if our dresses were as fine, as smooth, as bright colored as our neighbors'." But the pioneer era has passed and not for the better. "I cannot help thinking of these things," Mary says, "when I see my sisters robed in 'purple and fine linen,' with their voluminous skirts sweeping the dust from the sidewalks." Are those sisters better off? No, for she hears them complain of "their privations and hardships"[19] (fig. 4). Another woman speaks in favor of a healthy pioneer style. "Tell me not that a pale white face is pretty and lady-like; away with such vitiated nonsense."[20] She prefers a blooming complexion.

But there is no doubt that fashion and refinement are desired and even embraced by the women. The home manufacture of the Payson Relief Society, as presented in a beautiful display, featured luxury goods—"quilts in all varieties of patterns, carpets, rugs, tidies, laces, flowers, and ladies' mitts, gloves, vail, etc. . . . some . . . very nice indeed."[21]

Determining the proper and acceptable level of refinement is an important call, as refinement is certainly desirable. At the quarterly conference of the Relief Society, John Taylor urged politeness and courtesy.[22] C. E. H. urges mothers to have a "refined and gentle nature," to cultivate thoughts and abilities, to live a pure, religious life so that they could influence their children to be "pure, amiable, charitable, benevolent, patriotic sons and daughters of God possessing true moral force and sterling worth." A mother with "chaste manners and refined tastes" would persuade others of "the correctness of her arguments, and the clearness and beauty of her views."[23] The dividing line between the commendable and the undesirable is cost. The women were to be as refined as possible without emptying the coffers of Zion. Jemima Brown writes to tell the sisters to cease following the "fashions of Babylon." They should make their "dresses neat and comely" to fit them for the "society of holy angels."[24] Clothes distinguish the suitably refined.

With this division in mind, we can study the *Exponent*'s page of ads to see which business people were willing to advertise in a paper preaching thrift, women's rights, and home industry. I did a quick, superficial analysis of one page to see what was being offered (see fig. 5). The eighteen ads could be divided roughly into three groups: ten ads keeping with the message of frugality and industry, six ads for the proscribed fashionable stuff, and two professional listings—one for a genealogist and another for Romania B. Pratt, physician and surgeon. Among the suitable ads was one for silkworm eggs, four dollars per ounce with mulberry starts at five to forty cents each, as well as ads for a home industrial straw manufactory, for the Lamb knitting machine agency, and for Lamb knitted socks and stockings. Dry goods were available from ZCMI; Schwartz Store, featuring the "best and cheapest dry goods"; and Teasdel's, which sold a choice stock of groceries including currants and raisins. David James, a tinner, sold fittings and pumps. Home-manufactured goods (mostly yardage) were available in the Old Constitution Building, and homemade boots and shoes at another location.

Among luxury goods are such items as French hairpieces in curls, braids, and switches; Auerbach's new fall stock of embroideries, ruchings, kid gloves, and ribbons; "the fine arts"—chromotypes and hand-colored photographs; pianos and organs; H. Dinwoodey furniture featuring baby carriages, feathers, and wallpaper; and even the intimate merchandise of Mrs. C. E. Dye, who kept the Palace of Fashion, where she sold ladies' hair and millinary, the "most exquisite

FIG. 4. Describing the clothing challenges of earlier years, the "Pipsey Papers" correspondent mildly chastises her sisters for complaining of their "privations and hardships." (June 15, 1878.)

ness and beauty of her views. A noble, true woman can ever soothe the poor sufferer on his bed of sickness, calm the aching heart, cheer the despondent, and hallow a joy or success. Within her own home she is the crowning joy of all its inmates; there each heart turns to her for solace and comfort. If there is any sorrow she is the first to modify or allay it; if any pleasure, her presence enhances it; her influence is felt for good wherever she is. What would home be without a gentle, sweet-tempered woman there, to arrange everything for the family? To prepare some little elegant surprise, or pleasure? Without her elevating and refining influence there would indeed be a cheerless void.

And the aged grandmother, in her quiet corner, is like a ray of light from above. Her counsel is always esteemed, and her advice acknowledged to be good. Yes, woman's influence is great! How careful, then, should she be that it is not of a low and degrading nature, but an influence that will tend to make all better, and more worthy of the love they receive from God; that it may make all around her aspire to be great and good, to live intelligently and honestly, to strengthen their abilities, enlarge their capacities, brighten their intellect, and understand their individual traits and the principles of divine truth.

Oh, sisters! strive to be all that you profess, always study to do good, and let the Spirit of God dictate all your actions.

C. E. H.

PIPSEY PAPERS.

A noted author says there are two things necessary for a writer: first to have something to say and, secondly, to know how to say it. Lacking the first there is much skill needed to use the second with ability. Our Society is much interested in collecting means for the Welsh Mission, we have already donated thirty-five dollars towards their emigration. No doubt as a general thing we are not thankful enough for the blessings we enjoy. We make poor faces and complain when we have bread in the cupboard, and health in the family, forgetful of the days when we were glad to get wool to spin for our dresses; when we spun and wove all day and cut our cloth at night, and made it up for the family comfort. We had good servicable dresses then, that lasted several years; the first year they were usually kept for best, after which they were taken for everyday wear, and new ones made for Sundays. Do you remember sisters how much pains was taken in dyeing, how carefully the sage brush was boiled in the big kettle and set with alum or copperas to make the requisite shades for plaiding; and how proud we were if our dresses were as fine, as smooth, as bright colored as our neighbors'. Then our dainty feet were encased in good homemade, valley-tan calfskin; one pair of shoes lasted a year; they were put on in the fall and the lady who kept hers the longest, was the envy of her less fortunate sisters. Some of the ladies had ingenuity enough to make their own summer shoes, with a little help, perhaps, from the village shoemaker who would sew on the soles in the evening when his day's work in the field was done, if he was industriously inclined, in view, perhaps, of a nice roll of butter for his holiday dinner.

My reminiscences may be considered in bad taste, but I cannot help thinking of these things when I see my sisters robed in "purple and fine linen," with their voluminous skirts sweeping the dust from the sidewalks, and hear them find fault and complain of their privations and hardships. We should thank God for every blessing and carry our small annoyances as lightly as possible, for we never know when misfortune may overtake us. My neighbor, Mrs. Ezra Oakley received a letter from her husband, at Leeds saying that he was well, and doing well. The next day the word came flashing over the wires that he was dead; died of pneumonia and heart-disease at the age of twenty-six, leaving a wife and child, a mother and two sisters wild with grief at the unexpected bereavement. How small the common worriments of life seem compared to such a sorrow!

Speaking of our daily crosses, brings to mind a dream I will relate, hoping my sisters may profit by its teachings as I have done.

I thought I saw a child buried in very beautiful robes. After the friends had gone away I said to a woman standing by, what a pity it was for such beautiful clothing to be hidden and rot in the ground when something plainer would do as well; let us take it up and keep the clothing ourselves, which we accordingly did, putting some plainer things upon the body and burying it again. When fairly through our task we began thinking what we had done and what dreadful consequences would follow if it was discovered. An awful terror come over us insomuch that we concluded to take the child up and put the clothes back. When we tried to do so some one came by and we waited for them to pass, and others came and hindered us until we were called away and it was not accomplished. I awoke in grief and tears, and the interpretation was given me then. It meant that if we had troubles or disagreements when they were settled and past, we should let them lie buried and not bring them forth to annoy us, for it was difficult to have them replaced. So whenever I thought of a past grievance I remembered my dream and said nothing about it. When you are disposed to bring forward old troubles to torture or distress you, just remember it will be hard to bury them as they were before and let them alone. I have seen much happiness since I took that for my motto, and let my troubles lie buried.

MARY.

MEADOWVILLE.

This place is surrounded by gentle sloping mountains covered with beautiful green verdure to sustain animal life; and as Autumn approaches every variegated color one can conceive, attracts the eye. The meadows lying east of the town, fenced in for hay and pasturage afford an abundance of the best quality of hay, equal to tame grass; it grows two to three feet in height wet seasons. Butter is made here of the best quality, yellow, rich and hard, through the summer season; I have churned butter in the month of July, and it would be as hard as in other climates in the winter. Had we oak firkins, and pure salt, our butter could not be surpassed for sweetness and solidity. If some one would take an interest in setting out a few acres of the oak, what great advantage could be derived therefrom. Here we have one of the most beautiful and romantic springs, the largest in the Territory, forming a creek three miles in length, which empties itself into Bear Lake. In this spring the trout came up to spawn from the Lake. From this

Parisian styles to the cheapest American products."[25] We must assume that advertising paid off for these merchants, indicating robust sales for fashionable goods.

TENSION BETWEEN GROUPS. I find few indications of tension between men and women in these pages. When Eliza R. Snow urged women to save beans as well as wheat, she "advised the sisters to use their utmost influence with the brethren."[26] (I am surprised that bean saving did not go further as Sister Snow reported that mice and weevils do not like them and that refined New Englanders considered bean porridge and bean soup healthy food.[27]) There are hints of tension in Jane S. Richard's comments on male opposition to Relief Society. Some men think that "there is no necessity for Relief Societies—some of our good brethren even would rather their wives would not attend, think[ing] their only duty lies at home."[28]

Notably, I see nothing of romantic or sentimental attachment between genders. The party line, one definitely intended for eastern consumption, is of honor and respect: "Nowhere are women as a class treated with the respect and equality that they are among the Latter-day Saints. Here they are the honored wives of good and intelligent men, having no doubts of their husband's fidelity."[29] The other note, when any relationship with spouses is mentioned, is of cooperation. An unsigned report valorizes women, noting that "the peculiar exigencies, and experiences of Mormon life have had a tendency to make women self-helpful, and self-reliant, and have given them indomitable energy, and undaunted courage." Such a report might go on to discuss a gender war; instead, cooperation is stressed. The women are "fully aware that any antagonism or defiance towards men, would hinder instead of helping them, that both must co-operate together for the mutual benefit of all."[30]

If little tension between the adult genders is noted, tension between mothers and daughters, particularly over the gentility issues, is frequent. Girls "fret and whine away their existence . . . because God has not given them wealth to luxuriate in. They become chronically morbid." They suffer from unhealthy recreation, tight lacing and shoes, unhealthy clothing, scattered and desultory thoughts, and a

FIG. 5. In this page of classified ads, the *Exponent*'s message of frugality and home industry is supported by ten ads. Six items advertise luxury goods, and two are professional listings. (March 1, 1878.)

"don't carishness" in general.[31] Would that these girls follow the fashion dictates of virtuous B. M. from Richmond, Cache County: "Cannot we middle-aged sisters lay aside every form of dress except that which is neat, economical, pleasant to the eye and comfortable to the wearer. If we do this, our young folks after awhile will follow in our footsteps, wisdom will assume her power over us, and we may soon become what we desire, a pattern to all nations."[32] Their young folks were not likely to follow them anywhere. Sister Snow "exhorted the mothers to use their influence with the young people against night excursions and evening parties to public grounds or gardens," which had dangerous results.[33]

Most surprising to me is the gender gap concerning plural marriage. The young sisters are repeatedly instructed "not to speak a disrespectful word of this holy principle, but if they did not understand it, to pray to the Lord for wisdom"[34] (fig. 6). Such injunctions would only have been urged if negative comments about polygamy were being voiced. Meanwhile, Eliza R. Snow is "impressively" urging "upon the young people the necessity of entering into these holy covenants," exhorting them to "hold this principle sacred, and never upon any account speak evil of it."[35] Those "don't carish" girls, off on their evening pleasure-parties in their tight shoes and fashionable dresses, wanted love and romance and were less interested in the delayed gratification their mothers had chosen. One such mother blames herself: "Why do we hear the Latter-day Saints speak evil of each other and the holy principles of the Gospel? . . . I think if we mothers would examine ourselves, we would see where the evil springs from." She urges patience and virtue on her sisters. "If we could exercise a little more faith in God, the little troubles that come up in our way from time to time, would not annoy us. . . . I truly know my sisters if we honor this pure principle, we will be numbered with the honorable daughters of Zion, when the Lord comes to make up his jewels."[36] Blessings will come in the future, something less interesting to girls.

Another interesting tension is between boys and girls. The girls are shown modestly memorizing scriptures while the boys are shown playing cards and attending parties "with their hair uncombed, wearing their dirty overalls, without coats, and their breath smelling horribly of whiskey and tobacco." Gipsy Golden marvels that such boys could consider themselves "worthy of our pure, refined, cultured girls, and expect to marry them and make them

R. S. REPORTS.
———

NORTH JORDAN, SALT LAKE CO.,
Jan. 3d, 1878.

EDITOR EXPONENT:

Minutes of the meeting of the Young Ladies' Improvement Association, held at North Jordan Ward, Mrs. Mary A. Haigh presiding. Meeting commenced with usual exercises; after which Counselor Eliza Bennion stated that she was happy to meet with so many of her young sisters, but felt her inefficiency to instruct them in the things pertaining to the kingdom of God. She advised the girls not to speak evil of one another, but try to obtain the confidence of the sisters, and by their good actions to retain it. Alice Harker felt her incapability of fully expressing her gratitude for the innumerable blessings she had received during the past year. She realized that our actions were not so commendable as they might be, but thought it our duty individually and collectively to meet together and make our Association as interesting as possible. Select reading by Miss Isabella Webster, entitled, "A Voice from Dixie Land."

Sister Angeline Spencer bore testimony to the goodness of God; felt that if we had the spirit of this work our meetings would not lack interest, and stated that we ought not to neglect our meetings, for, by attending them, we obtain spiritual blessings, which are essential to our life and salvation. Sister Eliza Spencer, President of the Relief Society, gave some very excellent advice to the young sisters, among which were some instructive remarks on storing grain, and sericulture. She was much pleased at the advancement the young ladies were making, and realized that we were progressing favorably; advised the young ladies to obtain a testimony for themselves that this was the true Church, and not rely upon the testimony of others. Her hope of heaven and future life were far dearer than all earthly blessings.

Sister Moses spoke on the law of Celestial Marriage, and advised the young sisters not to speak a disrespectful word of this holy principle, but if they did not understand it, to pray to the Lord for wisdom, and He would reward them by answering their petitions. Recitation by Alvina Harker, entitled "Hate of the Bowl." Remarks were made by other sisters, and a good spirit prevailed. Meeting closed by singing and benediction.

MARY A. HAIGH, President.
HATTIE HARKER, Secretary.

Courtesy BYU Archives

FIG. 6. YLIA meeting minutes for North Jordan. (April 1, 1878.)

happy." She does confide that she has no sons of her own.[37] This rhetoric prepared the way for the Primary Association, organized at this time to teach and cultivate the little boys of Zion—an effort to bring young men in under the protecting umbrella of gospel living. The philanthropic leaders wanted to teach "a love of principle, a regard for truth, a respect for virtue and honesty, and a remembrance for keeping the Sabbath holy."[38]

Is it possible that the everyday Mormon woman, rather than the one prescribed, is in many instances the one the leaders were counseling her against being? The tensions between what such a woman was encouraged to do and what she was actually doing reveal a created reality. If she was urged to be busier at the silkworm tray, she had been ignoring it. If she was told not to complain about polygamy, she had been speaking ill of the practice. If the young women were counseled against fashionable clothing, they had been wearing it. As in photography, the negative images are one step closer to actuality than the positive prints produced from them.

IMAGE FOR NATIONAL CONSUMPTION

In the national arena, the Mormon women interacted with the United States in a social space of women's rights. Utah women were given the elective franchise between 1870 and 1887 and from 1896 on; their eastern sisters secured the complete franchise only after Constitutional amendment in 1920. Mormon women had more rights, yet they related to eastern women as unpopular suppliants, urging help from the power group in the East. Suffrage was a serious issue, for Utah's woman's vote was then under attack. As the two groups interacted and the Mormon women represented themselves to the larger nation, the Utah women created themselves in new forms for eastern consumption. While this transculturization usually works both ways, the Mormon women made the most effort to negotiate the space between the groups— rather than being directly written to the Mormon women, articles from the East were mostly copied from other publications.

The general message is that Mormon women have benefited and improved from suffrage; losing it would throw them behind. Their statements are implicit pleas for help to maintain their rights. They aim to be worthy of the voting privilege. Their civic activity has been incorporated into their religion. For example, Mrs. Howard of the Fourteenth Ward urges all Utah immigrants to become naturalized citizens, saying that instructing the sisters according to their temporal interests is the legitimate work of the Relief Society.[39] The women illustrate how the vote has expanded their sphere of usefulness. The domestic wives of the past were filling "positions of honor and trust in the various callings and avocations of life." Women who gave no thought to public duties before suffrage was extended to them saw "the benefits derived."[40] This message of improvement was widespread. Mary of Grantsville notes that eastern powers had cried that "the women of Utah were such down-trodden slaves to men that it was necessary to give us the right of the ballot box to free ourselves," and they have "improved rapidly since receiving that blessing; so much so as to astonish any thinking mind. . . . The franchise here in Utah is developing powers in women that will astonish the world,"[41] to which she is speaking. All this is familiar women's rights rhetoric. Both the before and after pictures are exaggerations.

Mary also asserts that, in contradiction to widely circulated lies, Mormon women are among the "most law-abiding and virtuous women on the face of the earth," and she is grateful for any help from women of the States to stop a bill that will deprive them of their rights. She closes with a slightly veiled threat: "If they should take the right of Franchise from us, it will be the death blow to the women of the States ever obtaining that right."[42] She insinuates the Mormon women into the greater women's rights struggle, even though most eastern women would ignore them, threatening that the voting future of eastern women will depend on their support of the Utah struggle.

A surprisingly tough message came from Franklin, Oneida County, Idaho. This piece counters the unspoken argument that voting Utah women are their husband's pawns. The writer asserts her independence. Acknowledging male opposition to suffrage or to reform work in the cities, the correspondent humbly opines that "woman has been too yielding, and it will take all the ability of what is termed the 'strong-minded women' to assist the weaker and teach them to act with more independence of character, and I believe it is in the power of woman to bring about a great reform in this respect."[43] The message here is a call to eastern women to join with independent women of Zion to improve society.

The *Exponent* reached out to, encouraged, and rewarded friends and supporters, featuring them as examples to the less committed. The Honorable Mr. Sargent, senator from California, had shown his "nobility of character" by upholding the women's cause in Congress, knowing "how unpopular said cause is."[44] Mrs. Spencer, of Washington, D.C., spoke for those in Zion at women's conventions in the East, saying that "the women of Utah desired to be one with them in asking constitutional protection of their rights as citizens." Mrs. Spencer asked no thanks for supporting the cause, "for if she did not oppose such legislation she ought to be stricken with instant paralysis." She did, however, appreciate kindly feelings in Utah, having "lost many friends and made hosts of enemies in [their] defense." Her request— "Can you not send me the Exponent? I need material to work with, knowing so little of your people"—was heeded and quoted.[45] Here was the perfect audience for which the distant voice of the *Exponent* was created, an audience that sought information and sacrificed to help.

What Mormon women had to cope with, and were indirectly speaking against, was the unflattering eastern view of Mormons. Many easterners did not care to recognize Mormon women as sisters. Lillie Devereux Blake, quoted in the *Exponent,* asserted the perceived bald truth that "the ballot is practically almost useless in the hands of both men and women in Utah under Mormon rule." Speaking on the proposition to disfranchise the women of Utah, she objected only on gender grounds, proposing that all polygamists should be disfranchised instead of just the women. She objected to the absurd idea that men protected women as they represented them. "Yes, as tyrants represent slaves, as hawks represent doves, as wolves represent lambs."[46] The editor differs with her views but copied the article.

What we have is a picture of a united phalanx of Mormon women religiously devoted to the suffrage cause, working in tandem with a larger eastern movement. The everyday actuality was less heroic. The unity with the East was realized only with a few national leaders like Elizabeth Cady Stanton and Susan B. Anthony, noted for their fraternization with questionable suffrage friends. Many in the East considered Mormon woman suffrage an aberration—almost an embarrassment to the cause—which had failed to confront Church patriarchy and polygamy.

The *Woman's Exponent*, then, despite its wide world of awareness and acceptance of many voices, successfully produced a clear image of preferred behavior at home and women's rights unity beyond. The reality, as always, was much more complicated, much less unified, much less decided in its views, when we acknowledge the difficulties and discouragements skated over by the hopeful presentation of the women in the 1870s.

Claudia L. Bushman is a researcher and writer who also teaches American Studies at Columbia University.

NOTES

1. Think of Winston Churchill in his radio addresses to the English nation during the Battle of Britain, when barrages of German bombs daily hammered London. When he told his beleaguered people that they would never give up, that this was their finest hour, he spoke not only to them, but to Franklin Delano Roosevelt in Washington to convince him that England was not a lost cause and that the United States should speedily enter the war. Churchill had a purpose beyond his words, as did the *Woman's Exponent*.

2. "Notes and News," *Woman's Exponent* 7 (July 1, 1878): 17.

3. Hannah T. King, "Jacob's Pillow versus Pillar," *Woman's Exponent* 7 (July 1, 1878): 17.

4. "Notes and News" (July 1, 1878), 17.

5. "Another Wonderful Cave in Kentucky," *Woman's Exponent* 7 (July 15, 1878): 29.

6. "Protection to Wives," *Woman's Exponent* 7 (July 15, 1878): 30.

7. "Notes and News," *Woman's Exponent* 7 (August 1, 1878): 33.

8. Mary Jane Crosby, "Woman and Her Opportunities," *Woman's Exponent* 7 (July 1, 1878): 23.

9. Ellen Parker and Elizabeth D. Gardner, "R. S. Reports," *Woman's Exponent* 6 (April 1, 1878): 162.

10. Mary L. Woolfe and Mary E. Griffith, "Correspondence," *Woman's Exponent* 7 (June 15, 1878): 15.

11. E. Davis, "The Sisters' Visit North," *Woman's Exponent* 7 (June 1, 1878): 3.

12. Sarah Sudweeks, "Woman's Voice," *Woman's Exponent* 7 (June 1, 1878): 6.

13. "Discourse by President Brigham Young: Delivered in the Tabernacle, Ogden," *Woman's Exponent* 6 (January 15, 1878): 125.

14. P. S. Hart, "Correspondence," *Woman's Exponent* 6 (March 15, 1878): 157.

15. "R. S. Report," *Woman's Exponent* 6 (April 1, 1878): 167.

16. "Home Affairs," *Woman's Exponent* 6 (March 15, 1878): 156–57.

17. H. M. Gunnison, "Should We Glean?" *Woman's Exponent* 7 (August 1, 1878): 35.

18. "Home Affairs," *Woman's Exponent* 7 (July 15, 1878): 29.

19. Mary, "Pipsey Papers," *Woman's Exponent* 7 (June 15, 1878): 14.

20. Hannah T. King, "Desultory Thoughts," *Woman's Exponent* 7 (June 1, 1878): 1.

21. "Home Affairs," *Woman's Exponent* 7 (June 1, 1878): 4.

22. "Quarterly Conference of Salt Lake Co. Relief Society," *Woman's Exponent* 6 (April 1, 1878): 163.

23. C. E. H., "The Influence of Woman," *Woman's Exponent* 7 (June 15, 1878): 14.

24. Jemima A. Brown, "Woman's Voice," *Woman's Exponent* 7 (July 15, 1878): 27.

25. "Classifieds," *Woman's Exponent* 6 (March 1, 1878): 152.

26. "R. S. Reports," *Woman's Exponent* 7 (June 1, 1878): 2.

27. "Home Affairs" (June 1, 1878), 5.

28. E. Howard, "Third Quarterly Conference," *Woman's Exponent* 7 (July 1, 1878): 18.

29. M. Elizabeth Little, "Woman's Advancement," *Woman's Exponent* 7 (July 1, 1878): 23.

30. "The Women of Utah," *Woman's Exponent* 7 (July 1, 1878): 20.

31. "Practical Capabilities," *Woman's Exponent* 6 (April 1, 1878): 164.

32. B. M., "There Is Much to Learn," *Woman's Exponent* 7 (August 1, 1878): 35.

33. "R. S. Reports," *Woman's Exponent* 7 (June 15, 1878): 10.

34. Mary G. Haight and Hattie Harker, "R. S. Reports," *Woman's Exponent* 6 (April 1, 1878): 162.

35. "Home Affairs," *Woman's Exponent* 7 (June 15, 1878): 12.

36. C. M., "Plural Marriage," *Woman's Exponent* 7 (July 15, 1878): 29.

37. Gipsy Golden, "Hints to Mothers," *Woman's Exponent* 7 (June 15, 1878): 9.

38. "Home Affairs" (July 15, 1878), 29.

39. "R. S. Reports," *Woman's Exponent* 6 (March 15, 1878): 154.

40. "Women of To-day," *Woman's Exponent* 7 (August 1, 1878): 36.

41. Mary, "Remonstrance," *Woman's Exponent* 6 (January 15, 1878): 123.

42. Mary, "Remonstrance," 123.

43. Elizabeth Fox, "R. S. Report," *Woman's Exponent* 6 (April 1, 1878): 167.

44. "Notes and News," *Woman's Exponent* 6 (January 15, 1878): 121.

45. "R. S. Reports," *Woman's Exponent* 6 (March 15, 1878): 154.

46. Lillie Devereux Blake, "The Proposition to Disfranchise the Women of Utah," *Woman's Exponent* 7 (June 15, 1878): 15.

Life Cycles

East side of Main Street between First and Second South Streets, Salt Lake City, 1862. Marsena Cannon, photographer. This view has been cropped to highlight the center portion of the photograph.

Pioneer children, ca. 1853. Three unidentified children stare into the camera not long after the Latter-day Saints established their home in the Great Basin. Marsena Cannon, photographer.

Growing Up in Pioneer Utah: Agonies and Ecstasies

Susan Arrington Madsen

Somewhere along the Platte River in the summer of 1841, there occurred an ox-bouncing competition:

> Boys from one of the earliest parties along the Oregon Trail came across a dead ox, it's paunch swollen tight with gasses of decay, and somehow they discovered that if they jumped against the animal's bloat, it would fling them vigorously back. Champions rose and fell as the boys ran faster, jumped harder and bounced farther. Finally, Andy, a long-necked redhead, backed off a great distance, lowered his head, sprinted, leaped—and plunged deep into the rotting carcass. His friends pulled him out, though with some difficulty, and the contestants went on their way, the observers with a good story, Andy with a deeply entrenched memory.[1]

Although hundreds of thousands of children took part in the westward expansion of the United States during the nineteenth century, historians have paid little attention to their lives, their challenges, and their contributions. The experiences of children and adolescents in American history, and certainly in Utah's history, remain a largely unexplored gold mine.

As a mother of four daughters, I spend much of my time trying to look at life through my children's eyes, delighting in their unique and refreshing perspectives. When my youngest daughter, Rachel, was ten years old, she sat at our dining-room table and heard her older sister, who was twenty-one, tell me how hard it was to tell a young man that she really did not like him and that she did not want to go out with him anymore. Worse yet, she agonized over her need to turn down a marriage proposal from another young man she had been dating. Rachel seemed surprised. She said to her older sister in a voice that was almost cavalier, "I tell boys at school *all the time* I don't like them!" Often the innocence of youth produces great courage. As one nineteenth-century immigrant wrote of the adventure of making the trek west, "There is an old proverb which says 'Them that knows nothing, fears nothing.' We feared nothing."[2]

REASONS FOR STUDYING THE LIVES OF PIONEER YOUTH

Let me suggest four reasons why we would do well to honor the pioneer youngsters of our past. First of all, to ignore the children in our history is to disregard the experiences of one of the largest of all minority groups. Elliott West, professor of history at the University of Arkansas, has written:

> Until its children are heard, the frontier's history cannot be truly written. The story of westward expansion has been a national inspiration and a global entertainment. It is a key to understanding America's precocious rise to power. But since its first telling, the story has been incomplete, and thus distorted. In all the human striving, failure, and accomplishment, a large portion of the actors have been left out.[3]

Consider these statistics: during the winter of 1847, historians estimate, there were 1,611 pioneers living in the Great Salt Lake Valley. Recent demographic studies have shown that an astonishing 53.2 percent of those individuals were under the age of nineteen and 25 percent under the age of eight.[4] Sheer numbers alone insist we pay attention to Utah's nineteenth-century children and adolescents.

A second reason to study the lives of Utah's youngest settlers is to give credit where credit is due. One pioneer mother said it well: "When all is said and done, man alone never settled a country, never built an empire, never even stayed 'put' unless accompanied by wife and children. . . . The unconquerable spirit of man may subdue, but it never yet has settled a new country; the family does that."[5]

Pioneer children and adolescents carried a heavy load on their relatively small shoulders. Although their fathers' work in settling the West has long been celebrated and their mothers' efforts have been more recently recognized, the backbreaking, relentless work accomplished by pioneer girls and boys has been virtually ignored. Their contributions included washing, spinning, plowing, making soap and candles, churning butter, preserving fruits and vegetables, gathering eggs, milking, and building homes, schools, temples, and barns. Sons were sometimes found doing women's work, and far more often, young girls moved into the realm of men—herding, harvesting, and hunting. It would be difficult, in fact, to find any part of a family's labor that children did not fully participate in.

Flora Robertson Brimhall, who grew up in Spanish Fork, wrote of how she contributed to the family's income:

> At the age of thirteen I served as nurse maid to a four-year-old boy in the Goodwin family, Salt Lake City. Mr. Goodwin was editor of the Salt Lake Tribune. I stayed four months in that family. My wages were a dollar and a half per week. At the end of the summer I presented our family with a practical gift—a sack of sugar and a box of laundry soap.
>
> [Later,] my sister, Grace, and I bent our energies toward home manufacture. We learned to operate Sam's knitting machine. We furnished hose for the family, the community, and Provo Woolen Mills. During one year I made two thousand pair of men's hose. To taper, narrow and heel the sock required special manipulation of the knitting machine. It was necessary also to count the rounds. There was a needle for every stitch and a little hook for convenience in case of dropping a stitch. One "red-letter day" I made two dozen pair of socks.[6]

To be sure, the work assigned to pioneer children was often exhausting and tedious. But they could be inventive in finding ways to speed up "quitting time." John Staheli, who was born in 1857 and immigrated to Utah at the age of four, is a case in point:

> A great part of our time was spent in making molasses during the fall and early winter months. Having the only mill in town we had to work almost continually day and night. I often became so sleepy and tired I could hardly work. On one occasion I asked Father if I could go to bed when the roosters began to crow. About twelve o'clock I began crowing which started the roosters in the neighborhood to crowing, so Father told me to go to bed.[7]

The children of early settlers often wrote of the impact their hardworking parents had on their own work ethic. George Theobald, who grew up in Hinckley, Utah, wrote:

> Father made a plow out of a big forked stock and we boys held it in place while our father pulled it. The stock plow was made of quaking aspen. He fastened it to himself by a strap. We plowed two and a half acres that way, and planted wheat. I always remembered that picture of my father doing the work of a horse.[8]

A third reason we should not ignore the experiences of our young pioneers is, simply, that frontier children and adolescents are worth watching. Seeing life and history through their eyes can bring fresh, unique insights to events we have generally viewed from adult perspectives.

For example, young people provide some unusual descriptions of important historical events. T. Samuel Browning, born in Ogden in 1860, remembers the first train coming to Ogden when he was nine years old:

> A number of us boys had heard that it was coming, so we went out to the south end of town and climbed over a bank and heard it whistle. It frightened us very much. We hastened back to the station where quite a large crowd of people had gathered to see it. There was a large slough on the south side of the station. When the train came in to Ogden, and whistled, people were so frightened they ran in all directions. Several people fell into this slough and had to be pulled out. It caused quite a commotion.[9]

Another youngster, Regina Mary Simmons Christensen, tells of her own brush with Utah history while living in Park City at age ten:

> The houses were made of wood and built so close together that when a fire started it was a serious thing indeed. Both mills would blow their sirens so loud it was terrible. One morning, in January, 1896, just as I was getting dressed, the sirens started to scream. I ran outside with only one shoe on, through the snow, down the steps, across the bridge, and into the store where Father had already gone to work. I must have been a sorry sight, with my uncombed hair flying, shoe untied, etc. Everyone in the store laughed at me. It was not a fire nor the end of the world, but the noise was because Utah had become a state![10]

The fourth reason is that the enthusiasm and optimism of the children contributed significantly to the well-being of the group. Christopher Alston, for example, celebrated his eleventh birthday just days before he entered the Salt Lake Valley in 1864. He had made the trip from England without his parents; his mother had remained in England, and his father was deceased. His first impressions of the Salt Lake Valley sparkle with the exuberance of youth:

> About 11 o'clock, we came out of the mouth of Parley's Canyon, where we were met by a number of men and teams. The first words of greetings I heard were, "Come here my boy and hold your cap." I came near the wagon from which this voice came. There was a man kneeling in the bottom of the wagon on some straw, and the wagon was nearly filled with peaches. He scooped up his double hands full of peaches and put them into my cap, then scooped up

another handful and put them into my cap also, and it was full of lovely peaches, the first I had ever tasted in my life. "There" he said, "now eat those." He kept handing out peaches until his load was given away. I ran to our wagon where my brother lay very sick and gave him some peaches, then divided the remainder with the teamster and my custodian, John Ollerton, who had brought me from England, then I ate the rest. Now imagine, if you can, an eleven-year-old boy who had walked 1,100 miles and had an 1,100 mile appetite, and had never tasted a peach before in his life, having half a dozen nice peaches to eat!

We traveled down the Sugarhouse street for four miles. There we were met by my uncle who took us home to his place where they were threshing, and where a thresher's dinner had just been served. We washed and sat to a table—the first time since leaving England—and ate a most glorious dinner not sitting on the ground and eating out of a camp skillet with a butcher knife. Someone gave me a big section of a luscious watermelon to eat. I thought "This is Zion;" most truly and I was in ecstasy.[11]

PIONEER CHILDREN'S CONCERNS

Children often seemed much less concerned about the overall picture of the settling of the West than they were with the everyday, ordinary tasks at hand. From their accounts, we can learn about those tasks and something about children's relationships with adults. The simple challenge of learning to make candles is described through the eyes of William Shipley Burton, who was born in 1850 in Salt Lake City:

One day a little girl, whose family was a recent arrival, came to our house and said [to my mother], "Sister Burton, Mother would like very much to borrow your candle molds if you would please let her have them."

Mother handed the candle molds to the little girl. In about 10 minutes the same little girl came again. "Sister Burton, Mother wants to know if you have a ball of candle wick that you will loan her. She hasn't any." The ball of candle wick was handed over.

In about 10 minutes the same girl was back. "Sister Burton, Mother has no tallow. Could you please loan her some?" The tallow was produced and delivered. In a few minutes the same child appeared at the door.

"Sister Burton, Mother does not know how to make candles, could you please come over and show her?" Mother went.[12]

Another practical matter that occupied the thoughts of Utah's youngest settlers was the constant need to find something to eat. Their ingenuity and their willingness to "do what needed to be done" to obtain a few mouthfuls of food contributed to the vitality of the whole community. Lorenzo Hadley describes an afternoon in West Weber at a nearby river:

> My parents had gone to attend a fast day meeting, which was then held on Thursday. My brother and I were down at the Weber River and the thought came to me how we could catch some fish. We went home and I got some needles and linen thread that my parents fetched from England. I took two or three of the needles and heated them so that I could bend them and make hooks. I then took two lengths of the thread and put it through the eye and bent the eye to hold it fast. We used grasshoppers for bait and my brother and I caught eight or ten fish before we heard daddy whistle for us to come home. He was sure pleased.[13]

Harrison Sperry wrote of his efforts one day to provide a meal for himself and his sister:

> The toughest meal we ever had was an old hawk. I had been out hunting all day and couldn't find any greens or game, but coming home I spied an old hawk perched up on an old stake. I crawled up close to him, as near as I could. I fired and down he came. I took him home and my sister said, "Harrison is this all that you could get?" I told her yes so we prepared him for the pot. When supper time came my sister went to take him up out of the pot but he was so tough she could hardly stick the fork into him. We had to put him back into the pot and boil him the greater part of the night. However we managed to eat him the next morning.[14]

Alma Mineer Felt, who spent much of her childhood in Mt. Pleasant, writes of the lengths to which she and her family went to add variety to their diet:

> We raised squash and hung this out to dry in chunks strung on strings. Then we used it in the winter by putting it in water to soak and baking it or mashing it like sweet potatoes and serving it with butter. Another food we enjoyed very much was pigweed. This grew in abundance between the sagebrush and we could gather all we wanted of it for the pigs and also for ourselves. It is more delicious than any spinach you ever tasted and just as good for you.
>
> There were also very large mushrooms that grew around the corral. After a rainy night they would pop up like magic—great big ones, the size of a saucer. I would go out and gather these in the

morning after it rained. We would clean them and peel off the out-side, then fry them in butter and pour cream over them just before serving. Oh, how we enjoyed those big whoppers![15]

Young people, too, felt the deep emotions involved in settling a new territory, braving the elements, and experiencing the daily drama of life and death in the West. At the age of thirteen, Martha Cragun Cox sat up all one night in 1865 in St. George with a widow's dying infant so that the exhausted mother could sleep:

> After some time had passed I perceived the child was dying. It was an awful task to me to call the mother to see her baby die. I [agreed] to go out at her request to call in her neighbors but was held in check at the door by their dog, a large fellow who had been howling on the steps for some time and who seemed to have suddenly become fierce, and [he would not let either] of us go out.
>
> The time we sat by that dying child seemed very long to me, while the dog never ceased to howl. When it was all over, the mother asked me if I would . . . perform the next sad rites. I could not refuse as there was no other way.
>
> The mother completely worn out with her long nights and days of watching and caring for her little one laid down with her other children on a ragged bed in the corner and fell into a sleep. I did the best I could but suffered under the ordeal. . . . When I had washed the little fellow and wrapped him in a piece of an old white window curtain I laid him out on the flat top of an old chest. By this time the only candle the widow had was burned down and it began to flicker and then flare up for a moment as the spirit of the little child had seemed to do and then fell down and went out forever as he had done. There was a pan of chips by the fireplace and these laid on the coals one at a time kept the little light I needed to sustain my reason. I dared not look at the dark door-less hole that led from the room into the cellar underneath the floor. This reminded me so much of an open grave.
>
> The wind blew hard and rattled the windows and whistled thru the openings in the chamber above. . . . During the short intervals in which the wind seemed to lose his breath I could hear the mice or rats scampering on the floor above making the dust fall down on my head. It was with the utmost economy that I made my chips last through the remainder of the night. As daylight appeared the dog left his post by the door. The wind and the rain ceased. The shad-ows of the night departed and a glorious morning was ushered in. I could afterward assist in the care for the dead without the feelings I had had before.[16]

When J. Martin Allred was fifteen years old, a severe drought forced his father and him to drive their livestock from their home in Wallsburg, Utah, to winter on the Uintah Reservation. After a long winter of sometimes lonely cattle herding, Martin was anxious to see his mother and siblings. Returning home a few weeks before his father, Martin experienced this reception:

> We hadn't heard one word from home all winter and when I got within about one mile from home I met an old neighbor by the name of John Purcell. He began telling me of the children that had died in [Wallsburg] during the winter from diphtheria. I thought every second he would tell about some of my brothers and sisters dying, but thank the Lord there were none of them seriously sick with that dreaded disease.
>
> When I got to our front gate Mother met me and said, 'Martin, you mustn't come in as some of the children are in the worst stage of the disease.' Then mother told me there had been 32 children die there during the winter, as many as five in one family. I was only fifteen years old, hadn't seen Mother all winter long and was so homesick to see the rest of the family. I wanted so much to take her in my arms and hug and kiss her, but she wouldn't even shake hands with me for fear of leaving a germ and I might be exposed. You can imagine my feelings at that moment and also hers.[17]

Martin's mother decided he should go away and work for another two or three months. She did not let him return home until the rest of the children were well.

CHILDREN AND RELIGION

The context into which we must place these experiences of work, play, life, death, and putting food on the evening dinner table is religion. It was, after all, the force which had brought the pioneers to the Great Basin in the first place.

Many frontier children had sacred experiences that would influence them for the rest of their lives. Many such experiences were neither sought nor expected at the time they happened. Alice Minerva Richards, at the age of eight, attended the dedication of the Salt Lake Temple and saw angels on the ceiling. She later recalled, "I have always been grateful for the privilege of attending on that sacred occasion."[18]

Eva Christine Beck, born in 1851, was deeply touched each spring to kneel alongside her parents and siblings and hear her father bless the seed wheat that each kernel might grow and bring forth an abundant harvest that they might have bread to eat.[19]

Sometimes, however, the spiritual impact of the occasion escaped the children, and they remembered the more temporal aspects of the moment. One young man who went to the dedication of the Salt Lake Temple returned to his home in Hyrum remembering only one thing:

> When we got down to Salt Lake they had a big yard where there was a big barn. We slept in the barn. I can remember when we got to bed and got asleep, a kid came hollering "Hot Tamales." He was selling them. So we had to buy a hot tamale and that was the first time I ever ate a tamale.[20]

Even the seemingly sacred experience of baptism can take on a whole new meaning when seen through the eyes of a frontier child. Here is the description of the baptism of Vera Blain Larsen in Spring City:

> This day [in November] that I was to be baptized my mother thought it was such a cold day that she put a winter dress on me. It had bands of velvet on it for trimming. When I got down in the water and it got soaked up with water, I had to be hauled out of there.[21]

Then there is this description from the life history of Rulon Francis Thompson, who grew up in Richmond, Utah:

> I was baptized north of [Richmond]. Several boys were baptized that day. I remember how cold the water was. It took your breath [away] as you waded out into the river to where we were to be immersed. The water came almost up to our shoulders. When one of the boys, LaFayette Tibbets, came up out of the water he said, "Hell, that's cold!" He was immediately immersed in the water again. When he came up the second time, he kept his mouth shut.[22]

As is the case today, example usually spoke louder than words when it came to the religious education of Utah's Mormon pioneer girls and boys. Perhaps my favorite story of the power of a father's example on his young son is from the life story of James William Nielsen, who was born in 1887 in Fairview, Utah:

> There was a piece of ground on Father's side of the homestead that was ideal clay for brick, so we all decided to go in together and build a kiln of brick. Father did the book work and kept account of all the time each put in, and Uncle George [Davis—actually James's brother-in-law] was in charge of the brick kiln, its building, and burning. Father and George did the molding of the adobes; the rest of us helped mix the mud for the adobes, turn them, and wheel them to the kiln.

We all worked our spare time during the summer, and in the fall the job was completed. The wood for burning was hauled and stacked around the brick kiln until Uncle George said we had enough. We used cedar wood, and the surrounding hills were full of cedar.

There were seventy-five thousand adobes in that kiln of bricks, our whole summer's work. How happy we all were when the fires were started in the arches and the job was nearing completion.

As well as I can remember, it takes three weeks to burn a kiln of bricks. They must be kept at a certain heat and watched continually night and day. How Uncle George stood the ordeal, I don't know; he was the one that watched night and day. If he ever slept it was only a cat-nap. He watched that brick kiln like a cat watches a mouse.

We took turns helping him, cutting the wood and firing the arches then the rains came. It rained night and day for a week, and we finally ran out of wood. We had burned every stick of wood we [could] find on the place—corrals, fence post, an out-house—everything.

We couldn't get off the place for a load of wood as the whole country would mire a saddle blanket. I shall never forget the dis-couraged look on Uncle George's face when he put in the last stick of wood, looked at the color of the arches, and said, "It will be noth-ing but a pile of smoked mud."

Father was not a brick maker, but he insisted we seal up the arches as though the kiln was completed and that we all go home to get some sleep.

The next morning, George and I were sitting by the brick kiln moaning the blues, when we missed father and went looking for him. We found him on the east side of the kiln with hands above his head, blessing the kiln of bricks. He was just talking to the Lord and telling Him how we had all worked and did everything we possibly could, and he sealed that kiln into the hands of the Lord.

George and I quietly withdrew; father never saw us, but the effect it had on us, and has again when I write this story, I shall never forget.

When the time was up to open the kiln, most of us were depressed, but father never turned a hair. They opened up the top, and the bric was beautiful, and rang like a bell when clicked together; they were highly colored and sold like hotcakes. They even bought the broken bricks and hauled everything away.

Uncle George said, and most people thought, that the wet weather held the heat in and completed the job, but we children know that it was done by the priesthood father held and the power of prayer.[23]

One of the intriguing aspects of history is that there is always a new perspective from which to study the events of the past. It is a terrain that will never be completely discovered, a canvas that can always be painted using different colors, techniques, and styles.

I once asked my father, Leonard Arrington, if the day would come when all of history will finally have been written: "Will we simply run out of things to say about the history of the West, the United States, or any other geographical area or culture?" Grinning, he told me to ask my husband, Dean, a music professor at Utah State University, if the day would come when all music will have been written.

Thankfully, that day will never come. There will always be a new symphony to write, a new painting to create, and a new angle from which to understand our past. I suggest that the study of Utah's youngest settlers provides a perspective that will enhance our understanding of our past. When the voices of our children are heard, some of history's most interesting actors and actresses will have their turn at center stage, and our history will be more complete, more interesting, and more true.

Susan Arrington Madsen is a wife, mother of four, and author of two best-selling books on nineteenth-century Latter-day Saint children.

NOTES

1. Jesse Applegate, *Recollections of My Boyhood* (Roseburg, Ore.: Press of Review Publishing, 1914), 21.

2. Chester Dutton to Rodman, June 20, 1878, Yale Class Records, 1938, Manuscripts Archives Division, Yale University Library.

3. Elliott West, *Growing Up with the Country* (Albuquerque: University of New Mexico Press, 1989), 245.

4. Pioneer Demographic Study, Research Information Division, The Church of Jesus Christ of Latter-day Saints, 1996.

5. Margaret Marshall, Reminiscence, Kansas State Historical Society, l.

6. Flora Robertson Brimhall, Autobiography, dictated to Minnie I. Hodapp, typescript, Special Collections and Manuscripts, Harold B. Lee Library, Brigham Young University, Provo, Utah.

7. John Staheli, "Mormon Diaries, Journals, and Life Sketches," Special Collections, Merrill Library, Utah State University, Logan, Utah (hereafter cited as USU Special Collections). Typescript of autobiography in Archives Division, Historical Department, The Church of Jesus Christ of Latter-day Saints, Salt Lake City (hereafter cited as LDS Church Archives).

8. George Theobald, "Mormon Diaries, Journals, and Life Sketches," USU Special Collections.

9. T. Samuel Browning, "Mormon Diaries, Journals, and Life Sketches," USU Special Collections.

10. Regina Mary Simmons Christensen, Autobiography, typescript, USU Special Collections.

11. Christopher Alston, Autobiography, in *Our Pioneer Heritage,* comp. Kate B. Carter, 20 vols. (Salt Lake City: Daughters of Utah Pioneers, 1958–77), 8:35–38.

12. William Shipley Burton, A Biographical Sketch and Some Things I Remember, typescript in possession of Janet Seegmiller, Cedar City, Utah.

13. Lorenzo Hadley, Autobiography, typescript, Utah State Historical Society, Salt Lake City.

14. Harrison Sperry Sr., Autobiography, typescript, LDS Church Archives.

15. Alma Mineer Felt, Journal, in *An Enduring Legacy,* comp. Lesson Committee, 12 vols. (Salt Lake City: Daughters of Utah Pioneers, 1977–89), 7:193–232.

16. Martha Cragun Cox, "Biographical Record of Martha Cox: Written for My Children and My Children's Children, and All Who May Care to Read It," holograph, LDS Church Archives, typescript available at Utah State Historical Society and at Brigham Young University.

17. James Martin Allred, Autobiography, typescript, USU Special Collections.

18. Alice Minerva Richards Tate Robinson, personal record in possession of George F. Tate, Orem, Utah.

19. Eva Christine Beck Zimmerman Harrison, Autobiography, in *Our Pioneer Heritage,* 8:50.

20. David Osborne Nielsen, Reminiscences, typescript, privately published and distributed, in possession of Lon Bower, Hyrum, Utah.

21. Vera Blain Larsen Downard Sorensen, Reminiscences, in *Life under the Horseshoe: A History of Spring City,* written and edited by Kaye C. Watson (Salt Lake City: Publishers Press, 1987), 44.

22. Rulon Francis Thompson, Autobiography, typescript, privately printed and distributed by the family.

23. James W. Nielson, "Blessing the Brick Kiln," in *Voices from the Past: Diaries, Journals, and Autobiographies,* comp. Campus Education Week Program under the direction of Division of Continuing Education, Brigham Young University, Provo, Utah, 1980.

"Heigh, Ho! I'm Seventeen": The Diary of a Teenage Girl

Davis Bitton

Just as women were long absent from the historical record, so have children and teenagers been largely ignored. Since the 1970s, some effort has been made to fill in the gaps, dramatically in the case of women, more modestly for children and youth.[1] I opened up the subject of young people in Mormon history in a pioneering article titled "Zion's Rowdies: Growing Up on the Mormon Frontier," and Susan Arrington Madsen has recently compiled anecdotal childhood experiences of young pioneers.[2] In the pursuit to learn more about the youth in Mormon history, demographers can help us with birth and death statistics; diseases and accidents are assumed to be inevitable parts of childhood. On the other hand, diaries can provide the texture of daily living, activities both ordinary and extraordinary, and, above all, personal, emotional reactions. Several years ago, I published an article based on the diary of a teenage boy from Brigham City.[3] Here I want to look at the life of a Salt Lake Valley girl—she lived on a farm by the Jordan River—who kept a diary that is delightfully frank and uninhibited.

Age Sixteen

In 1886, at the age of sixteen, Amelia Cannon, daughter of George Q. and his plural wife Martha T. Cannon, was given a new, blank diary by her mother, who instructed her: "Now Milly, I want you to take particular pains and write well in this. Do not scribble as you did in your former diaries. Also write nothing foolish in it."[4]

Amelia did not always do as she was told. "Oh, this journal! It makes me sick to look at it!" she wrote a few months later. "Why, oh why haven't I taken more pains with my writing? Better that I should write a little each day, and be careful than to leave my diary for months and then

Courtesy Mary B. Pearson

George Q. Cannon (1827–1901), age 65, First Counselor in the First Presidency of Wilford Woodruff.

Courtesy Mary B. Pearson

Martha Telle Cannon (1846–1928), George Q. Cannon's fourth wife.

come blooming out with such plentiful scrawls. But I am all theory and no practice! Why not <u>do</u>, instead of resolving and never acting?"[5]

A week earlier when she had attended the "matinee"—presumably at the theater—she had borrowed a new gingham dress belonging to her twin sister, Hetty (Hester). Now Amelia watched the baby while her mother made Amelia a new gingham. It was the time of year for such things as the start of school was just around the corner.

Like the other Cannon children, Amelia had the privilege of learning to play a musical instrument—in her case, the piano. She and her sister Zannie (Rosannah) enjoyed performing duets: "Baby Bye, Here's a Fly" ("a comical simple thing") and the more beautiful "Warblings at Eve." The two girls also sang the duet "There's a Sigh in the Heart." When Hetty joined them, they had a trio.

Amelia was a reader; she particularly enjoyed Louisa May Alcott's *Old-Fashioned Girl* and Mrs. A. D. T. Whitney's *We Girls*. At age nine, she had read *Jolly Good Times; or, Milly's Farm Life*. Now she read Alcott's *Rose in Bloom*. "It is an interesting story but not one I would advise any young friend of mine to read," she wrote. "'Tis not a story having a high moral." Although she was not strictly following her father's advice to avoid fiction, she shared some of his concerns. Later she read *The Girls at Quinnemont* and enjoyed it so much that she read it again:

> I have a perfect passion for reading story-books. Not love stories: I hate them, they are always so sicky, but young folk's storys [sic]. I never will read an instructive book, while there is a story book around.

Here this forenoon I went and read "The Girls at Quinnemont" again, after I read it just the other day.

What a waste of time. What a foolish expenditure of opportunity!

I can't help it. I love tales of girls at boarding schools so well, that I would neglect anything for such stories.

Whenever I read an interesting book, I always wish that the story were true and that I could mingle with and become acquainted with the characters of it. But no hope for that, for likely all of the best stories are concocted out of the imagination, with the assistance of everyday incidents and scenes of ordinary life.[6]

Courtesy Mary B. Pearson

Amelia Telle Cannon (1870–1937), daughter of George and Martha Telle Cannon.

Even though she worked hard on the farm, Amelia found time to read. During their noon break, she and Hester would spread a shawl on the grass and read. One story they liked was "A Midsummer's Madness" by Rosa Terry Vook.[7] When Amelia read *A Seaboard Parish,* she justified herself by noting that the author was a minister and that she read the novel "from a religious standpoint."[8] Reading *Memoirs of Aaron Burr* was a break from this diet of fiction.[9]

Amelia's diary allows us to follow some of the emotional swings of an ado-

Courtesy Mary B. Pearson

Hester Telle Cannon (1870–1936), daughter of George and Martha Telle Cannon. Amelia's twin sister.

lescent. She wrote silly poetry, then burned it up. One night she got up and filled pages, writing "about everything and anything." When upset at somebody, she would take it out on him or her in writing and later burn the pages. One afternoon, as she put it, "I got a freak of spinning off lover-sick poetry." Feeling moody, she tried to get Hetty to go for a walk. When Hetty refused, Amelia sat on the steps of the schoolhouse in the shade and in her "Scribble Book" wrote "A Declaration of Love." "Oh such sicky stuff as I wrote!" But eventually she got her sister Emily to join her. She asked Emily to write her thoughts and then they would read each other's, which they did until dark. At least Amelia had some sense of what she was doing. She signed these "sicky effusions" with the pen name "Fried Pickle."

Attendance at church meetings was a repetitive feature of Amelia's life. Resolving to keep the Sabbath day holy, she made the following observation:

> There are so many persons who make the Sabbath a day of pleasure. I, myself, formerly spent my Sundays in amusement. It was when we used to go to the Farmers' Ward S. Schools and Mutuals. There mutuals come on Sunday evenings. Well we girls used to go over early Sunday evenings, then we and the Farmers' Ward girls and boys would play "Pomp" or "Auntie-i over." I tell you it had a demoralizing effect on us, going to the Farmers' Ward. In the class, where we girls read the bible, we would all put our heads together and tell ghost stories.[10]

Amelia sometimes failed to attend fast meetings on Thursday evenings. Despite her father's repeated instructions, there was more than a little laxity. "I wish I could go to the Fast Meetings," she wrote, "but the boys wouldn't think of going unless Pa told them expressly about once a month that they must take the carriage. . . . the boys haven't taken the team once this summer. I've been to only two or three fast-meetings in my life, but its not my fault for I have gone whenever I've had a chance."[11]

When school started, Amelia found that it was not easy: "School is not a bit nice so far! The studies which H. and I have registered for are, German, Physics, Ancient History, and Drawing." Having had "home schooling," she and her sister would have to demonstrate their competence. They could either take classes in physics and history or be tested by a board of examination. They chose the latter course. Their drawing teacher was George T. Ottinger, who inspired them by saying that "anyone who practices drawing ½ hr. each day for a year or 1 hr. per day during ½ year. will become so proficient that he or she can draw anything which is seen."

She describes her classes as "higher" branches or sometimes as "university" classes. Not having applied herself as diligently as she might have during the previous year, Amelia faced tough challenges:

> Study, study, study all the time! That's what H. and I have! . . .
> We studied steadily all day yesterday on our Geography and we

have to study even on Sundays. . . . Oh dear! I am going to undergo an examination in four branches, this month. They are: Geography, Arithmetic, Elocution, and Writing. I have to study up for them all. The examination in Geography comes next St. Oh, I do dread it! There are going to be questions given in Mathematical, political, physical, and descriptive Geography.

Am I not a big dummy? Last year I took all of these branches; but I didn't pass on account of neglecting my lessons. . . .

Oh, they are so strict at the University this year. One has to submit to an entrance examination before taking any study, except in Drawing. And then every three or four weeks all in the classes are examined to see if they are capable of remaining in the class.

I would be studying now, stead of writing only H. is downstairs taking her bath and I am waiting for her to come up, so that we can persue [*sic*] our Geography together. My, I wish she'd hurry![12]

By dint of hard study, Amelia was able to pass all these exams.

Attending "public" school jolted the Cannon girls into another reality. "There are some girls going to school who think they are too good to speak to any one except those who wear fine dresses of silk, &c. They will not condescend to notice any that are not of high or wealthy families." The cruelty of childhood and youth; its stupid, but painful, snobbery; the inhumane, not to say unchristian, treatment of other human beings were alive and well in the 1880s. Happily, Amelia's values seem to be sound. "Thank goodness, there are not many who crave their company! Who would think that girls raised in Utah would act thus?"[13]

As a teenage girl, Amelia was naturally concerned about her appearance. One day she wore her hair bobbed on top of her head. "I had to go into the Dressing room every little while to comb it over in order that it would look decent." On another occasion, she took her hair down in order to braid it.

Oh such a terrible snarl as it got into! I could do nothing with it. Couldn't even part it. Had to braid it in a great snarl and rush off to school with it so. It was the same way yesterday and this morning. Well this evening I resolved to rid my hair of its snarl or die in the attempt. I brushed and combed brushed and combed until my arms fairly ached. Well, after I had drowned my head in oil, so the snarls would come out easier, and had broken off enough hair for a wig, I got my hair free from its entanglements. There was so much of my hair which came out that now it is about twice as thin as it was.[14]

Courtesy BYU Special Collections, Harold B. Lee Library

Early trolley in Salt Lake City, ca. 1878. Amelia was familiar with the trolley cars in Salt Lake City, for the first trolleys, known euphemistically as "horse cars," began service in Salt Lake City in 1872. By 1883, there were forty-one cars, nine miles of track, eighty-four mules, and thirty employees. In 1889, one line was electrified, and soon there were more than one hundred miles of tracks crossing the city.

She and her twin sister had their spats. Once Hetty hid a piece of Amelia's music. Amelia poured her heart out in her diary:

> I have cried myself nearly sick, just over a trivial matter too. Hetty has hidden my favorite piece of music, i.e. "Remember Me" and she won't tell me where it is. I shall want it very much tonight, for Pa will most likely call on me to play, and that is the only piece that I would risk, because I haven't practiced my others lately. Indeed I haven't practiced <u>that</u> one for the last week or two. I wanted it this afternoon to practice, but H. said she wouldn't tell me where it was. I then came up stairs, locked myself in the closet and cried.[15]

Almost as an afterthought, she added the following: "I suppose I must tell both sides of the story. I hid a piece of Hetty's first."

Of course, these twin sisters were very close. They studied together, roomed together, and talked and talked. "Last night Hetty and I sat up 'till after 12 talking. When we once get started to talk it seems as though we can never stop. We will neglect our lessons even, to talk."[16] One winter Sunday morning, Amelia got up at 2 A.M., thinking it was 6 o'clock. In the moonlight, she walked on stilts through the snow. "When I had been up an hour or so, H. got up and we both walked all over on our stilts, then went onto the pond and pushed each other on the sled until the arrival of morning forbid it. . . . I tell you we had a jolly time."[17]

She recorded what she called her "health routine": "Every night I take a bath. Eat none but coarse food. Wash my head once or twice a week. Try to take plenty of daily exercise. Change my clothes often and air them thoroughly. Wear nothing at night which I wear during the day, &c."[18]

Age Seventeen

When Amelia turned seventeen, in early 1887, she was taking the following subjects in school: botany, zoology, German, modern history, and drawing. "I tell you, I have a tussel [*sic*] to keep on in them," she wrote. Finally, music lessons seemed too much, and she stopped, although Hester continued to study and Amelia joined her in learning duets. Probably for financial reasons, the decision was made that the two girls discontinue their public schooling the following year and go instead to work in the *Juvenile Instructor* office. They would continue to take private lessons in several subjects. "We shall start to earn money next spring," Amelia wrote. "Oh, I shall be so glad. I don't like to be dependent upon my parents."[19] She accepted the work with a good attitude, but a few months later, she was able to quit:

> I am thankful to say I have quit work at the Juvenile Office. It seemed as though my perceptions were getting dull and that I found no pleasure whatever in life while working there. To use strong language, it seems like stepping right from hell into heaven to cease going to the J.I.O. bindery. Who could enjoy life while being penned up in a low, damp, bad-odored illy-ventilated book-bindery ten hours every day?[20]

Now that she was seventeen, she felt she had to act in a grown-up manner. "I am afraid to act at all girlish. . . . for fear it will be beneath the dignity of seventeen. . . . Since my birthday I have been as grave and dignified as an owl."[21] Quite conscious of her new maturity, she was also still partly a girl. "I believe that I will go now and wade in the ditch or else go in bathing before dinner. It's very undignified for a girl of seventeen to wade, but I don't care. I'll do it if I can without being seen."[22]

Amelia's father hovers in the background. By the spring of 1887, the family did not attend meetings in the Farmers Ward but instead met at home. Although hiding on the underground, George Q. would join them:

> His visits are kept very secret though, and no one out of the family knows about them. We always meet together Sunday evenings for

prayers. Then we have music until the guard comes to accompany pa to his retreat which by the way is fifty miles distant. So papa has a long ways to travel to meet with his folks. I always have to play on the piano for him in the evenings. Papa is so fond of music. I have had to perform so much on Sabbath evenings, that I have used up all of my prettiest pieces. Last Sunday I played "Woodland Echoes" and "Evening Parade."[23]

At the end of June, George Q. came to the farm for health reasons. Amelia stayed home from work in order to watch the baby while her mother cared for "papa." He had the "sistace" in his left leg, which had turned lame, and now sought to heal it by having his wife bathe it in sage tea.[24]

By the holiday season, Amelia, having now quit her job at the bindery, was busy taking care of infant Espey and making a "daisy tidy" for a Christmas present. Here is her description: "On a square of red groagrain [grosgrain] silk there is a cross of cherry satin ribbon, along which are double rows of daisys. There are pon pon balls clear around the edge of the square of silk, of cardinal and old gold alternately. I never saw such an odd beautiful piece of fancy-work as it makes."[25]

On Christmas Amelia's presents were "a fine set of Shakespeare, a silk handkerchief, a cotton one, a music book and an embroidered night dress." On New Year's Eve, two parties were held, one in the afternoon for the children, another in the evening for the "young folks." Sixty or more guests were invited. In planning for this evening party, sixteen-year-old David, Amelia's half-brother, asked George Q. Cannon, "Well, what about some round dances?"

"I would rather there would be none," Cannon answered, "for the example would not be a good one."

Amelia was disappointed, to say the least. "So we are doomed to have none but dreary monotonous square dances," she wrote. "Until I attended a University party recently, I was content with square dancing; but I imbibed a taste there for round dancing. It has remained with me ever since."[26]

Actually, the party turned out rather well for Amelia. Each of Cannon's families provided enough of one kind of refreshment to serve everyone. Martha brought cream puffs. Cannon furnished the lemonade. "I danced as much as I desired," Amelia wrote. "In this I was agreeably surprised, for I did not expect to dance much, or to enjoy myself."

Then Amelia reveals the main reason for her elation. "In the last dance (the Madly)"—apparently a round dance reluctantly conceded—"the <u>model</u> boy was my partner. His name is Willard Croxall. He is a good conversationalist, he is agreeable and gallant. He is very religious, however his face is not drawn down with a pious, long-suffering expression as some peoples' countenances are." Croxall was not "shocked" by round dancing but was "quite proficient himself in the forbidden pleasure."

"I am not adept in round-dancing, so you must excuse blunders," he said.

"There was no need for his saying that," Amelia wrote, "for he dances well, he glides along so lightly. Indeed he had to partly teach me the steps and pull me along the right way."

She had a good time.

George Q. knew how to make a hit with his teenage children. "Papa has filled my heart with joy," Amelia wrote, "by saying we are to have a series of parties this winter, one at the beginning of each month."

Amelia did not marry the smooth dancer Willard Croxall, but she did marry William Henry Chamberlin, who went on to become one of Mormonism's leading intellectuals in the first generation of the twentieth century.[27] With maturity, naturally, came greater responsibility and greater seriousness. Happily, Amelia Cannon Chamberlin did not feel it necessary to destroy the record of her youthful feelings.

INSIGHTS FROM THE DIARY

Besides amused chuckles, a diary such as this provides the historian and the student of history with valuable insights. I would suggest the following:

First, public figures come across as less formidable. The marble statue—George Q. Cannon—assumes some of the lineaments of humanity when viewed through the eyes of a daughter.

Second, the internal dynamics of a family come through to some extent. Although admittedly other family members would describe things differently, we are allowed to see the family, not stiffly posed for the photographer's camera, but in the give-and-take, the mood swings, and the tensions of daily living.

Third, schooling and self-improvement are revealed as central concerns, but again instead of reading a simple statement, we are allowed to observe the daily study, the frustrations, the examinations, the successes, and the failures. Who would deny that these loom large in the experience of young people? Yet how, in the absence of a personal record, are we to gain access to this fundamental part of life?

Fourth, work is revealed as an insistent, unavoidable demand. It is not always easy to determine, for adults or for children, what the work experience really was in all of its seasonal variety. We know that young people were called upon to work in the home and on the farm. But how revealing it is to follow someone like Amelia Cannon as she cares for children, keeps house, and takes employment in a bindery. Like teenagers now, she was subject to many simultaneous pressures but was never allowed to simply abandon work responsibilities.

Fifth, recreational pastimes are revealed in their colorful variety. It is one thing to say that certain activities were available; it is another to accompany the young person to the theater, to birthday parties, to the pleasure gardens, and onto the dance floor. The prohibition of round dancing is an illuminating case study of generational tension, which I have written about elsewhere.[28] But it is through a diary like Amelia Cannon's that we are enabled to view this tension with a teenager's perspective.

Sixth, the religious side of life is far too complex to be encapsulated by labels such as "Mormon" or "Methodist" or "active" or "inactive." It is valuable, I submit, to discover that young people, even in families of prominent Church leaders, were not always pious, that attendance at meetings was not impeccable, and that classes were sometimes boring or disrupted by disorderly behavior. To be sure, we do not celebrate this discovery, but it was part of life and gives us a picture of Mormon religiosity somewhat different from the earnest sermons delivered at general conference. Even people who were not exactly models of righteousness could be loyal Latter-day Saints in their way, could rise to acts of faithfulness, and could mend their ways. The trajectory, as we well know, could also move in the opposite direction. It is better always to see the whole picture and see it plain.

I have listed six areas of everyday life opened up by this diary, which has verve and color, concrete detail, and human interest. For someone interested in the sights and sounds of everyday life in territorial Utah, the rhythm and hum of life as it was experienced, the teenage diary of the vivacious Amelia Cannon is not trivial at all. It is a treasure.

Davis Bitton is Professor Emeritus of History, University of Utah.

NOTES

1. Joseph F. Kett, "Adolescence and Youth in Nineteenth-Century America" and John Demos, "Developmental Perspectives on the History of Childhood" are both reprinted in Theodore K. Rabb and Robert I. Rotberg, eds., *The Family in History: Interdisciplinary Essays* (New York: Harper and Row, 1971). Many articles are found in *History of Childhood Quarterly*, but often they are marred, in my view, by unconvincing psychohistorical interpretations. Three significant recent studies are Carolyn Steedman, *Strange Dislocations: Childhood and the Idea of Human Interiority, 1780–1930* (Cambridge: Harvard University Press, 1995); Hugh Cunningham, *Children and Childhood in Western Society since 1500* (London: Longmans, 1995); and Jacqueline S. Reinier, *From Virtue to Character: American Childhood, 1775–1850* (New York: Twayne, 1996).

2. Davis Bitton, "Zion's Rowdies: Growing Up on the Mormon Frontier," *Utah Historical Quarterly* 50 (spring 1982): 182–95; revised version in Davis Bitton, *The Ritualization of Mormon History and Other Essays* (Urbana: University of Illinois Press, 1994), 54–68; Susan Arrington Madsen, *I Walked to Zion: True Stories of Young Pioneers* (Salt Lake City: Deseret Book, 1994); Susan Arrington Madsen, *Growing Up in Zion: Young Pioneers Building the Kingdom* (Salt Lake City: Deseret Book, 1996).

3. Davis Bitton, "Six Months in the Life of a Mormon Teenager," *New Era* 7 (May 1977): 44–49.

4. Amelia T. Cannon, Journal (1886–87), typescript, George Q. Cannon Archives, Geneva Steel, Orem, Utah; Amelia T. Cannon, Diary 1892, holograph, Archives Division, Historical Department, The Church of Jesus Christ of Latter-day Saints, Salt Lake City (hereafter cited as LDS Church Archives). This relatively short diary is briefly summarized in Davis Bitton, *Guide to Mormon Diaries and Autobiographies* (Provo, Utah: Brigham Young University Press, 1977), 56. The details of Amelia Cannon's life following this paragraph are from her journal-diary.

5. Cannon, Journal, June 25, 1887.

6. Cannon, Journal, June 28, 1887.

7. Cannon, Journal, June 28, 1887.

8. Cannon, Journal, October 30, 1887.

9. Cannon, Journal, November 1, 1887.

10. Cannon, Journal, August 29, 1886.

11. Cannon, Journal, September 1, 1886.

12. Cannon, Journal, October 3, 1886.

13. Cannon, Journal, September 7, 1886.

14. Cannon, Journal, October 21, 1886.

15. Cannon, Journal, September 19, 1886.

16. Cannon, Journal, December 14, 1886.

17. Cannon, Journal, December 14, 1886.

18. Cannon, Journal, October 31, 1886.

19. Cannon, Journal, February 23, 1887.

20. Cannon, Journal, October 30, 1887.

21. Cannon, Journal, March 8, 1887.

22. Cannon, Journal, June 28, 1887.

23. Cannon, Journal, May 9, 1887.

24. Cannon, Journal, June 28, 1887.

25. Cannon, Journal, November 1, 1887.

26. Cannon, Journal, December 29, 1887.

27. Ralph V. Chamberlin, *The Life and Philosophy of W. H. Chamberlin* (Salt Lake City: Deseret News Press, 1925).

28. Davis Bitton, "These Licentious Days: Dancing among the Mormons," *Sunstone* 2 (spring 1977): 16–27; revised version in Bitton, *Ritualization of Mormon History,* 98–114.

GARBAGE!

All persons are forbidden to deposit garbage, offal or rubbish of any kind on the streets except in such places as shall be designated by the Street Supervisor.

Extract from ordinance relating to

CRIMES AND PUNISHMENTS.

SEC. 25. Any person who shall throw, cast or lay any ashes, offal, vegetables, garbage, dross, cinders, shells, straw, shavings, dirt, filth, or rubbish of any kind whatever, in any street, sidewalk, ditch, lane, alley, or public place in this city, except at such place as shall be designated by the Street Supervisor, shall be liable to a fine not exceeding twenty-five dollars for each offence.

Let all parties take due notice and govern themselves accordingly.

ANDREW BURT,
City Marshal.

SALT LAKE CITY,
April 11th, 1878.

Adopted or Indentured, 1850–1870: Native Children in Mormon Households

Brian Q. Cannon

Long before Mormon settlers arrived in the Salt Lake Valley, Indians in the region became involved in a lucrative slave trade. Capturing or buying women and children from rival bands, they bartered the captives to traders who transported them to New Mexico, where they became servants or slaves.[1]

Recognizing a potential new market, Indian traders approached the Mormons shortly after they arrived in the Salt Lake Valley and attempted to sell some of their captives. John R. Young recalled:

> Soon after we moved on to our city lot, fall of 1847, a band of Indians camped near us. Early one morning we were excited at hearing their shrill, blood-curdling war whoop, mingled with occasional sharp cries of pain. Father sent me to the Fort for help. Charley Decker and Barney Ward, the interpreter, and others hurried to the camp.
>
> It was Wanship's band. Some of his braves had just returned from the war-path. In a fight with "Little Wolf's" band, they lost two men, but had succeeded in taking two girls prisoners. One of these they had killed, and were torturing the other. To save her life Charley Decker bought her, and took her to our house to be washed and clothed.[2]

Thus commenced the Mormon practice of purchasing Indian children in Utah.

The Mormons continued to buy Native American children although they had no legal basis for doing so until 1852. In that year, bent upon eliminating the Mexican slave trade but recognizing that the Utes relied upon it, the territorial legislature passed a law providing for the purchase and indentured servitude of Indian women and children. The legislators fixed the maximum period of servitude at twenty years and required "any white person" who acquired "any Indian prisoner, child, or woman . . . whether by purchase or otherwise" to file an indenture agreement with county officials. The law mandated schooling for all indentured children between the ages of seven and sixteen and required masters to clothe them "in a comfortable and becoming manner."[3] Brigham Young, who had earlier encouraged the Mormons in southern Utah "to buy up the Lamanite children as fast as they could,"[4] exulted, "This may be said to present a new feature in the traffic of human beings; it is essentially purchasing them into a freedom, instead of slavery."[5]

For two decades following the passage of this law, hundreds of Paiute, Gosiute, Shoshone, and Ute children were taken into Mormon homes.[6] What circumstances surrounded the purchase of Indian children during that period? What motivated Mormon settlers to acquire a child, and how did the children react to their new living arrangements? Finally, how did the children and other members of their adoptive households relate to each other? Were the children primarily servants, linked contractually to their masters, or adopted children, bound to members of their white families by emotional ties?

Circumstances Surrounding Purchases

Mormons acquired Indian children under a variety of circumstances. Many children were purchased from warriors and raiders; livestock, food, weapons, blankets, and clothing valued between $25 and $100 were commonly used as payment. James Martineau, for instance, traded a rifle worth $40 for a girl.[7] Jacob Hamblin "bought" a six-year-old boy for "a gun and blanket [and] some amunicion [sic]."[8] In 1858, John Bennion gave a group of Indians "the horse I was riding" for a three-year-old boy,[9] and in 1869, Bennion sent his wife $45 "to buy a Piute Indian boy."[10]

While some children were purchased from traders, others were obtained as compensation for stolen goods or were taken as prisoners of war following battles or skirmishes. Some children were found who had been abandoned, and others were sold by their own parents or other relatives. Christopher and Caroline Arthur, for instance, purchased a child from its mother, who had abandoned her husband for another man. In order "to accellerate [sic] their speed" in fleeing from the husband, the couple decided to sell the baby.[11] Although parents often placed a price upon their children, Danish settler Christian Nielsen believed that most parents loved their offspring but "necessity forces them often to sell them."[12]

Motivations

Their testimony may have been exaggerated, but many claimed that their friends and relatives who bought children did so in order to rescue them from torture, neglect, or the threat of death.[13] John Young graphically described how one girl whom the Mormons purchased had been abused by her captors: "They had shingled her head with butcher knives and fire brands. All the fleshy parts of her body, legs, and arms had been hacked with knives, then fire brands had been stuck into the wounds. She was gaunt with hunger, and smeared from head to foot with blood and ashes." Young explained that the girl was purchased in order "to save her life."[14]

Similarly, Zemira Draper Jr. recorded that his parents bought a boy "to save him from being killed by a hostile tribe."[15] Charlotte Maxwell Webb wrote that her parents obtained a three-month-old orphan because she was about "to be abandoned,"[16] and Betsy Hancock Shurtliff explained that her father paid a high price for a nine-year-old girl "through sympathy for the child."[17] James Martineau referred obliquely to potential danger in describing his purchase of a young girl whose "little brother had been killed by the Indians a few days before because they could not sell him."[18]

Although some captives, particularly prisoners of war, were horribly abused by their Indian captors, Brigham Young told Elizabeth Kane that stories of cruelty were sometimes exaggerated.[19] In light of Young's assessment, it is significant that few settlers who purchased a child recorded doing so in order to rescue the child from harm. Thus, although some Mormons purchased children to save them from physical harm, abuse was not as prevalent as some stories might suggest, and most who bought children offered other reasons for doing so.

Many Mormons opened their homes to children because they were directed to do so by community leaders following military engagements or other armed conflicts. For instance, Lorenzo Brown recorded that in 1856 a militia company marched into Utah after a two-week campaign, bringing "a number of squaws & children prisoners" who "were distributed amongst the citizens here who feed & clothe them."[20] William Hull, whose parents cared for a Shoshone child following the Bear River massacre, explained that he discovered the girl as he was surveying the massacre site and rescuing the wounded under assignment from his bishop. He found "two little boys and one little girl about three years of age [who] were still living. The little girl was badly wounded, having eight flesh wounds in her body." Hull and his companions conveyed the wounded by sleigh back to the village, where the children "were given good homes."[21]

Religious beliefs inclined others to open their homes to Indian children. As Brigham Young observed, purchasing a child offered Mormons an unparalleled opportunity to "teach them the Gospel."[22] Acting upon this belief, President Young's associate Wilford Woodruff purchased a six-year-old Paiute boy for forty dollars, hoping "to Educate him & prepare his mind that He may some day be useful in preaching to his tribe."[23] Spiritual convictions likewise induced Jacob Hamblin to buy a ten-year-old boy. "One day, in my rambles, I came to a lodge where there was a squaw, and a boy about ten years old," Hamblin explained. "As soon as I saw the boy, the Spirit said to me, 'Take that lad home with you; that is part of your mission here.'"[24]

Others purchased children hoping to "civilize" them. In an address in which he described his views of two Shoshone children being reared in his home, Ezra T. Benson preached, "It is our duty, brethren and sisters, to go to work and bring these natives to an understanding of the principles of civilization. . . . In a short season we shall be rewarded for all that we do to civilize this lost and fallen race."[25] George A. Smith phrased similar sentiments more succinctly, observing that he had obtained a boy in order to "ma[k]e a man" of him.[26]

Emotional and psychological reasons impelled others to purchase a child. Christian Nielsen explained that he and his wife Maren, who had no children of their own, bought a child "to fill her [Maren's] longing for children."[27] Susanna Rogers Keate, who had two sons but was unable to bear any more children, took an Indian girl into her home partly because she had "always wanted" a daughter.[28]

Economic considerations strongly influenced other purchasers. As noted previously, some Mormons obtained a child as compensation for stolen goods; William K. Rice, for instance, took a small boy in exchange for a stolen horse and pack.[29] Even some who were not seeking compensation for stolen goods may have purchased a child for economic reasons. They parted with valuable horses, ammunition, clothing and other commodities in buying a child, recognizing that in a frontier setting where labor was scarce, Indian children could be put to work. Thus, Jacob Hamblin wrote that he purchased a six-year-old "that I might let a good Man hav[e] him that would try and make him yousefull [*sic*]."[30] Some masters did profit handsomely from their purchases. Zadoc Judd attested that his Indian girl Matilda "was very useful and handy with her work,"[31] and Jacob Hamblin acknowledged that his livestock "increased and prospered" under his foster son Albert's care.[32] Similarly, Christopher Arthur found that his Indian boy Sam "was a useful helpe[r] on the farm and choring at home"; after Sam left home, Arthur's income declined.[33] The economic motives of some purchasers particularly stood out when a child ran away. Christopher Merkeley valued his twelve-year-old Paiute boy so highly that he promised to "liberally reward" anyone who retrieved the boy.[34] Not content to allow his boy Lemuel to depart, John D. Lee visited with Chief Coretio, who was harboring the boy, and chastised him for not "sending [him] home" to his "proper owner."[35]

Whether humanitarian, religious, emotional, economic, or other considerations were paramount, a combination of these factors motivated many buyers. James Keate purchased an Indian girl, Corra, primarily to save her life, but as we have seen the purchase also satisfied his wife's longing for a daughter.[36] Likewise, although Wilford Woodruff wrote when he purchased a six-year-old boy that he had done so hoping the boy would one day convert his people, he later appraised the boy's worth in terms of his dependability as a laborer.[37]

Measures Taken Following Purchase

Regardless of their reasons for buying the children, most Mormons soon attempted to bathe them, cut their hair, and dress them in Euro-American clothing. Nine-year-old Tanequickeup, "being very lousy, was taken to the log stable, all her hair cut off, and all her clothing burned," her foster sister Betsy recalled.[38] Manoma Andrus was "sickened," she told an interviewer, at the sight of an "utterly dirty and unkempt" four-year-old boy that her husband brought home. Her niece heated some water; then she took the boy into a cornfield, where she "scrubbed [him] to the point of shining" and dressed him in some old, but clean, clothing before bringing him back to the house.[39] On the same day that he bought a three-year-old boy, John Bennion cropped the boy's hair with a pair of shears, accidentally cutting the squirming child's left ear in the process.[40] Settlers cut the children's hair, bathed them, and dressed them in new clothes primarily for hygienic reasons, but doing so also removed physical reminders—such as distinctive clothing and long hair—of the children's former culture.

REACTIONS OF THE PURCHASED CHILDREN

As they arrived in their new homes, children reacted in a variety of ways, depending upon their age, personality, and previous circumstances. Unfortunately, the children did not record their memories of these initial experiences, and the record that is available from adoptive parents may have been distorted by the passage of time. Some parents recalled that the Indian children wailed or wept frequently or kept to themselves and made no noise at all. One four-year-old "moan[ed] for his own people" for weeks and "grew almost ill before he would accept food and make friends," his foster mother recalled.[41] When he arrived at the home of James Brown, Alma Shock ran into the corner in terror, turned his face to the wall, and buried his face in a blanket. Only gradually did he learn to trust his new family.[42] Other children attempted to run away from their new homes. In order to prevent two children whom he had purchased from running away en route to Salt Lake City, Simon Baker tied them to a mule.[43]

Whereas some children struggled to adjust to their new living arrangements, others seemed relieved by or even pleased with their new homes from the outset. According to Jacob Hamblin, a ten-year-old Gosiute readily left his mother and followed Hamblin although the mother "appeared to feel so bad, and made so much ado, that I told the lad he had better go back." The boy "would not do so," however, and "became very much attached" to Hamblin.[44] George A. Smith recorded the sale of another boy who "immediately followed Brother Empey seeming much pleased."[45]

DEGREE OF SUPPORT OF CULTURAL HERITAGE

As the children were adjusting to their new living arrangements, adoptive parents or masters also struggled to adjust to the children. Some despised the children's culture and desired to eliminate it. Ezra T. Benson found it "repugnant to my feelings to have to put up with their dirty practices." Admitting that his Shoshone lad "yet has some of his Indian traits," Benson was heartened that his "mind is becoming clear and perceptive" and looked forward to the day when his Indian traits would be "all erased from his memory."[46] Eliza R. Snow, who cared for and lived with a girl named Pidash, was disgusted that "at first she cronched [sic] bones like a dog." Snow was satisfied, though, that under her tutelage Pidash "very soon became disgusted with her native habits,—became neat and tasteful in dress, and delicate in appetite."[47]

Although some despised "native habits," others sanctioned or even nurtured the children's cultural identity. Some adoptive parents learned to speak haltingly in an Indian tongue. "We . . . might as well learn Indian, since we more often talk that, than have an opportunity to speak to the Americans," Danish immigrant Christian Nielsen recorded. "We are beginning to speak a little of both, our children speak English and/or Indian all the time."[48] Many others who had purchased a child from its relatives permitted relatives to visit the child periodically, thereby perpetuating ties to the children's past. For instance, Fanny Gardner's brother Muchikee visited her several times,[49] and Zaidee Modiwak Hunter's father and brother visited her "quite often."[50]

"A Member of the Family"

Whether or not they approved of the children's cultural heritage, white masters commonly regarded Native American children as members of their families. Christian Nielsen informed his brother that he and his wife intended to rear an Indian girl "as our own child."[51] Similarly, Christopher Arthur viewed his Indian boy as "a member of the family."[52] So strong was the affinity between Ellen Draper and Ammon, "an Indian boy that had lived with us for a long while and was dead," that she had the boy "sealed to Mr. Draper and myself" in the Manti Temple.[53]

Those who regarded Indian children as members of their families often treated their white and Indian dependents equally in most outward respects of daily life. Kanosh Bennion "was treated the same as the rest. He went to school, bathed, dressed, ate and slept, and was mother's boy, just the same as the rest of us," recalled Israel Bennion.[54] Likewise, John Maxwell "was always treated as one of the family," his foster sister Charlotte recalled.[55] Indian children in some households may have been relegated to the most arduous or unpleasant tasks, but it appears that in most households Indian and white children shared the same tasks.[56]

Masters who viewed Indian children as members of their families delighted in the children and their progress. "It gives me much pleasure to see Lemuel doing so well in his schoolwork," noted Abraham Hunsaker.[57] Of his Indian girl Larinea, Christian Nielsen wrote, "She is a good, obedient and friendly girl; she pleases us very much; she is always happy and cheerful."[58]

Adoptive parents and Indian children in such circumstances often developed loving relationships. Referring to an Indian boy who lived with her parents, Charlotte Maxwell recorded, "Mother loved him and he was devoted to her."[59] Zettie Nebeker Kearl wrote that her father "legally adopted an Indian boy . . . and we loved him very much."[60] Likewise, Christopher Arthur believed his Indian boy "loved them [his wife and children] and they loved him."[61] After her adoptive daughter, Corra, had grown and married, Susanna Rogers Keate reflected that Corra had "been a great comfort" to her.[62]

In their own statements, some Indians confirmed that they regarded their masters as loving parents. Zenos Hill told a journalist in 1937, "The only parents I ever knew were Mr. and Mrs. George Hill of Ephraim," and he praised his adoptive parents for giving him a better education than most white children in the community had received.[63] As an adult, Frank Sagwich Warner corresponded frequently with his adoptive parents, expressing his desire to one day return to live near them.[64] In a letter to her adoptive mother, Lucy Meeks likewise expressed her affection for her adoptive family. "Dear Mother, . . . We are all well and I hope that thes few lines will finde you the same," she began. Lucy told her mother that she and her daughter Sylvia "would like to see you[.] Silva ses tell gany momy to come home." Closing her letter, Lucy asked her mother to "give my love to the familey."[65]

One of the more distinctive facets of relations between white adoptive parents and their Indian children involved the marriage of at least three children—Rose Daniels,[66] Eliza Hamblin,[67] and Pernetta Murdock[68]—to their adoptive fathers. According to family stories, another girl, Ellen Hamblin, rejected her adoptive father Jacob's proposal.[69] With the exception of Daniels, who married her alcoholic adoptive father after his wives divorced him,[70] these marriages were polygamous unions.[71]

White children as well as their parents developed close ties to Indian children in their households, even experiencing normal sibling rivalry. Zemira Draper recalled that he, his younger sister, and an adopted Indian named Ammon vied for special privileges. The family "had an old flat, iron spoon" that the three children prized. As the dinner was being set on the table, "the three of us would race to the cupboard for the spoon, and when one would get it, the other two would sit up and sing a psalm that would not sound as nice as other music I have heard."[72]

While they might regard one another as rivals on some occasions, many Indian and white children loved one another. Israel Bennion called Kanosh "my 'brother'" and praised him for being "clean, sweet, loyal, brave and sensitive."[73] Leo Rallison remembered his mother "hugging and kissing . . . her Indian sister."[74] Although apparently no Indian child married a white foster brother or sister, at least one, Nellie Benson, fell hopelessly in love with her adoptive parents' son Frank.[75]

SOME DISILLUSIONMENT AND TENSION

Despite the warmth that characterized relations between Indian children and their adoptive parents and siblings in many Mormon homes, some well-intentioned parents felt burdened and disillusioned because of their children's behavior. Although such disillusionment is common for parents of teenagers, the fact that these parents had chosen to open their homes to these children compounded their resentment and disillusionment. Sam Arthur "made us a great deal of trouble in raising him," his adoptive father, Christopher, recalled. As a teenager, Sam was "a great help" in the home and "a useful helpe[r] on the farm," and his father counted heavily upon his labor. When he was 17, Sam defied his parents and moved in with "unprincipled men," abandoning his moral training for "a dissolute life." His departure occurred at "a bad time" for the Arthurs because they had counted on his labor for the farm, and Christopher never forgave the boy. After several years the prodigal returned, begging his father to take him back, but Christopher "refused to take him" although he did later assist him economically.[76]

Wilford Woodruff likewise became discouraged and felt betrayed by his Indian children. In 1857, Elder Woodruff purchased Sarakeets, a "smart, active[,] good" boy who was six years old. With the lofty purpose of preparing the boy as a missionary, he sent the boy to school and cared for him.[77] When Sarakeets was kicked and seriously injured by a mule, his foster father washed and dressed the wound.[78] When Elder Woodruff returned home on New Years Eve in 1866 and found the boy suffering from an intense headache, he pronounced a healing blessing upon him.[79] The boy worked alongside Wilford's own children, planting, watering, and harvesting crops; herding livestock; shearing sheep; and cutting wood.[80]

During his teenage years, Sarakeets began to cause his foster father trouble. When he was thirteen, the boy took twenty dollars from Wilford's wallet and "spent most of it among the stores." Wilford, who was ill, devoted his birthday to "searching out the matter."[81] When he was seventeen, Sarakeets failed to return home on time after taking his horse up a canyon for a load of wood. After five days, Wilford dispatched a man to look for the boy.[82] Sarakeets returned and resumed his work for Wilford.

Four months later, the boy unintentionally endangered one of Wilford's sons through negligence, bringing the father's innate parental ties to his own offspring into conflict with his moral duty toward the Indian boy. Sarakeets had been working at the cane mill boiling molasses but "quit his work" at midday and returned to the house. Needing someone to take Sarakeets's place, the other workers assigned Elder Woodruff's "little son Asahel ownly [*sic*] 5 years old to feed the mill." Asahel's hand became caught in the mill, and the rollers severed his thumb, two fingers, and the upper part of the remaining fingers on his right hand. The next day, as the five-year-old writhed in pain, Sarakeets moved out. Referring to Sarakeets and another Indian who had once lived in the home, Wilford lamented, "I have raised two of them nearly from Childhood up But they have made me a good deal of trouble. They are vary uncertain help."[83] Notwithstanding his feelings of resentment, he permitted Sarakeets to return eventually. By 1870 the boy was again living with Wilford and working for him.[84] In 1880, Sarakeets, who was now twenty-nine years old, was boarding with another family in the valley and working as a teamster.[85] He remained in contact with his foster father, though, and in 1888, Wilford recorded with pleasure that Sarakeets had visited him.[86]

Although problems between white and Indian family members arose in probably every household, relations in some homes were bitter much of the time, unlike the relationships in the Woodruff and Arthur homes. Some white and Indian siblings consistently despised one another. Betsy Hancock Shurtliff, who was eight years old when her father purchased a nine-year-old girl named Tanequickeup, resented having to "share my clothes with her." To make matters worse, Tanequickeup sometimes took Betsy's shawls and bonnets without asking and neglected her chores, leaving extra work for Betsy. "She was the only [family member] I ever contended with, and she would aggravate me until I would strike her, then she would hit or scratch me with her long fingernails," Betsy recalled. Betsy's father "punished her [Tanequickeup] severely at times" for her mischief, but to Betsy it seemed that "it did no good." Eventually Tanequickeup ran away.[87]

In some households, tension and distrust divided not only Indian and white children, but also white adults and Indian youth. Nicaagat, or Captain Jack, an indentured Gosiute boy, reportedly ran away because his master called his dark skin a curse and whipped him.[88] Sam Benson accepted his foster parent Ezra T. Benson's directives but refused to submit to Benson's wife Adeline. After Ezra died, Sam quarreled with his foster mother and left home, swearing that he would not be bossed by a woman.[89] After living in a Mormon home for fourteen years, Shem Parkinson pulled a knife on his adoptive father during a heated argument and had to be restrained by neighbors. Although it is possible that the boy reacted in the heat of the moment, some who knew him believed that he had always despised white people, including his caregivers, because he was "believed to have been orphaned" by American soldiers in the Bear River massacre.[90]

The fact that some masters sold children who had lived in their homes for months or even years to someone else also suggests that relations between some Indian children and masters were tenuous. Susie Pulsipher, who was purchased at age five by Dudley Leavitt, was sold at age ten to William Pulsipher. Leavitt's daughter Hannah explained matter-of-factly, "Father kept her five years and let Brother William Pulsipher have her for a span of oxen."[91] Similarly, Z. N. Baxter, a resident of Nephi, purchased a nine-year-old boy in 1853 but a year later sent the boy to live in J. L. Heywood's home.[92]

CONCLUSION

To summarize, some Indian children and their white masters may have never developed affectionate ties, and some whites purchased children largely for selfish reasons. In such households, Indian children were treated and viewed as servants. Nevertheless, to the extent that it is representative, the evidence presented here suggests that most whites who opened their homes to Indian children did so primarily for altruistic, humanitarian reasons. Some by their purchase rescued children from the threat or the perceived threat of hunger, neglect, abuse, or death. Many others purchased children to promote their spiritual welfare or to educate them. Their perceptions of the children's best interests were colored by their conviction that tribal culture was inferior to Euro-American lifeways, but they sincerely desired to improve the children's lives. These altruistic attitudes helped to provide a foundation for positive, caring relations between many white families and Indian children.

Although many children initially feared or distrusted their white owners and although many masters despised the children's mannerisms and tribal culture, over time most—but not all—children became well integrated within white households, working, studying, eating, and playing alongside other members of the household. There were limits to their integration within these families: few were sealed through Mormon temple ordinances to their white families, for instance. Nevertheless, many remained in contact with their adoptive families, and some remained in the homes of their adoptive parents well into adulthood. When one considers the sibling rivalry and love that developed between Indian and white children plus the emotional ties between Indian children and white adults, *adopted* more clearly expresses their situation than the term *indentured* does.[93]

Familial relationships between Indian children and white Mormons developed while many white settlers and Native Americans were competing for scarce resources, a contest that sometimes culminated in brutal raids, massacres, and battles. In the history of interracial relations on the Utah frontier, the positive relationships resulting from the purchase of Indian children deserve consideration alongside accounts of dramatic conflicts. Such relationships were facilitated by the fact that Indian children were immersed in Euro-American and Mormon culture as a result of adoption; the differences separating whites and adopted or indentured Indian children could be bridged much more readily than the differences that divided most Native American adults from white Utahns.

Differences between the children and their adoptive families did exist, and they were reinforced by widespread, pejorative stereotypes. Nevertheless, the outcomes of the Mormon indenture program demonstrate the power of sustained interpersonal interaction in combating the prejudice, racial stereotypes, and racist hierarchies that were common among nineteenth-century whites. Daily interpersonal interaction between Indian children and white Mormons in individual households helped some participants to pierce the stereotypes and to recognize and celebrate the shared humanity of whites and Native Americans. Thus, James Martineau came to realize that his Indian girl Cora Colorado was "as smart and intelligent as any white girl,"[94] and Priddy Meeks discovered that Lucy Meeks "made a nice smart woman as anyone."[95]

Utah society at large failed to adopt such progressive views, and many Utahns likely would have rejected such attitudes even if Indians had lived in their homes. Nevertheless, the integration of whites and Native Americans within individual households is remarkable in light of the prejudice of the era. Thus, the Mormon indenture program serves as an intriguing counterpoint to interracial conflicts in the history of race relations in pioneer Utah.

Brian Q. Cannon is Associate Professor of History at Brigham Young University.

NOTES

1. For information on this slave trade, consult Ramón A. Gutiérrez, *When Jesus Came, the Corn Mothers Went Away: Marriage, Sexuality, and Power in New Mexico, 1500–1846* (Stanford, Calif.: Stanford University Press, 1991), 180–90; Leland Hargrave Creer, *The Founding of an Empire: The Exploration and Colonization of Utah, 1776–1856* (Salt Lake City: Bookcraft, 1947); Sondra Jones, "Pedro Leon: Indian Slavery, Mexican Traders, and the Mormon Judiciary" (master's thesis, Brigham Young University, 1995); and William J. Snow, "Utah Indians and Spanish Slave Trade," *Utah Historical Quarterly* 2 (July 1929): 67–75, 81–90.

2. John R. Young, *Memoirs of John R. Young: Utah Pioneer, 1847* (Salt Lake City: Deseret News Press, 1920), 62; see also Peter Gottfredson, ed., *History of Indian Depredations in Utah* (Salt Lake City: Skelton Publishing, 1919), 15–16.

3. *Acts, Resolutions, and Memorials, Passed at the Several Annual Sessions of the Legislative Assembly of the Territory of Utah* (Great Salt Lake City: Joseph Cain, 1855), 171–74. The system prescribed by Utah law provided a legal status for Indian captives remarkably similar to the customary status held by Indian servants in New Mexico. As Lafayette Head, the Ute Indian agent at Abiquiu, New Mexico, reported in April 1852, Native American children were purchased by New Mexican families, "but not for slaves—they are adopted into the family of those who get them, are baptized and remain & trusted as one of the family— The head of the house standing as Godfather. The Prefect has the right to free them whenever maltreated. The Indian has the right to choose a guardian— Women are freed whenever married—say from 14 to 16—Men ditto from 18 to 20." Lafayette Head, "Statement of Mr. Head of Abiquiu in Regard of the Buying and Selling of Payutahs—April 30, 1852," doc. no. 2150, Rich Collection of Papers Pertaining to New Mexico, Huntington Library, San Marino, Calif., quoted in Jones, "Pedro Leon," 69. As Jones notes, Lafayette's description was optimistic, but it was "reasonably accurate as to the integration of Indian children into the families and society."

4. Journal History of the Church, May 12, 1851, Archives Division, Historical Department, The Church of Jesus Christ of Latter-day Saints, Salt Lake City (hereafter cited as LDS Church Archives).

5. Brigham Young, "Governor's Message," *Deseret News,* January 10, 1852, 2.

6. The fullest scholarly studies of Indian adoption in Mormon communities are Juanita Brooks, "Indian Relations on the Mormon Frontier," *Utah Historical Quarterly* 12 (January–April 1944): 1–48; and Robert M. Muhlestein, "Utah Indians and the Indian Slave Trade: The Mormon Adoption Program and Its Effect on the Indian Slaves" (master's thesis, Brigham Young University, 1991). My paper differs from Brooks's and Muhlestein's studies in its heavy reliance upon statements made by the Indian children and their adoptive parents and siblings and its focus upon relations between Native American children and their adoptive families.

7. James Henry Martineau, Autobiography, typescript, 16, Special Collections and Manuscripts, Harold B. Lee Library, Brigham Young University, Provo, Utah (hereafter cited as BYU Archives).

8. Jacob Hamblin, Journal, typescript, 27, BYU Archives.

9. John Bennion, Diary, September 17, 1858, BYU Archives.

10. Bennion, Diary, June 26, 1869.

11. Christopher J. Arthur, Autobiography, in "Records of Christopher J. Arthur, 1860–1900," typescript, pt. 2, 15–16, BYU Archives.

12. Christian Nielsen to Carl Nielsen, April 27, 1856, published in Jorgen W. Schmidt, *Oh, Du Zion i Vest: Den danske mormon-emigration, 1850–1900* (Copenhagen: Rosenkilde og Bagger, 1965), 67, partial translation by Gerald Haslam, in author's possession.

13. Such humanitarian motives would have been consonant with the intent of the territorial legislature in legalizing the purchase of children. As the legislators noted, captive children were "larietted out to subsist upon grass, roots, or starve; and . . . frequently bound with thongs made of raw hide, until their hands and feet become swollen, mutilated, inflamed with pain, and wounded." The legislators reasoned that it was incumbent upon humane, Christian individuals to rescue children from such torture by purchasing them. *Acts, Resolutions, and Memorials,* 172.

14. Young, *Memoirs of John R. Young,* 62.

15. Estella Draper Burt, Journal, in *Our Pioneer Heritage,* comp. Kate B. Carter, 20 vols. (Salt Lake City: Daughters of Utah Pioneers, 1958–77), 3:451.

16. Charlotte Maxwell Webb to Anthony W. Ivins, February 5, 1929, microfilm, LDS Church Archives.

17. Melva Shurtliff Green, "Betsy Jane Hancock Shurtliff," in *Chronicles of Courage,* comp. Lesson Committee, 8 vols. to date (Salt Lake City: Daughters of Utah Pioneers, 1990–), 1:56.

18. Martineau, Autobiography, 16.

19. Elizabeth Wood Kane, *Twelve Mormon Homes Visited in Succession on a Journey through Utah and Arizona* (Philadelphia: n.p., 1874), 44.

20. Lorenzo Brown, Diary, typescript, 2 vols., 1:55–56, BYU Archives.

21. William Hull, quoted in Newell Hart, *The Bear River Massacre* (Preston, Idaho: Cache Valley Newsletter Publishing, 1982), 185.

22. Journal History, May 12, 1851.

23. Scott G. Kenney, ed., *Wilford Woodruff's Journal, 1833–1898,* 9 vols. (Midvale, Utah: Signature Books, 1983–84), 5:40–41.

24. James A. Little, *Jacob Hamblin: A Narrative of His Personal Experience, as a Frontiersman, Missionary to the Indians, and Explorer Disclosing Interpositions of Providence, Severe Privations, Perilous Situations, and Remarkable Escapes,* Faith Promoting Series, book 5, 2d ed. (Salt Lake City: Deseret News Press, 1909), 32.

25. Ezra T. Benson, in *Journal of Discourses,* 26 vols. (Liverpool: F. D. Richards, 1855–86), 3:64, July 13, 1855.

26. George A. Smith, Journal, typescript, 12, BYU Archives.

27. Maren and Christian Nielsen to Carl Nielsen, August 21, 1859, published in Schmidt, *Oh, Du Zion i Vest,* 113, partial translation by Gerald Haslam, in author's possession.

28. Susanna Keate to Eliza Johnson, November 17, 1895, reprinted in Jane Rae Fuller Topham, *In Search of Living Water: Biography of Susanna Mehetable Rogers Sangiovanni Pickett Keate, July 5, 1813–January 9, 1905* (n.p.: Privately printed, 1995), 213.

29. Martineau, Autobiography, 9.

30. Hamblin, Journal, 27.

31. Zadoc Knapp Judd, Autobiography, typescript, 41, BYU Archives.

32. Little, *Jacob Hamblin,* 93.

33. Arthur, Autobiography, pt. 2, 21.

34. "Ran Away," advertisement in *Deseret News,* September 18, 1852, 3.

35. Robert Glass Cleland and Juanita Brooks, eds., *A Mormon Chronicle: The Diaries of John D. Lee, 1848–1876,* 2 vols. (Salt Lake City: University of Utah Press, 1983), 1:162, 168.

36. Keate to Johnson, 159, 213.

37. Kenney, *Wilford Woodruff's Journal,* 5:40–41; 6:437.

38. Green, "Betsy Jane Hancock Shurtliff," 1:56.

39. Manomas Lavina Gibson Andrus, "Pioneer Personal History Interview by Mabel Jarvis," microfilm, 10, BYU Archives.

40. Bennion, Diary, September 17, 1858.

41. Andrus, "Pioneer Personal History Interview," 10.

42. Elva A. Christiansen and Elizabeth C. Munk, "Alma Shock Brown," in *Heart Throbs of the West,* comp. Kate B. Carter, 12 vols. (Salt Lake City: Daughters of Utah Pioneers, 1939–51), 1:157–58.

43. Smith, Journal, 50.

44. Little, *Jacob Hamblin,* 32.

45. Smith, Journal, 12.

46. Ezra T. Benson, in *Journal of Discourses,* 3:64, July 13, 1855.

47. Maureen Ursenbach Beecher, ed., *Personal Writings of Eliza Roxcy Snow* (Salt Lake City: University of Utah Press, 1995), 30–31.

48. Christian Nielsen to Carl Nielsen.

49. Delila Gardner Hughes, *The Life of Archibald Gardner* (Draper, Utah: Review and Preview Publishers, 1970), 68.

50. William E. Hunter, *Edward Hunter: Faithful Steward,* ed. Jannath Russell Cannon (Salt Lake City: Publisher's Press for Mrs. William E. Hunter, 1970), 247.

51. Maren and Christian Nielsen to Carl Nielsen.

52. Arthur, Autobiography, pt. 2, 16.

53. Ellen Albina Wilhelm Draper, "A Pioneer Mother Describes Life in Early Utah," in Leonard J. Arrington and others, eds., *Voices from the Past: Diaries, Journals, and Autobiographies* (Provo: Brigham Young University Press, 1980), 95.

54. Israel Bennion, "Indian Reminiscences," *Utah Historical Quarterly* 2 (April 1929): 44.

55. Webb to Ivins.

56. Two diarists who document extensive shared work of Indian and white children are John D. Lee and Wilford Woodruff. Betsy Jane Hancock Shurtliff recalled that she and her Indian foster sister worked together on tasks including washing the clothes. Green, "Betsy Jane Hancock Shurtliff," 1:56.

57. "Indian Lemuel—A Member of the Piede Tribe," in *Chronicles of Courage,* 5:410.

58. Maren and Christian Nielsen to Carl Nielsen.

59. Webb to Ivins.

60. Zettie Nebeker Kearl, "Rich County Indians," in Carter, *Our Pioneer Heritage,* 8:100.

61. Arthur, Autobiography, pt. 2, 16.

62. Keate to Johnson, 212–13.

63. *Spanish Fork Press,* [about August 12, 1937], quoted in "Zenos W. Hill, Indian," in *Treasures of Pioneer History,* comp. Kate B. Carter, 6 vols. (Salt Lake City: Daughters of Utah Pioneers, 1952–57), 4:374.

64. Glen F. Harding, *A Record of the Ancestry, Life and Descendants of Amos Warner* (Provo: BYU Printing Service, n.d.), 8.

65. Lucy Meeks to Dear Mother, June 17, [1871,] Priddy Meeks Correspondence, BYU Archives.

66. Ann Curtis, "Rose Daniels," in *An Enduring Legacy,* comp. Lesson Committee, 12 vols. (Salt Lake City: Daughters of Utah Pioneers, 1978–89), 7:43–44.

67. Brooks, "Indian Relations," 42–44.

68. Endowment House Records, June 26, 1859, International Genealogical Index Marriage Records, AncestralFile version 4.17. Pernetta Murdock is referred to in some historical records as Burnette or Benetty.

69. Brooks, "Indian Relations," 42–44.

70. Curtis, "Rose Daniels," 7:43–44.

71. Although there is no record of his marriage to Alace or Alnora Lee, John D. Lee wrote that Elder Amasa Lyman instructed him to marry the girls "to throw a shield of Protection around them, &c." While marriage to their adoptive father would have shielded these two young girls from other potential suitors, it also may have been encouraged to bolster Lee's own safety inasmuch as Indians had sometimes spared the lives of whites who had an Indian spouse. Cleland and Brooks, *Mormon Chronicle,* 1:214, 327 n. 62.

72. Zemira Terry Draper, quoted in Burt, Journal, 3:451.

73. Bennion, "Indian Reminiscences," 44.

74. Hart, *Bear River Massacre*, 191.

75. Donald Benson Alder and Elsie L. Alder, comps., *The Benson Family: The Ancestry and Descendants of Ezra T. Benson* (Salt Lake City: Woodruff Printing, 1979), 49.

76. Arthur, Autobiography, pt. 1, 18; pt. 2, 15–16, 21, 33; pt. 4, 25.

77. Kenney, *Wilford Woodruff's Journal*, 6:388. The name Sarakeets is also spelled Sarraqueets, Sarokeets, Sarrowkeets, and Sarroqueets. At times he is referred to simply as Keets.

78. Kenney, *Wilford Woodruff's Journal*, 6:400.

79. Kenney, *Wilford Woodruff's Journal*, 6:310.

80. Kenney, *Wilford Woodruff's Journal*, 6:167–68, 406.

81. Kenney, *Wilford Woodruff's Journal*, 6:159.

82. Kenney, *Wilford Woodruff's Journal*, 6:411–12.

83. Kenney, *Wilford Woodruff's Journal*, 6:436–37.

84. Kenney, *Wilford Woodruff's Journal*, 6:522, 531, 536, 583; 7:5.

85. Census Bureau, 1880 U.S. Census, Salt Lake County, Utah, Ft. Harrison Precinct, dwelling 57, microfilm.

86. Kenney, *Wilford Woodruff's Journal*, 8:524.

87. Green, "Betsy Jane Hancock Shurtliff," 1:56.

88. Jones, "Pedro Leon," 180; Al Look, *Utes' Last Stand at White River and Milk Creek, Western Colorado in 1879* (Denver: Golden Bell, n.d.), 12.

89. John Henry Evans and Minnie Egan Anderson, *Ezra T. Benson: Pioneer—Statesman—Saint* (Salt Lake City: Deseret News Press, 1947), 283.

90. Lester Parkinson Taylor, *Samuel Rose Parkinson: Portrait of a Pioneer* (Provo, Utah: Claymont, 1977), 70–71.

91. Brooks, "Indian Relations," 44–45.

92. Brooks, "Indian Relations," 34–35.

93. The Mormon indenture program was less effective in minimizing racist sentiment in society at large. As these children matured, they encountered social and economic obstacles that helped to consign many to the margins of white society—reminders of the persistence of strong racial prejudice in the general population. For a brief discussion of the life course of these children, consult Brian Q. Cannon and Richard D. Kitchen, "Indenture and Adoption of Native American Children by Mormons on the Utah Frontier, 1850–1870," in *Common Frontiers: Proceedings of the 1996 Conference and Annual Meeting* 19, ed. Donna R. Braiden and Susan Gangwere McCabe (North Bloomfield, Ohio: Association for Living Historical Farms and Agricultural Museums, 1997), 131–44.

94. Martineau, Autobiography, 16.

95. Priddy Meeks, Journal, typescript, 62, BYU Archives.

Courtesy LDS Church Archives

In this 1868–69 view of the Brigham Young family compound can be seen the octagonal bell tower and the roof of the family schoolhouse. Exceptionally well equipped for its time, the school served both the family and some of the townspeople. Its pupils remembered it fondly for the bell calling them to school at 8:45 A.M. and the apples roasting on the ledge around the stove. Savage and Ottinger, photographers.

Everyday Life in Utah's Elementary Schools, 1847–1870

James B. Allen

Elementary education in pioneer Utah was a study in contrasts. Some children had no formal schooling at all while others obtained a rather complete education for the times. Some attended school in tents, crude and ill-equipped log huts, or private homes while others enjoyed well-built schoolhouses with adequate desks and all the latest texts. Some learned little more than the three R's while others obtained skills that helped them support themselves and their families and also prepared them to earn a living later on. Some, no doubt, cared little for school while others could hardly get enough. Some found themselves the objects of severe and sometimes painful discipline while others enjoyed loving teachers who seemed never to use force.

Heber J. Grant, born in 1856 to a widowed and poverty-stricken mother, began his formal schooling at the Doremus School in Salt Lake City. There, in addition to whatever he learned, he was the object of at least one sound thrashing by the schoolmaster. Later he went to a home school, taught by Sarah Elizabeth Foss Cowley (mother of Matthias F. Cowley). At age eight, he attended Brigham Young's private school, perhaps the most well-equipped school in the territory. The following year, he moved with his mother to St. George, where he went to school in a tent, but before long he was back in Salt Lake City, where he came under the tutelage of some of Utah's best and most famous early schoolmarms: Camilla Cobb and Mary and Ida Cook.[1]

Ellen Burton was not so fortunate. In 1866 her family arrived in Utah and settled in Kaysville. Out of necessity, it fell to Ellen to help clear the farmland of oak brush, fight crickets, and plant and tend a garden and orchard. Though anxious to go to school, she could not do so except during parts of two winters because her help was needed at home. At harvest time, for example, it was her job to cut the grain with a scythe, then bind it in bundles. "I used to make myself miserable by wanting to go to school," she later recalled. "I felt that my parents and family were unfair for not making some arrangement for me to attend school. We had a neighbor with two girls about my age, Clara and Sarah Beazer. They went to school all the time and were always asking me why I didn't go. This made it harder than ever for me to stay home and work."[2]

Slightly more positive was the story of Elvira Elanor Coombs of Cedar Valley. In 1863, at age six, Elvira was left an orphan along with several brothers and sisters, from whom she was soon separated. Taken in by a Mrs. Spiken, a schoolteacher, she was severely mistreated, but she was soon relocated to the home of Robert Birkbeck, where she was adopted and she changed her name to Ella. She was not allowed to attend regular school, though the Birkbecks taught her at home. At age fifteen, she was apprenticed to a shoemaker. Later she went to a telegraphy school and became one of the first telegraphers in the territory.[3] Such practical education was not uncommon for Utah's young women, who often had to help earn a living both before and after they married.

These and myriad stories like them represent the widely contrasting experiences of Utah's pioneer school-age children, who are the focus of this paper. The discussion concerns the problems, challenges, and activities connected with everyday life in elementary school during the difficult first quarter century after the Latter-day Saints arrived—1847 to the early 1870s.[4]

MORMON ATTITUDE TOWARD EDUCATION

The importance of education was one of the fundamental values promoted by The Church of Jesus Christ of Latter-day Saints.[5] Therefore, in addition to whatever natural desire for knowledge they may have had, Church members often felt a religious commitment to learn all they could and to have their children do the same. One such parent was Marin Kristin Nielson, an immigrant from Denmark who settled with her husband, Andrew Christian Nielson, in Sanpete County. After she learned English (it is not clear whether she went to a school), she decided to teach her children in her own home school. The quest for intelligence became the family motto:

> While I was settling myself in America, I read something that stayed with me through the long years and short ones to follow.

Framed on the wall where I usually spent my busy hours was a short verse stitched in black letters on muslin. I asked Sister Oveson, the lady of the home where we were staying, what the words said. "Why that is the motto of our Church. *The Glory of God is intelligence,*" she explained, and added that we were the only people in the world who belonged to the true Church, and we must show the world that we are the learned people. . . .

As the children grew older, it became more difficult to keep them at home. In the evenings when we always had one hour of home school, one of the boys called it "skull practice." "Why do we have to study every night?" This was the usual complaint. When this outburst came, and it came often, I told the children that because we were the chosen children of the Lord, we must develop ourselves spiritually as well as physically; that we must read as well as work. Then I would always point to the embroidered motto hanging on the wall and ask, "Don't you want to be one of God's chosen?"[6]

Nevertheless, such religious commitment was often accompanied by a pragmatic view of education, reflected in the words of Orson Spencer, chancellor of the Board of Regents of the University of Deseret. Rebuking those who, he said, subverted spiritual knowledge to the learning of men, he exclaimed, "The boy that drives an ox team from Council Bluffs [Nebraska] to Salt Lake acquired more amplitude of intellect, than by two years of drilling in dead Latin."[7]

Furthermore, not all parents were as committed as Marin Nielson. As late as 1868, Robert L. Campbell, territorial superintendent of schools, complained of the "reprehensible" "apathy and indifference" displayed by local school trustees, many of whom failed to visit their schools even once a year. Equally disturbing, he went on, was the fact that "parents do not visit the schools as often as they should, so that there is but little stimulus to the indifferent schoolteacher and but little encouragement to the energetic and faithful."[8] High enthusiasm among some parents coupled with apparent apathy on the part of others and a wide range of conditions that affected both the quantity and quality of a child's schooling are only a few of the multitude of problems and issues that influenced the progress of education in pioneer Utah.

THE BEGINNING OF PIONEER SCHOOLS

The story of Utah's schools begins with sixteen-year-old Mary Jane Dilworth, who at the request of Brigham Young opened the territory's first school just three months after the vanguard pioneer company reached the Salt Lake Valley in 1847 and only three weeks after Mary Jane herself arrived. School was conducted in a tent inside the newly constructed fort. A few sections of logs served as seats for the nine children in attendance, and the teacher's desk was a camp table. The first day's lesson consisted of psalms from the Bible. Later, during the winter, Mary Jane moved her pupils into a small log house just completed by William Bringhurst as one of the buildings making up the fort. Its roof was piled high with dirt, and its floor was hardened clay. The one small window opening was covered with thin, oiled cloth, for no glass was available. A wagon box was broken up to provide benches and crude desks, and a fireplace provided heat.[9]

There were no free, tax-supported schools during the early years of Utah's pioneer history, but, as was the case in Salt Lake City, a privately supported school of some kind was usually available within a few weeks or months of the founding of each new community. The ecclesiastical organization of the Church proved to be a perfect vehicle for the establishment of these schools. By 1850 plans were under way for the construction of schools in each of Salt Lake City's nineteen wards. Bishops took the initiative in organizing them and finding teachers, and classes were conducted in the same buildings as those used for church meetings.

Something similar happened in each community throughout the territory, though in the rudimentary stages of colonization the facilities were sometimes even more primitive than those of Salt Lake City's first school. In the settlement that became Parowan, for example, George A. Smith opened a grammar school on February 21, 1851, only five weeks after the arrival of the families called to the Iron County Mission. It was an evening school, held in Smith's wickiup—a makeshift shelter composed of three wagons, a few wooden slabs, and some brush. The five children in attendance shared one grammar book, learned by the light of a campfire, and shivered in the cold. However, according to Smith, they seemed eager to learn. As he wrote in his journal six days later, "My scholars assembled round the camp fire, freezing one side and roasting the other, listened earnestly to my lecture on English Grammar."[10]

EARLY EFFORTS AT TERRITORIAL SUPERVISION AND FUNDING

In 1850 the territorial legislature placed the supervision of all education under the control of the regents of the University of Deseret.

Even though there was little money to support schools locally, the regents visited the various communities regularly and made every effort to improve the quality of education. They attempted to control subject matter, approved teachers, selected textbooks, and constantly urged the improvement of physical facilities. In 1851 the territorial legislature created the office of territorial superintendent of schools. An 1852 law provided for the establishment in each town of at least one school supported by local taxation. When the office of county superintendent of schools was created in 1860, the territory had in place a legal system for establishing and supervising all the schools.

Despite the fact that territorial law allowed Utah's cities to levy taxes for school purposes, most communities were slow to do so. In the rare instances where public money was raised, it was used for constructing schools and not for paying teachers. In 1866 the town of American Fork became the first community in Utah to provide a free public school where taxes were used both to maintain the physical facilities and to pay teachers.[11] At times, public funds were used also to pay for educating children from impoverished families.

AMOUNT OF SCHOOLING: HOW MUCH WAS ENOUGH?

As with everything else in pioneer education, the answer to the question of how much schooling was enough (or, frequently, how much families could afford) varied with the winds of circumstance. Many children finished most of the elementary grades, and some went on to secondary schools, but the formal education of many others was meager. Some had only a few years or months of schooling, many attended only irregularly, and some had no formal schooling at all. Statements from some pioneer leaders suggest an unusually high level of education at the time, but their claims were usually more rhetoric than substance. As Fred Buchanan, a careful modern student of Utah educational history, has observed,

> although [Brigham] Young's history records that in 1849 a number of schools were established in Salt Lake City to teach Hebrew, Greek, Latin, French, German, and Tahitian as well as English, there is no evidence to support the notion that such schools were anything other than the attempts of a few individuals trying to prepare the Mormon missionaries for the task of converting the world.[12]

In reality, "book learning" often had to take a backseat to such immediate challenges as supplementing meager resources, creating homes and farms, contending with drought, dealing with the Native Americans, and confronting the U.S. army in the 1850s.

In the early 1860s, Superintendent Campbell held high hopes for the future. "As a Territory," he reported to the legislature in 1863, "we have peace, and extensive ability exists with the people, to establish and sustain good common schools in every ward and district, not only three or six months in a year, as appears at present most common; but ten or eleven, wherein every child, no matter how poor, may find admittance."[13] Reality, however, fell far short of Campbell's ideal. Even those children who attended school did so only sporadically, and on any particular day, well over half of those eligible were not in school at all. The statistical data reported to the legislature was incomplete, but in 1860 the two counties with the most complete information reported that not even a third of their children attended. Davis County was the home of 1,020 children ages six to eighteen (the report did not distinguish further with respect to age), but only 362 (35 percent) of those were enrolled in school, and only 235, or 24 percent of the whole, attended on a daily basis. At the same time, only 562 (43 percent) of Utah County's 1,286 children were enrolled, and only 386, or 30 percent of the whole, attended regularly.

Eight years later the picture was improving, but it was hardly up to Campbell's expectations. Davis County's enrollment had increased to 56.5 percent, and attendance was up to 40.5 percent of the total number of children, while Utah County had jumped to an enrollment of 65.5 percent with an attendance record of 44 percent. The territory's most populous county, Salt Lake, had an enrollment of only 46 percent and an attendance record of 36 percent, while the territorial average was 56.5 percent of the school-age children enrolled with 39 percent of the total attending regularly.[14]

Underlying these averages were a multitude of differing circumstances and experiences. Some families could barely afford to send their children to school for even a short time. Children in many, if not most, families, could attend only sporadically, for they had to spend at least part of their time working on the family farm or elsewhere in order to keep the family solvent. In many cases, schooling was cut short at a very early age. Michael Peter Monk, for example, went to work at age ten, effectively ending his formal education.[15] Poul and Niels Pederson, who emigrated with their mother and stepfather from Denmark in the 1850s, obtained only one month of American schooling—in Salt Lake City.[16] In 1857 at age nine, Margaret Simmons emigrated from

London with her parents. Anxious to go to school but having no money, she spun yarn and knitted socks for the teacher in order to pay tuition. Her schooling lasted for only six weeks, however, after which she went to work at a variety of jobs, earning $1.50 to $2.00 per week and giving it all to her mother, who had six children to care for.[17] Alma Platt Spilsburg's parents were called by Church leaders to settle in southern Utah in 1862. The move to Grafton (now St. George) ended Alma's schooling when he was only twelve years old, for from then on he had to help his parents with their work.[18] Caroline Pederson, who grew up in Holladay in the 1860s and 1870s, learned to read, write, and spell, but she did not have access to the books needed to broaden her education beyond the rudiments. At age fifteen, when her mother became seriously ill, she dropped out of school entirely.[19]

Christopher Alston also faced educational challenges, but in an effort to gain all the learning he could, he often worked all day and then went to night school. He described his limited schooling, obtained in Sugarhouse in the 1860s, as follows:

> I attended school with no books, excepting a primary grammar brought from England; Paul Leichtenburg was my teacher. I went into the canyon with a yoke of oxen to take out logs to sell for fuel etc., to help make a living for my mother and fatherless brothers and sisters, I being the eldest of the five children. Later, I attended school at night, Professor Lucien W. Peck being instructor. He gave me special permission to come in late when I did not get home from the canyon in time for the opening class work.[20]

Other students also made special accommodations in order to attend school as much as possible. Joseph Openshaw went to the Seventeenth Ward school, then the Twentieth Ward school, then to a private school conducted by two women in their home, then back to the Twentieth Ward. Later he and his brother George took turns attending Karl G. Maeser's school, each going every other day. They needed money for tuition and other school expenses, so between the two of them they held down a daily job, Joseph working one day while George attended school, then trading the next day.[21]

In Smithfield, Lucy Smith was eager for an education, but the poverty of her family made obtaining one difficult. Nevertheless, she often arose early in the morning to help with the family wash and other tasks and then trudged off to school. In the wintertime, she had to wrap her feet in rags to protect them from the snow and cold. Fortunately, she was able to stay in school at least until she was sixteen.[22]

Such stories were not unusual in pioneer Utah, as families struggled the best they could to eke out a living and, at the same time, give their children the education desired. Clearly, with some, the question was simply how much schooling was essential when compared with the other demands of pioneer life.

GOING TO SCHOOL: PHYSICAL FACILITIES

As might be expected, the physical facilities enjoyed by those who attended school varied greatly according to both time and location. The children among the first settlers of Utah's various communities often found themselves huddled together in tents or wickiups, such as those used by Mary Jane Dilworth and George A. Smith in Salt Lake City and Parowan, or sitting beneath a willow bowery that doubled for church and school. Some were fortunate enough to go to school in the home of a friend, relative, or some other local citizen attempting to use his or her talents to earn a living as well as provide some cultural improvement. Part of David Layton's schooling, for example, took place in his father's house in Kaysville, where his oldest sister, Maggie, was the teacher.[23] Ada Arvilla Burke Earl wrote of her early schooling in Farmington:

> The first school we attended was in the home of Apostle Amasa Lyman and his wife Paulina was the teacher. We started school at a very early age and I remember carrying bread and a jug of milk for our lunch and Mrs. Lyman would give us dishes and spoons to eat our bread and milk in. She taught us the alphabet by having us sing it. . . . We sat on benches around the walls of the room. . . . We studied from McGuffey's and Wilson Readers.[24]

Very quickly, however, especially in Salt Lake City, Church and civic leaders set about constructing schoolhouses in each ward, most of these buildings also serving as meetinghouses, community centers, and theaters. In Huntsville, the "Old Rock House" served as a school and civic center. There Edward Anderson went to school, Sunday School, musical events, choir practice, and every other kind of gathering.[25] Students attending the first school in Hatton, Millard County, were taught in the largest and best room of the home of Peter Robison. Later they went to a new building that served as both a schoolhouse and a church.[26]

Many of the early Utah schoolhouses were one-room log or adobe buildings, although by the 1870s these were giving way to more substantial and commodious frame, brick, or rock buildings. The first schoolhouse in Spanish Fork was built during the winter of 1856–57 from adobe taken from the abandoned fort at nearby Palmyra. The floor consisted of slabs sawn from logs taken out of the canyon by George A. Hicks when the snow was two feet deep. The single, sixteen-by-twenty-foot room boasted six twelve-pane windows and had a fireplace in one end.[27] By the summer of 1862, Salt Lake City boasted twenty-four school buildings, described by George A. Smith as "about 20 by 30 feet" and "well finished."[28] Children in the Twelfth Ward in Salt Lake City attended what O. H. Riggs called the "best fitted up schoolhouse" in the territory. Built of adobe, it had six windows, ceilings and walls that were plastered and whitewashed, and painted woodwork.[29]

Open fireplaces provided heat in some schools, but cast-iron stoves were more often employed. In Huntsville each family was asked to haul one to three loads of wood to the "Old Rock House" in order to heat the combination school and civic center during the winter.[30]

Most buildings were simply not adequate for long-range needs, and many soon suffered from lack of maintenance. In 1874, for example, the territorial superintendent described two particularly bad schools. In one, a basement was used by the primary department, but, reported the superintendent, "it was immediately apparent that ventilation was not neglected, for the schoolteacher complained that about one-third of the panes of glass were broken." Not far away was another school, described as "small, poorly lighted, and entirely destitute of ventilation."[31]

For some children, sheer discomfort no doubt added to the problems of learning. Unventilated, often-crowded classrooms were bad enough, but uncomfortable seats were even worse. Early school furniture was usually homemade, for importing it seemed much too costly for the pioneer economy. The furniture differed from school to school, but some general patterns were common. In the early stages of community development, children sometimes sat on portable stools, if not on the floor or ground. Later they sat on slabs fastened to the four walls of the classroom, and still later they used backless planks set in the center of the room so that everyone could face the teacher. The highlight came when they began to sit on individual seats that were attached to desks.

In 1857 children in some southern Utah communities sat on high, backless slab seats designed to accommodate their parents but not the children, whose feet were left dangling in the air. In Holladay, students entering the first schoolhouse saw only one desk, which ran the entire length of one side of the room. The thirty-five scholars who attended the first year could not all sit there at the same time, so they had to take turns doing their written work.[32] Anna Starr began school in a one-room building in Cottonwood, where she sat on wooden benches but also, along with other students, used a desk near the teacher's when practicing writing.[33] Students in the first schoolhouse in Spanish Fork sat on benches consisting of wooden slabs, smooth side up, with two legs on each end and one in the middle for extra support. Their writing desks were equally crude.[34] By contrast, children in the Twelfth Ward in Salt Lake City enjoyed individual, stationary seats and desks, much more comfortable than the slabs their southern Utah cousins squirmed on. Later, however, the cousins themselves enjoyed new schoolhouses furnished with backed, finished-plank seats and long writing desks around the walls.[35]

Learning tools varied from school to school. In some, such as the school attended by Peter Monk in Spring City's stone fort, students used charcoal or chalk to write on slates.[36] In other cases, paper and ink were available, and students wrote with quill pens. Some schools had practically no books, maps, or other visual materials while others enjoyed many such conveniences. In the Salt Lake City First Ward school, each child was fortunate enough to possess a slate and a few books,[37] but textbooks at other schools were often at a premium. Peter Monk had one book to learn from, a blue-back speller.[38]

In the town of Palmyra in the 1850s, a student was considered well equipped if he or she owned a McGuffey's reader, an elementary spelling book, and a copy of Smith's arithmetic. According to George A. Hicks, a former pupil, Palmyra students used the New Testament and the Book of Mormon or "most any kind of book we could get." The teacher, Silas Hillman, owned the only grammar book in town, "Kirkham's Grammar,"[39] and taught from it orally. Young George "graduated" at the end of his first quarter under Hillman with "high honors," being able to read in the New Testament or Book of Mormon "without making many mistakes in the pronunciation of the words—with a very limited knowledge of arithmetic and none whatever of grammar or history."[40] Although the availability of learning tools improved over time, in 1874 the territorial superintendent discovered that only half the children in attendance at one school had books and there were no charts or other visual aids to help the teacher.[41]

Though Utah's pioneer teachers enjoyed few material resources for their classes, they were often innovative with what they had. Ogden's first teacher, Charilla Abbot, described how she began:

> The colony wished me to keep school, which in our meager circumstances I undertook. Finding a chicken feather, I made a pen, and I made a trial at it. . . . We had to collect letters from scraps of papers and from old books. These we pasted on paddles. We also made letters on the inside and outside of our hands. In this way the children learned to read and write.[42]

The fireplace provided charcoal for writing on their hands. In Alpine, Elsie Booth's geography lessons were conducted on the floor of the classroom. While the younger children were at recess, the older ones sprinkled and swept the floor in preparation for what would happen next. When class reconvened, wet and dry places were used to represent the land and water surfaces of the earth, as students were asked to point out various locations they had read about in the textbook.[43]

Amy Adams began school in the Salt Lake City First Ward, under the tutelage of Susan Eliza Savage Angell. With precious few teaching materials available, Mrs. Angell wrote the numerals, including Roman numerals, and the letters of the alphabet on strips of cardboard that she handed around the room so that the children could copy them to their slates. Some of the cardboard strips also contained mottoes for the more advanced students to copy, such as "Many birds of many kinds, many men of many minds."[44] Such austere school buildings, furnishings, and teaching materials were commonplace in the early history of most Utah communities, though they gradually gave way to more commodious facilities and better teaching supplies.

Unusual Family Schools

Among the best schools in early Utah were a handful of family schools founded by men such as Brigham Young and Heber C. Kimball, who, as a result of their plural marriages, had over fifty children each. These schools, also open to other people, were well equipped and well taught and tended to offer the best in educational opportunities during the pioneer period.

One of the finest school buildings in early Salt Lake City was Brigham Young's private school, built of adobe in 1853 but later enlarged and dedicated on Christmas Day 1860 (see p. 358). A fine-looking piece of architecture, it boasted an octagonal bell tower above

School desk designed by Brigham Young, Salt Lake City, ca. 1865. Brigham designed these sturdy desks to match the sizes of the children attending the family schoolhouse thereby providing a degree of comfort unusual in Utah schools. This desk was used by Brigham's daughter Susa.

the vestibule. Students entered through the vestibule, which was about eight feet square, where they were undoubtedly tantalized by the bell rope hanging from the ceiling but just out of their reach. The main room, which they entered through double doors, was square with about an eighteen-foot ceiling. Two high, oblong, vertical windows on each side and in the front provided plenty of light. In the center of the room was a large, round cast-iron stove, with "yards and yards" of stovepipe stretching to the chimney corner. In sharp contrast to the crude, rough-sawn desks in some other schools, those in the Brigham Young school were sturdy and well built. Painted green, they also had spacious compartments under their drop lids for storing books and belongings. Available teaching tools included slates and pencils as well as wall charts—something few early schools could afford.[45]

The bell at Brigham Young's school rang each morning at 8:45 A.M. to call students to school. At 9:00 it rang again to signal that school was in session. The students were not always attentive, for, as one of Brigham Young's daughters recalled, the lids on their desks were sometimes used to hide behind as they clandestinely munched an apple or read a note from a boy. Nor could she forget the two-inch ledge surrounding the stove in the middle of the room, for there each morning the students placed apples that slowly baked until lunch time. The delicious aroma of the sizzling apples made it nearly impossible to wait until noon. On each Friday afternoon, regular classwork was suspended, and scholars found themselves engaged in giving orations, participating in spelling bees, playing organ solos, singing, and reading the school paper.[46] However, such a school experience was clearly the exception to the rule in those early pioneer days.

THE INDISPENSABLE TEACHERS

Like everything else about school life in the nineteenth century, the teachers under whose tutelage Utah's pioneer students sat were a varied lot. Teachers' ages ran the possible gamut, and both women and men taught. The sixteen counties that turned in statistics in 1868 reported a total of 134 female and 164 male teachers.[47] Some were well-trained professionals while others were hardly trained at all. Efforts to establish training programs for prospective teachers were largely unsuccessful in the period under consideration, though a normal department was added to the University of Deseret in 1869.[48] But whatever his or her training, the teacher was at the heart of whatever

Plain City School, ca. 1884. Teachers (on the left, William S. Geddes, and on the right, George H. Carver) pose next to an adobe building with their (mostly) female students in the Mormon pioneer settlement of Plain City. One little boy sits on the second row by a girl who appears to be his sister.

Plain City School, ca. 1884. The same teachers pose with most of their male students—at least one and maybe two boys sat with the girls. Some young person is hiding around the building's corner. The variety of clothing, ranging from that of the fully suited boy on the left to the barefoot boy seated on the bench, may indicate differences in resources that often affected the amount of schooling a child received.

educational experience a pioneer child had. Unfortunately, he or she was also too often unsung.

Some teachers lived at home; others came from out of town and boarded from house to house, frequently at the homes of their students, where they were usually given the best bed to sleep in. At times they taught school in the homes where they stayed. In 1875, for example, eighteen-year-old Leona Mortensen began teaching in Elsinore. Having a total of ten students, she lived and taught in one house for about a week and then moved on to another.[49]

Some teachers changed schools often, trying to find a position where they could be secure and earn a comfortable living. It was difficult, however, for they were usually responsible for collecting their own pay, which often consisted of produce rather than cash and was sometimes not forthcoming. Their work was hard and frequently went unthanked by communities preoccupied with other things and apathetic to the problems of financing good education. Even when they were paid in cash, their incomes were meager, with tuition fees ranging from three to six dollars per quarter in 1868.[50]

Though teachers varied in quality, many pioneer students were blessed with outstanding ones. They included Camilla C. Cobb, who began the first kindergarten in Brigham Young's private school and is credited with being the founder of Utah's kindergartens; Mary Jane Dilworth Young; Mary and Ida Cook; Karl G. Maeser; Robert Campbell; and Warren and Wilson Dusenberry.[51]

When he began teaching in Provo, Wilson Dusenberry recorded some of his reactions. A few excerpts from his diary illustrate the frustrations faced by many teachers as well as something about the children they taught and the ultimate satisfaction that often came at the end of a series of struggles.

> [February 20, 1863]: Brother Warren sick so I had to teach his school. The little brats were determined on having a spree. I checked their cheer a little, however.

> [March 26, 1863]: Learned that a schoolteacher needs a false face, so that he can laugh! Some of the scholars told me they did not like me as well as Warren. Children are the personification of candor, but how necessary it is for us to forget it when we grow up.

> [April 20, 1863]: Penned a pig for the seventh time. Returned from school very hoarse—cause—incessant talking.

> [August 4, 1863]: The people of Provo are too unconcerned or too lazy to visit the schools. I know that the scholars have learned something!

[November 5, 1863]: At school all nearly are sick. Tried to sink into an oblivious sleep but could not with the "botherations of the school."

[November 6, 1863]: The last day of school. I'm pleased and sad. The little cards of merit and prize books were held in a "sacred light," judging from the clasp of their little hands as they passed out with their "Goodby, school master." Who can teach school without forming ties of affection! Not I.[52]

Despite the fact that there were many fine teachers in the territory, Superintendent Campbell constantly complained about the persistent lack of quality, urging both improved pay and better training facilities as the answer. In his 1863 message to the legislature, he was particularly concerned with poor teacher salaries. He urged the legislature and other citizens to use their influence to pay schoolteachers liberally "with sufficient of that kind of pay which would enable them to procure ample clothing for themselves and families."[53] In other words, payment-in-kind was simply not adequate for teachers trying to raise families. He also urged the legislature to appropriate funds to defray the tuition of students who had mastered their elementary education and were willing to declare in writing their intention to qualify themselves as teachers.[54]

THE CURRICULUM: A STUDY IN PRAGMATISM

Some of Utah's pioneer schoolchildren may not have seen much difference between school and Sunday School, for the LDS Church influenced the course of study in many ways. Although a number of teachers who were not Latter-day Saints were employed in various communities, especially after the 1860s, for the most part those who taught in the period under consideration were believing Latter-day Saints who taught their church's values. In 1857 the teachers in the Twelfth Ward school in Salt Lake City were Bishop L. W. Hardy and his assistant Miss E. R. Bunnell. They taught their students to read with the Bible, the Book of Mormon, and the Doctrine and Covenants as texts, although they also taught writing, arithmetic, geography, and grammar.[55]

The Bible and the Book of Mormon were used as textbooks in early Utah schools not only because these scriptures were the most readily available readers but also because teachers and administrators saw no problem in using the school to instill the religious values of the community. Superintendent Campbell wrote as late as 1873:

Our lot has been cast in lands favored with the Bible. We have been taught from our infancy that "the fear of the Lord is the beginning of wisdom;" and shall our common schools be the first place to ignore this sentiment. . . ?

Are we not apt to be narrow in our educational ideas, and to give undue weight to intellectual culture. . . . Any educational system that fails to give due prominence to religious and moral training is defective. . . .

The common school code of Utah does not require nor AUTHORIZE educators to inculcate RELIGIOUS TENETS, but all teachers are advised to open their schools by prayer, and to inculcate the "fear of God," and morality, both by precept and example.[56]

At first the territory had no prescribed curriculum—teachers taught what they thought best. Eventually, the territorial legislature suggested certain subjects for study, such as spelling, reading, writing, geography, grammar, arithmetic, bookkeeping, mathematics, astronomy, history, languages, music, and art. Considerable time passed, however, before all these subjects were offered to most pupils, including those in Salt Lake City. Neither was there a uniformity of textbooks in the period under discussion, although the educational committee's 1861 report to the legislature indicated that the most commonly used texts were "Webster's Elementary Spelling Book, McGuffey's Series of Readers, Smith's Grammar, and Ray's Arithmetic."[57] During the next decade, the territorial superintendent recommended various other readers and texts that were popular throughout the nation. He also recommended that curricula be expanded to include drawing, sewing, and vocal music.

What was actually taught usually depended on the interests of the teacher, which often included the practical skills necessary to making a living in the pioneer economy. In 1862, A. P. Welchman advertised the opening of a juvenile day school in the Salt Lake City Ninth Ward, boasting that there he would provide more satisfactory progress than schools of "mixed grades." His view of the practical needs of the community was revealed when he announced that his curriculum would include land surveying, perspective drawing, and fortification.[58] At age seven, Anna Maria Dorius began to attend a regular school in Ephraim, but she also went to a special school conducted by a Mrs. Otterstrom. There she learned to embroider, braid straw hats, and make straw trimmings and ornaments. These skills served her usefully throughout her life.[59] In the 1850s, Hannah Hood Hill attended Sister T. D. Brown's home school in Salt Lake City, where she learned sewing and other kinds of needlework.[60]

In 1858 a Mrs. Cooke advertised the opening of a school for girls in her home in the Salt Lake City Fourteenth Ward. There, for $5 students could take advanced English, for $4 they could attend the primary class, for $12 they could take lessons on the melodeon (a small reed organ), and a $3 charge was made for the use of Mrs. Cooke's books and instrument.[61] Mrs. Watmough, an English immigrant, taught about fifty students—all in one room—whose educational level ranged from beginners to the eighth grade. "We used to have some nice times at school," recalled Joseph Openshaw, who started in her school in the 1860s in the Salt Lake City Seventeenth Ward. The older students studied plays, which they presented on Friday afternoons, while the younger students gave songs and recitations.[62]

In Alpine, around 1860, English immigrant Elsie Booth helped her husband teach in the regular school during the winter, but she concluded that children could also profit from a short-term summer session rather than being left to wander the streets. Apparently many of the families in Alpine (or, as it was called then, Mountainville) were better off than pioneers elsewhere who had to keep their children working year-round. For several years, therefore, Elsie conducted a ten-week summer school in the meetinghouse, teaching geography, reading, writing, spelling, and singing.[63]

In the 1850s, the curriculum in Ann Jane Wilden's school in Cedar City included sewing, something Ann dearly wanted to learn. She asked her mother for some quilting pieces, but her mother had none, so Ann found some old rags and also obtained a few pieces of cloth from some girls at school. Her mother refused to let Ann take her only needle to school, but desperate to learn, Ann took it anyway and promptly lost it. She took the punishment meted out at home, but later her mother was able to secure enough needles for both of them. However, they had no thread, so Ann resourcefully went to the barn, obtained some horsehairs, and sewed with them. Whatever else she learned in school, the fact that she ultimately became an expert at quilt making was the most practical long-range result.[64]

For a time beginning in the early 1860s, some teachers attempted to teach the Deseret Alphabet, a curious system of phonetic characters intended to help foreign immigrants learn to speak English. Devised by George D. Watt, the alphabet had the enthusiastic endorsement of Brigham Young as well as Superintendent Campbell. A few readers as well as sections of the Book of Mormon were printed in this alphabet, but few people seemed to take it seriously. After Brigham Young's death, it became little more than a curiosity.[65]

Some pioneer children might have been surprised if asked what grade they were in, for their schools had no such distinctions. Rather, schooling usually meant learning along with children of different ages and sometimes even with adults. In Springville, for example, the oldest children of Jacob Houtz went to school with their father's new wife, Bridget Daly Houtz.[66] In 1857 an average of seventy students, ranging in age from four to twenty-five, attended the Twelfth Ward school in Salt Lake City. The younger students, about a third of the total, comprised the "infant class."[67] When Mary Elizabeth Lightner Rollins taught school in Minersville in the 1860s, she had married men in her classes.[68] Because age did not correlate with ability but the readers were graded, teachers sometimes kept track of students according to the reader they were studying rather than by age.

Of Hickory Sticks and Kindness: The Problem of Discipline

Although their parents often reminded them that they were God's chosen people, at times pioneer scholars did not seem to act as if they were. Tardiness, truancy, and various kinds of mischievousness were not unheard of. Some teachers were exasperated to the point of sheer frustration while others calmly took it in stride. To correct the problems, they employed various disciplinary devices, from the hickory stick to unexpected kindness. Many seemed convinced that the adage "Spare the rod and spoil the child" was just as scriptural as "The glory of God is intelligence" (D&C 93:36) and that students could be helped along on the path toward "light and truth" by a stinging backside.

Territorial officials frowned on physical punishment, but many schoolchildren were hardly aware of that. All they knew was that if they did not behave they were in for something serious. When O. H. Riggs visited one school in 1874, he found a "venerable matron" in charge who was over sixty years old. "The substantial ferule held in her hand demonstrated that she had not been careless in acquiring the means of correction," he noted with apparent disapproval.[69] The teacher may have felt intimidated, however, by the fact that she was in charge of a hundred pupils, seventy-two of whom were in attendance that day in a room too small to adequately accommodate forty.

In 1875 students in Orderville were under the tutelage of Robert Marshall, an Irish Protestant minister who seemed to know little about effective discipline. When he went in search of a switch to help along the education of a disobedient scholar, it was reported, the rest of the class "sure had a good time while he was gone." At times Marshall felt obliged to go in search of an absentee. When one student playing in the street was asked why he was not in school, he simply replied that Mr. Marshall had not yet come for him. Meanwhile, back at the school, as Marshall hunted down truants, the other students did what seemed only logical: they left.[70]

Other forms of discipline sometimes varied in degree with the frequency of the offense. In Palmyra, Silas Hillman required an offender to do nothing more than stand in the middle of the room after the first infraction. After the second offense, the student had to stand on one foot for a designated period of time; after the third, he stood on one foot with one arm raised; and after the fourth, the hapless scholar could expect to stand on one foot with one arm raised holding a stick. The next offense brought the humiliation of the dunce cap.[71] In Salina rowdy or uncooperative students were sometimes imprisoned under the platform used to elevate the teacher's desk, though some of them escaped by tunneling out the back way.[72]

Some teachers, however, seemed incapable of harshness and found other ways to impose discipline. In Ogden, Alice Tucker was caught chewing on the hard sap she found under her rough log seat, a practice forbidden by the teacher. She was required, therefore, to sit in the window, where she promptly went to sleep. This was hardly severe punishment, but at least she remembered it.[73] In Cottonwood, a teacher named Mrs. Andrus took the opposite tack. Instead of punishing poor behavior she tried to reward the good. Every Friday, students who had earned such a reward were invited to her home, where she entertained them with her singing and piano playing.[74]

A PERIOD OF TRANSITION

A number of changes came to Utah education in the latter part of the century, including the founding of several Protestant schools as part of an effort to combat Mormon influence and, in response to those schools, the establishment of increasing numbers of Latter-day Saint academies. In addition, as Charles S. Peterson has observed, a class of well-trained professional teachers arose.[75] After 1874 territorial taxes were allocated for school purposes. These changes all enhanced educational opportunities for Utah's children, resulting in a period of transition from the often makeshift pioneer education described in this paper to the more highly structured educational establishment of the late nineteenth and early twentieth centuries. In 1890 the legislature enacted a law providing for free public education (no tuition was to be charged), but only in the early twentieth century was that goal finally achieved.

Conclusion

Some writers have been exuberant in their praise for early Utah education,[76] but the fact remains that educational achievement varied greatly in the first quarter century of Utah's territorial history. Whether formal schooling was part of everyday life for pioneer children depended on the winds of circumstance, and for those who did attend school, daily life in the classroom varied according to the place, the school, the curriculum, and the teacher. Learning was sometimes inhibited by uncomfortable and inadequate furniture as well as inadequate learning tools, but even under these circumstances it was often enhanced by dedicated and skilled teachers.

Much of the education offered was directed toward the practical needs of a pioneering economy, which called for reading, writing, and arithmetic as well as various practical skills. Most school-age children in Utah needed little more to survive. Farming, merchandising, mining, and other common pursuits simply did not require more formal education, though they usually required on-the-job training. Girls often learned sewing and other practical skills, not only because they wanted to, but also because such training would help them provide for the family. Some went to telegraphy schools for the same reason. Some young men and women went on for professional training of various sorts, but they clearly were the exceptions more than the rule. In the sense, then, of providing the necessary preparation, rudimentary pioneer education was perhaps as adequate for its time as advanced education is for modern times.

Although education beyond the basic skills was not necessary to survival, pioneer Utah was not a cultural backwash. Many teachers, some of whom were unusually well educated, worked hard to instill in their students a love of learning and of the cultural arts, and many students took advantage of the opportunities thus provided. In 1913, George H. Brimhall, then president of Brigham Young University, remembered with fondness his own childhood schooling, which began toward the end of the period under discussion:

The mothers of that epoch had ambitions—not so much for themselves as for their children, and these ambitions were reenforced by the religious conviction that education is salvation,—it was part of their creed.

. . . Education in Utah has had no backwoods era. Fifty years ago this winter my teacher in the little hamlet of Cedar Fort was the honorable Zerrubbabel Snow, a member of the first supreme court of the territory of Utah. . . . Over forty years ago, in the little town of Grafton, on the Rio Virgin, it was my good fortune to come under the training of one of the best teachers I have ever known, in the person of Henry I. Young. In makeup he seemed to me the prototype of the author of the Monroe Doctrine, whose picture was in my geography, and in disposition I thought of him as I did of Washington. In my early teens the great man of our town was my teacher, Silas Hillman, a man of eastern training. He was justice of the peace and a general legal adviser of the town folk.

Then later I had the good fortune to become educationally intimate with Robert Campbell, a scholar of whom it is said, "He worked all the time. . . ."

[Then, after listing many more excellent teachers who influenced his life, Brimhall remarked:] Glancing back over this line-up of departed educators, with the famed philosopher and mathematician, Orson Pratt, at their head, and seeing also the community leaders still with us who have retired from teaching, and then viewing the multitude of trained teachers at this noblest of all tasks, it can be said of Utah, "She has had no cause to plead pedagogical poverty."[77]

Though education in pioneer Utah may not have reached the standard enjoyed in some other parts of the country, the valiant efforts of the teachers in that era helped lay the foundation for what Charles Peterson describes as "the flowering of learning and education in the last quarter of the nineteenth century which itself became one of several important points of embarkation for remarkable achievements by Utahns in the twentieth century."[78] Equally important, those who took advantage of the best their pioneer communities had to offer, even for a short time, remembered it as an important contribution to their lives and, because of it, passed on to those who followed a heritage greatly enriched.

James B. Allen is Senior Research Fellow at the Smith Institute for LDS History. The author expresses appreciation to Analise Ahlstrom, a student in his History 490 class, for research assistance on this paper.

NOTES

1. See Heber J. Grant, "My Days in School," *Improvement Era* 44 (November 1941): 665, 681–82; Ronald W. Walker, "Heber J. Grant," in *Presidents of the Church,* ed. Leonard J. Arrington (Salt Lake City: Deseret Book, 1986), 219–21.

2. Ellen Burton Beazer, Autobiography, in *Our Pioneer Heritage*, comp. Kate B. Carter, 20 vols. (Salt Lake City: Daughters of Utah Pioneers, 1958–77), 10:51–52.

3. Irene Branch Keller, "The Coombs Story," in Carter, *Our Pioneer Heritage,* 3:522–24.

4. While several previous works have traced the history of education in Utah, none have considered in detail the everyday life of pioneer schoolchildren. Unless otherwise noted, for basic historical information, including some administrative details, I have relied upon John Clifton Moffitt, *The History of Public Education in Utah* ([Salt Lake City: Deseret News Press], 1946); and Bruce L. Campbell and Eugene E. Campbell, "Early Cultural and Intellectual Development," in *Utah's History,* ed. Richard D. Poll (Provo, Utah: Brigham Young University Press, 1978), 295–315.

5. There is a plethora of literature on this subject, but Milton Lynn Bennion, *Mormonism and Education* (Salt Lake City: Deseret News Press, 1939), still provides one of the best treatments of general Mormon attitudes toward education.

6. Maren Kirstine Nielson, Autobiography, in Carter, *Our Pioneer Heritage,* 11:303–4; italics in original. The motto is taken from Doctrine and Covenants 93:36.

7. "Address," *Deseret News,* August 3, 1850, 63, quoted in Frederick S. Buchanan, "Education among the Mormons: Brigham Young and the Schools of Utah," *History of Education Quarterly* 22 (winter 1982): 446.

8. Robert L. Campbell, "Annual Report of the Superintendent of Common Schools for 1867," in J. C. Moffitt, comp., *Reports of the Superintendents of Schools of Utah, from 1861 to 1896* (Provo, Utah: n.p., 1941), 21, typescript.

9. "First Schoolroom in Western America," in *An Enduring Legacy,* comp. Lesson Committee, 12 vols. (Salt Lake City: Daughters of Utah Pioneers, 1977–89), 6:85–86; Emma P. Anderson, "Mary Jane Dilworth Hammond," in *An Enduring Legacy,* 6:86–87. See also N. G. Morgan, "Pioneer Adobe Homes in the Salt Lake Valley," in Carter, *Our Pioneer Heritage,* 1:118–19.

10. George A. Smith, Diary, quoted in Moffitt, *History of Public Education,* 20.

11. "The First Free School in Utah," in Carter, *Our Pioneer Heritage,* 10:14–15.

12. Buchanan, "Education among the Mormons," 446.

13. Robert L. Campbell to the Legislative Assembly of the Territory of Utah, January 14, 1863, quoted in Moffitt, *Reports of the Superintendents,* 3.

14. Moffitt, *Reports of the Superintendents,* 1, 29–30.

15. "Michael Peter Munk—101 Years," in Carter, *Our Pioneer Heritage,* 7:348.

16. "The Christian Christiansen Company," in Carter, *Our Pioneer Heritage,* 1:45.

17. "The Christian Christiansen Company," 1:43.

18. Della Tucker and Ruby S. Brown, "Alma," in Carter, *Our Pioneer Heritage,* 3:227.

19. "Sailed on the *Kenilworth,*" in Carter, *Our Pioneer Heritage,* 12:69.

20. "English Pioneers," in Carter, *Our Pioneer Heritage,* 8:37–38.

21. Joseph Openshaw, Diary, quoted in Carter, *Our Pioneer Heritage,* 16:199.

22. "Lucy Smith Cardon," in Carter, *Our Pioneer Heritage,* 7:419.

23. Zipporah L. Stewart, "David Edwin Layton," in Carter, *Our Pioneer Heritage,* 7:457.

24. Ada Arvilla Burke Earl, Diary, 1, quoted in Moffitt, *History of Public Education,* 258.

25. "Huntsville, Weber County," in Carter, *Our Pioneer Heritage,* 8:464–67.

26. "Millard County," in Carter, *Our Pioneer Heritage,* 13:514.

27. Maud Lewis, "Early School Teacher of Palmyra and Spanish Fork," in *Heart Throbs of the West,* comp. Kate B. Carter, 12 vols. (Salt Lake City: Daughters of Utah Pioneers, 1939–51), 2:143.

28. George A. Smith, "Historical," *Deseret News,* August 6, 1862, 3, quoted in Moffitt, *History of Public Education,* 259.

29. O. H. Riggs, *Territorial School Report, 1874–75,* quoted in Moffitt, *History of Public Education,* 263.

30. "Huntsville, Weber County," in 8:464–67.

31. Robert L. Campbell, *Territorial School Report, 1871,* quoted in Moffitt, *History of Public Education,* 263.

32. Emily Carlisle, "Holladay," in Carter, *Our Pioneer Heritage,* 1:158.

33. Bertha Hansen, "Anna—100 Years," in Carter, *Our Pioneer Heritage,* 7:392.

34. Maud Lewis, "Early School Teacher of Palmyra and Spanish Fork," in Carter, *Heart Throbs of the West,* 2:143.

35. Riggs, *Territorial School Report, 1874–75,* 263.

36. "Michael Peter Monk—101 Years," 7:348.

37. Laura P. Angell King, "Susan Eliza Savage Angell," in Carter, *Heart Throbs of the West,* 2:138.

38. "Michael Peter Monk—101 Years," 7:348.

39. Samuel Kirkham, *English Grammar in Familiar Lectures . . . : Designed for the Use of Schools and Private Learners* (Rochester, N.Y.: Wm. Alling, 1829), was extremely popular, going through many editions.

40. Maud Lewis, "The Early Schoolteacher of Palmyra and Spanish Fork," in Carter, *Heart Throbs of the West,* 2:142–43.

41. Campbell, *Territorial School Report, 1871,* quoted in Moffitt, *History of Public Education,* 263.

42. Mildred Hatch Thomson, comp., *Rich Memories: 1863 to 1960,* quoted in "Early Elementary Schools," in *An Enduring Legacy,* 5:271. See also Ivy Williams Stone, "Early Public Schools of Ogden City, Utah," in Carter, *Heart Throbs of the West,* 2:128.

43. May Booth Talmage, "Elsie Edge Booth," in Carter, *Our Pioneer Heritage,* 1:35.

44. King, "Susan Eliza Savage Angell," 2:138.

45. Clarissa Y. Spencer, "Brigham Young's School," in Carter, *Heart Throbs of the West,* 2:120–21; Catherine Britsch, "Camilla C. Cobb, Founder of the Kindergarten in Utah" (Ed.D. diss., Brigham Young University, 1997), 109–11; "President Brigham Young's Private School," in *An Enduring Legacy,* 5:274–75; a photograph of the school is found on page 275.

46. "President Brigham Young's Private School," in 5:274–75.

47. Moffitt, *Reports of the Superintendents,* 29. There were more female than male teachers in only Salt Lake County (thirty-seven women and twenty-nine men) and Box Elder County (nine women and eight men).

48. Normal schools (or departments) typically offered a two-year program preparing their students to be teachers.

49. Myrtle F. Marquardson, "From Sevier County," in *Treasures of Pioneer History,* comp. Kate B. Carter, 6 vols. (Salt Lake City: Daughters of Utah Pioneers, 1952–57), 1:88.

50. Campbell, "Annual Report of the Superintendent of Common Schools for 1867," 19.

51. For discussions of these and other outstanding teachers, see "Pioneer Schools and Schoolmasters," in Carter, *Heart Throbs of the West,* 2:113–48; "Schoolteachers," in *An Enduring Legacy,* 6:85–128; Britsch, "Camilla C. Cobb"; Frederick S. Buchanan, "Robert Lang Campbell: 'A Wise Scribe in Israel' and Schoolman to the Saints," *BYU Studies* 29 (summer 1989): 5–27; Jill Mulvay Derr, "The Two Miss Cooks: Pioneer Professionals for Utah Schools," *Utah Historical Quarterly* 45 (fall 1975): 396–409; Alma P. Burton, *Karl G. Maeser: Mormon Educator* (Salt Lake City: Deseret Book, 1953); and Jill C. Mulvay [Derr], "Zion's Schoolmarms," in *Mormon Sisters: Women in Early Utah,* ed. Claudia L. Bushman (Cambridge, Mass.: Emmeline Press, 1976), 67–87.

52. "From the Diary of Wilson Howard Dusenberry," in Carter, *Our Pioneer Heritage,* 1:234–40.

53. Campbell to the Legislative Assembly, in Moffitt, *Reports of the Superintendents,* 4.

54. "Annual Report for 1865," in Moffitt, *Reports of the Superintendents,* 12.

55. "One Hundred Years Ago," in Carter, *Our Pioneer Heritage,* 1:8.

56. Robert L. Campbell, *Territorial School Report, 1872–73,* quoted in Moffitt, *History of Public Education,* 268–69.

57. "Report of Committee on Education," in Moffitt, *Reports of the Superintendents,* 1.

58. "Education—1862," in Carter, *Our Pioneer Heritage,* 6:8.

59. "Anna Maria Dorius—1863," in Carter, *Our Pioneer Heritage,* 7:54–55.

60. "Hannah Hood Hill Romney," in Carter, *Our Pioneer Heritage,* 5:264.

61. "Girl's School," in Carter, *Our Pioneer Heritage,* 2:54.

62. Joseph Openshaw, Diary, 16:199–200.

63. Talmage, "Elsie Edge Booth," 1:35.

64. "Ann Jane Willden Johnson—1852," in Carter, *Our Pioneer Heritage,* 13:234–35.

65. See Douglas D. Alder, Paula J. Goodfellow, and Ronald G. Watt, "Creating a New Alphabet for Zion: The Origin of the Deseret Alphabet," *Utah Historical Quarterly* 52 (summer 1984): 275–86; "The Deseret Alphabet," *Utah Historical Quarterly* 12 (January/April 1944): 99–102; S. George Ellsworth, "The Deseret Alphabet," *American West* 10 (November 1973): 10–11, 53; Leah R. Frisby and Hector Lee, "The Deseret Readers," *Utah Humanities Review* 1 (July 1947): 240–44; S. S. Ivins, "The Deseret Alphabet," *Utah Humanities Review* 1 (July 1947): 223–39; Samuel C. Monson, "The Deseret Alphabet" (master's thesis, Columbia University, 1948); Samuel C. Monson, "Deseret Alphabet," in *Encyclopedia of Mormonism*, ed. Daniel H. Ludlow, 5 vols. (New York: Macmillan, 1992), 1:373–74; Douglas Allen New, "History of the Deseret Alphabet and Other Attempts to Reform English Orthography" (Ed.D. diss., Utah State University, 1985); Elizabeth Cottam Walker, "Brigham Young's Deseret Alphabet," *Montana* 24 (October 1974): 54–57; and Larry Wintersteen, "A History of the Deseret Alphabet" (master's thesis, Brigham Young University, 1970).

66. Veloy B. Bailey, "Bridget Daley Houtz," in Carter, *Our Pioneer Heritage,* 2:335.

67. "One Hundred Years Ago," 1:8.

68. "Mary Elizabeth Rollins Lightner," in Carter, *Our Pioneer Heritage,* 5:322.

69. Riggs, *Territorial School Report, 1874–75,* 163.

70. "History of the First School in Long Valley," in Carter, *Heart Throbs of the West,* 2:122.

71. Robertson, "Silas Hillman," 2:144.

72. Charles S. Peterson, "The Limits of Learning in Pioneer Utah," *Journal of Mormon History* 10 (1983): 71.

73. "Alice Rose Tucker Berryessa Blair—1864," in Carter, *Treasures of Pioneer History,* 3:60.

74. Hansen, "Anna—100 Years," 392.

75. See Charles S. Peterson, "A New Community: Mormon Teachers and the Separation of Church and State in Utah's Territorial Schools," *Utah Historical Quarterly* 48 (summer 1980): 293–312; and Peterson, "Limits of Learning," 65–78.

76. See Levi Edgar Young, "Education in Utah," *Improvement Era* 16 (July 1913): 877–94.

77. George H. Brimhall, "Evolution of Education in Utah," *Improvement Era* 16 (July 1913): 896, 900–901.

78. Peterson, "Limits of Learning," 78.

B. T. Higgs (1858–1939) and Susannah Summers Higgs (1861–1929) in Ogden, Utah, about 1885 as photographed by Adams Brothers. Married in 1876, B. T. lived longer than and his wife less than the average for married people in the second group studied by Bean, Mineau, and Smith.

THE EFFECT OF PIONEER LIFE ON THE LONGEVITY OF MARRIED COUPLES

Lee L. Bean, Geraldine P. Mineau, and Ken R. Smith

Those of us who would like to know how the length of our deceased forebears' lives compares to that of others in their community will find that such information is not commonly available. Peter Laslett notes that historical statisticians tend to focus on discovering how long people at birth could be expected to live, or they devote attention to analyzing infant and child mortality because those rates so dramatically determine the overall level of life expectancy. These limitations underlie Laslett's view that many historical studies of longevity are too narrow and need to be expanded. He explains that "expectation of life at every age . . . rises or falls in its duration, the probability at one birthday of reaching a particular later birthday, are all crucial aging phenomena on their own account, both for the individual and for society at large, in our own day and assuredly in the past."[1] In addition to recommending analyses of longevity at different ages, Laslett also emphasizes the importance of studying the longevity of particular localities and social groups.[2]

RATIONALE FOR THE STUDY

This paper addresses three of the concerns expressed by Laslett. First, our study details longevity at later ages, specifically the longevity of married couples. This study differs from the many studies that compare the fate of married individuals with that of single or divorced individuals. We study only married couples, not just married individuals. Our study, therefore, includes comparisons of pairs of husbands and wives.

Second, the analysis attempts to identify changes in longevity by comparing cohorts, or groups of individuals, who married during a

sixty-year interval—from those who married in the relatively early pioneer days of Utah to those who married in the first two decades of the
twentieth century. We extend our study to the first part of this century
to provide a comparison in order to understand the ways in which
the rigors of frontier settlement affected the likelihood of survival in the
adult years. The period covered is important because it encompasses
the development of hospitals, changes in attitudes toward medical practice, increasing numbers of medical specialists, improved sanitation,
and increasing development of public health programs.

Third, this study addresses Laslett's call for broadening historical
studies of longevity. We study the population in a specific region—Utah
primarily—and of specific groups, identified in this study by gender
(husbands and wives), regions of residence, and religion.

We are able to address these areas of historical research only
because of the availability of the records comprising the Utah Population Database (UPDB). The central core of this database is drawn
from the unusually large and comprehensive collection of genealogical records of the Utah Family History Library. The core has been
expanded with the addition of and linking of vital statistics from the
State of Utah as well as other records. The UPDB therefore provides
an increasingly complete record of the survival of large segments of the
population of Utah beginning with the pioneers. Because the population represented in the UPDB is not homogeneous, it is possible to
contrast husbands and wives, residents of more urban versus more
rural communities, and individuals distinguished by religion.

There are important reasons for focusing on these groups. First,
differences between the survival rates of men and women are well
known. For example, the 1993 life tables for the United States report
the life expectancy at birth of males in the United States as 72.2 years
and the life expectancy of females as 78.8 years. We accept higher
survival rates of females as the norm, but this norm is not universal.[3]
A wide range of studies conducted in developing societies show
higher female rates of mortality than male rates in the early years of life,
indicating a female disadvantage.[4] In addition, until recent years the
life expectancy of females was lower than the life expectancy of males
in some developing countries. But that difference was assumed to be
due to the higher rates of childhood mortality for females resulting
from the differential treatment of boys and girls in societies with a
strong "son-preference." A few studies, however, have also shown

adult females to have higher rates of mortality than males in the same age group.[5] Such cases represent societies where labor demands for both men and women are intensive and health conditions are poor. In addition to sharing some common risks with men, wives carry an additional burden where family size is large, the pace of childbearing rapid, and the births typically occur at home. Many of these conditions are to be found among the frontier population of Utah. Therefore we begin our analysis by contrasting the age at death of husbands and wives married between 1860 and 1919.

Second, we examine proximate rural-urban differences because of the long history of mortality differences between these two types of areas. Perhaps the earliest systematic study of mortality differences was conducted by John Graunt in the seventeenth century.[6] One of his generalizations is that cities are population-consuming areas and rural areas are population-producing areas—mortality rates were systematically higher in London than in outlying areas. This rural-urban mortality difference became a general truism in demographic studies, but there is evidence of a reversal in developing nations in the second half of this century, when investments in public health and health care facilities disproportionately benefit the populations of urban areas, especially capital cities.[7]

Therefore we examine community effects by distinguishing between the more urban and the more rural communities of Utah. We recognize that the early urban centers of Ogden, Salt Lake, and Provo did not face the problems of heavy industrial pollution, crowding, and the limited sanitary facilities found among major industrial cities of Europe and the northeastern and north central cities of the United States in the nineteenth century. Nevertheless, population density was far higher than in the rural areas of the state and thus provided a potential basis for rapid spread of infectious diseases.[8]

Third, we examine religious differences. The life expectancy of the population of Utah has been among the highest in the nation. Reasons often cited are favorable environment and ecology[9] and the lifestyle of the majority of the population. The avoidance of alcohol, tobacco, and caffeine drinks as mandated by the LDS Word of Wisdom has played a major role because of their contribution to specific causes of death. Although our data do not provide the opportunity to do a detailed study of mortality differences by cause of death,[10] the records available do allow us to examine mortality differences for different levels of religious commitment.

In summary, our primary focus is on the adult mortality of those who lived long enough to marry,[11] and the study is organized to utilize the strength of the UPDB—the ability to examine demographic changes over time for sequential marriage cohorts. That is, our study focuses on the adult survival differences of four groups: couples married between 1860 and 1874, between 1875 and 1889, between 1890 and 1904, and between 1905 and 1919.

THE STUDY POPULATION

The Utah Population Database contains several linked files: genealogies, the Utah Cancer Registry, the 1880 U.S. Census of Utah entered from the manuscript records, and Utah Death Certificates from 1957 to 1992. The genealogical records represent one million individuals from approximately 185,000 "Family Group Sheets" selected from the Utah Family History Library. Details regarding the selection, coding, and verification procedures for the records have been described in a number of previous publications.[12]

To reduce the number of confounding effects, a specific set of records was selected for analysis of adult mortality.[13] Marriages were the first marriage for each spouse. If later marriages for the husband were polygynous, the couple was excluded from the study. Wives first married between ages 12 through 49 and husbands 12 through 69 were selected. Husbands had to be no more than 10 years younger than their wives nor more than 25 years older than their wives. A small number of divorced couples were also omitted. Finally, consanguineous marriages were excluded in order to eliminate any possibility of a shared genetic risk of death.

As reported in an earlier analysis of this selected subset of records, "death dates for spouses are available from the genealogy whether the death occurred in Utah or not and are nearly complete through the 1960s. Death dates are also available from Utah death certificates (1957–92) linked to the genealogy."[14] Late death dates for individuals who died outside of Utah are, however, seemingly missing in a large number of cases. Late death dates are often provided by the linked vital statistics, but these cover only Utah. Therefore additional controls were adopted. All cases where either the husband or the wife of a couple died outside of Utah were excluded from the analysis reported in this paper. The sample thus consists of four marriage cohorts of individuals who are likely to have died in Utah (or who may have been living in 1992). Even with these constraints, numbers will vary slightly from one table to another. For example, death dates for husbands may be missing in some cases, and death dates for wives missing in other cases. Therefore the number of cases for couple comparisons will be smaller than the number of cases for husbands or wives alone. See table 1 for the number of cases included in the final sample.

Table 1 Couples by Date of Marriage		
Date of Marriage	Number	Percent
1860–1874	4,980	12.1
1875–1889	9,079	22.0
1890–1904	12,280	29.8
1905–1919	14,879	36.1
Total	41,218	100.0

The most important feature of the selected population is that its members are survivors. They are individuals who survived the high mortality risks of childhood.[15] At the time of marriage, they were, on average, between 20 and 25 years of age. (See table 2.) There is little variation in the age of marriage for husbands and wives across the four marriage cohorts, but these variations result in a systematic decrease in the mean difference in the husband-wife age at marriage. For the years 1860–74, the mean difference was nearly five years (4.89), and for 1905–19, slightly more than three years (3.16).[16]

Table 2 Mean Age at Marriage and Difference of Age at Marriage, Husbands and Wives, by Marriage Cohort				
Age at Marriage and Age at Marriage Differences	Marriage Cohort			
	1860–1874	1875–1889	1890–1904	1905–1919
Husband				
Mean	25.28	24.54	25.24	24.70
SD	(5.73)	(4.67)	(4.59)	(4.46)
Wife				
Mean	20.40	20.23	21.17	21.55
SD	(4.17)	(3.32)	(3.35)	(3.40)
Difference				
Mean	4.89	4.42	4.07	3.16
SD	(5.68)	(4.65)	(4.34)	(3.97)
N	4,980	9,079	12,280	14,879

Most of the variables used in this study refer to specific events—birth, marriage, and death—as well as to the time and place where they occur. From these variables, two others are readily computed: duration of marriage and duration of widowhood. Two additional variables are constructed and require explanation.

To identify rural-urban differences, the following geographic classifications were used. Wasatch Front communities (Utah, Salt Lake, Davis, and Weber Counties) were selected to represent the more urban regions of Utah, and all other counties (Other Utah) to represent the more rural regions. As noted above, the sample was restricted in order to insure maximum accuracy in the identification of age at death by using both genealogical data as well as Utah vital statistics information.[17] Therefore the sample includes only husbands and wives who died in Utah or who are presumed to be living. The deaths of individuals, therefore, could be assigned to the more urban or the more rural communities. The largest proportion of wives and husbands died in the same regions. In 92.2 percent of the cases, if the wife died in the Wasatch Front, the husband did as well. If the wife died in another area of the state, 84.6 percent of the husbands died in the same region. Consequently, place of death is used as an approximation of overall community influences.

Inferring religious affiliation and commitment is difficult because the information is limited to only the date of baptism and date of endowment.[18] In several previous studies, however, it has been shown that a reasonable predictive scale can be generated from these variables.[19] In this study, we have classified the individuals as follows:

Active LDS: baptized and endowed before death

Inactive LDS: baptized before death, but no record of endowment during the lifetime of the individual

Non-LDS: no evidence of baptism or endowment for either spouse

Husbands and wives were classified separately because of husband-wife differences (table 3) and because we wanted to test the separate effects of husbands' or wives' religious commitment on longevity. Most couples (90.7 percent) share a common religious code, and approximately three quarters are classified as Active LDS.[20] The approximately ten percent of couples for whom there are differences of religious coding arise from several situations. For example, a small number of individuals are endowed while the spouse is not because endowment takes place in a second marriage. This study examines only first marriages, but remarriage does occur frequently following the loss of a spouse, particularly if death occurs at an early age. Other differences arise from the fact that a husband or wife may have been baptized but the spouse has no recorded association with the LDS Church.

Table 3 Religious Classification of Husbands and Wives		
Religious Classification	Husbands	Wives
Active	73.1	79.0
Inactive	21.2	10.1
Non-LDS	5.7	10.5
Total	100.0	100.0
N	41,218	41,218

SURVIVAL OF MARRIED COUPLES

This section examines both independently and in combination the age at death, or survival rate for men and women, rural-urban populations, and various categories of inferred religious commitment.

The average age at death of husbands and wives and couple differences in age at death for each of the four marriage cohorts are reported in table 4. The top panel examines husbands and wives independently, and the bottom panel considers couple differences. The couple difference is computed by subtracting the age of death of each wife from the age of death of her first husband. Therefore a positive value indicates a wife died at an earlier age than her first husband, and a negative value indicates that a wife died at a later age than her first husband.

The individual data indicate that the mean age at death increases for both husbands and wives with each succeeding marriage cohort as the more recently married couples had access to improved public health facilities and medical care programs. The increase is greatest for the wives, reversing a pattern of earlier mean age at death for the wives in the first two marriage cohorts to the more modern pattern of later age at death of wives relative to husbands. It is important to note that the variance in the age at death for wives is much greater than for men. This finding suggests that the difference in the means is in part due to some extreme values for wives, including a number of early deaths that are probably due to maternal mortality. The shift from a relatively earlier mean age at death to a relatively late mean age at death for women is demonstrated by both forms of data presented in table 4—but there are differences. The couple data show that the reversal from an earlier to a later age of death for wives occurs among the 1890–1904 cohort. Again one should note the extreme variation around the mean.

Table 4
Mean Age at Death, Husbands and Wives and Mean Difference of Death,
Husband-and-Wife Couples, by Marriage Cohort

Age at Death and Couple Differences	Marriage Cohort			
	1860–1874	1875–1889	1890–1904	1905–1919
Husbands				
Mean	70.57	70.66	70.76	72.02
SD	(14.47)	(14.35)	(14.78)	(15.38)
Wives				
Mean	68.63	69.46	71.40	74.70
SD	(17.40)	(17.53)	(17.77)	(17.39)
Couple Differences				
Mean	1.94	1.20	–.65	–2.68
SD	(22.36)	(22.65)	(22.45)	(22.80)
N	4,980	9,079	12,280	14,879

Is this seemingly unusual pattern of mortality among women married before the last decade of the nineteenth century consistent across regional and religious groups? We first examine the mean age of death of husbands and wives by place of death as a proxy measure for community influences during the lifetime of the couples. (See table 5.) There are clearly community differences.

Table 5
Mean Age of Death of Husbands and Wives by Place of Death and Marriage Cohort

Place of Death	Marriage Cohorts							
	1860–1874		1875–1889		1890–1904		1905–1919	
	Hu	Wi	Hu	Wi	Hu	Wi	Hu	Wi
Wasatch Front								
Mean	71.29	70.29	71.39	71.12	70.94	73.65	73.36	76.50
SD	(13.79)	(16.34)	(13.99)	(16.56)	(14.22)	(16.08)	(14.89)	(15.98)
N	2,392	2,443	4,423	4,743	6,420	6,812	8,642	9,010
Other Utah								
Mean	70.65	67.60	70.09	67.96	70.76	70.04	72.58	74.55
SD	(14.33)	(17.64)	(14.53)	(18.02)	(15.21)	(18.87)	(15.57)	(17.89)
N	2,148	2,140	3,481	3,323	4,342	4,281	5,130	5,046

Mean age at death for husbands and wives is lower for the Other Utah category than for the Wasatch Front category, suggesting a substantial rural-urban difference. The rural-urban difference is much greater for wives than husbands, further suggesting some females were more disadvantaged if they lived and died in rural communities. Over time, that is, across the four marriage cohorts, mean age at death for husbands and wives who died in a Wasatch Front community increases, and the increase is substantially greater for wives than husbands. Consequently the reversal from earlier deaths for wives relative to husbands occurs in the 1890–1904 cohort. The apparent rural female disadvantage is shown by other rural-urban comparisons. The difference of the means for husbands and wives is much greater for the rural category, and the reversal does not occur until the most recent marriage cohort of 1905–19. [21] In this case, one also finds greater values of the standard deviations for the rural women relative to the urban women and for wives compared to husbands.

For the analysis of religious differences (table 6), separate religious codes for the husband and the wife have been used. Religion also has a major impact on survival. Husbands and wives classified as Active LDS (baptized and endowed before death) live substantially longer than the Inactive and the Non-LDS. The Latter-day Saint advantage does not affect husbands and wives equally. The mean age at death of wives is earlier than the mean age of death of husbands among the first two marriage cohorts for each of the three groups classified as Active, Inactive, and Non-LDS. The reversal occurs among each of the three categories in the 1890–1904 marriage cohorts of the Active LDS, although the differences are small.

Interestingly, the Non-LDS live longer than the Inactive LDS. A possible explanation for the earlier age of death of Inactive LDS men and women relative to the Active and Non-LDS is that they may have been concentrated among the group classified as rural. This concentration could have affected both religious classification and longevity. Extreme rural isolation might have prevented the individuals from having access to a temple for endowment purposes. In addition, extreme rural isolation might mean less access to health-care resources.

Table 6
Mean Age at Death, Husbands and Wives, by Religious Commitment and Marriage Cohort

Religious Code	Marriage Cohort							
	1860–1874		1875–1889		1890–1904		1905–1919	
	Hu	Wi	Hu	Wi	Hu	Wi	Hu	Wi
Active								
Mean	71.46	69.83	71.65	70.41	72.33	72.63	73.79	75.79
SD	(13.85)	(16.76)	(14.06)	(16.84)	(14.34)	(16.79)	(14.70)	(16.63)
N	3,875	3,827	6,585	6,637	8,508	8,736	11,145	11,456
Inactive								
Mean	67.26	64.56	67.71	66.38	66.70	68.00	65.02	70.58
SD	(16.25)	(18.75)	(14.77)	(18.97)	(15.09)	(18.87)	(16.08)	(19.45)
N	883	839	1,996	1,916	2,978	2,815	2,881	2,751
Non-LDS								
Mean	68.36	64.89	69.34	68.56	69.11	69.82	72.57	73.08
SD	(15.59)	(18.99)	(14.80)	(18.35)	(15.23)	(18.67)	(14.92)	(18.43)
N	222	314	498	526	794	729	853	672

It is true that more Inactive than Non-LDS died in rural communities, but more Active than Inactive died in rural communities. For example, 40.1 percent of the Active wives died in the more rural communities, 37.0 percent of the Inactive, and 33.4 percent of the Non-LDS. A further test can be made by examining simultaneously the effects of residence and religion.

There are three comparisons that are possible based upon the data presented in table 7: changes over time for each residence and religious group, region-of-death differences over time for each religious group, and husband-wife differences over time for each religious group. One would anticipate that the age of death would increase with each marriage cohort, with the lowest age at death being among those married during the earlier pioneer period. The expected trend of a rising age at death is evident among those who died in the more urban

Table 7
Mean Age at Death, Husbands and Wives,
by Place of Death, Religious Affiliation, and Marriage Cohort

Place of Death of Wife and Religious Affiliation	Marriage Cohort							
	1860–1874		1875–1889		1890–1904		1905–1919	
	Hu	Wi	Hu	Wi	Hu	Wi	Hu	Wi
Wasatch Front								
Active								
Mean	71.99	71.00	72.40	72.10	73.62	74.99	75.01	77.52
SD	(13.54)	(16.01)	(13.68)	(15.84)	(13.77)	(15.22)	(13.85)	(15.21)
N	1,819	1,853	3,117	3,342)	4,355	4,754	6,478	6,905
Inactive								
Mean	64.89	67.65	68.73	68.14	67.64	70.15	66.89	72.91
SD	(14.70)	(17.19)	(14.22)	(18.34)	(14.57)	(17.48)	(14.96)	(17.89)
N	459	424	1,040	1,078	1,579	1,571	1,598	1,681
Non-LDS								
Mean	69.70	69.06	69.97	70.88	70.83	71.85	72.73	74.08
SD	(14.23)	(17.16)	(15.22)	(16.46)	(14.05)	(17.64)	(14.64)	(17.80)
N	114	166	266	323	486	487	566	424
Other Utah								
Active								
Mean	71.44	68.97	70.99	68.98	72.27	71.31	74.40	75.63
SD	(13.62)	(17.19)	(14.37)	(17.43)	(14.76)	(18.07)	(14.62)	(17.03)
N	1,722	1,680	2,580	2,514	3,090	3,145	3,898	3,955
Inactive								
Mean	67.27	63.05	67.02	64.38	66.95	66.26	64.99	69.95
SD	(16.57)	(18.45)	(14.83)	(19.40)	(15.38)	(20.61)	(17.15)	(20.56)
N	337	336	720	648	1,004	941	994	870
Non-LDS								
Mean	68.19	61.26	69.42	66.43	67.38	67.62	74.56	73.36
SD	(16.34)	(18.98)	(14.01)	(19.45)	(16.67)	(20.09)	(14.25)	(18.63)
N	89	124	181	161	248	195	238	221

areas with the exception of the inactive males. In their case, the mean age at death is lower among the last two marriage cohorts compared with the 1875–89 cohort. The lower values for the last two cohorts suggests there may be some loss-to-follow-up (missing death dates) for some Inactive males. That explanation carries some weight because a similar pattern is found among the Inactive rural males. In general, however, the pattern is one of improvement—increasing age at death—over time, and the pattern is more consistent and regular among the wives.

Reflecting the data presented in table 5 above, the mean age at death is generally higher for the more urban husbands and wives than for the rural husbands and wives. In the aggregate, there remains evidence of lower age at death for wives among several categories, but the difference is more clearly indicated by comparing age at death of couples (husbands and wives) in table 8. The female disadvantage marked by an earlier age at death is essentially a rural phenomenon that is reversed among the last marriage cohort. The time factor, however, is important because in the first marriage cohort we find evidence of wives living on average longer than their husbands only among the Wasatch Front Inactive LDS. With that exception, among the 1860–74 marriage cohort, wives on average died at an earlier age than their husbands.

Table 8				
Couple Differences in Mean Age at Death by Place of Death, Religion and Marriage Cohort				
Religion and Residence at Death of Wife	Marriage Cohort			
	1860–1874	1875–1889	1890–1904	1905–1919
Active LDS				
Wasatch Front	0.25	–.64	–2.84	–4.08
Other Utah	2.70	2.72	1.67	–1.32
Inactive LDS				
Wasatch Front	–.43	–.92	–4.40	–7.85
Other Utah	3.67	3.33	0.56	–4.65
Non-LDS				
Wasatch Front	1.61	–.64	–2.12	–3.52
Other Utah	7.57	3.65	1.59	–.99

Summary and Discussion

Mortality among the early pioneer married couples and those married during the early part of this century indicates that the early pioneer experience reduced average age at death. However, the mean age at death for both husbands and wives may appear to be surprisingly high when contrasted with life expectancy in the United States at the turn of the century. For men and women of all races in 1900, the calculated life expectancy at birth was 46.3 years for men and 48.3 years for women.[22] However, for 1900–1902 in the limited number of states where deaths were registered, white males who reached the age of 25 could expect to live an additional 38.5 years, or to the age of 63.5 years, and women at age 25 could expect to live and additional 40.0 years, or to age 65.

If one focuses on life expectancy at birth, between 1900–1902 and 1993, life expectancy of males in the United States increased by 24.9 years, and life expectancy of females by 28.4 years. Life expectancy at age 25 increased by 11.1 years for men and 15.5 years for females. These figures provide a basis for comparing and interpreting the mortality experience of Utah married couples. For the pioneers of Utah who survived to marry, the average number of years husbands and wives might expect to live is only a few years less than contemporary men and women in the United States. The average age of death of men who married in 1860–74 was 72.0 years, and the average life expectancy at birth for white males in the United States based upon 1993 data is 74.6 years; for women the ages are 74.7 versus 80.3. The male-female differences are substantial: 2.7 versus 5.6. These improvements are consistent with our findings that it was the females rather than the males who gained between the first marriage cohort and the last marriage cohort.

A second major finding of our study is that among selected groups women experienced a mortality disadvantage. Especially in the rural areas, women on average died at an earlier age than their husbands. An earlier age of death is more common among the Inactive LDS and the Non-LDS, especially for the rural women. We are not in a position to provide a complete explanation, but there are several possible reasons.

We have noted that the variation around the mean is much greater for wives than husbands. The lower mean values may be in part due to some early deaths associated with maternal mortality—deaths associated with childbirth. In this initial, and preliminary, analysis of gender differences in mortality, we are able only to pose that explanation as a hypothesis to be explored in more detail in the future, although it must be studied indirectly for the women who died before death certificates that included cause of death became available in Utah. For those dying prior to that time, linking time of childbirth with time of death will provide an indicator of what is assumed to be a major factor accounting for the early death of many wives. There are, however, a number of important social factors that also warrant further consideration.

First, the rural population was less likely to have access to improvements in medical facilities and medical practitioners. Second, women carried a disproportionate risk because of the need for shared labor in the rural communities coupled with the burdens of many pregnancies, often close together. Third, women would be expected to bear the major responsibilities for the home and for child care, carrying them out in an environment where the women, more than men working outside of the home, would be exposed to contagious diseases introduced into the household. These conditions may have applied to all women, but the Inactive LDS and the Non-LDS probably experienced greater social isolation and therefore less access to social support systems in the community. Certainly religion was an important factor. The Active LDS men and women lived longer than the Inactive, and the differences are substantial. Lifestyle would certainly have been important, but in addition, community support systems in the case of illness in the family were more likely to have been available to the Active LDS.

The careful as well as the older, casual observer of Utah communities is likely to find the evidence that some groups of women died at an earlier age than their husbands unusual; the number of widows observed in these communities is obvious. Those observations are correct at the same time that the data presented in this paper are correct.

In table 1, we showed that wives were between five and three years younger than their husbands at the time of marriage. Among those groups in which the average age at death of wives was less than the average age at death of husbands, the mean would have to exceed the mean difference in the age at marriage for wives to actually die before their husbands. The point can be made by examining the number of widows and widowers. These numbers are presented in table 9 along with the mean length of potential widowhood for husbands and wives. We use the term potential widowhood because its length is measured between the time of death of the first spouse and the time of death of the husband or wife. Some would have remarried during the years following the loss of the first spouse.

The data presented in table 9 indicate that about 60 percent more wives will die after their husbands, although the age at death may be earlier because of age-at-marriage differences. The data also indicate that either the husband or wife will live for a number of years after the

Table 9
Mean Length of Potential Widowhood, Husbands and Wives, by Marriage Cohort

Husbands and Wives	Marriage Cohort			
	1860–1874	1875–1889	1890–1904	1905–1919
Husbands				
Mean	17.62	17.65	16.89	16.94
SD	(14.50)	(14.89)	(14.23)	(15.32)
N	2,094	3,844	4,922	5,550
Wives				
Mean	17.87	18.37	19.21	19.42
SD	(14.20)	(14.01)	(14.22)	(14.22)
N	2,883	5,231	7,345	9,310

loss of the first spouse. The time spent as a widower declines between the first and fourth marriage cohorts, while the years spent as a widow increase systematically. The difference in these two trends is almost entirely determined by the increasing survival of wives rather than husbands.

The limited amount of data available on the socioeconomic characteristics of the population and the ongoing process of linking death certificates to the files makes the analysis of mortality differences less complete than will be possible in the future as the UPDB is extended. At this time, however, it is clear that the mortality experience of married couples was strongly influenced by four factors: time, gender, residence, and religion. In contrast to modern patterns, pioneer women, especially rural pioneer women, were more seriously disadvantaged by the difficulties associated with the frontier experience. On average, women died at a younger age than their mates, but the changes occurring across our four marriage cohorts indicates that women have experienced a greater improvement in survival rates. The female disadvantage among the pioneer women was, however, more common among those who died outside of the Wasatch Front.

When religious categories are compared, the lifestyle associated with being an active member of the LDS Church is reflected in the fact that the Active died at a later age than the Inactive LDS and the Non-LDS.[23] One may assume that the lifestyle of these latter individuals was much more at variance with the dictates of the LDS Church, which eschews the use of tobacco and alcohol, substances that increase mortality risks.

To summarize the findings in more general terms, one should refer to the data presented in tables 7 and 8. Aggregate statistics such as those presented in table 1 underestimate the cost of the early pioneer experience. The statistics in table 7 present a more accurate picture. A comparison of the data for the 1860–74 marriage cohort with that for the 1905–19 marriage cohort suggests that the pioneer experience cost men who lived long enough to marry approximately three years of life and cost women who lived long enough to marry about seven years of life. The female disadvantage, however, was much greater among the more rural population and, in general, weighed more heavily on the Inactive and Non-LDS during the early settlement years.

Lee L. Bean is Professor Emeritus, Department of Sociology, University of Utah; Geraldine P. Mineau is Research Associate Professor, Division of Public Health Sciences, Department of Oncological Sciences, University of Utah; and Ken R. Smith is Professor, Department of Family and Consumer Studies, University of Utah. The authors wish to thank the Pedigree and Population Resource of the Huntsman Cancer Institute, University of Utah, for providing the data and valuable computing support. This work was also supported by NIH grant AG 13478 (Kinship and Socio-Demographic Determinants of Mortality).

NOTES

1. Peter Laslett, "Necessary Knowledge: Age and Aging in the Societies of the Past," in *Aging in the Past: Demography, Society, and Old Age*, ed. D. I. Kertzer and P. Laslett (Berkeley: University of California Press, 1995), 11.

2. Laslett, "Necessary Knowledge," 27–30.

3. Patterns different from the prevailing pattern of higher male than female mortality are often referred to as "excess female mortality." Ingrid Waldron, "Patterns and Causes of Excess Female Mortality among Children in Developing Countries," *World Health Statistical Quarterly* 40 (1987): 194–210.

4. Based on their analysis of Demographic and Health Surveys, Kenneth Hill and Dawn M. Upchurch, "Gender Differences in Child Health: Evidence from the Demographic and Health Surveys," *Population and Development Review* 21 (March 1995): 127–51, provide the most extensive comparative study of female mortality disadvantages during the childhood years.

5. Lee L. Bean, Masihur Rahman Khan, and A. Razzaque Rukanuddin, *Population Projections for Pakistan: 1960–2000*, Monographs in the Economics of Development, no. 17 (Karachi, Pakistan: Pakistan Institute of Development Economics, 1968), 13, 54–55, 58–61.

6. David V. Glass, "Graunt's Life Tables," *Journal of the Institute of Actuaries* 76, part 1 (June 1950): 60–64.

7. For example, data from the various demographic and health surveys conducted in Egypt show death rates among the young have declined significantly in recent years. However, infant and child mortality rates are higher in the rural areas and especially in the less-developed region of upper Egypt relative to the rates in the urban governorates of Cairo, Alexandria, Ismailia, and Port Said.

Fatma H. El-Zanaty and others, *Egypt Demographic and Health Survey: 1992* (Calverton, Md.: Macro International, 1992), 126.

8. It was not until the 1870s that hospitals were opened in Salt Lake City, and the first public health officer was appointed in the last decade of the nineteenth century. Ralph T. Richards, *Of Medicine, Hospitals, and Doctors* (Salt Lake City: University of Utah Press, 1953), 25, 146. For a summary of medical practices and facilities in America during the late nineteenth century, see Samuel H. Preston and Michael R. Haines, *Fatal Years: Child Mortality in Late Nineteenth-Century America* (Princeton: Princeton University Press, 1991), 3–48.

9. A particularly eloquent description of advantages of living in Salt Lake City is provided by L. Fowler, *In the Shadow of Moroni* (New York: Souvenir Guide Company Publishers, 1895):

> Being a compendium of the various advantages to be derived by living in this Rome of America; in this land of Perpetual Sunshine; the Home of Lilac and Rose vine; the Bower of Mysterious Night Fairies whose soft voices woo one to sweet slumber all the Year 'round.

10. Cause-of-death data from Utah vital statistics are being added to the database, and cause-of-death studies will be possible in the future.

11. A substantial body of literature indicates marriage itself is related to longevity. Among the studies, see Noreen Goldman, "Marriage Selection and Mortality Patterns: Inferences and Fallacies," *Demography* 30 (May 1993): 184–208; Yaunreng Hu and Noreen Goldman, "Mortality Differentials by Marital Status: An International Comparison," *Demography* 27 (May 1990): 233–50; Ellen Eliason Kisker and Noreen Goldman, "Perils of Single Life and Benefits of Marriage," *Social Biology* 34 (fall–winter 1992): 135–52; and Linda J. Waite, "Does Marriage Matter?" *Demography* 32 (November 1995): 483–507.

12. Lee L. Bean, Geraldine P. Mineau, and Douglas L. Anderton, *Fertility Change on the American Frontier: Adaptation and Innovation* (Berkeley: University of California Press, 1990), 98–101; Lee L. Bean, Geraldine P. Mineau, and Douglas L. Anderton, "Residence and Religious Effects on Declining Family Size: A Historical Analysis of the Utah Population," *Review of Religious Research* 25 (December 1983): 91–101; Geraldine P. Mineau and others, "Evolution Differentielle de la Fecondité et Groupes Sociaux Religieux: L'Exemple de l'Utah au XIX Siecle," *Annales de Démographie Historique* (1984): 219–36.

13. The subset of records has been used in other studies: Ken R. Smith and Geraldine P. Mineau, "Effects of Childbearing Patterns on Parental Mortality for Marriages during 1860–1919" (paper presented at the Annual Meetings of the Population Association of America, New Orleans, 1996), copy in possession of Geraldine P. Mineau; Geraldine P. Mineau, Ken R. Smith, and Lee L. Bean, "Has Survival among Widows and Widowers Improved? Trends from 1860–1965" (paper presented at the Population Association of America Meetings, Washington, D.C., 1997) copy in possession of Lee L. Bean. Marriages before 1860 were excluded for several reasons. Most important as a factor related to longevity is that individuals before 1860 included a substantially large number of migrants

who may have been more rigorous, having survived the difficult migration during the early settlement years.

14. Smith and Mineau, "Effects of Childbearing Patterns," 8.

15. Katherine A. Lynch, Geraldine P. Mineau, and Douglas L. Anderton, "Estimates of Infant Mortality on the Western Frontier: The Use of Genealogical Data," *Historical Methods* 18 (fall 1985): 160.

16. The variation (standard deviation) in age at marriage for the first marriage cohort is much higher than among the later cohorts, suggesting that the pool of individuals within which mates were selected may have been quite limited and resulted in both husbands and wives marrying across a wide range of ages.

17. The selection procedure does not unambiguously guarantee that each of the individuals died in Utah. The selection procedure excluded cases in which at least either the husband or wife died out of state. There are some cases in which a spouse died in state but there is no indication of date of death or place of death for the other spouse. These cases are found primarily among the last marriage cohort, and it is assumed that such individuals were still living in 1992. For this reason, the number of cases will be different for husbands and wives in some of the cells of the tables presented in this paper.

18. For a discussion of the use of baptism and endowment as the basis for a scale of religious commitment, see Bean, Mineau, and Anderton, *Fertility Change*, 100–101.

19. Mineau and others, "Evolution Differentielle," 219–36; Bean, Mineau, and Anderton, "Residence and Religious Effects," 91–101.

20. A substantial number of couples—both husbands and wives—were baptized and endowed by proxy after death. These individuals are classified as Non-LDS.

21. A possible explanation for the difference between these groups of women is that women, more than men, might move to an urban community after the loss of a spouse. To eliminate such a possibility, the data were also analyzed only for those couples who died in the same type of community. There is no variation from the pattern demonstrated by the data presented in table 5.

22. Donald J. Bogue, *The Population of the United States* (Glencoe, Ill.: Free Press, 1959), 188.

23. Fox studied mortality during the early decades of the twentieth century using vital statistics and records from the LDS Church to "cull out highly specific diseases" and to show these diseases are low in the Mormon Church because of the avoidance of "smoking, unchastity, or bolting hot beverages." Karl August Fox, *A Critique of Mortality Statistics with Special Reference to Utah* (master's thesis, University of Utah, 1938), 41.

Fig. 1. Wheeler and Child served the needs of the people of Springville, Utah, supplying headstones and undertaking services. Walter Wheeler (left) was a mortician, and his father-in-law, Thomas Child (right), was a monument engraver. Family members in the business over the years include A. H. Child, whose name can be seen on some of the gravestones illustrating this article.

Mormon Cemeteries: History in Stone

Richard H. Jackson

As early as 1693, after one of his frequent visits to a local cemetery, the famed New England minister Cotton Mather reported, "The stones in this wilderness are already grown so witty as to speak."[1] Mather was referring to the effusive praise recorded on the headstone of a fellow clergyman, but he was also implicitly recognizing that the information found in the monuments of a cemetery literally "speaks" to us of past times and people.[2]

As one modern geographer has noted, "Nowhere else . . . is it possible to look so deeply into our people's past."[3] Indeed, each cemetery is an ever changing volume that records the history, values, and dreams of a people and place, and each stone records the life of a real person—a person who lived and loved, laughed and played, cried and prayed, and left behind memories that reverberate through succeeding generations. To those outside the family who erected a specific gravestone, the message from that memorial may be unclear. Nevertheless, careful examination of the entirety of a cemetery provides important clues to our past.

A few articles have analyzed isolated messages from Mormon cemeteries in the Intermountain West.[4] This study documents the full "voice" of the Mormon cemetery and examines its change during the time the Mormons in the Great Basin created their own idiom within the American scene. Examples are drawn primarily from the core area of Mormon settlement in Utah, but other cemeteries in Mormon towns across the West are remarkably similar regardless of their distance from Salt Lake City.

Messages from Cemetery Platting, Condition, and Location

A window into the Mormon culture can be obtained by an analysis of the platting, condition, and general location of Mormon cemeteries.

Like the Mormon village,[5] the Mormon cemetery reflects the Latter-day Saint belief that God is a god of order (see D&C 88:119, 90:18, and 94:6), and Mormon cemeteries, like their cities, are platted in a regular gridiron pattern oriented to their cardinal directions. Literally "cities of the dead," their morphology not only reminds us of the Mormon penchant for order, but also tells something of Mormon eschatology. Cardinal orientation insures that the deceased can be laid to rest with their heads to the west. Mormons, like many other Christian denominations, believe all people will be resurrected, and on resurrection morning, when the dead come forth from their graves, they will face the east, from whence the Savior will come.[6]

The actual condition of the cemetery tells us little more than something of the relative abundance of the resources of a particular area within the Mormon cultural region. Where water is abundant, the cemetery is planted with grass and trees and is landscaped. Where urban growth has resulted from the growing economic strength of the West, the cemetery is maintained by professionals hired by the city. However, in smaller rural communities, upkeep is apt to be solely a labor of love by individuals and families in association with the local Mormon stake or ward.

Cemetery location is another factor that tells us something of a people and their times. The cultural roots of Mormon settlers of the West were predominantly in New England or western Europe, especially the British Isles and Scandinavia. During the sixteenth to early nineteenth centuries in New England and western Europe, cemeteries tended to be located in town, normally in association with the parish church. This location reflected a number of factors, including the concept of the church as a community of Christian believers whose faith included life after death and a spiritual reawakening. In such a milieu, the deceased members of the community appropriately shared the sacred space of the churchyard itself.[7]

Moreover, community life of the time necessitated having the burying ground nearby. Members of the congregation were in many cases charged with the duty of digging a grave, a task that they had to add to their daily labors in fields, shops, or factories. Lack of professional morticians and embalming techniques necessitated a quick burial; because transportation was limited and slow, accessibility of the burial place was important. Finally, the burying ground was used frequently. Life expectancy was low, especially for children, so the graveyard had to be in close proximity—in town for town dwellers, on the homestead for frontier farmers.

While the Mormons were attempting to establish homes and settlements in New England, Ohio, Missouri, and Illinois, a new phenomenon was developing in terms of cemetery location: creation of a burying ground outside of town that was larger and more spacious than the crowded churchyard. Mount Auburn Cemetery, adjacent to Cambridge, Massachusetts, was the first American example. It was modeled after the garden cemeteries that had opened in Paris in 1804 and later in London and Vienna.[8] Similar cemeteries were created rapidly in other U.S. communities. By the time the Saints fled to Salt Lake Valley in 1847, the cemetery was quickly replacing the church burying ground. The change in location also signified a change in the view of death. In fact, cemetery means "sleeping place," and the new American cemeteries were adorned with trees and grass and became places of contemplation and Sunday walks.[9]

Pioneer cemeteries in Utah followed national trends. In Salt Lake City, a large cemetery was located in the foothills to the east, outside the town's platted lots; it is still occasionally used.[10] The first burial in Salt Lake City's variant of the garden cemetery was that of a child: Mary E. Wallace, buried in 1848.[11] Assessment of the location of the remaining pioneer cemeteries reveals little commonality in geographic location except for a preference for elevated locations. The first cemetery was sometimes located within a few hundred yards of the center of the incipient settlement, as at Springville or Spanish Fork, Utah, but not in conjunction with a church. Other times, it was located outside of the community as much as a mile away on a raised elevation, as at Meadow or Spring Lake, Utah. Wherever it was located, each community tried to adapt elements of the garden cemetery, such as trees, paths, roads, and whenever possible a general parklike appearance.

TYPES OF HEADSTONES

The general appearance of the headstones themselves reflects Mormon adoption of eighteenth-century American funerary customs. The headstones can be categorized on the basis of their age, shape, and iconography. The oldest are typically in a tablet form, either as a simple rectangle, a rectangle with rounded top corners, or a rectangle topped with some variant of a semicircle.

The art and text associated with these early headstones is typically part of the American frontier funerary art that Mormon pioneers brought with them from the Midwest. Typical art forms include standard

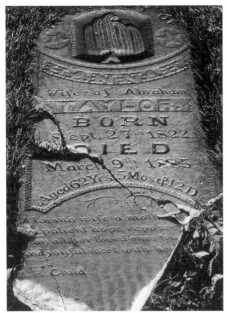

Courtesy Richard H. Jackson

FIG. 2. A willow tree signifies peace, rest, or heavenly protection on the gravestone of Hannah Taylor (1822–1885). The old Springville cemetery.

Christian icons like the lamb (innocence); flowers, especially lilies or roses (for a male or female respectively, although there were departures—either some Mormon survivors were less concerned about funerary practice than about the preferences of the deceased or themselves, or the carver was unfamiliar with the gender association of each flower); willow trees (signifying peace, rest, or protection, as in the Lord covering them; fig. 2); doves (peace); a hand with the index finger pointing to heaven (indicating the deceased's destination); an open book (Bible); clasped hands (fellowship, lasting union); and occasionally gates (symbolizing the entrance into paradise).

A general acceptance of the broader United States customs is revealed also by an analysis of headstones according to the age of the deceased. Whenever the lamb is used as a symbol in the Mormon West, it is restricted almost uniformly to the graves of little children (fig. 3). Very rarely is it found commemorating an adult. Unlike the broader Victorian society of America and western Europe, however, Utah society did not extensively romanticize the child as a symbol of innocence and as the antithesis of the urban industrial world then emerging in Europe and the eastern United States.[12]

The relative frequencies with which other symbols appear indicates that the selection of a specific gravestone symbol was a function of both the time the headstone was erected and personal idiosyncrasies. Headstones for adults buried during the prerail era in Utah tend to be simple tablets rather unadorned by symbols. Most commonly they were engraved with floral or plant symbols accompanying the basic vital statistics of the deceased. Since these headstones were generally the product of local artisans (often the local stonemason who quarried the stone blocks used in home or temple construction or who provided stone fireplace hearths), they tend to surpass other headstones in the variety of lettering styles and carving techniques. But almost all use the symbols found in the eastern United States or other areas settled by British immigrants. Common symbols are a rose or lily, a willow tree, or a garland of ivy or other leaves. Generally, the symbols are small and concentrated at the top of the monument, but over the years, some of the designs became rather ornate. One of these later designs is a double headstone, commonly for husband and wife, adorned with a variety of common American funerary symbols such as the willow, flowers, garlands, and clasped hands (fig. 4).

Courtesy Richard H. Jackson

FIG. 3. A lamb symbolizes innocence on the headstone of a child, Hannah Cook (1863–1866). The old Springville cemetery.

After 1870, obelisks begin to compete with simple tablets in Mormon cemeteries. Obelisks (four-sided gravestones that are wider at the base than the top and that are miniature adaptations of Egyptian obelisks brought to England)[13] are often in several sections (figs. 1, 7). The first is a rectangular base some twelve to eighteen inches wide by eight to twelve inches high. The obelisk's shaft is the second section. Modifications to the obelisk form over the years made them ever more ornate, as the top changed from a simple pyramid form to gabled eaves or rounded shapes and then became a third section forming a representation of a roof extending over the obelisk column proper. One adaptation to the obelisk form is the addition of a granite urn as the topmost ornament. It was either attached via a rod extending into the obelisk or simply cemented onto the gravestone. The urn has a long history in funerary practices; the Greeks placed an honorific

FIG. 4. This double headstone for W. J. Stewart and his wife features flowers, clasped hands, and a willow tree. The old Springville cemetery.

urn at the grave, and the Romans stored the ashes of the deceased in an urn. Urns were widely used on seventeenth- and eighteenth-century English grave markers and became common in the U.S. in the nineteenth century.[14]

Examples of floral or other plant symbols became a part of increasingly ornate headstones as the railroad made mass-produced materials, including headstones, available in Utah after 1869. While symbols such as clasped hands and the upward-pointing finger to indicate that the individual had gone to rest in heaven are occasionally found on hand-carved headstones in Utah before 1869, they are more common after this time. Clasped hands had many meanings in American cemeteries, from the eternal union of husband and wife to the fellowship of a fraternal lodge to the benediction of the church upon the deceased (fig. 5). This American funerary art may have been adopted by some Mormons as a symbol of the eternal nature of marriage and is a widely used symbol on Mormon gravestones, especially those of the late nineteenth century and first half of the twentieth.[15] The clasped hands, which looked about the same from headstone to headstone, are only one of a broad array of funerary symbols that proliferated in Mormon cemeteries as eastern granite quarries began producing headstones with basic artwork for the general American market.[16]

While the Mormons adopted the clasped hands and other examples of American funerary art for their gravestones, they ignored several major cemetery-related trends from the Victorian era. The first was the transformation of the cemetery into a formal, parklike setting in which Victorian ladies and gentlemen could stroll and in which large, impressive monuments became the norm.[17] Mormon cemeteries generally retained a more utilitarian air, with roads, grass, and trees but no curving paths, lakeside vistas, and benches like those in the grandiose cemeteries of the eastern United States. Likewise, the ornate funerary art, sculpture, and structures of Victorian cemeteries in nineteenth-century America are absent. For whatever reason, the Mormons who settled the West adopted primarily those symbols easily reproduced on gravestones while ignoring the more elaborate or ornate statues, sculptures, and structures used elsewhere.

Courtesy Richard H. Jackson

FIG. 5. Clasped hands, a symbol conveying such meanings as eternal marriage, lodge fellowship, and church benediction upon the deceased, varied little in design (compare to the clasped hands in figure 4). These are on the gravestone of John Frischknecht (1829–1894), Manti cemetery.

Notable for their almost complete absence are pictorial representations of the deceased and sculptures or large burial or commemorative structures. Large urban cemeteries of the Midwest and South commonly have sculptures commemorating the deceased or ornately carved stone structures at the gravesite. Depicting infants, soldiers, and other figures, many of these are beautiful art pieces in their own right. Even simple headstones from the nineteenth century in New England or the Midwest often include a likeness of the deceased represented in profile.[18] Mormon cemeteries rarely indulged in such ostentation. Not only were the people themselves characterized by frugality, but they also did not have the requisite cash incomes throughout most of the Mormon occupation of the West. The lack of large expenditures for grave markers may also represent the Latter-day Saint conviction that the deceased has departed for an immortal life, leaving behind only the shell of the body to molder in the grave.

Some early Mormon cemeteries include a few examples of the deceased's idiosyncrasies, such as one grave marker in Manti's old cemetery. Carved like a tree, the stone is an example of the Victorian funerary convention of symbolizing the life of a faithful Christian cut down by death. In the Manti case, however, it is used to commemorate the man's lifework as a logger.

Missing from early Mormon gravestones is the wide use of distinctively Mormon icons, such as the Book of Mormon, angel Moroni, or temples.[19] However, with the completion of the St. George Temple in 1877, temples began to be utilized as a symbol on Mormon gravestones. Dedication of the Manti Temple in 1888 augmented the use of temples on headstones in the southern and central Utah areas. In northern Utah, the same trend occurred with the completion of the Salt Lake and Logan Temples, although clasped hands and other symbols readily available on tombstones imported into Utah Territory continued to be the most common symbols on Mormon headstones until after World War II.[20]

The sheer number of people along the Wasatch Front of course led to the Salt Lake Temple being the most distinctly Mormon symbol on headstones, but the nature of nineteenth-century transportation in Utah expanded the Salt Lake Temple's influence. Until the highway improvements of the 1930s and later, the railroad made it easier to get to the Salt Lake Temple from places such as Fillmore than it was to get to nearer temples such as Manti. Consequently, the Salt Lake Temple is found on gravestones even in cemeteries closer to other temples than to the Salt Lake Temple (fig. 6).

Not until the last half of the twentieth century did customizing headstones with the temple or other personally important symbols begin to dominate gravestone art. Early stonemasons used patterns available in the nineteenth and early twentieth centuries, patterns that depicted traditional Christian funerary art. Thus early use of the temple as a symbol on headstones is relatively rare, and each depiction of the temple is very individualistic.

MORMON EPITAPHS

Epitaphs on the early Mormon gravestones convey a typically Christian message of hope. The most common are simple statements, "at rest," for example, or such statements concerning the deceased's earthly work as "Faithful unto her [his] trust even unto death." Because these are stock sentiments still found in the books of epitaphs available at cemetery monument companies (today's preferred name

Courtesy Richard H. Jackson

Fig. 6. Although relatively rare for this period, the Salt Lake Temple appears more frequently on gravestones than do the other Utah temples. This depiction is on the headstone of Adelaide Bertha Riche (d. 1913), Price cemetery.

for merchandisers of gravestones), they do not reveal whether some untoward events made a person particularly deserving of rest or whether a heroic effort resulted in his or her untimely death.

Longer poems as epitaphs are very common in the nineteenth and early twentieth centuries. One found on many Mormon gravestones of mothers and young children is the following (fig. 7):

> A precious one from us has gone
> A voice we loved is stilled
> A place is vacant in our home
> Which never can be filled.[21]

The pathos of losing a loved one is evident in this verse, perhaps explaining why it is so often chosen. Interestingly, it does not offer any statement about reunification or eternal life, perhaps suggesting that for Mormons, as for other bereaved individuals, the immediate sense of loss is the dominant emotion when epitaphs are chosen. Another epitaph simply states of a six-year-old son, "We miss the bright eyes of our darling child, and the sweet lips that so oft on us smiled."[22]

Other epitaphs suggest more reliance on divine sources for reconciling the death of a loved one. One common verse reads:

> Weep not that her toils are over
> Weep not that her race is run
> God grant we may rest as calmly
> When our work like hers is done.[23]

FIG. 7. On the base of Anna Cederland's gravestone is this commonly used verse: "A precious one from us has gone / A voice we loved is stilled / A place is vacant in our home / Which never can be filled." This headstone is an excellent example of the obelisk style and hometown specifics: "Born at Mapleton Nov. 21, 1891, Died at Springville, Oct. 31, 1903." The old Springville cemetery.

This message clearly incorporates Christian beliefs in life after death and in a divine being, elements that are found in many stock epitaphs used among Mormons as well as members of other faiths (fig. 8).

Christian beliefs are particularly evident in the epitaphs placed on young children's gravestones, a relic of the Victorian emphasis on the innocence of little children:

> A little flower of love
> That blossomed but to die
> Transplanted now above
> To bloom with God on high.[24]

This verse is rich with symbols, from the view of little children as flowers planted in a garden to be nourished and protected by loving parents, to the idea that such little ones are transplanted to a safer "nursery" under the care of God, the ultimate wise and loving parent. Variants of these beliefs are also found on many gravestones of individuals who died in maturity. Such epitaphs emphasize the fundamental Christian doctrines of death, the Atonement of Christ, and the resurrection and eternal life of faithful Christians:

> Here I'm sleeping in the dust
> Till the resurrection of the just
> When my savior Christ shall say
> Arise ye Saints and come away.[25]

Another epitaph has a different Christian emphasis:

> Dearest Mother [or Father] thou hast left us
> And thy loss we deeply feel

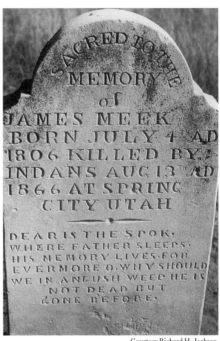

Courtesy Richard H. Jackson

FIG. 8. Mourners often found consolation in their belief in life after death, as revealed in this epitaph. (See also fig. 9.) Also an example of the inclusion of death details, this epitaph for James Meek (1806–1866) expresses how fragile life could be on the frontier of Utah in the 1800s. Spring City cemetery.

But it is God that has bereft us
He can all our sorrows still.

Common in many gravestones, this sentiment implies both fatalism and hope: it was God's will that the deceased died, but He also can help the family deal with the pangs of sorrow.

Other epitaphs reflect the Victorian penchant to use the gravestone as a permanent expression of the deceased's or their survivors' perception of life experiences. For example, one states:

The pangs of life are past
Labor and sorrow ceased
And life's warfare closed at last
His soul is found in peace."[26]

Whose views are represented by this inscription cannot be determined, but clearly life was a challenge if "warfare" is the best adjective to describe it.

Other markers include more specific inscriptions, including information that today might even result in a lawsuit for defamation of character. The Hall obelisk in the Springville cemetery says of their son Nephi (July 29, 1852–November 27, 1872):

Died Nov. 27th from a pistol wound
Inflicted by the hand of Charles Bouldan[27]
Vengeance is mine saith the Lord
AND I WILL REPAY

Either the family believed their son was murdered and the perpetrator was not adequately punished, or they wanted all visitors to know of the vicious deed done to their son. Capitalizing the entire last line of the epitaph emphasizes the family's belief that their son's killer would receive punishment in due time. Without further research, it is impossible to know why he was killed, but the family gives a clue in an ode on the base section of the obelisk:

Angry words are lightly spoken
Bitterest thoughts are rashly shared
Brightest links of life are broken
By one single angry word.

Anger is not the only sentiment commemorated in epitaphs. The gravestone of Edward Koyl Sr. (August 12, 1833–1893?) bemoans the loss of his youthful love and his unhappiness since. The inscription has no date of marriage or death:

The epitaph of Professor Koyl
Sixty years I have wandered,
My life in despair by the loss of
A lover in my 20th year. Four
Trips I have made to California
and the Pacific. Back to Utah I
came to the joys of my youth.
Only to increase the pangs of my
Pain. Farewell to earthly friends
I bid you adieu. My lover on the
Other side I intend to persue [*sic*].[28]

That the author of this epitaph missed someone from his youth is clear, that his life since had not been all that he wanted is apparent, but the epitaph is like an unfinished story—it piques the readers' curiosity, then leaves them hanging. What did the author hope readers would take from the epitaph? That he was a professor? (If so, a professor of what?) Did the loss of his "lover in my 20th year" preclude his marriage? Again it is not clear, for buried next to him are three individuals: "Edward, son of E. and Unice Rosetta Koyl (June 18, 1865–August 15, 1902), Harriet L., daughter of E. and Unice Rosetta [indecipherable], and Rosetta, daughter of E. and Martha Koyl, Jr. (Dec. 2, 1890–Dec. 25, 1908)." Was Edward the son of "Professor" Koyl? If so, was his mother the mysterious lost lover? The age of Edward Koyl would place his birth in the twenty-second year of Professor Koyl. Is there a discrepancy caused by poetic license in referring to "in my 20th year," when in actuality the senior Koyl was in his twenty-first or twenty-second year? Was Unice the name of the "lost lover" or of another wife for whom he cared so little that she was not listed on his headstone? The stone remains silent, refusing to provide any more details to this little mystery from nearly 150 years ago.

By contrast, some epitaphs clearly state the relationship of man and wife, celebrating in immortal stone their lifetime journey together, along with the fervent prayer of their children to once again join them:

They bravely crossed the ocean wide
And here they slumber side by side
This monumental marble stands
Love's tribute from their children's hands
When all the storms of life have passed
May we all meet in heaven at last.[29]

A few epitaphs are distinctively Mormon, primarily because of some unique aspect of Latter-day Saint belief. The graves of two of the four wives of Cyrus Sanford in the Springville cemetery suggest the friendship of polygamous wives, stating, "As wives devoted, as mothers affectionate, as friends ever kind and true." They share a double-arched gravestone, with a willow at the top of one and a finger pointing up to heaven on the other.

GRAVESTONE MESSAGES ABOUT GENEALOGY AND FAMILY HISTORY

The distribution of Mormon gravestones reflects Mormon adoption of eighteenth-century folk customs. Typically, a family plot was purchased at the time of either the cemetery's creation or the death of the first family member. Consequently, even in the oldest Mormon cemeteries, various gravestone types and ages are mingled together.[30] Mormon visitors are thus reminded of the link between the living and the dead.

Gravestones contain more than epitaphs. Cemetery readers will also find information on the vital statistics of the one commemorated, including name, age, and sometimes even a birthplace. The exact details included on the stones vary by time period, reflecting changing custom, cost, and community age. Gravestones of many individuals in the nineteenth and early twentieth centuries record the birthplace of those they commemorate, especially if they were born outside of the United States.

Nineteenth- and early-twentieth-century gravestones in Utah often tell of birthplaces in foreign countries but also reflect a strong regionalism that is evident in statements specifying birthplaces in counties in the Northeast, South, or Midwest (fig. 9): "born in Clinton, Ohio" (Hannah Cox, 1829–96); "born in Livingston County, Illinois" (George A. Gifford, 1867–91); "born in Decalb, St. Lawrence Co., New York" (Happylonas Sanford, 1824–67); "born in Addison Co., VT" (Cyrus Sanford, 1813–1900); and "born in Jamestown, Russell Co., Ky." (Nancy E. Hall, 1826–90). Interestingly, some gravestones contemporaneous with those just cited specify the parts of Utah in which the deceased were born. "Born at Mapleton Nov. 21, 1891, Died at Springville, Oct. 31, 1903" (Anna Cederland, fig. 6), or "born June 18, 1865 in Fountain Green, Utah" (Edward Koyl), are typical references to hometowns that were apparently important.

Birthplace information indicates that most of the early foreign-born immigrants to Utah were from England and western Europe. Bambury, Oxfordshire, England, and Bradford, Yorkshire, England, typify the numerous references to English place names. Other European countries are less frequently cited, reflecting the dominance of British converts to the Mormon Church in its formative years. The British influence is carried over even in the numerous references to birth in "Upper Canada," a reference to the British part of Canada along the Upper St. Lawrence River, as opposed to "Lower Canada," which was French.

Other European countries are less frequently mentioned on gravestones in early Mormon cemeteries unless one is visiting an area that under Brigham Young's guidance was a destination for specific groups of arriving immigrants. References to Iceland as a birthplace are concentrated on gravestones in the Spanish Fork cemetery; the cemetery for the

Courtesy Richard H. Jackson

FIG. 9. Reflecting a strong regionalism, Isaac Allred's gravestone lists the county where he was born in South Carolina. It also expresses a belief in peace hereafter. The old Springville cemetery.

city of Wales in central Utah has many references to the country of Wales; and Sanpete County cemeteries have greater concentrations of references to Scandinavian birthplaces.

Large numbers of markers in some Utah cemeteries, such as those in Helper and Price, mention southern European countries. Many coal miners in Carbon County in the late nineteenth and early twentieth centuries, who were not members of the LDS Church, came to the United States at a time when immigration was dominated by people from southern and eastern Europe. "Born in Montenegro on July 25, 1895" means little to most Americans today, but until it was assimilated by Yugoslavia, Montenegro was a kingdom located just north of Albania. Other indications of southern and eastern European origin include specific place names such as "Corio, Navese, Italy"; inscriptions written in Greek or a Slavic or Romance language, with such text as "Tuka

J Pociva Miru Alois Petrik Rojen, June 20 Leta, 1889, Umarl V Explosion March 8, 1924"; and personal names such as Erramouspe.

A unique early cemetery in Utah is that found at Iosepa, west of Grantsville. Founded in the late nineteenth century as a home for Polynesian immigrants to Utah, Iosepa existed only into the first two decades of the twentieth century. The names on the gravestones there include such distinctive surnames as Hoopiiaina, Nawahine (fig. 10), and Kalauao. The headstones themselves are generally simple but have the traditional early Mormon symbols of clasped hands and floral and other plant motifs. Other than the names themselves, the only distinctive elements are the use of small stones mounded over the grave and the shell necklaces left at the graves by the immigrants' descendants or other visitors. The names themselves are so distinctive that even a casual passerby cannot help but wonder about the story behind the presence of a Polynesian settlement in the Utah desert. Fortunately, the LDS Church has erected a monument, fenced the Polynesian cemetery, and provided a bronze plaque that outlines the history of the settlement.

An unusual message of some early Utah gravestones resulted from a passing fancy of some survivors not only to inscribe the birth and death dates of the deceased in the gravestones, but also to indicate their precise age when they died. "In memory of Thomas Hebbert, born April 10th, 1826, died Mar. 7th, 1898, aged 71 years 10 months and 27 days." Were the survivors concerned that we know that Thomas was almost 72? Or were they just sticklers for detail? Happylonas Sanford died in 1867, "aged 42 yrs. 9 mo & 20 days," while her sister wife in a polygamous marriage died in 1872, "aged 61 yrs 6 mo 29 days."[31] Unlike these two wives, the first wife is remembered only by the dates of her birth and death, leaving the observer to determine for themselves her exact days, months, and years of life.[32] Similar explicitness in age is found in early cemeteries across Utah.

Fads and idiosyncrasies are sometimes revealed in the names recorded on headstones. Elvira, Elmina, Saphronia, Olive, Ovanda, Myrtle, Unice (or more commonly Eunice), Lydia, Rhoda, Tabitha, or Rosetta are rarely heard today, but in a previous century, they competed with Elizabeth, Mary, Margaret, Nancy, and Hannah as names for little girls. Boys' names seem to have elicited less originality, with John, William, Joseph, Samuel, Edward, Richard, George, Thomas, Raymond, and Charles being only occasionally replaced by a Rupert, Cyrus, Warren, or Amos.

Fig. 10. In the desolate Iosepa cemetery, the gravestone of Polynesian immigrant Cecelia Nawahine (1869–1910) teases us with hints of the story of Pacific islanders settling in Utah's west desert.

In boys' names, tradition also exerted a stronger pull than the distinctive names of the role models available to many of the early Utah settlers. Rarely do Book of Mormon names replace biblical or stock European names. It is fairly obvious why the names of wicked figures such as Laban, Lemuel, or Korihor would not be selected by a faithful Latter-day Saint, but even the names of the heroic Nephi, Moroni, Helaman, Mormon, or Abinadi are rarely seen. Names of males and females in early Mormon cemeteries overwhelmingly reflect the broader culture. This reliance on traditional names may reflect the fact that many gravestones in early Mormon cemeteries are those of converts. Their parents used the names of their culture, and even converts may have named their children before joining the LDS Church, perpetuating the traditional Mary, Ruth, Martha, John, Mark, Matthew, or other biblical names.[33]

Visitors are also provided a graphic lesson on genealogy and interesting tidbits of history by simply reading the varied gravestones in a family plot. For example, a headstone in the old Springville cemetery includes on one side of a four-sided stone for Thomas Child (February 11, 1825–November 8, 1910) the following:

> Father, Mother, 4 brothers, 2 sisters are buried in the Methodist Chapel Yard Idel. [*sic*], near Bradford, Yorkshire, England. About 50 rods from the above are laid Lorenzo D. Barnes, First Elder of the L.D.S. Church that died in a foreign land, Dec. 20th, 1842, at Thomas Cordinglys, who came to Springville and was buried in the cemetery in the Spring of 1858. Thomas Child has a brother buried in Bradford Old Churchyard. A sister in American Fork Grave Yard. Also a brother in Salt City Cemetery.[34]

The rest of this headstone includes information about Thomas's wife, Tabitha (June 3, 1824–March 30, 1903), and some memorial verse to remind visitors of the positive view of death held by Thomas or those descendants who erected Tabitha's headstone:

> Shed not for her the bitter tears
> Nor yield to Sorrows regret
> Tis but the casket that lies here
> The gem is sparkling yet

Even the casual visitor cannot but be impressed by the sense of history that caused Child to record the details of the location of his family members' graves. His attention to the death of the "first Mormon missionary" to die in a foreign land is even more interesting. Was Child serving with this missionary? Was that why Thomas Cordinglys later came to Springville to die and be buried? Answers to these questions are not included in the stone, but Child's concern for recording facts about both Elder Barnes and Brother Cordinglys suggests a strong commitment to the LDS Church and its missionary program.

Another message about life in the nineteenth and early twentieth century is unwritten in gravestones but is nonetheless evident to the interested observer—the fragility of life in an earlier age. Birth and death dates for children indicate that their lives were often tragically short (fig. 11). A cursory examination of three headstones in one cemetery revealed the following life-spans: February 18, 1855–February 18, 1855; February 12, 1873–December 24, 1878; 1888–1890; 1887–1893. Individuals die at any age, of course, but in nineteenth-century America, most families could expect to lose children in infancy. Even more poignant to the observer are the clusters of deaths of children in a family or community, as common childhood illnesses claimed the lives of multiple victims within days of one another.

Susan (June 15, 1831–March 9, 1907) and Ira Sanford (September 1828–November 19, 1878) of Springville buried their daughter Sylvia (September 28, 1862–September 1863) after she had lived less than one year but were later blessed with three boys: George (May 22, 1865), Frank (May 8, 1867), and Asa (June 18, 1869). Tragically, all three died in early December 1878 when some disease claimed first Frank (December 1), then George (December 7), and finally Asa (December 11). Was it the same illness that had killed their father two weeks earlier in November? The stones are mute on this point, leaving us only to ponder the pathos that must have marked Susan's next thirty years without her husband or children. Similar personal tragedies abound in the early graveyards of the Mormon West, but intermingled with them are the gravestones of individuals who lived a long, full life, leaving behind numerous children.

Little is generally recorded about the accomplishments of those buried in Mormon cemeteries. Whether the choice of the individual or family or the result of the more or less egalitarian nature of frontier life, few epitaphs note individual interests or positions. Even when such facts are mentioned, the observer cannot always determine what the significance of membership or position in a fraternal organization implies. Eliza Hatfield Thompson (March 11, 1867–November 13, 1908) has on her gravestone that it was "erected by the Women of Woodcraft: Courage, Hope, Remembrance." What was the significance of the "Women of Woodcraft" in the late nineteenth and early

Courtesy Richard H. Jackson

Fig. 11. Life-spans of children were often tragically short, as seen in this headstone for Ovanda Child (1888–1890), "another little angel before the heavenly throne." The old Springville cemetery.

twentieth century? The stones do not say. Occasionally a stone will record that the deceased was a bishop in the LDS Church, seemingly the only position worth noting in most Mormon communities. Presidency of a Relief Society or elders quorum is not mentioned, but rank of any type in a military or a paramilitary organization for men is almost always noted.

Ironically, grave markers of some nineteenth-century Mormon settlers are now being replaced or supplemented by more ornate gravestones or granite slabs that recount each accomplishment of a perceived famous ancestor. "First mayor," "first Marshall," "first teacher," and "Bishop" reflect the braggadocio of a new generation, whose pride in their ancestor's achievements may blind them to the fact that perhaps that individual did all of those things not to glory in them, but to be of service, and that to the ancestor the public display of such accomplishments might have been embarrassing.

Conclusion

Utah headstones and cemeteries are essentially variants of the broader American experience at each time period. Like other cemeteries, they tell us about those buried there, their age, perhaps something of their origins, and, when the deceased were old enough, something of their accomplishments as fathers and mothers, soldiers, and sons and daughters. There are few references to Church accomplishments (perhaps because there are few individuals of heroic stature in the LDS Church, only heroic offices through which good people rotate), and only the symbol of the temple gives visitors a clue to the deceased's Latter-day Saint convictions. The temple has become the distinctive Mormon funerary icon, the litmus test for transmitting the message of Church commitment to descendants. The temple provides eternal proof of faithfulness and an intergenerational permanence to either comfort surviving family members or to eternally validate the deceased.

Early graves were recognized by the settlers of Utah as a place to leave a brief message about their feelings for the deceased and to state something significant about them. Significance might be reflected in the epitaph about a loving mother or child, the missing presence of a child or other loved one, or reference to the birthplace, either to remind the visitor that the individual was not originally from Utah or to express a wish that the survivors recognize their origins.

A frontier economy in Utah did not provide for frills, and large, imposing gravestones or sepulchers are not found in early cemeteries. Utah gravestones, like those of the Midwest, are basically simple. Economics, isolation, and practicality precluded Mormon adoption of the ornate statuary and structures of the Victorian era in funeral art in America. But the messages engraved thereon continue to "speak" to those interested enough to listen.

Richard H. Jackson is Professor of Geography at Brigham Young University.

Notes

1. Quoted in Harriette Merrifield Forbes, *Gravestones of Early New England and the Men Who Made Them, 1653–1800* (1927; reprint, New York: Da Capo Press, 1967), 7.

2. Richard E. Meyer, "Introduction: So Witty as to Speak," in *Cemeteries and Grave Markers: Voices of American Culture,* ed. Richard E. Meyer, American Material Culture and Folklife, ed. Simon J. Bronner (Ann Arbor, Mich.: UMI Research Press, 1989), 1.

3. Terry G. Jordan, *Texas Graveyards: A Cultural Legacy,* The Elma Dill Russell Spencer Foundation Series, no. 13 (Austin: University of Texas Press, 1982), 7.

4. Richard and Susan Oman, Allen D. Roberts, and Richard Poulsen have published short articles that examine the symbolism associated with Mormon structures, some of which are reproduced on gravestones. Richard G. Oman and Susan Staker Oman, "Mormon Iconography," in *Utah Folk Art: A Catalog*

of Material Culture, ed. Hal Cannon (Provo, Utah: Brigham Young University Press, 1980); Richard G. Oman, "Exterior Symbolism of the Salt Lake Temple: Reflecting the Faith That Called the Place into Being," *BYU Studies* 36, no. 4 (1996–97): 6–68; Allen D. Roberts, "Where Are the All-Seeing Eyes? The Origin, Use, and Decline of Early Mormon Symbolism," *Sunstone* 4 (May–June 1979): 22–37; Richard C. Poulsen, "The Handclasp Motif in Mormon Folk Burial," in *The Pure Experience of Order: Essays on the Symbolic in the Folk Material Culture of Western America* (Albuquerque: University of New Mexico Press, 1982), 45–55.

Carol Edison has focused on aspects of headstone symbolism found in Mormon cemeteries or in specific subregions of the West where Mormons comprise the majority population, especially the use of the temple on headstones as a fairly recent folk expression of the Mormon religion. Carol Edison, "Motorcycles, Guitars, and Bucking Broncs: Twentieth-Century Gravestones in Southeastern Idaho," in *Idaho Folk Life: Homesteads to Headstones,* ed. Louie W. Attebery (Salt Lake City: University of Utah Press, 1985), 184–189; Carol Edison, "Mormon Gravestones: A Folk Expression of Identity and Belief," *Dialogue: A Journal of Mormon Thought* 22 (winter 1989): 88–94.

5. Richard H. Jackson and Robert L. Layton, "The Mormon Village: Analysis of a Settlement Type," *Professional Geographer* 28 (May 1976): 136–41.

6. This same belief has resulted in the main doors of Mormon temples being located on the east side of the building, although the main entrance for temple patrons is elsewhere.

7. Edmund V. Gillon Jr., *Victorian Cemetery Art* (New York: Dover Publications, 1972), v.

8. Gillon, *Victorian Cemetery Art,* vii–ix.

9. Gillon, *Victorian Cemetery Art,* vii. The concept that the deceased were resting or sleeping was reinforced by use of both a gravestone at the head of the grave and a smaller plain stone to mark the foot of the grave. Over time, the gravestone became popularly referred to as the headstone, signifying the head of the symbolic "bed" wherein the beloved family member rested.

10. Brigham Young maintained his own family cemetery on the hill immediately north and east of Temple Square; his grave is located there.

11. Interest still exists for stories of the Salt Lake Cemetery. See Dale J. Neilson, "Cemetery Sagas," *Deseret News,* May 25, 1997, L1–L2.

12. Ellen Marie Snyder, "Innocents in a Worldly World: Victorian Children's Grave Markers," in *Cemeteries and Grave Markers,* 11–29. Snyder discusses the symbolic importance of children and how their innocence reinforced the importance of the home in an ever more material world. Ironically, in Victorian thought, a child's death ensured his or her eternal innocence. "Dead children were safe children; ultimately and wholly pure and innocent" (14). Given the high death rate for children in the nineteenth and early twentieth century, of course, such a view provided some comfort for grieving parents.

13. Diana Williams Combs, *Early Gravestone Art in Georgia and South Carolina* (Athens, Ga.: University of Georgia Press, 1986), 95–96.

14. Combs, *Early Gravestone Art,* 92–95.

15. Loren N. Horton, "Victorian Gravestone Symbolism on the Great Plains," *Journal of the West* 33 (January 1994), 70. Horton discusses the symbolism of the clasped hands in the Plains states, giving an example from an 1881 Red Cloud, Nebraska, headstone. I have photographed headstones with the clasped hands in many places, including New Zealand. All date from about the same time period, beginning in the last decades of the nineteenth century and continuing into the twentieth.

16. Poulsen, "The Handclasp Motif in Mormon Folk Burial," 45–55, discusses Mormon use of the clasped hands. Roberts, "Where Are the All-Seeing Eyes?" 22–29, points out that the all-seeing-eye symbol was probably of ancient Egyptian or Hebrew origin and was used extensively in Masonic ritual.

17. See Blanche Linden-Ward, "Strange but Genteel Pleasure Grounds: Tourist and Leisure Uses of Nineteenth-Century Rural Cemeteries," in *Cemeteries and Grave Markers,* 293–328.

18. John Gary Brown, *Soul in the Stone: Cemetery Art from America's Heartland* (Lawrence, Kans.: University Press of Kansas, 1994), provides excellent photographs of Victorian cemetery art. The significance of this art is noted by Dr. Oliver Wendell Holmes (nineteenth-century poet and physician), who stated, "I always take off my hat when I stop to speak to a stone-cutter. 'Why' you ask me. Because I know that his is the only labor which is likely to endure. A score of centuries has not effaced the marks of the Greek's or Roman's chisel." From a pamphlet at the Exhibit of Barre Granite, World's Columbian Exhibition 1893, Chicago, Illinois., as quoted in *Focus* 44 (spring 1994): 34.

19. Victorian funereal art in the United States often includes a side view of an angel flying, although such are not found on Mormon gravestones. Pictures of the angel Moroni figure used on the Nauvoo Temple show a statue carved in a horizontal flying position almost identical to those found on headstones of the time. Don F. Colvin, "Nauvoo Temple," in *Encyclopedia of Mormonism,* ed. Daniel H. Ludlow, 4 vols. (New York: Macmillan, 1992), 3:1001–3, claims that this horizontal position was "doubtless inspired by the prophecy in Rev. 14:6–7." This prophecy refers to another angel flying in heaven and may well be the origin of the idea of an angel flying, but the angel Moroni's remarkable similarity to the angel Gabriel (presumably . . . an angel at least) on headstones of the region may be an equally likely source for the inspiration of the artist who created the angel on the temple. Completion of the Salt Lake Temple more than fifty years later was associated with adoption of a very different view of the angel Moroni, who now appears in a standing position blowing his trump.

20. Edison maintains that "gravestones featuring an image of a Mormon temple. . . began to appear around 1910" and that "the first temple stones displayed a recognizable Salt Lake Temple," but that "for the next fifty years, aside from an occasional metal plaque, the image of the temple was not commonly used on gravestones." Edison, "Mormon Gravestones," 90.

21. A casual stroll through one corner of the Springville [Utah] cemetery revealed this verse on the headstone of both Anna Cederland (November 21,

1891–October 31, 1903) and Hannah Cox (March 6, 1829–October 3, 1896). The author has seen it in many cemeteries both in Utah and elsewhere in the United States.

22. William O. Packard, October 10, 1887–February 17, 1893, old Springville cemetery.

23. This epitaph is found on the graves of many people. A particularly well-preserved example is on the gravestone of Martha Eaton Boshardt (April 23, 1833–January 11, 1907) in the Springville cemetery.

24. This sentiment is found on numerous gravestones in the United States in the late nineteenth and early twentieth centuries. The decline in infant and children's death rates in the post–World War II era makes them less obvious today, yet the couplet is still available in modern funerary art books.

25. William Brumull (Jan. 15, 1852–June 1, 1873), Springville cemetery.

26. From the gravestone of Willard Y. Child (1849–1903) in the Springville cemetery. The gravestone is in poor condition near the ground, making the inscription very difficult to decipher.

27. Or Charles Bouldin; due to weathering, it is impossible to tell if the last vowel in the surname is an *a* or an *i*.

28. Headstone of Edward Koyl Sr., Springville cemetery.

29. Samuel Carter (June 22, 1815–March 6, 1888) and Hannah H. Carter (June 2, 1806–July 24, 1876), Springville cemetery.

30. Unfortunately, newer additions to Mormon cemeteries in the United States reflect the growing cost of labor for maintenance and resultant mechanization of lawn mowing—mechanization that results in standards that dictate use of low or flat monuments that can either be mowed over or easily circumvented. Set in concrete, these stones have the additional advantage that they are difficult targets for vandals who sometimes tip over tall or columnar gravestones.

31. Springville cemetery. The double gravestone appears to date from later than either of the wives' deaths. The husband died in 1900 at age 87, and his first wife died in 1912 at age 97. They share a large ornate obelisk, while Happylonas and Olive share a lovely double-arched, white marble slab that probably dates from the late 1870s or 1880s.

32. Listing the precise days, months, and years of life is found in other America cemeteries in the late nineteenth and early twentieth centuries. It is unclear why this fad emerged or why it subsided.

33. Noel Reynolds cites two studies showing that early Mormon converts emphasized the Bible rather than the Book of Mormon, in part because they did not receive formal training in the Book of Mormon as they had in the Bible. Noel Reynolds, "The Coming Forth of the Book of Mormon in the Twentieth Century," *BYU Studies,* forthcoming.

34. Without checking Church or other records, of course, it is uncertain whether the information given on the headstone about Elder Barnes is correct. The detail included in this epitaph suggests, however, that Thomas Child had some record he or his descendants used in completing the headstone.

PIONEER LIVES

Street scene of Manti, Utah, about 1888–89. George Edward Anderson, photographer.

Fifty Years Building Utah: Joseph Horne's Pioneering Contributions

Harriet Horne Arrington

Building the kingdom and establishing Zion in the Great Basin challenged many talented, innovative men and women, who by their competence, skills, and mastery over the forbidding frontier actually won it. One of these early builders, Joseph Horne Jr.,[1] an 1847 settler in Salt Lake Valley, participated in exploring and colonizing expeditions, helped lead fourteen groups to the valley, rendered service in Salt Lake City ecclesiastical and civil governments, and applied his remarkable skills with tools and animals to clearing land, building homes and meetinghouses, and providing goods needed by early settlers. His well-documented assignments and activities during the fifty years that followed his initial pioneer trek enable us to better understand what was required to settle the Great Basin.

Abraham Hoagland, who traveled across the plains with Joseph and later served as his bishop with Joseph as counselor,[2] admired Joseph's ingenuity and mechanical skill:

> Whatever Bro. Horne's eye can see, . . . his cunning right hand can fashion. . . . Brother Horne was immediate in resource as to the remedy of the ills and ailments to which vehicles and implements are subject, but also marvelously skillful in making the most workmanlike repairs out of the most unpromising materials. In short, a pioneer of pioneers, a worker in wood without a peer.[3]

In spring 1847, about the time that Brigham Young and his advance company left to go west, Elders John Taylor and Parley P. Pratt returned from their missions to England and prepared to take a second group of Saints west in the wake of the vanguard company. Joseph Horne Jr., who had joined the LDS Church in 1836 in Upper Canada, was appointed captain of the first fifty wagons of the second group of one hundred pioneers, the group in which Elder Taylor, his "most precious friend,"[4] would be traveling. To prepare for the trek west, Horne went to the settlements in Missouri and purchased provisions for his family and also for the family of Elder Taylor.

This second pioneer company, led by John Taylor and Edward Hunter, started the journey west on June 17, 1847.[5] The 1,553 people in the company were outfitted with 556 wagons, eighteen months' provisions, seeds, tools, and considerable livestock—2,213 oxen, 124 horses, 587 cows, 358 sheep, 716 chickens, and some pigs.[6] The Horne wagons carried English immigrants Robert and Elizabeth Holmes and the Horne family of six—Joseph, age 36; his wife, Isabella, 29; Henry, 10; Joseph, 5; Richard, 3; and Elizabeth, 1. Robert Holmes had been hired to drive one of the Horne wagons. Because Joseph's trail responsibilities kept him busy, young Henry had to drive Isabella's wagon with two yoke of oxen much of the way across the plains.[7]

Upon reaching the Sweetwater River in Wyoming, the company met Brigham Young and most of the first pioneers, who were returning to Winter Quarters for their families. John Taylor and Edward Hunter "suggested that a feast be made in honor of the Pioneers." Although it was early in the fall, snow fell while the women roasted a steer and cooked other food over the open campfires and while the men "improvised a rude table" by clearing the land upon which the "feast" was laid. The sisters served the meal on their dishes, unpacked for the occasion. Providentially, the storm abated before the meal was served. Isabella recorded that "we had a feast indeed, spiritual as well as temporal," for they enjoyed sermons as well as dancing and food. The leftover food was distributed to Brigham Young's company.[8] The Taylor-Hunter company continued west.

On October 6, 1847,[9] Elder Taylor, who earlier that day had gone ahead into the Salt Lake Valley, returned to assist with the wagons and teams of the Horne group in the final stage of their trek—the dangerous descent down Emigration Canyon. The pioneers had dust on their faces, as Elder Taylor pointed out, and the women's skirts were tattered from rocks, brush, and tree stumps, but the group's exultation about arriving in the valley dispelled any anxiety over their appearance. Although they had no constructed road to follow, the flickering glow of campfires at Pioneer Square across the valley beckoned them warmly as they picked their way over the uneven desert floor in the twilight. The newcomers greeted their friends who had arrived earlier and offered prayers of thanks for their preservation during the arduous

Joseph Horne Jr. (1812–1897). In 1895, when he was 83, Horne posed for a University of Utah art class where his daughter-in-law, Alice Merrill Horne, was a student. He had, she said, "the head of a statesman." She drew this portrait in charcoal on paper 18" x 14". Photograph by Stephen H. Moody.

journey.[10] They were now residents in "The City of the Great Salt Lake," which a "public assembly [had] resolved to call the city."[11]

THE FIRST YEAR IN THE VALLEY

The Horne family lived in their wagon boxes and tents for a few days while Joseph went into a nearby canyon and cut logs to construct a two-room shelter in the fort. Initially the home had dirt floors, a sod roof, and no doors, although it did have two windows, which Joseph had carried across the plains in one of his wagons. Both the Horne and Holmes families lived in this building for the first year, the Holmeses leaving after the harvest in 1848.[12]

Being one thousand miles from a market demanded that growing food receive priority, so Joseph cleared four acres of land and sowed fall wheat. Unfortunately, the family lost one ox and a cow a few days after they came into the valley, and during the winter, the Native Americans took two more oxen. But the settlers were blessed with a mild winter, and they were able to find food by digging up sego roots and wild parsnips in the foothills.[13]

In the meantime, the family furnished their new home, using both imported and improvised materials. On the trek west, the Hornes had brought a small rocking chair and a stove for cooking. Joseph constructed their cupboard by hanging a "large packing box" on poles that extended from holes bored in the walls. In this cupboard-box, lumber shelves were laid to hold supplies. Their cupboard was placed up high so that in a flood the food would be safe. Such a precaution proved wise after a "cloud burst up City Creek Canyon" flooded the cabin's floor with a couple of inches of water. The family also made tables, beds, and stools supported by poles inserted into holes in the wall. A 6' x 4' x 2' bedstead consisted of "strips of rawhide . . . stretched, crossing side to side and head to foot" forming a substantial square base upon which the mattress and coverlet could be laid.[14]

Additional touches to the cabin included calico curtains and "paint" made from lamp black, yellow ochre, and a little skim milk. Isabella used a rag as a brush and "painted" the door and window frames, "which made them more homelike." For light the family used "a little grease in a saucer with a twisted rag in it" to hold the flame.[15]

Without lumber mills in the valley, lumber was scarce. In order to plane lumber by hand, the men dug sawpits: "[They] were made by digging a trench ten feet long and five feet deep, above which trestles were built. The log to be sawed was laid on these trestles. One man stood on top of the log and another in the pit, and pulled the saw up and down." This labored method of forming boards explains why board floors and doors were slow in being added to the cabin.[16]

The ground was full of mice. Isabella remembers that rodents "ran over us in our beds, ate into our boxes, and destroyed much valuable clothing." The Hornes used mousetraps, but they were grateful to pay fifty cents for a cat, which was more effective at control.[17]

Another distraction was the sod roof's tendency to leak for several days following a rainstorm. It was not unusual "to see a woman holding an umbrella over her while attending to her household duties," and after a storm, the surrounding area "presented a ludicrous appearance" with clothing and bedding hanging out to dry. To alleviate the problem, Joseph fastened a wagon cover to the roof over the bed to keep it dry, and he tacked a protective oil cloth above the table when the family ate.[18]

In the spring of 1848, a man from California came through the valley with potatoes. Joseph Horne purchased four small potatoes for fifty cents, cut the potatoes up for seed, and planted the pieces. He used the resulting crop for more seed, finally producing a crop abundant enough for both food and seed. Another traveler came from California with sugar for sale. As Isabella had no sugar, she waited with other women for an hour and a half, succeeding in purchasing a pound of brown sugar for one dollar.[19]

Joseph planted twenty-two acres. His wheat crop was very light, but he raised good crops of corn, oats, and beans. Beets, turnips, carrots, and onions were raised in the gardens. The harvest of 1848 brought an abundant crop of melons, from which Isabella made preserves. From pumpkins and squash she made a syrup, and from cornstalks she produced molasses in her washboiler.[20]

Harvesting grain was a primitive experience on the frontier. Lacking threshing machines and a gristmill, the pioneers threshed and cleaned the grain by several means, including the use of flails. Another method was having horses and oxen walk on grain placed on wagon covers that had been laid on the ground. To winnow and clean the wheat, pioneers would again use the wagon covers, pouring the grain onto them on a windy day. The wind would blow the chaff away, and the heavier grain would be saved.[21]

Joseph's daughter-in-law, Alice Merrill Horne, later wrote of the efficiency of his harvesting skills: "Joseph Horne admitted he could beat his compeers in cutting, cradling, and handling wheat and hay with the 'hand scythes.'" He claimed that "only the Prophet Joseph Smith could chop wood faster than he or could cut, cradle or handle wheat, and hay faster than he could manage it."[22]

The pioneer's hand mills for grinding grain produced a rough product. Leonora Taylor, wife of John Taylor, solved the problem by using a piece of cloth for a sieve to prepare a "fine flour."[23] Resourcefulness, economy, and home industry helped to sustain the Hornes and other pioneers in this early period in the valley.

Isabella Horne recorded one of the few pioneer accounts of the famous cricket episode when seagulls saved the settlers' crops. She recounted, "It appeared all would be destroyed." In their distress, "the Saints united in calling upon the Lord in mighty faith, and He came to the rescue by sending large flocks of seagulls to devour the crickets and save us from starvation. It was one of the greatest miracles of this dispensation."[24]

In the fall of 1848, Elder John Taylor proposed a "harvest feast of thanksgiving and praise to God for His blessing and protection over us in these valleys." The pioneers constructed a bowery, under which the long tables were set for their banquet, and they gathered from their fields decorative sheaves of wheat and corn, which they garnished with wild flowers. Their meal consisted of beef and fresh fruits and vegetables, all of which gave the settlers a representative harvest banquet. At the head of each of the four tables presided one of the pioneer leaders—Presiding Bishop Edward Hunter, Elder John Taylor, Joseph Horne, and Lewis A. Shurtliff. Far from civilization but justly at "home," the pioneers were properly thankful.[25] Joseph felt grateful that he not only had provided adequate food for his family, but also had kept them in shoes he had made himself.[26]

The land that Joseph cultivated in 1848 was partly city and partly Church property that those agencies now desired to use, so Joseph was given fifteen acres west and northwest of the Church farm. He proceeded to clear and cultivate his land, and in March 1849, he moved his log rooms in the fort out to his city lot, which was two blocks southwest of Temple Block. This move placed them in the Salt Lake Fourteenth Ward, which had been organized the month before. The ward contained nine ten-acre blocks, and its boundaries were North Temple, Main Street, Third South, and Second West. Members of the Fourteenth Ward in 1849 included seven Apostles: Parley P. Pratt, Orson Pratt, John Taylor, Wilford Woodruff, Willard Richards, Amasa M. Lyman, and Franklin D. Richards. The first bishop of the Fourteenth Ward was John Murdock, who was succeeded by Abraham Hoagland. In 1852, Hoagland appointed Joseph Horne one of his counselors, a position Joseph held until 1861.[27]

The Fourteenth Ward saw the first Sunday School in the valley organized on December 9, 1849, at the home of Richard Ballantyne. Joseph Horne actively assisted Ballantyne in preparing the special facilities for this Sunday School—a large room with special benches—and in teaching the weekly lessons, which formally educated the frontier youth in the scriptures and Christian concepts. Two of Joseph and Isabella's sons were in the initial class and, along with the other students, provided their own scriptures. The Sunday School was so successful that attendance grew to fifty within a year, too large a number to handle in Ballantyne's schoolroom. The students were divided into separate classes, and the Sunday School was moved into the Fourteenth Ward meetinghouse when that building was completed in 1852.[28]

EXPLORATIONS

President Brigham Young "intended to have every hole and cor-ner from the Bay of San Francisco to Hudson Bay known to us."[29] These words formed the core of Brigham's Young's assignments to the "frontiersmen" who were called to explore the Great Basin. Immi-grant converts were on the seas and on the plains, and the Church needed to identify areas for settlement to receive the immigrants when they arrived. The frontiersmen were to map and evaluate potential sites for settlement. Such exploring parties became part of the rhythms of pioneer life.

In August 1849, Joseph Horne, Dimick B. Huntington, W. W. Phelps, and Ira Willis were appointed to explore the Sanpete Valley. On this trip, the explorers both determined the site for the settlement of Manti, 123 miles from Salt Lake City, and dedicated the land for that purpose.[30] Settlers were sent to Manti the subsequent November.[31]

On November 20, 1849, Horne set off again, this time with Parley P. Pratt's exploring company, which was comprised of five units of ten men each. Their mission was to explore "southward, to the outside of the Rim of the [Great] Basin."[32] Joseph Horne was selected captain of the third ten.[33] Many of the company's daily experiences as de-scribed in the journal of Isaac Haight were copied into the Journal History of the Church:

> Friday, Nov. 23 [1849]. The Southern Exploring Company, numbering about fifty persons, met at John Brown's residence on Cottonwood Creek and organized. . . . The company had with them 12 wagons, 1 carriage, 24 yokes of cattle, 38 horses and mules, an odometer to measure distances, a brass field piece, small arms, 7 beeves, also 150 lbs. of flour to each man, besides crackers, bread, and meal.[34]

By December 3, the company had traveled along Hobble Creek, descended into Juab Valley, where they noted rich feed,[35] and arrived at the new settlement of Manti:

> [December 3, 1849] Snowing nearly all the past night. . . . At 1 P.M. arrived at the San Pete settlement, which consisted of one house, and about 46 families in wagons and tents. Fired off the can-non and sang "Some fifty Sons of Zion," "All is well," and "Come all ye Sons of Zion," while passing the wagons and tents. Crossed the creek, 13 feet wide, 15 inches deep, rocky bottom, and camped on the south bank.[36]

They continued onward, following "Indian trails and [Charles] Shumway's track" until reaching their camping place on the Sevier River. Haight made these observations of the area:

> Many willows and some feed. . . . The Sevier is a noble river, several feet deep, with a sluggish current, and having much the appearance of the Jordan, but considerable larger. It is apparently navigable for small steamers, but its valley and the country . . . is mostly a desert.

> Captain Walker and another Indian rode into camp. [Walker] told Parley P. Pratt not to pass over the mountains southeast, as there was no good country over there.[37]

On December 10, they recorded twenty-one degrees below zero and the river frozen. They crossed the mountains and "found a good ford, . . . with more and better feed and dry bushes for fuel."[38]

On December 12, they descended into Mary's Vale: "No Indian nor Spanish trail was visiable [*sic*] to the company," but some hunters said it was a great deer country. The company found deer tracks and "put up a board marked '200 miles from G. S. L. City.' "[39] By December 16, the company were proceeding toward the Little Salt Lake Valley in subzero temperatures. The trail was difficult, broken up by "a succession of canyons." When faced with snow and "places [where] the horses could not pass," the men "had to dismount and make a track by stamping" in order to proceed. By nightfall, "the brethren were cold and tired with wading through the deep snow, holding the wagons back, and pulling the oxen and wagons up steep pitches."[40]

On December 18, the wind was piercing, "nearly tear[ing] off the wagon covers." The company continued to traverse steep mountains and ravines, where the snow was deep and drifting. Their sufferings were intensified by the lack of water and feed for the animals. They felt forlorn:

> Parley P. Pratt, Richard Campbell, Dan Jones, and William Wadsworth assembled in the carriage, and sang and Parley prayed the Lord to forgive The camp for their vanity, folly and wickedness and not to hedge up the way, but enable them to find a pass and get out of the mountains and to ask him also to treat the camp kindly, for the sake of those among them who kept his names sacred and sought to fulfil their missions. Schyler Jennings swore at Capt Jones, in God's name, telling him to take his horse from his wagon, and threatened him with club in hand.[41]

On December 23, they "struck [the] California road" and decided that the area could be the home for fifty to one hundred families. A part of the camp went down to the Rio Virgin. Joseph Horne and Isaac Haight on December 30 explored a main canyon, finding that "the bottom was wide and practicable for a good road, having a gradual ascent to the head of the canyon" and that it contained "pine timber fit for any purpose." On December 31, the company reported:

> The Wahsatch [*sic*] range . . . terminates in several abrupt promontories, the country . . . showing no signs of water or fertility, . . . a wide expanse of chaotic matter presented itself, consisting of huge hills, sandy deserts, cheerless, grassless plains, . . . and various other elements lying in inconceivable confusion—in short, a country in ruins.[42]

Haight records that in the evening David Fullmer "made some very good remarks on the necessity of laying aside our folly and living in such a manner that we should not be ashamed to have angels come into our midst and behold our acts." In the same entry, the journalizer reveals, "We are in the habit of meeting every evening for prayer and singing, upon which occasion we enjoy ourselves as well as we can deprived as we are of the company of our wives and children." Some Native Americans served as guides as they explored the Santa Clara area.[43]

On January 8, 1850, a liberty pole was erected in what they called the Little Salt Lake Valley. There they had a dinner, described by Isaac Haight: "It was truly an interesting scene in the wilderness where white men's foot had never trod before to see a table spread with roast beef, mince and pumpkin pies, and apple sauce, etc."[44] The men had accomplished their mission and were ready to return.

Two weeks later, Parley P. Pratt and about twenty men, including Joseph Horne, left the main camp on Chalk Creek (present-day Fillmore) and started for Great Salt Lake City. The remainder of the company were to spend the winter at Chalk Creek.[45]

Parley P. Pratt's journal describes the difficulties Horne and his compatriots suffered on the return journey. January 22, 1850: "Commenced our wallowing in the snow. We made about nine miles." January 23: "The men went ahead on foot, the entire company, men and animals, making but one track. . . . Camped in a mountain pass, thirteen miles south of the Sevier River." January 24: "Waist deep in snow. . . . We made fires, spread our blankets, and sank down to rest, being entirely exhausted—our animals tied either to cedar bushes without food, or wallowing up the hills in search of bare spots of bunch grass." January 25: "We passed through Round Valley [now Scipio]. . . . It was still snowing." January 26: "In the morning we found ourselves so completely buried in the snow that no one could distinguish the place where we lay. . . . I raised my voice like a trumpet, and commanded them to arise; when all at once there was a shaking among the snow piles, the graves were opened, and all came forth! We called this Resurrection Camp." January 27: "Our provisions being nearly exhausted, [an advance group hurried on to Fort Utah (now Provo)] some fifty miles distant. . . . We started at daylight, breaking the way on foot. . . . Camped at eleven at night on Summit Creek, extremely hungry and feet badly frozen. We built a small fire." January 28: "Arose long before day . . . entered Provo at dark; raised a *posse* of men and animals, with provisions, and sent [them] back same night."[46]

Rushing a rescue party back proved to be wise, for the day before they were rescued on January 29, Isaac Haight, who had remained with the Chalk Creek camp, wrote the following: "Thermometer registered 30 deg. below zero. We almost perished with cold. . . . Had a little flour stirred in boiling water." Upon returning to Provo, Haight wrote, "Our hearts burned with gratitude to God for delivering us from starvation and death."[47]

On January 30, Horne and the others arrived safely in Salt Lake City; they found their families alive and well. "So the Lord has brought us safely home after suffering much hardship," wrote one participant.[48] As soon as he could, Joseph began to build an adobe house for his family, getting lumber from the canyon and completing their home in summer 1850.

The following November, Horne was called to go with a company under the leadership of Apostle George A. Smith to establish the Iron County Mission settlement at Parowan. The group consisted of 119 men and some families.[49] Arriving at Fort Utah on December 15, George A. Smith assembled the group around the campfire to instruct them on how to conduct themselves:

> I hope our ears will not be saluted with any profanity . . . or taking the name of the Lord in vain, or gambling, etc. We are going to build up the Kingdom of God; prepare the way for the gathering of the Saints and establish Zion. We should act as consistent [with principles] as though we were preaching the Gospel. The Sabbath should be observed. . . . We do not want a mean man to settle in Iron County.[50]

At his request, all Saints settling in Parowan were rebaptized, a not uncommon practice among LDS colonizers.

The full company of the Iron Mission arrived at Parley P. Pratt's liberty pole on January 13, 1851. On January 14, an exploring party including Joseph Horne departed, traveling to Summit Creek and meeting Captain Jefferson Hunt, who was returning from California with seven or eight brethren. Friday, January 17, 1851, an election was officially held in Little Salt Lake Valley with Joseph Horne elected as assessor and collector. The men proceeded to build a fort, clear land for farming, and "build a city." George A. Smith advised the settlers "to only fence the land you were going to farm." Joseph Horne promptly built a log house, the first house in Parowan, which was the name given to their settlement. It was immensely satisfying to Joseph that he was able, as required several times in his life, to "go into the woods with a saw and axe, chop down trees, set up logs on a predetermined lot and presently step out of the door of my own house built entirely with my own hands with the aid only of that good saw and stout axe." He sold his first house in Parowan to another settler whose wife was ill and built a second house, cultivated fifteen acres of land, and fenced it.[51]

When Brigham Young arrived on a visit to Little Salt Lake Valley in May 1851, he advised Horne he could exchange his improvements in Parowan with someone who wished to take a family there. He could then return to Salt Lake City for the birth of his ninth child. Joseph did exchange his property for Jonathan Pugmire's property in the Salt Lake Seventh Ward. As Joseph's improvements in Parowan—grain and land and buildings—were valued at $500, Joseph also paid Pugmire $450 in livestock and cash.

Because Horne had rented his Salt Lake City farm for the year 1851, he went to work as a mason and built a house for John Taylor's family, paid through the tithing of Elder Taylor's friends, as Taylor was on a mission in France. Joseph completed the house that fall. During winter 1851–52, Horne hauled wood from the canyon, made shoes, and worked on construction. In the spring, he resumed farming and did some masonry work during the summer.

The Sugar Enterprise and Public Works

When Elder Taylor returned from his mission in August 1852, he commissioned Joseph to go east to meet the Deseret Sugar Company train, which was en route to Utah with equipment purchased in France.[52] Joseph started August 20 on horseback, met the train at Independence Rock, found they needed more teams, returned to Salt Lake City, reported the situation, and went back to the train with fifty yoke of cattle. He made a second round trip to the city for additional teams and provisions to help the group with the steam boiler, meeting them near Bear River.

With the equipment in the valley, Elder Taylor engaged Joseph to superintend the business of installing and working the machinery to manufacture beet molasses on Temple Block. Joseph was occupied with this work during most of the winter of 1852 and 1853. During this period, he was also elected a member of the Salt Lake City Council.

In the spring, Joseph was again engaged in farming. In June, Brigham Young called on him to substitute for A. O. Smoot in building a sugarhouse about four miles south of the city. Smoot had been seriously hurt by an explosion of a keg of gunpowder, which prevented him from attending to the sugarhouse for several weeks. After Smoot's recovery, Joseph resumed his own business.

In November 1853, Brigham Young asked him to prepare a house on Temple Block for a beet-molasses manufacturing operation. Joseph worked on this project during the winter of 1853–54.

Joseph continued his work on public projects in 1854. He spent some time at the sugarhouse during the winter of 1854–55 and then returned to Temple Block, where during the years 1854–58 he superintended the tithing labor and teamwork. In April 1856, Joseph, still on the city council, was appointed city watermaster. Horne remained at the Public Works until winter 1858 and continued as a member of the city council until January 1858.[53]

Joseph Horne was also a supporter of many enterprises in which he was not personally involved. For example, Brigham Young decided to establish a series of way stations to assist the thousands of immigrants who "gathered" to the Salt Lake Valley each summer and fall. The Brigham Young Express and Carrying Company, as it was called, secured the government contract to carry the mail to Utah, established a pony express system, and built way stations at six new locations. The heavy investment of men, livestock, and provisions was funded by donations from many private citizens. Among the four hundred persons listed in the company's ledger as making donations in 1857 to further the enterprise was Joseph Horne, who made several donations, including $50 of tithing-office pay.[54]

PLURAL MARRIAGE

In the fall of 1856 occurred the often misunderstood Mormon Reformation, when Church leaders urged moral and spiritual principles with great intensity and when individual members were asked to search their souls to discover and cast out sources of evildoing and thinking. Hundreds of sermons were delivered throughout the territory, individual homes were visited, and members were catechized on their worthiness. Nearly everyone was rebaptized, and officers exacted pledges of conformance with Church practices. As a result, that year many men who previously had resisted plurality were sealed to one or more plural wives.[55] Joseph Horne was of these men.

On November 30, 1856, after twenty years of marriage to Isabella and with Isabella's approval, Joseph married Mary Park Shepherd; Brigham Young officiated. A second woman, Elizabeth Ashford, was sealed to Joseph Horne, perhaps on the same day, but this may not have been a connubial marriage—there were no children from that marriage, and Elizabeth had apostatized and left the territory by 1860.[56]

Twenty years old at the time she married Joseph, Mary Park (her godmother's name) was a recent immigrant from England. Shortly after arriving in the valley, she had gone to work for the John Taylor family at their home at English Fort (Taylorsville). It was there that she met Joseph Horne, who visited the Taylors frequently. Joseph built a home for Mary on the corner of First South and Second West in the Fourteenth Ward, next to Isabella's home.[57]

William Wallace Horne, a grandson, said concerning these neighbor wives, "Life was not easy for either Mary or for Isabella, under the new conditions, or for Joseph, either. . . . Both of these women were proud and independent, intelligent, refined, yet resourceful, . . . patient and kind."[58] Mary Shepherd bore Joseph Horne ten children; Isabella had fifteen children, including three sets of twins.

THE HEBERVILLE MISSION TO GROW COTTON

In 1858, Joseph Horne was placed in charge of a group of eighteen men sent to southern Utah to establish an experimental cotton farm at the junction of the Santa Clara and Virgin Rivers, near present-day St. George. The company left on January 26, 1858, with a letter of instructions from Brigham Young and also letters to the bishops in the southern settlements asking them to supply Horne's company with provisions, horse feed, and supplies. Joseph kept a diary of this assigned experiment to raise cotton, which occurred well before the Cotton Mission of 1861 to 1867.[59]

Joseph located his expedition at the site of Heberville, constructed a corral for stock, and was visited and helped by friendly Native Americans. He put in a dam, cleared land, planted crops, hauled logs and rock for a house, built a bridge, and set out peach trees. He detailed in his diary some of the other tasks facing the new settlement: the effort to get water on the land; the harvest of vegetables, cotton, corn, and sugarcane; and the production of molasses. He directed celebrations, held a religious conference in Santa Clara, and in November 1858 delivered 575 pounds of ginned cotton and 160 gallons of molasses to the General Tithing Office in Salt Lake City. While there, Joseph joined a prayer circle presided over by Elder Taylor. Whenever the Apostle was requested to meet with the First Presidency in their prayer circle, he put Joseph in charge of the John Taylor circle.

Horne returned to Heberville with eight men and his plural wife Elizabeth on March 18, 1859. They built a house, replaced the dam and canals that were filled with mud and trash, survived malaria, and returned to Salt Lake Valley with more cotton and molasses on November 30. Horne's two-year cotton mission was a success—cotton could be successfully produced in Utah's Dixie.

The next winter and spring, Joseph built a molasses mill in Salt Lake City and superintended the erection of a schoolhouse, of which he was trustee. He built a cider mill and for a period, as a trustworthy Latter-day Saint, was in charge of the city's brewing company, which made alcohol and brandy for medicinal purposes and visiting officials.

On June 4, 1860, Horne accompanied Brigham Young and other Church officials on about a three-week tour of northern Utah settlements. They visited Farmington, Ogden, Brigham City, and Cache Valley. The company included thirty carriages, one hundred men, and some women and children. During the remainder of 1860, Horne spent time at the sugar factory. He produced molasses and also erected another schoolhouse, perhaps this time for John Taylor's family.

On April 5, 1861, Horne was called to be in charge of a company sent out by the Church to meet immigrants at the Missouri River and take them to the Salt Lake Valley. He left April 24, accompanied by his son Richard S. The company numbered 54 wagons with four or five yoke of oxen to each. On May 19, they reached Independence Rock, where they camped for the night. He completed his mission, returning the immigrants to Utah by fall. He was captain of another company that conducted a similar "down and back" trip in 1862. He told his daughter-in-law Alice Merrill Horne he completed fourteen assignments "recrossing the Plains" for the Church. He said of these trips, "One might think it was hard but there was such a great deal to be learned from the many highly intelligent emigrants in the companies I headed."[60]

THE LAST YEARS

Information about Horne's last thirty years is sketchy. As a member of the Nauvoo Legion, he took part in the Black Hawk War of 1865–67. Joseph Horne was made a member of the Salt Lake Stake High Council June 4, 1873, which appointment he held until he was ordained a patriarch by the First Presidency on March 18, 1890. In 1878 he was elected as Salt Lake City justice of the peace and judge of the Petty Court, an office he held for six years. He also was chaplain of the State of Deseret legislature for a period. In 1888 he moved to a new home he had built at 146 Third Avenue. With the move, he left the Fourteenth Ward for the Eighteenth Ward.[61]

Because his cattle and horses were fat and sleek, Salt Lake community leaders appointed him estray pound keeper, a position he held four years. He commented that "the owners of lost stock were quite willing to pay for the keep of their stock when they were returned in good condition."[62]

In a recently discovered document, Joseph depicts his life from 1887 to 1888. At seventy-five, Joseph Horne still wrote with a firm, steady hand. He mentions the concern of his family for his safety in eluding the government agents seeking to prosecute polygamists. He busied himself with letter writing and projects in whichever house or region he was temporarily residing, biding his time until he could return home but keeping wholesomely active. He began to mention the effects of trigeminal neuralgia, a major facial nerve pain, which he refers to during the two-year period this holograph covers, mentioning that when the pain was acute he could still get some sleep with the help of morphine pills.[63]

In February 1888, upon returning to Salt Lake City from travels to San Francisco, the Utah town of Oasis, and other locations, Joseph Horne mentions his return to activity in the John Taylor prayer circle, which usually held meetings each Sunday. During the total period of his membership, he attended 1,070 of the circle's 1,852 meetings in spite of absences due to calls to serve outside of the valley and to his self-imposed exile. In 1895 "in commemoration of his long and faithful association therewith and of his retirement from the active Presidency thereof in his old age," Joseph was presented with a document, *A Token of Love from the Members of the John Taylor Prayer Circle to Patriarch Joseph Horne, in commemoration of His Long and Faithful Association Therewith, and of His Retirement from the Active Presidency*

Thereof in His Old Age, detailing the history of the prayer circle and his long membership.[64]

Horne died in 1897. He had spent fifty years in the Great Basin supporting civic projects, serving in the government, and building the kingdom of God. At his funeral services on Temple Square, President George Q. Cannon, who crossed the plains in 1847 in Joseph Horne's fifty, offered this eulogy: "I thought Joseph Horne was the most remarkable man I had ever known, and I have never changed my mind. . . . He was the most intelligent and best informed man in the company."[65]

Harriet Horne Arrington, a great-granddaughter of Joseph and Mary Park Shepherd Horne and granddaughter of George Henry and Alice Merrill Horne, is a biographer and historian in Salt Lake City.

NOTES

1. The principal sources on the life of Joseph Horne are Andrew Jenson, *Latter-day Saint Biographical Encyclopedia: A Compilation of Biographical Sketches of Prominent Men and Women in The Church of Jesus Christ of Latter-day Saints,* 4 vols. (Salt Lake City: Andrew Jenson History, 1901–36), 1:806–77; Clara Horne Park, *Joseph Horne: Pioneer of 1847* [Salt Lake City: Privately published, 1961]; Alice Merrill Horne, "Joseph Horne, Utah Pioneer of 1847," typescript in the author's possession; Frank Esshom, ed., *Pioneers and Prominent Men of Utah* (Salt Lake City: Utah Pioneers Book Publishing, 1913), 942; Joseph Horne, Diary, 1858–1861, holograph, Archives Division, Historical Department, The Church of Jesus Christ of Latter-day Saints, Salt Lake City (hereafter cited as LDS Church Archives); and Joseph Horne, Diary, 1887–1889, typescript of holograph, in the author's possession. These are the sources for all the material in this paper except those items given separate reference. Direct quotations will be referenced in these and other sources from which they came.

2. Park, *Joseph Horne,* 26.

3. Park, *Joseph Horne,* 28.

4. Alice Merrill Horne, "Joseph Horne," 4. John Taylor had been Horne's neighbor in Upper Canada. In Nauvoo he had adopted Horne by having him sealed to the Taylor family. See Gordon Irving, "The Law of Adoption: One Phase of the Development of the Mormon Concept of Salvation, 1830–1900," *BYU Studies* 14 (spring 1974): 294–95. See also Nauvoo Sealings and Adoptions, 1846–1857, Book A, microfilm of holograph, Family History Library, The Church of Jesus Christ of Latter-day Saints, Salt Lake City.

5. "They Came in '47," in *Heart Throbs of the West,* comp. Kate B. Carter, 12 vols. (Salt Lake City: Daughters of Utah Pioneers, 1936–51), 8:424; Park, *Joseph Horne,* 13.

6. Park, *Joseph Horne,* 14; William E. Hunter, *Edward Hunter: Faithful Steward,* ed. Janath Russell Cannon (Salt Lake City: Mrs. William E. Hunter, 1970), 91; B. H. Roberts, *The Life of John Taylor* (1892; reprint, Salt Lake City: Bookcraft, 1989), 188.

7. Park, *Joseph Horne,* 14; "They Came in '47," 8:424; Alice Merrill Horne, "Joseph Horne," 3.

8. M. Isabella Horne, "Pioneer Reminiscences," *Young Woman's Journal* 13 (July 1902): 293. Isabella's recollections contained in this article are reprinted in Preston Nibley, comp., *Faith Promoting Stories* (Independence, Mo.: Zion's Printing and Publishing, 1943), 65–71; Hunter, *Edward Hunter: Faithful Steward,* 94–95; Roberts, *Life of John Taylor,* 190.

9. Isabella Horne, "Pioneer Reminiscences," 293; Mary Isabella Horne, "Home Life in the Pioneer Fort," in *Our Pioneer Heritage,* comp. Kate B. Carter, 20 vols. (Salt Lake City: Daughters of Utah Pioneers, 1958–77), 9:107. "They Came in '47" says they arrived September 29 (see 8:424).

10. Isabella Horne, "Home Life in the Pioneer Fort," 9:107.

11. The name was decided in a meeting held August 22, 1847. Edward W. Tullidge, *Life of Brigham Young; or, Utah and Her Founders* (New York: n.p., 1877), 183.

12. Isabella Horne, "Home Life in the Pioneer Fort," 9:107; Mrs. Joseph Horne [Mary Isabella Horne], "Migration and Settlement of the Latter-day Saints," manuscript, Bancroft Library, Berkeley, California, 11. I have access to the eighteen-page typescript Leonard Arrington has made.

13. Isabella Horne, "Home Life in the Pioneer Fort," 9:109.

14. Isabella Horne, "Pioneer Reminiscences," 293.

15. Isabella Horne, "Pioneer Reminiscences," 293.

16. Isabella Horne, "Pioneer Reminiscences," 293.

17. Isabella Horne, "Pioneer Reminiscences," 294; Isabella Horne, "Home Life in the Pioneer Fort," 9:107.

18. Isabella Horne, "Pioneer Reminiscences," 294.

19. Isabella Horne, "Pioneer Reminiscences," 294.

20. Isabella Horne, "Pioneer Reminiscences," 294.

21. Isabella Horne, "Pioneer Reminiscences," 294–95.

22. Alice Merrill Horne, "Joseph Horne," 4.

23. Isabella Horne, "Pioneer Reminiscences," 295.

24. Isabella Horne, "Pioneer Reminiscences," 294. This article is taken from a speech presented by M. Isabella Horne, "Their First Year in the Valley," at the World's Congress of Representative Women, which was held May 15–21, 1893, at the Columbian Exposition in Chicago. Jeanne Madeline Weimann, *The Fair Women* (Chicago: Academy Chicago, 1981), 531. One of the sessions was conducted by the LDS women representing the Relief Society. Isabella was one

of the speakers of that session, appointed by the Relief Society General Board to represent their charter-member organization in the National Council of Women. See also Carol Cornwall Madsen, "'The Power of Combination': Emmeline B. Wells and the National and International Councils of Women," *BYU Studies* 33 (1993): 650–54.

25. Isabella Horne, "Pioneer Reminiscences," 295; Roberts, *Life of John Taylor,* 194–96.

26. Alice Merrill Horne, "Joseph Horne," 4.

27. Jenson, *Biographical Encyclopedia,* 1:806–7; see also Lynn M. Hilton, *The Story of Salt Lake Stake, 1847–1972* (Salt Lake City: Salt Lake Stake, 1972).

28. Conway B. Sonne, *Knight of the Kingdom: The Story of Richard Ballantyne* (1949; reprint, Salt Lake City: Deseret Book, 1989), 45, 52.

29. Tullidge, *Life of Brigham Young,* 179.

30. Jenson, *Biographical Encyclopedia,* 1:807. Jenson erroneously gives the date as 1850. See also Andrew Love Neff, *History of Utah, 1847 to 1869,* ed. Leland Hargove Creer (Salt Lake City: Deseret News Press, 1940), 155–57.

31. Neff, *History of Utah,* 155.

32. Journal History of the Church, November 20, 1849, LDS Church Archives.

33. Journal History, November 25, 1849.

34. Journal History, November 23, 25, 1849.

35. Journal History, November 27, 29, 1849.

36. Journal History, December 3, 1849.

37. Journal History, December 6, 7, 1849.

38. Journal History, December 10, 1849.

39. Journal History, December 12, 1849.

40. Journal History, December 16, 17, 1849.

41. Journal History, December 18, 1849.

42. Journal History, December 23, 24, 30, 31, 1849.

43. Journal History, December 31, 1849; January 1, 1850.

44. Journal History, January 8, 1850.

45. Journal History, January 21, 22, 1850.

46. Journal History, January 22, 1850.

47. Journal History, January 22, 1850.

48. John Brown, February 2, 1850, quoted in Journal History, January 22, 1850.

49. Morris Shirts, *The Iron Mission* (Provo, Utah: forthcoming); Journal History, December 21, 1850, 1.

50. Zora Smith Jarvis, comp., *Ancestry, Biography, and Family of George A. Smith* (Provo, Utah: Brigham Young University Press, 1962), 148–49.

51. Jarvis, *Family of George A. Smith,* 152, 153; Alice Merrill Horne, "Joseph Horne," 4.

52. The story of the Deseret Sugar Manufacturing Company is told in Samuel W. Taylor, *The Kingdom or Nothing: The Life of John Taylor, Militant Mormon* (New York: Macmillan, 1976), 169; see also Leonard J. Arrington, *Great Basin Kingdom: An Economic History of the Latter-day Saints, 1830–1900* (Cambridge: Harvard University Press, 1858), 116–20.

53. Jenson, *Biographical Encyclopedia,* 1:807.

54. Arrington, *Great Basin Kingdom,* 164–65. See also Express and Carrying Co.'s Ledger, manuscript, LDS Church Archives.

55. Paul H. Peterson, "The Mormon Reformation of 1856–1857," *Journal of Mormon History* 15 (1989): 59–87. See also William G. Hartley's article in this volume. The number of plural marriages in relation to population was 65 percent higher in 1856–57 than in any other two-year period in Utah history. Stanley S. Ivins, "Notes on Mormon Polygamy," *Western Humanities Review* 10 (1956): 231.

56. Park, *Joseph Horne,* 36.

57. Park, *Joseph Horne,* 35–36.

58. Park, *Joseph Horne,* 36–37. One of Mary Park Shepherd Horne's sons, George Henry, became a prominent Salt Lake banker and churchman; his wife, Alice Merrill Horne, became a legislator, president of the Daughters of Utah Pioneers, member of the Relief Society General Board, prominent leader in the international peace movement, and Utah's leading art entrepreneur. Mary Park Shepherd Horne often went to the home of George and Alice for Sunday dinner. Mary Park died in Salt Lake City in 1924 at age eighty-seven.

59. Joseph Horne, Diary, 1858–1861. This overlooked holograph gives new insights into this early mission to grow cotton in Heberville, Utah, 1858–59, three years before the Cotton Mission of 1861–62. I have used it freely in the following paragraphs.

60. Arrington, *Great Basin Kingdom,* 205–11; Jenson, *Biographical Encyclopedia,* 1:807; Alice Merrill Horne, "Joseph Horne," 1.

61. Jenson, *Biographical Encyclopedia,* 1:807.

62. Alice Merrill Horne, "Joseph Horne," 2.

63. Joseph Horne, Diary, 1887–1889. The nineteen-page typescript copy goes from April 13, 1887, to July 22, 1888.

64. *A Token of Love from the Members of the John Taylor Prayer Circle to Patriarch Joseph Horne, . . .* (Salt Lake City: [John Taylor Prayer Circle], 1895), copy in the LDS Church Archives. This document confirms Joseph Horne's abiding love for John Taylor. See also D. Michael Quinn, "Latter-day Saint Prayer Circles," *BYU Studies* 19 (fall 1978): 79–105.

65. "They Came in '47," 8:424. The eulogy is quoted in Park, *Joseph Horne,* 23; and Alice Merrill Horne, "Joseph Horne," 5.

ESTRAY NOTICE.

I HAVE in my possession:

One bay HORSE, 4 years old, branded Q on left thigh;
One light bay MARE and colt, 7 years old, branded L S on left thigh.
One dark bay MARE and colt, 4 years old, branded H on right thigh.
If not claimed by the 20th inst, they will be sold at the Estray Pound in Tooele City, at 2 p. m.

LORENZO KELSEY,
District Pound Keeper.

Tooele City, April 10, 1878.   dsw

A wooden peg projects beyond an upright in this 1968 close-up of the interior of the barn owned by John Welch Jr. The large crosswise timbers—the beam is roughly sixteen inches wide—are about ten feet from the floor. John W. Welch, photographer.

John Welch:
A Pioneer in Paradise, Utah

John W. Welch

Prologue

In 1968 my brother James and I stopped in the quiet town of Paradise, Utah. For over sixty years, my great-grandfather John Welch, one of my namesakes, had owned a barn there. It was ninety-nine years old—pretty good for a barn in these parts but still not quite antique. On its face, the pioneer past seemed not so long ago.

Like the pioneers who had built it, this barn's rough, hand-shaped timbers were solid and rugged. No veneer hid their essence. Through the cracks between the planks that protected this inner space from not only the weather, but also the outside world, brilliant fingers of light streamed in, illuminating the barn's irregular but solid construction. Its dirt floor felt like it belonged to another world—at least it seemed alien to the soles of the shoes of a young returned missionary who had grown up in Los Angeles. The smell was a rich, warm, humid, earthy mulch of vapors rising from the ordinary processes of daily life and death.

I looked past the lofts above me and beyond to the ceiling timbers. I had stood in many Gothic cathedrals in Europe, but I had never looked so intently upward as I did in this templed pioneer structure. I marveled at the ingenuity of the pioneer builders with their derricks and pulleys. I noticed the sharp wooden pegs driven through the criss-crossing beams. I stooped down, ran my fingers through the dirt, and found a rusted, hand-pounded, square-shafted nail. Whose blows had shaped that nail? I put it in my pocket.

I looked around and noticed old tools that needed repairing and old equipment that might someday come in handy. A pioneer never threw anything away. How many times growing up had I heard this pioneer-family imperative: "If it's broken, fix it. If you can't fix it, make it do. If you can't make it do, do without."

This barn was more than a shelter for cattle and sheep, wheat and hay. It was a reflection of the men who built it and worked it. My great-grandfather John Jr.; his father, John Sr.; and his son Johnny worked in it for over seventy-five years.

The roof of the barn sagged a little, like a swaybacked horse, but the barn's corners and posts were still solid, standing firm on their foundations. More than simply staking a claim of ownership on the land, this pioneer barn squarely defined an oriented domain, a *Sitz im Leben,* a place of life.

JOHN WELCH, PIONEER JOURNAL KEEPER

Fifty years ago, the Days of '47 centennial parade in Logan honored eighty-three-year-old John Welch as a "pioneer." His personal experiences tell a broad story of pioneer life in Utah. From 1908 until his death in 1948, he faithfully kept a series of twelve journals recording his daily routine and steady pace of life.[1] I will focus in this paper mainly on the ordinary events he recorded for the years 1908 and 1909. Although those years are late in the pioneer period, life had changed little in Paradise over the preceding decades. Automobiles had not yet arrived in Paradise; wagons were still horse drawn. Electricity, running water, and radios were still a decade or more in the future. Life in Paradise in those years was still basically the life of an isolated, self-defined, Mormon pioneer village, connected through its citizens' excursions to the hubs of higher education, Church organization, and commercial services in the larger Cache Valley.

John was the oldest son of John Welch Sr. (1823–1910) and Eliza Billington (1825–1907), both of whom had been converted to the LDS Church in England and had immigrated to Nauvoo. Born at Three Mile Creek, Box Elder County, on September 5, 1864, John Jr. grew up working in a brush factory and then turned to carpentry. He started school at an early age and attended high school in Brigham City. In 1884, John Sr. bought some property previously owned by Alvin Monteith in Paradise, and at the age of twenty, John Jr. moved to Paradise.[2] John Jr. married Ann Rebecca Shaw three years later in the Logan Temple. Their first child, John Shaw Welch, was born in 1888, and at the same time, John Jr. purchased eighty acres of dry land from John Sr. for seven hundred dollars. On this land stood the barn, built in 1869, that John Jr. would use throughout his life. The barn's foundation contained thirty-five hundred cubic feet of rock and mortar.

Courtesy John W. Welch

John Welch Jr. in the 1890s.

John Jr. was an ordinary member of The Church of Jesus Christ of Latter-day Saints. In 1899, at age thirty-five, he was called to serve a mission in the Northwestern states, and for over two years, he labored in Montana and Oregon away from his wife and their five young children. On his return, he served as a member of the Hyrum Stake MIA Board. He acted as president of the 118th Quorum of Seventy for twenty-six years. He also served as first counselor in the Paradise Ward MIA organization, as first assistant in the ward Sunday School, and as a longtime Sunday School teacher. He was a member of the stake Old Folks committee for four years, chaired the ward Old Folks committee for eight years, and served four times as a stake home missionary. Late in life, he was proud to have been a continuous subscriber to the *Improvement Era* since its first publication in 1898 and a steady subscriber to the *Deseret News* for fifty-nine years. He filled several terms as a school trustee. In April 1907, when Paradise was incorporated, he was chosen a member of the first town board. Twice he was elected board president, the equivalent of town mayor, and for twenty-seven years served as town clerk.

Solidly grounded in the restored gospel, John Sr. conveyed a strong testimony of the gospel to his son John Jr., who admired the keenness of mind his father maintained, in spite of his increasing frailty, until his death in Paradise in 1910. The revered memory of his father's life remained a significant part of the ordinary life of John Jr. On January 6, 1926, John Sr.'s birthday, John Jr. wrote in his journal, "Another birthday of my noble sire has rolled around. May I ever appreciate and strive to live worthy of my parentage and birth, and my heratage [*sic*] among the people of God." Five years later, on January 6,

1931, he wrote again, "This is father's birthday. I have been thinking today, as I often do, of some of the wise counsel and advise I received from him in the years long since passed." John Jr. remembered how his father, schooled in cutlery, "made a beautiful pocket knife and p[r]esented it to the prophet Joseph Smith."

John remembered particularly that his father had taken "great pride in having all his tools and implements clean and bright, having a place for everything and everything in its place. . . . It was considered a serious offense to unhitch from a plow and leave any dirt adherring [*sic*] to it, or to put a shovel or other tool down without cleaning it. He also earnestly counseled us to keep ahead of our work and 'Never put off till tomorrow what can be done today' " (January 6, 1931).

The Village of Paradise

Paradise was a small pioneering settlement in Cache Valley, twelve miles south of Logan.[3] The first settlers arrived in Paradise in 1860, and in 1861, Elder Ezra T. Benson and the Presiding Bishop, Peter Maughan, organized it as a town. Apostle Benson was charmed with the country and in his large-hearted impulsiveness gave the place the name of Paradise.

Due to the abundance of timber in nearby canyons, lumber became an important industry in Paradise. Paradise was also an early dairy center in Cache Valley, boasting the most modern and finest dairy equipment west of the Mississippi.

The town placed great emphasis on education. In 1865 a Sunday School began in Paradise. Fifty students attended Paradise's day school, under the teaching of Henry Shaw, the father of Ann Rebecca (born in Paradise, April 7, 1868, to Henry's second wife).

To a large extent, the community lived an order of honesty, sharing, and sufficiency. A local history of Paradise reports that "a mutual feeling of common interest and willingness to assist each other are notable conspicuous [*sic*] to a person who has lived in the city. Mills, mines, machinery, and a store owned by a cooperation of laboring men, and everything else go to prove that this Paradise is not a place of departed spirits."[4]

A new meetinghouse was constructed at Paradise in 1876. This ward chapel was lighted by kerosene lamps, which were cleaned and then filled with oil by the deacons, who also put out the lights by blowing through a pipe attached to the end of a stalk. The deacons also helped the ward by chopping wood for the stove that heated the building.

At the turn of the century, the Paradise Ward consisted of 739 souls, including 2 patriarchs (Henry C. Jackson and John Welch Sr.), 15 high priests, 32 seventies, 68 elders, 2 priests, 13 teachers, 49 deacons, 329 lay members, and 229 children under the age of eight.

DAILY LIFE IN PARADISE

John Jr.'s grandson, named John Stanley Welch, was born in 1920 and spent much of his childhood in Paradise and a neighboring town, Mendon. John Stanley Welch knew and occasionally worked beside his grandfather John Jr. in his daily routines, which he describes as follows:

> The pioneer man needed to be a jack-of-all-trades. He was carpenter, axeman, blacksmith, wheelwright, machinist, mason, horseman (and oxman, too), cowboy, leather worker, dog trainer, veterinarian, farmer, well digger, dairyman, chicken rancher, horticulturist, and butcher, among others.
>
> It was a hard life. They worked six days a week, twelve hours a day. They rose in the dark, fed the stock, milked the cows, harnessed the teams, went out and plowed, harrowed, planted, mowed hay (at first with scythes and later with horse-drawn mowers), raked, loaded, and stacked. At first, they also cut the grain with scythes, and tied bundles to be fed into the thresher (steam driven) when it came; later they had horse-drawn binders that cut the grain and bundled it. They grew sugar beets, thinned bent over at the waist, using a back-breaking short-handled hoe; they watered, weeded, topped, and loaded the beets into racks and hauled them to the railroad siding. They went into the mountains and cut 6–8 inch maples with axes, loaded them onto an axle, and dragged them down to the town where they cut them into firewood for their fireplaces and stoves. They logged out pines and firs from the mountains and used them for timbers for barns and sheds. Early on they built saw mills to make lumber for houses. They dammed streams and dug irrigation ditches. They built water-driven grist mills near the streams.
>
> They traveled by horse, on horseback, in buggies, and wagons most of the year and with sleighs in the winter. During the winter months, they mended fences, repaired harness, sharpened tools, hauled manure to the fields, cared for the stock, carpentered, slaughtered and butchered, hunted, milled, and kept very busy. Weather was just something that happened. You went out in it. You got cold and hot—of course.
>
> They furnished their own entertainment. They were not too tired to do that. They were musicians, with choirs, bands, and orchestras; they put on plays, memorized and gave readings (declamations), played parlor games, and read to each other.[5]

Daily Data from 1908

The 1908 journal of John Welch Jr., the earliest of his journals, which he began keeping after the death of his mother, provides a wealth of information about the daily life of this ordinary pioneer. John was forty-four years old in 1908. He was a farmer with a wife and six children (ages eight to twenty). Record keeping was a major part of his life: he kept the minutes of church meetings, the monthly prayer circle, town meetings, and other functions.

First, this journal shows that an important part of John's daily routine was writing in the journal. One wonders when and how he did this. Apparently, it happened at the end of the day, when it was somewhat dark. No radio or television interrupted this nightly reflection on the day's activities. Typical of these entries are those of the first week:

Monday January 6$\underline{\text{th}}$ 1908.

I took Johnny and Myrtle [John Jr.'s two oldest children] back to Logan this morning, where they will resume their studies at the B. Y. College.

Since the new year came in several of the family have suffered slight attacks of lagripp.[6] We are having lovely weather but hardly enough snow for slaying [sleighing].

John Miles [neighbor] went to College Ward for a few days visit.

Tuesday Jan. 7th

Thora [daughter] is quite poorly. She has a very bad cold. I am not doing much except daily chores.

Wednesday 8th

Thora is considerable better. I had a little visit with old father and sister Price. They are both quite feeble though able to look after themselves.

Gene [son] and I hauled a load of straw this evening after school.

Thursday 9th

We are having a rough blustery day, some little snow has fallen. Ann has gone to a surprise party up to Luella Bickmore's.

Friday Jan. 10 –08

I did some visiting, soliciting subscriptions for fuel for the meeting house and the poor.

Johnny came home this evening but Myrtle remained in Logan.

Saturday 11th

We hauled hay and corn all day. In the evening I attended a meeting of the Town Board.

Sunday 12th

I attended Seventies meeting, Prayer Circle, and sacrament meeting. also an evening meeting held by Elders J. H. Mitton and Jos. P. Welch [stepbrother].

Sister Shaw [Ann's mother] and her folks were visiting with us.

The data from the 1908 journal, supplemented with quotes from other years, can be divided into ten subject categories:

1. FARMING. The most common topic mentioned in John's journals is, as one would expect, farming. In 1908, 293 entries deal with various farming topics. John wrote 221 entries about crops: work (97), wheat (39), hay (38), corn (21), garden (14), straw (11), oats (1). He made 72 comments about animals: horses (37), pigs (15), cows (11), lambs or sheep (7), dog (1), goat (1). Farm work included numerous daily chores, lots of hauling (gravel, hay, or anything else), plowing, helping other people haul or plow, repairing fences, preparing to plant, planting, weeding, working with cement, looking for or working with horses, building additions to barns, taking crops to market, and so forth. John kept a herd of cows and a few pigs and sheep, but his main concern with animals was his horses, which were used to pull plows, wagons, sleighs, and carriages.

Farming, of course, depended largely on weather: "A good rain would be a fine thing as the ground is getting very dry" (April 21, 1908). "Rain, rain, rain. It is impracticable to do any outside work so we did some repa[i]ring in the barn" (June 17, 1908). Water was crucial for irrigation. On August 8, 1908, John bought two shares of water from the Shaws at twenty-five dollars each—more money than he would pay for a cow.

Education about farming was limited but appreciated. On January 8, 1909, while riding a train from Logan to Hyrum, John attended two lectures in cars "which have been equip[p]ed and sent out by the A. C. [Agricultural College] of Utah as a Farmers institute on wheels." He reported that the lectures on dairying and dairy breeds "were very interesting and instructive."

During a few months in the spring, John would occasionally look for "pet lambs"—motherless lambs out on the countryside—and would bring them home for his children. Often he would take some of his children with him to look.

2. FAMILY. The second most frequently mentioned subject is family life, especially the health and education of family members.

John was often involved with his children—John Shaw (born in 1888), Myrtle (1891), Florence (1893), Nicholas Eugene (1896), Harry LeRoi (1898), Thora (1904), and Louis (1909). Three others had died as infants (one in 1903 and twins in 1906).[7]

The subjects of the 266 entries regarding the family in 1908 break down as follows: his wife, Ann (44); Johnny (83); Myrtle (41); Flossie [Florence] (33); Gene [Nicholas Eugene] (39); Harry (22); and Thora (4).

Dealing with illness was a common and frustrating part of daily family life. When Ann was ill, John helped her do the washing every Wednesday. On March 8, 1908, John went to priesthood meeting but remained "at home in the afternoon so Ann can go to meeting. Flossie[8] is too sick to be left alone." On March 12, 1908, Flossie was ill with "quite a sore throat," which actually turned out to be diphtheria:

> Flossie dont seem any better. Sister Shaw came up and took her tempreture found it 101. Ann telephoned to doctor Cantril and he advised to bring her down to his office.
>
> She asked if there would be any risk and he said, none whatever. Sister Shaw thought it would be allright so I hitched up and took her down. When the doctor examined her he and I were thunderstruck to find that she had diphtheria of the worst kind. He injected 8000 unites of antitoxine and I brought her home. The trip didnt seem to hurt her, but, of course, if we had had any idea she had dip[h]theria we would not have taken her out for the world.

The doctor visited frequently during Flossie's illness, and the Primary children fasted and held a meeting in her behalf. Neighbors looked after the other children and stayed with the Welches to help them tend Flossie until she recovered.

Other activities John enjoyed with his family included taking Ann and Thora to Logan to do errands and to have Thora's picture taken (April 6, 1908), going to MIA parties (see May 1, 1908), and taking the younger children to Brigham City to see *Rip Van Winkle* at the "electric theatre" (August 6, 1908).

In September, John took a trip to Bear Lake[9] to sell produce. He took Harry (aged nine) with him. They camped by the side of the road at night or stayed with friends in nearby towns along the way: "We reached Garden City before dark and put up with Thomas Sims, still raining. I managed to keep Harry reasonably dry and he is quite cheerful" (September 24, 1908). John reported that they were glad to get home after ten days away but that they had had "a very nice time and quite a profitable trip" (October 1, 1908).

John spent many days taking his two oldest children to Logan. Johnny and Myrtle went to school there and lived at a boardinghouse during the week, then returned home for the weekends. All the work paid off: on May 28, 1909, Johnny graduated from the Brigham Young College in a class of fifty-seven students. John recorded, "It is a great satisfaction to know that he is in the front ranks of his class altho[ugh] he has been to the disadvantage of not being able to get to school in the fall until from one to six weeks after school work had begun." Four days later, on June 1, Myrtle took the teacher's examination and soon began teaching school, earning forty dollars per month. A few years later, John remembered those school days:

> In bringing Johnny and Myrtle home it seemed like old times. I was forcibly reminded of many trips to and from Logan with them when they were attending school. They came home nearly every week end when the weather was not too awful bad. How fondly I looked forward to Friday. Those were truly happy days and I often live them over again in my mind. (December 23, 1916)

3. NEIGHBORS. Associating with neighbors is the third most frequently mentioned item in John's 1908 journal. The 216 entries deal with general visiting and teaching (26) and visiting specific people: Ann's parents, the Shaws (52); John Miles (20); John Sr. (16); Lofthouse (15); Melissa Howell (11); Price (10); Parley Welch (8); Luella Bickmore (7); Holbrook (6); Joseph Welch (5); J. P. James (5); Housley (5); Jack (5); J. T. Roberts (4); Hansen (4); President Oldham (3); Pearce (3); and Hyrum Miles, William Humphreys, T. F. Jackson, Shirley, Elder J. H. Mitton, Williams, Hammond, Rae and Ella Welch, Henry Johnson, and Wilford (1 each). Only once did John specifically record receiving assistance from others.

John's journal depicts close ties among community members. John kept a faithful watch over those in his community who were older or ailing or ill. He frequently mentioned if someone felt poorly or if they were improving, and he and Ann often visited the sick. On many occasions, neighbors helped each other out; John did not say just why he needed to plow in the middle of the winter, but it seems as though he liked to follow a job through until the end: "John Miles went to the field with me and we plowed a few furrows around the piece of ground in the bend accross [*sic*] the ditch. It was rather disagreeable work plowing through six or seven inches of snow but I did it to finish up the job" (December 1, 1908). These pioneers watched out for each other, day and night. On February 24, 1909, John wrote:

> Ann awoke about 1–30 this morning and discovered Miles' house was on fire. I ran across and wakened T. L. Obray and then went to the fire. We got there before it had made much headway and had little trouble in putting it out.
>
> Had we been a few moments later the house would certainly have went up in smoke. The old folks were sleeping in the other end of the building and Mrs Miles is so badly crippled up with rheumatism she is unable to help herself at all.

4. WEATHER. With 179 entries, weather is the fourth most commonly mentioned subject in the 1908 journal. The comments are usually brief. John nearly always noted the coldest day of the year. He made general remarks (118 times), and took note of good weather (41 times), bad weather (9), and sleighing weather (11). Sleighing was important for hauling loads over firm, frozen ground.

The weather determined what John would do each day—whether indoor chores, planting, working in the fields, working with the animals, or traveling to another town. It also determined whether his children would come home on the weekends from school in Logan: "Another beautiful day. The nights are quite cold. Myrtle came home this evening and Johnny went to College Ward" (February 21, 1908). "A fine day but the children didnt come home from Logan on account of the bad condition of the roads" (March 6, 1908).

John also noted unusual occurrences: "Two slight earthquake shocks were felt, about 8 oclock" (October 5, 1909). He mentioned two lightning strikes: one hit and killed a sixteen-year-old boy of another town; the other struck a neighbor's team of oxen.

5. CHURCH. Church-related entries are very common, totaling 120. Mentions of meetings were the most common: seventies meetings (46), sacrament meeting or afternoon services (23), prayer circle meetings (9), general conference (4), ward conference (2), stake conference (2), priests/teachers meeting (2), quarterly conference (1), Relief Society conference (1), Sunday School conference (1), and district convention of seventies (1). Other topics are the meetinghouse (5), MIA (4), Joseph F. Smith (2), Heber J. Grant (2), missionaries (2), Relief Society (1), Primary (1), traveling home missionaries[10] (1), Tithing Office (1), and temple (1).

John mentioned Church every Sunday, and he almost always recorded the seventies meetings as being "firstrate" or very interesting.

John noted that the seventies began using B. H. Roberts's *Seventy's Course in Theology* as a priesthood study manual (November 8, 1908). He also attended a lecture on "the Bible as literature" given by "Professor Larsen of the A. C. of U. [Agricultural College of Utah]" (December 6, 1908).

John frequently administered to the sick of his community: "I was called to assist in administering to John Shaw [Ann's father]. He is very sick and seems terribly discouraged. Afternoon Ann and I went up to see Jack and found him feeling considerable better" (February 27, 1908). "I called to see John Shaw. He is improving nicely" (March 4, 1908). In 1923, John "attended a special fast meeting" and reported that "in accordance with president[i]al proclamation[11] services are being held throughout the land and contributions taken up for the benefit of the poor and needy in the 'Near East'" (December 2, 1923). Other Church duties involved visiting the neighbors: "Jos. Welch [step-brother] went with me and we visited several families in the capacity of teachers" (March 4, 1908). John was careful to differentiate clearly between the roles of the various offices of the priesthood.[12]

Funerals were often held on Sundays. "[I] attended the funeral of sister Christiansen [Ann's cousin Amy]. altho[ugh] it was a cold stormy day the services were largely attended and all the speakers spoke in the highest terms of the noble character of deceased" (May 31, 1908). The one time John mentioned attending the Logan Temple that year, he recorded that he did so in behalf of Henry Howells; presumably John performed a proxy endowment (February 14, 1908).

John took advantage of his close proximity to Church leaders by attending conferences and lectures as often as he could. On March 22, 1908, he wrote, "Quarterly Conference in Hyrum yesterday and today. Three months ago we had a scarlet fever flag and six months ago I was over to Bear Lake. It seems a long time since I attended conference." He always attended local conferences. At one conference, "Elder David O. McKay of the quorum of apostles delivered an excellent discourse" (April 24, 1909). John tells of traveling to Logan to listen to President Joseph F. Smith talk at the Brigham Young College:

> At 9–40 went to chapel in the B.Y.C. The occasion being a visit from Prest. Smith and the board of trustees. . . . Prest. Smith and party, headed by the college band, marched down through, and the assembly room was quickly filled to its capacity. We had the privilege of listening to good singing by the choir, fine music by the band and excellent addresses by prests. Smith and R. W. Young. (February 7, 1908)

In a rare trip to Salt Lake City, John attended a reunion of the Northwestern States Mission and went to general conference: "Prest. Smith, his counsel [counselors?] and some of the Apostles have done the talking and, thus far, the principal topics have been temperance, the Word of Wisdom, and prayer" (October 5, 1908).[13]

6. HEALTH. For pioneers, death was never far from awareness. John mentioned health matters 99 times: illness (48), good health (12), funerals (10), administration to the sick (9), doctors (7), deaths (7), dentists (3), and old age (3; plus mentions of John Sr.). Ailments included diphtheria, smallpox, old age, colds, aches, "lagripp," "dropsy," "erysipelas," and rheumatism of the heart.[14] During 1909 many houses had to be quarantined because of sickness—smallpox, scarlet fever, whooping cough, etc. John was often in charge of marking each affected house with a flag that alerted neighbors to the quarantine.

7. TRAVEL. Travel, even to a nearby town, was a major undertaking. In 1908, John logged seventy-seven trips to various places. About two days a week, on average, he was away from Paradise: Logan (54), Hyrum (15), Brigham City (7), Avon (3), Wellsville (3), Bear Lake (2), and Hyrum Canyon, Montpelier, Salt Lake City, Little Basin, George Town, Bennington, and College Ward (1 each). On December 17–18, 1908, John recorded one journey as follows:

> There is hardly enough snow for good sleying [sleighing]. Quite cold. "Sun dogs"[15] were in evidence both this and last evening. I have always heard they are an indication of cold weather.
>
> . . . We had a very cold trip [to Logan]. The sun dogs, certainly, have not disappointed us this time.

8. COMMUNITY. Community service and community activities were major concerns for John and the others living in Paradise. John noted community involvement on 38 occasions during 1908: participating in town board meetings (19), working on the Old Folks committee (8), attending parties or dances (7), attending county conventions (2), attending events at Brigham Young College (2), going to the theater (2), working on Beaver Dam (1), seeing traveling minstrels (1), going to the Barnum and Bailey circus (1), attending school meeting (1), going to the Republican primary (1), and participating as school-election judge (1).

John was much involved with a group called the Old Folks, consisting of the married couples and the elderly in the area.[16] After many days of planning and gathering money and supplies, he reported:

The "Old Folk's" and married people's reunion was held today. Quite a number remained at home on account of sickness, but fully two hundred came out and, apparently, enjoyed themselves to the limit. The affair was pronounced highly satisfactory. We had an old time dance in the evening which was also considered a grand success. (January 23, 1908)

He expended similar efforts in fulfilling his community assignments that year, including participating in a local co-op store (September 17, 1908), being appointed delegate to the county Republican convention (October 12, 1908), being appointed by the board of education to be judge of the school-board election (November 26, 1908), and participating in a trial of a community member who had been caught stealing cows (May 26, 1909).

Throughout this time, the community held many meetings to discuss "the feasibility of lighting the town with electricity" (January 21, 1909). Searching for the best deal, the community wrote letters to different electric companies and ended up bargaining with one that agreed to do the job for a lower price if the people of the town would volunteer their labor and time: "The Telluride Power Co. agree to put up one fourth of the expence and if the commissioners make an appropriation the citizens will donate considerable work" (July 2, 1909). Both John Jr. and Johnny put in many hours on this project.

9. HOLIDAYS. In his journal, John notes that he observed twelve holidays and other important milestones in various degrees during 1908: Bear Day[17] (February 2); Washington's Birthday (February 28); Arbor Day (April 15); Mother's Day; Decoration Day (May 30); Flag Day (June 15); Fourth of July, or Independence Day; Twenty-fourth of July, or Pioneer Day; the fair in Salt Lake City (October 6); election day (November 3–4); Thanksgiving; and Christmas.

Some interesting journal entries regarding holidays are as follows:

I celebrated my birth day strengthening a bridge for the steam thrasher to cross the canal on. Afternoon I hauled wheat from the machine for Melissa Howell's. In the evening I attended a meeting of the Town Board. (September 5, 1908)

This is known as "bear day." There is an old saying that the bear comes out on the 2nd of Feb. and if there is no sunshine he concludes spring has come and remains out, but if he can see his shadow he goes back to his nest and we will have six weeks more of winter. (February 2, 1909)

On June 15, 1909, John observed the tenth anniversary of his LDS mission in the Northwestern States.

He often noted that time passed rather quickly. By September 2, 1909, he had spent twenty-five years in Paradise, and on September 5, 1909, he wrote, "This is my birthday, 45 years of age. Hardly seems possible but it's a fact nevertheless."

Obviously important to him throughout his life were Mother's Day and his parents' birthdays, as he remarked twenty years later:

> The beautiful custom of honoring "Mothers" on the 2<u>nd</u> Sunday in May each year was fittingly observed in our ward.
>
> An appropriate program was rendered in Sunday school, and in sacrament meeting along with several musical numbers. Prest. Jos. R. Shepherd of the Logan Temple delivered an inspiring discourse. Nearly all mothers in our ward were present and quite a number of fathers and young people. I noticed those who's mothers have passed to the "great beyond" seemed the most interested in brother Shepherd's talk. . . .
>
> I thought, previous to my sainted mother's death, that I was performing my duty pretty well. I didn't know that I was causeing her any particular sadness. (I was thoughtless) As I grow in years and get more of a parent's viewpoint of life I can see where, by little attentions that I could easily have given, I might have increased her happiness very much.
>
> The older I become the more I appreciate her kind, loveing and patient disposition.
>
> I never read the Apostle Paul's definition of charity, (and I refer to it quite frequently) 1st Cor. 13:4, 7 but what I feel in my heart, if ever a human being measured up fully to that standard, she did. (May 13, 1928)

One 1908 entry describes the town's Decoration Day:

> Decoration Day. Quite a croud [crowd] of people turned out and fixed up, very nicely, the graves of their dead and in the afternoon services were held at the cemet[e]ry, a game of ball on the square between Hyrum and Paradise boys which resulted in a victory for the home team. (May 30, 1908)

The Fourth of July that year consisted of a sunrise flag ceremony, cannon salutes, celebration as usual, a meeting in the morning, a children's dance, ice cream, an oration, and a band. These festivities usually finished by noon, and John was able to work on his farm the rest of the day.

Pioneer Day in Paradise was much more important than the Fourth of July. John always woke up early on Pioneer Day and hoisted the flag "just at sunrise" in the town square assisted by his children. The town celebration included a meeting, bands, pageants (put on by the Primary), a pioneer celebration, and a parade representing the pioneers of 1847, early life in Utah of both "the white and red man," and contemporary Utah.

Thanksgiving celebrations included services in the meetinghouse. In his journals for other years, John frequently mentioned that members of the family were missing:

> Our family members are all home enjoying good health which is a great satisfaction to me. I feel that we have much to be thankful for, while our crops fell short and we are a little "hard put" for cash, yet we are fairly well provided for and we have a comfortable new home which, I believe, we all appreciate. (November 24, 1910)

> Rather a dull thanksgiving. . . . Ann and Florence prepared an excellent dinner but it seemed there was somewhat of a lonesome feeling at not having more of the family at home. We are trying to appreciate the blessings we enjoy for truly we have abundant reason for thanksgiving especial[l]y when we consider conditions in the war strickened nations of the earth. There seems to be no indications of peace. (November 30, 1917)

> I feel that we have abundant reasons for thanking the "giver of every good and perfect gift."

> While some of our farm crops were almost a failure, we have plenty to eat, drink and wear and the health of the family has generally been good. (November 25, 1926)

Christmas consisted of spending time with the family, giving and receiving gifts, having a visit from Santa Claus, attending services in the meetinghouse, and visiting neighbors. Often the community had a dance for the children in the evening.

10. OTHER. Occasionally, John mentioned other items of entertainment, education, or economics. He bought a white-top Studebaker wagon from Andrew Hansen for seventy dollars on October 16, 1908. Temple garments were five dollars for two pairs (January 19, 1909). He often kept track of money he spent for purchasing equipment or animals for the farm and of money gained from selling grain, coal, and animals.

THE PARADISE PRAYER CIRCLE

Another facet of the rhythm and cycle of routine life for John in pioneer Paradise was the prayer circle.[18] Only two prayer circles were organized in the Cache Stake. The Paradise circle functioned from May 12, 1907, to January 1, 1911, beginning with about fifteen male members and gradually declining to five, at which point it was discontinued due to lack of attendance. Participants initially met twice a month on Sundays in a special room in the ward house. They later met only on fast Sundays. The bishop was president of the circle.

Attendance requirements were stipulated to maintain membership, and great efforts were made to contact and encourage those not attending. John once recorded that "there were too many vacant chairs in our prayer circle room and [we] felt that some of our brethren remained away with out any excuse. We meet here for our own good and also for what good we can do to others" (Sunday, November 1, 1908). Members were required to ask themselves if they were full-tithe payers and if they obeyed the Word of Wisdom. Most of the time, members paid a full tithe, but some acknowledged that they did not fully obey the Word of Wisdom; many found it difficult to abstain from the use of tobacco and alcohol.

Each meeting began and ended with a song, most often "We Thank Thee, O God, for a Prophet." Minutes and roll were kept for each meeting; John served as secretary for the last two years. Instructions were given, a prayer was offered, oil was consecrated, some sick or infirm were anointed, and encouragement and various remarks were given. The purposes of the meeting were to seek basic spiritual benefits and to pray for those in need. At one meeting, the president "suggested that we have some object in praying," and the members of the circle discussed the matter: "It was decided to pray for those who were sick, also those who were on the shady [disreputable] side of life, and for the preservation of our crops and the things which God had blessed us with. Also the preservation of our young, and the faithfulness of our priesthood" (August 25, 1907). On September 6, 1908, one member "spoke of the spirit of hoodlumism which seemed to be prevalent among some of the youth of our community." At another meeting, it was reported that "some of the members at the ward had testified that they had been blessed by being prayed for" (November 10, 1907).

Significant counsel was often given, such as "we should always make it a point to be at peace with every one" (November 10, 1907). On December 8, 1907, the members were exhorted "not to use vain repetition in repeating our Heavenly Father's name, but to mention his name when we commence and when we finish our prayer to ask it in the name of Jesus Christ." On June 6, 1909, he recorded, "Several of the brethren spoke urging the necessity of elders acquainting themselves with the requirements of the gospel and preparing to officiate in the ordinances there of in an intelligent manner." On November 7, 1909, the brethren were urged to perform temple work to "do something for those departed," and on January 2, 1910, the brethren were encouraged "to be faithful in times of prosperity as well as adversity."

Epilogue

Not long ago, the old Paradise barn was torn down. It had fallen into disrepair and was no longer used for much. While it was the oldest structure from pioneer Paradise still standing, the gray-planked barn was too ordinary, too plain, and too wooden to be preserved as a historical landmark. No particular ceremony, no fanfare, no heraldry attended its demolition. The unsightly and unsafe barn was removed to make room for some unknown future progress.

But maybe the old barn was unsightly only to those who lacked a view of its daily past and a vision of its pioneer spirit. Perhaps the old barn was unsafe, as they said, as a physical hazard; but it may have seemed more subtly unsafe to a modern mentality that had grown out of sorts with the extraordinary personal and community values that characterized the ordinary life of the everyday pioneer in Paradise. John Welch was a typical, rural, faithful, and decent man involved in the routines of life in pioneer Paradise, Utah. He is an example of the hardworking and dedicated men and women who comprised an agrarian culture that is part of the foundation of our own lives.

John W. Welch is the Robert K. Thomas Professor of Law at Brigham Young University and Editor in Chief of *BYU Studies*.

Notes

1. These journals are catalogued by Davis Bitton, *Guide to Mormon Diaries and Autobiographies* (Provo, Utah: Brigham Young University Press, 1977), record number 2660. The holograph is in the Archives Division, Historical Department, The Church of Jesus Christ of Latter-day Saints, Salt Lake City.

2. This biographical summary is based on a thirteen-page personal history written by John Welch Jr. in 1933, with supplements in 1940, 1943, and 1946 and additions by Myrtle Welch Hatch, and on a four-page anonymous tribute

written thirty-one years after John became town clerk. Both are in the possession of the author.

3. This historical sketch of Paradise is based on Viola Welch, "Paradise Was Chosen as the Name of This Pretty Place," *Logan Herald Journal,* March 25, 1956; "History of Paradise," typescript, in possession of the author; and "Paradise," typescript, in possession of the author.

4. J. Smith, *Deseret News,* clipping in possession of the author.

5. John Stanley Welch to John W. Welch, January 1997, in possession of the author. To keep all these Johns straight, the family refers to John Sr. as I, John Jr. as II, John Shaw as III, John Stanley as IV, John Woodland as V, and my son John Sutton as VI.

6. This was probably a flu of some sort.

7. John Welch and Rebecca Shaw family group sheet, Family History Library.

8. In 1908, Flossie was fifteen years old.

9. About two days' travel from Paradise by wagon.

10. John Jr. did not explain the difference between "traveling" missionaries and "home" missionaries. Perhaps the former were full time, and the latter the equivalent to stake or local missionaries.

11. John Jr. did not indicate whether this was a Church "presidential proclamation" or a national one.

12. For information about acting teachers, see William Hartley's article in this volume.

13. This conference was a historic event in the Latter-day Saint application and observance of the Word of Wisdom.

14. John Welch did not give descriptions of these ailments in his journal.

15. They are refractions of the sun glistening on the horizon in a luminous halo of bright spots.

16. The Old Folks movement was important in early Utah. See Joseph Heinerman, "The Old Folks Day: A Unique Utah Tradition," *Utah Historical Quarterly* 53 (spring 1985): 157–69; and Brian D. Reeves, "Hoary-Headed Saints: The Aged in Nineteenth-Century Mormon Culture" (master's thesis, Brigham Young University, 1987). The "married people" in Paradise were probably included in whatever activities were held for the Old Folks.

17. I assume this was the equivalent of Groundhog Day.

18. Prayer-circle meetings were commonly held by LDS members throughout the territory. For more information, see George S. Tate, "Prayer Circle," in *Encyclopedia of Mormonism,* ed. Daniel H. Ludlow, 5 vols. (New York: Macmillan, 1992), 3:1120–21; and D. Michael Quinn, "Latter-day Saint Prayer Circles," *BYU Studies* 19, no. 1 (1978): 79–105. John Welch was the last secretary of the Paradise prayer circle; the information in this section of this article comes from the Paradise Ward prayer-circle minutes, copy belonging to the Welch family.

In Quest of Betterment: The Lee Roy and Priscilla Arrington Family

Leonard J. Arrington

President J. Reuben Clark paid tribute fifty years ago to the meek and lowly mothers, fathers, and children of the last wagon of the pioneer train, the unhonored but lovingly revered who followed their leaders in building the kingdom of God.[1] I would like to add a further dimension to his tribute and write about a family who came after 1869 in a freight train, as did some others because of the discounted fare—a family who moved to Utah seeking to improve their lot spiritually and economically. A family who along with many others around the turn of the century had difficulty making a living despite sweat and sacrifices. Who suffered misfortune, tragedy, and illness. Who nevertheless remained faithful, trying to make the best of circumstances, trying to do what the Lord wanted them to do.[2]

In North Carolina and Tennessee

This family originated from an unlikely area for Latter-day Saint pioneers: the valleys and hillsides of the Great Smoky Mountains in western North Carolina and eastern Tennessee. This colorful region was speckled with Scotch-Irish settlers who had gone from England and Scotland to settle in northern Ireland in the seventeenth century and had come to the United States in the eighteenth century, just before the American Revolution. Some of these people joined George Washington's army. The people were poor, subsistence farmers. They did not own slaves and in fact rarely saw Blacks. They grew cotton, tobacco, vegetables, and fruit. They usually had a horse, a cow, some pigs and chickens, and perhaps some sheep. They owned muskets and used them to hunt squirrels, wild turkeys, razorbacks, raccoons, opossums, and deer. Most of them belonged to the Freewill Baptist Church and were reconverted at frequent revivals.

Courtesy Leonard J. Arrington

Eastern Tennessee home of the Arringtons at Read Hill, Cocke County, until 1900, when they moved to Spanish Fork, Utah. Photographed by Leonard J. Arrington in 1946, the house may have been added to by later residents. On the hill to the left of the house is the burial site of Lee's father, Silas.

One of these families, the Lee Roy Arrington family, lived on some bottomland on a slope of the Blue Ridge Range of the Great Smokies. Within a few miles of their cabin was a church they had helped build, a school, and perhaps a dozen neighbors. Lee's ancestors had come to Virginia in the 1600s, then moved to North Carolina when it was opened for settlement after 1680. Their descendants moved to the mountains of western North Carolina when land there could be settled, about the time of the Revolution. Three Arrington generations grew up on Bulls Creek, Madison County, North Carolina. There Lee Roy Arrington married Priscilla Jane Brisendine, a descendant of an early pioneer of Jamestown, Virginia, and the couple crossed the French Broad River into Cocke County, in the hills of eastern Tennessee. The area they settled was called Read Hill, twelve miles from Del Rio, Tennessee. Lee's father and mother, Silas and Mary Arrington, joined them at Read Hill, and Silas became the volunteer, unpaid, Baptist preacher.

In most families in the area, the girls often did not go to school but stayed home to help their mothers cook, spin, cut wood, and sew. This was true of Priscilla, who, though she lived to be ninety-six, never learned to read or write. But she was intelligent, believed in education, and saw to it that her three daughters, along with her six sons, went to school. Lee Arrington, however, could read, and he read the Bible to his family daily. He conducted legal and other business in the nearby town of Marshall, North Carolina, and later in Newport, Tennessee.

Mormon missionaries finally wandered into these hills in 1892. They were not received well by the area's citizenry, but Lee Arrington had a strong sense of justice. He was the squire (or justice of the peace), and he refused to sanction any mobbing or hanging. When the missionaries were arrested for disturbing the peace, he paid their five-dollar fine and took them to his home for both supper and a place to stay the night. The missionaries had vigorous discussions with the family, which Lee may have won because he was well acquainted with the Bible, probably more so than the young missionaries. The family enjoyed these discussions, and the missionaries stayed several days. Missionaries came the next year, and the next, each time staying with the Arringtons. Finally, in 1896, over the objections of Lee, who did not want to offend his father and mother, Priscilla (always called Siller) joined the Church. The next year, her sixteen-year-old daughter, Lee Anner (always called Sis), joined. Lee's sister Betty and her husband, Anderson Cook, also joined, and they lobbied Lee to be more permissive.

To Spanish Fork and Back

In 1898, Anderson and Betty Cook decided to move to the San Luis Valley, in southern Colorado, where other southern Saints had established Mormon communities. When Anderson became ill, they moved on to Spanish Fork because that is where "their" missionaries lived. The Cooks wrote back invitingly, although ward records show they did not do well and survived primarily by handouts from their neighbors and the ward.[3] In fact, Anderson Cook became severely ill and died in June 1899. Regardless, having been urged on by the Cooks, the Arringtons decided in 1899 that they would go West.

To earn money for train fares, the family quit drinking coffee. The boys spent an entire winter stripping oak trees and gathering the huge piles of bark, which they dried and sold to the Newport tannery. This money, together with proceeds from the season's crop of tobacco, was kept in a leather pouch for a while and at other times put in a box buried somewhere on the farm. Whenever the whole family left the house, they would toss the pouch into a corner with some old clothes and rags so no thief would think to steal it. Priscilla and the daughters cured ham and put up preserves until they had readied large boxes of food to take on the train. By early spring 1900, they were ready to go. The farm and house were left in the keeping of Silas and Mary. The outgoing family consisted of Lee and Siller, each 44; Bruce, 20; Lee Anner, 17; Grover, 15; Jake, 13; Noah (my father), 11; Callie, 9; Glenn, 7;

Earl, 5; and Pearl, 2. This was the first time any of them had been out of the hills.

Always going by freight train because of the cheap fare, they headed first for Vibbard, Missouri, where Lee had acquaintances. The only land available was mountain farmland, which was not to Lee's liking. They went on to Florence, Colorado—on the Arkansas River in central Colorado—where their money gave out and where Lee came down with Colorado tick fever. Bruce found employment to support the family for several weeks, during which time they wrote to the elders in Spanish Fork who had taught them the gospel and who promptly sent them enough money to get to Salt Lake City. One of the elders, now a Salt Lake banker, met them at the depot, took them on a tour of Salt Lake City, and put them on the Denver and Rio Grande Western to Spanish Fork. They arrived in early summer, and their former missionaries helped them find a place with a cheap home, garden space, and a ward that would assist them in obtaining employment.

Spanish Fork in 1900 was three years short of seeing its first automobile. The streets were unpaved, and the few sidewalks were boardwalks. The only telephone in town was at Robertson and Argyle's Drug Store. With a population of about three thousand, Spanish Fork was primarily a farming community, but a few other industries were sprouting here and there—saw and flour mills, a foundry, a molasses and honey mill, and a shoe factory. The best farmland lay on the east bench, but farmers just starting out there had a rough time due to a water shortage—established users lower down had first rights to local water, and there was not enough to share.[4]

The home the Arringtons rented had a very large garden, and planting it was one of the first things they did. From the fruit trees on the lot, the family obtained a fine crop of apricots and plums, and from the garden, a bountiful supply of tomatoes. Canned tomatoes and dried fruit provided practically their total diet for several months during the winter. They learned that nothing grew there without watering; in the summer, a Utah farmer's life revolved around irrigation, which quite shocked this southern hills farmer who had never had to worry about drought.

Besides harvesting their crops, the family supported itself by putting everyone to work who was old enough. At first they could find work only on local farms, where Bruce, Jake, and Grover worked topping sugar beets. One week they worked on a farm belonging to a brother of Bishop John H. Koyle of Dream Mine fame and later a bishop of Leland Ward, Palmyra Stake. The brother had been very close to Anderson and Betty Cook. But wages for farm laborers were low, and soon Lee and Bruce went to the Union Pacific Railroad employment office in Salt Lake City and hired out as section hands for the Utah Central branch. On July 1, Bruce was sent to Rock Springs, Wyoming, with a grading outfit and later to do construction in Cumberland, Wyoming.

When winter came, most of the children enrolled in the district school. For Callie, this was her first schooling, and for Noah and the older children, the school was quite different from the Read Hill school on their grandfather's corner of their Tennessee farm. This district school was graded—students went into different rooms according to their skills in reading, writing, and arithmetic—and even more remarkably, the school furnished free paper and pencils. As soon as the snows came, Bruce quit his railroad job and returned to Spanish Fork, where he enrolled in high school. His attendance was irregular, as he had obtained a job driving a Benjamin Creamery delivery wagon from Spanish Fork to the Tintic mining district. He made this two-day trip twice a week until the creamery man himself took over the deliveries, and Bruce went to school full-time, winter and spring. When the man later offered Bruce a steady delivery job at $35 a month, Bruce turned it down, thinking an education would be "more beneficial." As soon as spring came, the boys again worked thinning sugar beets.

During the fall and winter of 1900, the members and neighbors were very friendly to the Arringtons, although only Priscilla and Lee Anner were members of the Church at the time. Two families who were especially friendly were the Holts and the Jexes. Jesse P. Holt, the ward clerk, had been on a mission to the southern states, although he had not known the Arringtons there. William Jex and his wife, Eliza, had converted to the Church in 1853 in Norfolk, England, emigrated to Utah the next year, and settled in Spanish Fork. In 1900, William was sixty-nine years old and a member of the Spanish Fork City Council, a school trustee, and a watermaster. Eliza, two years younger, had eleven children, carded and spun clothes for her own family, and was a Relief Society officer.

Another family the Arringtons knew well was an elderly couple, Joseph E. Beck and his wife. The Arringtons used to go over to the Beck home, where Sister Beck would make up a huge plate of cottage cheese for them, and Brother Beck, who was ninety in 1900, would tell how he had once given money to the Prophet Joseph Smith in Nauvoo. (This story is family lore; a check with sources reveals he did not join the Church until 1847.)

In September 1900, the Arringtons' tenth child was born and named Silas, after his grandfather. About this same time, Lee Anner and Earl became ill with inflammatory rheumatism; Callie, seven years old at the time, remembered the elders coming to administer to them. This illness was only the beginning of the family's troubles. During the winter, the entire family came down with smallpox, catching the tail end of an epidemic that had closed churches and schools the previous winter. Not all family members suffered as severely as others, but the house was quarantined, and they had no income. When Lee recuperated quickly, the city appointed him "watchman" to see that no one left or entered the house. The family very nearly starved this winter, saved only by their dried fruit, tomatoes and whatever else Priscilla had been able to can and by the help of ward members and friends. One man brought half a beef. Elder Mueller, who had baptized Priscilla, brought a large box of Christmas food and clothing, including a dress that Sister Mueller had made for Priscilla; the family remembered it as "a pretty dress and a nice one."

During the winter, while the family was quarantined for smallpox, a controversy developed throughout the state when the state Board of Health ordered the local boards to require smallpox vaccinations of all school-age children. The *Deseret News* in Salt Lake City complained about the state's physicians making a "supreme effort" to force vaccination on parents. But, said the *News,* "the citizens of the State are massing against this usurpation of statutory power." In Spanish Fork, the local Board of Health and school board refused to obey the edict, and the Spanish Fork correspondent for the *News* insisted: "Our people do not believe in compulsory vaccination." However, he indicated a willingness to "submit to all necessary regulations to preserve the public health."[5] Had vaccinations been required earlier, some of the Arringtons and others might have avoided smallpox.

On March 9, 1901, baby Silas died of hemorrhage of the bowels and was buried in the Cook family lot in the Spanish Fork Cemetery. It may have been just after little Silas' death that the family moved into the Third Ward.

In the new ward, Callie attended Primary and MIA, even though she was only seven. The Arringtons were welcomed to the Third Ward and on one occasion received help from the Relief Society in the form of some cash and merchandise.

Sometime in the spring, Lee received word that Grandfather Silas Arrington had died several days before baby Silas. The news meant that only Mary was left to care for the farm and houses in Tennessee, so the family decided to return to their former home. Their decision was influenced by other factors. One was that they could see no economic future in Spanish Fork. Farm wages were low, railroad wages better but not good enough to meet the needs of a father of ten, and good farmland was virtually not available anymore along the Wasatch Front even if Lee had had the money to buy a farm. Their entire savings had been consumed getting to the valley, and they had no credit in Utah.

Some descendants see the decision as fortuitous, for after returning to the South, Lee finally became converted, now that his father would not be embarrassed. Some believe the deciding factor in the return was that Lee could not adjust to irrigation. The effort and expense of raising a crop on dry Utah ground did not seem worth the crop a man harvested. Fifteen years after they left Spanish Fork, when the family moved to Idaho, Lee did not turn to farming but kept only a garden alongside his pasture land.

So in late summer 1901, the Arringtons packed up fewer boxes than they had brought and boarded the train for Newport, Tennessee. No details about that return trip remain; it must not have been memorable. Their attempt to get out of the Tennessee hills and better themselves had failed, and back home things would never be the same, for Lee's father had died. They had no money and no prospects. Probably their return tickets were purchased by Bruce, who had resumed working for the railroad that summer and did not return South with them. He was a laborer and assistant foreman on an "extra gang" for the Denver and Rio Grande Western Railroad. Bruce worked on Utah railway jobs for six years, sending much of his salary home to help his family.

Back in Read Hill, Lee settled the estate of his father, who, if he left a will at all, had not registered it. Silas had been buried, as he wished, under a certain tree above the spring on one of the hills of his little farm. Lee never intended to occupy his farm when he returned to the South; instead he rented it out and brought his mother and his sister Lucinda Harper to live with him in Sweetwater in southeast Tennessee, about eighty miles southwest of Newport. Sweetwater was a factory town where Lee's sister had lived; in her letters, the place had sounded good. Lee rented a house in town and a farm on the outskirts, where he worked while the older children went to work in the cotton mills. The children too young to work attended grammar school during the winters, but at other times, they helped in the fields. The whole family worked and saved, trying to accumulate enough cash to purchase a farm.

The four years spent in Sweetwater proved to be disappointing. The family did not come close to starving as they had in Spanish Fork, but neither were they able to accumulate savings. Priscilla had a large garden northeast of the house where the family raised all their table vegetables. Their land contained a "long place" for the cabbage to be pitted, as well as separated pits for the sweet potatoes, Irish potatoes, red beets, and turnips. Parsnips were left in the ground until spring. The family continued their self-sufficient hill custom of making their own kraut and molasses by the barrel. They made soap once or twice a year. A few days beforehand, Priscilla would pour water over hardwood ashes in the ash hopper to start the lye dripping. When the lye was running fast, she would set a bushel-sized iron pot with legs under the hopper to catch it. They also killed, salted, and smoked four or five hogs a year.

For a Mormon family, Sweetwater was not a hospitable environment. A few years before the Arringtons arrived, Mormon missionaries had been driven out of Sweetwater with rotten eggs. Immediately afterwards, a terrible storm, with thunder and lightning and hail, "punished" the people, but since that time, the elders had been barred from Sweetwater. Not only could the family have no contact with their church, but they themselves were the objects of derision. In the end, Lee and Priscilla decided to look for a new home, one where the mills paid better wages and they could associate with other Mormons.

In Oklahoma

This was in 1905, when a large tract in the Indian Territory (later Oklahoma) was being opened to homesteaders. Talk of virgin soil at minimum cost was everywhere—in the newspapers, corner stores, lecture halls—and Lee had heard of it. The family did not know exactly where in Oklahoma they wanted to settle, but they knew it offered opportunities. Lee set off alone to Chattanooga to purchase train tickets.

When the railroad agent informed Lee it would be cheaper to wait until fall to travel, since the land rush in Oklahoma was over anyway, Lee decided to stay in Chattanooga temporarily. He wrote to his family, asking them to join him. Almost immediately after their arrival in Chattanooga, they rented a home in Rossville, just over the line into Georgia, where several new mills had opened. Six of the children went to work, the boys in the knitting mill, the girls in a woolen mill. The four younger ones earned 25 cents a day, Noah (age sixteen) 45 cents for a ten-hour day as operator of a spinning mule, and Lee Anner 50 cents a day as a weaver. Lee worked as a teamster. On payday of each week, the children handed their wages over to their father.

When they first arrived in Chattanooga, the family asked around and learned that the Southern States Mission headquarters of the LDS Church was located there. Lee contacted President Ben E. Rich, who sent elders to Rossville to "work" the family. After six months of cottage meetings and discussions, Lee and all the unbaptized children except Bruce, who was in the West working on the railroad, and Grover, who decided he was not worthy of it at the time, agreed to be baptized. On October 15, 1905, the father, three brothers, and one sister were baptized by Percival C. Winter and James H. Wallis in a nearby Tennessee river. That same day they took a streetcar into Chattanooga, where they were confirmed. The next day, the family left on the train for Oklahoma City.

They located a farm in what was called Faxon, just above the Texas panhandle in southern Oklahoma. They raised cotton and corn, and the boys worked on wheat farms in the region, particularly in Kansas. They remained there ten years. The younger children went

Courtesy Leonard J. Arrington

Priscilla and Lee Arrington and their family, probably taken in Lawton, Oklahoma, in 1906. *From left to right, front row:* Jacob, 18; Priscilla, 48; Lee, 48; Pearl, 7. *Second row:* Callie, 14; Glenn, 12; Earl, 10; Noah, 16. *Back row:* Lee Anner, 22; Grover, 20; Bruce, 25.

to school. Occasionally, the family attended church meetings in the region, but generally they waited for visits by elders. The family did reasonably well; Lee acquired some good horses, and they had plenty to eat and plenty of work.

In 1913, Noah Arrington, the fourth son and fifth child, was twenty-three. He fell in love with his next-door neighbor, Edna Corn, an eighteen-year-old, red-headed girl just finishing high school. Her parents were staunch Methodists, did not like Mormons, and were opposed to a marriage. Noah and Edna determinedly escaped to Lawton, Oklahoma, where they were married by a Presbyterian preacher. The couple (my parents) lived in a farm shanty for three summer months while they grew a crop, and in September 1913, they set out for Idaho on a freight train.

In Idaho

Noah's older brothers, Grover and Jacob, while working on the railroad in Nevada, had heard about the opening of the Twin Falls, Idaho, tract, which opened in 1905, when Milner Dam, a private dam, was built on the Snake River and brought 250,000 acres of desert land under canals. This seemed a good opportunity. Grover and Jake found jobs as carpenters in the area, and they encouraged Noah and Edna to settle there as they had decided to do. The couple did. Noah did farm work, did some butchering, and worked for the beet sugar factory, which was built in 1916. In 1918, just after Leonard, their third child, was born, Noah and Edna bought a twenty-acre farm three miles east and three-fourths of a mile north of the Washington School on the southeast edge of Twin Falls.

The rest of the family were impressed with the news from Grover, Jake, and Noah, and in 1916, Lee and Priscilla, Callie, Pearl, Glenn, and Earl came to Idaho. Lee had a pasture and small acreage; Priscilla had an orchard and garden and sold fruit and fresh vegetables; Callie and Pearl worked for a local music store. Jake opened a small grocery store and built cabins for transients; Grover and Glenn did carpentry and operated a dairy; and Earl attended the University of Utah, served in the United States Army in France, and finished an M.A. in history at the University of Chicago.

Noah was only a nominal Mormon after his baptism in 1905. He went to meetings when it was possible, but not often. In Twin Falls, however, there were faithful Saints who befriended Noah and Edna. They talked to them about the gospel. They gave them literature. And finally, in 1914, Edna joined. She prodded Noah into praying, going to meetings, paying his tithing, and meeting his LDS obligations. In 1917, Noah was ordained an elder, and he and Edna went to the Salt Lake Temple to receive their endowments and patriarchal blessings.

In 1919, when the Twin Falls Stake was formed by the new Apostle, Melvin J. Ballard, Noah was ordained a high priest and made an assistant high councilor. He was soon advanced to the high council.

In 1924 the Church was soliciting missionaries to go preach the gospel. In those days, they took married men, even married men with families, so they called Noah, the high councilor, to go to the

Courtesy Leonard J. Arrington

Edna Arrington and family in their backyard shortly after the birth of baby Wayne, about June 1925. Edna, 30; Wayne; Leonard, 7; Marie, 6; LeRoy, 11; Ken, 1½. Noah was serving a mission in Virginia.

Southern States Mission for two years. By the time he left (December 1924), he had a family of four living children (a girl, Thelma, had died in 1919, and an unnamed baby had died at birth): LeRoy (10), Leonard (7), Marie (5), and Kenneth (3). Another was on the way; Asa Wayne was born in May 1925 while Noah was in the mission field. Noah returned after his two years, having been president of the Virginia, North Carolina, and Florida conferences. He returned to the high council, having never been released. Four additional children were born to him and Edna in the following years: Doris (1927), Don (1929), Ralph (1931), and Ross (1934).

Noah's farm was well managed. The family worked hard, lived frugally, and survived the depressed 1920s and '30s until the coming of agricultural prosperity during World War II. Noah was energetic and imaginative. He built markets for his hay and potatoes in the Midwest. He did well financially, bought more land, and improved machinery and equipment.

Noah was a remarkable Latter-day Saint. Full of faith and fervor, willing to forego anything to advance the work, his primary Church accomplishment was activating several hundred "senior Aaronics" who had not been stalwart. He was released in 1936 from the high council to become bishop of the Twin Falls First Ward, remaining in that calling until he became bishop of the Twin Falls Third Ward in 1946. He held that position until 1953, serving as bishop for a total of seventeen years. During those years, he bought the Twin Falls Stake welfare farm—personally standing most of the cost—farmed the welfare farm, and personally did most of the tractor work, irrigating, and harvesting. He served as president of the Twin Falls Stake high priests for another eight years after his release as bishop.

Bruce, who married an active Presbyterian and woman's club leader, did not become a Mormon, but his oldest son, a leading contractor in Idaho, built the Idaho Falls Temple and served several years as a bishop and high councilor. Grover served a mission in Pennsylvania and was a counselor in a bishopric. Glenn was a ward and stake clerk. Callie was a noted teacher in her ward, and her daughter and son-in-law have been mission presidents and Church representatives in Argentina. Jacob was an active Seventy president and lived to be 105. Hundreds of grandchildren and great-grandchildren of Lee and Priscilla Arrington have served missions, been ward and stake officers, become professors, builders, and artists. Leonard Arrington was Church historian for ten years, Woody Arrington was the general contractor who built the Idaho Falls Temple, and Randy Sparks was a popular folk singer and founded the Christy Minstrels.

The family, then, was a product of the insistent Latter-day Saint missionaries in the Tennessee mountains in the 1890s; of Ben E. Rich, the forward-looking mission president at Chattanooga in 1905; of the few missionaries that passed by the Arrington cabin in Faxon, Oklahoma, from 1905 to 1913; and of the loving early settlers in Twin Falls who "took them in" from 1913 to 1918. The Arringtons were also pioneers who traveled by freight train in quest of greater spiritual and economic possibilities. I admire them, respect them, pay tribute to them. Above all, I pay tribute to my old grandmother, the one who could not read or write, who loved all the rest of us into Mormonism—into the restored gospel of Jesus Christ.

Leonard J. Arrington is a former LDS Church historian, was the first director of the Smith Institute for LDS History and a director of the Charles Redd Center for Western Studies, both at Brigham Young University.

Courtesy Leonard J. Arrington

Lee and Priscilla Arrington in Twin Falls, Idaho, about 1946. Both were in their 90s.

NOTES

1. J. Reuben Clark Jr., "They of the Last Wagon," *Improvement Era* 50 (November 1947): 704–5, 747–48. Reprinted as "To Them of the Last Wagon," *Ensign* 27 (July 1997): 34–39.

2. The principal source for this article is Leonard J. Arrington and Rebecca F. Cornwall (now Bartholomew), *A History of the Noah and Edna Arrington Family to 1933* (Salt Lake City: Published in typescript by the family, 1976). The principal writing of this 167-page book was done by Rebecca, for whose research and writing I am grateful. Fully documented, the work provides sources for the facts given in this paper.

A history of Noah and Edna Arrington is provided in Leonard J. Arrington, *Magic Valley Pioneers: A Photographic Record of N. W. and Edna Corn Arrington* (Salt Lake City: Historian's Press, 1991). The story of Priscilla Arrington is told in Leonard J. Arrington, "Priscilla Jane Brisendine Arrington, 1857–1949," typescript in author's possession, 1989.

3. In February and March 1899, the First Ward deacons furnished eggs, soap, pork, matches, and fifty pounds of flour to "Anderson Cook who had come from the states." Then Anderson died on June 16, 1899, and Betty must have had a hard winter. In March 1900, the ward again furnished her one hundred pounds of flour plus pork and soap. See First Ward Deacons Record, July 1892–August 1904, Spanish Fork First Ward Minutes, 24, Archives Division, Historical Department, The Church of Jesus Christ of Latter-day Saints, Salt Lake City (hereafter cited as LDS Church Archives).

4. On Spanish Fork, see Elisha Warner, *The History of Spanish Fork* (Spanish Fork, Utah: Press Publishing, 1930).

5. Journal History of the Church, January 24, 1901, LDS Church Archives.

Epilogue

Street scene of Richfield, Utah, 1870.

The Folk Speak: Everyday Life in Pioneer Oral Narratives

William A. Wilson

As we look at the everyday life of common people in pioneer Utah through the lens of folklore, we should make sure that we understand what kinds of images will be reflected by that lens. A common misperception holds that the study of folklore is useful primarily for illuminating the past. Just the opposite is true. To be sure, folklore is born in the past and relates events that occurred at earlier times, but it lives in the present. It will give us a picture not so much of what "really happened" in pioneer Utah, but rather of what those of us living in the present believe happened.

The reason for this circumstance is simple. Folk narratives are kept alive and are passed from person to person by the spoken word, by people who hear stories, like them, and then tell them to other people. As they participate in this process, narrators of the stories change them—not consciously, in most instances, nor in any attempt to deceive, but in response to the cultural imperatives of the moment. Like most of us who tell stories about events important to us, these narrators will selectively remember details from the past, will highlight and sometimes embellish those that appeal to them, and will leave others in shadow. Through this process—a process folklorists call "communal re-creation"—the stories come in time to reflect the attitudes, values, and beliefs of the people keeping them alive and lose at least some of their credibility as accurate accounts of the past. That is, the narratives will tell us much more about those who relate them than they will about the events they recount. What Elliott Oring has said about the truth value of folksongs can be applied equally well to the stories we tell about nineteenth-century Utah:

> If a song is to continue, a generation must find something in it worth continuing while altering aspects which are no longer consonant

with its own values and beliefs. . . . A song cannot be adequately conceptualized as the reflection of some ancient past [or in our case, the pioneer past]. At any point in its history, the song is the distillation of generations of cumulative modification. If it can be said to reflect any group at all, perhaps it can only reflect the group in which it is currently sung—that group which has (for conscious or unconscious reasons) maintained and transformed elements from the past in the creation of a meaningful, contemporary expression.[1]

Applied to the stories contemporary Mormons tell about the practice of polygamy, for example, Oring's dictum would suggest that these Mormons would remember and relate narratives about plural marriage in terms meaningful to them in the present. And that, indeed, is the case. In those families that hold positive views of polygamy, narratives of harmony and cooperation between the families of plural wives circulate. In families that hold a less sanguine view of the practice, stories of heartbreak and discord, like the following, predominate:

> A kind and mild man received instructions to get another wife. The first wife, knowing that this was a principle of the gospel, willingly accepted the situation and helped prepare for the wedding. She prepared the nuptial chamber and the wedding dinner. [Her husband] . . . and his new wife went upstairs, and [she] . . . was left to do the dishes. Then something happened. As she was doing the dishes and thinking things over, she got madder and madder. She went outside, picked up a hatchet, rushed upstairs, and chopped down the door. The new wife was so terrified she left and never returned.[2]

Historians are sometimes dismayed by what they perceive as folklorists' lack of interest in the truth about the past. Truth is an illusive creature, seldom fully capturable, but folklorists are as much interested in it as are any other scholars. They simply seek different kinds of truth—truths of the human heart and mind. Folklorists understand that it is not what really happened in the past that captures the attention of most people and moves them to action, but what they "believe" happened. And they know that one of the best ways to get at what people believe is to examine the stories they tell about former times. If, for instance, one wants to know what polygamy was really like, one will be much better off relying on standard historical sources. But if one wants to know what contemporary Mormons believe polygamy was like, how this belief could influence the manner in which the historical record is interpreted, or, perhaps more important, how this belief reflects and shapes present attitudes and influences current behavior, then one would do well to turn to folk narratives like the one above.

So it is with stories of the pioneer era in general. Many people, most perhaps, do not learn of life in nineteenth-century Utah by reading historical treatises. They learn what life was like "back then" by listening to stories—stories told in their homes, at family reunions, in Sunday School classes, in seminary classes, and occasionally across the pulpit. While these stories may have originated in actual historical happenings and may at times square with historical reality, they will have developed, through the processes of communal re-creation described above, into accounts that reveal how the common people of contemporary Utah view the everyday lives of Utah's common people of yesteryear. More important, the stories will have become something other than mere reflectors of beliefs about the past. As usually occurs in the process of myth formation (and I use the word in its positive sense), the narratives have become projections onto the past of what we value in the present, historical constructions, as it were, after which we hope to conduct our own lives.

In saying this, I should make clear that, while folklore is communal in nature and reveals concerns common to a group, it would be a mistake to assume that a folk community is some sort of monolithic body whose members all think and act alike. No two members of any group will ever see the world through quite the same lenses. Still, the stories collected and submitted to the BYU Folklore Archives over the past four decades—the stories upon which this paper is based—present a fairly uniform view of the past held by those who have told the stories.

It should come as no surprise that this view is heroic. Most people seeking in their lore historical warrant for present-day action will see the past in heroic terms. Mormons are no different. The dominant theme in their pioneer narratives is struggle—struggle against nearly insurmountable forces of nature and humankind, carried on by valiant men, women, and children who do not yield to opposition. They may suffer severe deprivation and even death, but they do not falter or waver in the faith, and they remain ever true to their vision of the kingdom of God restored. They and their stories thus serve as exemplars of the way we should confront the challenges of our lives in our contemporary world.

Though the stories cover a broad range of subjects, they tend to cluster around three major themes: struggles on the trek West, struggles with Native Americans, and struggles to survive in a new land.

The Trek West

Although accounts of the migration to Utah lie generally outside the focus of this symposium, the telling and retelling of these stories was very much a part of the life of nineteenth-century Utah, as settlers in a new world sought courage to face present hardships by remembering the price paid to get to their new homes. One storyteller, for example, noted that his grandmother had told him trek stories when he was young "to impress on his mind the suffering of his ancestors to get across the plains and enable him to be born and raised in a Mormon environment."[3]

Some of the most poignant trek stories tell of the travails of children on the trail:

> Grandma would tell the stories about walking the long, long way across the plains and some of the hard and frightening experiences of being at Winter Quarters and burying loved ones on the plains. She'd also tell of evening, as they were stopped for the night. Wagons and handcarts in a circle. Parents trying to keep warm by dancing the Virginia Reel and little children playing tag or Ring-around-the-Rosie or, if they needed to be quiet and rest, to just try to catch the sunbeams in their aprons.[4]

Unfortunately, the stories reveal few sunbeams in the children's lives. Many tell of the youngsters' tragic deaths:

> My great-grandmother . . . was a member of one of the numerous pioneer companies that came across the plains to Utah. One night, when the company was within the region of Wyoming, my great-grandmother slept next to a little girl. The weather was especially bad and the temperatures that night went far below zero. When they awoke the next morning, they found that the little girl had frozen to death and my great-grandmother's long hair was frozen to the stiff body. The only way they could get them separated was to cut my great-grandmother's hair. The pair of scissors they used has been passed on from generation to generation since that time and are now in the possession of my aunt.[5]

Other stories tell of children mourning parents' deaths:

> My great-great-grandmother . . . decided to go to Salt Lake with the hand carts. But she died along the way and was buried on the plains. Her little girl cried and cried. The rest of the company got ready to go after the burial, and started off. When they camped for the evening, they noticed that the little girl was not with them. They sent back some scouts to see if they could find her. They retraced

the entire day's journey and found the little girl crying on the grave of her mother. . . . They took her with them back to camp and eventually to Salt Lake.[6]

Still other stories tell of both parents and children attempting to show love and affection for each other in ways made more difficult by life on the trail. When a little girl lost her "precious doll that she had taken care of since her family had been forced to leave Nauvoo," she was heartbroken. Her mother, "sad to see her daughter so sad, . . . made a new doll with a face made out of an apple core and a dress made of an old rag."[7] Another girl, wishing to give her mother a birthday gift but having no means to do so, "would pick the flowers that she thought were prettiest along the way and dry them somehow. When they finally reached the valley, she had a lot of flowers. She pressed them in a glass frame and gave them to her mother for a birthday present."[8]

The stories about the suffering of adults focus on their hunger, their chills, their weariness, and their deaths. The following story is representative of tales that are legion:

As one of the early wagon trains was nearing Utah, . . . their provisions were already nearly exhausted, and the people themselves were near exhaustion. During the storm, three members of the party died. After the storm had passed, their relatives and loved ones made arrangements to bury them. The ground, however, was frozen so hard that the poor pioneers were unable to dig the necessary graves. The people were faced with the problem of not knowing what to do but of having to do something fast. They had only a few blankets, but from those few they took three. They wrapped the bodies in these blankets. They hung the bodies from trees with ropes. They were high enough so that the wolves could not get to them. Thus, the wagon train continued on its journey toward the promised land, leaving their loved ones and friends taken care of as well as possible.

Some of these pioneers, once arrived in their promised land, carried marks of the journey throughout their lives. "Grandma could never understand," said one narrator,

why anyone would want to cultivate a cactus plant. She and her husband had both walked across the plains as children, and as they made their journey West there seemed to be so many thorny weeds and rocks. Grandpa said, "My feet were torn and bleeding and many times I could hardly walk." His widowed mother . . . had brought the fatherless family through to Payson, Utah. She had done her very best to keep her family as clean as possible, but the little boy's feet had healed with dirt still under the skin. When he died of cancer at age 67, his son stood by the bedside. The nurse said, "I wonder why the bottoms of his feet are black?" His son said, "It is all right. He is carrying the soil of the plains with him, even to his grave."[9]

According to the above story, the widowed mother brought the family through the trek West to safety. Another account states:

> While Sarah Jane Matthews and her husband were crossing the plains with a handcart company, the husband developed arthritis to the extent that he could not ford the streams and rivers without a great deal of pain. Sarah carried him across the remaining streams. This is a literal example of supporting the priesthood.[10]

Though this story is recounted somewhat tongue-in-cheek, it nevertheless points to the fact that in story after story, pioneer women emerge as some of the strongest characters in the narratives. One good sister lost her husband soon after the trek to Salt Lake had begun, and three of her six children died on the way. The first year in Salt Lake Valley, the three remaining children were caught in a storm and froze to death. "This would seem to be the end of the story," said the narrator, "but this woman went on to get married again and start her life all over. She never gave up."[11] Contemporary Mormons, both women and men, could scarcely find greater examples of courage to face present challenges than is to be found in these stories of rugged pioneer women who never gave up.

NATIVE AMERICANS

Once in Utah, the Saints faced new dangers from the original inhabitants of the region. Though the pioneers had encountered Native Americans on the trek West, few accounts in the archive give details of these encounters. Once the pioneers had arrived in Utah, however, numerous stories developed recounting struggles between settlers and Native Americans.[12] Though the Mormons probably treated the Native Americans better than did most western settlers and consequently had fewer violent encounters with them, the events that have caught the fancy of later storytellers have been the hostilities and conflicts. These narratives are full of dramatic intensity and once again characterize the pioneers as bold and heroic. Unfortunately, they also paint an uncomplimentary and dehumanizing picture of the Native Americans. Told entirely from the settlers' point of view, the narratives refer to Native Americans again and again in pejorative terms, as "bucks" or "squaws," and depict them as less than fully human—vicious, depraved, dirty, lazy, smelly, and stupid. One can only wonder how some of the stories discussed below might sound told from the perspective of the Native Americans.

Many stories of Indian raids and ruthless murders closely resemble accounts of the savagery perpetuated against the Mormons in Missouri a few decades earlier, suggesting that the Saints at times viewed both Missourians and Native Americans in a similar light. For example, one of the Missouri persecution narratives states:

> It was at the time of the Haun's Mill episode,[13] and during this time some of the Saints had a warning before the disaster struck. H. Lee's mother put him into or under a huge grate in the fireplace just before the mob came into her house. They [the mob] saw the mother with the baby, and they killed his mother by shooting her. They took the baby and bashed him against the stone fireplace until his brains were running out. All this was witnessed by this young boy.[14]

A narrative from Sanpete County tells of a local massacre in almost parallel terms:

> These boys [hired to help with the grain harvest] were just about to this farm, and they could hear these Indians whooping and carrying on, so they got down and crawled through the grass over to where they could see this ranch. The father must not have been at home at that time, and there was the mother and a little boy and then a baby. The little boy had run and hid and got away from them, . . . but they took the mother and tied her across a horse and whipped the horse and made it run with her. They took the baby and swung it around and hit its head on a tree and killed it. Then they set fire to the farm. . . . The way they had put [the mother] . . . on the horse had killed her too.[15]

In similar narratives of brutality, the Native Americans cut off the arm of a man traveling to his home in Bountiful and beat him to death with it,[16] completely wipe out a group of settlers on the way to Manti,[17] kill and scalp a young boy herding cattle,[18] and kill a father and son from Circleville on their way home from cutting wood, filling their bodies with arrows and then stealing their wagon and oxen.[19]

In numerous accounts, Native Americans attempt to kidnap the children of the settlers, especially if the children are fair haired. But they display their assumed depravity most clearly in accounts of how they treat other Native Americans, sometimes children kidnapped from other tribes, sometimes their own:

> Granddad . . . was out working in the field one day and looked up, and two buck Indians had a little Indian girl they had stolen from another tribe, and they made him understand they wanted to trade the girl for some of Granddad's prize heifers he had secured to help build his herd. Granddad hesitated, and they placed her head on a chopping block and indicated they would chop her head off unless Granddad gave them the heifers. To save her life, he went along with their request.[20]

In one instance in Cache Valley, an Indian father threatened to kill his own daughter if a family of settlers would not allow him to exchange her for food. The settlers took the little girl in and raised her as one of their own. When she was fifteen, her father came back after her. "She refused to go with him. She said that she loved her white parents better than her parents who would trade her off for food."[21]

Intrepid fighters themselves, the Native Americans in some stories are claimed to have greatly admired white men who resisted their attacks with fierce courage. According to one account, "a stage driver from Eureka was surrounded by warring Indians. He valiantly held them off for a great while, but was finally . . . captured. After he was killed, the braves cut out his heart and ate it because they wanted some of his great courage."[22] According to other accounts, the Indians actually released, rather than killed, dauntless foes.

But even more than they admired brave men, the Native Americans supposedly respected feisty pioneer women who would stand up to them with fire in their eyes. In narratives describing such encounters, the pioneer housewife is not unlike her predecessor in Missouri, who, as in the following story, fearlessly confronted mobsters:

> The Saints knew they were in danger, so it was not unusual for grandmother to have her gun close by when she was alone. One day two men came up to the door and said they were supposed to collect all of the weapons and they wanted her gun. She looked down the barrel at them and said, "All right, but I intend to unload it first." They rode away and didn't make any attempt to take it by force.[23]

In a similar fashion, as the following three narratives indicate, spunky Utah pioneer women stood their ground against marauding Indians:

> My grandmother was a little teentsy woman only about five feet tall and real light, and she wouldn't take guff from anybody. One day when she was baking bread, a buck Indian came just as she was taking a loaf out of the oven. I guess he asked for some, but when she

said no, he said he'd take it anyway. Well, she was building up a fire and had put the poker and fire shovel right in the fire while she talked. Now the Indian was only wearing a little breech cloth and when he went to take a loaf, she jerked the red-hot shovel right out of the stove and smacked him on the bare behinder. He pulled his knife and said, "I'll kill you." She took her shovel and said, "I'll burn you," and chased him out of the house.[24]

The husband [of a newly settled farm] had gone off to get supplies. The wife and children were left by themselves. One night some Indians came and started bothering them. Finally the Indians camped right out in front of the cabin. The wife could not sleep because she knew the Indians were planning to kill her and her family. She got on her knees and prayed; after that she knew what she must do. She gathered her children, marched outside and spread their bedding out right in the middle of those Indians. She got her children to kneel down and had a family prayer. Then they all crawled into bed and slept as much as they could under the circumstances. The next morning the Indian in charge told her they were planning on killing her and her family, but when they saw how brave she was they decided not to.[25]

One evening as a certain woman was finishing milking the cows and making cheese in the milk house, there suddenly appeared at the door a small band of Indians. These Indians were very fierce looking and demanded to have the milk and cheese which was there. This pioneer lady, being a fiery-tempered woman refused to give these Indians what they wanted. Instead she grabbed an axe which lay nearby and began swinging it around her head warning the Indians that the first to attempt to steal the milk and cheese would be very sorry. After contemplating their situation for several moments the Indians began to shrink back away from this woman and toward the door leading to their safety. The woman kept brandishing her weapon, threatening these intruders, and even sermonizing to them, saying that if they had come to her and asked in a gentle manner for something to eat she would gladly have given them what they requested. The Indians left. Later, however, they returned, this time in a different spirit. They asked the woman in a polite manner for some milk and cheese. She gave it to them, and from then on the Indians were very friendly to this "heap brave white squaw."[26]

In some of the stories, resourceful pioneer women move beyond winning respect of the Native Americans through plucky acts of courage and instead diminish their humanity by reducing them to buffoons. In one account, a housewife sicced her dog on Indians who had come begging for bread, causing them to flee in terror.[27] In another, a girl hid from approaching Indians in a flour barrel. Unable to breathe, she emerged from the barrel a ghastly white just as her unwelcome visitors burst into the house. They "took one look at her, thought she was a spirit sent to punish them, and they hurriedly backed out of the door and galloped away on their ponies."[28] And in still another example, a plucky pioneer girl turned a threatening Native American into a complete fool:

> [This family] lived quite close to the hills and Indians were camped quite close to the foothills. This girl was washing; she had a washing machine that was an old wooden one that had a wheel that would turn. This Indian brave came down and he had long braids. He came down and he started acting smart to her and talking smart to her and she couldn't understand him. He wanted different things than she had here at her home. . . . When she wouldn't give them to him, he grabbed her and started throwing her around. She grabbed one lock of his hair, his braid, and hurried and put it into the wringer and wound it up tight and fixed it so it couldn't run back, and then she turned and fled while he was tied to the wringer.[29]

After relating an account of a battle in Diamond Fork Canyon between settlers and Indians who had stolen the settlers' cattle and scalped and cut off the right hand of one of the their men, one storyteller added, "The men were called out on such occasions many other times to fight for their land and protect their families."[30] I have no reason to doubt this story. Battles did occur, with casualties on both sides. But the statement gives not the slightest hint that the Native Americans who had occupied these valleys before the arrival of the Saints might also have been fighting for their land and to protect their families. Nor do any of the stories berating the Native Americans for begging for food suggest that they might occasionally have been reduced to such action because they had been driven from their homes and hunting grounds.

In defense of the pioneers and especially of those who have kept narratives about them alive, I should add that most people who tell the stories do not necessarily do so to deprecate Native Americans; they tell them to illustrate the heroism of their ancestors in taming this land and establishing a new Zion. But in order to achieve these ends, the settlers had to displace the area's original inhabitants. Stories that depict these inhabitants as savage, dishonest, and shiftless have made the task seem more justifiable. Unfortunately, even today the stories have helped keep alive attitudes that might otherwise have disappeared long ago.

A New Land

Fortunately, an occasional story presents the Native Americans in a favorable light. In one story, for example, when the food supply of a southern Utah family was exhausted, a group of Native Americans appeared on the scene. They demanded food. When the mother, whose husband was absent, protested that they had none, the Native Americans opened a sack of clover seed, thinking it was flour, and began eating. They found it so bitter they spit it out and then left. The next morning, the mother "found fresh deer meat at the front door. The Indians had felt so sorry for the children having to eat nasty clover [that] they gave them something good to eat."[31]

This account leads us to the third category of popular pioneer stories—those illustrating struggles to survive in an inhospitable physical environment, where not only the Native Americans, but the Saints as well suffered severe deprivation. These narratives are in many ways similar to the tales of hardship and struggle experienced by the Saints on their trek West, except now the suffering arises not from the difficulties of the journey, but from trying to survive in a hostile land at journey's end. Once again, the tellers of these tales find in them examples of courage and fortitude we would do well to follow in our contemporary world. The stories are, as one narrator points out, "monument[s] to pioneer virtue."[32]

Many of the stories, like the following, tell of both severe hunger and self-reliance:

> Things got really hard. There would be lean years on the farm, but ... [this fellow's] dad would never accept charity or help of any kind. One day he was so hungry because he would share what he had with the children that he fainted in the store. Everyone thought that that was such willpower and remarkable that a man ... rather than accept charity would be so hungry that he would pass out in the store. They fed the family, and the next year things were better and he paid it all back again. He always paid his tithing, and he wouldn't take charity either.[33]

Other stories tell how the pioneers suffered from lack of material goods and from the harshness of frontier living:

> When Grandma Gurr was a child, her mother told her of the hardships endured by those who settled in Orderville. They had no houses, so the settlers had to dig holes in the ground. These they covered with brush. When it rained they had to leave, and she said

as soon as it would start to drizzle, the people would begin to pop up like prairie dogs. They were all very poor and could not afford shoes, so in the winter they would take a hot board with them when they went to school. They would run as fast and as far as they could, and then they would put the board down and stand on it to warm their feet and then begin over again. Granddad Gurr was sixteen before he had a pair of shoes.[34]

And again:

My grandfather . . . raced over those hot desert rocks [at Rockville, Utah] on feet that had grown tough as shoe leather, and a good thing too, for he had never had a pair of shoes. It must have been icy enough in mid-winter that he had to have makeshift shoes along with all the other makeshifts, for the hot, dry land produced little, and they were very poor.[35]

Numerous stories tell of heartbreak caused by sickness and death. One narrative tells how a couple lost two children to diphtheria and then had to remain isolated so others would not catch the disease:

Nobody could go to the home and help take care of the sick. The poor mother and dad had to [care for them], and finally the children died. . . . Some of the . . . young fellows in the town went and dug the grave in the cemetery. Then they had to go stand on the other side of the fence clear away, while the parents put the two children in boxes. They had to build the boxes themselves and dress the children's bodies. They put them into the boxes all by themselves, took them down to the cemetery in their own wagon all by themselves, and put them in the grave—the mother at one end and the daddy at the other—and covered them over so no one else could get close to the plague. . . . Then the mother and daddy got in the wagon and drove home all alone.[36]

This story demonstrates, says the collector, how the people carried on "in the face of great personal sorrow."[37] The clear implication is that in the struggles we face in our lives we should do likewise.

During the pioneer era of hardship and trial, one major narrative cycle rose to prominence—stories of the Three Nephites, those ancient Book of Mormon disciples of Christ who were granted their wish of "tarrying in the flesh" until the second coming of the Savior to "bring the souls of men unto [Christ]" (3 Ne. 28:9). Throughout the second half of the nineteenth century and still today, narratives have circulated throughout the Mormon West telling of one or more of these disciples appearing to the pioneers and assisting them through difficult times.[38]

Though the stories are interesting for their own sakes, for our purposes they provide further insight into what contemporary Mormons perceive to have been the major trials in the pioneers' lives. The narratives cover a broad range of subjects, but their main themes roughly parallel those already illustrated in the stories cited above—struggles with the harsh natural environment, with illness, and with grinding poverty. Three examples will have to suffice. In the first, a Nephite helps a man escape death in a severe snow storm; in the second, two Nephites heal the child of a woman isolated from adequate medical assistance; in the third, a Nephite provides material assistance to a widow and her impoverished family.

> This story was told to me by my father about his uncle, reported as having occurred in the 1880's during the time when settlers from Sanpete County, chiefly Fountain Green and Fairview, were moving over the mountain to settle Emery County. Circumstances had required Uncle Milas to cross over the mountain on foot, since the majority of the people didn't have . . . riding horses in those times. As he got on top of the mountain, a storm hit, the temperatures dropped, it became very cold. He was unable to move on and unable to find much in the way of shelter, and he realized that unless he could find some and build a fire he would freeze. He did find some sort of sheltered place and attempted to start a fire but was unable to get one going successfully. The wood was damp and the wind and things just generally prevented the fire from burning. He was becoming more and more desperate, more and more hopeless of success. At last he did succeed in getting a tiny little ember going—a small flicker—but it was evident that it was not going to catch on. In fact it was dying out when suddenly someone stepped up behind him and threw something from a bucket onto the fire which made it immediately blaze up and begin to burn the wood vigorously. Uncle Milas turned about to see who had done it since he hadn't been aware of anyone else anywhere near him, and there was no one there. And he searched and called and was unable to find the person. And he always interpreted it as having been one of the Three Nephites who had helped him in a time of need.[39]
>
> There was a lady that had a child that was very sick, and she didn't live very close to neighbors. She was alone with the child—her husband wasn't home at the time. She was afraid the child was going to die, and she prayed earnestly that help could come some way to

her, and she knelt down and prayed. Shortly after, there was a knock came to the door, and there was a man standing there at the door. He said he had been told to come there, that she had a sick child. He had a partner with him, and if she liked they would come in and administer to the child. She told him she would and didn't give it a thought that he was a stranger. . . . The two men came in and administered to the child. The child was healed almost instantly. She asked them to come in and sit down, but they couldn't stop. But her child was made well. She didn't see where they went. She thought the two men were the Nephites. She never did know where they went. [40]

My aunt, who lived in Rock Point, Summit County, Utah, was left a widow with a large family. She just wondered how she was ever going to manage, and one day an elderly man came to her home and asked for bread. She said, "Oh, I wonder what I'm going to do! I just have this big family and all." But anyway she gave him a meal and brought him in and fixed him up, and when he left he said, "Sister, you'll be blessed. You'll never see the bottom of your flour bin." And she looked for him when he went out the door, and she couldn't find him anywhere. And she always felt that this visit was from one of the Nephites. She had looked and looked and not any of the other neighbors had ever seen him. And she said as long as she lived she never did see the bottom of her flour bin. [41]

In this last story, the Nephite gives assistance to the widow because, following the teachings of the Savior, she willingly shares her last meager provisions with a stranger. This pattern is followed again and again throughout the Three Nephites canon. The Nephites come to the assistance of those who, in spite of overwhelming hardships, strive to live gospel principles. As the stories continue to circulate among us today, they testify that those of us who follow the examples of our valiant pioneer ancestors will be similarly blessed.

The last two stories given above are interesting for another reason: the subjects are women. Indeed, in story after story the righteous person a Nephite visits is a woman—in many instances a woman struggling to care for her family by herself, because her husband is dead, on a mission, or simply away from home working. These are strong women, tough women, women who do not waver in the faith and who willingly sacrifice themselves for the benefit of their families. For women struggling today to overcome different, but equally challenging, obstacles, the stories encourage faithful perseverance as they face their trials.

Other pioneer women emerge from a variety of non-Nephite narratives who also serve as role models, but for other reasons—not just because they are faithful but because they are plucky, resourceful women with take-charge attitudes. One good widow sister, for example, worked hard to support her children by taking in washing. She was thrilled when a neighbor gave her a sack of seed peas one day in exchange for her work. She carefully prepared the hard, sagebrush-covered ground for planting, made furrows, and then, on hands and knees, placed "each precious seed the right distance apart." When she had completed the task, she stood up satisfied, turned around, and discovered that their old rooster had followed closely behind and had eaten every pea. She did not wring her hands in despair. She immediately killed the rooster, reclaimed and replanted the peas, and then ate the tough old bird. When summer came, she and her children enjoyed many meals from the pea patch.[42]

In another instance, a sister in Spanish Fork used her old copper clothes boiler until it finally wore clear through and was completely useless. New boilers were available only in Salt Lake City. Her husband was too busy plowing to make the trip to buy a new boiler, and because the family horse was being used in the plowing, the sister could not make the trip herself by buggy. Undaunted, she

> walked the sixty miles from Spanish Fork to Salt Lake City, bought a copper boiler, and carried it sixty miles home. This in itself was an impressive feat, even in those rugged pioneer days. But the thing that made the 120-mile hike really amazing was that when she made that grueling journey, . . . [she] was seven months pregnant.[43]

CONCLUSION

As I look back over the stories discussed in this paper, I am aware that they seldom picture the routine, daily events of everyday life in pioneer Utah. To be sure, they tell us of the hardships endured and of the faith and unyielding courage to withstand these hardships. But they do not tell us what the people ate, what they wore, how they made their food and clothing, how they built and furnished their homes, how they educated their children, how they entertained themselves, how they worked, how they worshipped. My grandmother, the wife of a homesteader in Idaho, baked eight loaves of bread for her large family every other day; my mother felt she had successfully passed the rite of passage to womanhood when she first cooked for threshers all by herself; my grandfather followed the yearly agricultural cycle of dry-land wheat farmers. Such details do not appear in these pioneer stories.

Discussing how the stuff of ordinary life gets transformed into legend, folklorist Richard M. Dorson writes:

> There would be little point . . . in remembering the countless ordinary occurrences of daily life, so the legend is . . . distinguished [from regular discourse] by describing an extraordinary event. In some way the incident at its core contains noteworthy, remarkable, astonishing, or otherwise memorable aspects.[44]

Freshly baked bread appears often in pioneer stories: Native Americans come begging for it; Nephites deliver it to starving missionaries. But the baking of the bread or the cooking for threshers or the planting and harvesting of crops does not seem noteworthy, remarkable, or astonishing enough to have made its way into the stories we tell of our pioneer ancestors. We prefer instead dramatic stories of conflict, struggle, and heroic action.

And this observation takes us back to the point made at the outset. We have remembered the past in terms meaningful to us in the present. We have taken the actual events that gave rise to the stories discussed in this paper and, through the process of communal re-creation, have dropped some details, embellished some, and added some. In the process, we have created narratives that reflect ourselves—our values and attitudes—at least as much as they do the events described.

This is certainly not a process unique to Mormons. I have spent considerable time studying nationalistic movements.[45] Many scholar/patriots, in attempts to create for their countries a national spirit and a sense of national purpose, have sought in the stories of their people's past historical models for what they want the nation to become in the present. Speaking of this process as it relates to living history exhibits in our own country, Mark Leone observes:

> As a visitor, you take all this folklore and all this symbol mongering and imagine yourself to be the native of Williamsburg or Mesa Verde. . . . And because the data are relatively mute . . . , they are then more easily made to give the messages of those who do the reconstructing. . . . The tourist [at Williamsburg] does not really become immersed in the real eighteenth century at all; he is spared the shock of the filth, degradation, and misery common to that era, and is led into a fake eighteenth century, a creation of the twentieth. While in this altered frame of mind he is faced with messages—the reinforcement of standard modern American values like those surrounding the myths of our own origin as a nation—that come out of today, not two centuries ago.[46]

What Leone describes comes close to the process we follow as we tell and re-tell, and in the telling create and re-create, the stories of our pioneer past. I would not use Leone's word "fake." I see nothing pernicious, or even conscious, in the communal re-creation of our past in folklore. I would use instead the word "constructed." The stories give us a constructed past, a mythical past, a past shaped, as Leone suggests, in terms of our contemporary values, in terms of what we want ourselves to be today.

In saying this, I wish in no way to detract from or diminish the importance of our pioneer heritage. My own roots are too firmly embedded in that heritage for me ever to disparage it. Of my eight great-grandparents, six of them crossed the plains before the coming of the railroad, four of them in wagon trains, two of them in a handcart company. One of them participated in the united order experiment in Brigham City. Another participated in the skirmishes designed to delay the advance of Johnston's army. All of them played important roles in establishing Mormon communities in Utah. The blood of the pioneers courses through my veins, and I am immensely proud of these ancestors. My regard does not change the fact that the stories many of us have grown up hearing construct a picture of Utah's past that focuses on the heroic and leaves in shadow the living, breathing human beings, with all their human foibles, who have made possible our being here today.

If we have in our folk narratives created a picture of the past that is in large measure the image of what we value and want to become, what is that picture? With the exception of those narratives that reflect and continue to strengthen demeaning stereotypes of our Native American brothers and sisters, it's a pretty good picture. In the stories, we find both women and men who, inspired by their unwavering faith in the restored gospel, live always by their principles. We find men and women who will not be swayed from their course by persecution, the ravages of nature, unrelenting poverty, illness, or death. We find women and men who, no matter what trials this life may bring, believe that, if they persevere, in the end all really will be well. I have the feeling that if my pioneer fathers and mothers were shown this picture they might smile a bit and then say, "Well, we weren't quite like that, but we hope you will be."

William A. Wilson is Professor Emeritus of English, Brigham Young University, and Adjunct Professor of English at Utah State University.

NOTES

1. Elliott Oring, "On the Concepts of Folklore," in *Folk Groups and Folklore Genres: An Introduction,* ed. Elliott Oring (Logan: Utah State University Press, 1986), 10.

2. Collected by Barbara Campbell in 1970, Brigham Young University Folklore Archive, 191.4. Subsequent references to archive items will give the name of the collector, the date the item was collected, and the number of the item in the archive. For more on the folklore of polygamy, see William A. Wilson, "The Lore of Polygamy: Twentieth-Century Perceptions of Nineteenth-Century Plural Marriage," *Weber Studies* 13 (winter 1996): 152–61.

3. Marion Wixom, 1975, 453.5.

4. Patricia Bryant, 1972, 181.2.

5. Mary Strong, 1965, L3.5.2.2.2.1.

6. Shirley Tometich, 1967, L3.5.2.2.8.1.

7. Leesa Steed, 1984, L3.5.2.0.15.1.

8. Holly Sue Smith, 1982, L3.5.2.0.14.1.

9. Patricia Bryant, 1972, 181.14.

10. Laura Dene Card, 1971, L3.5.2.3.3.1.

11. P. K. Anderson, 1967, L3.5.2.2.4.1.

12. Austin and Alta Fife have argued that "the lore of every Mormon family includes stories about [Native Americans]." Austin Fife and Alta Fife, *Saints of Sage and Saddle: Folklore among the Mormons* (Bloomington: Indiana University Press, 1956; reprint, Salt Lake City: University of Utah Press, 1980), 64. The Fifes overstate the case, but the stories were once immensely popular and still comprise the largest section of pioneer narratives in the BYU Folklore Archives.

13. See Leonard J. Arrington and Davis Bitton, *The Mormon Experience: A History of the Latter-day Saints* (New York: Alfred A. Knopf, 1979), 45.

14. Don Bryner, 1970, L3.2.2.1.8.1.

15. Doris Blackham and Susan Christensen, 1971, L3.2.1.5.22.1.

16. James A. Ball, 1992, L3.2.1.5.1.30.1.

17. Doris Blackham and Susan Christensen, 1971, L3.2.1.5.1.27.1.

18. Doris Blackham and Susan Christensen, 1971, L3.2.1.5.1.24.1.

19. Linda Lundell, 1974, L3.2.1.5.1.26.1.

20. Genevieve Larsen, 1974, L3.2.1.4.4.2.

21. Jillian A. Woodhouse, 1975, L3.2.1.3.5.1.

22. Kathleen J. Roberts, 1974, L3.2.1.5.1.17.1.

23. Enid McCauley, 1971, L3.2.2.1.6.1.

24. Randall Sabin, 1961, L3.2.1.3.1.1.

25. Janett McDonald, 1984, L3.2.1.5.1.6.2.

26. Gordon Rees, n.d., L3.2.1.3.13.1.

27. Doris Blackham and Susan Christensen, 1971, L3.2.1.3.12.1.

28. Charlotte Easten, n.d., L3.2.1.5.1.8.1.

29. Doris Blackham and Susan Christensen, 1971, L3.2.1.5.2.2.1.

30. P. K. Anderson, 1967, L3.2.1.5.1.23.1.

31. De Anne George, 1982, L3.2.1.3.14.1.

32. Ema Carson, 1973, 194.7.

33. Ema Carson, 1973, 194.7.

34. Maren McDaniel, 1972, L3.6.2.1.1.

35. Enid McCauley, 1971, L3.6.2.2.1.

36. Ema Carson, 1973, 194.4.

37. Ema Carson, 1973, 194.4.

38. See Hector Lee, *The Three Nephites: The Substance and Significance of the Legend in Folklore,* University of New Mexico Publications in Language and Literature, no. 2 (Albuquerque: University of New Mexico Press, 1949). Stories of Nephite appearances continue to be told today; see William A. Wilson, "Freeways, Parking Lots, and Ice Cream Stands: The Three Nephites in Contemporary Society," *Dialogue: A Journal of Mormon Thought* 21 (autumn 1988): 13–26.

39. Janet Geary, 1968, N341.

40. Marion King, 1945, N1092.

41. James D. Browne, 1969, N246.

42. Mary Strong, 1965, L3.6.2.3.1.

43. Steven C. Walker, 1964, L3.6.2.4.1.

44. Richard M. Dorson, *Folk Legends in Japan* (Rutland, Vt.: Charles E. Tuttle, 1962), 18.

45. See William A. Wilson, *Folklore and Nationalism in Modern Finland* (Bloomington: Indiana University Press, 1976); and William A. Wilson, "Sibelius, the *Kalevala,* and Karelianism," in *The Sibelius Companion,* ed. Glenda Dawn Goss (Westport, Conn.: Greenwood, 1996), 43–60.

46. Mark P. Leone, "Archeology as the Science of Technology: Mormon Town Plans and Fences," in *Research and Theory in Current Archeology,* ed. Charles L. Redman (New York: John Wiley and Sons, 1973), 130–31.

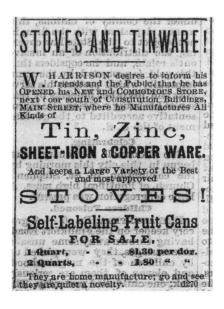

INDEX

*The numbers for pages with illustrations appear in **boldface**.*